The Green Howards in the Great War

This book is dedicated to the memory of the officers, warrant officers, non-commissioned officers and men of the 8th and 9th (Service) Battalions of the Green Howards 1914–18, but in particular to my grandfather, 13093 Private Walter Sheen, B Company, 8th Battalion.

The Green Howards in the Great War

8th and 9th Battalions A.P.W.O. Yorkshire Regiment

John Sheen

Pen & Sword
MILITARY

First published in Great Britain in 2024 by
Pen & Sword Military
An imprint of Pen & Sword Books Limited
Yorkshire – Philadelphia

ISBN 978 1 39908 094 1

A CIP catalogue record for this book is
available from the British Library

Typeset by Mac Style
Printed in the UK by CPI Group (UK) Ltd, Croydon, CR0 4YY.

Pen & Sword Books Limited incorporates the imprints of After the Battle, Atlas, Archaeology, Aviation, Discovery, Family History, Fiction, History, Maritime, Military, Military Classics, Politics, Select, Transport, True Crime, Air World, Frontline Publishing, Leo Cooper, Remember When, Seaforth Publishing, The Praetorian Press, Wharncliffe Local History, Wharncliffe Transport, Wharncliffe True Crime and White Owl.

For a complete list of Pen & Sword titles please contact

PEN & SWORD BOOKS LIMITED
47 Church Street, Barnsley, South Yorkshire, S70 2AS, England
E-mail: enquiries@pen-and-sword.co.uk
Website: www.pen-and-sword.co.uk
or
PEN AND SWORD BOOKS
1950 Lawrence Rd, Havertown, PA 19083, USA
E-mail: uspen-and-sword@casematepublishers.com
Website: www.penandswordbooks.com

Contents

Foreword

As I grew up in the 1950s, on my grandmother's sideboard stood photographs of my father and his brothers in battle dress. The group was enlarged as uncles Geordie and Rory went off to do their National Service. I was always intrigued by the one on the extreme left with his legs in bandages; my grandfather, Walter. I asked many times about him but always got the same answer from my gran, 'He was in the Green Howards, By! Them lads could fight but not like the Tyneside Irish.' From my father and the 1914–15 Star, I knew his number was 13093 and he served with the 8th Battalion of the Green Howards. I was brought up where the streets are named after County Durham men who were winners of the Victoria Cross, where Wakenshaw has a road, Cooper his square, a crescent is named after Bradford, while Heaviside and McNally have their 'place', too. It is small wonder I grew up to be interested in military history.

In the mid-1960s there was a second-hand book shop in the old part of Durham where I would go to look at the old military histories and if they were reasonably priced could buy them. I was able to purchase a few rare books in there, but one in particular I had to have. At the price of two shillings and six pence a copy of *The Official History of the War, France and Belgium 1916, Volume II*. At last! I could read about the 8th Green Howards and their part in the taking of Contalmaison on 10 July 1916. Many years later I discovered that Great Uncle Jimmy was there too with the 9th Battalion, Green Howards.

So having written about the Northumberland Fusiliers and the Durham Light Infantry, here is my humble attempt to tell the story of the 8th and 9th Battalions of Alexandra, Princess of Wales's Own Yorkshire Regiment. I hope that I have done them justice and if the likes of my grandfather, Billy McNally and others are looking down they will say, 'Well it's not too bad'.

John Sheen
Durham, November 2023

Acknowledgements

Thanks are due to many people, and this work could not have been completed without the support of the Trustees of the Green Howards Museum.

Also Zoe Uttley and Steve Erskine at the Green Howards Museum; their help has been most greatly appreciated.

Pam and Ken Linge of the Thiepval Project, who passed on photos.

Mr Charles Fair for Francis Dodgson's letters to his fiancée and mother.

The Yorkshire Regiment Remembrance website.

Edward Nichol, Yorkshire Regiment WW1 Remembrance website.

Elaine Miller, Murton Local History Group.

Also those relatives who loaned photographs of their soldier relatives.

Last but not least my wife, who has put up with my obsession with the First World War over the years since we married.

Chapter 1

Your Country Needs You

Assassination

On the bright sunny morning of Sunday, 28 June 1914, the visit of the Archduke Franz Ferdinand and his wife, Duchess Sophie, to Sarajevo, the capital of the Austrian province of Bosnia-Herzegovina, was to set Europe alight. It was a National Fête Day and the streets were decked with flags and thronged with people as the royal train arrived at the station. Security arrangements began to go wrong almost immediately: when the royal cars left the railway station, the security detectives were left behind and only three local policemen were present with the royal party. The Archduke with General Oskar Potiorek, the Military Governor, travelled in an open-top sports car, which, at the Archduke's request, travelled slowly so he could have a good look at the town.

As the car drove along Appel Quay, near the Central Police Station a tall young man named Čabrinović threw a hand grenade at the car. The grenade bounced off the folded roof and exploded under the following car, wounding

Archduke Franz Ferdinand visited Sarajevo on 28 June 1914.

several officers. Despite the threat, Archduke Ferdinand ordered a halt to find out who had been injured and it was now that it was discovered that a grenade fragment had grazed the Duchess. The Archduke arrived at the town hall in an outrage and decided to visit one of the wounded officers who had been taken to a nearby military hospital; he would then continue with the visit to a local museum as arranged. The cars left the town hall and went back along Appel Quay, this time at high speed, but the drivers had not been told of the unplanned visit to the military hospital. The first two cars turned right at the corner of Appel Quay and Franz Josef Street but General Potiorek shouted at the driver of the third car that he was making a mistake. The driver, obviously confused, braked sharply and brought the car to a halt, in the worst possible place. Standing right at the spot was a young Bosnian, Gavrilo Princip, who emerged from the crowd only some three or four paces from the Archduke's vehicle. Drawing a pistol, he fired two shots into the car; the first mortally wounded the Archduke and the second struck Duchess Sophie in the abdomen. The car raced to the Governor's official residence but the bumpy ride only made matters worse and the royal couple were pronounced dead shortly after arrival. If Austria-Hungary was to continue as a world power this outrage could not go unchallenged.

Gavrilo Princip fired the shots that started the First World War.

If Austria-Hungary declared war on Serbia, this would bring in the Russians, but Austria was allied to Germany and as early as the beginning of July the Kaiser, who was a personal friend of the Archduke, is reported to have said: 'The Serbs must be disposed of.' Then, on 23 July the Austrian Government sent a strong memorandum to the Serbs listing ten demands, the strongest of which was that Serbia allowed Austria to suppress local agitation and subversion directed against Austria. Although the Serbs accepted most of Austria's conditions, Austria deemed it inadequate and declared war. The nations of Europe rushed to mobilise: the Tsar, Nicholas II of Russia, tried to maintain peace but the Russian Army mobilised on 31 July. To counter this Germany declared war on Russia, having first offered France the chance to stay out of the conflict and remain neutral. The French, however, remained true to their treaties and refused the German offer; the Germans therefore declared war on France. Having declared war on France, on 3 August the Imperial German Army crossed the border into Luxembourg and threatened to move into Belgium. Belgium had mobilised on 2 August and the Germans sent an ultimatum on the pretext that the French had crossed the border into Belgium. The French in fact had retired so that they could not give any cause for such an accusation. The note said that if the Belgian Army could not stop the French the Germans would, and if the Belgians resisted then it would be considered an act of war. The Belgian border with Germany was covered by a line of forts and the key to these was the fort at Liege on the river Meuse. The main invasion of Belgium began on 4 August, although a cavalry patrol had crossed on 3 August. The German cavalry moved quickly through the frontier towns and villages, their task to capture the bridges over the Meuse before the defenders could blow them up. They also had the task of providing a screen in front of the advancing infantry and carrying out advance reconnaissance.

Meanwhile, in England mobilisation had been ordered. In July, more by luck than planning, the majority of the Territorial Army were on their annual camp. At Deganwy in North Wales, the York and Durham Brigade, consisting of the 4th Battalion, East Yorkshire Regiment, 4th and 5th Battalions of the Yorkshire Regiment (The Green Howards) and the 5th Battalion of the Durham Light Infantry were in camp. The Deganwy camp was situated on the sloping grass land dominated by the Vardre Hill overlooking Conwy Bay on which are the remains of the castle around which many fierce battles were fought.[1]

The various units were recalled to their home drill halls. At Saltburn the possibility of war did not prevent thousands from spending a happy afternoon beside the sea. The crowds were able to witness the departure of the West Riding Brigade, who had been in camp at Marske, making their return to their home drill halls.[2] Meanwhile, in Wales the 4th Battalion, Green Howards (4/Yorkshire Regiment), recorded that:

> The last two days of the first week of training were full of alarms and excursions of all kinds, and on 3 August the battalion camp was broken up and each company proceeded at once to its own headquarters.[3]

The experience of the 5th Battalion (5/Yorkshire Regiment) was slightly different. On arrival at Deganwy the battalion was ordered to provide a Special Reserve Section, which at once returned to Scarborough. On Sunday, 2 August a second Special Reserve Section was dispatched to the North Yorkshire town. The next day the camp was struck but owing to the congestion on the railway, the battalion did not entrain until 2.30 p.m. There then followed a long journey as the train made its way via the various company locations, finally arriving at Scarborough at 2 a.m. on 4 August.

The Belgians had a treaty with England and when the German Army crossed the Belgian frontier, Britain sent an ultimatum to Berlin. No reply was received so the British Empire declared war on Germany on 4 August 1914. On the night of 5 August a German ship was arrested in the Tees. The arrest was reported in these words:

> GERMAN SHIP SEIZED IN THE TEES
> Shortly after midnight last night there was a rather exciting scene at Messrs T.R. Dent's wharf at Middlesbrough. In the silent hours there was heard the tramp, tramp of a posse of police in charge of a number of officials including the Chief Constable. Arriving at the *Emma Minloss*, the order to halt was given and they marched up the gangway and arrested the ship and the ship's company in the King's name. At about 03.00 hours she proceeded in the charge of a Tees pilot to the Middlesbrough Dock, where she is now moored.
>
> The crew had made themselves scarce but on enquiry they were found to consist of ten Germans, two Russian Finns, two Assyrians and one Black man, a British subject.[4]

New Armies

The British Regular Army at home in England and Ireland had been organised as an Expeditionary Force of six infantry and one cavalry divisions and at a meeting of the principal ministers, including Lord Kitchener, who became Secretary of State for War on 6 August, the decision was taken to send four infantry divisions and the cavalry division to France on 9 August. The other decision taken by Kitchener was to raise New Armies, each army of six divisions of civilian volunteers, and on 7 August he appealed for 100,000 recruits. He launched his poster 'Your Country Needs You' and the recruiting offices were packed with men, over 10,000 enlisting in five days.

Most Territorial units were moved quickly to their war stations guarding vulnerable points on the coast and along railway lines and docks. It was stated in the Middlesbrough press that of 4/Yorkshire Regiment, 94 per cent had volunteered for foreign service. Likewise, 81 per cent of 5/Yorkshire Regiment had done the same.[5]

Throughout the locality the news of Lord Kitchener's appeal appeared in the local press and this was added to by owners of collieries and iron and steel works offering inducements to their workforces to enlist.

In Seaham on the Durham coast Lord Londonderry had the following statement printed:

THE WAR
THE LONDONDERRY COLLIERIES LIMITED
Lord Londonderry desires to intimate that for the present he will make the following allowances to the families of such of his workmen as may be on active service as members of the Regular Army, the Reserve Forces, the Territorial Force or the Yeomanry, as an augmentation of the allowances or pay made by the Government and the Soldiers' and Sailors' Families Association. But his Agents may at their discretion alter all or any of the proposed allowances, either generally or in any particular case to such extent as circumstances may in their judgement render necessary.

The first weekly payment will be made on Friday next the 11th inst.

Scale in addition to the provision of house or rent and coals free of charge the following weekly allowances:- Wife and five or more children not earning wages, 8s; wife and four children not earning wages, 7s; wife and three children not earning wages, 6s; wife and two children not earning wages, 5s; wife and one child not earning wages, 4s; wife only, 2s.

The places of all men on military service in any capacity will be kept open for them.

While other firms were not quite so generous, they did offer incentives for men to enlist:

J Newhouse and Co., Limited. Middlesbrough suggested that as the call for Volunteers is now very urgent, all their eligible employees who are not already at the front should offer their services. The firm are willing to reinstate any employee so doing at the end of the war.

Miners and boys with a pit pony and tub. Hundreds of men and boys from the Durham Coalfield enlisted in Kitchener's Army.

Likewise, Colonel Chaloner of the Guisborough estate gave instructions to his agent Mr Clarke that:

> All men renting cottages on the estate who have volunteered are to have their cottages rent free whilst away on service and if any of his estate employees who are married have been taken their wives and families will be properly looked after.

Richard Chaloner let his workmen have their cottages rent free while they were serving.

At the same time at South Bank, the firm of Alexander Cross and Sons Ltd were prepared to pay a £5 bounty to the first fifty men who offered and were accepted for enlistment into Lord Kitchener's Army, and they further undertook to find employment for all such men on the termination of the war. Furthermore, the North Eastern Steel Company Ltd of Middlesbrough stated that all men employed by them who had already been called up to join the colours or who responded voluntarily to Lord Kitchener's appeal for recruits could rely upon getting the same jobs back immediately on their return. The company said it had taken the necessary steps to see that all dependants left by men on service

Blast furnace men at Bolckow's works in Middlesbrough.

would not suffer want. In many cases the fact that their families would be cared for eased the difficult decision regarding enlistment and soon after the newspapers were reporting the departure of men to regimental depots far and wide. On 31 August, the *Middlesbrough Daily Gazette* reported that:

> Enthusiastic scenes were associated with the departure from the mining areas of Cleveland today. About thirty from Lingdale, Skelton and Boosbeck left amid the cheers of a large crowd. Whilst a further sixty departed from Loftus and Skinningrove, receiving an equally enthusiastic send off. At the coast in Saltburn it was reported that the recruits were also heartily greeted. Those congregated at the station included, Major Hamilton and officials of the Cleveland Miners Association. The area of East Cleveland responded well to Lord Kitchener's appeal with a further batch of twenty-four men leaving Guisborough on the morning of 31 August with more to follow.[6]

Indeed, all over the region the work of recruiting continued at speed. In Stockton a new recruiting office was opened in the Borough Hall, opening at 9 a.m. The work went on until 9 p.m., although the numbers reported as enlisting were low. Across the river in Thornaby, Sergeant Major Gibson and two clerks worked in a recruiting office at 48 Mandale Road, where over sixty men had enlisted. Further along the River Tees in Darlington, recruiting was described as 'brisk', but more ex NCOs were required. Corporals up to the age of 42 and sergeants up to the age of 45 could re-enlist and be given their old rank back.

Recruiting notice published in the *Middlesbrough Daily Gazette*, September 1914.

In East Durham, miners were reported to be flocking to the colours. On the night of Sunday, 30 August a train left Horden with ninety men on board and when it stopped at Easington a further twenty got in. Over that weekend the coastal colliery villages provided some 300 men to the various regimental depots. Up the coast at Seaham Harbour, some 250 men volunteered and in the local Territorial unit, the 1st (Durham) Battery, Royal Field Artillery, every man had volunteered for overseas service. A Mr Horsley of West Hartlepool organised a fleet of cars, which toured all the colliery villages and conveyed many volunteers to the local recruiting office. At Blackhall railway station, where the train only stopped on a Wednesday, a number of men were waiting for a car to take them to Hartlepool, however the promised vehicle did not turn up. A telephone call was made to the recruiting office but no transport was available, and furthermore the recruiting office stated that they 'had more recruits than they could deal with'. An effort was made to get a car from Sunderland but to no avail. Mr J.J. Prest, the chief agent of Horden Collieries Ltd, desperate to assist those wishing to enlist, sent a telegram to the War Office as follows:

> Kitchener, War Office, London.
> Hundreds of young miners physically fit and excellent recruits, unable to join your army at Hartlepool or Sunderland owing to inefficient arrangements of recruiting staffs.
> Prest, Castle Eden, Durham.

In fairness it has to be said that a car did eventually turn up and took some men to Hartlepool, although ten others went by train from Horden to Sunderland and a local contractor took another ten in his lorry to Sunderland.

Hamar Greenwood, MP for Sunderland, gave a recruiting speech in the White Lion Hotel.

Further inland the MP for Sunderland Captain Hamar Greenwood gave a recruiting speech in front of the White Lion Hotel. In what was described as a 'stirring address', 'he appealed to those men who had the physique and were not debarred by other causes, that they could best serve their country by joining the army'.[7]

On 1 September at Bolckow, Vaughan and Company's Cleveland Iron and Steel Works, a meeting of over 3,000 workmen heard stirring and eloquent addresses from local dignitaries. Speakers included the Mayor of Eston, Councillor Trevelyan Thompson and the Vicar of South Bank, Reverend H. Robson. The upshot of the meeting was that some 250 men indicated their readiness to join the colours.

Thursday, 3 September 1914 was the day that over 33,000 men across the country enlisted. At the Assize Court in Durham large groups of men gathered in lines in front of tables, each recruiting for a different regiment or corps. Those joining the Northumberland Fusiliers, the Durham Light Infantry and the Royal Field Artillery were sent away by train to Fenham Barracks in Newcastle later that morning. Others joining the cavalry left for the Northern Command Cavalry Depot, at Burniston Barracks, Scarborough. Those who enlisted into

Durham North Road Railway Station, 3 September 1914.

the Yorkshire Regiment gathered at North Road Railway Station around 1 p.m. waiting for a train to Richmond, where they would join the Regimental Depot.

It was reported in *The Durham Chronicle*:

> That some excitement was caused as the young men who had enlisted marched through the streets to the railway station. Thursday 3 September had proved a capital day for enlisting and consequently there was a record number dispatched to their regiments. At the Railway station there was a scene of much enthusiasm. The men who were on the point of departure sang popular songs such as, 'It's a Long Way to Tipperary', and 'In the Evening by the Moonlight.' And their friends joined in with them. A gentleman, kindly provided 'tabs' and the supply was augmented by a 'gathering', i.e. a whip round with all present donating what they could. Cheers were given for the donors and the leading military and naval figures of the present campaign were lustily cheered. The Kaiser was not forgotten, but boos and groans and not cheers were the tribute he received.
>
> Mrs Morant, the wife of the Chief Constable, and Mr H Bottomley arranged for some food for the waiting men.

Before they departed a photographer took a photograph of the large group of men.

The depot at Richmond had been very busy initially absorbing and fitting out the Regular Reservists as they re-joined. During the first three days over 950 arrived at Richmond and on 6 August the first draft of 300 were sent off to join the 2/Yorkshire Regiment in Guernsey, followed the next day by a further 250. As the 'Kitchener men' began to arrive the available accommodation began to overflow and empty houses had to be requisitioned for the troops. Any available halls and the old married quarters in the castle were soon taken over. The local population were active in supplying blankets, rugs and all manner of comforts for the men, while the local gentry and farmers supplied straw for beds where needed. The depot was soon so overcrowded that the Commanding Officer was instructed to send 500 men home on furlough. To achieve this, those residents of Sunderland and Middlesbrough were selected and they were paid at their respective town halls weekly by an officer from the depot until called for. It was soon time to start dispatching men to their training areas to form the new Service Battalions of the regiment. The first to leave were those sent to Grantham to form the 6/Yorkshire Regiment. They were followed by 7/Yorkshire Regiment on 7 September and their departure was recorded as follows:

> LIVELY SCENES AT RICHMOND
> In the old garrison town of Richmond on Monday night and early this morning there were some lively scenes when 1,100 soldiers left by special trains – one about midnight and one at 7 a.m. They had a hearty send off. The men heartily appreciated the generosity of the people of the town for providing amusements and suppers for them at the various institutions.[8]

On Saturday night, 11987 Private Edward Burton, a 27-year-old miner from Eston, was found near Gilling with a large wound in his throat, evidently inflicted with a pocket knife. He was also very wet, revealing that he had spent some time in a river or stream. He had gone to Richmond to enlist and it was stated that he had broken out of barracks. He was taken to the Richmond Workhouse, where he was said to be seriously ill. The outcome was that Edward was medically examined, during which he stated he had been drinking heavily, but the Doctor noted that there was no history of habitual intemperance and there was no history of sunstroke or head injury. The main cause seemed to be strain and alcoholism. There did, however, appear to be a family history as one brother had committed suicide and another was in an asylum. Further statements indicated he was depressed, dull and slow of speech and had delusions. He was removed to the North Riding Lunatic Asylum on the grounds he had attempted to commit suicide by cutting his throat. Then on 17 October his case was brought before a Medical Board and he was discharged as unfit on 20 October 1914.

Army Order No. 388 of 1914 authorised the formation of another six divisions, thus creating a third New Army. These divisions were to be numbered 20–26.

In an appendix to the order it was stated that the 23rd Division was to consist of the 68, 69 and 70 Infantry Brigades. It also stated which battalions would form each brigade and that 69 Brigade would consist of the 11th Battalion West Yorkshire Regiment, the 8th and 9th Battalions of the Yorkshire Regiment (Green Howards) and the 10th Battalion, West Riding Regiment (Duke of Wellington's Regiment). The 23rd Division would be commanded by Major General Sir J.M. Babington KCB KCMG, with 69 Brigade being commanded by Brigadier General F.S. Derham CB.

We are going down south

It wasn't until 18 September that the 8 and 9/Yorkshire Regiment were ordered to move. Although the regimental history records the date as 28 September, the *Surrey Advertiser* confirms it as 18 September in its issue of 19 September, when the paper reported as follows:

> FRENSHAM
> GREAT MILITARY CAMP
> A great military camp has been formed on Frensham Common which has been chosen for the training of twelve divisions (battalions) just added to the Army and yesterday (Friday) the troops entered into occupation, coming from the depots of Yorkshire regiments at Leeds, Halifax, York, Pontefract, Richmond and Sunderland. They are mostly recruits and the

A large, tented camp sprang up close to the lake at Frensham.

The inside of one of the large marquees at Frensham.

majority are without any uniform. With but few exceptions all belonged to the working classes. One or two of the colliers gave evidence of their calling by carrying pit lamps. Several had musical instruments of the accordion type and one fondled a kitten. As a whole they are a muscular lot of men

A different view of the camp.

> and when 'licked into shape' should prove an excellent reinforcement to the allied troops. Many of them entrained on Thursday night and reached Farnham station yesterday morning. The others followed in the afternoon and all on reaching the camp were served a substantial meal, consisting of curried stew, potatoes and bread. Messrs J Lyons and Co of London is the caterers and the meals are served in large marquees. Four of the structures are of extraordinary size, each accommodating a thousand men. There are upwards of five hundred bell tents. The total population of the camp is over eight thousand men.[9]

The camp was described in these words, 'Frensham Common near Farnham, one of Surrey's beauty spots has been chosen. It is a picturesque spot, rolling hills of heather stretching for miles, with backgrounds of pine trees and in the centre two lakes, one two miles and the other a mile in circumference.'[10]

A very large percentage of those who joined 9/Yorkshire Regiment were married men over 30 years of age. The majority came from Middlesbrough and North Yorkshire with the exception of D Company, who were mainly County Durham and Tyneside men. The men in D Company were primarily coal miners, while the other companies had a fair portion of ironstone miners and iron and steel workers from the banks of the Tees.

Chapter 2

Training in the South of England

Frensham was a tented camp and both Green Howard battalions and the rest of the brigade were accommodated in long lines of bell tents, each holding thirteen men, with larger marquees providing cover for the cookhouse, dining tent and quartermaster stores, company and battalion headquarters and a guardroom. For a long time there were no tent boards available so the men had to sleep on the ground. Fortunately the missing boards were issued before the weather broke. The battalions were hampered by two main shortages; firstly there was a lack of trained instructors. This difficulty was overcome by the War Office advertising for ex-NCOs to re-enlist to serve as drill instructors, with no liability to serve overseas if they were over 45 years of age. Secondly, there was a real shortage of equipment; khaki uniforms had run out rapidly after the formation of the first New Army. There were also shortages in equipment and weapons, all of which had to be overcome to complete the training of the New Armies. For a number of weeks the men paraded in their own civilian clothing, which owing to the nature of the training was wearing out rapidly, as

Blue uniforms had been issued, but no caps.

were the men's boots. Owing to this lack of uniforms and equipment, training was somewhat limited to route marching, squad drill, physical training, running and entrenching.

Major E.G. Caffin arrived at Frensham with no other officers, one sergeant major and one quartermaster sergeant and 1,070 other ranks. So, if there was a shortage of NCOs, the shortage in officers was even greater. There were insufficient regular officers for there to be one in each battalion of the 23rd Division, and in at least one case the command of a battalion was given to a retired officer, commonly known as a 'dug out'. Command of 8/Yorkshire Regiment was offered to Colonel C.J. Spottiswoode, formerly of the 2/Green Howards, but almost immediately he had to resign owing to ill health, the baton being passed to Major A.J. Stephen from the 11/West Yorkshire Regiment. Along with those already mentioned the officers that arrived in September were Captains J. Rikey (B Company), S. Robson (D Company), Lieutenants T.L. Webb (A Company), F. Dodgson (C Company), Second Lieutenants J.D. Dellus, J. Tilly, G.M. Whitehead, A.R. Thompson, C.S. Simpson, R.F. Nicholls, E.N. Player, A.J. Peters, B. Jessop, and R. Evers. Captain A.C.W. Cranko was adjutant with Lieutenant C. Ridsdale as quartermaster.

The regimental history also records those officers that initially joined 9/ Yorkshire Regiment at Frensham. Command was originally given to Colonel H.C.F. Vincent CMG, late Indian Army, but after the move to Frensham Major H.G. Holmes of the Reserve of Officers of the Green Howards assumed command with the rank of lieutenant colonel. At that time other officers include

As equipment became available the men began to look more like soldiers.

9th Battalion officers at Frensham. Standing L to R: 2/Lt G.K. Thompson, 2/Lt E. Collier, 2/Lt F. Hermiston, 2/Lt A.C.L. Parry, 2/Lt R.H. Tolson, 2/Lt R.G. Pettle, 2/Lt W.F. Greenwood, Seated: 2/Lt A.B.H. Roberts, Capt H.A.S. Prior, 2/Lt P.M. Courage. (*Green Howards Museum*)

Major C.E. Ross (late Indian Army), Captain H.A.S. Prior (from 4/Yorkshire Regiment), Lieutenants L. Crawley-Boevey (late 2/ Yorkshire Regiment) and W.F.C. Beckett, along with Second Lieutenants A.C.L Parry, E. Collier, W.T. Wilkinson, W.F. Greenwood, F. Hermiston, R.G. Pettle, G.K. Thompson, R.H. Tolson, C. Barraclough, A.B.H. Roberts, P.M. Courage and A.C. Barnes, with Lieutenant R.E. Wall as quartermaster.

During their free time the men made their way into Farnham to have a look round the town and to find a hall where they could read and write letters home. Many made inquiries as to the location of the 'Free Library'. Coming from the industrial north they were used to reading rooms and miners' welfare halls, but these were not to be found in the rural villages of Surrey and Hampshire. Thanks to the efforts of Morton Latham JP of Frensham, the National School at Frensham was opened to the soldiers. Pen, ink and writing paper was provided free of charge. It was reported that the men were most respectful and showed a keen sense of the regard thus displayed for them, and were repaying the kindness shown by their magnificent behaviour. In Farnham E. Kempson, Chairman of the Urban District Council, convened a public meeting in the Corn Exchange to raise funds for a recreation room for the use of the troops on Frensham Common. It was estimated that £100 to £150 would be required. The motion being passed, the Reverend F.G. Webster, chaplain to the troops at Frensham, thanked the meeting on behalf of the men.

It was also related that the men were especially pleased with the catering arrangements of Messrs J. Lyons and Co. who had provided sausages, brawn, tinned meat and boiled eggs for breakfast and at tea time bread, butter, jam and cake. Furthermore, the dinners were just as good with plenty of everything. The firm chartered a special train every day to bring foodstuff and supplies from London. Additionally, a number of footballs were provided, which were kicked around the common followed by huge crowds of players, enough to make up thirty or forty teams.

In glorious weather on Sunday afternoon the men at Frensham basked in the sun. There was a respite from training and at 3 p.m. religious services were held. The largest assemblage was that of the Church of England, which was conducted by the Reverend F.G. Webster. The troops were marched from their battalion lines and formed a square in which a local brass band accompanied the singing of hymns.

The men of 69 and 70 Brigades had scarcely been at Frensham two weeks when His Majesty King George V, accompanied by Queen Mary, made an inspection of the tented camp. Their Majesties passed down the ranks and visited the kitchens and mess tents. In the kitchen the King spoke to Mr Lee, the manager of Messrs Lyons and Co. Ltd, and asked a number of questions and expressed delight in all he saw. Their Majesties were particularly interested

Officers of 9th Yorkshire Regt at Frensham 1914–15. L to R: 2/Lt A.B.H. Roberts, 2/Lt W.F. Greenwood and 2/Lt A.C. Barnes. (*Green Howards Museum*)

Inspection by King George V and Queen Mary.

in the methods of cooking, most of which was done by steam. In the course of the inspection the King and Queen spoke to several men and after shaking hands with the chief officers motored back to Aldershot amid the ringing cheers of the troops.

Photographic evidence shows that some of the men on parade had been issued with red jackets and blue trousers but the vast majority were still wearing their civilian clothes. In one battalion a separate squad had to be formed of all those with no seats in their trousers. These men were tactfully lined up with their backs to one of the large marquees. That afternoon a further 1,000 men from the depots in Pontefract, Richmond and Newcastle arrived to bring the battalions stationed at Frensham up to strength.

There was now a need for more men as some of the earliest enlistments were found to be unfit. Men such as 14443 Private George Hall a 22-year-old seaman, from Whitby of 8/Yorkshire Regiment; 13017 Private Charles Allan, a 30-year-old labourer, from Linton, Lincolnshire, of 9/Yorkshire Regiment; and 11408 Private George Allan, a 25-year-old bottle maker from Sunderland serving with 8/Yorkshire Regiment, were all found to be unfit and unlikely to become efficient soldiers, and were therefore discharged under King's Regulations paragraph 393iiic, during October 1914. It is no reflection on the men themselves as at this stage the route marching and physical training were arduous and some loss of men was to be expected. However, the late Brigadier Holmes then commanding 9/Yorkshire Regiment, wrote in the *Green Howards Gazette* in 1924, 'In these early days there was little difficulty in eliminating "wasters", and "non triers", whether they were officers, non-commissioned officers or men, and after two or three months the battalions gradually got into shape.'[1]

He also wrote: 'Soon however platoons were to be seen doubling in extended order across the common, or digging hard at some trenches which were supposed to be constructed on the very latest principles from France, while in the distance some particularly keen or ambitious Company Commander might be seen leading his men in an attack on the Devil's Jumps or Kettlebury Hill.'[2]

Another amenity supplied by the people of Farnham was hot baths. Eight baths were installed by Messrs Mardon and Mills above the skating rink in Castle Street, where for 2d a soldier could get a hot bath between 1400 and 2000 on a Saturday and a Sunday, and from 1600 to 2000 on a weekday. Donations for fuel for heating the water was made by Messrs Taylor and Anderson Ltd. Mr H.J. Wells and Mrs Andrews donated towards the purchase of soap and the Farnham Swimming Club provided towels. The townsfolk also organised concerts and the Corn Exchange was filled with soldiers when a number of ladies gave recitals and an orchestra played for the men.

However, not all the locals at Frensham were kindly disposed to soldiers, as reported under the heading:

> ASSAULT ON A SOLDIER
> Thomas Chiverton of Headley was summoned for assaulting 11235 Private Hugh McMillan of the 9th Yorkshire Regiment. The Private stated that whilst returning to camp at Frensham at 10 p.m. on 3 October, he overtook the defendant and asked him for a ride in his wagon. Thereupon, defendant struck him on the head with an iron hammer. Two comrades of the complainant corroborated. Defendant an old man said he was pestered with requests for a ride on the way home from Farnham. Complainant was clambering into the wagon when he struck him. Mr Chiverton was fined ten shillings.[3]

The same day as the court case, 3/9110 Sergeant Edward Henderson, 9/Yorkshire Regiment, a 46-year-old miner, died in hospital at Aldershot. His body was taken home to Ferryhill, County Durham, where he was interred at Duncombe cemetery in the village.

As time went on uniforms became available, not the khaki of the Regular Army that the new recruits hoped for, but blue serge, which today is known as, 'Kitchener Blue'. However, the issue of these uniforms meant the men were starting to look a little more like soldiers. One soldier of 'Kitchener's Army', writing home to Chester-le-Street, told his family, 'We are expecting to get our uniform. It will not be khaki. It will be plain blue with no red stripe on the trousers; it is thought the caps will be the old Glengarry style. This uniform will be used until we are ready for the front, when it will be changed to khaki.'[4]

This was followed with the issue of pieces of old Slade Wallace leather equipment: a belt; two straps, an ammunition pouch and a water bottle. Some Lee-Metford rifles were also issued, which allowed some arms drill to take place. The weapons were handed from one squad to the next squad of men to begin their training.

Kitchener man wearing old Slade Wallace leather equipment, braces belt and a single ammunition pouch.

Meanwhile, the depot kept sending men south to join the battalions. On 14 October, fifty-two men were sent to the 8/Yorkshire Regiment and nine days later, on 23 October, forty left Richmond bound for the 9/Yorkshire Regiment.[5]

One area of training that instructors or officers could not improve on was the men's ability at entrenching. With the majority of men in all the battalions of 69 Brigade being miners, they would be 6ft beneath the surface before the officers could explain the task to them. This would hold them in good stead when they arrived in France. In the middle of November the weather changed and the camp turned very muddy, but the worst happened during a gale on Wednesday, 11 November:

> During the gale of Wednesday evening one of the Y.M.C.A. tents at Frensham Camp was blown down. There was danger from the fact that the tent was lighted by oil lamps which fell, but owing to the canvas being saturated no damage was done, the soldiers quickly stamping out the flames. There was sufficient warning for most of the occupants to escape, but Mr Edmonds, who was in the centre of the tent at the time, was enveloped in the folds of the canvas. He was, however, rescued uninjured. Postal orders and cash were scattered about the tent, but were recovered by the soldiers.[6]

The bad weather, however, spelt the end of Frensham Camp, and it was decided to move the whole of the 23rd Division into barracks at Aldershot.

The departure of the troops from Frensham was a matter of general regret in the district, where the residents had found great pleasure in ministering to their comfort. Local residents had been instructing the men in French and German with classes well attended. Both 8 and 9/Yorkshire Regiment were squeezed into Ramillies Barracks in Aldershot, which was only designed to accommodate one battalion. Uncomfortable as it was, it was preferable to being under canvas at that time of year.

The effects of the weather and the move into Aldershot were passed to his fiancée by Lieutenant Francis (Toby) Dodgson:

> 3 December 1914
> Ramillies Barracks
> Aldershot
>
> Dear Marjorie
> Your letter arrived just before we left Frensham where we certainly did have rather a poor time of it during the last three weeks or so. The end was quite dramatic as the camp was partially wrecked by that gale last Sunday night. The hospital and part office tents being blown down and two of the large mess tents each seating about 1,000 men collapsed the next morning. As it pelted incessantly from Saturday till Tuesday morning you can imagine it wasn't very pleasant. We had to arrange to get the men fed somehow in their own tents. I never in all my life saw such a quantity of mud: it was a forlorn sight and looked very much as if the much talked of air raid had actually taken place! Thank goodness it was fine the day we moved in here where we [are] in the most comfortable quarters. I can't tell you how luxurious it seems to see a fire again and to be able to see what you are doing during the dark hours.[7]

Lieutenant Francis Dodgson, 8th Battalion.

The early part of December was given over to route marching but training was moving on and for the purposes of battalion training 69 Brigade moved to billets in the area of Eversley, Blackwater, Bagshot and Camberley. In Camberley no occupied houses were requisitioned but several larger public buildings were taken over including the Drill Hall, the Odd Fellows Hall and St Michael's parish rooms. A number of unoccupied residences were also taken over by the authorities. As the bad weather continued the local heaths were waterlogged and flooding made the delivery of rations difficult, but the work continued and battalions progressed in their training.

However, with Christmas approaching authority was given to send the men away by companies, this being done to ease the strain on the railway companies. Each man being given seven days leave and a return warrant, it took the best part of a month for everyone in a battalion to get home. The 8/Yorkshire Regiment put up some good shows in the cross-country races organised by the Southern Counties Cross Country Association for units based in Aldershot and the surrounding area. A report of a race held on Saturday, 3 January 1915 was printed in *The Sportsman* the next day:

> A most successful military team race was arranged on Saturday afternoon. Torrents of rain made the going, however, dreadfully heavy, but the adverse conditions were not sufficient to affect the spirit of the competition for out of ninety-seven starters who left the post at All Saint's Church on the 5½ mile spin only ten of that number failed to finish. A most satisfactory issue when the dreadful nature of the country much being under water was allowed for. The officials were Lieutenant R Norman 6/Leicestershire Regiment, referee; Messrs W.F. Pearce and J.A. Cotterell Southern Counties Cross Country Association, Judges, C.O. McBrien; timekeeper; Garrison Sergeant Major Clarkson, clerk of the course. The conditions of the race were that the winning team should be the one with the first six of their men home and this proud position fell to 6/Leicestershire with 73 points. 12/King's Royal Rifles came in second place with 110 points and 8/Yorkshire Regiment took third place with 170 points.[8]

A report in the same newspaper printed on 24 January placed a Private Teebody of the 8/Yorkshire Regiment among the medal winners, however, no soldier with this name has been traced.

On 12 January, from his billet in Sandhurst, Toby Dodgson sent the news of their return to Aldershot:

> We leave these billets on the 14th and go back to Ramillies for one night then go out into billets again at a place called Eversley somewhere in this part of the world. I expect we shall be there about ten days, anyhow the Aldershot address will find me all right.[9]

This was followed on 20 January by another letter giving news of a change to the battalion movements; 'We are not moving into billets till Saturday owing to an inspection by Kitchener and the French Minister of War which is to take place the previous day.'

This event occurred on 22 January after they returned to Aldershot. It was a parade on Queen's Parade when the whole of the 23rd Division was inspected by Lord Kitchener and M. Millerand, the French Minister for War:

> It was a day few who took part in it will ever forget. The inspection was timed for 2.30 p.m. but M Millerand had unfortunately been delayed and did not arrive until 3.30 p.m. Snow fell during the morning and was lying four inches deep on the parade ground at 12 noon, when heavy rain set in. The men in their blue-serge uniforms and civilian great coats were soaked to the skin. The infantry armed with D.P. rifles were formed up in line of battalions in mass. It was a trying day for all concerned.[10]

On 16 January Major E.G. Caffin left 8/Yorkshire Regiment and took over as second in command of 9/Yorkshire Regiment. Battalion training was resumed and 69 Brigade was again moved to billets in the training area, with 8/Yorkshire Regiment being allocated the village of Eversley for their accommodation. The 9/Yorkshire Regiment were billeted in Camberley. Then, when company training ended, the whole battalion assembled at Stratfield Saye and were quartered in barns and farms on the Duke of Wellington's estate.

The remainder of January and most of February was spent in perfecting the battalion training and near the end of February the long-awaited issue of khaki uniforms began. However, the whole of the 23rd Division was ordered to the Maidstone area. This was to be done in three brigade columns. Men who had enlisted into the various battalions of the division had formed the 23rd Divisional Cyclist Company and on 25 February 1915 they were transferred to the Army Cyclist Corps. One such man was 12123 Private George Bostock, a Middlesbrough resident who had enlisted in 8/Yorkshire Regiment but was renumbered 3490 in the Army Cyclist Corps.

Lieutenant Toby Dodgson again let Marjorie know of his intended movements:

> Monday, Plans are altered again this morning. Now we are to leave Aldershot next Sunday and march to Folkestone; they are arranging for us to do about fourteen miles a day so that we shall not be idle, as there will be all the billeting to make each day. We are expected to get down there the following Sunday and if we have anything like decent weather it should be quite good fun and very instructive.[11]

9th Battalion on the march to Folkstone.

The march to Folkestone was mentioned briefly in 8/Yorkshire Regiment notes in the May 1915 issue of the *Green Howards Gazette*:

> On 23 February and the five succeeding days we marched down to Folkestone. On this trying march, the Battalion quite upheld its fine reputation; for on arrival at Folkestone it had done exceedingly well both as regards the condition of the men and the number of those who had fallen out.[12]

Then again, Lieutenant Toby Dodgson was able to give much more detail about the march to the coast:

> It feels quite strange to be settled down again in one place after all that tramping which seems rather like a dream, a little blurred, and it is quite an effort sometimes to remember even what the places looked like! I thought Dorking a ripping spot, I was billeted with some people who lived in the knoll Road off Horsham Road, but didn't see anything of them, as they

> were dining out and we had left the house by 0730 the next. That twenty-five miles to Edenbridge was the most strenuous day we had, but oh! Such glorious weather, it was a curious old place as sleepy as they make them, quite pretty and about twenty years behind the times. The fourteen miles to Tonbridge was the best of all, including as it did Chiddingfold and Penfold, both ideal little villages and an almost uninterrupted series of scenic effects, culminating on top of the Hog's Back just outside of Tonbridge, when we had the whole of the Vale of Kent spread out beneath us. I enjoyed it immensely right up to the end, though I tremble to think what it might have been like if the weather had been wet and beastly, instead of frosty and sunny. We only had half an hour's drizzle the whole way down except at Folkestone when we were greeted by a regular Arctic blizzard, with thick snow for about an hour or so just as we were marching in.[13]

The march of 9/Yorkshire Regiment was recorded in the Regimental Journal in this way:

> Our destination Folkestone was reached … so that the whole march was completed in a week the average distance covered each day being over 16 miles, though one day we were called upon to do as much as 25 miles at a stretch. That the march was so successfully accomplished was largely due to the energies of the Billeting Officer, his Sergeants and the Quartermaster, who must be thanked respectively for the admirable way billets were allotted and the supplies distributed at each successive halting place. The march was to a large extent intended to be a test of efficiency and it is greatly to the credit of the Green Howards that a Brigade, which contains two battalions of the Regiment, was able to publish the following notice:
>
> > *The G.O.C. Brigade wishes to express his appreciation of the fine spirit shown by the Brigade and its excellent conduct on the march from Aldershot to Folkestone. The march was a higher trial than any which the Brigade has so far had to undergo; and the manner in which it acquitted itself gives great promise for the future.*
>
> Converted boarding houses have provided most comfortable billets for the men; the chalk downs furnish a more interesting manoeuvre ground than Long Valley; and all seem to find life at a seaside resort a pleasant contrast to barracks at Aldershot.[14]

At Folkestone and the other brigade billeting areas they came under command of Headquarters Shorncliffe Garrison. This headquarters issued, 'Instructions to be observed in connection with Land taken into use by the Military Authorities':

> Under the provisions of para 3a, Defence of the Realm Act No. 2. Every endeavour must be exercised by all ranks to reduce to a minimum the amount of damage done during Company, etc., training.

There followed twelve major instructions to which the men were to strictly adhere. The main points were:

1. Camping Grounds, not to be taken under these powers except for a few nights bivouac.
2. Trenches, be of a temporary nature and should be reinstated at the earliest opportunity.
3. Crops and Tillage, should be treated with the greatest respect.
4. Livestock, should not be disturbed or frightened.
5. Gaps, should not be made in hedges, railings or other fences, except by order of an officer.
6. Training Gallops, may be crossed by Infantry and Cavalry in extended order at a walk, Golf Greens are not to be crossed by wagons or mounted troops.
7. No Fires, are to be lighted near farm buildings.
8. Parks and Woods, may be entered except those marked out of bounds.
9. Rubbish, tins, cartridge-cases, waste paper, bottle etc must be collected. It must not be buried.
10. Unnecessary damage to roads, must be avoided in every possible way.
11. Spectators, are to be kept well away from the troops during operations. Officers and NCOs must cooperate with the Civil and Military Police. Offenders are to be handed over to the civil police.
12. Compensation, [This was a very long paragraph detailing the appointment of Compensation Officers and how claims would be settled and on whose authority it fell to pay amounts of cash.]

Each paragraph went into much more detail about the subject heading and in some ways it is surprising any training was carried out without upsetting local farmers and landowners.

The arrival of the Yorkshires in Folkestone was commented upon by 'The New Journalist' in his column in the *Folkestone Express*:

> Just now we have a large contingent of the Yorkshire Regiment in Folkestone, and I have met and talked with them – keen, hard headed miners who have left berths in which they were well off, simply because they are patriots and the appeal 'Your King and your country want you', has not been made to them in vain. One of them said, 'We nivver grumble at nowt sin we joined the t'Army.' He was earning nine shillings a day in a coal mine working six hours a day. Now he gets a shilling, subject to deductions. What terrible experiences they have had marching right through England, first to Aldershot and then to Folkestone. In most inclement weather, taking off wet clothing and putting it on wet next morning. Many will never see their homes anymore and others will return no longer able to wield pick and shovel. They are patriots – all honour to them.[15]

The interesting thing about this article is how the reporter has mixed the Durham and Yorkshire mining dialects in his comment by the soldier.

The soldiers of the Green Howards were witness to several tragic events during their stay at Folkestone. On Friday, 12 March two members of the Royal Field Artillery were having a struggle in Dover Road when one fell in the road and was run over by a motor bus. There was a number of witnesses, one of whom was 15032 Private Thomas Jobling serving in 8/Yorkshire Regiment. At the inquest he made this statement:

> I am at present billeted at 3 Bouverie Square. On Friday, between half past eight and a quarter to nine, I was walking up Dover Road, Opposite the Church I saw the prisoner and the deceased on the pavement. The prisoner was trying to get past the deceased, who got in front of him. The prisoner then put his hand up and shoved the deceased away and caused him to fall. I could see they both had been drinking. If the man had been sober I do not think the shove would have made him fall. The deceased wheeled round and staggered before he fell over. The prisoner shoved the deceased between the shoulder and the neck. I did not see the prisoner strike the first man. The prisoner had no hat on at the time as the deceased fell. I saw the car go over him.[16]

One morning in mid-March Privates Taylor and Winwood of 8/Yorkshire Regiment, who were billeted at 24 Darby Road, Folkstone, were taking an early morning walk along the beach. In the sea they spotted a body floating about 70 yards west of Mr King's boathouse. Taylor went for the police, while Winwood remained to watch the body. The body, that of a woman in her twenties, was recovered and taken to the mortuary. At the inquest the Coroner's Officer said the body was that of Miss Alice Cole, being identified by Miss Charlotte King, who was employed at the same house. In a long article in the newspaper there was a description of the postmortem. However, as there was no evidence of how she got into the water, the jury returned a verdict of death by drowning.[17]

As would be expected in a Garrison town, sooner or later soldiers would appear in court owing to excessive drinking. One such unfortunate was a Middlesbrough man, 11933 Private James Conway of 9/Yorkshire Regiment. Charged with being drunk and incapable on Grace Hill he pleaded guilty. PC Fox proved the case. The prisoner said he had been teetotal since Christmas but on Saturday night he met two Canadians and had a drink out of a bottle of rum which they had. The Chairman of the court gave him some advice and then told him he would be discharged.[18]

Sporting notes also appeared in the local press, which included a football match between 8/Leicestershire Regiment and the 9/Yorkshire Regiment:

> Excellent weather prevailed on Saturday 13 March when a football match was played between 8th Leicestershire Regiment and the 9/Yorkshire Regiment on the Folkstone Grammar School Ground, Cheriton Road. There were a fairly large number of spectators, who enjoyed a very exciting match. The Leicester's triumphed with several goals to the good. The play throughout was keen and capital shots were witnessed.

The report stated that the Yorkshire backs were in good form and the wing play was admirable. 'The goalkeeper, although he let some shots through, played a good game as the Leicester shooting was splendid. The final score being 6–1 to the Leicester's.'[19]

The 9/Yorkshire Regiment team was as follows; Sergeant Parkins, Hospith and Carr, McCluskey, Vitch, and Hay; McCall, Sergeant Potter, Appleyard, Gosnold and Wilson. Of the Yorkshire team only 15792 Private John McCall from Tynemouth and 14929 Sergeant George Potter from Leeds can be identified. Of Parkins, McCluskey, Carr and Wilson there are too many men of that surname for positive identification. No mention can be found of the others.

On 18 March the division was inspected by the GOC Southern Command, Major General Sir Leslie Rundale. This parade was made very memorable for the men of 9/Yorkshire Regiment for an event that could have led to a major disaster:

> While marching to the parade ground, the horses drawing an old van which had been brought from Aldershot and which was the only transport vehicle the battalion possessed, – took fright. They careered off at a gallop down Sandgate hill through the whole of the battalion. Luckily, however,

neither the driver nor any of the troops were injured, the wagon eventually being brought to a standstill in the village.[20]

Fortunately, this happened out of the view of the inspecting officer. It is not difficult to imagine the battalion scattering in all directions to avoid the galloping horses and the wagon behind them.

On Saturday 28 March, the officers of 8/Yorkshire Regiment gave a smoking concert at the Hotel Metropole, Folkestone. The Mayor of Folkestone, Lieutenant Colonel Sir Stephen Penfold J.P., was among those present and there was a large attendance of officers and NCOs. Local young ladies Miss Palgrave-Turner and Miss Kathleen O'Nane sang in splendid style, and Miss Dorothy Varick rendered musical sketches at the piano. Lieutenant Maurice Besly of the battalion gave several songs at the piano, among them a clever one of military interest that related the amusing doings of a newly joined subaltern. Miss Marjorie Hayward gave two charming violin solos. The accompanist, Miss Mary Carmichael, was described, as excellent.[21]

The next few months were taken up with more hard training and frequent inspections by senior officers. On 8 and 9 April the infantry were inspected by Major General L. Drummond, the inspector of the infantry, who expressed himself as, 'pleased with the progress made'.

On Wednesday, 14 April the body of a soldier, later identified as Private Benjamin Wheetman of 8/Yorkshire Regiment, was found on the beach at

Unidentified platoon of the 8th Battalion in Folkstone, 1915.

Folkestone. The deceased's throat had been cut and the circumstances pointed to suicide:

> The inquest was held on Thursday afternoon by the Borough Coroner (Mr G.W. Haines) at the Town Hall. Mr Bert Fagg of 10 Bridge Street, a mariner, said that on Wednesday morning about 6.20. a.m. he was on the beach opposite the bathing establishment when he saw the soldier lying on the shingle, and he went up to him to wake him, as he thought he was asleep. As he got nearer he saw the blood on his face and as he got alongside his feet he saw the most awful gash in his throat he had ever seen in his life. Close to the right hand of the body an open razor was lying on the beach. The razor was bloodstained and the box of the razor was lying close by and the deceased's cap was close alongside it. The shingle at the spot was covered with blood. He went for a policeman and fetched him to the spot.
>
> Mr E.J. Chadwick of the coroner's office said that about 6.30 a.m. he went to the beach opposite the west end of Marine Gardens. He went about seventy yards over the beach and about a dozen yards from the high water mark he saw the body of a soldier fully dressed lying flat on his back alongside a boat with his head towards the Harbour and his feet towards Sandgate. The body was on the west side of the boat. He saw the deceased had a deep wound in his throat and he appeared to have been dead for some hours. The cut started about two and a half inches from the left ear. P.C. Thorne and the last witness were there. The constable handed witness the razor produced and said he had found it near deceased's right hand. It was covered with wet blood. The case of the razor was near deceased's feet. Deceased's cap was close by. Witness removed the body to the Mortuary and on making a search of the clothing found a letter, in the left hand ticket pocket. It was unsealed and addressed to Mrs B Wheetman, 32 Cromwell Street, West Hartlepool. In it was written, '*My Dear Wife, - May god help you for I am done.*' There were two religious books an three pence half penny in bronze. There was also a piece of paper containing the names of two soldiers, a knife, three boxes of matches and some string. There were no other marks on the body. The left hand was open and the other was clenched. He searched deceased's kit but found no other letters.

Lance Corporal Copeling (probably 13873 Robert W. Codling), of the Yorkshire Regiment, billeted at 21 Alexandra Gardens, said he identified the body as that of Private Benjamin Wheetman of the 8/Yorkshire Regiment.

> He was aged 35. He enlisted on 5 January, his home being 32 Cromwell Street, West Hartlepool. He was working as a smelter when he enlisted. He was billeted with the witness and six other men at 21 Alexandra Gardens. Witness had known him six weeks and he had been all right until the last week. He received letters from somewhere that seemed to cause him a lot of trouble. He received the last one on Monday morning, so far as witness knew. The witness did not know who they were from and deceased did not speak about them. On Tuesday night deceased should have been indoors at 9.15 p.m. but he did not return. The witness reported him as absent. The deceased had been drinking heavily during the past week, since he received the letters and the witness had to check him about it. He had a family of three daughters and one son, the eldest being nine years old. The razor produced was the man's own. The men in the billet saw deceased writing on Tuesday evening the letter found in his pocket.

A verdict of 'suicide during temporary insanity' was returned.[22]

The unfortunate Private Wheetman was laid to rest in Plot O, Grave 270 in Shorncliffe Military Cemetery. Buried eight graves further on is 3/9295 Sergeant Joseph Henry Lanagan who died on 11 May. He was an old soldier of the regiment who had re-enlisted, and was posted to 9/Yorkshire Regiment aged 60, determined to do his bit.

At a court in Folkestone, Albert Edward Harrold, a private in the 'New Army', was charged with stealing six shirts. On Saturday night, 17 April at 8.30 p.m., 13816 Private Michael Nolan, 8/Yorkshire Regiment, was acting as a Regimental

A military funeral in England, 1915.

Policeman in Tentine Street, Folkestone, when he saw the defendant going along the street towards the harbour. The accused was a bit drunk and had under his arm a parcel. Nolan followed him and stopped him. Harrold dropped the parcel on the ground. When asked about the parcel, which contained six shirts, he replied that he did not know anything about them. Private Nolan handed him over to a picket, who escorted him to the police station. In court he pleaded not guilty and an officer from his regiment stated that he had a very good character and did not drink, Harrold was discharged.[23] Michael Nolan became a corporal and died at Messines in June 1917.

The Victoria Pier Pavilion was crowded on the night of Monday, 19 April when Councillor Robert Forsyth presented another of his popular military boxing tournaments:

> Very good boxing was witnessed and the audience which mainly consisted of soldiers of the various regiments stationed in Folkestone and the neighbourhood, who enthusiastically supported the members of their regiments who took part in the contests, Regiments taking part were the 3rd Hussars, 3rd Reserve Cavalry Regiment, Royal Field Artillery, 32nd Battalion Canadians, Army Cyclist Corps and 10th West Riding Regiment. However, Driver Langton Royal Field Artillery knocked out Private Armstrong of 9/Yorkshire Regiment Yorkshire Regiment in the third round of their bout.[24]

On Thursday, 22 April just before 7 p.m. evening 3/9022 Corporal Thomas Hawkswell of 9/Yorkshire Regiment was walking in the Sandgate Road with some companions when he was in collision with a boy named Marsh of 11 Albion Road, who was riding a bicycle. Hawkswell fell heavily on his head on his head on the road and was rendered unconscious. He was transferred to the Royal Victoria Hospital, where he was detained suffering from slight concussion.[25]

With training so advanced the division was able to hold large-scale field days. During the latter part of April and in early May the various battalions were employed digging a defensive line for the defence of London should the Germans decide to invade.

The battalion scribe of 8/Yorkshire Regiment noted the following in the *Green Howards Gazette*:

> Our stay on the South Coast has been very instructive and enjoyable. The time has been spent with Battalion training. We are quite ready for Brigade training which we expect to begin soon in 'fresh fields and pastures new.' Of course under present conditions there is practically no time for socialising.

8th Battalion officers in Folkstone, 1915. (*Green Howards Museum*)

> Last month however, a chance presented itself and invitations to an At Home and Concert were issued to Officers of the Brigade and prominent townspeople by Colonel Stephen and the Officers of the Battalion. This function arranged by Major Paget and Lieutenant Besly was a great success from every point of view.[26]

It was now time for the 23rd Division to complete their training, although much had been done in the field during company, battalion, brigade and divisional training, hardly any musketry had been carried out. On 24 May the division entrained for the Borden area of Hampshire. Throughout their sojourn on the coast the general behaviour of the troops had been described as exemplary, so much so that General Babington received a letter from the Mayor of Folkestone:

> Town Hall, Folkestone, 21st May 1915,
> Dear General Babington, – Now that the troops who for the past few weeks have been billeted in Folkestone are leaving, I should like to express for myself and the inhabitants of the town our appreciation of the exemplary behaviour of the men whilst they have been among us.
>
> Their earnest yet cheerful demeanour has aroused our admiration and we are deeply grateful for all that they are doing and are prepared to do for their King and Country.
>
> May God bless and protect them in all their dangers yours very faithfully.[27]
>
> Stephen Penfold, Mayor.

On arrival in the Bordon area, divisional headquarters and 70 Brigade were accommodated in the barracks in Bordon, whereas, 68 and 69 Brigades went into hutted camps at Bramshott.

Toby Dodgson had spent nearly all of May and some of June at a course for officers at the Staff College in Camberley, so it wasn't until 10 June that he wrote to Marjorie from his battalion location:

General Babington, commander of 23rd Division.

> 8th Yorkshire Regiment,
> Bramshott
> Hants.
>
> After 10 June we start our firing and as that goes on all Saturdays and Sundays it knocks all leave on the head.
>
> It is very hot down here but otherwise very pleasant and the huts are excellent. All our men have rifles now and they are also going in batches on a week's leave, so it really looks rather like business. It is rather pleasant and cheery being back with the regiment again and that did a good deal to counteract the depressing effect of saying good-bye to you.[28]

It was at this time that 8/Yorkshire Regiment swapped its bugle band for a full brass band:

> Yorkshiremen are nothing if not musical. It is therefore with peculiar satisfaction that we hail the formation of a brass band to take the place of our old friend the bugle band. This has been rendered possible by the generosity of Major Paget, who has very kindly provided the necessary instruments.[29]

On 11 June 1915, 13347 Private Robert Wynn, a 27-year-old labourer from Sunderland, serving in B Company, 9/Yorkshire Regiment, went absent without leave. However, on 9 July he re-joined and was placed in confinement awaiting trial by District Court Martial. On 19 July he was sentenced to fifty-six days detention. Moreover, as embarkation was so close the sentence was remitted at the time of embarkation. Almost one year later on 14 June 1916 he absconded again and was declared a deserter.[30]

Later, at the end of June, Toby wrote again describing the camp and some of his work:

> The officers' lines are under some splendid pine trees on top of a hill at the bottom of which there is a splendid pond for bathing, but just the thought of it makes me shudder now.
>
> It is a strenuous life here: up at 5.30 a.m. then on the ranges in the morning from 7.00 till 1.00 and shoals of musketry returns to be sent in before the evening. Oh such silly, stupid army forms!
>
> I am fed up with this place: six hours on the range, and then four or six more writing up returns when you get in, soon becomes rather wearisome and I have not been outside the camp yet.[31]

During June 1915 a number of officers of the 23rd Division went out to France for a three-day visit and compiled notes on the operations of their respective arm of service. In each report there was a number of points that were of interest to all officers. On their return all the various notes were written up and issued as a booklet, 'Notes derived from report of officers of 23rd Division who visited Flanders in June 1915'. These notes were lengthy and covered almost every aspect of trench life in 1915. However, experience and necessity would change many of the ways things were done later in the war.

The training of 8/Yorkshire Regiment received a small mention in the *Regimental Gazette*:

> The fact is this is a war of specialists would be driven home by anyone visiting our camp. Musketry, bayonet fighting, bombing, sniping are

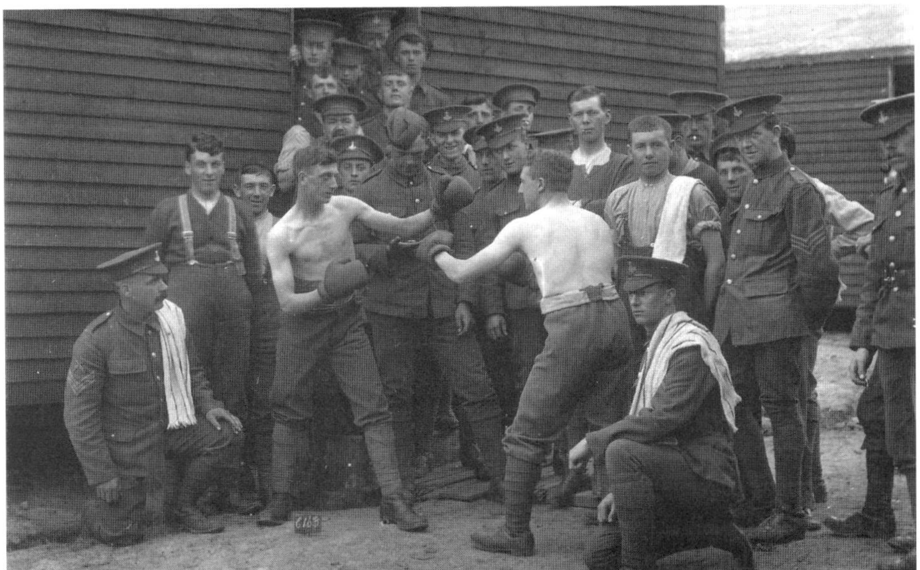

8th Battalion at Bramshott, 1915.

9th Battalion washing dishes at Bramshott.

> all in full swing. In one corner the President of the Suicide Club (The Battalion Bombing Officer) daily instructs its members in the art of working their handy little weapon and we hope in the art of praying. In another, a squad of stretcher-bearers at drill reminds us that brief life here our portion.[32]

The time was getting near to embarkation and mobilisation stores were issued. The transport sections were equipped with G.S. wagons and smaller two-wheeled limbered wagons. The same sections practised loading wagons and horses onto railway trucks.

On 19 July 1915, Battalion Orders of the 9/Yorkshire Regiment contained:

> Orders for the move No. 2.
> If the Battalion is ordered to move then the following routine will be substituted for that already issued,
>
> 1. Ammunition. O.C. Companies will draw 20 rounds per man ball ammunition, each 20 rounds will be issued in a cardboard box, which will be put into one pouch and kept intact. Ammunition weights will be handed in to Company Quartermaster Sergeants.
> 2. Waterproof sheets and Blankets. One waterproof sheet will be taken and carried by the man. Orders as regards blankets will be issued later.

3. Kits. Field kits will be taken by Officers NCOs and Men and will be as laid down in the Field Service Pocket Book, pages 182 to 193. O.C. Companies will be responsible that all articles are packed and carried as therein laid down. Men's kit bags will be taken and will be carried to the station by each man and taken into the carriage with them. Officers' kits will be stacked outside the Quarter Maters stores at the head of the Officers lines.
4. Rations. The Quartermaster will draw and arrange to carry three days preserved meat and groceries. A haversack ration will be carried by all ranks.
5. Composition of Trains. The first train will be composed as under: – Major E.G. Caffin. Quartermaster. Medical Officer. Signalling Officer. Servants and Grooms to above officers. Transport Sergeant. A & B Coys.

2 Wagons A.S.C.	4 Horses
2 Cookers	4 Horses
1 Watercart	2 Horses
6 Limbers	12 Horses
1 Maltese Cart	1 Horses
Riding or Pack horses	14*
	Total 37 Horses.

* To include chargers of Major Caffin, Quartermaster, Medical Officer, Transport Sergeant and O.C.s A and B Companies.

No. 1 Machine Gun Section under Lieutenant M.G. McCall will also proceed by this train, the guns being packed on their limber wagon on this train.

SECOND TRAIN.
Commanding Officer, Adjutant, Transport Officer, Servants and Grooms to the above Officers, Sergeant Major and Batman, Orderly Room Sergeant, C and D Companies.

2 Wagons A.S.C.	8 Horses
5 Limbers	10 Horses
2 Cookers	4 Horses
1 Water Cart	2 Horses

1 Officers Mess Cart 1	2 Horses
Riding or Pack Horses 16	* Total 37 Horses

* To include Chargers of C.O., Adjutant, Transport Officer and O.Cs, C and D Companies

Signallers will be in the ranks of their companies.

Leave for the men did not take place until the end of July and on into August. On 10 August 12034 Private Thomas Gallacher was on his embarkation leave on his way home to William Street, Middlesbrough. He had however, partaken of alcoholic drink and had become inebriated. A statement was made against him by the Station Master Mr E. Essame and two other soldiers:

Statement of Evidence.
12036 Pte T H Gallacher. D Comp 8th Service Batt
Yorkshire Regiment, Bramshott.

Sir,
At Grantham, on the 10th instant about 11.30a.m. I was on duty at the Guildhall when in response to a telephone message from the Station Master of the Great Northern Railway Station; I went to the above station. On arrival of the 9.50 Express from King's Cross, I saw the above named soldier,

Officers of 9th Battalion at Bramshott. (*Green Howards Museum*)

he was drunk. He was accused by Mr E Essame for making improper use of the communication chain there by stopping the train at Offord. Pte Gallacher alleged that someone had stolen his cap badge and threatened to assault him so he pulled the chain.

11/8/15 E Patley Sergt M.M. Police (Military Mounted Police)

I have read and corroborate the above statement,

24304 Pte William Sergeant 17 S.B. Kings Liverpool Regiment.

On his return to Bramshott, on 19 August, Private Gallacher appeared in the unit Orderly Room in front of Major J.B. Paget. His punishment was the award of ten days confined to barracks and the forfeit of five days' pay.

A story told in the *Green Howards Gazette* at this time concerned a service battalion that was about to embark for France:

Lt Col H.G. Holmes and the Warrant Officers and Sergeants of the 9th (Service) Battalion, the Yorkshire Regiment, at Bramshott in August 1915. Back row (l to r): Sgts W. Elliott, A. Scott, N. Gornall, F. Dent, T. Parsons, W. Gatehouse, S. Crute, J. Petch, J. Dolan, Thompson, Taylor. 4th Row (l to r): Sgts H. Friend, A. Goulder, C.E. Remison, D. Muncaster, R. Oglesley, P. Turnbull, F. Hardisty, A. Eaves, W. Bennison, J. Riley, S. Waugh. 3rd Row (l to r): Sgts H. Smith, T. Benton, G. Bird, G.A. Lightfoot, J. H. Armstrong, W.N. Close, F. Mitchell, B. Ankers, A.C. Carter, G. Normandale, W.H. Musgrave, L/Sgt J. Wilson, G. Hunt, S. Cockcroft. 2nd Row (l to r): CSM G.T. Londen, Sgts J. Murphy, E. Nash, J. Goodison, CQMS H. Parkin, CQMS W.T. Tait, CQMS A.P. Jackson, CQMS A. Murray, Sgts W. Overend, R. Beckwith, E.E. Mayes, J.J. Marsh, C/Sgt J. Buxton. Front row (l to r): CSM G. Potter, Lt and QM R.E. Wall, CQMS Westgarth, Capt W.T. Wilkinson, Capt W. Whittington, Sgt Maj F. Bannard, Lt Col H.G. Holmes, Lt and Adj G.N. Hunnybun, QMS J. Wadsworth, Capt A.C.L. Parry, CSM M.H. Mason, Capt A.C. Barnes. (*Green Howards Museum*)

> Sergeant to Company Commander 'Sir, Private ------- would like to speak to you.'
>
> C.C, 'Well Private ----------- what is it?'
>
> Private, (holding the top half of a set of false teeth which the benevolent Government had thoughtfully provided for tackling bully beef and biscuits): 'Please, Sir, they are broken.'
>
> C.C, 'Well I'm not a dentist. I can't mend them. How did you do it?'
>
> Private: Well, Sir, you see I took 'em out to ave me dinner and trod on 'em when I'd finished.'

After all ranks had returned to their various units, on 16 August the 23rd Division paraded for His Majesty the King on Hankley Common. Lieutenant Toby Dodgson related this as follows:

> Thursday
>
> We have been inspected by the King today and had a grilling time of it as the inspection ground was about ten miles from here in the neighbourhood of Frensham. The whole Division was there and it was quite an impressive scene. We left here at 6.00 and did not get back till 4.30. and such a hot day. Princess Mary was there on horseback, really looking very attractive, she is evidently escaping Mama's influence![33]

On the next day embarkation orders were received. The Brigade HQ War Diary records that on 20 August the brigade was to hold itself in readiness to move. All officers and men were recalled from leave in readiness for embarkation.

9th Battalion sergeants' mess (*Yorkshire Regiment remembrance website*)

Chapter 3

The Western Front, August–December 1915

9th Battalion on parade prior to embarkation. (*Green Howards Museum*)

The Brigade War Diary records that the advance parties of both battalion transport and machine gun sections of 8 and 9/Yorkshire Regiment left Liphook by train and moved to Southampton bound for Havre.[1] Conversely, the War Diary of 8/Yorkshire Regiment records that on 26 August 1915 they marched in two parties, Battalion Headquarters, C and D Companies followed by A and B Companies. On arrival at Folkestone at 9.45 p.m. the first party embarked immediately and after a safe crossing arrived in Boulogne at 11.20 p.m. A and B Companies arrived shortly after midnight and after disembarking the whole battalion marched out to a rest camp, where they arrived at 2.30 a.m.[2] Likewise, 9/Yorkshire Regiment, who had left on 25 August in two trains, one at 6.55 p.m. carrying 15 Officers and 455 men and the second at 7.35 p.m. with twelve officers and 434 men bound for Folkestone.[3]

Lieutenant Toby Dodgson recorded the crossing of 8/Yorkshire Regiment:

> Our crossing of the Channel was short and sweet. It was such a beautiful night and there was a fresh breeze, which was most pleasant after the heating start. We had rather a long wait on the quay side but eventually marched off to our camp (tents) pitched on the downs about three miles away: quite a sound spot. By the time we were all settled down there, there wasn't too much time for sleep. The next day was very hot and was spent it doing odd jobs in the camp which we left that afternoon.[4]

Francis (Toby) Dodgson waits to entrain. (*Charles Fair*)

At 3.15 p.m. 8/Yorkshire Regiment marched out of their camp and when the train arrived to carry them nearer to the front they found that the battalion transport and machine gun sections were already on board.

The diarist of 9/Yorkshire Regiment recorded that on arrival they marched to Ostrahove, a large camp, where they arrived at 2.30.a.m. Their time there was described as 'more or less uncomfortable for a few hours', before they boarded a train for the Saint-Omer area.[5]

Unfortunately one man was left behind sick at Boulogne when the battalion marched out of the tented camp at 8.10 p.m. to Pont aux Briques railway station, where they arrived at 9.30 p.m. They had to wait until 11.35 p.m. to entrain for an unknown destination.

Lt E.M. Besly, 8th Battalion, at Liphook Station, 25 August 1915. (*Charles Fair*)

> After the comfortable carriages of English trains the large box trucks of France labelled 'Hommes 40 Chevaux 10' seemed to be a real sign of being on active service at last.[6]

The diary of 69 Brigade headquarters records that the strength of the battalions was as follows:

> 11/West Yorks 24 Officers, 900 Other Ranks.
> 8/Yorkshire Regiment 28 Officers, 985 Other Ranks.
> 9/Yorkshire Regiment, 29 Officers, 986 Other Ranks.
> 10/DWR, 29 Officers, 872 Other Ranks.

Both battalions of the Green Howards detrained at Watten. The 8/Yorkshire Regiment marched off to billets in the village of Monnecove. The 9/Yorkshire Regiment did not arrive until 3.45 a.m. on 28 August and were split between the villages of Mentque and Nortbécourt. In this last-named village 9/Yorkshire Regiment buried their first fatality on French soil. No. 9114 Private James W. Agar, an ironstone miner from Boosbeck, was driving a limber when the two mules pulling it took fright and ran away down a steep hill. Unfortunately Private Agar was killed in the incident and was buried in the local churchyard.

Men of the 8th Battalion entraining. (*Charles Fair*)

The journey and the billets of 8/Yorkshire Regiment's officers were recorded in a letter from Toby Dodgson to Majorie:

> We left that afternoon and continued our journey by train again, packed like sardines and the average rate of progress about ten miles an hour. On detraining we found we had about four miles to march to the village where we are billeted, the men in barns, which are numerous and good. I together with the other C Company officers and Besly and Tilly am at the local pub: such a nice clean looking place, long and low with a simple whitewashed front which is pleasing to the eye. Here we got boiled eggs and the most delicious bread and butter, coffee and some vin blanc (1.50F the bottle) all of which we devoured greedily and then retired to bed fairly

> tired out. Six of us are sharing a loft under the roof, approached by a most dangerous trap door which I quite expect to end my days down before the shells get me! Today is broiling hot again and there does not seem to be much chance of the dust getting any less … The country round here is a pleasant surprise: this village is on a slight rise and one sees a large expanse of open undulating land, all well cultivated. The hay harvest, which for most part is gathered, appears to be a very good one. They seem to have a perfect genius in this part of the world for planting trees in just the right place and one cannot help being reminded of the Dutch painters. So far we have not seen a sign of an English newspaper, which is very boring and makes one feel very much in the dark. Nor do I expect to get any letters for some time as probably our postal arrangements will take a little time to get settled down.[7]

The battalions remained in these locations for just over a week and continued training. Specialists were sent away on machine gun, bombing and signalling courses, while the rifle companies carried out route marching and tactical exercises. Then at 9.15 a.m. on 5 September 8/Yorkshire Regiment marched out of Monnecove. The route taken was via Saint-Omer and Arques to Wallon Cappel, a distance of 17 miles, described as, 'over very indifferent roads and the weather exceptionally hot, in consequence a large number of men fell out, but all were reported present that night'.[8]

The 9/Yorkshire Regiment were travelling about twenty-four hours behind 8/ Yorkshire Regiment and left their billets at 5.30 a.m. on 6 September and took over the billets that the 8th vacated that morning. At 9.30 a.m. that morning 8/Yorkshire Regiment left and marched via Hazebrouck, a distance of 14 miles in equally unfavourable conditions, to billets near Oultersteen.

Toby Dodgson was faithfully recording his march up to the front line in his letters home and gives lasting impressions of the countryside and the billets he and his fellow officers occupied. Alas he provides little information on the conditions for the men:

> 7 September 1915
>
> Since I last wrote we have been very busy. We left the billets we were in early on Monday morning and had a very sweaty day of it, marching something like eighteen miles. The first part was along a good straight road, but the going through the towns was a terribly slow business, perpetual checks and the pavè, of which most of the roads are made in these parts is perfectly damnable to march on. We spent the night in a nice little village (Walloon) right in the country. My company had quite a decent farm and the officers

> had the parlour which was a cheery old room with good wooden beams in the ceiling. The lady of the house was a jolly sort of body and looked after us. One thing we are very lucky in is the weather, after all the rain last week. Sunday turned out a beautiful day and I went for a delightful walk. There was a hill about two miles away from our billets, quite like a small Martinsell, of course on a very reduced scale, but all the south-east slope up to the top was one large cornfield and there was a clump of trees on the top. The view from the top was delightful and one could see a long way: on the left there was a large stretch of forest. Everything was so peaceful and quiet and agriculture so very much in evidence everywhere that one could not believe that out there towards the east there was an ugly great scar across the country that you come up against something that prevents you going any farther.[9]

By 10 September 9/Yorkshire Regiment moved up to Rue Delpierre and had come under command of 2/Cameron Highlanders and 1 Royal Scots for instruction in the trenches. The 2/Cameron Highlanders' War Diary records that the CO, Adjutant and Company Commanders came up that evening to visit the trenches and at 7 p.m. two companies came up and were distributed among the Highlanders two platoons to a trench. Then at 7.15 p.m. on 11 September the other two companies of 9/Yorkshire Regiment along with the machine gun section relieved the first two companies in the trenches and the relieved

Artist's impression of the Bois-Grenier Reserve Line.

companies returned to billets in Vieux-Berquin and from there to Rue de Biez, where they were in billets.[10]

The front of this sector, which had a length of 4,500 yards, extended from Ferme Grande Flamengrie to the Armentières–Wez Macquart road. It was regarded a peaceful sector, ideal for teaching new formations the routine of trench warfare. The front line was mainly a built-up breastwork except for on the right where a short section of trench existed; a close support line with dugouts for some of the front-line garrison was not far behind and 1,000 yards in the rear lay the Bois-Grenier reserve line. Six main communication trenches ran forward from the reserve line and between the support and front line were many short communication trenches. Also in the rear were a number of fortified posts that allowed for switches to the Bois-Grenier Line.

On the morning of 13 September, 2/Cameron Highlanders were shelled heavily before the CO, Adjutant and Company Commanders of 8/Yorkshire Regiment arrived for a visit to the trenches. At 7 p.m. it was the turn of A and B Companies of 8/Yorkshire Regiment to enter the trenches for the first time. The next day they were relieved by C and D Companies. Then on 15 September 8/Yorkshire Regiment relieved the 2/Cameron Highlanders and took over the front line for the first time. During this tour the first casualties occurred. Second Lieutenant William V. Fenton, who hailed from Heston, Middlesex, was seriously wounded and died from his wounds the following day. He was buried in Bois-Grenier Communal Cemetery. He had joined the Universities and Public Schools Battalion in September 1914 and was gazetted to the 8/Yorkshire Regiment on 8 February 1915. At the time of his death he was the battalion machine gun officer. The battalion also had its first other rank casualty when one man was wounded. Nothing of major interest occurred but the casualties started to mount slowly. Each day a man was wounded and then on 19 September the battalion's first other rank fatality occurred when 23-year-old 13243 Lance Corporal Henry Hoggett, a blast furnace labourer from 96 Bessemer Street, Grangetown, was killed accidentally.[11]

The 9/Yorkshire Regiment had in the meantime sent C and D Companies up to the third-line trenches, known as the Bois-Grenier line. They were followed by Battalion HQ and A Company on 20 September. The next day the British artillery commenced firing at 9 a.m. and this went on all day, however there was very little return fire from the enemy gunners. The bombardment was carried out in preparation for an attack by the 8th Division as a diversion to the large-scale attack to the south at Loos. On Wednesday, 22 September B Company moved up to join the rest of the battalion in the third-line trench. The British bombardment drew some hostile fire in return, but 8/Yorkshire Regiment escaped with little damage.

Indeed the damage was to the A Company cooker only and the loss of some tea that was being prepared on it. This loss of tea was not, however, much grudged by A Company for they were fully compensated by watching from the safety of their trenches the amazing sight of their cooks headed by Pte McCarlty (McCarthy?) make a somewhat hurried exit from the barn in which the cooker was concealed and in which a shell had burst.[12]

Having stood by to assist 10th West Riding Regiment if they advanced it was not until 27 September that 9/Yorkshire Regiment moved into the La Basée sector, where they relieved 8/Yorkshire Regiment.

Whereas, 9/Yorkshire Regiment had been in reserve for the last week, 8/Yorkshire Regiment had been having a lively time holding the front-line sector, Casualties were beginning to mount steadily. Each day men were reported wounded and then on 22 September, 14961 Private Matthew Hewison, a 22-year-old miner from Penshaw, County Durham, was killed.

Two days later another three were wounded and two more, 12254 John Ashfield, from Feversham Street, Middlesbrough, and 14579 John Berry from Dee Street, Jarrow on Tyne, were killed by enemy shell fire. Intermittent fire was kept up on the enemy trenches with rifle and machine gun fire, to which the enemy replied immediately, shelling the British front line for about thirty-five minutes, but doing little damage.

About this time many men were sending home their first impressions of life in the front line. On 16 September, Lieutenant Toby Dodgson wrote to his mother as follows:

> Dearest Mother,
> Just a line to let you know that we are in the trenches amongst the 'whizz-bangs', snipers etc. However, the Hun is not doing very much in these parts apparently and I think he is not keen on trying too much 'strafe'. The worst part of this life is the lack of sleep which is very trying. Would you get me a periscope? I only want quite a simple affair – a couple of mirrors on a stick; only it is no good having mirrors too small and one wants something not too bulky to carry about. Also I should like my canvas washing basin, but don't send the wooden frame.

He followed this letter with two more that give details of going behind the lines for a lecture and the condition of the trenches:[13]

> 22nd September 1915
> We are still in the trenches and there is the devil of a noise going on. I got out for the day yesterday to go to a place about three miles back for a

lecture – practical illustration in the use of the gas helmet! I wasn't sorry to get away for the day and to get a fairly decent lunch which we got in a local *estaminet*.[14]

Two days later he wrote:

> Just a few lines to let you know that we are still in the trenches and beginning to feel it is about time we were relieved. Last night there was a thunder storm but, although the lightning was very vivid it never came really close to rain, which lasted on and off for a couple of hours, was of a very ordinary kind. Even so, the whole place is a quagmire and I would never have believed that so little rain could make so much mud. It must be the most extraordinary soil, as it was as dry as a bone previously. The result is that we are all smothered in mud and have the greatest difficulty in keeping our feet owing to the intense slipperiness. What it can be like after a proper spell of wet I can't conceive.[15]

On the right of 69 Brigade, troops of the 8th Division made an attack on the German lines and the brigade was to cooperate with support fire and be prepared to assault the enemy line to exploit any success with an assault on the trenches opposite. Zero hour was to be at 4.50 a.m. on 24 September. Six minutes later a smoke barrage was to be laid along the whole front and was to be maintained for about half an hour. To lay the smoke barrage a giant catapult was employed, described as an ingenious device borrowed from the Romans, but of greater terror to the operator than to the enemy. Although the troops of the 8th Division took the enemy front line they could not hold on to the position and by 10 a.m. the firing had died down.

At 7.30 p.m. on the night of 26 September 9/Yorkshire Regiment relieved 8/Yorkshire Regiment in the front line. The 8/Yorkshire Regiment then began moving back to the reserve trenches in the Bois-Grenier Line. On the way back Second Lieutenant Charles Crichton was wounded and a Middlesbrough man, 13200 Private Edward Chelton, was killed. His obituary appeared in the *Middlesbrough Daily Gazette* on Friday, 15 October:

> Beloved husband of Lily Chelton, 5 Robert Street, and eldest son of Mr and Mrs Chelton, Inness Street, Middlesbrough, aged 31 years.
>
> Respected by all who knew him, deeply mourned by his wife, child, mother, father, sisters and brothers, also Aunt Emily.[16]

These notices appeared in the vast majority of regional newspapers throughout the nation, expressing family grief at the loss of a loved one far away in a foreign land.

Having, arrived safely back in the reserve line, in the early hours of 30 September Toby Dodgson sat by the light of an oil lamp, or more likely candlelight, to write a long letter to Marjorie:

> 2.30 a.m. 30 September 1915
> We were moved out of the front two nights ago, but instead of going back into billets as we had hoped, they have only sent us back to the second line, which is rather more than half a mile behind our former position. Of course it is a good deal quieter here: you are immune from anything except shell fire; nor are one's nerves stretched out to the extent they were, but against all those very good points is the fact that these trenches are only about half made and in consequence there is practically no cover. More than half the men have to bivouac out in the open under a waterproof sheet with a blanket and there are only two dugouts built so far for us, as compared to six which we had in the firing line. The weather has been vile, soaking wet ever since we came to these trenches, so that everyone is thoroughly moist if not actually wet through. And the mud – it defies description – I thought I knew what a clay soil was, but I never saw the like of this stuff. Naturally the weather makes all the digging twice as hard and, Heaven only knows we have enough to do here anyhow. Certainly from the point of view of comfort there is no comparison. I had an awfully cosy dugout up in the front line, with a jolly comfortable bed too, but there one never had the chance of appreciating it. Now here, when one could get a decent uninterrupted night's rest there is nothing to sleep on – ugh! And owing to a muddle with the transport I have not yet got my valise, so I am left with just the one blanket that I took up to the firing line, which makes a very poor bed with nothing but the hard damp clay to support it. And I had been so looking forward to sleeping really soundly without having to get up at all sorts of odd hours during the night. Never mind tonight it really will be here and I'll be able to snuggle down into my flea bag with a delicious sense of luxury. The very essence of bed is that warmth and personally I can't sleep when my feet are numb and there is a nasty

Charles J.W. Crichton was wounded in September 1915.

> breeze blowing round your back all the time; hence this scrawl and I feel much warmer already.[17]

This part of the letter highlights the social difference between the classes in Kitchener's Army. Many of the other ranks in the battalion, particularly those from the Durham coalfield, would never have had a bed to themselves. Often they would have been top and tailed into a large double bed with a number of siblings until they reached an age where they left home and lodged with another family, but even then, although they may have had a bed to themselves, they would have shared the room with other lodgers. In some cases they may have shared a bed with someone on a different shift, so as one went out to work, another came in.

Nevertheless, the letter continued in a similar vein, this time highlighting that the officers set up a bath house for themselves:

> Yesterday in desperation we managed to fix up a bath in a shattered farmhouse behind these lines. They are a dreary sight, these farmhouses, not much more than a mass of debris out of which arise the remains of walls supporting the roof, all of which have large shell holes through them and look rather unsafe. Inside they have been utterly gutted, every piece of furniture having been taken. A good deal is to be found in the dugouts: beams have been sawn off; tiles from the floor removed wholesale together with doors and windows, all of which there is a great demand for our amateur homes, in this particular one there are two fairly decent rooms, i.e. they have floors and walls intact. One we use as the officers' cookhouse and owing to a brainwave yesterday afternoon, we used the other as a bath house. We found a round wooden tub, which after much scrubbing made a very tolerable bath, just room to sit down. The hot water we got from the company cooker. Imagine then, as dusk drew on, your beloved seated in a round wooden tub in the middle of a desolate room, lighted by one flickering candle, a ground sheet hung over the entrance in place of a door and another one over the window to hide the eyeless socket and help keep out the reeking damp atmosphere. It was an anxious moment when I took off all my clothes but it's all right, there were no signs of life! (Lice) I did enjoy that bath; you can't imagine what it means to have your clothes on solid for a whole fourteen days.

Here again we see the social difference between the officers and men. The vast majority of the soldiers, indeed all of the miners, would have been used to sitting in a tin bath in front of the fire, with wife, mother or sister pouring hot water over their back and getting stuck in with a scrubbing brush to remove the coal dust.

Toby then went on to tell Marjorie about the trenches:

> What you have heard about our trenches is quite correct; they are the trenches of the British Army and quite wonderful. I should like you to see them. Of course they aren't really trenches at all here but breastworks, as they have never been dug out more than two or three feet below ground level, the parapet being built up with sand bags. The parapet is from eight to ten feet high and quite sixteen feet thick, in many places much more, so that what it really amounts to in this part of the line is a gigantic Roman wall with a trench slotted into it all along its length and it looks as if some enormous mole had been at work, the sort of beast you might meet in Wells's 'Food of the gods'.[18]

The 9/Yorkshire Regiment spent until 2 October in the line but their War Diary is very uninformative, with comments such as 'Nothing of importance to report', and 'Nothing to record'. But on 29 September there is 'One man slightly wounded by shrapnel'. There are no names or clues to who the soldier was. In the meantime 8/Yorkshire Regiment had moved to rest billets at Fort Rompu. Here they learned quickly that rest meant the exact opposite in France and for the first time the words 'Working parties were furnished', appeared in the War Diary. Furthermore, training by those not on a working party was undertaken, while bomb throwing, trench warfare and bayonet fighting continued and route marches were carried out. Four new subalterns arrived during this period: Second Lieutenants Larner, Oakley and Watson reported for duty on 7 October and Second Lieutenant Blunden on 9 October.

Having commented on his own bathing arrangements, Toby now found time to tell Marjorie about the arrangements for his men. This was normally undertaken by companies one at a time in rotation:

> 7 October 1915
> We went to the divisional baths the other day and I can tell you I was not sorry to get the men a real hot bath and plenty of soap! What used to be the local laundry has been well adapted by the military for bathing purposes and they bath over a thousand per day: this includes ironing and disinfecting their khaki while they are in their bath and exchanging all their underclothing for a clean set, so that part of the establishment still fulfils its old functions and is run by a staff of most wonderfully industrious French girls. There is, I fear a certain amount of laxness as to the conventions

> owing to the fact that the washing rooms for clothes can only be reached through the room used as a dressing room by the men, so that a sergeant has to be stationed at the door and whenever any of the fair workers want to pass through there is a furious blowing of whistles and shouts of 'cover up!': all of which I think the immovable natives regard as an absurd piece of prudery: anyhow they seem not a whit embarrassed and the men thought it no end of a joke. Yesterday I played in a football match on a very muddy ground with the result that today I feel so stiff that I might be about sixty. I don't know at all about our movements will be but I will send you a p.c. signed 'Francis Dodgson' when we go into the trenches again.[19]

Then, a few days later on 10 October, he wrote a very long letter to his mother:

> I promised to write and try and give you some account of my experience and what trench life is like. Not being a genius there is no chance of my succeeding but however here goes.
>
> You remember the final stage of our march up to the firing line brought us to some fields about two miles behind where we were bivouacked out in the open. Our Division was to relieve a regular one, and during the two or three days we spent there we visited the trenches and saw how they ran things and generally spent all our time getting as much information and as many tips as possible from them. We took over trenches from a well-known Scotch regiment and I can't tell you how nice they were and what a lot of trouble they took to help us in every way. They had an awful time at Ypres and one of the other big shows. They regarded these trenches as a kind of rest cure, and I believe it is a fact that they are considered the best and most comfortable trenches in the British lines.
>
> They were known as the 'Daily Mirror trenches' at one time who, in their turn spoke of them as the 'Garden City'. It is a literal fact that we have in our section of trench two very fine gardens: real flower beds, actually trimmed with grass and beautiful neat paths for which the wooden trench floor boards come in very handy. There were two standard rose trees and some excellent flowers of which the mignotte was the best.
>
> Well, on the evening we were to take over (it is always done at night) we started for the trenches just as it was getting dark. The country is absolutely flat and divided into a regular chess board by numerous roads. These and ditches half full of water, form the boundaries between the fields, there being comparatively few hedges. The land is all cultivated and it is extraordinary how they go on working, even now, quite close up to the firing line. There are endless farmhouses dotted about all over the place and as we marched

down we must have passed any number in various states of dilapidation, but generally speaking it struck one how little damaged they were. About half-way there we went through a bit of a village – a long row of squalid-looking cottages still occupied by women and children; then some more of these black and deserted, the street looking horribly desolate. By now it is nearly dark; the crack of rifles sounds distinctly nearer and the glare of the flares shot into the air like small rockets from the trenches, lights up the surrounding country. We turn to the right and are heading now direct for the firing line, past another group of houses evidently occupied by the R.F.A. (Royal Field Artillery) and very strongly fortified, until we finally reached the beginning of the communication trench. This is by a farmhouse – or rather what remains of it – and a more hopeless appearance of utter confusion is difficult to imagine. There are our men filing into the trench from the road which is blocked with transport dumping rations; R.E. wagons full of timber and wire waiting to be unloaded, and a pair of mules starting to kick and attempting to destroy the last vestige of any order. It is all pitch dark. Everybody is swearing and cursing and no one knows who anyone is or where they are. I stick to the side of the canny Scot who has at length found No. 11 Platoon and is to guide us to our section of the trench. After much halting and waiting, we at length get under way up the communication trench which is as a matter of fact, more like a miniature Devonshire lane, being on average eight or nine feet broad. The sides are boarded up the whole way and half the ground space is occupied by the trench floor-boards, indispensable on account of the mud. Every ten or twenty yards it takes a violent turn, first one way then another, so that by the time you've been walking for twenty minutes or so you've not the very least idea which way you are facing. It is a slow business getting the men up with their equipment and full packs, as there is a constant stream of men coming the other way, carrying various impedimenta of the Regiment we are to relieve; and tiring too, as the surface is very rough and it takes all ones time not to slip off the boards. I think what strikes the novice most is why the Huns don't shell the horrible medley disentangling itself at the dumping point, and what an awful mess there will be if one does come!

At last we are in or rather behind our sector of the fire trench … it has all come to be greatly elaborated, regular forts being built at some points, dug-outs, cookhouses etc. all being built into and connected up to the main trench by a maze of secondary trenches. So you can imagine that to get one's men into these trenches is no simple matter for the first time, chiefly on account of the darkness. At length however, the thing straightens out: somehow our men are all in and the Jocks lined up in the rear ready to

> file away. They go and you realise that this bit of the line depends entirely on your Regiment.
>
> I am not going to attempt to describe our feelings on that first night, but the men were as jumpy as could be and there was a general feeling of insecurity. The trenches are about three or four hundred yards apart in that part of the line, so there is a large tract of 'no man's land' consisting of what were once fields with a fair number of trees dotted about. The German snipers were particularly active that night and it was this more than anything else that upset the men who, by about 1 a.m. were seeing a sniper in every bush. One man declared that a Hun was creeping about at the bottom of our parapet and had even climbed up and looked over!! Anyhow, everybody was jolly glad to see daylight, but not for long because the shelling started as soon as the light was good enough, and we had learnt to respect shells the morning before when we were going round the trenches. It was just after lunch, which we had in the trenches, when the Hun started putting a few shells over. The first two went well over and burst among some trees about thirty-five yards back. Personally, I didn't mind a bit and was chiefly interested in watching the effect, being inclined to regard the whole performance as a sort of firework display. However the third shell got the range and burst just behind the trench and caught poor Fenton, who was walking from one dug-out to the next. He was badly wounded in the head and died that night. It really was rotten luck. So our Company was short-handed from the very start.
>
> But after the first two days everybody had quite settled down. The routine is more or less as follows: – everybody 'stands too' early in the morning before it starts to get light and that is the beginning of the day. When it is bright daylight one carries on with rifle inspection, etc. then probably breakfast, after which working parties to be seen to, filling sandbags, repairing and improving sections of the trench etc. then letters to censor – a long horrible job. After lunch one tries to get some sleep.[20]

The 69 Brigade now took over the left sector of the divisional front and on 11 October 8/Yorkshire Regiment relieved 11/Sherwood Foresters. During this four-day tour, 'Nothing unusual occurred', that is, apart from three men being wounded and two killed. John Davies was a Welsh miner resident at Haswell Plough, and Clement Rose, from Monkwearmouth, was at the time of the 1911 census a butcher's boy aged 14, so it appears he had added a year or two in order to enlist. They were buried side by side in Desplanque Farm Cemetery, La Chappelle-d'Armentières.

Toby Dodgson's letters continued and on 12 October he wrote:

The weather has been much better again this last week and the ground has dried up a lot but I'm afraid it can't last long. We are in the trenches again now and a little further up the line; a rather more interesting spot too, as the Huns trenches are only about seventy yards away just here. This seems very close after the respectful distance at which our last trenches were built. We've not had any sausages or bombs over yet but expect to be introduced to these armaments before long. They had a pretty busy day yesterday but I think Fritz is prepared to dig in for a rest. It is a perfect autumn day and it seems a shame to spend it in these absurd trenches. These are much more battered about by the fortunes of war than those we were in before (no flower gardens here).

I am sharing a very excellent dug-out with another man. It was built by the R.E. when they were up here a lot sinking a mine which has since to be abandoned as they could not cope with the water. This gives one a certain sense of safety, as if we can't mine neither can the Hun. The point is, however, that in consequence this hutch is very well and strongly made and even has a nice stove in it.[21]

After four days in the line, on 15 October the battalion were relieved by 9/Yorkshire Regiment and marched back to billets in Rue Marle:

We are in billets just behind the firing line for a few days and I expect we shall settle down to the regular routine of four days in the front line, four days second line, four days support billets, until it comes to our turn to go back further for a rest. I went into the town near here yesterday – rather a queer experience. It is quite a good sized place as big as St Albans I should think, but quite deserted except for the military, a few shopkeepers and that part of the population which was, I suppose literally too poor to go away. There is absolutely no traffic on the streets and not much of that in daytime. All the big houses are barred and shuttered and several of the better class residential streets are just a mass of weeds. It seems so strange to be in such a large place and find all so quiet. What shops that are open are very good but charge exorbitant prices, with the few exceptions such as the tea shop where you can get a first class tea for 1.50F – delicious eclairs such as only the French can make.[22]

This proved to be a trying tour for 9/Yorkshire Regiment. The battalion War Diary records that they had seven men killed and one wounded. However, the number of dead conflicts with the Commonwealth War Graves Commission, whose records show five dead and one man who died of wounds. Two were killed on 16 October, 17955 Private William Collinson and 15344 Lance Corporal Albert Walters. Two on 17 October, 15360 Lance Corporal William Bayliss and 13050 Private John Graham, followed on 19 October by the death of 12078 Private James Keany. The wounded man, 12857 Private John Burke, was hit in the jaw and the head; he was evacuated to 70 Field Ambulance and from there to No. 3 Casualty Clearing Station (No. 3 CCS) at Bailleul, where he died from his wounds on 20 October.[23]

A notice of Lance Corporal Collinson's death appeared in the *Middlesbrough Daily Gazette* on 31 October. It stated simply: 'Killed in Action somewhere in France Lance Corporal William Collinson (17955) 9th Yorkshire Regiment son of Mr and Mrs Collinson of 30 Harford Street, Middlesbrough. Ever remembered by all. Memorial Service Durham Street Mission Sunday 31 October.'[24]

However, not all those evacuated were suffering from battle injuries. The same volume of admissions to No. 3 CCS shows that one day earlier, two 8/Yorkshire Regiment men, 17241 Private Edward Curry, a miner from Horden, and 14381 Private William Almond, were both admitted suffering from impetigo.[25]

On 18 October a change in the Divisional Order of Battle occurred when 70 Brigade was swapped with 24 Brigade of 8th Division. The idea was that the regular battalions of 24 Brigade would stiffen the Kitchener Battalions of 68 and 69 Brigades. To this end 1/Sherwood Foresters replaced 10/DWR in 69 Brigade, the latter battalion joining 24 Brigade. In November this decision was reversed and 10/DWR re-joined 69 Brigade with 1/Sherwood Foresters returning to 24 Brigade.[26]

On the evening of 19 October 8/Yorkshire Regiment left their billets in Rue Marle and went into the front line, where they relieved 10/DWR. Yet again they spent another four uneventful days, the enemy being described as, 'very quiet throughout the period'. The casualty list recorded was officers nil, other ranks, three wounded. Two of the wounded, 15048 Corporal Malcolm Mackay, who had a gunshot wound (GSW) to the left arm, and 11995 Private William Waters, suffering from a GSW to the left thigh, had been wounded on the way into the trenches or shortly after takeover. They had arrived at No. 3 CCS from 70 Field Ambulance and were evacuated the next day on No. 9 Ambulance Train.[27]

Likewise, 9/Yorkshire Regiment moved back to the front line, where they relieved 11/West Yorks on the night of 20 October. Once again four days in the line with the only comment being 'four casualties all other ranks'. Once more the records of No. 3 CCS help with the story as 3/8916 Sergeant James Dent was admitted with a GSW to the left leg. He would go on to be awarded the Military Medal. Posted to the 2nd Battalion, he was killed in action in October 1918. Relieved by 8/Yorkshire Regiment on the night of 24 October, 9/Yorkshire moved back to billets in Rue Marle. They were still there when on 4 November a German shell hit a billet occupied by men of the battalion. Fortunately no one was killed but thirteen men were wounded. They were all evacuated to 70 Field Ambulance and from there to No. 3 CCS at Bailleul. They are named in the Admission and Discharge Register of No. 3 CCS as follows:

Number	**Rank**	**Name**	**First**	**Wounds**
15903	Private	Fearon	John	L Leg, Face
14095*	Private	Hodgson	W	L Leg.
19342	Private	Helm	Ernest	R Hand, R Foot
15898	Private	Ward	James	Foot, Chest
15624	Private	Cuthbert	George	Head, Foot
14542	Private	Jones	George	Contusions R Leg
13118	L/Cpl	Chaney	Samuel	Contusions R Side
15971	Private	Smith	Job J	GSW Back & Head
17252	Private	Maughan	John	GSW Back, Head & Chest
13229	Private	Holmes	Alexander	L Leg
17702	Private	Harding	Robert	Head
15762	Private	Lynch	James	L Leg
19341	Private	Wilson	John	L Foot

Marked 14095*, Private W. Hodgson is recorded as such in the *Green Howards Gazette*, yet no medal index card for a man with this name or number can be traced. Furthermore, no medal roll sheet can be found.

The time between 27 October and 2 November was the quietest tour for 8/ Yorkshire Regiment so far. No casualties, although they furnished some working parties for the Royal Engineers (RE) and they did some improvement to the trenches. However, Toby Dodgson wrote to his mother when he reached the billets behind the line:

> 4 November 1915
> We came out of the trenches on Tuesday night after a pretty rotten time, as it rained without ceasing during the last forty-eight hours and it was still pelting on the night we came out. We had a six mile march to a house. I am glad to say I managed to get a billet as I have been feeling pretty rotten with a perpetual stomach ache. I have been in bed all today and the doctor has been up and given me some pills and told me to eat nothing but slops. He was not our own man, who is ill himself, but a very nice chap from the field ambulance.

However, on 9 November 13178 Corporal Francis Whittle was wounded in the left hand, evacuated and eventually discharged in December 1916. On 10 November 9/Yorkshire Regiment had moved into the Bois-Grenier Line, where they took over from 8/Yorkshire Regiment, who in turn moved to the billets in Rue Marle and then moved into the line and relieved 2/East Lancashire Regiment. They spent a quiet four days, having only four men wounded. They moved back to the billets in Rue Marle on 12 November and training began again the next day, with the now normal routine of bomb throwing, trench warfare and bayonet fighting continuing. However, on 13 November there was an accident at the 69 Brigade Bomb School, which was located in the Brasserie, Chappelle d'Armentières. Four wounded men, namely 12121 Lance Corporal Alfred Winch from Middlesbrough; 14303 Private William Judson, who came from Seaham; 13337 Private George Smithson, a miner from Hetton-le-Hole; and a Halifax man, 13745 Private Alick Lee, were wounded, and 11258 Private Charles Townend was killed.

A Court of Inquiry was assembled at the headquarters of 9/Yorkshire Regiment on Monday, 22 November to investigate the circumstances under which NCOs and men were killed or wounded by the bomb explosion in the Brigade Bomb School. The President of the Inquiry was Major H.A.S. Prior, 9/ Yorkshire Regiment, and the members were Captain R.C. Grellet and Second Lieutenant N. Rowley, both 8/Yorkshire Regiment. When the Court assembled witnesses were called and evidence was taken.

The first witness was Second Lieutenant W.A.L. Kerridge 10/DWR, who stated:

> On the afternoon of 13 November 1915, a bomb party proceeded to the Brasserie, Chapelle D'Armentières, which is the 69 Brigade Bomb School, with instruction to Lieutenant Hume-Wright 8/Yorkshire Regiment, who was in command, that the sergeant instructor should carry on with detailing grenades and that arrangements should be made for un-detonation of a supply of bombs returned from the trenches. At 2.45 p.m. I had just reached the school with the other party when I heard an explosion therein and on entering found that Sergeant Instructor C McCusker and one man had been killed and several wounded, one of whom died shortly after. I ascertained from those present that a bomb had exploded while the instructor was showing how to make it up.
>
> W.A.L. Kerridge Second Lieutenant
> 10/DWR
> O.C. 69 Brigade Bomb School

The next witness required to give evidence was Lieutenant Maurice Hume-Wright, 8/Yorkshire Regiment, whose evidence was as follows:

> On the afternoon of 13 November I was in charge of the 69 Brigade Bomb School. I had instructed Sergeant McCusker to carry on detailing and then went down to the cellar to see about un-detonating the bombs which had arrived from the trenches. About 2.45 p.m. I heard an explosion just above me and going upstairs found that a bomb had exploded and had killed and wounded several men. I had been into this room 2 minutes previously and had warned the instructor to be especially careful.
>
> M.G Hume-Wright
> 8/Yorkshire Regiment

Having called the officers, the next witness was 15849 Private Robert W. Rotherforth, 11/West Yorks, who was a 33-year-old coal miner from Stanley near Wakefield. His statement read:

> On the afternoon of 13 November I was a member of the class under Sergeant C McCusker. He was giving us instruction on the No. 12 Square-box bomb and telling us to be very careful when setting it in a trap, when the bomb suddenly exploded killing him and two others and wounding several. This occurred about 2.45 p.m. At the time of the accident Sergeant McCusker was just telling us to be careful not to shove the lighter too far on to the detonator. This is all I know of the case.
>
> R.W. Rotherforth
> 11/West Yorks

The fourth witness was another coal miner, from the small mining village of Shadforth near Durham. No. 13661 Private James Champley, aged 39, was serving with 8/Green Howards and said:

> About 2.45 p.m. on 13 November I was a member of a class under Sergeant Instructor C McCusker. He had a No. 12 Bomb which he was explaining to us. He first showed us it with a five second fuse, then how to set it as a trap with the fuse out. Whilst showing he told us to be very careful of the lighter and the detonator and to be sure not to pull the pin out, just at that moment the bomb exploded killing the Sergeant and two others and wounding several. This is all I know of the case.
>
> James Champley
> 8/Yorkshire Regiment

The three battalion Commanding Officers, Lieutenant Colonel F.W. Evatt 11/West Yorks, Lieutenant Colonel H.A. Stephen 8/Yorkshire Regiment and Lieutenant Colonel H.J. Bartholomew, 10/DWR, all added identical statements that the men of their battalion were on duty and in no way to blame. Brigadier General F.S. Dereham, commanding 69 Infantry Brigade concurred with them.[28]

Of the four wounded men, all who appear to have been evacuated through 70/ Field Ambulance, Alfred Winch had the most severe wounds, to his knee and eye. From 70/Field Ambulance he was sent to No. 4 British Red Cross Hospital at Boulogne and then onto the Anglo-American Hospital at Wimereux, from where his next of kin were notified that he was seriously ill; it was not until 11 February that he was admitted to a hospital in Guilford. After over a year in hospital, he was discharged on 17 April 1916 as 'no longer physically fit for war service'. Private Alick Lee, after being evacuated to No. 3 CCS and then to No. 13 General Hospital at Boulogne and No. 1 Convalescent Depot, re-joined the battalion on 24 February 1916. Both George Smithson and William Judson went on to re-join the battalion after a short spell in hospital.

On 14 November the 8/Yorkshire Regiment again relieved 2/East Lancashire Regiment. Yet again there was 'nothing unusual to report', just three wounded. However, one of the wounded, 14379 Private William Bycroft, having reached a hospital on the French coast, was evacuated on HM Hospital Ship *Anglia.* On the morning of 17 November HMHS *Anglia* left Boulogne for England. On board, as well as ship's crew and nursing staff, she carried 366 wounded men, of whom 166 were 'cot cases' carried in beds or on stretchers. A German submarine, *UC-5*, had been laying mines in the channel and as HMHS *Anglia* approached the gap in the British defences just after noon, she struck a mine. The explosion ripped a hole in the port side just ahead of the bridge and the ship began to go down by the bows, listing to port as she did. Two of the hospital wards flooded immediately and it was in one of these that William Bycroft lost his life, just one of the many fatalities. 'The nurses of the *Anglia* worked with splendid devotion. They gave no thought to their own safety, but laboured with the men to transfer their patients to the waiting boats.'[29] Of the four nurses on board, only one, Staff Nurse Mary

HM Hospital Ship *Anglia*, mined 17 November 1914.

Rodwell, lost her life. She was last seen alive shortly before the explosion of the mine, when she came up from the ward to get some warm clothing for her patients.

Meanwhile, at the front, the 23rd Divisional sector of the front line was extended to the left and 69 Brigade took over the right section of the divisional front, the front line being held by 8/Yorkshire Regiment in the left sub-section and 9/Yorkshire Regiment in the right sub-section. Machine gun sections and signallers were sent into the line in advance of the companies to take over machine gun emplacement and signalling stations, and other personnel went in to take over trench stores. The Brigade Bombing Officer also issued additional green rockets to 8/Yorkshire Regiment and red rockets to 9/Yorkshire Regiment. After a spell in the line both battalions were relieved by battalions of 68 Brigade and moved to positions well in the rear, where the inevitable training began again.

The cycle of four days' rest and back in the line continued, with 8/Yorkshire Regiment replacing 10/DWR in the left subsection of the left sector on 12 December. The trenches were in a very bad condition owing to the continuous rain and the activity of the German artillery. The parapet was knocked down in a number of places and the trenches full of water. Toby Dodgson had been lucky to get leave to England on 4 December and on his return he wrote about the conditions of both the return journey and the conditions at the front:

> The railway journey took over six hours. On arriving at the railhead we found there was nothing to meet us and so we had a long weary tramp to the transport lines, nearly four miles away. The final straw was finding the farm completely surrounded by water, even on the road it was about two feet deep, and in the fields round about more than waist high, so reluctantly we splodged on through it. My boots proved an immediate success and I arrived with quite dry feet. The whole state of the country is indescribable and they say that the floods have not been so bad for twenty years. Curiously enough no one has heard a word from Cranko, my company commander, so I suppose he must have been sent back to England. Player, after being out of hospital three days, has only returned apparently with an attack of nerves: he seems to have been most peculiar, very rude to everyone and quite impossible.

That night the men in the line started repairing the parapet and at some time while they were at work 11976 Private Harry Ryder from Hull was killed and one other soldier was wounded. The 9/Yorkshire Regiment too were back in the line but their diary gives no other details, however, the Brigade War Diary records that 'two officers and 100 men moved to Croix Du Bac where they received special training for a proposed offensive operation'.[30]

The 8/Yorkshire Regiment were also being offensive. On the night of 21 December, Second Lieutenant Eric Wellesley and a number of men went out to patrol the wire opposite the front line. The officer was subsequently reported missing. The patrol apparently threw some bombs at the German trenches and as they made their way back to the British lines came under fire. Two of the party were wounded. No. 13873 Private Robert Codling from Tyne Dock, was awarded the Distinguished Conduct Medal for his actions that night; 'For conspicuous gallantry near Rue de Bois on December 21st 1915 when under heavy fire and in the face of rifle grenades, he returned to a wounded comrade and brought him in. Later in the day, he joined a patrol and searched, under heavy fire, for his platoon officer who had failed to return.'

Lieutenant Wellesley was reported as missing but there was a question mark about whether he was a prisoner or had been killed.

On 24 December, Captain Archdale Parker, Second Lieutenant Wellesley's next of kin, received the usual telegraph message from the War Office:

> Regret to inform you that 2/Lieut E.G. Wellesley, Yorkshire Regiment reported Missing 21 December. This does not necessarily mean he is killed or wounded.
>
> Secretary War Office

To try and ascertain the facts, the Red Cross interviewed a number of men from the battalion during the next few months. These witness statements are included in Wellesley's personal documents held at the National Archives.

The first statement was made on 18 January by 13386 Private Christopher Blenkey, a labourer from Middlesbrough, at Coulter Hospital, Grosvenor Square, London. His statement was taken by F.E. Craik, who recorded the following:

> At Armentières 2nd Lt Wellesley, to whose company he belonged, made a night sortie with twelve bombers (the distance to the German trenches being about 500 yards). The men returned without their officer. Next day they looked as well as they could without leaving the trench, but could not see him. At night a party went out to search, but in vain. Two days later the East Lancashire Regiment reported they had picked him up dead. They found the body in a small dyke. This was formerly reported to Lt Wellesley's company and accepted by them. If this is reported to the family I should like them to know how the informant's face lighted up when he spoke of his officer and described how brave he was. 'He did not know what fear

> was … he was almost too daring'. He described him as quite young and very tall. Asked if his effects had been sent in informant did not know.

The next statement was made by 13059 Private John Dale, who served with XII Platoon, C Company. On 27 February 1916, when he was a patient in Brook War Hospital, Woolwich. He stated:

> In December at Armentières it was reported in the Batt., that Lt Wellesby [*sic*] went out with a wire cutting party and was wounded – this was one day in December in the early morning – they would be in 'no-mans-land'. He was given up by the Regiment. Under the idea he was a prisoner. I was told later his body had been found afterwards by another Regiment. I do not remember who told me or what Regiment it was said to be.

The same day at No. 3 General Hospital, at Le Tréport, 9024 Company Sergeant Major (CSM) Henry Brown of B Company said, 'He was in D Company. Captain Gillett of D Company, now with the regiment, is the most likely man to give information.'

On 2 March, Second Lieutenant Carr gave this information to C.B. Collard of the Red Cross:

> Informant states that:
> On Dec 21st/15, this officer and men were ordered to investigate result of our bombardment on the German barbed wire. Lieut Wellesley went with two bombers and two riflemen. On getting half way back, by a stream which flowed between our trenches and the German trenches Lt Wellesley asked his bombers to go back with him and bomb. They went and threw two bombs and the Germans commenced rapid machine gun firing. One bomber was wounded and the other bomber picked him up and carried him back. Lt Wellesley was seen to fall. The first bomber returned to bring Wellesley in but he had disappeared. (N.B. the affair was on a dark night.)
>
> Next night a patrol was sent out to find Wellesley and they encountered a strong German patrol on the spot. Informant holds the theory that the Germans had taken Wellesley prisoner on 21 Dec 1915 and expected that we should send out a patrol on the following night to find him, and went to meet us. Wellesley was never seen again. The first bomber got his D.C.M. for going out to try to bring Wellesley in on 21 Dec. It was just getting light.

Five days later at the Northumberland War Hospital, Newcastle-upon-Tyne, 14292 Private William Berry from South Shields had this to say:

> In December at Armentières Mr Wellesley went out bombing with three men. They reached the enemy trenches successfully and did their work without any casualties, but halfway back two of the men were hit, the third man Pte Codling of 13 Platoon D Coy carried them in one after the other. He had imagined that Mr Wellesley had got safely back to our own lines, but on finding out this was not the case went out again to look for him. He could find no trace of him. He was last seen near a stream which ran between the two lines of trenches, but informant did not know on which side of it. If he had been hit on the far side of it, he might, even if he had been able to crawl away, have found it impossible to cross. One of the wounded men said he saw Mr Wellesley standing unhurt near a tree, the other stated that he had seen him fall. The ground was searched the following night but no trace could be found.

Then on 4 April at No. 1 General Hospital, Étretat on the French coast, two further men were interviewed. The first informant was 14611 Sergeant John Parkin from Horden. He was the Platoon Sergeant of XV Platoon and stated:

> He was in D Company in command of XIII Platoon. He went out on the morning of 21 December about 4.15 a.m. with a bombing party of eight or nine men and a Sergeant Barbinson [no trace of a man with this name] and a L/Cpl McCrachen (since killed.) They went right up to the German barbed wire and heard talking in their trenches. Then the L/Cpl threw two bombs and the Germans opened machine gun fire. Private Codling who afterwards got the D.C.M. carried Private Dent, shot through the side into our trenches. The Sergeant called to Lieut Wellesley but the latter was hit. I cannot say where. Later I and a lot of others went out to try and find him and the Germans called out they had got the officer. This was in 64 Trench at Armentières just to the left of Bois-Grenier. He was the pick of the Regiment and anybody in the Platoon would go anywhere for him. He lived in London.

The second witness that day was 14082 Private William Tate, who came from Easington. His presence at No. 1 General Hospital is accounted for by a gunshot wound to the right arm on 29 March. He stated:

> Lieut Wellesley was in charge of a Bombing Party which went out from our first line trench at Armentières. Codlingham (Codling) of D.C. (D.C.M.) at present with the regiment may be able to give full particulars. Also Murphy of D Co was one of the party of bombers and was brought back by Codlingham.

2/Lt. Eric George Wellesley, 8th Battalion, went missing on 21 December 1915.

At Endell Street Hospital in London, on 5 April, 13950 Private John Perkins, a miner from Washington Station, was questioned by Mostyn Price of the Red Cross Enquiry Section. His short statement just confirmed what was already known:

> On 21 Dec at Bois-Grenier three and a half miles from Armentières it was generally stated the 2nd Lieut Wellesley went out with a bombing party about 3 a.m. to throw bombs into the German front line. When the party returned to our own lines before it became light Lieut Wellesley was missing. Two search parties went out as soon as night came on and they found a strong German patrol occupying the ground where Lieut Wellesley was last seen. That is all that is known about him.

On 15 April at No. 2 Canadian General Hospital, 11855 Lance Corporal Charles Roberts made the following statement:

> He started out with a bombing party of six men near Bois-Grenier. They threw their bombs all right but the Germans almost immediately fired on the party and Mr Wellesley called out to the men to make back to our own trench. They got a little separated. After they got a good distance back he got them together to see if anybody was missing. One man Murphy was missing. And Mr Wellesley went back to search. Meantime Bradley, his servant, had found the missing Murphy up against our own barbed wire, the others all got back to the trenches. When Mr Wellesley failed to return search was made two or three times afterwards. It was for bringing in Murphy and going out by day to search for Mr Wellesley that Pte Codling received the D.C.M. There was a deep ditch running between our and the

> German lines and it is just possible that being wounded Mr Wellesley might have fallen in or got into the ditch which had about five feet of water in it.

In a statement made at the Royal Free Hospital, Grays Inn Road, London, Lieutenant C. Barraclough, who came from Leeds, declared that:

> On or about 21 December, he was close to Wellesley who went out with a fairly large party to patrol at night. It is thought that a German patrol was encountered and that Wellesley divided his men into two parties to try and surround the Germans. This they apparently could not do and Wellesley then tried to bomb the German trenches. Most of the men returned, but Wellesley and a Sergt (name not known) (but in his company) did not return: a search party went out but could find nothing (i.e. not Wellesley wounded nor dead). It was thought by everyone in the Regiment at the time that he must have been taken prisoner.

This last statement is open to a number of questions. On the night in question the informant's battalion were holding the right sub-sector in trenches numbered I.57 to I.61, while 8/Yorkshire Regiment were in the left sub-sector. The battalion War Diary records that Lieutenant Wellesley's patrol left from I.26. So how was Lieutenant Barrowclough near Wellesley, this seems unlikely. The second point is if he was near Wellesley how did Barrowclough get the size of the patrol so wrong. Three men is not a 'fairly large party'. Furthermore, where does the missing sergeant from D Company fit in; certainly 8/Yorkshire Regiment did not report any senior NCO missing that night.

The statement by Private Blenkey was completely dismissed by the Officer Commanding 8/Yorkshire Regiment, who replied to a query about it, that 'the statement, by Private Blenkey is absolutely untrue and without the smallest foundation'. It is highly probable that Blenkey picked up what was a 'latrine rumour' and repeated it for the benefit of the interviewer. Moreover, he appears to have had a genuine fondness for the officer, as noted by the interviewer. These statements show the lengths that the Red Cross were going to trace those missing in action. Names of the missing were circulated in the prisoner of war camps in Germany in the hope that some information might be obtained. But the statements also show how distorted facts became in the trenches.

It is highly probable that many of the battalion officers wrote home with the story of Second Lieutenant Wellesley's loss. Toby Dodgson told Marjorie in these words:

> We had one very unfortunate incident during our last spell in the trenches, which resulted in the loss of Wellesley. He was sent out on a reconnoitring patrol to inspect the enemy's wire and having done this quite successfully without being spotted by the Hun at all, he needs must go and start throwing bombs into their trench, after which they had, of course, to make a hasty retreat at the beginning of which he must have been hit. This all happened at about six in the morning just before it got light, which is all the more foolhardy, as it was impossible to send anyone out to look for him until the following evening. We spent a miserable day wondering if he was lying out there wounded and able to do nothing. However, the next night no trace of him could be found and the Huns were waiting all ready for our patrol, so it looks as though they must have got him, though whether alive or dead it is useless to speculate. Personally, I shall miss him very much as I used to see a lot of him and we had many a cheery game of cards together and the battalion can ill afford to lose officers such as he.

The last piece of information was sent to the next of kin on 3 October 1916:

> Sir,
> I am commanded by the Army Council to thank you for your letter of 21 September to the effect you have received no further information concerning 2nd Lieutenant E.G. Wellesley, 8/Yorkshire Regiment, The Yorkshire Regiment.
>
> The Army Council are in consequence regretfully constrained to conclude that this officer died on or since 21 December, 1915, and I am to express their sympathy with you in your bereavement.
>
> I am to add that the council regret that no information has reached them which would confirm the story that there are any camps of Prisoners of War in Belgium from which British Prisoners of War, officers or men are over any considerable length of time prevented from writing home.

Both battalions were relieved in time to spend Christmas 1915 out of the line but neither War Diary records any mention of a special meal for the men or anything of a festive nature.

The 23rd Division did, however, produce a Christmas magazine named *The Dump*, which was produced by members of the division with a talent for art, poetry and comic writing. It is a reflection on the humour of the times.

Toby Dodgson sent his copy home with these comments:

The Dump magazine was mentioned in Lt. Dodgson's letter.

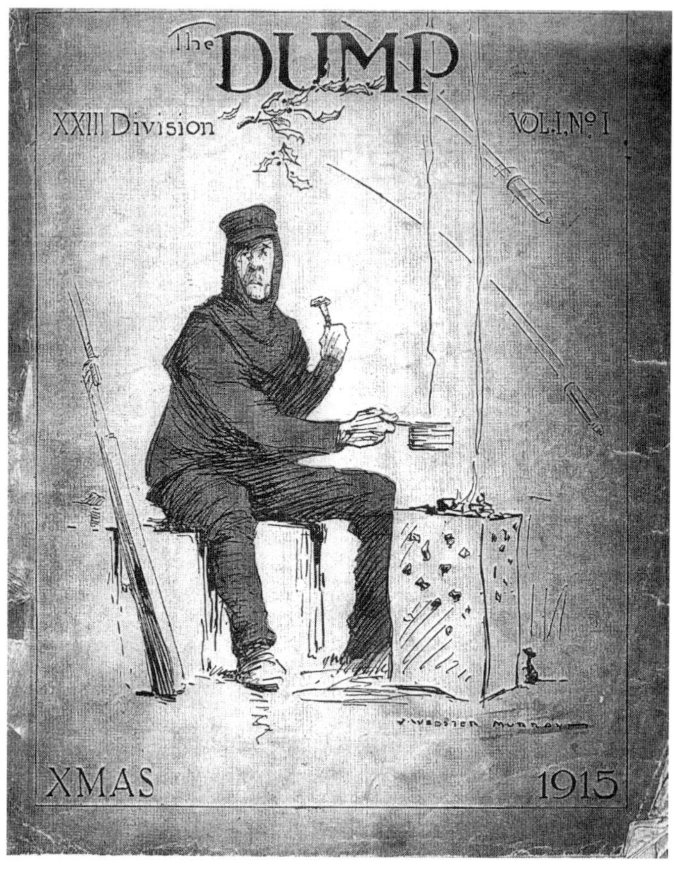

> *The Dump* won't amuse you much, I expect as it is so topical and a lot of it is bad at that. Will you pass it on to Mother; she might like to see it and I have not got another copy.

Some of the officers of 8/Yorkshire Regiment had their arrangements upset by the news they were going back into the line:

> We had arranged to have a select little dinner at Lucienn's tonight – Besly, Simpson, Thompson and myself, but we are in the trenches, so that is off; rather sickening, as it would have been good. I and the red headed Rowley are together in the remains of a farm a few hundred yards behind the front line. There is only one room left inhabitable and in that the rain comes through the ceiling, as there is no roof and the only means of entrance is through the shattered windows which one has to scale as they are some six or seven feet above the ground. The furniture consists of a few relics amongst which we sit with a couple of candles and a smoky brazier.

In preparation for a trench raid, 9/Yorkshire Regiment sent a reconnaissance patrol out under the command of Lieutenant Ronald Tolson, who was wounded, as was 19627 Corporal Matthew Casey. The latter was born in Dublin but resident in South Shields when he enlisted. Unfortunately, he died from his wounds on 29 December at either No. 8 or No. 53 CCS. Both were based in Bailleul, where he is buried in the Communal Cemetery Extension.

On the last night of the year, 17808 Private Thomas O'Neill from Middlesbrough of 8/Yorkshire Regiment died of his wounds at 70 Field Ambulance and was buried in Erquingham–Lys Churchyard extension. So ended the year 1915.

Chapter 4

France, January–June 1916

New Year 1916 started with a bang for 9/Yorkshire Regiment. The two officers and 100 men who had been away from the battalion training for a special operation carried out a raid on the German trenches. For several days prior to the raid the divisional artillery had been employed on wire cutting and bombarding the enemy parapet all along front held by the 23rd Division. Reconnaissance parties noticed that the enemy were becoming more and more alert, and at the risk of the wire not being completely cut, the artillery wire cutting was stopped for two nights prior to the raid:

> The night of 31 December–1 January was still and starlit, the German trenches were about 250 yards from the point of exit from the British trenches. The enemy were very alert and were using, in addition to numerous Very Lights, three searchlights.
>
> At 9.30 p.m. on 31 December a wire cutting party under Second Lieutenant Armitage crossed to the enemy's lines and successfully cut a lane about five feet wide through the enemy's wire. The wire cutting party was left at the wire and the officer returned to our own trenches at 11.30 p.m. and reported that the way was clear to the enemy's parapet and there would be little difficulty crossing the borrow pit.
>
> At 12.15 a.m. the raiding party left our trenches and proceeded to a place of assembly in front of our line. From here the parties crawled very slowly towards the enemy position and on nearing it were met by the wire cutting party, who guided them to the lane which had been cut.
>
> It was necessary in order to ensure success that the raid and the accompanying artillery support should be simultaneous.

2/Lt. William Armitage.

It had consequently been arranged that the infantry attack and artillery should act in accordance with a pre-arranged timetable. The artillery barrage started at 1.33 a.m. and at this moment the enemy's trenches were successfully rushed by the raiding parties. As the parties entered the enemy lines they proceeded at once to bomb right and left of the point of entry.

The right party under the command of Second Lieutenant Gibson found the trench lightly held. This party killed four Germans either with the bomb or the bayonet.

The left party, under the command of Captain Thompson was attacked by the enemy with bombs, but the hostile bombers were driven off. Fifteen Germans were reported to have been bayonetted by the party and it is thought that probably five or ten more were killed exclusive of others who took flight and were driven into the artillery barrage.

About thirty-five of our men in all entered the enemy's trenches. This number was found to be quite sufficient. The parties left the enemy's trenches at 1.48 a.m. bringing their wounded (seven in all) with them. No men were killed. The enemy was undoubtedly surprised and only offered feeble resistance. A password was used and this was found very useful.[1]

One additional fact mentioned in the War Diary of HQ 23rd Division is that three prisoners were reported to have been captured; however, they tried to escape and were killed.[2]

One sad fact about the raid is that a party of Royal Engineers was to accompany the infantry. Earlier that afternoon Lieutenant Rowse, in charge of the sappers, was busy priming the bombs in preparation for the raid. Somehow there was an accident and a bomb exploded. It killed the officer and four men and wounded many others, also destroying the vast majority of the explosive required for dugout destruction. The result of this was that no engineers accompanied the raid.

In his report on the raid the Brigade Commander Brigadier F.S. Dereham wrote:

I consider that the manner in which the attack was carried out reflects great credit on Major Prior who planned it and supervised the training of the men; Captain Thompson, who led the assaulting party; on Lieutenants Laycock and Roberts and all NCOs and men who took part in it. I consider the enterprise has had a very good effect on the men.

Signed F.S. Dereham
Brig. Genl.
Commanding 69th Inf Bde.[3]

The April 1916 issue of the *Green Howards Gazette* contained the news of the issue of gallantry medals to various members of the Raiding Party.

Captain George E. Thompson, Second Lieutenant William H. Armitage and Second Lieutenant Arthur B.H. Roberts all received the Military Cross for their part in leading the raid. For acts of gallantry and devotion to duty in the field the following NCOs and men received the Distinguished Conduct Medal for their part in cutting the wire: 13364 Sergeant E. Crowther, 13272 Private J. Dixon, 11984 Private J. Gething and 11546 Private C.W. Kett. Furthermore, for their work in the enemy trenches, 17889 Corporal W. Hodgson and 14496 Private E.E. Brick received the same medal.

The casualties for the raid are stated to be seven, however, the Battalion War Diary gives one officer died of wounds, one officer wounded, one other rank killed and fourteen other ranks wounded, for the period in the trenches. The dead officer must be Second Lieutenant Bernard Wilkins, who died on 6 January 1916 of wounds received in the retaliatory bombardment. The other rank was 15925 Private Joseph Husband, a 20-year-old who lived at Lingdale, Boosbeck. The only 9/Yorkshire Regiment man traced as wounded is 12151 Private C, Robinson, who arrived at No. 3 CCS on 3 January from 71 Field Ambulance with a GSW in the right shoulder. He was evacuated to the coast on No. 24 Ambulance Train. At the same time, 13476 Private Samuel Somervile of 8/Yorkshire Regiment was admitted with a GSW of the right thigh. On the other hand, not all the wounded were battle casualties. The same day the raid took place, 13777 Private Thomas Hamer, who although born in Manchester had been living and working in South Bank, found himself in confinement awaiting trial by Field General Court Martial for Neglect to the good order of military discipline in that he negligently wounded himself. He was sentenced to fifty-four days field punishment and the second toe of his right foot was amputated.

Having taken over the line from 11/West Yorks and held it for four days without any casualties 8/Yorkshire Regiment, on being relieved, moved back to billets at Rue Marle. While they were out of the line the battalion had a visit from General Babington, who presented the ribbon of the DCM to Private Codling for the gallantry he displayed when on patrol on 21 December.

On 10 January the British artillery placed a barrage on the German lines at 12 noon and at 4.10 p.m. Around 100 high-explosive rounds were fired at the German front-line and support trenches. As soon as the British stopped firing the German guns replied. At 12.20 p.m. they wounded eight men of 8/Yorkshire Regiment. One of the wounded, a Middlesbrough man, 11986 Private James Walsh, arrived at No. 3 CCS in Bailleul from 71 Field Ambulance with a GSW in the buttocks and was evacuated the next day on No. 22 Ambulance Train.[4]

During the same period that 9/Yorkshire Regiment were interchanging with 10/DWR, the reliefs were routine and nothing major occurred until 27 January, when the Germans began intense firing on the trenches at I.31.1 to I.31.4, which was said to be to celebrate the Kaiser's birthday. During the barrage Lieutenant Barrowclough was wounded in the head and during their time in the line four other ranks were killed or died of wounds. All four were buried in Brewery Orchard Cemetery, Bois-Grenier. Another officer wounded at this time was Captain Freeman Atkey, who had been hit in the arm.

The 8/Yorkshire Regiment had a new appointment as Commanding Officer when Lieutenant Colonel E.L Lowdell assumed command on 17 January. However, three days later, on 20 January, he went on leave to England and command passed to Major Vaughan of 1/Worcestershire Regiment.

The appointment was mentioned in a letter to Marjorie from Toby Dodgson:

> We have a new Colonel definitely appointed, who appears to be quite a good sort, though I've not met him personally yet. He was in the Navy in earlier days. Everyone was quite sorry to lose Lush, who really went out of his way to be pleasant. I was playing a poker round with D Company the other night. It's a fine game and has almost entirely taken the place of 'Vingty' amongst us. Incidentally, Besly had some rather nice new tales. 'Do you know why all the nurses are leaving Egypt? They are afraid of becoming mummies!' Secondly … but he told me I couldn't tell you this yet; however it tickles me so I shall though if I thought I should remember it I should keep it till we met. Well, to continue: 'a dear little girl is showing her trousseau to her best friend. Who is much impressed by the wondrous ribboned underwear etc. She 'My Dear these nighties are simply too too, but why do you have all that fur round the bottom?' The dear little girl (replied) 'Oh that's to keep my neck warm.'
>
> They have started a Divisional Theatre now, with a combined cinema and variety show which I went to last night; really awfully well done and all real talent. There are two sergeants who are evidently comedians in civil life and they made everyone scream with laughter. It's a great thing for all the Tommies and it was packed full.

Having moved out to rest they started training bombing and wire-cutting parties with a view to carrying out a possible raid. During the time out at rest the battalion had no casualties at all. Nevertheless, when they took over the line from 2/Northamptonshire Regiment on 22 January they had two killed and two wounded. The two men killed were 12540 Thomas Hornby, who was aged 23 and an iron works bricklayer. The other man was 12542 Robert Hornby. Both were born in Eston and enlisted in Middlesbrough, but it is believed they were not related. The same day at Camiers on the coast in No. 20 General Hospital, Royal Army Medical Corps (RAMC), 13235 Private James Cannell, who was 26 years of age and a labourer in a blast furnace in Grangetown, succumbed to the wounds that he had received some days earlier. On 27 January 8/Yorkshire Regiment were relieved by 10/DWR and moved to billets in Rolanderie.

The same day at the Second Army Grenade and Trench Mortar School based in Téteghem, 13722 Private Joseph Kirkup, who came from Croxdale, near Durham, serving with the 9/Yorkshire Regiment attached to 69/Light Trench Mortar Battery, was loading a Stokes mortar. Also present was a group of English and Italian officers. There was a premature explosion of a bomb. Kirkup made this statement:

> On Saturday 27 January I was firing rapid from a Stokes Trench Mortar at the School, Teteghem, when the first or second shell burst on leaving the gun, wounding me in the face and hands. There were several British and Italian officers present at the time of the accident. [Signed] J. Kirkup.

As in all cases of accidental wounding, a Court of Inquiry was assembled and a medical officer had to write a report, to see if there was any blame on a particular individual. Major W.R. Armstrong, RAMC, No. 15 CCS, wrote the report in this case:

> The above man states he received orders to fire six rounds rapid.
> He was acting No. 1 of the Gun Team.
> He placed the first shell in the gun and it was fired.
> He was placing the second shell into the gun when he was wounded.
> He is of the opinion that he may have placed No. 2 shell into the gun too quickly or, that the cartridge container may have burst.
> He has been on the same kind of gun for six or seven months. And has never had any accident before.
> He has been on Trench Mortars since March 1916.
> I removed this morning from his face the enclosed which seems to be the cap of the cartridge used in this gun.
>
> W.R. Armstrong
> Major
> R.A.M.C
> For, O.C. No. 15 C.C.S.

The Court of Inquiry assembled on 28 January 1917. The President of the Court was Captain F.J. Thompson, 1/East Surrey Regiment, with Captain C.E.L. Watkins, 2/KOYLI, and Lieutenant B. Clarke, 17/Sherwood Foresters. They called three witnesses who were present at the time.

The first witness was Lieutenant E.S. Porter, 12/King's Liverpool Regiment, who stated:

> At Teteghem on the afternoon of 27th, I was in charge of the N.C.O.s and men of the Trench Mortar wing which paraded at 2 p.m. for live firing. About 3.20 p.m. we were proceeding with the rapid firing practice and Private Kirkup was loading the mortar. I was standing about ten yards away and on the first round being fired I heard an unusual noise in addition to the explosion of the cartridge. I saw that Private Kirkup had received slight injuries on the left side of the nose and in the left hand. There was a premature explosion of the shell and the gun was not damaged in any way. This practice was being carried out at a range of 360 yards. I afterwards recovered a blind round which had fallen 100 yards from the mortar – the top of the guide of this round had a small piece of metal snapped off it. E.S. Porter 12/King's Liverpool Regiment.

The second witness called was L/13667 Acting Company Sergeant Major William Spencer, 1/Royal Fusiliers. He added this testimony to that of the lieutenant:

> At Teteghem, on the afternoon of the 27th inst. I was in charge of the squad to which Private Kirkup belonged. We commenced the rapid firing practice at about 3.20 p.m. The gun being loaded by Private Kirkup. After firing the first shell, Private Kirkup shouted, 'get out,' I then perceived he was wounded and went to assist him. Six rounds were prepared for this practice but though I only heard the report of one round being fired four rounds only were found in the emplacement after the accident.

The third witness was 24757 Lance Corporal George W. Slater, 13/DLI attached 68 LTMB. His statement was to the point:

> At Teteghem on the afternoon of the 27th inst: about 3.20 p.m. I was performing the duties of No. 2 of the detachment to which Private Kirkup belonged. It was my duty to hand the shells to Private Kirkup who loaded the mortar. On the word 'Fire,' being given Private Kirkup had one shell in his hand loaded the mortar. I handed him a second shell which he

> appeared to load too quickly. I heard Private Kirkup shout, 'get out,' and then noticed that he was wounded and went to his assistance. I heard the report only being fired and there was no premature explosion.

The final statement was made by the President of the Court of Inquiry Captain Thompson:

> The Court having carefully considered the evidence, are of the opinion that the accident was due to the impact of the two shells carried by Private Kirkup's attempt to load the mortar too quickly and that no blame can be attached to anyone.
>
> F.J. Thompson Capt President
> 1/E Surrey Regt

Private Joseph Kirkup was evacuated from No. 15 CCS to No. 13 General Hospital at Boulogne and from there on the Hospital Ship *Brydel* to England, where he went to Highfield Auxiliary Military Hospital at Knotty Ash, Liverpool. Here he spent seventy-four days before he was sent to the Command Depot at Ripon. Eventually, he re-joined the regiment on 1 August 1917.

Also on 27 January, 14205 Private Herbert Little, a coal miner from Willington, was outside a dugout that had two other men inside. A shell landed very close to the post and blew Herbert over; it also buried the two men in the dugout. Herbert picked himself up, and although he was shaken, he immediately set to and started to dig them out. He was eventually awarded the Military Medal, the following October, for his action that day in showing great coolness and devotion to duty under fire. On the night of 30 January, the battalion was stood to and ordered to be ready to move as 10/DWR were going to raid the German trenches. The enemy, however, had patrols out the raid was cancelled. Then on 31 January 8/Yorkshire Regiment took over from 10/DWR in the front line. This tour was quiet, although they did have three men wounded, one of them self-inflicted.

On 2 February, Toby Dodgson now sent word home that he was leaving C Company:

> You will be interested to hear that I have been appointed second in command of B Company. I don't know whether it will mean a third star: probably not, as they have a nasty way out here of giving you a job without the accompanying kudos. Anyway it is a change for the better. Of course I was sorry to leave C Company as I had been there ever since the start and knew all the men, but the Mess was awful. Captain Richardson commands

2/Lt. Harry L. Oakley's pictures were published in *The Bystander* in 1916. He became a well-known artist after the war.

> this company – a funny old bird, an awful grouser and a terrific bore. There are only three other members at present: Miller the signalling officer, Oakley (who draws and did those silhouettes amongst other things) and another harmless sub. We are in the trenches again and the weather has gone much colder, though it is still wonderfully fine.

He only had to wait a month and on 4 March 1916 he was gazetted as a captain and got his third star.

The 9/Yorkshire Regiment started February in the front line, where between 1 and 4 according to the War Diary they had two killed and two wounded. However, *Soldiers Died in the Great War* shows that 14738 Private Joseph Davies from West Hartlepool fell on 2 February. Furthermore, 3/8805 Private John Boyle from Middlesbrough and 13502 Private Robert Trotter, a Ryhope resident, were both killed the next day. All three lie today close together but not side by side in Plot III of Brewery Orchard Cemetery, Bois-Grenier. On relief by 11/West Yorkshire Regiment the battalion went into billets at Rue Delettree and from there four days later to Jesus Farm.

The 69 Brigade was now the Divisional Reserve. The 8/Yorkshire Regiment, having been replaced in the line by 10/Northumberland Fusiliers, moved back to Hallobeau, where they started a bomb and machine gun school. On 14 February the move south began, and that day the whole of 69 Brigade marched to

Vieux Berquin, en route to Army Reserve. Two days earlier, on 12 February, 8/Yorkshire Regiment had sent a billeting party, under command of Lieutenant Pickering, to report to the staff captain of 102 (Tyneside Scottish) Brigade in Steenbecque. His party consisted of his batman a cook, a storeman and five NCOs. They would take over the billets for the battalion and lead the various companies to the right place on their arrival. The battalion paraded at 8.45 a.m. and marched off fifteen minutes later. Each battalion was allotted an additional five general service wagons for extra baggage and four blanket wagons. They arrived at Vieux Berquin by 3.45 p.m., and when compiling the War Diary the Adjutant was pleased to report that 'there were no stragglers'. The route march continued the next day to Steenbecque, where they arrived at 12.30 p.m. Here they had trouble in obtaining billets. What had the billeting party been doing? Here the bathing and sanitary conditions were bad and they had to spend time putting things right. The usual training programme commenced and as they were further back now a battalion run was included. On 17 February Second Lieutenant M.G. Hume-Wright reported for duty.

Of 9/Yorkshire Regiment during this period nothing can be written as their War Diary simply states, 'Camp' or 'Billets'.

On 22 February the old Long Lee Enfield rifles of 8/Yorkshire Regiment were at last replaced with the Short Lee Enfield and the long bayonet. They then marched to Neuf Berquin in a snowstorm.

At this stage of the war the Germans had launched their offensive against Verdun and their daily efforts were increasing, so much so that General Joffre came to the conclusion that the Germans were attempting to break through. Joffre then asked for a relief of the French Tenth Army in the 10 miles from Ransart–Arras-Vimy Ridge–Souchez, which was taken over by British divisions. This was achieved by 14th and 5th Divisions extending the left of First Army northwards and the 23rd, 46th and 51st extending the right of Third Army southwards. From the point of view of the 23rd Division, they had been moved from the Bois-Grenier sector into Army Reserve and were now under orders to move again.

The comfortable life in Army Reserve came to an end on 28 February when orders were received at brigade headquarters that 69 Brigade would move to the Bruay area the following day. The orders for such a move are quite lengthy and complex, and in order that the reader may understand how such a move is organised are produced below:

69 Infantry Brigade
OPERATION ORDER No. 35
Secret 29/2/16

1. The Brigade and unmounted personnel of 101, 102, and 128 Field Companies, R.E. will move today 29th February by rail from STEENBECQUE Railway Station to the BRUAY area in accordance with the attached Time Table 'A'.
2. Advance billeting parties consisting of 1 Officer and 1 O.R per Battalion will assemble at Brigade Headquarters at 7.a.m. today the 29th inst and will proceed to BRUAY by Ambulance wagon and on arrival will report at Headquarters IV Corps (near Bruay) Three additional billeting parties of 11 West Yorkshire R, 8th Yorkshire R and 9th Yorkshire R.; each will proceed by the first train and report on arrival at destination to the Brigade Major 69th Infantry Brigade.
3. Each man will carry one blanket, the second blanket and surplus baggage will be packed ready for removal by 8 a.m. this morning, at which time a motor lorry will be available for each unit to convey baggage etc, to STEENBECQUE Railway Station where it will be loaded on a goods train and will follow the Brigade. Each Unit will leave a loading party of 1 N.C.O. and 8 men who will travel to Bruary in the goods train. The loading parties will be under the command of an Officer to be detailed by the 8/Yorkshire Regiment; he will report at Brigade Head Quarters at 7 a.m. today.
4. Transport will march as follows:-
   Starting point J.2.a.1.7. (Map 36a). The head of the column will pass the starting point at 8.45 a.m.
   Order of march:-
   (a) 1st Line Transport and riding horses of units of the Brigade in the following order :-
       10th West Riding R.
       11th West Yorkshire R.
       8th Yorkshire R.
       9th Yorkshire R.
   (b) The riding horses and the whole of the Transport of the Brigade Headquarters.
   (c) 2nd Line Transport of Units same order as above, the head passing the starting point at 9 a.m.

The Brigade transport Officer will himself be in charge of 1st Line Transport and will detail an officer to be in charge of 2nd Line.

Route:-

ST VENANT – LILLERS – BRUARY

Billeting Area for Transport:-

HESDIQUEL – HALLICOURT- RUITZ

5 A motor bus will call at Head Quarters of A/69 Trench Mortar Battery at 8 a.m. today, it will take all the ammunition of the Battery to the Ordnance Dump at MORBECQUE.

Hand carts in charge of Battery will be returned to the Dump at 7.30 a.m.

Hand carts in charge of the Battery will be returned to the Ordnance Dump at 7 a.m. today, the men taking them there will proceed direct to the Station on completion of duty and rejoin their Units there. The officer Commanding A/69 Trench Mortar Battery will report at Brigade Head Quarters at 7.30 a.m. today.

6. Rations for today may be carried on the man or on a cooker (the distance to BRUARY is about 29 miles).
7. The Officer Commanding the 9th Yorkshire R. will detail a Captain to be present at STEENBEQUE Railway Station to superintend the entraining.
8. The G.O.C. will travel on the first train.

Capt A/Brigade Major
69th Infantry Brigade

As the orders stated, 8/Yorkshire Regiment entrained at 8.30 a.m. and after a short train ride detrained at Camblain-Châtelaine at 10.10 a.m., they then had a three-hour trudge along the French Pave. They arrived in Ruitz at 1 p.m., where the 8th and 9/Yorkshire Regiments were both billeted, taking over from 1/King's Royal Rifles. The battalion transport, which had travelled by road, eventually re-joined at 6 p.m. The next day, 1 March, was spent cleaning equipment and doing some musketry. That day Toby Dodgson wrote home again:

> I am afraid letters will be rather erratic at present as we are on the move again – no peace for the wicked! Thank goodness the weather has improved and yesterday was a ripping fresh day with quite a warm sun. There are some quite pleasant hills around here and the march yesterday after the train was quite exhilarating. It is a relief to see some decent country after the eternal flatness of our last environment.

Having moved into a new corps, the IV Corps Commander, Lieutenant General Sir Henry Wilson, carried out an inspection of 69 Brigade.

On 3 March the training continued but the Brigade Commander and three of the battalion Commanding Officers went up to the line held by the 17th French Division. Two days later the Company Commanders went up to the sector they would take over. This happened on 6 March when 9/Yorkshire Regiment took over from the French in the left sub-sector of the Souchez sector. During their four days in the line here they had two men wounded.

In the meantime, 8/Yorkshire Regiment moved to billets in the Servins District with headquarters and two companies in Gouy-Servins and the other two companies in Petit Servins.

Yet again the letters of Toby Dodgson shed light on the battalion movements at this time:

> 6 March 1916
> We marched away from our last place this morning, with snow falling quite heavily, but after about quarter of an hour it cleared up and the sun came out and made us very warm. I enjoyed the tramp very much, about half way we climbed up along hill which gave us a splendid view from the top, where we halted for lunch on the outskirts of a wood.

Later in the letter he described his new billet:

> We are now billeted in the most extraordinary place that must, once upon a time have been a fine chateau, but all the windows have been bricked up, every sort of fixture, down to the mantelpieces, removed and generally it looks as though no one has inhabited it for years. It is fitted up with makeshift beds and has the appearance of a very dirty barracks. I am fed up with this snow. It does make everything in such a mess and it came down like anything just as we were getting here.[5]

The next day they were to take over the centre sector of the brigade front. In this part of the line the 23rd Division had three battalions in the line and one in support, unlike Bois-Grenier where it had been two battalions in the line, one in support and one in reserve. At 7 p.m. that night, in a snowstorm 8/Yorkshire Regiment moved out of their billets and proceeded up to the line. The takeover was completed by 3 a.m. Each man was carrying 300 rounds of ammunition and the battalion had been issued with 2,000 grenades. The brigade held the line from Ersatz Trench on the right to the Souchez River and was disposed as follows:

Right Battalion	11/West Yorkshire Regiment
Centre Battalion	8/Yorkshire Regiment
Left Battalion	9/Yorkshire Regiment.[6]

Over the next few days, the German infantry were inactive but their artillery shelled the trenches during the morning, and on 9 March caused three casualties. In a short letter home Toby quickly gave a very brief description of conditions: 'We are again in the trenches and having a fairly thin time of it. All this snow is the limit and makes it bitterly cold. Our present bit of the line is as big a contrast to what we had previously as you could imagine. It makes me realise to the full how good our old trenches were.'

The command of 69 Brigade changed on 8 March when Brigadier Dereham handed over command to Lieutenant Colonel T.S. Lambert from 2/East Lancashire Regiment, who was very soon promoted to brigadier. That morning 9/Yorkshire Regiment was relieved by 10/DWR and moved back to billets in Villers-au-Bois, where they spent two days prior to replacing 1/Sherwood Foresters in the support lines at Notre Dame de Lorette.

Likewise, at 9 p.m. on the evening of 10 March, 8/Yorkshire Regiment were replaced in the line by 2/East Lancashire Regiment. They proceeded to the billets at Gouy-Servins and spent two days cleaning up both men and equipment. This gave Toby Dodgson time to write a long letter home, giving descriptions of the conditions in this new sector:

> We got out of the trenches a couple of days ago after a rotten time. It was the most arduous time we've had and a great change from anything we'd done before. The weather was awful: we left our billets at about six in the evening with snow falling fast and were not in position until about 2.30 a.m. and the snow had not stopped even then. It was about a six mile march. Along the road and then a communication trench over two miles long and hilly at that. We finally found ourselves in a trench (so called by courtesy only) perched on top of a hill, with the Bosch sitting also on top of a hill about fifty yards, and in some places only ten yards away. Morning disclosed that we were in 'some' position. It looked just like Switzerland and they would have been fine skiing slopes. From where we were we could see a tremendous way, as the ground fell away sharply behind us and to our left, so that we looked right down on top of the line. The trench was the worst thing I've seen: our accommodation for five officers was one hole in the ground, about twenty feet below ground level, which you had to descend to backward down a sort of mineshaft. The said hole was certainly not more than 6' x 10' and here we slept and did everything. You couldn't cook,

except on a Tommy cooker and water was very scarce, as every drop had to be carried from the bottom of that damned hill. The men had a rotten time as there were practically no dug outs for them and many of them never got a drop of hot tea all the time they were in. It snowed again the second day we were in and thank goodness they relieved us on the fourth night and that was about as bad as the rest of it. We got back to these billets at 5 a.m.! Heavens! Bed was nice and I slept without winking from six till four in the afternoon and got up for dinner.

Yesterday, Besly and I went over to the chateau at the other place we were and damn me if some blasted Hun didn't bomb us from the skies and fairly put the wind up us. We were riding through a village and saw five aeroplanes high up. The first bomb fell quite close and made the most hideous noise coming down. I may mention that this visit was for the benefit of Besly entirely! Anyhow we do manage to enjoy ourselves when we are out of the trenches, and I have been quite liking the war since we came to these parts: the people are so much more pleasant than those sour looking Flemish. Later, we moved again today and are now back where we were before. It has been a splendid day – hot and sunny. It is a treat to feel some warmth in the air. Have you seen,[7] Oakley's silhouettes in the 'Bystander' of 8 March? You will recognise Jennings leading his platoon up a communication.[8]

As Captain Dodgson stated, on 12 March the battalion marched to Bruay, where company and platoon training was carried out and the Divisional Bath Unit was available to the men. They left Bruay at 12 noon on 18 March and marched to Hersin. From there, the next day, they moved into the left sub-sector of the Angres III sector where the trenches were taken over from 24/Royal Fusiliers. This relief was conducted in daylight, and furthermore without casualties. Toby Dodgson got a letter away to Marjorie about the billets they had just left:

We weren't a bit keen on coming into the firing line again, as we had had a cheery time at the last place. We were billeted next door to one of the mines which was most convenient, as they have splendid hot baths, which I was very glad of as I'd not had one since I left England! Then we made the acquaintance of the engineer of the mines, who was very friendly and had two daughters who had been to school in England and spoke English quite well. They had a hard tennis court which we went to play on. It wasn't too good and the net had no tape and the balls did not bounce, but it was good fun all the same. (This was at Bully).[9]

However, having taken over during the afternoon, the Germans started firing rifle grenades into the British trenches; this resulted in three men being wounded. Two of them, 14140 Corporal William Barker, who when he enlisted was resident at Easington, and 14686 Private George Shakeshaft from South Bank, having been evacuated to No. 58 (West Riding) CCS, both died from their wounds.

Private Walter Henry Evetts, from Middlesbrough, was killed in action on 24 March 1916.

On 20 March the German Artillery shelled the British front line most of the day, and then at 3.05 p.m. British artillery and trench mortars replied with the result that the enemy ceased fire. That is until 7 p.m., when they opened a very heavy fire on the front line and battalion headquarters that lasted for half an hour. British artillery replied and by 7.45 p.m. all was quiet. Alas! The shelling had resulted in five more wounded. Although evacuated, 11529 Private Dennis Manning from Middlesbrough remained alive until he reached one of the Casualty Clearing Stations in Lillers, where he died from his wounds, 12704 Private Arthur Hawkswell from Whitby lived to make it to a general hospital at Camiers on the coast, where he too passed away. The improvement work to the trenches was hampered. First, on 21 March there was difficulty in obtaining RE material for revetments and duck boards for the trench floor. The next night rain fell and on the third night a heavy fall of snow hindered work even further. The two companies in the front line were relieved by those in support and reserve. The handover completed, a German rifle grenade landed in the trench and wounded three men and killed 13401 Private Walter Evetts, from South Bank, and 13748 Private Mark O'Brien, who lived in Grangetown.

On 23 March Toby wrote again once again, complaining about the weather and conditions in the trenches:

> We are in the front line again and, as luck would have it, there was a heavy fall of snow again. It was sickening to see all the roads wet and muddy again and now snow on the top. It is the limit.

More snow fell during the night of 25 March, which was followed the next day by the Germans shelling the British trenches throughout the day. Next day it was the turn of the companies in support to receive their share of the Germans' attention. The communications trenches were damaged and a machine gun and its post were put out of action. This German activity did not go unpunished and retaliation took place. Artillery, trench mortars, rifle grenades, all fired at the Germans. This action was repeated a few days later and instructions for this were issued by 69 Brigade Headquarters.

Minor Tactical Operations to take place on Friday 31 March
Object To intimidate enemy in Salient M.20.c and Northern parts of M.26.a. at a time they usually fire numerous in and around Bully craters.
Action
(1). Trench Mortars. Time 5.10 a.m.
(a) Two French Mortars fire 2 aerial torpedoes each,
Targets M.26.a.4.5.
M26.a.7.7.
(b) Three Medium Trench Mortars fire 3 round each,
Targets M.20.c.3.0. (two mortars)
M.20.c.7½.1.
(c) Three Light Mortars fire 5 rounds each.
Targets German Saphead, M.20.c.2.1.
German Saphead, M26.a.2.9.
Front parapet, M20.c.4½.2.
(2) Infantry Time 5.12 a.m.
Four grenades rifles (near M.20.c.1.2.) Target M.20.c. 4½.2
Four grenades rifles (near M.25.b.8.8) Target M.20.c.3.0

Each grenade rifle to fire 3 rifle grenades only.
All other personnel in Angres 3 except actual sentries to be under cover, ready for action if necessary.
The sentries in Bully Craters to be temporarily withdrawn under cover from 5 a.m. to 5.20 a.m.
(3) Artillery.
Battery will not fire unless assistance is asked for by O.C. Angres 3 in consequence of retaliation by Germans. Targets in each case will be M.20.d.1.2 to M.25.d.0.6.[10]

Captain,
Brigade Major,
69 Infantry Brigade.

The last mention of 9/Yorkshire Regiment was in support trenches at Notre Dame de Lorette. Here they were replaced by 15/London Regiment and moved to huts at Bois de Bouvigny, followed by a further move next day to Camblain-Châtelaine. They spent ten days here doing the usual training and it was on 25 March they relieved 10/DWR in Angres II sector. The trenches in this sector had been well laid out by the French; several excellent, long and deep communication trenches running from Bully-Grenay right to the top of hill to the front-line trenches. A fair number of deep dugouts had been excavated in the chalky soil.

Five days later 10/DWR returned and 9/Yorkshire Regiment moved to billets at Fosse 10.

After the bombardment on 31 March, the rest of the day was described as 'quiet' in the 8/Yorkshire Regiment War Diary. This gave Toby Dodgson a chance to write a very long letter to Marjorie in which he described in some detail the events of the month and in particular taking over from the French:

> I expect you have guessed from the information published in the newspapers a few days ago that at that we had an extra long relief and four rotten days in the trenches. We were taking over from the French in the Souchez sector. It was very interesting and at times distinctly amusing. The French are perfectly amazing; so utterly unlike us and they certainly have disadvantages. They are the dirtiest people you can imagine. I couldn't describe to you the filth of the billets we took over from them. Their sanitary arrangements are conspicuous both to nose and eye by their absence. Why they don't contract the most horrid diseases I can't imagine. But our experience of their trenches was a real eye-opener. I was very interested because we went over the country where there was all that tremendously heavy fighting last May, when the French advanced and took Carency, Souchez and the Notre Dame de Lorette Spur. It was an eerie feeling marching down that road where four or five miles back from the present line, the country is utterly blasted and desolate. It was all so cold and still in the snow, so utterly dead, while everywhere was that faint smell of decay which we are becoming so accustomed to out here. Souchez which anyone can see must have been a ripping little place, lying snugly in the valley, with a stream running through it and pleasant woods round about, is now nothing more than heaps of stones. There isn't an upright wall. Even what was once the road is now no more than a footpath between piles of bricks and rubbish? The whole valley made a great impression on me; not only were there no houses standing but all the trees were blasted and whole woods reduced to a collection of stumps.

The French guides who met us and showed us the way up to the front line were comical to a degree. The whole performance was reminiscent of some extravagant scene from a comic opera. They jabbered and laughed, lost the way as though it was the most natural thing in the world and explained in dramatic sentences the state of things prevailing in the trenches. 'Ne tirez jamais,' they kept on impressing on us.

It was not until the next morning that we could see our position. We found ourselves on top this damned hill which was a maze of trench and shell holes; our front line trench a rotten shallow ditch that exposed you from the waist upwards nearly everywhere, with the most feeble wire in front of it, You can imagine our amazement when, as the daylight came, we saw great fat Huns strolling about not more than fifty yards away and, in places where the listening post reduced the distance to ten or fifteen yards, there was soon a rapid exchange of questions and answers. It proved to be as the Frenchman said: no one fired off their rifle, and when they were going to let off torpedoes, etc., the Hun gave us the tip. I didn't like it a bit and felt much more unsafe than if we dared not put our heads above the parapet. Still, there was nothing else to be done until we had deepened the trench and made it reasonably safe. But aren't the French extraordinary? Apparently they just sat there and did damn all: then one fine day, when it suited him, the Hun would play dirty and the Frenchman would get his blood up and fight magnificently. The Hun is very anxious for English newspapers, so they threw him some over for his edification while he supplied our men with cigars, etc. One of their most bitter topics was the artillery: they would kill all theirs if we would do the same, etc.

Of course it's all different now and we've had pamphlets galore on fraternising with the enemy from the ……. staff! Yet at the same time they winked at it, knowing it was the only sensible thing to do under those circumstances and now they try and insinuate that the officers and men did not do their duty. I think our staff are utterly mad. I've never known such sheaves of pamphlets and ridiculous orders come round. Everybody is simply fed up to the teeth with it all. I am at last beginning to think we shall lose the war. Pages and pages of rot about whether a man wears his mess tins in his pack or tied on somewhere else, and another hundred other stupid footling similar things. We are in support trenches now, about five hundred yards behind the firing line. The Battalion is in the trenches for twenty-one days, two companies in the front line and two behind, so that we relieve each other. I shall be very glad when it's over and I hope we may get back to Bruary for a week or so.

April 1916 started with 9/Yorkshire Regiment still in billets at Fosse 10, where they remained until 4 April. At 8.30 p.m. they took over trenches in the front line on the right of 8/Yorkshire Regiment. That night 8/Yorkshire Regiment could hear lots of enemy transport on the move behind their lines. Either, on 1 April[11] or 2 April, at 3.25 p.m.[12] a French aeroplane was shot down by the German anti-aircraft guns and fell into the British lines about 600 yards behind 8/Yorkshire Regiment Headquarters. The pilot was found dead in the wreckage and the observer died a few minutes after being found.[13] On the evening of 2 April German artillery launched an intensive barrage on the Souchez sector, where they caught a battalion relief taking place. The 23rd Divisional howitzer battery replied for half an hour. The enemy barrage had inflicted six casualties on 8/Yorkshire Regiment. During their tour 9/Yorkshire Regiment recorded nine wounded. On 10 April 9/Yorkshire Regiment returned to the billets in Fosse 10, where the usual cleaning up and training took place. That day at 4.29 p.m. 68 Brigade laid smoke bombs across their front and the divisional artillery laid an intense barrage on the enemy trenches. During the day 8/Yorkshire Regiment had two more men wounded one of whom, 13209 Private Thomas Morrison subsequently died from his wounds. The next few days were generally quiet but on the third day the Germans were busy with their trench mortars. Then on 14 April one more soldier was wounded and two, 12307 Private Stephen Bennett from Grangetown and 15209 Private Frank Robinson, who came from Layerthorps near York, were both killed.

On the morning of 16 March German rifle grenadiers were busy and 15208 Private William Dale was killed and four other ranks wounded. In an unusual daylight relief at 2 p.m., 2/HLI arrived and took over the front line and 8/Yorkshire Regiment marched back to Coupigny, where they arrived at 6 p.m. They only spent one night here and at 12 noon the battalion marched off en route for Divion.

The 9/Yorkshire Regiment was also on the move. Leaving their billets at Fosse 10 on 16 April, they moved to Hersin, then on to Camblain-Châtelaine, or Charlie Chaplin as it was known to the troops. The period 20–25 April was spent in Reclinghem, where manoeuvres took place. Also available to the brigade were the divisional baths and a general clean-up of clothing and equipment took place. As part of 69 Brigade training a mock attack on the village of Romy was carried out. All levels of training took place, starting with platoon, then company and battalion on the training area. On 22 April, while the battalion were engaged in 'interior economy' and cleaning up, Toby Dodgson wrote to Marjorie:

> We got back to this little place a few days ago and very nice it is – quite out of the world surrounded by fine, high rolling country which reminds me rather of the Wiltshire Downs only every inch of it is cultivated. We are doing manoeuvres and so far they've not given us a moment to ourselves, which is pretty rotten after a long spell in the trenches. My hair is longer than most musicians and I am badly in need of a bath, which I don't see much prospect of getting. The weather has been vile; bitter cold winds and perpetual storms of rain so we have not been able to appreciate the country much yet.

He wrote again the next day and by now he was really sick of training:

> 23rd April 1916 (Easter Sunday)
> I am awfully fed up with life as we are having a stinking time doing manoeuvres (so called). Today, Easter Sunday, we shall have done the best part of ten hours parades by the time this evening's night operations are over. I think everybody is looking forward to the time when we get back into the trenches away from all this tommyrot.

On 25 April the move back to the front line commenced with 9/Yorkshire Regiment marching to Febvin-Palfart and then on to Hersin, where they spent eight days in billets. The 8/Yorkshire Regiment were also on the move; they marched to Pernes railway station and were carried to Barlin and from there on foot to Fosse 10, where they took over billets. The whole of 69 Brigade was then employed on working parties on the Maestre line and in the Souchez sector. As 8/Yorkshire Regiment left the training area on 28 April Toby Dodgson wrote to his mother:

> We had quite a pleasant week back at a delightful little village in very nice country, and the weather during the last four or five days has been too glorious. I am having a very strenuous time as we are so short of Officers again. What with people sick and away on courses of instruction, it is extraordinary how they dwindle down to nothing. My Company Commander is going on leave today, which will leave me in charge of the Company, without a single Subaltern.

The next day he wrote once more to Marjorie. In this letter he sounds really depressed and expresses his feelings for the Brigade Commander, who being a regular soldier was affecting the morale of his Kitchener volunteers:

> 29 April 1916
> We are having a rotten time or I should have written before this. This new Brigadier that we've got is a perfect fiend, a regular slave driver, and he never has a good word for anyone; nothing is ever right. Everybody is fed up to the teeth; it is knocking all the spirit out of the men and demoralising the officers. God, they are fools. We've not a chance of winning the war and they had much better make peace on the best terms they can. That little village, Lavies that we were at would have been delightful if only we had been left in peace, as it was right out of the way; no motor lorries or noises and the people were charming. I had a room in the local *'estaminet'*. 'Au Vin Blanc' and they brought me coffee in the morning and couldn't do enough.
>
> My Company Commander is going on leave today, lucky devil and I am left alone with the Company, all others being either sick or on courses of instruction, so don't expect much in the way of correspondence. We are in some miners' cottages near a pit (Fosse 10) which is just behind Bully: not altogether a healthy spot, as the Hun likes to drop nasty shells on the mine which, however, is still worked by night. We are supposed to be here till the 2nd and then go back to Bruay for a week and then the trenches once more.

On 29 April, 19591 Lance Corporal Arthur Malton, from Seaton Delaval, was killed. Or was he, for the War Diary states 'one other rank accidentally drowned'. This is confirmed in Annex VII to 69 Brigade War Diary for April 1916. However, no report or court of inquiry evidence has come to light.

Lance Corporal Arthur Malton was killed in action on 29 March 1916.

Some of those who had been wounded and evacuated made the final sacrifice far from the front. On 2 April 3/8779 Private Thomas Ivers died from wounds at home in Leeds and was buried in Leeds Roman Catholic Cemetery. On 19 April, 15920 Private John Sidwell, who was born at Adelaide, South Australia, died from wounds at No. 2 Stationary Hospital in Rouen. This was followed on 27 April by the death in an English hospital of 19812 Private Frank Green, who at the time of the 1911 Census was a baker's porter near his home in Bingham, Nottinghamshire. His body was taken home to be buried in the local cemetery.

German artillery was responsible for many casualties.

So April passed to May and the early part of the month was spent in billets behind the front. On 12 May 9/Yorkshire Regiment replaced 2/HLI in the trenches at Bully-Grenay. Here they noted that the sector was not so quiet as it had been previously. The German artillery was now concentrating on anti-battery fire against the British gun positions and billets in the rear.

During this tour two other ranks died of wounds, two were killed and nine suffered wounds. The first to be wounded on 12 May was 24400 Private Harry Wardman from Sowerby near Thirsk. He had not been in France very long, having arrived sometime after 1 January as a reinforcement. The second man to be wounded, on 13 May, 14619 Private John Owen Wright, was also from Thirsk. Both these men were evacuated to No. 22 CCS at Bruay, where they finally succumbed to their wounds. The next day 17747 Private William Ellmor from Silksworth, near Sunderland, was killed, and on the following day 14942 Private Alfred Jones from Leeds was another added to the battalion Roll of Honour.

The 8/Yorkshire Regiment too returned to the line on 12 May. That day they marched out of Coupigny at 9 a.m. and marched to Bully-Grenay. A Company went into billets at Corons d'Aix, B Company went to Mechanics Trench, while C Company and half of D Company had billets in Bully-Grenay. The remainder of D Company took over the trenches at Metro Cap De Pont. From these positions they sent working parties forward daily to assist those in the front line. Between 13 and 17 May the whole battalion less B Company were able to bath. On 17 May the battalion took over the Angres II sector from 9/Yorkshire Regiment. They recorded that the enemy were fairly quiet except at M.20.1, which they fired rifle grenades and trench mortars against. The 69th Light Trench Mortar Battery (68 LTMB) replied and suppressed the German fire. However, it was too late for 14821 Private Charles Claydon of South Bank and 15947 Private Joseph Smith of Jarrow, who were both killed in action. A third man, 10749 John Barnett of Whitby, reached a hospital at Le Havre but they were unable to save his life and today he lies in the town's Saint Marie Cemetery.

At 6 a.m. on the morning of 19 May the British fired a mine just in front of the German front line at a minute past the hour. Trench mortar batteries, Stokes guns and machine guns fired at pre-arranged targets, and one minute later four batteries of the divisional artillery fired three salvoes and at three minutes past the hour all ceased fire. There was no reply from the enemy, however, later in the morning there was trench mortar activity and shrapnel was fired into Bully-Grenay.

While 9/Yorkshire Regiment was out of the line in billets at Bully-Grenay on 22 May they were unfortunate to have a German shell hit one of the company officers' messes. One officer, Lieutenant William Armitage MC, was killed outright and Second Lieutenant Richard Bethell was badly wounded and subsequently died. The incident would have been worse if it had not been that others in the mess had just gone down to the cellar, as the room was completely wrecked by the explosion. It wasn't only the British that suffered casualties; at that time Bully-Grenay was still inhabited by a number of French civilians carrying out their ordinary occupations. During the barrage a number of them became casualties.[14] From Bully-Grenay the battalion moved to Verdrel on 30 May.

The 69 Brigade had now been in the Lens–Souchez area for around three months and had been fortunate to spend much of the time when not in the line in villages, where training could be carried out. Over the winter when they were in the Armentières sector hardly any training had been possible owing to the weather conditions and because when in support the battalions were required to supply working parties to support those in the line. In the present sector training opportunities were more frequent as the brigade was not constantly in the line.

Having spent time at Fosse 10, where they came under enemy shellfire and incurred some wounded, 8/Yorkshire Regiment were able to get all companies through the baths: A, B and C at Sains en Gohelle and D Company at Bully-Grenay. Then, on 26 May they returned to the Angres II Sector. The next day was described as 'fairly lively', the Germans firing guns, trench mortars and rifle grenades, which breached the British parapet in a number of places. This fire resulted in the death of 3/8637 Sergeant James Butler from Middlesbrough, who is buried at Aix-Noulette. Relieved by 1/Worcester on 30 May, they moved to Coupigny, where they went into huts and the officers into private billets. The next day fresh clothing was issued and the day was spent cleaning up and being inspected.

As May turned into June 8/Yorkshire Regiment began running classes in Coupigny. The bombers, machine gunners and signallers under their respective officers carried out specialist training, while those in the rifle companies paraded under company arrangements. An addition to the programme was wiring, which they would be doing a lot of in the future. All deficiencies in equipment were replaced as far as possible and the whole battalion was able to bathe.

Then, on 8 June, the battalion moved to the Lorette Spur, where they relieved 13/DLI. This section of the front was held with three companies in the front line. B Company, on the left, had three platoons in the front line and one platoon in support. In the centre was D Company, with two platoons in the line and two behind them in support. On the right lay A Company, again with two platoons up and two platoons behind. C Company was in reserve with battalion headquarters at Ablain-Saint-Nazaire. The battalion was put to work digging deep dugouts and each night 150 men were made available to the OC 128 Field Company, Royal Engineers, for any labouring tasks required. This work continued until 11 June, when Headquarters, C and D Companies of Anson Battalion of the Royal Naval Division replaced those of 8/Yorkshire Regiment. Command of the Lorette Spur passed to Anson Battalion and the relieved portion of 8/Yorkshire Regiment moved to huts in Bouvigny Wood. The two companies and the Lewis gun teams left behind were replaced on 12 June by 8/London Regiment and rejoined the battalion in Bouvigny Wood, and from there the next day to Bruay. Toby Dodgson was fortunate to be given leave from 22 May until 5 June and he sent a short note to his mother to let her know he had returned safely:

> 6th June 1916
> I got back to the Battalion yesterday morning and found everyone very cheery and in good form. We are back resting for a few days.

On 9 June 9/Yorkshire Regiment took over the trenches in Souchez I from 11/Northumberland Fus, where they spent four days. They were replaced in the line by 6/London Regiment and moved back to Fosse 10. They re-joined 69 Brigade and marched via Divion with them to the 1st Army training area, Meanwhile, 8/Yorkshire Regiment had moved again: HQ, C and D Companies to Tangry and A and B Companies to Sains-lès-Pernes. In these locations they spent a day cleaning up and had a clothing issue. It was here that Major P.E. Vaughan assumed command. Next day they were back on their feet trudging along the French pave to the next stop, billets in Estrée-Blanche. Here they started training as they were now in the Divisional area. At this time Toby Dodgson had more on his mind than battalion training; his marriage to Marjorie was utmost:

> I came back to find everyone very optimistic out here and talking about the war being over before next winter, but I still don't think so personally. All leave has been cut down to seven days again: Isn't it stupid? It will mean an awful rush if we are to be married in so short a time, and only about three or four days honeymoon.[15]

The 9/Yorkshire Regiment too was training and at this time they were described by Brigadier Holmes, the author of the manuscript held by the regimental museum, as follows:

> By the end of June the battalion was therefore a very fine fighting unit indeed and perhaps more efficient and better disciplined than at any other time. The Battalion was still to all intents and purposes the same personnel who had assembled at Frensham Camp nearly two years before. It had passed through a year's training at home and had spent ten months in France. The casualties which it had incurred during this period were negligible and had been replaced by drafts. Officers NCOs and men were all better acquainted with one another. Sections and platoons all possessed capable and experienced leaders.[16]

Brigadier Holmes wrote a history of the 9th Battalion in the 1920s, but it was never published.

Both battalions took part in both brigade and divisional manoeuvres, which consisted of assaulting trenches, then from 20–24 June they were at the Commanding Officer's disposal. For 8/Yorkshire Regiment this meant company training in the various available parts of the training area. The time spent in the training area allowed Toby Dodgson time to write home again:

> We are still in the same village and have had a very pleasant time here. The weather has recovered itself these last days and it has been very jolly having our lunch out each day and we've not been messed about

as we were last time. The C.O. we have got now is a good fellow, Major Vaughan. No one outside can realise what a relief it is to have someone at the head who knows his own mind and his job and is a gentleman.

The 9/Yorkshire Regiment War Diary, however, is very sparse and only states one man accidentally wounded on 16 June. Then on 24 June they marched to Berguette and entrained for Longau.

These journeys in troop trains were recorded for posterity in the *Regimental Gazette*:

The officers had carriages – not first-class it was true but still carriages. Dusty cushions were found in some and the ventilation was good, as most of the windows were broken and in some cases even a door was missing.

The men were accommodated in cattle trucks which bore the significant label: '*Hommes 40 Chevaux 8.*' Barely had we entrained when with a violent shock that threw everyone into a mutual embrace the train started. With many a creek and groan and jolt we got under way and were soon plodding along at a good five miles per hour. We wrapped ourselves up in coats and groundsheets and having come to a working agreement as to the disposal of our feet settled down to brood on the war and its accompanying discomforts. It is not very difficult to sort the 'new' from the 'old' soldier on a troop train. The veteran when he is not sleeping sits with his legs over the side of the truck surveying the scene with a jaundiced eye, a, 'Scott-what-a-boring-life' expression on his face. The view has no thrills for him. But the recruit gazes with wide eyed astonishment at the flattened homesteads, scarred trees and old shell torn, wire strewn trenches. At every halt he swarms off the train eager to get a closer view.

Having arrived behind the Somme front and before the battalion moved forward, Toby Dodgson wrote again:

27 June 1916

We were all rather sorry to leave that village, as the people were nice and friendly and the wenches très chaudes! I speak from hearsay of course.

We have had some drastic changes in the officers' staff of B Company with excellent results. (1) Our mess cook is cook no longer, he having seen fit to get blind drunk while we were out on a field day, so that when we got in, ravenously hungry it was only to find what was to have been our dinner sitting forlornly on the stove, burnt to a cinder. So he once more stands in the ranks and has to content himself with the food of Atkins –

silly fool. (2) The once faithful Humble[17] has fallen from his high estate and likewise lost his job – a fat and comfortable one. He, on the morning we left failed to wake me till 5.45 a.m. at which hour all kit was ordered to be packed and taken to the Q.M. stores. And then, when I told him off, he was most impertinent, for which latter offence there was nothing for it but to return him to duty. I have now got a lad named Alton[18] who is going to be a success I think. He is a nice quiet person, more refined than most of them, nice looking with the deepest brown eyes.

Our move here was a lengthy affair with a ride in the puff puff and a good long march each end. On the way I saw two of the most charming maidens in the world who were engaged in serving out tea to the Atkins at one of the stations en-route. It really gave me quite a shock as I went up to get the men back on the train, just before going on, imagining the ladies to be some worthy people doing their bit, when I heard the dulcet tones of a really beautiful English girl and looking up, was instantly captured. The vision was, unfortunately necessarily momentary but the impression remains and will do for some time. But we will get on, as I expect you have heard enough of that!

I had a very nice letter from Besly yesterday. He seems in great form and likes his new job very much. It certainly is a good one as he will probably never see a trench again, most of his work being done well behind the line.

We are rather crowded up in this village and beds are scarce, but luckily I have one and I am sharing a room with Tommy (Captain R Thompson). Yesterday we went into the town not so far away (Amiens) and had a very good time – excellent shops, where I was able to get some luxuries for the mess, including a magnificent duck pasty and some pàte de fois gras. We finished up with a good dinner and came away feeling very pleased with life.[19]

Chapter 5

July 1916, The Somme, Horseshoe Trench and Contalmaison

The 23rd Division, as we have seen, had been moved south to take part in the Somme offensive, which had been in the planning stages for many months. General Sir Douglas Haig had given the main part of the Somme Offensive to the Fourth Army commanded by General Sir Henry Rawlinson, and a smaller part, to the north, to the Third Army. The Fourth Army comprised from right to left XIII, XV, III, X and VII Corps. The III Corps was commanded by Lieutenant General Sir W.P. Pultney, who had under his command the 8th and 34th Divisions holding the line, with the 19th (Western) Division in reserve. Behind them, moving up to take their place in the line, was General Babington's 23rd Division.

Major General Ingouville-Williams' plan of attack for the 34th Division was relatively simple. The division would advance in four columns, each three battalions deep. The 34th Division had in the line 101 Brigade on the right and 102 (Tyneside Scottish) Brigade on the left, with 103 (Tyneside Irish) Brigade in reserve along the Tara–Usna line. The first objective of the leading battalions was the German front system consisting of four trenches. The fourth trench, requiring an advance of 2,000 yards, was to be reached forty-eight minutes after 'zero hour' at 8.18 a.m. The second objective was the German intermediate line, the 'Kaisergraben', in front of Pozières and Contalmaison villages. This line was to be reached at 8.58 a.m. and when this line was reached the 101 and 102 Brigades would halt and consolidate. The 103 Brigade, following close in the rear, would pass through the leading troops and capture Contalmaison village. Having captured the village, they would advance to the third and final objective, a line from the eastern edge of Contalmaison to Pozières, which would be reached by 10.10 a.m. However, these first-day objectives were not taken; the 34th Division advanced under a withering hail of enemy machine gun bullets and suffered the worst casualties of any division on that July day.

The survivors of 34th Division supported by fresh troops of the 19th Division kept the pressure on the Germans, particularly around La Boiselle. While all this fighting was going on 69 Brigade was moving forward and arrived in Bazieux Wood at 12.20 a.m., where they bivouacked for the night. The next day they moved up to Albert, where they bivouacked about three quarters of a mile north-west of the town. At 5.30 p.m. orders were received to take over the trenches held by 101 and 102 Brigades and their positions included Scots Redoubt. The 11/West Yorks were on the right and 9/Yorkshire Regiment were on the left, with 8/Yorkshire Regiment in the Tara–Usna line and 10/DWR in Bécourt Wood.

Having taken over from 101 Brigade HQ in the Tara–Usna line, dugouts 69 Brigade HQ now had communication problems. A wire had been laid to Scots Redoubt but it was continually being cut by artillery fire. The only means of communication was by runner and it was taking on average one and a half hours for each journey. The 10/DWR and 11/West Yorks both attacked but were driven back by strong counter-attacks.

On the night of 4 July A, B and C Companies of 8/Yorkshire Regiment dug a new communication trench from the old British front line to Sausage Redoubt, while D Company was detached to 9/Yorkshire Regiment. The latter battalion only recorded that they were in reserve trenches in the evening and took over the front line at night. Both sides made bombing attacks during the day and the Germans heavily counter-attacked 11/West Yorks. At 4 a.m. on the morning of 5 July 10/DWR made an attack assisted by 11/West Yorks but this was driven back by another counter-attack. At 10.a.m. the Germans launched a very heavy counter-attack on 11/West Yorks and the West Yorkshiremen, aided by 10/DWR, repulsed them but only after being driven back almost to Scots Redoubt.

That afternoon 69 Brigade Operation Order No. 63 was issued detailing orders for an attack on the Horseshoe Line. Details were given for the artillery barrage and the forming up positions for the infantry battalions involved. The brigade machine gun company allotted four guns to each of the assaulting battalions, and likewise the 69 light trench mortar battery allotted two Stokes guns.[1]

The attack of the other units was cancelled but 9/Yorkshire Regiment was to continue with their part. The battalion advanced promptly at 6 p.m. and fought their way into the objective.

An artist's impression of 2/Lt. Donald Bell winning his VC.

Serving his machine gun by himself under very heavy fire, 15908 Private Fred Collinson, of Hartford Street, Middlesbrough, 'with total disregard for his personal safety, thereby setting an example which enabled an enemy's flank trench to be cleared and a machine gun to be put out of action at a critical period during the assault'. He was awarded the Military Medal.[2]

On the flank a German machine gun was enfilading the battalion, causing a number of casualties. This gun was spotted by Second Lieutenant Donald Bell, who along with 15958 Lance Corporal Harrison Colwell from Hetton-le-Hole and 16748 Private Joseph Batey, who hailed from Spennymoor. As would be expected, both were colliers in the Durham coalfield. All three attacked the machine gun and Bell was able to put it out of action with a grenade. The 23rd Division headquarters released an intelligence report from midnight 4 July to midnight 5 July that stated:

> At 4 p.m. the Germans attacked Sots Redoubt, but were driven back by 1/DWR, 11/West Yorks and 8/Yorkshire Regiment. At 6 p.m. after an artillery bombardment of one hour all the regiments of 69 Brigade made a combined attack on the Horseshoe with the object of consolidating the line 04, 74, 35, 79 and then pushing on to 00 and 56. The attack met with immediate success by 6.15 p.m. 10/DWR captured the line X.22.a. 5.6. 04, 74, 56. Thence pushing patrols forward. 11/West Yorks and 8/Yorkshire Regiment captured the line X21.b.5.6 to 0.0 and 9/Yorkshire Regiment captured Lincoln Redoubt. The Germans made a determined resistance and their machine guns were very active. Realising that they were caught between our attacking parties on the Northern side of the Horseshoe they began to surrender fairly freely.
>
> In all about 200 unwounded prisoners were taken and heavy casualties were caused amongst the enemy, who were caught by our machine guns as they attempted to retire.[3]

Private Harrison Colwell was awarded a DCM.

The whole of the Horseshoe line was taken but at a cost. The 9/Yorkshire Regiment reported the casualties as three officers killed, four wounded and two missing. Among the other ranks, fourteen were killed, 144 wounded and twenty-eight missing. That night there was a German counter-attack on the battalions left flank that was driven off.

Of the officers, Captains F.A.H. Atkey and W.T Wilkinson are buried in Bécourt Military Cemetery. Lieutenants John Gibson and Frank Hermiston, along with Second Lieutenant Cyril Wyld, are commemorated on the Thiepval Memorial to the missing. The majority of the other ranks are commemorated on the Thiepval Memorial, twenty-nine to be precise. After the war, in October 1919 the bodies of 23513 Private Joseph Ashton from Sheffield and 3/8005 Sergeant Lawrence Pell, a Brotton man, were exhumed by the 21st Labour Company and reinterred in Gordon Dump Cemetery. The work of exhuming the remains of the dead went on and in 1929 14550 Private George Outram was found and reburied in Serre No. 2 Cemetery. Three years later 12891 Private Arnold Coultas and 14792 Private John Rowse were found and taken to the same cemetery for reburial. Of those wounded that reached the group of Casualty Clearing Stations at Heilly Station, three died from their wounds and are buried in the cemetery there.

Lieutenant John Gibson, from Hull, was killed in action on 5 July 1916.

Captain William Wilkinson, killed in action on 5 July 1916.

Captain William Wilkinson, who as was previously stated was killed on 5 July, was born in Hampstead on 6 November 1886. He was educated at University College School between 1900 and 1902 and was a keen member of the Officer Training Corps. He served with the 28/London Regiment, the Artists Rifles, from 1909 until 1912. On the outbreak of war he had enlisted into one of the University and Public Schools Battalions of the Royal Fusiliers and was commissioned on 22 September 1914 into 9/Yorkshire Regiment.

No. 14806 Private John Collins, who served in C Company and was most likely Captain Wilkinson's batman, wrote to his brother about the captain's death and received the following reply:

27 July 1916
Dear Collins,
It was very kind of you to write me about the manner of my brother's death. Your letter arrived soon after I had written to the Colonel to ask if he could give me more information than I had earlier received. Yours was a great relief to us in that it told us that his end was swift + that there could have been little or no pain + suffering. It was a hard blow for us all, as in spite of looking facts in the face + realizing that death was always at hand, it is almost impossible to be prepared fully when it comes.

In the loss of his young life we have to get what satisfaction we can out of the fact he died gallantly doing his duty. Thanks very much Collins for your offer to do anything you can but I do not know that there is anything I can ask of you except that later on when regulations allow we should like to know exactly where he was laid to rest + to know if it will be possible to locate it.

I remember you quite well + shall hope to see you safely returned from the war with all this trouble at an end before very long. My brother was very proud of his Battalion and his regiment was looking forward to doing useful work for a long time in it, and he also spoke well of you.

Thanking you again with our best wishes that you may come through well + safely.

Yours truly
J Sydney Wilkinson.[4]

Captain Freemen A.H. Atkey's obituary was published in the *Regimental Journal* and stated:

> He was the youngest son of F.W. Atkey of Sackville Street, London and was in his 34th year. He was a scholar of Pembroke College, Cambridge where he obtained a first class both in classics and history and was also a chancellor's Medallist. When the war began he was VI Form Classical Master at Marlborough College. Gazetted to the 9th Battalion he was promoted Lieutenant on 1 May 1915 and Captain on 14 August 1915. He had been at the front for nearly a year and had been wounded in February last.[5]

Captain Freeman Atkey, killed in action 5 July 1916.

Second Lieutenant Cyril Wyld had served in the Territorial Force prior to enlisting into the Sherwood Foresters in 1914 and as 14996 Corporal Wyld he had landed in France with 10/Sherwood Foresters on 14 July 1915. Promoted to sergeant, he was Mentioned in Despatches for gallant conduct and sent home to be commissioned, which he received in March 1916. He left a widow and one child.

2/Lt. Cyril Wyld was killed in action on 5 July. He has no known grave and is commemorated on the Thiepval Memorial.

Another who fell that day was the Battalion Medical Officer Captain J.C. Rix, Royal Army Medical Corps. After the action the battalion stretcher-bearers were bringing in the wounded to the Regimental Aid Post. The post was overflowing with wounded men and the doctor was outside treating newly arrived wounded in the open. A German shell burst very close and he was killed instantly along with two others.

Rix had been commissioned on 1 April 1915 and joined 9/Yorkshire Regiment some time before embarkation. He had done some magnificent work tending the battalion wounded around Armentières and Souchez and was a great loss.

As an officer in the RAMC, Captain Rix was killed in action while treating the wounded at the regimental aid post on 5 July.

At hospitals behind the line and in England wounded men were questioned as to if they had any information regarding those wounded and missing. On 26 July, three men, 12513 Lance Corporal Bee, 15927 Lance Corporal Robinson and 13271 Private English, were at a convalescent camp in Rouen and made the same statement that they had seen Lieutenant Hermiston fall between the two lines, but did not know if he was badly wounded. This was added to by 14496 Lance Corporal Ernest Brick on 11 August. At the time he was a patient at the Dudley Road Hospital in Birmingham and stated: 'I saw Lieutenant Hermiston killed at Albert about 6 p.m. on 3 July 1916 [*sic*] – by a German Machine Gun when attempting to get over the parapet in front of the German trenches. I saw him buried later on at the same time as Captain Wilkinson (C Company) was buried.' This last sentence conflicts with the statement by the other three, who clearly stated, 'he fell between the two lines'.

On 6 July 9/Yorkshire Regiment were replaced by 9/Welsh Regiment and moved back to bivouacs, from where Second Lieutenant Donald Bell wrote a short note with the news he was expecting an award for putting the machine gun out of action:

> 7/7/16
> Dear Mrs Nicky,
> I was delighted to receive your letter this morning as we have had very little chance of receiving mail this last few days. We are taking part in the great offensive and you will be pleased to hear that our battalion has made its name by capturing a very strong German position. I have had greatness thrust upon me because I was lucky enough to chuck a bomb on a machine gun which was mowing our fellows down & putting it out of action.
> The CO is highly delighted and I have also been congratulated by the Divisional General. He told me that I was to be recommended so there is a chance of me getting a military cross or something of that sort. Talk about luck! Fancy just chucking one bomb, even if it was a bullseye.
> I am sorry to hear that only 2 scholarships were won this year but if you still beat the other schools that's good enough.
> I must close now. Give my regards to all at school
> Yours v sincerely Don[6]

Donald Bell did a lot better than a Military Cross for he received the Victoria Cross and the two soldiers with him both were awarded the Distinguished Conduct Medal.

The next day the line was consolidated and 8/Yorkshire Regiment was relieved by a battalion of the DLI from 68 Brigade and moved back to Belle Vue Farm, where 69 Brigade became the Divisional Reserve. They moved up to positions in front of Bécourt Wood on the morning of 8 July and were shelled heavily that night. The next morning the battalion came under shell fire again and the Battalion Headquarters' dugout was blown in. Later on during the day the battalion returned to Belle Vue Farm. During the period 5–8 July, three officers had been wounded, one other rank had died of wounds, eighty-six had been wounded and one was missing. The 9/Yorkshire Regiment too had moved forward to reserve trenches as support for an attack. However, in heavy rain they returned to the bivouacs about midnight.

While back in this reserve position Toby Dodgson sent two letters home, the first on 7 July to Marjorie:

> So sorry this has not gone off before, but we've literally had no time. This pushing is the most strenuous business. Unfortunately the weather has been awful the last three days – torrents of rain, and the trenches are about back

> to winter conditions. Our Brigade did a bit of a push yesterday and bagged about two hundred Bosches who seemed only too glad to give themselves up. Richardson and another officer in this company got wounded – nice little ones that will just take them back to Blighty. Several pieces of shrapnel fell on me too, but none with sufficient force to make a puncture.

Then on 8 July he wrote a short note to his mother:

> Dearest Mother
> As you will see from the papers the 'push' has started. After the first two days' which were real summer ones, the weather has been perfectly awful – rain, rain and always more rain – and the trenches are as bad as in mid-winter. It doesn't improve bivouacking either, so you will understand that letter writing is rather impossible, but I will try and write a proper letter directly we get back under cover for a night.
>
> Your ever-loving Toby.

On the morning of 10 July, the brigade received word they were to attack Contalmaison. The village had been a first-day objective for the 34th Division when the Battle of the Somme commenced on 1 July 1916.[7] Although some soldiers of 103 (Tyneside Irish) Brigade, the 34th Division's supporting brigade, had reached the village they were not in sufficient numbers to change the outcome of the attack that day.[8] Furthermore, on 7 July the village had been entered again, this time by 1st Worcestershire Regiment. However, they were forced out when they ran out of bombs and ammunition.[9] The following day the General Officer Commanding III Corps, Lieutenant General Sir William Pulteney, spoke with the Commander of the 23rd Division, Major General James Babington, and ordered that 69 Brigade should make an attack on the village.[10]

The brigade was warned on the morning of 10 July it was to move off and attack Contalmaison.[11] Brigadier T.S. Lambert, Commanding 69 Brigade, prepared an order for the attack and placed two companies of 11th West Yorkshire Regiment on the left with 9th Yorkshire Regiment in the centre and 8th Yorkshire Regiment on the right. Furthermore, headquarters 23rd Divisional Artillery produced a comprehensive barrage plan that was to cut the wire and assist the infantry with the capture of the village.[12]

Many hours before the attack began, the 23rd Divisional Signal, Company Royal Engineers, had a very busy time. Lines were laid to connect 69 Brigade HQ with the Divisional Signals HQ. An armoured cable was laid on the surface to a point near the Willow Patch. Two core cables were laid for the use of the Artillery Forward Observation Officers. These were laid on the ground to a point on the right flank. This pair of cables crossed the trench leading to advanced Brigade HQ at Scots Redoubt, which was about 200 yards to the east. Here at the point of crossing the trench, lines from Advance Brigade HQ were tapped into these main lines, thus establishing communications with Divisional Headquarters. Visual signalling stations were also established using flags. As soon as 8/Yorkshire Regiment were in position the signalling stations established communication. As a back-up two orderlies each carrying a basket of four pigeons was sent to both battalion headquarters before the attackers moved off. However, owing to conditions in the trenches these orderlies did not arrive in time to accompany the battalion. They were left to follow the attack as best they could. With regard to wireless communication, two trench sets were available, one near Scots Redoubt and one near Willow Patch, both working to Brigade HQ at Bécourt Château. The final last resort was to use 'runners', with two men from each battalion attached to Brigade HQ. These two men supplied a runner service from brigade to their battalion HQ.[13]

Brigadier Lambert, 69 Brigade.

The orders for the attack were issued on 9 July; these gave locations for the attack and the equipment each man was to carry:

> The advance will be made in quick time in not less than four waves for each company and will be followed by searching and consolidating parties in similar formation.
>
> One day's rations and emergency ration will be carried on every man.
>
> Assaulting troops and reserves will carry at least four bombs and two sandbags each.
>
> Searching parties will carry at least six bombs and four sandbags each.
>
> Consolidating parties will carry tools, four sandbags each, wire and pickets.[14]

The attacking troops were deployed in the northern end of Horseshoe Trench, behind Bailiff Wood, some 2,000 yards due west of Contalmaison.[15] The 69 Brigade headquarters and both battalion headquarters were located at Scots Redoubt with an attached liaison officer from the Divisional artillery. Also located near Sots Redoubt were both Regimental Medical Officers, Captain

A German sentry keeps a sharp lookout.

Matson, RAMC, attached 8/Yorkshire Regiment, and Captain Blake, RAMC, attached 9/Yorkshire Regiment. In order to facilitate the swift evacuation of the wounded, they established their Regimental Aid Posts (RAPs) in old German dugouts close to both the brigade and battalion headquarters, which were in Scots Redoubt.[16] Lieutenant Colonel A.N. Walker, commanding 69 Field Ambulance, established his headquarters near Scots Redoubt in order to be in touch with the brigade and battalion commanders. The German forces opposite were 183rd Division, which held the ground to the British right. On the left was the 3rd Guard Reserve Division with the Lehr Regiment, which was in the northern part of the village.

With the orders issued the battalions started moving up to their start lines. The 9/Yorkshire Regiment reported that they left the bivouacs at 11 a.m. and, although they were shelled heavily on the way up, they were in their assembly trench by 4 p.m. The timings for 8/Yorkshire Regiment must have been similar for they were in position too, ready for the start time. Ten minutes before zero hour the advanced divisional headquarters received a message from the Forward Observation Officer attached to 8/Yorkshire Regiment that the British heavy artillery was dropping shells 200 yards short of Bailiff Wood. The German infantry were firing Very lights in abundance to call for artillery support. He also reported that the German artillery was placing a heavy barrage about the objective, and that the British infantry was moving forward.[17]

From Horseshoe Trench both battalions advanced over the open ground and came under shrapnel fire from the German artillery. However, they kept going and as they got closer they were fired upon by rifles and machine guns. At 4.52 p.m. the artillery observers reported that the Germans were running from their trenches north of Acid Copse. The 9/Yorkshire Regiment lost heavily to this fire. Although 8/Yorkshire Regiment found the enemy wire practically intact and it posed a serious obstacle, they did not let it hold them up for long. As they cleared this wire they began to prepare for the assault and came across a hedge that had wire netting in it. It was between these two obstacles that

German infantry in a trench in France.

about half the battalion's casualties occurred. Advancing here with B Company were 13101 Private Harry Inglis and 13093 Private Walter Sheen, part of a Lewis gun crew, probably carrying spare ammunition drums for the gun. They both lived in the same tenement at No. 1 Sidegate, Durham, and had enlisted together. All of a sudden there was an explosion and Harry disappeared; not a trace of him to be found. Another man blown up and shell-shocked was 13408 Private Matthew Braithwaite of D Company, 8/Yorkshire Regiment. One of the battalion's Lewis guns was destroyed by a shell. The only survivor of the team saw the gun blown up with the gunner, 13416 Private Frank Jerverland from Middlesbrough. A second Lewis gun was lost west of Contalmaison when all but one of the crew became casualties. These were the only Lewis guns lost by 8/Yorkshire Regiment during the attack. Some men had slight wounds, others quite serious or multiple wounds. One such man was 13339 Private William

German gunners in a well-made shelter supplied covering fire to the defenders of Contalmaison.

Savage, from Murton Colliery, serving in A Company, who had a wound in the right knee.

Casualties in 9/Yorkshire Regiment were very similar: 15955 Corporal Joseph Birtley, from Hetton-le-Hole, had a GSW to the right arm; 24466 Private John Cory, a Marske man who had joined the battalion in April, was wounded in the left arm; and 14631 Robert Kennedy, a Middlesbrough resident, was also wounded in the left arm.[18]

At 5.25 p.m. the forward observation post reported that the infantry were entering the village. Five minutes later a message from Headquarters III Corps said that 'If Contalmaison is taken it must be held at all costs.' Five minutes later the Forward Observation Officer sent a message that the infantry could be seen fighting in the south-west corner of the village and his next message stated that 'the enemy can be seen running from the north-east corner of Contalmaison and also from Contalmaison Villa'.[19] This was documented by Brigadier Holmes in the *Green Howards Gazette* in the November 1924 edition, when he wrote:

> The sight of the flashing bayonets was too much for the enemy, who ran in all directions, only to be shot down by the artillery and machine gun fire from guns placed beforehand on the flank of the village.

German machine gunners.

One of those with a gleaming bayonet was 14793 Lance Corporal Cuthbert Piper of 8/Yorkshire Regiment, from Middlesbrough, 'who showed great dash and daring leading his section, which accounted for several Germans, in the face of heavy firing at Contalmaison'. He too was awarded the Military Medal.[20]

Of the 8/Yorkshire Regiment, only four officers and 150 men reached the village, where they took part in some fierce hand-to-hand bayonet fighting. Evidence of this is found in the personal documents for 13783 Private Albert James Bail, serving with A Company of the battalion, as they record he had a bayonet wound in the chest.[21] Also fighting in the village was a party under the command of Captain Maurice Hume-Wright, who, under heavy fire, had just stopped and given a wounded 'Tommy' a drink of water. A few minutes later they turned a corner in the village and ran straight into a party of Germans. The captain was shot dead at close range. But his actions in the village had saved a critical position.[22]

Private George Hall Evans was killed in action on 10 July.

At 7.30 p.m. a party of German infantry was seen at the cutting but the men of 8/Yorkshire Regiment using a captured

German machine gun, opened fire and scattered them before they could start a counter-attack. At 9 p.m. another larger group of the enemy were seen to be forming up behind a hedge. This group, around a platoon in strength, opened fire and the position became critical. Major Western made a barricade across the road and reinforced it with men from 8/Yorkshire Regiment and some men from 9/Yorkshire Regiment. Further aid in the shape of a bombing party of 9/Yorkshire Regiment led by Second Lieutenant Donald Bell arrived. Under the cover of a Lewis gun firing from a house, they counter-attacked the Germans at the hedge and they were able to drive them out. Unfortunately the gallant officer was killed trying to bomb another German machine gun post.

Private William Kennedy was wounded on 10 July 1916. He is photographed here with his wife in the 1930s.

At 7.35 p.m. the Brigade Commander had reported to Divisional HQ that the brigade had suffered heavy casualties and in conversation General Babington told him he would send one company up to reinforce 69 Brigade. At 9.20 p.m. a pigeon arrived at the III Corps Pigeon Loft with a message from the Officer Commanding 9/Yorkshire Regiment asking for reinforcements, ammunition and bombs.[23] At 11 p.m. two companies, one from 11/West Yorks and one from 10/DWR, arrived and inserted themselves into the line and got in touch with the unit on the right, thus securing that flank. During the night the village was shelled heavily by enemy artillery, but no further counter-attacks were mounted. Both battalions had patrols out all night and some Germans that approached the cutting were fired upon and dispersed.

As has already been detailed, 8/Yorkshire Regiment were in greatly reduced numbers and they had the undoubted pleasure of capturing a force greater than their own, comprising some eight officers and 180 men of the *Kgl Wurtemburgisches Reserve Infantry Regiment 122*, which formed part of the 183rd Division.

The Germans described the conditions in Contalmaison under British bombardment: 'One dug out after another collapsed, one machine gun after another was destroyed, the cellars were full of wounded. … Scarcely more than a hundred men escaped to the second position.'[24] 'The troops were in a miserable state, lying in mud and water with many wounded and sick among them.'[25]

Excellent work was done by the pigeon orderlies, and the importance of this method of communication was clearly demonstrated. Four pigeons arrived at the same time as 8/Yorkshire Regiment headquarters party. They were brought up by 11837 Private Henry Smith of 10DWR, who had walked alone without special orders through a heavy barrage with his basket of pigeons and reported to Major Western. By his action the first news of the capture of the village was at Brigade HQ, from Divisional HQ via the Corps HQ Pigeon Loft. The second basket sent up to 8/Yorkshire Regiment failed to arrive.

Corporal Charles Walton, from Redcar, was killed in action on 10 July.

The casualties were evacuated to various aid posts and Dressing Stations manned by the staff of the 69th and 70th Field Ambulances. Once their wounds were dressed and they were fit to be moved they were placed on transport down the Lines of Communications (LOC) to a Casualty Clearing Station. The estimates for casualties during the Battle of the Somme required the number of battalion stretcher-bearers to increase from sixteen to thirty-two. Due to the exhausting nature of carrying a stretcher, a system of relay posts every 1,000 yards was established for stretcher-bearers.[26] The early intervention the casualty received would dictate the eventual outcome of his treatment and the arrest of bleeding as early as possible gave the casualty a better chance of survival. The first treatment a wounded soldier was likely to receive was:

Private Joseph Ainsley in hospital.

A. Self-help, the soldiers carried a First Field Dressing and an iodine capsule to put on the wound, the latter to assist in Tetanus prevention.
B. A comrade, using the wounded soldier's own field dressing, could have dressed the wound and dragged the man into a place of safety.

However, orders often prohibited advancing soldiers to stop and assist the wounded and they were left for the stretcher-bearers.

C. A battalion stretcher-bearer. Once the stretcher-bearers reached a casualty they would do what they could to arrest the flow of blood. They were trained to stop bleeding and where possible splint wounded limbs. They learned to handle the limb with gentleness, as a simple fracture may easily be converted into the much more serious compound or complicated fracture by rough handling.[27] Each bearer carried six field dressings and some shell dressings, a small bottle of iodine with a brush in a haversack. If the stretcher-bearer gave morphine tablets to the casualty a letter M would be marked on the casualty's forehead so the medical and nursing staff further down the LOC would be aware of the drug had been administered.

A stretcher-bearer going over the top was not aseptic as they were generally covered in mud. As Major William Blackwood RAMC observed, 'The stretcher-bearer is bound from his surroundings to be the most septic individual … consequently it should be impressed upon him that on no account is the wound to be touched.'[28] That was impractical; when a stretcher-bearer was stemming the flow of blood the wound must have been contaminated and any dressing applied would have needed changing as soon as possible.

The battalion stretcher-bearers were infantrymen, trained by the Regimental Medical Officer and under his command. They were ideally men of intelligence who were interested in their work.[29] According to Captain Fred Davidson RAMC, the RMO of 2/Cameronians, treatment could also include cutting away clothing in order to splint wounds:

Private Thomas Taylor, D Coy 8 Battaltion, was wounded in the hand on 10 July and evacuated to No. 34 Casualty Clearing Station.

> In the case of a fractured thigh or leg, the outside seam of the trousers should be split right up. Braces must be unfastened all round. There must be no dragging or taking off clothing. The leg of the cut trouser should be drawn very carefully to the inside of the injured limb, and the leg of the trousers of the sound limb can be pulled off. The

> sock should be cut off after the boot has been slit up the back seam, fully unlaced and removed. In a fracture of the arm, the jacket seam and shirt must be ripped up. They should learn to do this blindfold because better splinting will reduce death rates.[30]

Having arrested any bleeding and dressed and splinted any wounds, the stretcher-bearers' unenviable task was to get the wounded man back to the RAP. This could have been on a stretcher brought with them for the task. Or, if that had been lost or damaged, a stretcher would need to be improvised. Once Contalmaison had been taken both RMOs organised search parties to look for the wounded. In this work the battalion stretcher-bearers were assisted by bearers from the Bearer Sub Division of 69 Field Ambulance. This was the part of the Field Ambulance with the specific task of recovering and transporting wounded. Coupled with this, the Assistant Director Medical Services (ADMS) 23rd Division, Colonel R.J. Blackham, despatched 100 men of the Divisional Pioneer Battalion, 9th South Staffordshire Regiment, to act as extra stretcher-bearers. It is also probable that some German prisoners were employed as additional bearers. The use of prisoners of war was a common practice.

The Regimental Aid Post (RAP) was a temporary location, established as near to the front line as possible. However, it was not able to house the wounded. The main purpose was to enhance the emergency first aid and to stabilise the casualty for the onward transport on the LOC. The equipment of the post included a pair of medical panniers. One was a medical comforts pannier containing items such as meat extract, milk, tea and brandy. The second pannier contained basic medical equipment, for example, anti-tetanus serum, field and shell dressings, cotton wool and ointments.[31] Other equipment included a water bottle, with either a field companion or a surgical haversack containing scissors, forceps, chloroform and a supply of shell dressings and iodine.[32] The RAP was commanded by the RMO, who was an officer and doctor of the Royal Army Medical Corps (RAMC). One doctor, normally a captain, was attached to each infantry battalion. At the MO's disposal was a non-commissioned officer of the RAMC. Having, reached the RAP, the survivability of the casualty was now increased. Here dressings would be checked and if necessary replaced. However, Major W. Blackwood commented, the medical officer should see all cases and re-dress them except the most trivial cases.[33] However, it is likely that given the shortage of dressings in the front line, many RMOs would just check the wounded man's dressing and if they were satisfactory evacuate him as soon as possible.

Owing to the heavy rain on 8 July, the battlefield was waterlogged and movement through the trenches was very difficult, so most of the wounded were moved over the open and exposed ground. However, casualties were also taken straight out to the sunken road that ran from Fricourt to Belle Vue Farm. Because the road was relatively free of mud it was possible to use wheeled stretchers, on which the casualties were taken straight to the Advanced Dressing Station (ADS) set up by 69 Field Ambulance.[34]

As no records of the RAPs exist it is not known which RAP the individuals were evacuated through. However, as previously explained, the use of the sunken road meant a number of casualties may have bypassed the RAP and been taken straight down to the ADS.

On 6 July the ADMS 23rd Division received permission to establish additional ADS on the Fricourt–Belle Vue Farm Road and he went forward to select a location for the Dressing Station.[35] This was manned by 69 Field Ambulance. At the same time, a casualty collecting station was established at the head of the tramway on the Albert–Moulin Vivier Road. All arrangements were made to ensure the swift movement of casualties away from the battlefield. The arrangement also complied with the orders of the Deputy Director Medical Services (DDMS) III Corps, who directed that lightly wounded casualties should be evacuated to No. 34 CCS at Vecquemont.[36]

The ADS was primarily to triage, that is sorting the wounded into groups based on their need for or likely benefit from immediate medical treatment.[37] When the wounded man arrived at the ADS the wounds were re-examined and cleaned where possible. The wounds were re-dressed and a casualty label would be tied to the man's uniform giving details of wounds and any morphine injections. However, with modern blast injuries from shrapnel and high-velocity bullets, pieces of clothing dirt and detritus were very often embedded into the wound. Therefore, it was impossible for the Medical Officer at the ADS to clean the wound thoroughly. This could result in the onset of gas gangrene if the patient was not evacuated quickly and seen to at the Casualty Clearing Station. Although the ADS was better equipped than the RAP, it still did not hold casualties for long and when transport was available the casualty was placed on a waiting ambulance or lorry for onward transportation along the LOC. However, photographic evidence of medical units on the Somme shows lines of casualties on stretchers on the ground waiting for onward transportation. This resulted in delayed care, which then allowed the onset of gangrene to take place. However, in some life-threatening cases, an operation could be performed at the ADS. In other cases where the Medical Officer deemed it was impossible to save the casualty, he would be placed to one side of the Dressing Station, administered pain relief and allowed to die as peacefully as possible.

The lesson learned in South Africa and from the Russo–Japanese War was that speed of evacuation was paramount to saving a life. This highlighted the fact that the British Army Medical Services needed to overhaul the evacuation system for the wounded. In view of this, in 1905 six large semi-mobile 'clearing hospitals' were authorised for the Regular Army.[38] Casualty Clearing Hospitals were to have three distinct roles:

1. To receive and treat until fit for further transport those sick, wounded and seriously ill.
2. To expedite the immediate evacuation to the base of those fit to travel.
3. To retain for an early return to duty cases of wounds and sickness likely to recover within a few days.[39]

The methods of transporting the wounded were as follows:

A. Human, carried on a stretcher or on the back of a comrade, or on a wheeled stretcher.
B. Animal, on a light railway pulled by horses or mules or in a horse-drawn ambulance.
C. Mechanical, in a motor ambulance, or a supply or ammunition lorry or omnibus.

On 4 July III Corps headquarters placed a number of omnibuses at the Divisional Collecting Station at Dernancourt. These were augmented by lorries of the 23rd Divisional Supply Column, Army Service Corps (ASC). Both means of transport were for the evacuation of the lightly wounded.[40] At 08:30 hours on 11 July the Deputy Director Medical Services (DDMS) III Corps, Colonel Bruce Skinner, recorded in his war diary, 'Q [Deputy Quarter Master General III Corps] told me that supply lorries are not to be used for wounded. As a result, the 23rd Division called last night for more ammunition lorries.'[41] This highlights the confusion that was occurring at command levels about how the wounded were to be evacuated from the battle area. The DDMS III Corps Operation Order No. 2 is quite specific in the use of lorries. 'Walking cases will be despatched by motor lorries at night only to Frechencourt Medical Rest Camp. They will be reported as transfers to Casualty Clearing Stations, Vecquemont.'[42]

Depending on which ADS the soldier passed through, the method of transport was different. If they went to 70 Field Ambulance they came back via the light tramway to the Albert–Moulin Vivier Road. At Moulin Vivier, they would have transferred to ambulances of No. 21 Motor Ambulance Convoy (21 MAC). This unit over the period 10–11 July evacuated fifty-three officers and 998 other ranks.[43] For those arriving at the 69 Field Ambulance, the official medical history (W.G. Macpherson, *History of the Great War Medical Services General History*) shows that 20 MAC was operating in that area. Furthermore, some may have been transported in horse-drawn ambulances. Given the ground conditions and the constant German artillery fire at the time, the arrangements for the removal of the wounded could not have been better. Arguably, if more motor ambulances had been available the evacuation would have been faster. The use of supply lorries caused much unnecessary suffering to the wounded.[44] According to Sister Edith Appleton, 'the men on stretchers cried out with the pain caused by the jolting'.[45] Other methods of transportation, such as the handcart with bicycle wheels and the flat wagon used on the trench tramways, did not have springs and were just as uncomfortable for the wounded. All that could be done to make the wounded comfortable was done before onward transportation to the Main Dressing Station (MDS). At the latter facility pain relief and hot drinks were given, the dressings checked or changed before the patient was sent further down the LOC.

Having established the route that the wounded took on their evacuation journey, the numbers of dead and wounded, where they are buried or commemorated should be given some consideration. The casualties suffered by the brigade during 4–5 July in the attack on Horseshoe Trench and during 10–11 July in the assault of Contalmaison were heavy but not excessive considering the importance of the objective.[46] Furthermore, if compared to battalions that attacked in the area on 1 July they could be considered light.

Both battalion War Diaries record casualty figures for the day:

	Officers			Other Ranks		
	Killed, Wounded, Missing			Killed, Wounded, Missing		
8/Yorkshire Regiment	5	6	1	19	241	87
9/Yorkshire Regiment	3	11	-	13	192	24

The dead officers from 8/Yorkshire Regiment were all buried in Bécourt Military Cemetery. Of Captain Clifford Simpson, a brother officer wrote:

> He was killed in the thickest of actions at about 5.30 p.m. Nobody could have wished for a better or noble end. He was with Colonel Vaughan in the thick of it charging across the open to attack a village, which we took.

Another officer wrote, 'He died as he lived a very great and gallant gentleman.'

Second Lieutenant Raymund Binns was educated at Stoneyhurst School. The school magazine contains part of a letter from Lieutenant Colonel Vaughan to Mrs Binns regarding his death; 'He was a fine soldier who died whilst assaulting the enemy's position.' Another officer, most likely his Company commander, said: 'He was perfectly splendid and the men followed him wherever he went. The men of his platoon carried him back to Bécourt Cemetery outside Albert and gave him a burial any soldier might have been proud of. He was the bravest platoon commander I have had.' His soldier servant gave the information that he was killed instantaneously with a bullet through the head, when his men had just taken the first enemy trench. Second Lieutenant Alan Darling had served as 12080 Private in 9/Northumberland Fusiliers, landing in France with that battalion on 15 July 1915. Sent home to train as an officer, he was commissioned on 23 April 1916. The *Newcastle Journal*, reporting his death, stated, 'He was a popular member of the South Shields, Rowing Club.'[47]

Private George Lambert, killed in action 10 July.

The 9/Yorkshire Regiment only had four killed that day. The remains of Lieutenant Donald Simpson Bell VC were exhumed at 57d X16. d. on 9 April 1919 by 21 Labour Company and reburied in Gordon Dump Cemetery in Mash Valley. Three other officers' bodies were never recovered and they are commemorated on the Thiepval Memorial to the Missing. Second Lieutenant E.O. Hart was attached from the 13/Green Howards. The other two, Second Lieutenants T.J. Mitchell and G.H. Gorton, were both attached from 11/Green Howards. Further to these casualties, Major Victor Becket died at either No. 36 CCS or No. 38 CCS, both of which were stationed at Heilly Station where he is buried.

Private William Sargison, killed in action 10 July.

The other officer to die from his wounds was Second Lieutenant Thomas T. Wood. He had landed in France as a corporal with the King's Shropshire Light Infantry in September 1915 and was commissioned on 23 January 1916. Evacuated to England where he died, he was taken home and buried in St Andrew's Churchyard, Bebington, Cheshire.

Only one second lieutenant of 8/Yorkshire Regiment died from his wounds. Thomas Swain had only crossed to France on 16 June 1916 and was wounded on 10 July. He made it alive to a hospital in London, where he died from his wounds and was repatriated to Northallerton. He is buried in the local cemetery. He was 22 years of age and played football for Northallerton and Brompton juniors. Prior to the war he was employed at Messrs Oxendale and Barker in Northallerton.[48]

2/Lt. Raymond Binns, killed in action 10 July.

The one missing officer of 8/Yorkshire Regiment was Captain Francis 'Toby' Dodgson, whose descriptive letters have been followed from the formation of the battalion, through training and his time in France. Along with all his letters, those received after his death show the respect that was held for him:

> 26 July 1916
> Hospital for Officers
> 24 Park St W.
> Dear Mrs Dodgson
> I am writing to say how very sorry I was to hear that your son was missing.
>
> He was very popular with all the officers and men and we shall all miss him very much and I shall especially as he was in my company. I meant to have written before to tell you how sorry I was.
>
> Yours sincerely,
> Captain Arthur V Richardson.

Finally, on 28 July, Mrs Dodgson received a letter from Lieutenant Colonel Vaughan, the Commanding Officer, saying that he was definitely killed on 10 July:

> It is with the deepest sympathy that I write to you to say that I fear there is now no doubt whatever that your son was killed in the advance on Contalmaison.
>
> The ground we advanced over was quite open and the Battalion did magnificently led by your son and Captain Thompson.
>
> The advance was without cover: and advantage was taken of the numerous trenches or shell holes and your son was evidently killed and completely buried in one of the trenches or shell holes for we found no trace.

He died gloriously leading his men, and he lies with many others of his company, in the torn and shell swept valley just south-west of Contalmaison.

But that was not the end of the matter, for Lieutenant Colonel Vaughan wrote again on 4 August 1916:

Dear Mrs Fulton [Toby's mother had remarried]
We are again back in the line and I have since found out that your son's body was found and buried by the burial party. It was found as we thought in one of the shell holes and I have marked the place with a rough wooden cross. I have shown on the back of this where his grave is. It will I feel sure be a comfort to you to know that his body was found.
Believe me.
Very sincerely yours
Lt-Col Philip E Vaughan

Further details about how he died were sent to Marjorie by 14043 Private Norman Angus, a miner from Fencehouses, a Durham Colliery village:

No 1 Coy No. 5 Hut,
Yorkshire Regiment
Ballyvonare Camp
Buttevant
County Cork
Ireland

Dear Miss Secretan,
Sorry you have had to wait for an answer to your letter but with me coming straight to Ireland my mother had to send it on to me here. Yes, I was with the Yorks when we left Liphook two years ago and I have had the misfortune to be wounded twice, of course not too serious.

Well to give you all the help I can give you in regard to Captain Dodgson. Our first advance began on 8th July. Of course we came through alright with a few casualties. Of course we never sleep

Captain Maurice Hume-Wright, killed in action 10 July.

for one hour from the 1st up to the 10th where we caught pretty hot. We were ordered to take Contalmaison at costs and we had to advance over 1,000 yards of open ground. We arrived at the front line trench at 5.50 p.m. then we mounted the parapet at 5.55 every man as calm as water in a cup. Captain Dodgson leading and encouraging his men on like an old veteran, never once faltering, all this going on with our men falling on all sides but we had to get the village and we meant to have [it].

But just about 100 yards from the goal Captain Dodgson got hit in the head. Then we gave him a drink and made him as comfortable as possible under the circumstances. He wasn't dead then, but later on in the evening after we got the village someone passed the word up the line that Captain Simpson, Lieutenant Hume-Wright and Captain Dodgson had been killed, but I can tell you Captain Dodgson got hit leading his men over the open front.

Sorry I can't write more as I have no paper left. Hoping you will accept my greatest sympathy during your bereavement, but hope for the best until informed of his death.

I am yours truly
Private N Angus

Another private who wrote to the family was 16814 Anthony Maughan, another Durham miner who although originally from Usworth was living in Hetton-le-Hole. He had been Toby Dodgson's servant for a time and was wounded in the scrotum on 10 July:

Holnest Hospital
Nr Sherborne,
Dorset.
Dear Sir

I hope you will excuse me for taking the liberty of writing these few lines sympathising with you through the death of Capt Dodgson. I feel it my duty to tell you how much he was loved by the NCOs and men that were under him while he was in command of B Company. Although he was killed you can rest assured that he did not throw his life away through carelessness, as he was known to be one of the coolest-headed officers in the battalion.

I was in the officer's mess all the time he was in B Coy. He was the president, as you will no doubt know, and I was the caterer.

> I have never seen a man so cool as he was when we made the attack. I saw it in the paper about his death, so I will close.
>
> From your sincere friend
>
> Private A Maughan.

It has previously been explained that the Red Cross published lists of the missing and had interviewers speaking to wounded men in hospitals both in England and in France. On 11 August, L.M. Ashton, a Red Cross researcher, interviewed 11507 Private Timothy Boddy of Middlesbrough, who had been admitted to the Woodlawn Red Cross Hospital in Didsbury with a GSW to the left ankle. He stated:

> On 10 July 1916 at Contalmaison the Captain was just to the left of him in the trench and was shot outright just at the beginning of the charge. Informant saw no more as he went on and when he returned later with prisoners he was not able to make a further search. The Captain had just taken over command as Captain Richardson had been wounded a day or two before. The informant said Capt. Dodgson came from Liphook and he had been with him at Frensham from 1914 was B Coy.

Another soldier interviewed at the V.A.D. Hospital Eastcote, Middlesex, was 13697 Private William J. Lobban, originally from Huntly, Aberdeenshire. By 1911 he was employed in a marine boilermakers in Sunderland as a general labourer. He didn't say anything about Captain Dodgson but offered A. Hall, the Red Cross researcher, the information that, 'Private Maughan A, 16814 8th Yorks was orderly to Captain Dodgson and was most probably with him when he fell.'

A similar statement was made by another Sunderland man. Interviewed at No. 10 General Hospital, Rouen, 14564 Private Wilfred Tweddell said. 'Private John McKensie, 8th Bn A Coy, who is a great friend of mine, told me that the Captain of his company told him that Capt Dodgeson [*sic*] was killed at Contalmaison.'

Before he wrote to Marjorie, Private Norman Angus made a very similar statement as he wrote in his letter to P.L. Waterhouse when he was a patient in the County of London War Hospital, Epsom. However, the researcher recorded the statement, as made by Private Angus Norman, a relatively easy mistake to make in the circumstances.

One other statement exists in Toby Dodgson's file at The National Archives, made by 13793 Private William Campion, a labourer from Whitby, of 9 Platoon, C Company. He was at a convalescent camp in Rouen when he said: 'We began an attack at Contalmaison at about 5 p.m. on July 11th. I do not know how Capt Dodgson was killed but after the attack his body was found and brought in by the Pioneer Battalion of the S Staffs Regt. I think this is the 9th Batt. I do not know where they took it, nor could I say where Capt Dodgson was buried.'

Captain Francis Dodgson was killed in action on 10 July. His body was later recovered and buried in Serre Road Cemetery No 2, France.

On 14 December 1928 his remains were recovered and in the same place the remains of three other men were discovered, more about these below.

The other ranks are somewhat harder to track down. However, as the Commonwealth War Graves Commission now attach the exhumation records to a deceased soldier's online documents, tracing information about an individual is a little easier than some years ago.

Of those originally reported missing, seventy-five men of 8/Yorkshire Regiment and forty-four of 9/Yorkshire Regiment are recorded on the Thiepval Memorial to the Missing. Those exhumed in the years immediately after the war by the 21st Labour Company were reburied in Gordon Dump Cemetery, six from 8/Yorkshire Regiment and four from 9/Yorkshire Regiment. Those exhumed later were taken to Serre Road No. 2 Cemetery. On 9 April 1927 six bodies were recovered just outside of Contalmaison. However, only three were identified. All six were taken to Serre Road No. 2 Cemetery and reburied in Plot III, Row C. Nevertheless, on 14 December 1928, when the body of Captain Dodgson was recovered, the remains of 14772 Lance Corporal James Dixon were recovered in the same place. Along with him were two others, one corporal and a private, but they could not be identified. Given that it had been almost eighteen months since the other men had been buried, the cemetery had filled rapidly with recovered bodies and the four found that day were reburied in Plot XXVIII, Row K.

Others were buried close to the Dressing Stations and Casualty Clearing Stations where they were taken for treatment to their wounds, namely Heilly Station, Punchevillers and Abbeville. These war grave cemeteries all sprang up around medical facilities where wounded men died. Likewise, some men who were wounded during the attack on Contalmaison and reached hospitals on the coast died from their wounds and were buried near the hospital. Of course, others made it home to hospitals in England, Scotland and Wales, apart from 11755 Private George T. Clark, who died in Plymouth and is buried there.

Three others died at hospitals and were taken home to be buried. No. 12525 Private Walter Nice died in London and was transported back to All Saints Churchyard, Langley Park, for burial. In the same way, 11951 Lance Corporal Joseph Mann died at the Alexandra Park Hospital in Stockport. He too was carried home and lies in Linthorpe Cemetery, Middlesbrough. A third soldier, 13711 Private Albert Moss, lived until 24 July, when he succumbed to his wounds in Aberdeen. His body was conveyed to Houghton-le-Spring, where he is buried in Durham Road cemetery.

As has been previously stated, the DDMS III Corps had directed that the lightly wounded should be evacuated to No. 34 CCS at Verquemont. No fewer than 126 men of the 8/Yorkshire and 9/Yorkshire Regiments passed through this Clearing Station between 10 and 14 July 1916.

Given that their details are recorded in the ledgers, they provide information about the nature of the wounds and dates of admission and discharge. Hence, it has allowed a small degree of analysis of this group of wounded men.

A number of the casualties had wounds that no other man had, for example eye, face or neck. Others had multiple wounds such as lower jaw, lips and neck or right leg, right thigh and right arm:

1. Thigh Wounds

Eleven of the casualties of the group studied had thigh wounds. However, only one had a broken femur. In the first two years of the war, this wound was associated with a high mortality rate. However, by 1916, a programme of medical advancements had been made to reduce disabilities from thigh wounds.[49] Nine soldiers of the study group were evacuated on No. 22 Ambulance Train on 11 July. No. 11513 Private Ernest Wright was evacuated on No. 9 Ambulance Train on 12 July. It is assumed therefore that he did receive some form of treatment at the CCS. The remaining man, Private Matthew Richardson, who had been admitted before 6 a.m., remained at No. 34 CCS until 15 July, when he was evacuated on No. 16 Ambulance Train.[50] Given the length of time he spent at No. 34 CCS, it must be assumed that the medical staff had concerns and he was unfit to travel. However, he must have had some form of medical intervention before being sent further down the LOC. Furthermore, it is known that he soon returned to the front. Posted to 2/Yorkshire Regiment, he was killed in action on 31 March 1917.[51]

No. 19853 Private Robert Young was wounded in the right thigh with a compound fracture of the femur. He was evacuated on No. 22 Ambulance Train. In his case, he was a late arrival at No. 34 CCS.[52] When the ambulance train arrived at Rouen, Private Young was immediately taken to No. 1 Canadian

General Hospital, where his right thigh was amputated at the hip. For eight days Private Young was on the dangerously ill list but on 19 July Infantry Records York informed his next of kin he had been removed from the list and was improving.[53]

From the cases of Privates Richardson and Young it can be seen that early intervention and treatment saved limbs and lives. The late intervention led to amputations and in many other cases the death of the casualty. However, the question arises: was Private Young properly assessed before being placed on the ambulance train?

Lieutenant Colonel C. Gordon Watson RAMC stated; 'Within a few hours of the onset of physical signs of gas, extensive gangrene may develop in the wounds, and life will hang upon the slender thread of an immediate and rapid amputation.'[54]

No. 11942 Private James A. Woods was another casualty with a thigh wound but also a severe arm wound who reached No. 5 General Hospital at Rouen early on 12 July. Two days later he was evacuated to Bradford War Hospital. He was discharged on 24 November as no longer physically fit for war service owing to a compound fracture of the radius, a bone in the arm, and received a weekly pension of fifteen shillings and sixpence.[55]

Many articles regarding the search for an effective way of treating infected gunshot wounds were written by eminent surgeons serving in France. Colonel H.M.W. Gray recommended the use of tablet and gauze packs as early as April 1916:

> It is requisite that some dressing should be available which is effective in preventing severe sepsis, easy to carry, simple in application, economical of material and time, and so continuous in action that little attention is necessary during transport. Hypertonic saline dressing, especially in the form now known as the 'tablet and gauze pack', fulfils these desiderata better than any others applied.[56]

Moreover, given the lack of treatment evidence for the wounded men of the research group, it can be seen from the surviving documents that a number of them were back in England by 14 July. Therefore the 'tablet and gauze packs' may have been in use at No. 34 CCS in July 1916.

One man with a thigh wound was not evacuated through No. 34 CCS. No. 13337 Private George Smithson, who was wounded in the bomb accident in November 1915, was wounded in the thigh and his leg broken on 10 July 1916. He was treated at No. 13 Stationary Hospital at Wimereux and although they saved his leg it was weak and he was discharged on 31 May 1917.

2. Shell Shock

The term shell shock was invented during the First World War as a blanket descriptive term used to cover the various mental disorders of wartime. However, it became controversial as it was inaccurate and extremely damaging as it suggested a connection between the effects of a shell explosion and the development of neurotic symptoms.[57] Owing to the lack of understanding of shell shock, Medical Officers were reluctant to commit themselves to a diagnosis and cases were sent down the line labelled as shell shock (wounded). This arguably led to unnecessary evacuation to the base of patients suffering from fatigue and simple hysteria. By 1916 the treatment for minor shell shock casualties was to remove them to the Divisional Rest Station and to give them food, a warm drink and then, after a period of rest, return them to active duty. However, less than 10 per cent of the psychiatric casualties were consequences of the physical effects of explosions, the rest it was argued were emotional in origin.[58]

On 11 July ten of the soldiers in the study arrived at No. 34 CCS suffering from various types of shell shock. They were all evacuated to the base; seven of them were sent on 11 July on No. 22 Ambulance Train. The remaining three casualties were evacuated on 12 July: two were evacuated on No. 9 Ambulance Train and the last shell shock patient was evacuated on No. 25 Ambulance Train.

The most serious case was that of 16670 Private Thomas Lumley, a coal miner from Waterhouses, County Durham, who was blown up by a shell and buried on 10 July. Private Lumley was unconscious when he arrived at No. 34 CCS and was still in that state when he reached No. 12 General Hospital at Rouen. He was hospitalised for six days and was then evacuated to England, where he was sent to the 4th London General Hospital. He remained in the hospital for nine weeks. In his surviving service documents, the 'Army Form B 179 Medical Report on an Invalid', written by Captain Stephenson RAMC, the Assistant Registrar of the 4th London General Hospital at the time of Private Lumley's discharge from hospital states:

> Usual shell shock symptoms, Treatment in Neurological section, anaesthesia – generalised at first (now limited to right leg below knee 9/9/1916). Analysis, from six inches above to nine inches below the knee. Discharged from the hospital under Army General Instruction 1023/16 para 4 Section D.

Private Lumley was posted to the 3/(Reserve) Battalion Yorkshire Regiment at West Hartlepool. Then in January 1917, owing to further medical problems with the shell shock, he was examined by a Medical Board. It reported that:

> He complains of pains in the head and occasional loss of memory. Has pain in the back and constant numbness in the right leg. He sleeps badly and is troubled by bad dreams. The man has evidently received a severe shock which has undermined his nervous system. He has slight shaking of the head and constant tremors of the hands. The heart appears normal, pulse rate 70. Knee reflex seems slightly exaggerated.

The result of this Medical Board was that he was medically downgraded and was transferred to the Labour Corps in June 1917.[59] Despite being blown up and buried, on the Army Form D 400 compiled at the time of his discharge he stated that he was returning to work as a coal miner in his home village. Private Lumley died in 1934.

Another soldier, 17231 Private William Strong, was admitted to No. 34 CCS suffering from similar symptoms, although he was conscious throughout. Private Strong was a coal miner who came from Seaham, County Durham. His case is interesting because he is one of those young men who lied about their age in order to enlist. Private Strong enlisted at Sunderland on 28 November 1914, when he gave his age as 19 years and 9 months. This gives a birth date of 1895. On 11 July 1916 on admission to No. 34 CCS, he gave his age as 18 years. These conflicting age facts led to a search of the 1911 Census for Seaham, where he was found living with his parents and siblings. However, his age was given as 13 years. The 1939 Register gives his date of birth as 1 February 1898, which in effect means he was aged 16 when he enlisted. In his service file a medical report states that Private Strong suffered from:

> A tremor of hands and slight & stammering, headaches, memory defective some mental confusion, knee and ankle jerks slightly increased. Palpitation of the heart, no murmur.

It would appear from the entries in medal rolls that Private Strong did not return to France but went on to serve until 1919 in England. However, in 1919 he did receive a pension for shell shock, which continued to affect him in later years. This can be substantiated by further entries in his medical reports in 1920 and 1921, when he is reported as still suffering from 'pains in the head, he talks in

Private Billy Strong, from Seaham, served in B Company, 8th Battalion. (*Brian Scollen*)

his sleep, has war dreams and becomes easily excited. Furthermore, he avoids places of amusement and is self-conscious.'[60] After discharge, he returned to coal mining, and by 1939 he was still employed as a hewer in Dawdon Colliery, near Seaham.[61] William Strong died in 1976.[62]

Of the ten men researched who suffered from shell shock all survived the war. No. 24466 Private John Cory was transferred to Class W Reserve as a munitions worker and subsequently returned to work as an ironstone miner. No. 12677 Private Thomas Goodings was evacuated to No. 23 General Hospital and then on 16 July to the 3rd Scottish General Hospital at Stobhill, Glasgow, from where he was discharged in March 1917 as 'No Longer Fit for War Service'. Two remained in the infantry, with one man transferred to the Royal Defence Corps. Three were transferred at different times to the Labour Corps. However, the lack of treatment records for the remaining casualties prevents a reliable appraisal of their level of 'shell shock' treatment and further military service.

3. Head Wounds

In 1915 the British front-line soldier in France was wearing the Field Service Cap made of khaki serge material. However, Captain J.E.H. Roberts, RAMC, stated, 'The number of patients who arrive at the base hospitals with gunshot wounds of the scalp is large.'[63] To protect the soldiers in September 1915 the Army issued the 'Brodie' helmet but the supply was limited and they were designated as 'trench stores'.[64] As such, the helmets were handed over to the next unit when a relief took place in the front line. However, it was not until the summer of 1916 that steel helmets were on general issue. Arguably owing to the protective nature of the steel helmets, the incidence of head wounds in the study is relatively small as only five cases of such wounds are recorded.

No. 14423 Private John Earl, a locomotive fireman employed in the steelworks at Redcar, was evacuated to the East Leeds War Hospital with a shrapnel wound of the skull. He was a patient there from 13 July until 9 September, when he was deemed fit for overseas service and was posted to the 6/Green Howards in France.[65] Another casualty, 14564 Private Wilfred Tweddle, was evacuated with a gunshot wound of the head. When he arrived at Rouen he was transferred to No. 10 General Hospital, where he was a patient until 31 August. He was not evacuated to England and joined the 37th Infantry Base Depot for two weeks training before re-joining his battalion on the Somme.[66]

All of the five men researched were returned fairly quickly to active service. Four survived the war, although two were discharged owing to being wounded again later in the conflict. It can be seen that any treatment these casualties received was successful. However, 24395 Private Tom Lee, who before the war was a groom living in Stokesley, was posted to the 7/Green Howards and was killed in action on 5 November 1916.[67]

4. Wounds to the Extremities – Shoulders, Arms, Hands, Knees and Legs

The largest number of wounds in the study, 50 per cent, was to the shoulders, arms and hands. Those to the left of the body were twice as many as those to the right. It can be seen that advancing at the 'high port', which is with the rifle carried diagonally across the body, gave some protection to the chest. Of those whose documents have survived, the only amputations were of fingers and thumbs. Some of the wounds were relatively light, for example, 17539 Corporal John Riches was wounded with soft tissue damage to the right arm. Within two weeks he had re-joined his battalion, only to be wounded again. He was evacuated again to Vecquemont, where he died of wounds on 7 August.[68] There were four soldiers with wounds to the knees. One, 3/8489 Private Walter Williams, was discharged owing to his wounds in July 1917, while the others remained in the Army until the end of the war. After a period of treatment, rest and recuperation most of those with leg wounds were soon back at the front, often posted to another battalion.

5. Chest Wounds

There were only two soldiers with chest wounds among the researched cohort. The first was 19316 Private Thomas Henry Dunning. Before the war, he was a pony driver in a colliery near West Rainton in County Durham. The Green Howards' recruiting registers show he enlisted on 14 January 1915 at Houghton-le-Spring and was posted to the 11/(Reserve) Green Howards before joining the 9/Yorkshire Regiment on 4 March 1915.[69] No documents survived for this soldier, however, it is known from the medal rolls that he went back to France, probably in early or mid-1917, and joined 13/Green Howards. Coupled with this, his name appears in *The Times* casualty list of 23 October 1917. This would indicate a wound in early September 1917. Recovering from this wound, he was transferred to the West Riding Regiment and was reported wounded for a third time in the War Office Weekly Casualty List on 11 June 1918. He was discharged on 29 November 1918. However, the research is hampered by the lack of knowledge of Private Dunning's exact wounds. He returned to his home village, married, had children and was still working in a coal mine in 1939.[70] His death was recorded in the June quarter of 1969.[71]

The second man with a chest wound was 13783 Private Albert James Bail. His personal documents have survived in a burned format. However, they do show that there was hand-to-hand bayonet fighting in Contalmaison, as the document records. Bail had a bayonet wound in the chest.[72] This was quite significant and the only incidence of a bayonet wound in the research group. However, as Lieutenant H.H. Sampson, RAMC, wrote, 'bayonet wounds are rarely seen and must be rapidly fatal'.[73] However, Private Bail was again reported wounded in *The Times* casualty list on 27 December 1917.[74] By 1918 he had transferred to the Labour Corps and served with a number of labour companies. When the information for the 1939 Register was gathered he was working at a steelworks on Teesside, where he was employed as a bricklayer's labourer.

In summary, all the casualties evacuated from No. 34 CCS should have had their wounds cleaned and re-dressed prior to evacuation to hospitals on the French coast. From there they were either sent back to England or to convalescent camps for a period of recuperation before joining the base depot for reposting. However, the lack of treatment information can only lead to assumptions and speculation about their wound management and the treatment they received.

It was not long after the battle that stories from those who took part started to appear in the newspapers. Under the heading, 'Sheffield lieutenant in a great charge', The *Sheffield Daily Telegraph* printed a letter from Lieutenant Edmund G. Bingham, the youngest son of Mr and Mrs F.W. Bingham, 117, Upper Hanover Street, Sheffield, who was said to have been wounded on the 9th inst., and was resting at a little village away from the firing line until he regained his strength. In an interesting letter to his father and mother he said:

> I told you in my last letter on Sunday that we were out for a few hours' rest, but on Sunday night we got orders to proceed into the front line to take a strong position occupied by the Germans. No less than four attempts had already been made to take it, but had failed and with considerable loss. The attack was timed for 4.50 in the afternoon and punctually to the minute we got over the parapet and advanced across the open. The distance between us and the enemy was, roughly 1,000 to 1,200 yards. I shall never forget that advance. We were exposed the whole way to a galling fire from heavy shell, shrapnel, machine-gun and rifle fire, our fellows dropped all around, and at one time I thought the attack must fail. But it didn't. I got three fourths of the way across when I was bowled over by shrapnel in the arm and leg. One of the majors was shot through the back at the same moment. I managed to drag him and myself into a shell hole just by. Later, I succeeded in reaching the Boche trench. The Boches had then stampeded but they were captured in a village in the rear. We kept that position all night and the following day, when we were relieved at midnight. We have now come

out to get reorganised. The fame of the battalion is assured everywhere. The cost was enormous and regrettable, but we accomplished what we set out to do. I have had my wounds properly dressed at the hospital and I am progressing very favourably. I am not in hospital, but resting quietly in one of the villages. The Colonel was most anxious that I should stay in hospital but as I only have a flesh wound I didn't think this was necessary. I daresay you will think all this sounds very terrible, but I am alive and comparatively well, so one cannot grumble. I can assure you we gave the Boches something for their trouble. This is my first real action and I think after this I shall weather the storm, or at least, I hope so.[75]

Edmund Bingham was commissioned into the 11 (Reserve) Battalion on 29 January 1916. He landed in France on 15 June. Therefore, he was in France less than a month before being wounded.

Another man who had a letter printed in his local paper was Sergeant Thomas Parsons, who before the war had been employed at Cochrane's Works at Cargo Fleet but by 1916 was the machine gun sergeant of 9/Yorkshire Regiment. He wrote a letter to his local newspaper as follows:

Just a line or two from a few local lads who are now having a well-earned rest after chasing the Boche out of his kennel. I expect by now that the news of the Yorkshire Regiment will be old and 'No bon.' In all the papers we get here the story of our regiment's doing is conspicuous by its absence. I will bet a franc to a cing sous that there were more local lads – Middlesbrough, South Bank, Ormesby, Grangetown, Eston, Stockton and Durham went over the top at what we call the backbone of the 'Allemands' line than some think of. They all went over in broad daylight about five o-clock and took a line of trenches, a village and a line of trenches at the end of the village. Among them were our battalion and our pals, the Yorks [8/Yorkshire Regiment].

As our General told us after they went over as if they were on the parade ground at Richmond. Every man was a hero. I think I can honestly say that it was most hellish. Every man in the Boche line I think must have had a machine gun and I assure you he used it. They tried to stop us with a heavy fusillade of machine gun fire and all sorts of shells, but our lads never wavered for one moment. Some went over singing, some talking. I noticed one of our officers smoking a cigar. We lost some fine lads out of the two battalions. All that went over were out of the good old Yorks.

These two battalions are formed (along with others of course) out of the very first lot of Kitchener's. Men who came and sacrificed good homes, work and as Kipling said, 'Left their little ones behind.' It is exactly two years ago next month that these battalions were made up with these men. Men out of the mines, pits, foundries, blast-furnaces, etc. They all came at our great leaders' call. Do you know sir, no matter what paper the lads pick up the first thing they look for is the tribunals. The paltry excuses of these men who say their homes would be broken up. What about ours? We have left better homes than some of them. I myself left a good job, good money and one of the best homes in the world. We will send them a few francs if that is all they are thinking about. The Government will look after their homes for them. It is all rot. We are now well on the road for victory, and we will want a lot of good men yet. I can assure you that the Yorkshire Regiment has seen some bitter times, and a nice spell of a few days with our dear ones at home would be 'fort bien.' So round them all up and send them, so we can get to Berlin (We are on our way now). I would like to tell you where we broke the Boche line and took hundreds of them prisoner, along with over a dozen machine-guns. The Boche when you go for him merely whines 'Merci Kamerade.' The poor devils are in an awful plight. Our Artillery has put the fear of the devil in him.

He is half hungered. Some Boche officers' dug-outs were so full of food but the German soldier does not get it. They tell us they are glad to be caught. We have found lots of whips and cat-o-nine tails in their dug-outs. That is what the officers of Satan's mate (Kaiser Bill) do to their men. All our officers are our pals in the trenches, and share our hardships. That is all the difference. I will now close as I know how valuable our good old paper is, and as badly as this letter affects over a thousand local lads in the good old Yorks, not mentioning the two other regiments who are with us, and shares all our honour (this concerns the Yorks alone), I ask, on their behalf, to let us see it out here. We get sent every week the '*Herald*', the '*North-Eastern Daily Gazette*', and the good old 'Sports Gazette'.

So au revoir and the best of luck, and send the shells for our artillery to blow them to h.....

Keep all the good men on munitions – they are doing as much as us – but don't send us any conscientious objectors, as our C.O. will be disgusted and swear, and we will do the rest, via Berlin. You talk about seeing life. We do out here. The Yorks have, I think, been all over France bar Paris. So 'bon jour' and best wishes for 'Old Bird,' who we all expect to see at Ayresome Park this winter. – Machine Gun Sergt T Parsons (Proud of the Yorks.)[76]

Sergeant Parsons' letter is very much of its time. He is obviously proud of being an early Kitchener volunteer and proud of his battalion and regiment. However, his true feelings come through when he refers to those still at home and the feeling against the conscientious objectors. There is a feeling that any grounds, religious or moral, for not serving would have been dismissed without question. He also belittles the German soldier and exaggerates the number of whips and the like found in their dugouts. Nevertheless, it cannot be denied that he was a brave man for the following was reported in the same newspaper:

> Sergeant T Parsons 9th Yorks of 28 Aire Street, South Bank, son of Mr and Mrs Parsons of Upper Oxford Street, South Bank, has been awarded the Military Medal for exceptional bravery and devotion to duty on the field. His commanding officer reports that when the machine gun officer was shot, Parsons led the men and captured single handed a machine gun. He was the first British soldier to arrive in Contalmaison. Previous to the war Sergeant Parsons was employed at Cochrane's works. He was captain of the First South Bank Division, Boys Life Brigade and was also in the Territorials. He was keenly interested in all sports and often figured in amateur athletics.[77]

As well as the letters, the newspapers carried reports of the battle, of which, many stated that the German troops fighting in the village were the 'Prussian Guard', with headlines such as 'How the Prussian guard were cut up'. However, the overall command was in the hands of the 3rd Guard Division, and one of its units, the 'Lehr' Regiment, was holding their right flank. But the two

Wurttembergische Reserve Infantry Regiment 122 on parade before leaving for the front.

other regiments were normal infantry not guardsmen, who had been sent in as reinforcements. They were Schleswig-Holsteinisches Infanterie-Regiment Nr. 163 and the Wurttembergische Reserve Infantry Regiment 122.

The German View

It is useful to read and understand the German point of view of the battle. When RIR 122 arrived on the Somme on 6 July their historian made this observation:

> As it was daylight one could clearly see the rapid progress of our lines ahead. During the day you could clearly see the hustle and bustle of our front lines. The high [ground] south of Contalmaison was wrapped in black smoke from impacting shells and shrapnel of all sizes. From time to time earth fountains might be shot up, resulting from the hitting of the heaviest calibres.[78]

Having moved up to the line near Mametz wood, the commander of the III Battalion, Major von Zeppelin, was seriously wounded there by shrapnel, and died in a flash. Lieutenant Rostlin himself vividly described more details about the advance of No. 6 Company and the conduct of the fighting between Contalmaison and the Mametz Wood on 10 July in his report:

Infantrymen of Sachsen Infantry Regiment 163 at the front.

On the afternoon of July 9th I received the order to take No. 6 Company with two machine guns to reinforce the III Battalion in the section at Mametz wood with the instruction to bring a lot of food, hand grenades and light ammunition. Two guides of the III Battalion, who led us to the troubled position, were ordered to go to Martinpuich at 11.30 in the evening to go to the bivouacs. With the dusk drawing in, I left the reserve position with the company to go back to our bivouac and the ammunition depot in Martinpuich. I took this opportunity to put all the knapsacks down by the bivouacs in order to free us of any weight that could be dispensed with. Even with all the ammunition we still had enough to carry the cased hand grenades and food. Our meal at the kitchen was interrupted by shells suddenly striking in the yard in the middle of the local road, which scared our goulash horses [these horses pulled the goulash cannon, the German nickname for the field cooker] so much that they immediately took off with the kitchen at a gallop. Despite visible reluctance on their part, they had to endure with us after they were stopped again. At around 1 a.m. on July 10th, I gave the order to get ready to leave. I divided the company into three new roles. Then it went forward. When I was exploring the path in the dead of darkness, my compass did an excellent job for me. I didn't want to leave the men from the III Battalion placed on top of me as guides. Lieutenant Schmid, who had gone up to the III Battalion with the 5th company the night before, had his orderly, whom he had detached

The funeral of Major von Zeppelin, 12 July 1916.

from the company, direct me not to walk through the Mametz sections if I was going forward because he had already been there. It had already suffered severe damage from the barrage. I had therefore decided to proceed between the Mametz forest and Contalmaison in the rough shrapnel mill and avoid the forest itself. On the advance I first marched in rows, however, I soon found that the column was too long and when crossing the steep rift between Martinpuich and the south-western forest of Bazentin, more and more breaks, which wasted too much time, so I ordered group columns to be formed in which we better got ahead. Up to Bazentin, where we again passed the reserve position, everything went without a noticeable incident. Shortly afterwards, before crossing the Bazentin–Contalmaison road, the first shrapnel came rushing in, which immediately cost us losses. My orderly, who was walking close behind me, was the first to suffer a slight wound in the hand. While a large number of men from the company were still lying on the floor, some seriously wounded, including Sergeant Hopplich. The stretcher-bearers had plenty of work. The rest of us who remained intact had to keep going in order not to be caught off guard by the day. It was a difficult pretence, all the usual shrapnel came close and there were few wounded. We saw the whole space between the front trench and the second position, constantly being scattered by enemy artillery, and because of this barrage, which was particularly violent on the forest to our left, we had to go through it, if we wanted to go forward. When, in the opinion of the two guides from III Battalion, we were not far from the front positions, I stopped at a suitable place as well as I could, took cover and went and sent the two guides ahead with the question of HQ III Battalion. Where the company should be deployed.

After a long twenty minutes they came back with the decision that we were correct and that we were behind 10, 11 and 12 Companies. Immediately I found it easy to start again when something very unexpected happened for us. A machine gun came down sharply a few hundred metres to the right of us and the bullets pounded hard over our heads. Everything apart, there was a great deal of confusion. I ordered: 'All march, march into the ditch in front of us.' There it was still a good distance to run maybe 300 metres. I hurried ahead and was of the opinion that the whole company had heard my order and followed it. Whether some of the people were confused or had not heard my order due to the noise of machine gun fire, or perhaps they were surprised, we might have believed hours in front of an enemy trench, that the result of the surprise was only Lieutenant Roch and about with me 30 men of 6 Company instead of around 50 had reached the trench of the III Battalion after the

> wounded had moved. It was of course quite a while until this discovery, which for me was quite sad, and although I immediately asked one of my best people, Dengler to go himself, to bring forward the sections and mainly the two machine guns, this unfortunately failed. But at least I was reassured by Dengler's report that the people hadn't been buried in the MG fire, because in the whole area in question no one was to be found, including any wounded or killed. As can be determined later, after they had lost their sight of us once and no longer knew where to go, they had to call out to the broader position at dawn. Some of them remained lying in shell holes in the intermediate area all day and only returned in the evening after the second position.[79]

Having reached the position without enough men, Leutnant Roslin needed information and sought out the officer in charge of holding that portion of the line:

> Lieutenant Irion, who greeted me in the trench when I arrived, informed me that the English had broken through to our right tonight, i.e. on the high ground on the eastern edge of Contalmaison, and there must be an English nest with a MG on the high ground behind our right wing. Of course it was like that. This machine gun had shot at us when we broke into position and broke my whole company apart. It is a pity that we had not been instructed about this earlier in the rear, for example at our start point. From there we had begun to attack and dig in. Now it too late, because of the dawning day. The connection with the battalion commander Major von Zeppelin, whose battle tunnel on the southern edge of the Mametz forest was about 600 metres from us, could not be established at 4 a.m. because the gorge in between was in the fire of a fiendish machine gun. The real order of the battalion was to act independently without waiting for further orders. For the same reason it was not possible to find out what the situation was with the company that was in the positions to our left over the gorge across the south and east of the Mametz Wald, i.e. our 5th, 8th and 9th companies.[80]

This gives the reader a good idea of what things were like for the German reserves moving forward in relief. However, this was all to the south of the area that 69 Brigade was to attack at Contalmaison, held by 1 Battalion RIR 122. The German regimental history goes on:

The struggle for Contalmaison was of brilliant courage and perseverance for itself. Our people had to fight their way to the top. With hand grenades and bayonets they had to work their way through a maze of labyrinthine trenches which during the high point of the battle were filled with dead and wounded. At last the survivors had worked their way through to the southern tip of the village. They also had to be aware that they were kept secretly hidden. Machine guns across from them were now on both sides and from the front under fire imitated that was supported in an uncanny way by German hand grenade throws that suddenly protruded from the most unbelievable bursts. In addition, the bad weather increased as well. A pouring rain feasts on them down to their bones and as if struck with blindness by the storm and the bullets rattling down like hailstones they lost contact with one another. It was impossible to go any further under these circumstances. The utmost had been done and our people withdrew.

The infantry attack of the English began at 6 o'clock [pm German time on July 10]. They went ahead in 15–20 waves. Our artillery would only be very weak. The companies defended themselves desperately and with the utmost effort and also inflicted considerable losses on the enemy; but these were immediately replenished by the Division by sending reserves. There in the afternoon of July 9th, Inf Reg 183 attacked the Jagerhohe again; initially moving forward quickly, the attack met resistance in the high point of the western exit of Contalmaison. The attackers received a myriad of machine guns in such a way that they only stayed on the eastern edge of the Jagerhohe and some of them went back to Pozières. In connection with this success, the English tried to push through the hollow path and the abandoned battery positions towards the village. When they did not succeed, they opened a concentric MG fire at 7:30 in the evening against the 3rd company and the village. At the same time, a heavy hail of shrapnel set in there, and the heavy artillery was soon rucked back into the large shelter as quickly as possible, everything else was dead, buried, and badly wounded.

The Company Commander, Lieutenant d R [der Reserve] Heinzelmann, had the edge of the village occupied to the right and left of the shelter, since I did not have the position in front of the edge of the village. Smoke, smoke and dust filled the air in such a way that the approach of the English could not be expected. The company leaders sent up red flares to get Artillery support. One of the two exits of Heinzelmann's shelter collapsed, though the other large shelters also collapsed. The rubble rendered the machine gun unusable. On the shelter itself, hit after hit. A direct hit threw the wall around behind which was the Company Commander and his bugler observer, and the former fell. The bugler pulled him out and dragged him back into the reserve position; he was also wounded in the foot by the barrage. Lieutenant Hering took over the company and, when the English had already penetrated the village from the east, occupied a ravine with the remains of the company between the Contalmaison and the reserve position. The other companies of 1 Battalion RIR 122 had meanwhile been shot to pieces and no longer sprang up against the superior forces, especially against the concentric machine gun fire against the position and the edge of the village. The position in front of the latter was almost completely destroyed; their machine guns were out of action. Therefore, at 7:30 in the evening, the remnants of the 4 company and parts of the 1 company withdrew to the edge of the village. At 10 o'clock that evening the enemy advance on our right flank forced us to withdraw to the reserve position. The enemy, no longer effectively to be kept back, reached Contalmaison from the south-east, and took the battalion staff prisoner in Contalmaison Chateau and in the south of 2 Company, which was also held in the front by the enemy about 300 metres away. The remnants of 2 Company with parts of 1 Company remained in their position until 11.30 in the evening. But since they were more uncomfortable and the enemy began to get stuck in front of the company, they went back to the reserve position. The remnants of the regiment gathered on July 11th in Bertincourt, where the large baggage [the packs and equipment not required in the line] was also quartered. It was only a tiny village. The attitude of the officers, non-commissioned officers and men in these difficult battles was excellent. They fell on the post on which they were placed; others attacked the enemy, no matter how endangered the post was. There was never a lack of volunteer runners to go through the barrage. The regiment's position had been taken up at a fresh stage of combat; it was lost due to the overwhelming force of the attackers and was especially destroyed by the enemy artillery. On the right, Contalmaison hung completely in the air as a result of the loss of the Jagerhohe, and on the left, after the excess of the Mametz forest, the situation became untenable. All in all, the regiment, even if it failed to succeed, held a difficult bastion for a few days and forced the English to initiate an infantry storm, prepared by gunfire from artillery, against the weakly occupied position.

Schleswig-Holsteinisches Infanterie-Regiment Nr. 163 had been in the line since early in July. Their regimental history gives a quiet graphic account of the early fighting in front of Contalmaison:

Oberst Sick Commanding Inf Regt 163.

At I Battalion on the right wing, 3 Company, to which parts of 6 Company had been attached, had repulsed three English attacks. The first two were totally rejected. During the third, two groups, positioned on the right wing in the small square forest south of 4 Company position, were bypassed and for the most part defeated. The rest fell back until the forest edge 9/186 had joined 2 Company's decline. 1 Company was spared from English attacks. It was separated from the neighbouring company by a small ridge. It now began, under the leadership of its youthful officer Leutnant Ruge, to establish a 400 metre-long connecting trench to the south-western edge of Contalmaison. The company had significant losses to artillery. Nevertheless, before dawn they managed to dig 250 metres to a depth of about 1.5 metres. At first it was not noticed that the English had the previous evening entered the trench in front, and had occupied it on the right wing of the company. About 250 metres in front of our position still stood a machine gun from 190 I R, and it fired uninterrupted against the enemy. Lt Meyer with his division was pushed back into the old trench with hand grenades. Here the Englishmen who carried a machine gun were left dead and badly wounded, several with hand grenades and M.G. ammunition.

Major d Reserve Weede OC Inf Regt 163. Killed in action 4 November 1918.

The machine gun fired actively at the firing lines that appeared over the hill south of Fricourt, thereby preventing further progress. At 0900 Derling Meyer was relieved and returned to the Company. The replacement a platoon from Lehr I R. and machine guns were only in their position half an hour when there appeared to be a major enemy attack. The shelling of the company was constantly concealed. At

> noon Leutnant Melchior was wounded. Leutnant Ruge now determined that the left trench that the day before had been occupied by 2 Company was now occupied by the enemy. Our company was thus surrounded on all sides and covered with drum fire. Yet the position was retained. Only after dark did it become possible to bring the many wounded from the company and from 190 I.R. back to Contalmaison. At 0030 Leutnant Ruge went with the company back to Flers, where the people, who since the 3rd of July had neither eaten nor drunk, exhausted fell asleep, many without first having drunk the coffee that was ready for them.

On 9 July the regiment had moved back for a rest, but not for long:

> On July 10, there was rest, which was primarily used to get some sleep. Weapons were maintained and ammunition distributed. One went to bed early in the evening but the rest did not last long. On July 11, 0030,

The Guns of Contalmaison. Captured German weapons proudly displayed by those in charge. Taken from the *Green Howards Gazette*.

> the alarm went off. In a short time the Regiment was ready to march. From Army Group Stein, the following telephone signal had arrived: The regiment must be alerted immediately. The regiment marches to Le Sars, 6 km south-west of Bapaume, and occupies here as a stop line, the third line on both sides of the road.[81]

The battalions of 69 Brigade were relieved on the night of 11 July by units of 1 Brigade, 1st Division, and moved back initially to Belle Vue Farm, and then on 12 July to Franvillers supposedly to rest. However, the next day they were on the move again and marched to Molliens Au Bois, 8/Yorkshire Regiment proudly reporting, 'no stragglers'. Yet again the War Diary of 9/Yorkshire Regiment between 12 and 21 July simply states, 'in billets.' Furthermore, the GOC 23rd Division, Major General Babington issued a special Order of the Day:

> The G.O.C. the Division cannot allow the action of the 69th Brigade on July 10th to pass without special recognition. Nothing could have exceeded the steadiness and gallantry with which they carried out the attack and bore themselves in the hard fighting that followed. The example of gallantry and devotion to duty they set calls forth the highest admiration of all, and the Division are proud to possess such gallant comrades in their ranks.

On 14 July the GOC gave an address to the survivors of 69 Brigade in which he said:

> General Lambert, Officers and men of the 69th Brigade:-
> It was with confidence I trusted the capture of Contalmaison to this Brigade. It was not an easy task, in fact it was a difficult operation to carry out – very difficult, but most important, and it was with every confidence I entrusted it to your care.
>
> It is in a great measure due to the success of your efforts that the operations which began this morning were able to take place.
>
> In one area alone over 2,000 prisoners are reported to have been taken.
>
> It was not only important to take the place but also to hold it, and hesitation would have proved fatal.
>
> You never wavered. Nothing could have been finer. You have proved yourselves men and I have every confidence that if you have to face the same situation again, you will behave equally as well.
>
> I hope it will not be the last time I shall be called upon to offer my sincerest thanks to 69 Brigade.

The next day the Commander III Corps, Lieutenant General Sir W.P. Poultney KCB DSO, Commanding III Corps, arrived and also addressed the brigade in similar fashion. The one difference was that he included, 'the Artillery, the Trench Mortar Battery, Machine Gun Company, Signallers and stretcher-bearers'.

Congratulations also came, in the form of a Morse signal, from the Fourth Army HQ, which congratulated the whole division:

> 12/7/16 Following from FOURTH ARMY via III Corps, begins. Following, from General Rawlinson begins. Please convey to 23rd Division my hearty congratulations on their capture of Contalmaison. They have acquitted themselves right well and I desire to thank them most heartily for their gallantry and the fine fighting spirit displayed by all ranks. ends.

Chapter 6

The Somme Continued – Munster Alley and Le Sars

The 69th Brigade remained at Millencourt until 25 July. That day orders were received to relieve 2 Brigade the next day. This order was carried out and 69 Brigade became part of 1st Divisional Reserve. On 27 July 9/Yorkshire Regiment received a draft of six officers, with another six arriving the next day along with six for 8/Yorkshire Regiment.

In the evening of 29 July the 10/DWR began an attack on Munster Alley and, although they reached their objective, they were driven out by a counter-attack. The 10/DWR had quite a number of casualties, so on 30 July 9/Yorkshire Regiment took over the front line. It was now the German artillery started shelling Contalmaison and the Old German 1 and Old German 2 trenches with gas and tear shells, which lasted until 6.a.m. on the morning of 31 July. That morning 9/Yorkshire Regiment were increased by a draft of another four officers, then later in the day, 22-year-old 18391 Private Frank Stinger from New Brancepeth was killed. They held the front line on 1 August, losing one officer and four men wounded. One of those wounded, 14625 Private Henry Taylor, was evacuated to a CCS at Heilly Station, where he died from his wounds. That evening they were relieved by 13/DLI and moved back to trenches in Peake Wood. On the way out they had two killed, 23137 Lance Corporal John Bamborough and 16936 Private Robert Hobson, as well as eleven men wounded. Of the eleven, 20524 Private Henry Storey died in the Field Ambulance based in Albert.

Over the last few nights 8/Yorkshire Regiment had been providing large working parties to work on a new trench named 'Yorkshire Trench'. As many as 400 men were employed in this way. On the night of 29 July the Germans fired a large number of gas shells, which interrupted the work as the effects were felt strongly by those at work. On 31 July, 280 men were employed digging a communication trench from Contalmaison Villa to Yorkshire Trench, which was named 8th Alley. The battalion left its reserve position on 1 August and took over Scots Redoubt from 10/DWR, coming under the temporary command of HQ 68 Brigade. During the day one man, 17750 Private James Churchill, a coal miner from Ryhope, was killed. On 19 September 1919,

21 Labour Company exhumed at least fifteen bodies at 57d.X.22.d. The only one identified before reburial in Gordon Dump cemetery was James Churchill. Also on that July day five men were evacuated with shell shock, so heavy was the enemy artillery. On 3 August 10/DWR returned and 8/Yorkshire Regiment moved to billets in the Rue de Bapaume in Albert. While in Albert the battalion had the opportunity to have a bath and clean up. However, they were soon on their way back into the line for on the morning of 5 July they took over the front-line system from Munster Alley to Gloster Alley held by 13/DLI. On what was described as a hot and dusty day, they had hardly taken over when the Commanding Officer, Lieutenant Colonel Philip Vaughan, and Captain John Tilly were wounded and Major Western, East Lancashire Regiment attached, was blown down a dugout.

Sgt Edgar Burlison, D Coy, 8th Bn, was from Bradford. He was killed on 6 August 1916.

On 6 August the enemy artillery increased their shelling of Munster Alley and the front line.

At 4.15 p.m. 8/Yorkshire Regiment attacked Munster Alley after it had been shelled by British artillery. The attack was led by Lieutenant Lister with twenty picked bombers, all volunteers, of whom some carried picks, shovels and sandbags. Behind them came a platoon led by Second Lieutenant Watson. They had previously held the barricade in Munster Alley but had been withdrawn during the British barrage. One platoon under Lieutenant Cole with picks and shovels were to clear the trench, which had, in places, completely blown in. The orders were to carry and hold the junction of Munster Alley and Torr Trench and to establish double blocks in each trench at least 50 yards beyond the junction. If possible a further advance was to be made up Munster Alley towards the switch.[1] The attack was personally supervised by Major Western from the junction of Munster Alley and OG2.

Private Walter Sheen, B Coy, 8th Bn. He was evacuated from Munster Alley with shell shock on 6 August 1916.

At some stage on 6 August during the attack 13093 Private Walter Sheen, 21, was evacuated with shell shock to 70 Field Ambulance ADS, which was at the Red Cottage, Fricourt and then from there to the 23rd Divisional Rest Station in Baiseux.[2]

The DDAMS 23rd Division produced notes on the operations of the divisional medical units in which it stated:

> Function of the Divisional Rest Station during a battle
>
> The Divisional Rest Station is for sick and lightly wounded cases.
>
> Sick will be sent direct to the Divisional Rest Station and they will be shown as transferred by the Field Ambulance running the Divisional Rest Station. Lightly wounded of the Division will always be transferred to the Divisional Rest Station from Field Ambulances. Lightly wounded of other Divisions will be disposed of as directed in operation orders.[3]

The enemy were encountered near the junction of Torr Trench and Munster Alley and were at once driven back and pursued for 170 yards beyond the junction, two prisoners were taken and a number of Germans killed. Heavy opposition was met and the leading party were endeavouring to make a block when they were driven back for 20 yards. Here another block was made and two more further back. During all this time very heavy shell fire and counter-attacks were made by the enemy but were driven off with heavy loss. This went on until daylight on 7 August. Eventually two Lewis guns were brought up to cover Torr Trench and the bomb block in Munster Alley.[4]

One of the volunteer bombers was a Grangetown man, 12067 Private William Short, whose actions during the day brought him the posthumous award of the Victoria Cross. His citation testifies to his bravery:

> For most conspicuous bravery at Munster Alley on the 6 August 1916. He was foremost in the attack, bombing the enemy with great gallantry, when he was severely wounded in the foot. He was urged to go back, but refused and continued to throw bombs. Later his leg was shattered by a shell and he was unable to stand, so that he lay in the trench adjusting detonators and straightening pins of bombs for his comrades. He died before he could be carried out of the trench. For the last eleven months

Artist's impression of Private William 'Twigg' Short winning the VC.

> he had always volunteered for dangerous enterprises and had always set a magnificent example of bravery and devotion to duty.[5]

Better known to his friends as 'Twigg' Short, prior to the war Short had worked as a crane man at Messrs Bolckow, Vaughan and Co.'s Eston Steelworks. He was a well-known local footballer, and had formerly played for Grangetown Albion, Saltburn and Lazenby.[6]

Second Lieutenant Lister was wounded, so Second Lieutenant Watson assumed command in Munster Alley and completed the barricades and organised the defence with great ability. At 9 p.m. the company of 8/Yorkshire Regiment in Munster Alley, who had been attacking for eight hours, were relieved by a company of 11/West Yorks. The fighting continued through the night and between twenty and fifty Germans were taken prisoner. Unfortunately a good many of these men were killed by their own artillery as they made their way to the rear. These prisoners taken by 8/Yorkshire Regiment and 11/West Yorks were from three different regiments that had been sent in to support the 18th Reserve Division.[7] The following report from 69 Brigade HQ was passed to HQ III Corps via HQ 23rd Division:

> Enemy about thirty strong attacked from Torr Trench at 3.30 a.m. and later a party about forty strong again attacked from the same point. Enemy appeared to advance to the attack most unwillingly. They were easily repulsed on both occasions and suffered heavily from our rifle and Lewis gun fire. Our snipers have inflicted casualties on enemy who have afforded many targets.

On the left of 8/Yorkshire Regiment, the 45th Battalion, 12th Australian Brigade of the 4th Australian Division had provided much-needed support in the way of bombs, of which a vast number were required and used to good effect. Among the dead of 8/Yorkshire Regiment was the Officer Commanding B Company, Captain Eric Noel Player. Born at Blaydon on Tyne in County Durham, his family had moved to Clevedon in Somerset by the time he died.

Captain Eric Noel Player, killed in action 6 August 1916.

During 7 August, 8/Yorkshire Regiment and 11/West Yorks were relieved by the uncommitted portion of 11/West Yorks and three companies of 9/Yorkshire Regiment, while their Battalion HQ and the remaining company stayed at Scots Redoubt.

The War Diary of 9/Yorkshire Regiment records that on that day there were four killed and four wounded. However, the remains of 24248 Private George Brogden from Leeds were exhumed by a Canadian Burial Detachment on 13 June 1919 at 57D X.6.c.35.1. This position is well in advance of where the battalion was that day so it is highly likely that he was a wounded prisoner and died in German hands. The Battalion HQ and the company at Scots Redoubt were relieved by 6/Cameron Highlanders and the three companies in Munster Alley by the King's Own Scottish Borderers. They then moved back to billets in Bresle.

Likewise, the other companies of 6/Cameron Highlanders replaced those of 8/Yorkshire Regiment and they too moved to Bresle.

After the action the Brigade Commander, Brigadier General T.S. Lambert, wrote:

> I cannot speak too highly of the excellent arrangements and gallantry displayed by Major Western Commanding 8/Yorkshire Regiment and all ranks under him, including the Companies of the 11/West Yorks who joined in the operations.
>
> The actual objective was reached without serious loss, but great resolution was required to complete the consolidation of the position gained and to endure the incessant and very heavy shelling of the whole of the Brigade lines including those occupied by neighbouring Australian troops.
>
> At no time was there any hesitation or delay and all ranks deserve the highest credit for the determination displayed to win and hold on at all costs.[8]

Having assembled in the Bresle area, 69 Brigade was ordered to move north. Battalion transport sections, the Lewis gun sections and trench mortar batteries that employed handcarts were to move on foot, over two days, to the X Corps rear area. Furthermore, the infantry battalions were to move by train. On 10 August 8/Yorkshire Regiment marched to Méricourt and late at night entrained. Detraining the next morning at Pont-Remy, they marched to billets in Vauchelles. The 9/Yorkshire Regiment were travelling twenty-four hours behind them and when they arrived at Pont-Remy the battalion went to billets in Yaucourt-Bussus. One day was spent in billets on the usual cleaning up, washing uniforms and equipment and trying to look like soldiers again, before marching back to the railhead and entraining for Bailleul.

Private Edward Isaac Brough. Having served at Gallipoli with 6 Yorks, he joined C Coy 8th Bn with a draft in August 1916.

On 13 August the 8/Yorkshire Regiment detrained in Bailleul, where they marched to billets 6 miles away. However, it was not until 4.30.a.m. that they arrived at their final destination. Again one day behind, 9/Yorkshire Regiment detrained at Bailleul at 3.a.m. on the morning of 14 August and marched to accommodation in Schaeken. There they spent three days prior to taking over hutment from 21/King's Royal Rifle Corps at Papot.

Having had two days' rest, on 17 August 8/Yorkshire Regiment marched to billets near Steenwerck. They moved closer to the line on 18 August and then for three days provided working parties of 300 men for the Royal Engineers. On 22 August 9/Yorkshire Regiment came up and relieved 8/Yorkshire Regiment, who went back and took over the huts vacant at Papot. The next two days were spent doing company and platoon training to assimilate the new drafts into the way things were done in the battalion. Then on 25 August they moved up and took over the front line from 11/Sherwood Foresters of 70 Brigade. Here one other rank was accidentally wounded and Second Lieutenant Reginald Oakley, who had only joined the battalion after the fighting at Contalmaison, was killed.

Second Lieutenant Oakley was aged 21 and after he had been educated at Archbishop Holgate's Grammar School and St John's College York, he entered the teaching profession. He was described as a clever footballer and besides playing for his college team he occasionally turned out for York City FC. In a letter to his parents the Commanding Officer wrote:

> Second Lieutenant Oakley was killed by a rifle grenade, he had only been with the battalion a short time, but during that period he helped it to maintain the great reputation it won in the recent fighting. Your son was very popular with the non-commissioned officers and men in his platoon, and will be a great loss to the company and to the regiment.[9]

The weather turned wet at this time and although the enemy were quiet, the trenches were beginning to collapse owing to the rain. On the night of 30 August, 9/Yorkshire Regiment sent out two small raiding parties of one officer and ten men each, which were to try and enter the German lines and obtain identification of the unit opposite. The raiders were to be covered by artillery, Stokes mortars, Lewis gun and machine gun fire. One additional aspect of this attempted raid was that gas was used. Unfortunately, the raiding parties were unable to reach the enemy trenches. The gas released had an effect on one of the raiding parties and they were also held up by German machine guns. But the biggest obstacle was the enemy barbed wire, which was found to be undamaged by the British artillery fire. Given these circumstances the raiders had little option but to return to their own lines.

On 2 September 9/Yorkshire Regiment took over the front line from 8/Yorkshire Regiment, who moved back to the following positions: A and B Companies went into Hunters Avenue, C Company to Touquet Farm and D Company went to Ploegsteert Wood. During the handover or shortly afterwards 9/Yorkshire Regiment had 18114 Private Michael McElwee, a 22-year-old miner from Waterhouses, near Durham, killed and two other men wounded. After two nights in the line they were relieved by 7/East Lancashire Regiment and moved to II ANZAC Corps training camp at Bailleul. Here they spent two days cleaning up and resting. Meanwhile, in the rear positions held by 8/Yorkshire Regiment on the night of 2 September there was a report of 'gas' and the whole battalion 'stood to'. Somehow, whether he failed to answer or did not give the correct password, Second Lieutenant H.R.B. Bailey was bayonetted by a sentry. The alarm proved false and the battalion was 'stood down'. On 4 September 7/King's Own Lancaster Regiment (7/KORL) took over and 8/Yorkshire Regiment also moved to II ANZAC Corps training camp. This was in preparation for a move back to the Somme. On 5 September all the battalion transport sections of 69 Brigade set off by road. On the morning of the 6th the remainder entrained at Bailleul and were taken by rail to Saint-Omer.

On arrival at the last named station they set off on foot to another training area. The 8/Yorkshire Regiment marched to Houlle and 9/Yorkshire Regiment to Moulle. Here three more days' training took place. The War Diary of 8/Yorkshire Regiment records that this comprised company and platoon training on the first day and all companies were on the range firing, which also included the Lewis gunners. They also had the chance to have some bombing practice. On 10 September the day was spent resting ready for the move that night. The battalion left Houlle at 10.55 p.m. and entrained at Saint-Omer at 2.a.m. Likewise, 9/Yorkshire Regiment had entrained at Saint-Omer at midnight destined for Longueau.

When 69 Brigade arrived at Longueau they marched through Amiens to billets at Coisy, except two companies of 8/Yorkshire Regiment who billeted in Poulainville. No time was wasted here and at 8.a.m. they were marching back towards the Somme and into hutments at Hennecourt Wood, the whole brigade being settled in by 4 p.m. Rain fell on 14 September and the various units exercised in the vicinity of their huts. The day was described as exceedingly cold, then on 15 September orders were received for the whole brigade to move to Millencourt and when all units were in billets they were placed at one hour's notice to move. On 16 September, before 8/Yorkshire Regiment moved forward, there was a tragic accident while training with bombs. One bomb exploded and badly wounded 19334 Private Thomas Blunt from New Lambton, near Fencehouses. Soon after he died from his wounds and was buried in Millencourt Communal Cemetery Extension.

On 18 September 9/Yorkshire Regiment went into the line and took over from 8/Seaforth Highlanders. It is here there is some confusion occurs. The Battalion War Diary clearly states 'took over from 8/Seaforth Highlanders'. Yet a report in the 69 Brigade War Diary states that '9/Yorkshire Regiment relieved a Battalion of 150 Brigade in the advanced post.' That afternoon the advanced post was surrounded and heavily bombed causing a number of casualties. 9/Yorkshire Regiment made bomb blocks in both PRUE and STARFISH Trenches but later in the afternoon a heavier attack began with a large number of bombs thrown, by the enemy who came over the top and down both trenches. Later in the evening, after bombarding Prue Trench and the Starfish Line and Martin's Alley very heavily, the enemy delivered another stronger attack which succeeded in taking part of Prue and Starfish Trenches. At 10.30 p.m. a counter-attack took place which was successful and the trenches were recaptured.

At this time the 9/Yorkshire Regiment War Diary records that one officer 'died of wounds'. However, the only officer casualty at this time was Second Lieutenant Wilfred N. Halliwell from Bury, Lancashire, who died of wounds on 21 September. At the time of the 1911 Census he was a medical student living at home with his parents. Halliwell had only married twelve months earlier to Verna Twentyman of the Hall, Kirby Misperton, North Yorkshire. This was the second blow her family

Lieutenant Wilfred Newbold Halliwell, 9th Bn, died of wounds on 21 September 1916.

had received as her brother, Captain Denzil Twentyman of the York and Lancaster Regiment, was killed on 1 July 1916.

There were four other wounded officers and among the men twenty-nine were killed, fifteen Missing and ninety-four wounded. However, comparing these figures to the Commonwealth War Graves Commission (CWGC) figures it appears that the diary was written up some time later and the men were killed over a three- or four-day period. Of those killed, the vast majority are commemorated on the Thiepval Memorial to the Missing, However, five have known graves: 19824 Private Arthur Moon of Canterbury; 15651 Private John Smiles, who lived in Seaham; and 23136 Private Arthur Thompson are buried in ADANAC Cemetery. No. 8401 Private Joseph Ganner from Burslam, Staffordshire, was buried at Dernancourt, having died from his wounds. The last named body recovered was that of 24808 Private Herbert Steel from Hemsworth, near Tadcaster. His body was recovered by a Canadian Burial Detachment and reburied in Pozières Military Cemetery on 26 June 1919. One of the wounded, 12512 Corporal Watson Whitfield, who lived at Sacriston, was wounded by shrapnel in his lung. He arrived at No. 1 Canadian General Hospital at Étaples on 22 September and was able to send a message to his mother. 'Dear Mother I have been slightly wounded but I am going on well. I don't think I will get home with it. Don't worry. Love to all Watson XXX.'

Corporal Watson Emerson Whitfield, from Sacriston, was wounded on 22 September 1916 and died in October.

Later on 10 October she received a letter from Reverend C.F. Atherton, who was the Senior nonconformist chaplain at No. 24 General Hospital, Étaples. He wrote:

> Dear Mrs Whitfield,
> I have just seen Corporal Whitfield of the Yorks, who is lying in No. 1 Canadian Hospital. Many of our lads are unable to write, not having the same facilities as when free to move about the rooms. So whenever I can – I like most to drop a word to break a long silence. I know how you must feel when day succeeds day without a word from the loved one far away and in danger. I know how my own wife is if I miss 3 days she thinks that I must be wounded or killed or something worse. But there are many times out here – and I speak of a period that dates back to Aug

4 1914 – it is impossible to write although we are well in health. I will keep in touch with Whitfield + let you know how he progresses until he is able to write himself.

Most sincerely yours
C Forshaw Atherton

The same day the Official Army Form B 104-82 was posted to Mrs Whitfield stating that Watson had passed away on 10 October from his wounds. She also had a letter from the Canadian nonconformist padre attached to No. 1 Canadian General Hospital. As things turned out he was a Durham man and knew Durham and the local pit villages well:

Dear Mrs Whitfield,
Your son Corporal W.E. Whitfield passed away last night very peacefully. I did not know he was from Sacriston until I went through his personal effects this morning before sending them to the Base which is my solemn duty in this hospital. I wish I had known the district from which he came as I used to live in Durham myself and I have preached in Langley Park where I see some of his friends and one in particular [are from]. I am so sorry Watson has not pulled through. The Sister tells me he was a lovely boy and so cheerful to the end. I hope she will be writing to you about him.

I am sure you will feel your sorrow most keenly, but it will be a proud sorrow, for your son has given himself for the cause of righteousness and died a death than which there is none more glorious. The gloom which has been cast over your life is typical of many lives and homes throughout the world and will cause you to feel more than ever the need of that Comforter who never Faileth us and is always more truly with us when the clouds gather. May grace be given to Him who was moved with compassion at the funeral of Nain's son, the Christ who worketh all things for good.

I well remember Philip Hall and George Watson of Langley Park and I think they will remember me. If you should see them at any time give them my kindest regards.

Please write if there is anything I can do for you.
Yours very sincerely
Reginald Bailey

Bailey had a reply from Mrs Whitfield that must have told him the two gentlemen from Langley Park were going to write to him. She must have also asked some questions about her son. He replied on 17 November:

Dear Mrs Whitfield,
I have just received your letter dated 13 November and I am sorry your other letter has in some way gone astray.

Your son Watson was admitted to this hospital on the 22 September with a piece of shrapnel in the lung. Everything possible was done for him but he passed away on 10 October at 10.45 p.m. The sister tells me his heart was weak and could not stand the strain. However, from all accounts he did not suffer but very little discomfort and was quite cheerful up to the last. He was bright and cheerful all the time. The Sister says he was a loveable boy never complaining. I am sure you would be glad to hear this.

We buried him on 11 October in the Military Cemetery, Camiers Road, Etaples, where the slant of graves of so many of our heroes faces the chalk cliffs of Dover and is touched each night with the red glow of the sinking western sun. The cemetery is well kept and is a pretty sight in the spring and summer months.

The number of the Grave is G 213, and though we are not permitted to take a photograph of it, you will surely be able to obtain one after the war … Mr Rigg who was at Leadgate and who is well known to you, I think, called to see me the other day and we had a long talk about the 'Canny North'. Watson, I think used to work in his office and the latter was very disappointed to have missed the opportunity of visiting Watson while he was in this hospital. Mr Rigg is a Sergeant in the St John Ambulance Brigade Hospital next to this one.

With Kindest regards and heartfelt sympathy, Yours very sincerely
Reginald Bailey.

On first reading Bailey's letters it was assumed he was a padre working at No. 1 Canadian General Hospital, but that was incorrect. He was at the time a corporal in the Canadian Army Medical Corps. At the time of his enlistment on 1 March 1915, Bailey was a theological student resident in Winnipeg, Manitoba. He was also serving in the Canadian Militia with the 16th Cavalry Field Ambulance. His father was a minister living in Liverpool. Discharged as a sergeant in April 1919, he returned to Winnipeg.

On 21 September two companies of 8/Yorkshire Regiment arrived and relieved two companies of 9/Yorkshire Regiment, who moved to a reserve trench. That night those in the front line established contact with a unit of the 50th Division on the right. They also pushed patrols up Crescent Alley and were able to report it was unoccupied by the enemy.

The account of events in the War Diary of 8/Yorkshire Regiment states that B Company were sent up to support 9/Yorkshire Regiment followed by two platoons of C Company. Unfortunately, according to the War Diary two men of B Company were killed: 27585 Private Herbert Whitehead, from Saltaire, near Bradford, and 28791 Private George Goodall, a Kippax man, were buried together and exhumed at 57c. S7. B.8.3. They were identified by the cross over the grave, uniform, titles and boots on 26 June 1928. They were reburied in Serre Road Cemetery No. 2. A third man died that day. No. 10477 Private William King, from Bow, London, died of wounds in the Dressing Station at Dernancourt and was buried there. From the Reserve trench, 9/Yorkshire Regiment moved first to Round Wood, where they had three men accidentally wounded, and then to the cutting at Contalmaison, where they took over from 11/Sherwood Foresters.

Second Lieutenant J.P. Heron, 8th Bn, commanded a patrol on 22 September 1916.

In the meantime, the rest of 8/Yorkshire Regiment were engaged on working parties and carrying stores up to the line. During these tasks Second Lieutenants Hamilton Bush from Highgate, London, and Patrick Killacky, a Dublin man, were wounded. During 22 September two patrols went out from 8/Yorkshire Regiment. Each patrol consisted of one officer, one NCO and four men. Led by Second Lieutenant Alick Ross and Second Lieutenant John Heron, the latter officer had landed as a private with 4/Green Howards in April 1915 and was commissioned the following November.

Their patrol report reads as follows:

> Starting out at 11 a.m. they moved down the Eaucourt L'Abbaye road from Martinpuich with one party on each side of the road.
>
> Each party worked up onto the sloping ground from where they could get a view of the country on the opposite side of the road.
>
> The party on the right reached a point about M.27.b.9.2. The German trench south of the road in M.27.b was unoccupied. This party then saw a hostile working party at about M.28.a.4.7. at work with timber and sandbags on a new trench running from this point in a N.W. direction apparently joining up with hostile trench running from N.E to S.W. in

> M.21.d. This new trench continues south of the road and leads into trench running parallel to the road at M.28.a.7.5. They also saw another party of Germans apparently working at a dump about M.22.c.9.2. Three wagons came up to the dump with material. The party on the north side of the road reached a point about M.27.b.6.5. This party had a good view of the hedge running along the track from M.22d.6.2. to M.29.a.0.6. Germans were very busy working on this line and our artillery were seen to make some very good shooting here.
>
> A trench runs from this line at M.28.b.8.8. in a S.E. direction and apparently connects up with the trench mentioned above which runs into the road about M.28.a.4.7. Germans were seen moving about in this trench. They also saw a battery of guns in action at the old quarry M.22.d.30.0.6. A heliograph was also being used here. The party were sniped at, and later a few rounds of shrapnel were fired at them.
>
> The patrol returned and reached Martinpuich at about 2.45 p.m. No Casualties.
>
> From a point about M26.d.7.8. at about 3.30 p.m. a large gun was seen to be removed from Little Wood M.9.d. From the same point of observation a battery was seen in action about M10.c.6.2[10]

While the patrol was out Second Lieutenant William Swain was killed. His brother Thomas had died of wounds the previous July.

The eight days until the end of the month were spent resting and supplying working parties to the front line, and then on 26 September they replaced 9/Yorks and Lancs Regiment in Shelter Wood. Here they were in support and although there were some large working parties, some time was allowed to rest and clean up, although one man was wounded at this time.

On 1 October 8/Yorkshire Regiment took over from 9/Yorkshire Regiment at the cutting in Contalmaison, while they were moving daily by stages back to the front line. The next day saw them move up and take over from 11/Sherwood Foresters in OG 1 and 2, A and D Companies went into OG 1 and 2, B Company into a trench behind Destremont trench and C Company into Zig Zag trench. At this time the weather had changed and had turned wet. Once more the relief of 70 Brigade had taken a long time and was not complete until 7 a.m. on 3 October. Although the enemy were comparatively quiet, they enfiladed the trenches taken over and caused some casualties, added to which the condition of the front-line trenches and the communication trenches to the rear was appalling. It must have been at this time that 13093 Private Walter Sheen was wounded by a bullet in the left forearm. He was initially evacuated to the 1/3rd Northumbrian Field Ambulance, RAMC, which was located in

Bottom Wood, near Mametz. After having the wound accessed and dressed he was transferred to the 15th Divisional Rest Station. Here after examination it was decided it would be better to leave the bullet in the arm, and he was returned to the battalion on 4 October. (However, there is a sequel to this story. In the 1920s and '30s, when he was unemployed, if a job came up that he was to get, the left forearm would swell up and the bullet could be seen under the skin, then when he was employed the swelling would go down.)

The Germans shelled the battalion positions and the headquarters dugout had to be vacated. That evening C Company and the battalion bombers attacked the trench and sap in OG2 on the right of the Bapaume Road. On the left 10/DWR were attacking the same German trenches on the other side of the road. The 10/DWR attack failed, but that of 8/Yorkshire Regiment was successful and the position was consolidated and trench bomb blocks established. Three times the Germans counter-attacked and three times they were driven off. Early on the wet and stormy morning of 5 October, a fourth counter-attack was launched, which was again beaten off. The trenches were in a very bad state and those in the front line were exhausted from want of sleep. Even the battalions in support were not much better off. No shelter from gunfire or the weather was possible and there was the constant need for working parties, day or night, to supply the needs of the front line with water, food, bombs and ammunition. That evening between 6 p.m. and 8 p.m. the enemy shelled the battalion positions heavily, which caused the deaths of several soldiers. The majority of those who died are commemorated on the Thiepval Memorial to the Missing. However, four of those killed that day were exhumed on 22 November 1920 and reburied in ADANAC cemetery: 28933 Private George Durham, from Leeds; 11276 Private Stephen Flynn also from Leeds; 13774 Private Michael Higgins from Eston, Middlesbrough; and another Leeds man, 20575 Private Robert Wagstaff.

The shelling and casualties caused 8/Yorkshire Regiment to fall back to their original positions, which were handed over to 9/Yorkshire Regiment when they arrived to take over. This period in the line had been very trying for 8/Yorkshire Regiment. The weather was abominable, communication was very difficult and during the period nineteen other ranks had been killed, twenty-six wounded and five evacuated with shell shock, with one man missing Along with these casualties, five subalterns were wounded, including Lieutenant N.E.O. Storey, who had arrived in France as a private with the 13th Battalion Canadian Infantry, although by birth he was from Faynes in County Limerick. The others were Second Lieutenants R.F. Wilson; A.P. Jackson, a former colour sergeant; F. Ayton; and Alex W. Ross, who was from Sutton in Surrey.

On 6 October the weather improved a little but the hostile shelling continued very heavily all day and all night on all parts of the lines and headquarters in the rear. During that morning, Lieutenant Peter Courage and 17771 Private Charles Loughren from Wheatley Hill were in the front trench near the road and they saw some Germans enter the village. A Stokes gun was brought into action: this scattered the Germans and six of them ran forward to cover. Lieutenant Courage shouted to them to surrender but they would not do so. Private Loughren at once ran at them, followed by the officer, and the Germans surrendered and were brought back into the British lines. From these men much information was obtained. The men captured were a patrol of one NCO and five men of 5 Companie, Infantrie Regiment 361. They had been sent out to capture a trench mortar left behind by 69 Brigade when they evacuated a small portion of a trench under fire.

Tactical Dispositions:
A. Infantry:-
2/Bn 361st I.R. hold the support Flers Line to the NW of the Bapaume Road, all four companies are in the line.

The 1st Battalion 361st I R was in Galwitz or Warlencourt Line, two or three of its companies lining the Sunken Road which runs through M.10.d and M.16.b.

The Third Battalion was at rest somewhere behind Bapaume. It went into the front line when the regiment first came down south on Oct 1st and has suffered fairly heavy casualties.

B. Machine Guns:-
There was a machine gun battalion commanded by a Captain attached to the Regiment, It consisted of three machine gun companies of six guns each, 18 guns in all, Each battalion having one company attached to it. Of these two guns were according to the prisoner at about M.15.d.9.5. in the trench along the road running N.W. Orders had been given that this trench was to be continued in a S.W. direction, across the main BAPAUME ROAD to the SUNKEN ROAD about M.16.c,2.2. One M.G. was then to be placed in this trench on the N.W side of the main road about M.16.c.1.3. so as to sweep the road. It was said last night that heavy trench mortars were being sent up to the front line. In the event of these being sent, two machine guns were to be placed in the shrubs of the gardens on the S.W. side of the road about M.16.c.1.0. and one machine gun on the S.W. side of the main road about M.15.d.1¼.1½. again so as to sweep the road. It is possible of course that all six machine guns could be put into position.

C. Minenwerfers:-
Owing to the fact that we had greatly harassed the enemy with our trench mortars, the enemy were going to bring up (Prisoner thought they would be in position to-night 6th/7th) three or four heavy trench mortars, 2 which were to be placed in the trench running from M.15d.2.4 to M.21b.6.8. They intended to fire on our trenches heavily to-night if the mortars arrived.

D. Supports:-
There were no supporting troops in LE SARS. In fact no troops between the front line and the WARLENCOURT LINE, except in the sunken road in M.10.d and M.16.b. The prisoner thought that a platoon or so was usually in dugouts in the sunken road in M.16.c.

E. Dugouts:-
There were dugouts in LE SARS mostly strengthened cellars – which were used only by machine gunners, as far as the prisoners know. There were also dugouts in the Sunken roads in M.10.d., M.16.b and M.16.c. and along the bank in M.16.b.9.9 to 9.0. In the dugouts along the latter bank, prisoners thought that troops were quartered.

F. Headquarters:-
2 Battalion HQ Dugout about M.18.c.2.2.
Regimental HQ, Warlencourt at northern end of the village about M.10.d.8.4. (Prisoner was not certain of this).

G. Movements:-
On 30/9/16 prisoners regiment was relieved up at Ypres by 1/20 R.I.R 58th Division They came down by train and slept that night at VAULX N.E. of BAPAUME. On Sunday 1/10/16 they marched to the Reserve Line (Galwitz Line) where they relieved 393 R.I.R.

H. Morale:-
The prisoner stated that it was common talk in the trenches that bad times were in store for Germany. England had ample reserves of men and were vastly superior to them now in aviation and artillery. They seemed to think it quite natural that we should break through and that their western front would have to be shortened.

I. Officers:-

Divisional Commander:-	Lt General Werder.
Brigade Commander:-	Major General Mechau.
Regimental Commander:-	Oberst Leutnant C. Haumann.
1st Battalion Commander:-	Captain Ernst.

2nd Battalion Commander:- Major Andersohn.
3rd Battalion Commander:- Captain Brand.
5th Battalion Commander:- Leutnant Burshel.
6th Battalion Commander:- Leutnant Busch.
7th Battalion Commander:- Leutnant Stricker.
8th Battalion Commander:- Leutnant Geiser.

J. TROOPS SEEN:-
2nd Marine Infantry Regiment in Bapaume on 1st October.
360th I.R prisoners stated they believe they went into the front line – in the sector they (the 2/Bn) were now holding, on Oct 1st when the 2/Bn was in the reserve line.
16 Bavarian Res. I. R. on the road to the W of Bapaume on 1st October.

K. ORDER OF BATTLE
From, N.W. to S.E. prisoners thought the following was the order of battle.
Some Naval Battalion
361 I.R. 2nd Bn
Elements of Bavarian Res Inf Regt 1.
362 I.R.

NOTES
1. The 361 Inf Regt 2/Battalion went into the front line about 3rd October. Their relief is due therefore tonight (6th/7th).
2. The Bapaume main road has up to this date been a Corps and Divisional Boundary. The 362 I.R. were identified to the south of the road. The *361 I.R* have now been identified to the north of it, but since Bav Res. I.R 17 has suffered severe losses it is unlikely that a battalion of the 362 I.R won't temporarily reinforce them and that 4th Ersatz Division is going to relieve *7th Division*.

III Corps 'I'
W.W.T. Torr
6 October 1916
Captain G.S. III Corps.

Also during the morning of 6 October, Captain Lambert of 8/Yorkshire Regiment, who had already done much reconnaissance work, observed a German lamp signalling within the German lines. Captain Lambert read and translated a number of messages and the information he gathered enabled verification of some of the information that the prisoners had given. The signals also confirmed that an attack planned for the previous night had been postponed. The enemy had also been ordered to reinforce Le Sars and to hold the village at all costs.

Zero Hour for the attack on Le Sars was fixed for 1.45 p.m. on 7 October. Right on time the barrage lifted and 9/Yorkshire Regiment advanced rapidly to the assault. On their right 12 and 13/DLI were advancing, too. The left company of 12/DLI came under enfilade machine gun fire, which was maintained until 9/Yorkshire Regiment captured the crossroads in the village.

The 9/Yorkshire Regiment advanced through the south end of the village, so close to the barrage that an officer and some men were killed by their own artillery at the crossroads in the village. The enemy in Le Sars manned their machine guns and came out of their dugouts. Considerable hand-to-hand fighting took place at the crossroads. The machine gun posts were bombed and those who refused to surrender were either bayonetted or shot. Various parties were told off to search houses, cellars and dugouts and this work was carried out effectively. An enemy machine gun located near the crossroads was observed; the crew were shot down and the position was rushed and the gun captured. At the German battalion headquarters near the crossroads several officers were killed or taken prisoner and a store of valuable documents and a telephone station seized. The 11/West Yorks, advancing on the left of 9/Yorkshire Regiment, were met by artillery fire and very heavy rifle and machine gun fire from in front and from their left. This attack was unsuccessful and another attack had to be organised in conjunction with 9/Yorkshire Regiment, who were now holding the village under Major Barnes. This second attempt was successful and the enemy ran back across the open from the Flers support line.

Meanwhile, C Company of 8/Yorkshire Regiment was sent up to join 9/Yorkshire Regiment in Le Sars and assisted in consolidation, remaining with them until relieved. The remaining companies of 8/Yorkshire Regiment were employed in carrying stores forward. During the evening strong points were constructed in at least three positions in the village. Casualties during this period had been; Five Officers wounded, Other ranks, killed twenty nine, wounded 121; missing four; shell shock six. The 9/Yorkshire Regiment War diary at this time simply states: 'The Battalion took part in the attack on Le Sars which was entirely successful Casualties Officers killed two, wounded 3, O.R. killed fifteen, wounded thirty six, missing ten.' The work of the battalion Medical Officer, Captain Blake RAMC, was described as, 'Worthy of the highest credit'.

The work of the battalion stretcher bearers and those bearers of the 69/Field Ambulance was as always remarkable for their efficiency and personal bravery as all the wounded had to be carried over open ground. More than 300 men exclusive of Germans were brought out before the brigade was relieved.

In his report to HQ III Corps, the GOC 23rd Division, General Babington, made two comments about the part 9/Yorkshire Regiment played in the capture of Le Sars:

> The spirit of co-operation displayed by all ranks of the 9th Yorkshire Regiment was admirable and forms I think an excellent example of what can be done by quick appreciation on the spot of the value of flank fire.
>
> The advance of the 9th Yorkshires through the village was made as intended, close under the barrage and again exemplified the value of such action.

Brigadier Lambert, commanding 69 Brigade, was annoyed to say the least by the correspondent who worked for *The Times*. In his report to divisional headquarters he stated:

> In the description given by the 'TIMES' correspondent of the capture of Le Sars it was stated that the operation was effected without difficulty, the enemy surrendering freely; this description gives a totally wrong impression as the correspondent would have learnt had he spent the previous and succeeding days in the open country with the troops, in front of Brigade Headquarters and I should be glad if on a future occasion that correspondent might be invited to do so. The enemy only surrendered when compelled to do so and after suffering as much as he was able.
>
> D.S. Lambert Brigadier General
> Commanding 69th Infantry Brigade

On 9 October the 15th (Scottish) Division commenced the relief of the 23rd Division. In the front line 8/Seaforth Highlanders relieved 9/Yorkshire Regiment, who moved back to a camp in Round Wood in the early morning. They were then replaced by 6/Cameron Highlanders and moved to billets in Albert. The 8/Yorkshire Regiment were also on the move back to Albert. The next day all the men of the battalion bathed and were fitted out with new clothing.

The morning of 11 October saw the whole of 69 Brigade assembled for an inspection and address by the Commander III Corps, Lieutenant General Sir William Pultney, who congratulated and thanked the men for the work they had done during this second tour of the Somme. Further orders had arrived for another move, further north this time, to Ypres. As usual, the transport sections moved off by road on 11 October with orders to spend the night at Saint-Sauveur, while those on foot entrained at Albert for Longpre. When the trains carrying the various units arrived at Longpre they were met by motor buses, which conveyed the battalions to their billets. The 8/Yorkshire Regiment shared billets in Vauchelles with Brigade Headquarters, while 9/Yorkshire Regiment went to a village named Yaucourt. The next day was spent resting and cleaning up until the early hours of 15 October, when they marched to Conteville and entrained for Houpoutre.

> The Officer Commanding 8/Yorkshire Regiment was ordered to detail a working party of two officers and 100 men to travel on train No. 1 for duty at the detraining station The officer commanding the party was to report its arrival to the Railway Transport Officer by 7.40 p.m. on 14 October and should have its necessary rations.
>
> The Officer Commanding 9/Yorkshire Regiment was ordered to detail a working party of two officers and 100 men to report to the Railway Transport Officer Conteville by 5.25 p.m. This party will proceed by train No. 23 a 5.57 a.m. on the 16th inst.[11]

When the trains carrying 69 Brigade arrived at Houpoutre, the battalions detrained quickly and marched to billets in Poperinghe. Over the next week there were parades every day as well as many forms of working parties. Guard also had to be found for vulnerable positions and police duties carried out. Drafts joined the battalions and these had to be absorbed into those units. Men had to be examined, kits checked and allocated to companies.

On 21 October 69 Brigade issued the following orders:

1. The Brigade will relieve 68 Brigade in the Left Sector of the Divisional Front on the 23rd inst. Reliefs will take place as per attached table.
2. All details of relief are to be arranged between O.C. Units concerned.
3. Units will proceed by train from Poperinghe Station and will detrain near Ypres Asylum in H.12. Times of trains will be notified later.
4. Guides will be at the level crossing I.7.c.4.7 at 6.30 p.m.
5. All trench Stores, Gum Boots etc, will be taken over and lists forwarded to Brigade Headquarters by noon 24th inst.
6. Transport Lines will remain in their present positions.
7. Brigade Headquarters will close at Poperinghe at 7 p.m. and open at the Ramparts, Ypres, at the same hour.[12]

Further reference to the replacement of 68 Brigade by 69 Brigade was made in 23rd Division Order No. 77 dated 21.10.16. It outlined that the following would be the train arrangements for relief on 23rd instant:

(a) Move of 69 Brigade:-
Two trains will leave Poperinghe Station at 6 p.m. and two trains at 7 p.m.
These trains will reach railway crossing immediately west of Ypres at 6.20 p.m. and 7.20 p.m.

(b) 68 Brigade
Two trains will leave sidings at Ypres at 2a.m and two trains at 3 a.m. reaching Poperinghe respectively at 2.20 a.m. and 3.20 a.m.
Units will be at entraining stations half an hour before departure of trains.
Staff Captains of Brigades concerned will be at entraining stations half an hour before time of departure of trains and will report for instructions to the R.T.O.s
A train consists of 23 coaches each containing 5 compartments for 10 men, one coach for officers and a brake van.
Under no circumstance can any baggage be taken on these trains which are for conveyance of personnel only.

D.H.Q.
Major
21.10.16
D.A.Q.M.G.
23rd Division

Accordingly, at 6 p.m. on 23 October, 8/Yorkshire Regiment entrained at Poperinghe and detrained in Ypres. From there they proceeded on foot and relieved 11/Northumberland Fusiliers in the front line. B and C Companies took over the front line from I.18.4 to I.24.4, with D Company in reserve in Wellington Crescent, Maple Copse and Fort Street. A Company were in Rirz Trench. The battalion headquarters was located in the Tulleries. The relief was completed without casualties. Likewise, 9/Yorkshire Regiment moved up to the hospice in Ypres, where they replaced 12/DLI. However, on 26 October they changed their billets from the hospice to the infantry barracks. In the line, 8/Yorkshire Regiment reported that the Germans were extremely quiet and that as the trenches were very wet and damaged they had started work immediately to put things right. Wiring parties were out each night and the work draining the trenches continued until A and D Companies took over and B and C Companies moved into support positions.

Although during this tour in the line 8/Yorkshire Regiment had suffered no casualties, in hospitals at Havre on the coast on 15 October, 18392 Corporal Harry Leefe from Scarborough and 24660 Private Fred Thompson, who lived in Scorton, both died from their wounds and were buried close together in St Marie Cemetery, Le Havre. Later on 27 October in Manchester, Lance Sergeant Albert Graham passed away from his wounds and was taken home and buried in North Ormesby at 3.15 p.m. on 31 October.[13] Three days after he died, Private David Bell died in the New Infirmary in Perth, Scotland. His remains were taken home to Linthorpe Cemetery in Middlesbrough. His cortege left his home in Weir Street on Thursday, 2 November and all friends and neighbours were kindly invited. 'He died a hero.'[14]

On 29 October 9/Yorkshire Regiment relieved 8/Yorkshire Regiment and the latter battalion moved to the infantry barracks in Ypres. Here they rested during the day but each night working parties, 250 strong, were sent up to work on the front line, while others were employed in the endless task of carrying stores up to the dumps. Once again the War Diary of 9/Yorkshire Regiment gives no information on the happenings to that battalion. However, death still laid its hands on the battalion, for on 13 October, 14440 Private John Barron from Crossgate in Durham died from his wounds in Warrington War Hospital and was buried in St Cuthbert's Churchyard at North End, Durham. Further from home, in a hospital at Rouen on 16 October, 16360 Private John Walton, whose home was in West Cornforth, died from his wounds. Today he lies in St Sever Cemetery, Rouen.

German Infantry in a dry and well-made trench.

The first three days of November were described as quiet in the 69 Brigade War Diary, However, 8/Yorkshire Regiment reported they were still supplying the usual working parties. Furthermore, 9/Yorkshire Regiment related that they were holding the front and support lines in the left sector and that they had two men wounded.

On 4 November Field Marshal HRH the Duke of Connaught and Strathearn accompanied by General Sir H. Plummer commanding Second Army visited 69 Brigade Headquarters. However, with the battalions of the brigade in the line they did not visit the troops. Also that day, 9/Yorkshire Regiment were relieved by 11/Sherwood Foresters and moved to huts in Montreal Camp. At the same time, 9/York and Lancs relieved 8/Yorkshire Regiment, who entrained at Ypres and after the short ride to the rear area detrained at Brandhoek and marched to Toronto Camp.

The Army Commander had issued orders that no troops were to be billeted in Poperinghe, hence the use of the hutted camps outside the town. The conditions in the camps were very bad at that time. They were in fact so bad that the Director of Medical Services Second Army visited the camps. The ADMS of 23rd Division stated that the camps were in bad repair, comfortless and situated in a sea of mud. 'I am afraid it will react on the health of the men to send them from the trenches into these comfortless camps. Poperinghe had cinemas, shops and estaminets and the men love getting into a town and seeing what they call, "a bit of life", but I suppose the Army Commander knows best.'[15] They were, however, allowed to go into Poperinghe as a unit to use the baths having spent five days in Toronto Camp.

On 8 November 69 Brigade headquarters issued a warning order that the brigade would move forward and relieve 68 Brigade on the night of 10–11 November. The brigade frontage was in the right sector of the 23rd Divisional Front, from Fosse Way to Trench I.24.4; St Peter's Street being the boundary between the two battalions manning the front line. Slight differences in the orders came at this time. The 8/Yorkshire Regiment and 10/DWR, the battalions going into the line, were to take over the filled Lewis gun magazines of the unit they relieved in the line. They were to leave a similar number at the Lille Gate under guard to be taken over by the outgoing battalions when they arrived back in Ypres. The other instruction concerned control posts, observation posts and sniper posts, which were all to be taken over in daylight by trained observers and snipers and details of the personnel forwarded to Brigade Headquarters.

On the night 10–11 November 8/Yorkshire Regiment entrained at Brandhoek station as ordered and moved forward to the right sector of the divisional front, where they took over from 10/Northumberland Fusiliers. A, B and D Companies went into the front line and behind in support was C Company with platoons in Stafford Street and Halifax Street. During the day the Germans opposite were very quiet and the battalion had no casualties. Likewise, 9/Yorkshire Regiment moved to billets in the Hospice Ypres, where they took over from 11/Northumberland Fusiliers. They did unfortunately have one man wounded and two killed on 14 November, most likely on a working party. The two men were 28286 Private George Mark from Wortley, who enlisted in York, and 12151 Private George Wilkinson Robinson, aged 21, whose parents were from Middlesbrough but were living in Cardiff at the time.[16] Both men were buried in Bedford House Cemetery Enclosure No. 2.

On 12 November the front line was described as quiet until 4 p.m., when the enemy bombarded Canada Trench and St Peter's Street for almost two hours. The British replied with artillery and trench mortars, which caused the enemy to cease fire. Two men were wounded, two had shell shock and one man, 3/9580 Private James Ryder, was killed. Unfortunately his place of burial was lost in later fighting and he is commemorated on the Menin Gate Memorial to the Missing in Ypres. The following afternoon the Germans exploded a counter mine in front of B Company. This and the work the Germans were doing on their saps revealed they had plans for this sector. Consequently, wiring parties went out that night to improve the British wire entanglements. Apart from some sniping, the days were quiet until on the night of 16 November 9/Yorkshire Regiment took over the line and 8/Yorkshire Regiment marched to the hospice, where they billeted. During the period 17–22 November the whole battalion was employed on working parties. Then on the night of 22–23 the 8/York and Lancs relieved them and they went back to Toronto Camp. For the whole of their tour in the line the only information supplied by 9/Yorkshire Regiment was that they had six men wounded prior to 9/Yorks and Lancs relieving them.

Brigade headquarters issued a new Order No. 99 on 1 December in which the first paragraph was bad news for the infantry battalions. It stated:

> In future the Brigade will be sixteen days in the line and eight days in reserve. Inter Battalion reliefs will take place in accordance with the attached tables.

The instructions were fairly simple in that the battalions of the brigade operated in pairs and replaced each other on the dates and times specified.

During this period out of the line 8/Yorkshire Regiment found time to carry out some musketry practice and even some drill. They were only required to supply working parties every other day. Another activity they practised was wiring and it was carried out by companies. Their 'rest' did not last long and on the night of 28–29 November they were back at Brandhoek station, where they entrained and were moved up to Ypres. Once again they went into the right sector of the divisional front and took over the positions held by 11/Northumberland Fusiliers. This time only two companies C and D held the front, with B and A in support. Furthermore, 9/Yorkshire Regiment had moved up and took over the barracks in Ypres from 12/DLI. It is interesting that 8/Yorkshire Regiment said of this period at the beginning of December 1916, 'Usual trench life, both sides very quiet casualties nil'.

On 3 December 9/Yorkshire Regiment took over and 8/Yorkshire Regiment went back to the infantry barracks in Ypres. Here they provided large working parties each night. They were building up parapets along Warrington Street. The pattern of replacement changed at this time and instead of going back to the camps in the rear, on 7 December 8/Yorkshire Regiment went back to the front and took over from 9/Yorkshire Regiment. They placed A and B Companies in the line, with C and D in support. Battalion headquarters at the 'Tile Works' was fairly quiet the next day, until at 1.15 p.m. the enemy bombarded the battalion on the right with trench mortars.

Two more quiet days were spent until on the night of 11–12 November 9/Yorkshire Regiment returned to the line. Having returned to the infantry barracks in Ypres, 8/Yorkshire Regiment provided large working parties every day, until on 15 December they moved back to Toronto Camp and became the Corps Reserve. The same day 11/Sherwood Foresters replaced 9/Yorkshire Regiment, who moved to huts in Toronto Camp.

Over the next four days the battalions in the camps carried out Platoon and company training and, of course, formed large working parties. Owing to cold weather and falling snow, these proved harder than usual. The decision had been taken that battalions would have their Christmas dinner in rotation, therefore on 20 December 8/Yorkshire Regiment sat down to their meal. On 21 December, the Commander in Chief, Sir Douglas Haig, inspected 9/Yorkshire Regiment and 10/DWR. The two battalions were drawn up in two ranks on the Ouderdom–Vlamertinghe road at 12.40 p.m. When the inspection was completed the two battalions marched past in column of route. The next day 9/Yorkshire Regiment had their Christmas dinner.

On 23 December 69 Brigade went back into the line on the right of the divisional front, where they took over positions held by 68 Brigade. The 8/Yorkshire Regiment replaced 13/DLI as the left battalion, placing A, C and D Companies in the front line with B Company in support in Winnipeg Street and the Redan. Battalion headquarters were located at Dormy House. Meanwhile, 9/Yorkshire Regiment relieved 12/DLI in dugouts in the Bund at Zillebeke Lake.

The period over Christmas was very quiet, with nothing to report and the normal artillery trench mortar and machine gun fire.[17] On 27 December the 8/Yorkshire Regiment changed places with 9/Yorkshire Regiment and took over the dugouts at the Bund. On 30 December the south end of the Bund was shelled by German artillery, and then on New Year's Eve the two battalions changed over again. On the way out 9/Yorkshire Regiment had their last casualty of 1916 when one man was wounded.

Chapter 7

The Salient January–June 1917, The Battle of Messines

The start of 1917 was not kind to 8/Yorkshire Regiment in the front line, where both British and German artillery was busy. From 2 p.m. until 4 p.m. the enemy shelled the battalion positions with trench mortars and 77cm howitzers. At 5.30 p.m. British artillery bombarded the enemy trenches on the left. The whole salient burned up and the enemy, thinking they were under attack, opened up extremely heavy fire, adding 4.2cm guns to the trench mortars and 77s already in use. They bombarded the trenches held by 8/Yorkshire Regiment for over an hour and these were badly knocked about. The casualties were Second Lieutenant Frank Barrowcliff and nine men wounded along with 15642 Private George Frankland from Shotton, County Durham, and 20656 Private James Robshaw from 3 James Street, Holbeck, Leeds, who were both killed in action and buried in Railway Dugouts Cemetery. The next day was quieter as both sides were busy repairing the damage done the previous day. However, 3 January saw the artillery active again between 11 a.m. and 4 p.m., when the Germans shelled the British lines with high explosive and shrapnel. The battalion Lewis gunners had the satisfaction of breaking up a German working party and claiming two dead.

On 4 January 9/Yorkshire Regiment took over once again in the front line. Meanwhile, Ypres was being shelled heavily and some 5.9cm shells hit the dugouts at Zillebeke Bund, where 8/Yorkshire Regiment had one man wounded. On 8 January 9/Yorkshire Regiment moved back to Montreal Camp.

Here the battalion received some replacements from 3/Green Howards based in West Hartlepool, among them a young Darlington man, 38026 Private George Kidson, who wrote down some of his recollections for the Regimental Museum:

> I was called up on my birthday 5 September 1916, I was to report to Richmond, there I became a soldier. After about a fortnight I was sent to Hartlepool where we jogged before breakfast. Then we would go to the Rifle Range at Hart or bomb practice at Foggy Furze. I was on Guard duty the night the Zepplin [*sic*] was brought down on 29 November 1916. The next night we entrained for Folkestone then on to Boulogne. We slept in

> Bell Tents which had twenty-two sections, one man to each. From there we went by cattle trucks to Poperinghe then into huts at a camp called Montreal. We had to sleep on boards and had plenty of rats for company.
>
> Then the real war began.[1]

On 8 January 1917 8/York and Lancs arrived to replace them and they went back again to Montreal Camp. On 16 January they moved forward again and George Kidson recorded his impression of moving up the line:

> We marched to the trenches through Ypres under shell fire. Our front line was called Canada Trench; we would do four days and then be relieved. It was a severe winter, frost and snow. Every morning we had to rub our feet with whale oil to stop the frost bite. During the day we shaped barbed wire into gooseberry shapes. Then at night we took them into No Man's Land to place them between our trench and the Germans.[2]

When the battalion reached the front, they took over the left sector front and support lines from 13/DLI. Here, as George Kidson stated correctly, they spent four days before being relieved by 8/Yorkshire Regiment on 20 January.

While 8/Yorkshire Regiment had been out of the line they had sent thirteen NCOs away on local courses and the companies carried out a scheme of training, but as usual every night working parties were detailed for work wherever they were required. They also received a large number of reinforcements, which brought the battalion almost up to full strength. Having hardly any time to assimilate the new men, on the night 16–17 January the battalion entrained at Brandhoek for Ypres. There they relieved 10/Northumberland Fusiliers in the infantry barracks, where they were the Divisional Reserve. Each day over 200 men were employed on working parties. However, nothing was reported about enemy activity. The weather, indeed the amount of snowfall, brought comment as they were required to send out large working parties. The two battalions changed places again on 20 January and 8/Yorkshire Regiment placed C and D Companies in the front line and A and B in support, with battalion headquarters at 'Halfway House'. The only comment were that the nights were very cold and there was -10 to -15 degrees of frost. Artillery shelling increased and enemy aircraft were particularly active over the British lines. The usual relief took place on 24 January, with 9/Yorkshire Regiment taking over the front line again. During this tour there was shelling on almost every day and this resulted in six men being wounded and two men killed. The men who died were 17776 Private John Moran from Ludworth, a small village near Durham, and 29264 Private George Watkins, whose parents lived at 57 Everard Street,

Hartlepool.[3] Work on the trenches was impossible at this time owing to the frozen condition of the ground.

George Kidson recalled being in the line that winter:

> In the trenches each night we were told what to do. I was told to stand on the Fire Step. Whilst I was there one night about seven Germans walked past me, so near they could have picked me up, if they had seen me. I said to the Sergeant 'Should I fire?' he said 'No – not to give the position away' During the night we got a bombing party up. Next morning the bombs were flying, ours and the Germans. 'Tatie mashers' we called them. I got a splinter in the shoulder and said I was wounded. The Sergeant said, 'Get the hell out of it'. I was more frightened than hurt. After that I had the wind up as we called it.

On 28 January 8/Yorkshire Regiment took over again, this time placing A and B Companies in the line. The vicinity of battalion headquarters was shelled occasionally but the front line was left in peace. On the night of 31 January an SOS rocket was sent up by the battalion on the left. They had a German raid on their hands, which after a short firefight they were able to repulse.

Replacements that arrived were in the main young lads from training battalions in England, although sometimes returning the wounded brought some experience with the draft.

It was about this time that 9674 Private William George Johnson, a Regular soldier with five years' service, was evacuated. He had originally gone to Belgium with the 2/Green Howards in October 1914. In January 1915 he had been wounded in the head. After recovering from this wound he went back to 2/Green Howards, however he was in rather bad health and he was sent back to England. He went back again to France and was posted to 8/Yorkshire Regiment, but shortly after joining the battalion he was wounded in the foot. He was evacuated to the Northern General Hospital in Newcastle, where an abscess formed in the old head wound. The surgeons performed an operation but were unable to save him and he died on 5 February 1917. He was buried in Newcastle.

On the night of 1 February, 69 Brigade was relieved by 70 Brigade and went back to the huts; 8/Yorkshire Regiment to Toronto Camp and 9/Yorkshire Regiment to Montreal Camp. Owing to the hard condition of the ground, the parade ground could be used for drill and the 'recruits showed a marked improvement'. The 8/Yorkshire Regiment organised an inter-company football competition and then on the night of 8 February a very successful concert was organised in the YMCA hut in the camp. Also at this time two of the original officers, Second Lieutenants Harry Oakley and George Lister, re-joined from England. However, the time in reserve passed quickly and on 9 February Headquarters, C and D Companies left Toronto Camp and took over the front line from 13/DLI. They had a company of 9 Green Howards attached to them. In the meantime, A and B Companies of 8/Yorkshire Regiment proceeded to the 69 Brigade School for special training. During the move into the line the Germans bombarded the position with trench mortars and field artillery. This shelling caused the death of 27049 Private Alfred Harper, a Barnoldswick resident, who was buried in Railway Dugouts Cemetery. To this fire the British artillery replied and fortunately there were no further casualties. The 9/Yorkshire Regiment had also moved up. One company occupied the Cavalry Barracks in Ypres, one at Kruisstraat and one at the Zillebeke Bund. During this tour five other ranks were wounded. The company of 9/Yorkshire Regiment was relieved by B Company of 8/Yorkshire Regiment, who returned to join the battalion from the Brigade School.

Arthur Bielby, 9th Bn, from Hornby, Yorks. He was killed on 14 February 1917 and is buried in Transport Farm Cemetery.

On 13 February both battalions changed over and 9 Green Howards placed three companies in the front line. B Company, however, was sent back to the Brigade School. George Kidson remembered being on sentry duty at this time:

> I remember two of us on sentry duty looking over the top. We would take turns in looking. The other laid on the duckboards until it was his turn. Whilst I was laid there I remember a rat ran over my chest. The winter of 1917 was very cold, our coats were as stiff as boards and men's moustaches were frozen.

During their time in the line the battalion had four wounded and, according to the War Diary, three killed; however, only two are recorded by the Commonwealth War Graves Commission. They are 27255 Private Cyril Lazonby from Stockton-on-Tees and 42531 Private Percy White, who was born in Birmingham; he had enlisted in the Royal Field Artillery but was transferred to the Green Howards owing to a shortage of men for the Infantry. The 8/Yorkshire Regiment recorded ten other ranks wounded, one accidently wounded, two killed and one who died from his wounds during their last tour.

Out of the line they provided the usual working parties, including one for the Canadian tunnelling company working on the mines in preparation for the Battle of Messines. The infantry job was to carry the soil from far below ground and take it far behind the line for disposal. The 9/Yorkshire Regiment were employed on this work too, as George Kidson recalled:

> We were amongst working parties for the Canadian Sappers at Hill 60 and our job was to carry the soil out in sand bags. We had sand bags around our boots to prevent the sound on the duck boards. When we had finished we received a good rum ration from the Canadians, then we went back to Ypres.

On 17 February the usual inter-battalion relief took place and although the days were quiet at night 8/Yorkshire Regiment were actively patrolling no man's land. This patrol work cumulated on 20 February when Lieutenant F.C. Miller and twenty-eight other ranks carried out a raid on the German trenches. Using a Bangalore torpedo to cut a lane through the enemy barbed wire, they entered the enemy trenches. All the time they were there the British artillery kept a box barrage around the sector where the raiders were. The Germans had evacuated their lines, which were searched thoroughly for half an hour, but no identification of the unit holding that sector was obtained. When the order to retire was given the raiders came safely back to the British lines without casualties. At 5 p.m. the division on the right carried out a large-scale raid and in retaliation the Germans bombarded the line held by 8/Yorkshire Regiment, causing the death of one man. The raiders were congratulated for their efforts, with Brigadier A.R. Cameron at X Corps HQ forwarding a message from the Second Army Commander General Sir H. Plumer. 'I consider it reflects great credit on all concerned.' Furthermore, the Commander of 69 Brigade Brigadier Lambert added his compliments.

On 21 February 9/Yorkshire Regiment returned to the line and during their tenure they had Lieutenant H.G. Scott and four men wounded and three killed, namely, 42531 Albert Petit of Hurworth near Darlington on 23 February; 24371 James Watson of Yarm on 24 February; and 42481 Private Thomas Saunders, who was born in Bermondsey and was another of the draft from the Royal Field Artillery. Down on the coast, in one of the hospitals at Boulogne, 28274 Private Arthur Johnson a Scarborough man, died from his wounds. From the regimental numbers of the casualties, the change in the battalion from a pure 'Kitchener battalion' to one made up of Kitchener men, Derby Scheme volunteers and conscripts is seen.

The 69 Brigade was now replaced by 116 Brigade of 39th Division, with 11/R Sussex Regiment replacing 8/Yorkshire Regiment and 13/R Sussex Regiment taking over from 9/Yorkshire Regiment.

The two Green Howard Battalions marched back to their usual camps in the rear. They did not get any rest though for Brigade Operation Order 109 was issued:

1. The 69th Brigade Group will move to the Epperlecques Area, via the Houtkerque and Bollezeese areas by March Route as per attached Move Table commencing on 27th inst.
2. The Brigade Group will be comprised as follows:-
   69th Infantry Brigade
   128th Field Company R.E.
   69th Field Ambulance
   192 Company, A.S.C.
   9/South Staffordshire Regiment
   194 Machine Gun Company.
3. Billeting parties (as directed in 3rd Division No Q.S.132 dated 22nd inst.) will proceed to each billeting area 24 hours in advance of their unit.
   The same party will do the billeting for their unit throughout the move. They will each day hand over the billets as allotted by the Staff Captain to their Unit on its arrival in the area and will then rendezvous at a prearranged point and time to meet the lorry and proceed immediately to the next area. All first line Transport will march with units – 2nd Line Transport will proceed under orders of OC 192 Company A.S.C. Steps will be taken to ensure that baggage wagons do not block the roads leading to the starting point before the stated hour. This applies to first day only.
4. All troops will observe the strictest march discipline en route.
5. 10 minutes halt will be made at every 10 minutes before the clock hour. The march will resume at the clock hour.
6. On 28th inst., a halt will be made for dinners at 12.30 p.m. Animals will be watered and fed. The march will resume at 1.30 p.m. Cookers

where possible will be drawn clear of the road. Troops will be taken clear of the road if any ground is available at the halting place.

7. Billeting parties will be responsible for meeting their units before the latter arrive at their actual billets.
8. All units of the Brigade Group will immediately report on their arrival in Billets to Brigade Headquarters.
9. Brigade Headquarters will close at Poperinghe at 9 a.m. on 27th inst., at 8.45 a.m. at each of the areas en route and will reopen in each successive area on arrival.

Capt. for
Brigade Major,
69th Infantry Brigade.

	Order of March of Units	**Starting Point**	**Time**	**Route**	**To**
1	9/S Staffs Regiment	L.4.b.8.10.	10.10 a.m.	St Jan ter Beizen-Watou-Houtkerque	Herzeele Area
2	69 Bde HQ & Sig Sec	G.e.c.7.2.	9.40 a.m.	Switch Road - Poperinghe, St Jan ter Beizen-Watou-Houtkerque	Houtkerque
3	69 TM Bty	G.5.d.1.2.	9.20.a.m.	G.5.c.7.2. Then as above	Herzeele Area
4	128 Fld Coy RE	G.3.c.7.2.	10 a.m.	G.5.c.7.2. Then as above	Herzeele Area
5	69 MG Coy	G.5.d.1.2.	9.30 a.m.	G.5.c.7.2. Then as above	Herzeele Area
6	194 MG Coy	Vlamertinghe Church	9.50 a.m.	G.5.c.7.2. Then as above	Herzeele Area
7	11/West Yorks Regiment	G.5.d.1.2.	9.40 a.m.	G.5.c.7.2. Then as above	Houtkerque
8	8/Yorkshire Regiment	G.5.d.1.2.	9.49 a.m.	G.5.c.7.2. Then as above	Houtkerque
9	9/Yorkshire Regiment	G.5.d.1.2.	10.08 a.m.	As above to St Jan ter Biezen	Camp Y
10	10/DWR	G.5.d.1.2.	10.17 a.m.	As above to St Jan ter Biezen	Camp Z
11	69 Fld Amb RAMC	G.3.c.7.2.	11 a.m.	Above route	Herzeele Area
12	192 Coy AQSC	G.3.c.7.2.	11.5 a.m.	Above Route	Herzeele Area

The march table above shows the times that the individual units were to pass the start point and also how long it would take the whole column to pass by. The movement order and march table help us understand how the Army managed the movement of large units through the French countryside during the war. Each day of the march a new table was published with different timings and start points. Additionally, the order of march would change, for example on 28 February 8/Yorkshire Regiment moved off first at 8.45 a.m.

Meanwhile, at Toronto Camp 8/Yorkshire Regiment were busy fitting out ready for the move. At 9.40 on the morning of 27 February the battalion was on parade ready to move. Moreover, it is highly likely that the men had been there for a least twenty minutes. The parade was scheduled for 9.40 – Company Commanders would have added five minutes, so 9.35 – and the Company Sergeant Major, to ensure everything was correct, would have added his five minutes. So too, the Platoon Commander and Platoon Sergeants would add their five minutes, so the men would have fallen in outside their huts at 9.15. Over the years in the British Army this has become known as 'hurry up and wait'. The transport drivers and grooms too would have been working much earlier to feed, clean and fit harnesses to the draught horses and saddle riding horses. Finally, in time to march to the start point the order would have been given, 'In column of route quick march.'

The first day's march for 8/Yorkshire Regiment was 10 miles and the battalion diarist recorded; 'The Battalion marched excellently, no man falling out.' The next day at 8.45 a.m. the battalion marched to Millain, a distance of seventeen miles, where they arrived at 4 p.m.; 'again the battalion marched well'.[4] On 1 March they had a lie-in and did not start marching until 11.40 a.m., when they did a short march of 7 miles to Houlle and by 3.15 p.m. they were established in billets. Once more the diary of 9/Yorkshire Regiment gives no information except, 'moved to camp near Houtkerque'. However, the Brigade War Diary gives their location as Moulle.

After spending a day clearing up and resting, on 3 March the training started in the morning A and B Companies of 8/Yorkshire Regiment were on the rifle ranges, while C and D carried out platoon and company training. Then in the afternoon inter-platoon football matches and cross-country running took place. On 4 March a church parade was held and again in the afternoon recreational training. Other training consisted of physical training, platoon drill, bayonet fighting, and specialist classes for signallers, snipers and Lewis gunners. Wiring a position was another activity undertaken. Overnight snow fell but thawed during the day. Range work, extended order drill and skirmishing were also commenced on 6 March, with further sports that afternoon. The weather changed almost every day: on 5 March, 'a fall of snow', on 6 March Weather 'much brighter and mild', on the 7 March, 'very cold', then for two days, 'slight falls of snow'. Not ideal weather to be on the training area. By 12 March they were practising deployment and skirmishing, having carried out 'the attack on a village.' A boxing competition was also arranged. On 17 March the battalion bathed at Houlle baths and that afternoon A Company won the battalion inter-company football. That night the boxing continued.

On 18 March the move back to the front started, being an almost reversal of the march to the training area. On 21 March the 8/Yorkshire Regiment arrived in Camp Z, where more training was undertaken. The highlight of this period was the inter-battalion football match, when 8/Yorkshire Regiment managed a 1–0 victory over 9/Yorkshire Regiment. Several small working parties were also provided at this time.

On 28 March the Second Army Commander General Sir H. Plumer inspected 8/Yorkshire Regiment but no comments from the inspecting officer have come to light. It is presumed that 9/Yorkshire Regiment carried out similar training; however, their War Diary for the whole of March consists of three lines 'moved to billets' and in the margin the town where they were billeted.

By 1 April the battalions of 69 Brigade were in camps in the Proven area, well behind the lines. Over the next week some small working parties were provided and some men were able to take a bath. The usual training was also carried out, until on 6 April 8/Yorkshire Regiment returned to Toronto Camp. It is once again assumed that 9/Yorkshire Regiment returned to Winnipeg Camp as their War Diary states, 'Moved to camp in Divisional Reserve'. Various competitions that commenced in the training area were now completed. In the inter-battalion transport competition, 9/Green Howards took first place in the company turn-out class, which consisted of a cooker, a limber and a pack animal. Second place went to 11/West Yorks, who also won the water cart class. Also taking place was the Divisional Football Competition. In the first round 69 Brigade met the Divisional RFA and after a really hard-fought they beat them 3–2. Over the next week training was carried out and during the Easter weekend there was a number of church parades, with Roman Catholics using the local Catholic church. The weather turned colder and there were slight falls of snow.

On 14 April, after almost seven weeks out of the line it was time to go back to the war. That night 9/Yorkshire Regiment moved three companies to dugouts at the Zillebeke Bund and one to Railway Dugouts, where they became the Brigade Reserve. At 9 p.m. 8/Yorkshire Regiment entrained at Branhoek and detrained at Ypres. They then marched up to the front line, replacing 9/KOYLI and becoming the left battalion of the brigade front. These trenches were those that they had last held on 21 February. A and D Companies held the line with B Company in Halifax Street and C Company in Maple Street, while battalion headquarters took over 'Rudkin House'. At this time the headquarters 23rd Division Intelligence Branch were issuing a daily intelligence summary. The summary for 15 April contained information on the following:

1. Operations.
   This covered enemy artillery activity, the positions that had been shelled and the number and type of shells that fell. For example, Trois Rois received about 20 77mm shells. It also covered 23rd Divisional artillery activity.
2. Enemy Front and Support Lines.
   Comments on work that the enemy had carried out and where new work had been spotted.
   For example, J.31.a.26.67 A dump of new wood. There is a light tramway being constructed from this point.
   I.29.c.75.25. Recent shelling has exposed a concrete dugout in the lip of a crater.
3. Machine Guns.
   Enemy machine gun activity is above normal, especially at night.
4. Sniping.
   Enemy sniping activity is above normal. Fixed rifles are active against weak points along the front line
5. Enemy Movement.
   Considerable movement, about J.3.c.9.8. Some movement throughout the day on the road near Klien Zillebeke. Smoke from a train near Zanvoorde was seen at 3.15 p.m.
   J.32.c.7.0., Two men in full marching order approached a dug out here.
   J.32.c.7.0., Man in dirty clothes, probably a cook, constantly loitered near this point.
6. Miscellaneous.
   Lamp signalling was seen from a hostile balloon, which rose at 6.30 p.m.
   Enemy fired two red lights from opposite I.35.1. yesterday morning at 4.45 a.m. No apparent action followed.[5]

This is just a small sample of the information being disseminated from division down to the battalions in the front line, although the battalion observers and snipers would have been passing information back through the Battalion Intelligence Officer. Perhaps the most useful was the information about the train and the men in full marching order. Were the Germans replacing their front-line units?

On 14 April 8/Yorkshire Regiment had provided a working party for the RE, which came under hostile fire and suffered a number of casualties; Second Lieutenant A.G. Withington and seven men were wounded and 41992 Private William Shawcross who lived in Urmston, Manchester, was killed.

The 9/Yorkshire Regiment relieved 8/Yorkshire Regiment in the front line on 18 April, with two companies in St Peter's Street, the other two being in Halifax Street and Maple Street. The next couple of days were quiet. But on the night of 19–20 an officer's patrol located a suspected enemy sap, which was found to be a loop line from I.30.c.2.8 to the German front line. In one place it was within 6 yards of the British front line and the wire about it was very thick in most places. The patrol lay in wait outside the enemy wire for an extensive time but no enemy were seen or heard.[6] It was therefore planned to raid the position. This raid was to take place at 2 a.m. on the morning of 22 April, and as well as destroying the enemy sap would hopefully provide identification of the German unit opposite. It was to be led by Second Lieutenant M.G. Robson and consisted of two parties of one NCO and six other ranks wearing white bands on their arms each composed of: '1 NCO in charge, 2 Bayonet Men, 1 Bomber, 1 Carrier, 2 Fatigue men for carrying explosives shovels etc. These partied will be formed up in the British font line by 1.40 a.m.

The plan was that directly the Bangalore torpedo exploded under the enemy wire the above parties headed by the bayonet men would rush the enemy sap and work up the trench for about 30 yards, one party to the right and another to the left, until a spot was reached where the charges could be exploded. They would then withdraw to a safe distance. As soon as the charges had exploded a block would be made at the head of the trench communicating with the front line. This trench was to be dug as quickly as possible by a party detailed by Captain W.F. Greenwood for that purpose. They were to commence work directly the raiding party had left the British trenches. Two covering parties consisting of one NCO and three bombers were to proceed to points outside the enemy sap on the right and left and would be outside the hostile wire in order to bomb any enemy moving down the trench to the assistance of their party in the sap. These covering parties would proceed with the greatest caution and were to be in position by 1.45 a.m.[7]

The raid was unsuccessful owing to the fact that the Bangalore torpedo that was to blow the enemies wire failed to explode. The enemy were alert and started bombing the raiders. Four were wounded and 19004 Private Adam

Joyner from Goole was killed. One of the wounded was 14443 Private George Hall, an ironstone miner born in Leeds but resident in Guisborough. He had a bomb wound to the right thigh and reached No. 13 General Hospital, RAMC, at Boulogne before being evacuated to the Royal Infirmary in Derby. Owing to the nature of the wound he was eventually discharged as unfit. However, 14443 Private George Hall of 8/Yorkshire Regiment was mentioned earlier as being a seaman from Whitby and had been discharged in November 1914. On rechecking the two sets of documents at some stage after the second man was discharged, the mistake was noticed and he, although having been in France since August 1915, was given a new number, 46953.

The next day 70 Brigade started replacing the battalions of 69 Brigade, who moved back to the camps behind Poperinghe. The 8/Yorkshire Regiment moved to Toronto Camp, where one of the platoons was inspected by General Babington, and he carried out the same inspection of all the battalions. On 28 April the semi-final of the Divisional Football Competition took place in which 69 Brigade beat the Divisional Headquarters team 3–1. It was a very fine, hot day on 29 April, which saw 69 Brigade move to the Steenvoorde Area. The march was described as 'very hot and dusty' in the Brigade War Diary. Here time was initially spent cleaning up and sorting out equipment and making good any deficiencies.

The first four days of May were spent training in glorious weather in the Steenvoorde area. General Babington inspected units in fighting order and on the same parade presented the ribbon of the Military Cross to Second Lieutenant

No. 69 Brigade Football Team.

C.W. Jones of 8/Yorkshire Regiment. One exercise that was held involved A and B Companies under Captain Pearson attacking C and D Companies under Major Cranko. Also at this time a number of officers attended the Second Army Bomb school at Terdeghem. Three new second lieutenants joined that battalion on 4 May, namely J.T. Shaw, A.G. McCulloch and J.L. Armstrong. On 5 May 69 Brigade marched to the Reninghelst area, where they pitched tents in fields and then all battalions were employed on working parties. This work was carried out for X Corps RE and they worked in four-hour shifts, 4 a.m. until 8 a.m., 8 a.m. until noon, noon until 4 p.m., and 4 p.m. until 8 p.m. They were unloading heavy shells and stores, filling the dumps at Heksken, Reninghelst and Atlantic South sidings. This work went on until 12 May, but during that time 8/Yorkshire Regiment had some changes in officers. Lieutenant A.W. Ross and Second Lieutenant P.J Killacky re-joined from England having recovered from wounds. Major Mintoft went to Paris on leave and Major Cranko left the battalion to take up command of a prisoner of war guard company.

> On 8 May the final of the divisional football competition took place, in which 69 Brigade played 70 Brigade. The game was hard fought and the War Diary of HQ 70 Brigade states that just before full time the score was 1–1. However, in the last minute 69 Brigade were awarded a penalty. This was duly taken and scored, leaving 69 Brigade 2–1 winners. The War Diary of HQ 69 Brigade records the team as follows: Second Lieutenant Pontefract, Sergeant Hall, Corporal Sturdy and Private Anderson 10/DWR, Sergeant Sams, Private Layton and Private Shepherd 11/West Yorks, Corporal Gibson 8/Yorkshire Regiment and Sergeant Bee, Corporal Simpson and Private Dobson 9/Yorkshire Regiment.

On 13 May the battalion struck camp and marched to Winnipeg Camp. After resting, they marched to support positions in the salient. Two companies, A and C, went to the Bund and B and D marched to the Promenade dugouts in Ypres. The 9/Yorkshire Regiment in the meantime remained in Divisional Reserve in Montreal Camp. Second Lieutenant James Gregory and his platoon were detached from D Company to work for the 101/Field Company RE in Ypres and were given the opportunity to have a bath. However, while the second lieutenant was getting his men out of the baths, a stray shell landed and he was killed. In civil life he was a Bradford solicitor, was 40 years of age and was educated at the Edinburgh Academy. The two companies in the Promenade dugouts provided 120 men each to 101 and 102 Field Companies for working parties. The two companies at the Bund came under shell fire and 14825 Sergeant James Dwyer of Shiney Row near Houghton and 42879 Private Ralph Platt one of the RFA draft from Oldham were both badly wounded. Platt died at the Advanced Dressing Station at Railway dugouts, while James Dwyer lived until he reached the 71 Field Ambulance Main Dressing Station at Vlamertinghe Mill.[8] The medical instructions show he was moved by trolley or wheeled stretcher to the Lille Gate and from there by motor ambulance to Vlamertinghe Mill.

The 9/Yorkshire Regiment relieved 11/Northumberland Fusiliers on 18 May, when they took over in the left sector of the right brigade front with two companies in the St Peter's Street–The Gap trenches. The two companies in support were placed in Halifax Street and Maple Street. On the night of 20–21 May a small raid was carried out. Zero Hour was set for 1 a.m. and gaps had been cut previously in the hostile wire opposite Canada Street about I.30.a.8.1. The objective of the raid was to take prisoners and obtain information, identification and counteract the German strategy of raiding the British trenches. The raiders were divided into two parties. No. 1 party under Second Lieutenant M.G. Robson and sixteen men were to work their way to the right for about 50 yards. No. 2 party under Second Lieutenant N. Groom with ten men were to move to the left for 50 yards. They were to vacate the enemy trenches not later than 1.15 a.m. The respective parties were to form up in the front line no later than 12.15 a.m. All identification was to be removed before forming up. Fire support would be in the form of a box barrage, which would open at zero plus three minutes and would be intense until zero plus fifteen minutes and then continue at a slow rate of fire until ordered to cease fire by the Forward Observation Officer. Further support would come from trench mortars, Stokes guns, machine guns and Lewis guns, all firing on pre-arranged points in the enemy positions.

At 12.50 a.m. both raiding parties were in position 15 yards from the enemy trench and at 1 a.m. the signal to attack was given by Second Lieutenant Robson. In No. 1 party the officer and bayonet man entered the enemy trench without difficulty and at once moved to the right expecting to be followed by the rest of the party. There was no enemy to be seen but about 30 yards further on a communication trench was found, but as the other members of the party had not followed it was thought inadvisable to go any further. They returned to the entry point and three more men jumped into the trench. By now the box barrage had started and shells were falling short into the enemy wire. The Germans had also started to return fire with rifle grenades. With three more men the party again made their way to the right back to the communication trench, where they were held up. Second Lieutenant Robson climbed up onto the parapet and threw a grenade, to which the enemy replied with a shower of rifle grenades and bombs. One of the bomb carriers was wounded and had to leave the trench. Second Lieutenant Robson and one man them moved along the top of the parapet but owing to the artillery again falling short it was impossible to go further. It was now 1.12 a.m. so the decision was taken to evacuate the position and No. 2 party were informed.

Meanwhile, in No. 2 party, Second Lieutenant Groom and three men entered the trench at exactly the same time as No. 1 Party. Immediately they moved to the left. Two of them were hit by shrapnel from rifle grenades, which were falling all around. Second Lieutenant Groom and the remaining bayonet man moved for another 30 yards down the trench, when they saw a German soldier about to fire a Very light. The officer fired at him but he immediately ran away chased by the bayonet man for a short way. Second Lieutenant Groom then decided to return and guard the rear of No. 1 party. Both parties had left the enemy trench by 1.14 a.m. Although there were five men wounded, there were no fatalities. Those that did not enter the trench were caught on the hostile wire and were very troubled by rifle grenades and by British shells falling short.

Likewise, on 18 May 8/Yorkshire Regiment had moved to the Hill 60 subsector and took over from 12/DLI. The position was fairly quiet. However, on the night 22–23 May at 3 a.m. Lieutenant Hiley and twenty men from B Company attempted to surprise a German advanced post. Unfortunately, just as the raid was about to take place, the battalion on the left sent up an SOS rocket and the British shelling and the upcoming dawn made it impossible to carry on.

Planning the Battle of Messines

The initial idea of an offensive in Flanders had taken place as early as December 1914. Apart from the defensive action in November 1914 and April 1915 at Ypres, and the Battle of Mount Sorrel in June 1916, there had been no major actions in the area. However, the Admiralty were concerned about German submarines using the ports of Ostend and Zeebrugge and wanted a combined naval and army action to free the ports and eliminate the submarine threat. Sir Douglas Haig's plan was to advance north-eastwards from Ypres and leave the coastline until his main assault had made progress. There were many difficulties to overcome. The Germans held all the high ground to the east of Ypres, which sat in the centre of a bowl, with the Germans in a semicircle around it, able to observe all British movement in both the front line and back areas. The northern part of the semicircle was the Pilckem Ridge; beyond that the ground rises steadily to Passchendaele, Westroosebeke and Staden. In January 1916 it was thought to be important that the Gheluvelt plateau should be captured before the northern part of the offensive crossed the Steenbeek. However, General Sir H. Plumer pointed out before that could be done they would need to occupy the Messines–Wytschaete Ridge, which formed the southern rim of the saucer.

Plumer also pointed out that the preparation for this was well advanced. This included the tunnelling of nineteen mines, started in July 1915, under the German trenches. Throughout 1916 various plans were put forward, which failed to materialise for different reasons.

At a conference at Chantilly, General Joffre and Sir Douglas Haig discussed Allied plans for 1917 and considered various options for different offensives. General Plumer was again asked to submit plans for an offensive in Flanders. Plumer's plans were submitted on 12 December 1916 and were very much similar to those previously submitted. The offensive would begin by simultaneous attacks to take the Messines–Wytschaete Ridge, Hill 60 and Pilckem Ridge. Sir Douglas Haig held another conference with his army commanders on 7 May, where it was eventually decided the operations would continue in two phases, with the first phase being the attack on the Messines–Wytschaete Ridge. Several factors had to be taken into account though. Mutinies had taken place in the French Army and, furthermore, General Petain had taken command of the French armies in the north and north-east.

On the whole though, as this work centres on the experiences of 8 and 9/Yorkshire Regiment, the main thing that affected them in the planning was that all the nineteen mines would be blown together and the 23rd Division would be one of the assaulting divisions.

Preparation for the Battle of Messines

In the early hours of 25 May battalions of 70 Brigade commenced the relief of those of 69 Brigade. The 11/Sherwood Foresters took over from 8/Yorkshire Regiment, who marched to Brandhoek and entrained for Abeele. By 9 a.m. they were in billets 2 miles north-west of Abeele and the rest of the day was spent resting and cleaning up. Likewise, 9/York and Lancs relieved 9/Yorkshire Regiment, who moved to billets in Boeschepe area. The purpose of the move was so they could begin training for the forthcoming Second Army offensive. The preparation for this

Australians study a large model of the battlefield, which was also used by Imperial troops.

included the digging of practice trenches near Waton, just over the border in France. This was visited by officers and NCOs so they could familiarise themselves with the layout of the area they were to attack. Also, the opportunity was taken to view a large model of the battlefield made by the Australians.

HQ 23rd Division instructions were very detailed:

23rd Divisional Instruction No. 1
Artillery Supporting Left Division in Attack

1. The attack of the Right Brigade (69) will be supported by the following Artillery Groups:-

	18 pdr Guns	4.5" Hows
"A" Group (298 Bde)	24	-
"B" Group (102 Bde)	18	6
"C" Group (315 Bde)	24	6

The instruction goes on cover the artillery support for 70 Infantry Brigade and to outline command and control. It then covers the arrangements for the support fire of the 5th and 30th Heavy Artillery Groups with 8in guns and 9.2in howitzers. Also mentioned are the timings for the barrage and the lifts of fire onto the next line:

23rd Divisional Instruction No. 2
Fighting Kit
The Fighting kit to be carried will be as follows:-
Steel Helmet, Haversack on the back.
Water bottle filled, entrenching tool.
One large tool on the back of every other man, in the proportion 5 shovels to 2 picks.
Tube Helmet, Box Respirator.
Field Dressing.
Two sandbags per man.
Two grenades one in each top pocket to be collected by Section Commanders and used as a reserve.
Small Arms Ammunition, 120 rounds.
Two flares every other man one in each bottom pocket of the jacket.
One Iron Ration.
One days' preserved meat and biscuits.

All infantry officers must be dressed and equipped the same as their men. Sticks are not to be carried.

Specialists will be equipped as laid down in S.S.143 Part 1 para 3.

Attention is also called to Sections XXXI and XXXII of 'Instructions for the training of Divisions for Offensive Action' as regards to the distribution of wire cutters, very pistols, SOS rockets and distinguishing marks to be worn.

An amendment issued three days after the original added 'Waterproof sheet', to the list.

<u>23rd Divisional Instruction No. 3</u>

<u>Pioneers and Tunnellers.</u>

This instruction was for the attached platoons of the Pioneer Battalion (9/South Staffordshire Regt), who were to be employed constructing strong points at certain positions. These would then be strengthened by the RE.

<u>23rd Divisional Instruction No. 4</u>

<u>Liaison and Communication.</u>

This dealt with the provision of liaison officers and runners to be attached to neighbouring infantry brigade headquarters. Moreover, it also covered the attachment of artillery officers to brigade headquarters and for an artillery officer to be attached to each infantry battalion headquarters. Also provided for was the location of brigade and battalion headquarters and the various battalion command posts. Furthermore, routs for signal and telephone cables were laid down, along with instructions for the laying of new cables from captured trenches and positions. A relatively new idea was the provision of a wireless set working from a position in Larch Wood to a set near the divisional report centre. Further provision was made for additional electronic equipment, such as, amplifiers and power buzzers. In case all the relatively modern equipment failed there were sixteen pigeons available to 69 Brigade. An additional measure was the use of visual signalling stations (flags and lamps). Those for 69 Brigade were to be at the lip of the Hill 60 Crater and at the 8/Yorkshire Regiment Battalion Command Post. As a final resort, runner posts were to be set up, thirteen in all for 69 Brigade. The instruction also laid down the routes to be taken by runners. For example, a runner from 8/Yorkshire Regiment command post going to Brigade Forward Station would travel via Immovable Support trench, while a runner from the same HQ going to 'A' post would travel via Immovable Row and Swift Street. Runners were to travel in pairs 50 yards between each man. The lead runner was to carry the message and the second man was to take the message on if the lead man became a casualty.

Appendix 'A' to this instruction gives the code calls for the units of 23rd Division for use after Zero Hour. Those for 69 Brigade were:

69 Brigade HQ:	Z.F.I.
11/West Yorks:	N.W.Y.
8/Yorkshire Regiment:	H.Y.O.R.
9/Yorkshire Regiment:	I.Y.O.R.
10/DWR:	J.W.R.

23rd Divisional Instruction No. 5
Contact Aeroplanes.
This gives instructions for communication with contact aeroplanes. When called for the infantry were to light green flares to show their position.

23rd Divisional Instruction No. 6
Machine Gun Barrages.
In this instruction the timings and rates of fire were laid down for the machine guns of 68 and 194 Machine Gun Companies and 12 Motor Machine Gun Battery. It also provides instruction for the move forward to provide fire support for the third objective.

23rd Divisional Instruction No. 7
Arrangements for dealing with Prisoners and captured documents.
The collection and disposal of prisoners was clearly laid down. Officers and NCOs were to be separated from the other ranks. When searched any documents found were to be placed in sandbags, separated by regiment, and sent to Advanced Divisional Headquarters as soon as possible.

Four intelligent NCOs or men of each battalion were to search the battlefield and collect documents. They were to be issued a brassard with the word 'Intelligence' on it. Dead bodies, especially those of officers and NCOs, were to be searched thoroughly. Dugouts in the vicinity of Hill 60, especially those of the pioneers employed on mining, should be searched especially. Plans of all mining operations are urgently wanted.

23rd Divisional Instruction No. 8
Gas and Smoke.
This instruction applied to No. 3 Special Company, RE, which was responsible for firing lachrymatory and fatal gas shells into the German lines. It was dependent on the wind direction and the decision to fire was left with the OC No. 3 Special Company.

23rd Divisional Instruction No. 9
Concentration March.
This instruction provided a detailed march table with the routes and timings for each brigade and its battalions to move to the front.

23rd Divisional Instruction No. 10
Instructions for Tunnellers.
Half a section of 1st Australian Tunnelling Company and half a section of 2nd Canadian Tunnelling Company were allotted for work with 69 and 70 Brigades. Their duties consisted of the repair and construction of brigade forward stations, battalion headquarters and artillery observation posts. There followed a detailed list of map references for these posts.

23rd Divisional Instruction No. 11
Documents and Maps.
All ranks were warned that no documents or maps, letters, papers, orders or sketches were to be carried that in the event of their capture would give any information to the enemy.[9]

There followed additional instructions from HQ X Corps but as can been seen from the notes above, which provide only the initial points from each instruction, it is clear the operation had been well thought out:

We left the battalions in the rear area ready to start training for the coming battle. From 26–31 May they went over the practice trenches marked out on the training area. One day was given over to a complete brigade attack. With 8/Yorkshire Regiment, Lieutenant Oakley made a plaster model of the trenches that the battalion were to attack, which proved useful. The various companies carried out attack formations and bayonet fighting, and dinner was taken out on the training area. On 29 May Second Lieutenant Wheeler reported for duty. Hardly the best time to be joining the battalion. During the morning of 31 May another practice attack over the trenches was carried out and in the afternoon the battalion practised fighting in Beauvoorde Wood. That night the battalion held a very successful concert organised by the padre, Reverend Williams. The reason for the concert was to present the Commanding Officer with a souvenir of his wedding. Of the 9/Yorkshire Regiment nothing more was recorded than 'In billets training for 2nd Army offensive'.

The Battle of Messines

On 1 June 69 Brigade left the training area and moved to Busseboom. The next day there was a competition for the men who had been training with Yukon packs. These had been adopted for men to easily carry heavy loads over the broken ground. It is believed the idea had been adopted from the Canadians. The competition was won by 9/Yorkshire Regiment, with 8/Yorkshire Regiment in second place.

Over the following two days 11/West Yorks and 10/DWR moved up to the front line. The 8/Yorkshire Regiment moved to Scottish lines, where after a long trying march they took over huts. Training in making hasty wire entanglements and wire cutting took place, and the baths in Poperinghe were made available. They also issued all the extra equipment that would be needed during the assault, such as sandbags, bombs extra wire cutters and lots of other small items a soldier needed. For example, toilet paper is never mentioned but there would have been a great need for it. On 5 June the battalion made preparations to move into the trenches.

The 69 Brigade had issued its own instructions for the coming attack, which were almost identical to those of HQ 23rd Division. The main difference was that at section 11 it listed the formation for the attack. Thus 10/DWR would be on the right, 8/Yorkshire Regiment in the centre with 11/West Yorks on the left. Each battalion was to attack in four waves and supporting companies would consolidate the strong points in the German second line. They would also provide moppers up for the German front line and communication trenches. There would be 20 yards between lines, 50 yards between waves and 100 yards between companies. Company Commanders were to detail carrying parties to bring up sufficient material to construct strong points. The brigade orders specified that every platoon, every section and so far was possible every man were to be given a definite point to reach and work to do in each objective to be attacked. The determination to reach this personal objective and to consolidate it must be impressed on every man.

8/Yorkshire Regiment at Messines:

On the night of 5–6 June 8/Yorkshire Regiment moved out at 8.30 p.m. and marched up towards the trenches. On the way up they met heavy hostile shelling in places with intermittent bursts of lachrymatory and gas shells. Gas helmets had to be worn and the battalion had eleven casualties from this shelling on the way up. Battalion HQ, B, D and C Companies less two platoons of C went into the Larch Wood tunnels. A Company and two platoons of C Company went to S.P.9. The next day, 6 June, was uneventful and the assembly trenches were inspected. Platoons were given their exit points from the tunnels and as far as possible everyone rested. At 2 a.m. on 7 June A Company and the two platoons with it moved to Panama Canal and Jackson Avenue and at 2.30 a.m. the battalion was in its assembly trenches. The Commanding Officer made a point of going round and inspecting the men in these positions, presumably to let those going over he was there with them. By all accounts the men were in excellent spirits and morale was high. Shelling by both sides died down and by 3 a.m. it was almost nothing. However the enemy were constantly sending up very lights from Hill 60. Everything was ready:

> At 3 a.m. the men got out of the assembly trenches and lay down in front of them. At 3.10 a.m. the ground shook and trembled. All along the front the nineteen mines exploded and the guns opened fire. The advance was difficult owing to the darkness, but a steady advance was maintained. A and B Companies had made allowances for the lips of the craters being more extensive and accordingly made unnecessarily large detours. This however, they remedied on reaching the high ground. Both Captain Lambert M.C. and Captain Pearson M.C. handled their companies with great skill and gallantry. They broadened their front, changed direction half left and half right respectively and captured the RED objective with Great dash.
>
> Meanwhile, C Company under Captain Atkinson had been advanced direct on the two mine craters. Any enemy resistance was at once overcome and consolidation was commenced at 3.20 a.m. Battalion headquarters had started in front of the leading wave; but on reaching DEEP SUPPORT were so far in front of the battalion that a halt had to be made They pushed on again at 3.20 a.m. and by 3.30 a.m. were established on the eastern slope of Hill 60 at the Mound according to instructions received from Brigade. The Battalion signallers had followed with the fourth wave laying a wire as they advanced.
>
> In the meantime, A and B Companies with hardly a check on the Red Line had pushed onto the BLUE Line which fault the Commanding Officer attributed to the fact that the enemy ran from shell holes near the objective, and men could not be restrained from pursuit. Also the hostile trenches had been so destroyed that it

Private Thomas Dent Wright, 8th Bn, from Barnoldswick, formerly 29/469 29th Reserve Bn Northumberland Fusiliers. Killed in action 7 June 1917.

> was difficult to verify one's position. Both companies pushed out patrols according to orders; but these were beyond our own barrage for three hours.
>
> At 3 hours 40 minutes after zero hour, D Company passed through in artillery formation and occupied the BLACK Line with hardly a casualty and meeting practically no resistance. As, however, the troops on their left and right had not advanced so far, D Company accordingly withdrew and immediately got in touch with both flanks. The morning was spent in reorganising in depth, consolidating and putting strong points in a state of defence, carrying up material, stores, food water and ammunition.

As has come to be expected, the War Diary of 9/Yorkshire Regiment gives very little information; On the night 5–6 June a simple statement 'Moved to trenches preparatory to attack next morning, perfect weather'. Then on 7 June, 'Attack on Battle Wood. Perfect weather'. The War Diary does, however, have some appendices, which provide more detail. The preparation for the attack was 'all that could be desired'. The artillery preparation was 'successful beyond one's wildest dreams'. Assembly trenches and arrangements for evacuating the tunnels were excellent. Supplies, material etc were very ably organised.[10]

9/Yorkshire Regiment at Messines

Unlike the other battalions, 9/Yorkshire Regiment in support did not move forward until long after the battalions in the front line. Their report was as follows:

> REPORT ON THE ATTACK ON BATTLE WOOD ON 7 JUNE 1917
>
> The attack was made through the BLUE Line at 6.50 a.m. in two lines in small columns in Artillery formation, A Company on the right, C Company on the left, supported by B and D Companies respectively.
>
> About the first two hundred yards the advance did not meet with very great resistance and the troops kept close up to our barrage. After this the undergrowth became increasingly thick and snipers and machine gun fire caused many casualties. It was with great difficulty that touch was maintained with the troops on our flanks, and for some considerable time we were well in front of them and our advance was checked by flanking fire. The battalion was eventually forced to dig itself in on the southern edge of the wood owing to heavy machine gun fire from emplacements just beyond our objective, which made further advance practically impossible. I am of the opinion that the objective allotted to this battalion was situated in low ground in the very centre of a strong hostile position, and one

Private Fred Shaw and family, from Slaithwaite, Yorkshire. He was killed on 7 June 1917.

Captain Eric N. Lambert was killed on 6 June 1917 and is buried in Railway Dugouts cemetery.

which had been carefully organised for defensive purposes with concealed Machine Gun emplacements on the rising ground in front, and on our flanks. For reasons which are not clear to me these emplacements did not appear to have been dealt with by our artillery. The arrangements previous to the attack were quite efficient so far as I am in a position to judge, but signalling communication during the attack was very unsatisfactory. I found it impossible to get in touch with Brigade by this means until 7 hours after the attack was launched, although every effort to do so was made on our part. The Artillery Liaison Officer did not report to me at all on the 7th inst., and although our own guns were consistently bombarding the positions we had just captured, it was impossible to get in touch with the Artillery in order to get them to lengthen their range. I would suggest that in future a series of coloured Very Lights be used for this purpose.

The enclosed reports from companies make the situation on each flank more clear for information of the G.O.C.[11]

16/6/17

H.A.S. Prior
Lieut Colonel
Commanding 9/Yorkshire Regiment

Casualties, 7 June 1917

Second Lieutenant William Buckle, 8th Bn, died of wounds on 7 June 1917 and is buried in Lisjenthoek Military Cemetery.

The casualties were high in 8/Yorkshire Regiment, Captain E.N. Lambert and Second Lieutenant W. Buckle died from their wounds. The following officers were also wounded and evacuated: Captain B.L. Pearson, Lieutenant A.G. McCulloch, and Second Lieutenants C.W. Jones, J.L. Armstrong, J.T. Shaw, W.H. Mitchell. Second Lieutenants A.T. Dudley and H.J. Smith were both wounded but remained at duty. Of the other ranks, thirty-five had been killed or died from wounds, thirteen were missing and 191 had been wounded. Four were wounded but remained at duty, with one missing believed killed and one missing believed wounded. Both officers are commemorated in known graves, Second Lieutenant Buckle in Lijssenthoek Military Cemetery and Captain Lambert in Railway Dugouts Burial Ground (Transport Farm). Captain Lambert's family received a letter from a staff officer of the 24th Division saying that he was wounded on 7 June. He was taken to a dugout, where he had his wounds dressed but while this was being done a shell landed on the dugout and killed him and others.

This was the only report that the family had received up until that time. Consequently they wrote to the War Office and a request was sent out to France for more information:

> Could a special enquiry be made please to find out if Captain Lambert is alive or dead? As the relatives, are making urgent enquiries. I have seen the letter [From the Staff officer at HQ 24th Division]. R C Lilley Captain M.C. & Bar.[12]

There are two things that appear odd in this case. Firstly, the letter to the family comes from a staff officer in 24th Division. Is this a written mistake and should it read 23rd Division? Secondly, the letter states 'killed Captain Lambert and others'. When Captain Lambert's body was recovered what happened to the others. Only 26618 Private Edward Barwood is buried close to him; was he the only other man recovered?

Likewise, the casualties in 9/Yorkshire Regiment had also been high. Second Lieutenant F.W. Knott was killed, Captain W.R. Gamble was wounded but died on 12 June, Second Lieutenant G.C. Knowles was also wounded and died on 9 June and Second Lieutenant T.W. Dean died on 7 June shortly after being wounded. A number of other officers were also wounded: Captains W.F. Greenwood and R.H. Tolson, along with Lieutenant S. Blore and Second Lieutenants D.B. Almgill, H.G. Robson, R.T. Eaton, H.S Hobby and C. Read. Among the other ranks, sixty-seven were killed, 178 wounded and 9 were missing. Furthermore, over the next four days there was one more death and nine more wounded as well as one man missing on 11 June.

Private Thomas Outhwaite, 9th Bn, died of wounds on 19 June 1917 and is buried in Lisjenthoek Military Cemetery.

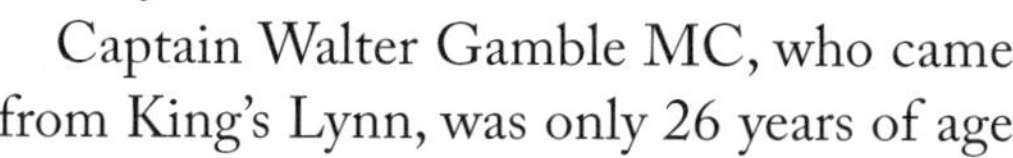

Captain Walter Gamble MC, who came from King's Lynn, was only 26 years of age and had enlisted in the 16th Royal Irish Lancers at the age of 19. He landed in France in August 1914. He was commissioned into the Green Howards on 6 February 1916. General Lambert, Commanding 69 Brigade, wrote to his parents:

> Will you accept from myself and all of the brigade our deepest sympathy in the loss of your son Captain W.R. Gamble in the recent operations. Both as Adjutant of his battalion and as a company commander he had proved of great value to the Brigade and we all miss him. From the first news I had of his being wounded I had hoped that his wounds were not so severe but he died as you know in a hospital. He was a man of great energy and character, whose experience was of much value to his comrades, who did his duty gallantly to the end, after following the fortunes of the brigade so long and whose memory will not be forgotten by those of us that knew him so well. I hope it may be of some comfort to you in your sorrow to know how much we all appreciated the example he gave us as a soldier.

The Commanding Officer of 9 Green Howards, Lieutenant Colonel H.A.S. Prior wrote:

> It is with the very deepest sympathy that I write to inform you that your son, Captain Walter R Gamble, died of his wounds at 11 p.m. on the night of the 12th inst. He was buried yesterday close to the hospital. He was shot through the chest by a sniper on the 7th inst, while gallantly cheering on his men. We shall all miss him and the battalion will feel his loss keenly. I feel I have lost a personal friend, as he was very much with me while acting as my adjutant. He always set a fine example of bravery and devotion to duty to his men. With renewed assurances of the deep sympathy, of all ranks with you in your bereavement.

Another letter arrived at the family home, this one from the Wesleyan chaplain attached to 69 Brigade, who wrote:

> I lived with his company for several days before they went into action and found him to be the perfect gentleman. He was always thoughtful and kind toward his fellow officers and the men. His company were proud of him. I also feel that I have lost a good friend. I am very sorry for you. His death after 2½ years of war will come as a great shock, but he laid down his life in a great cause and will not lose his reward.

One further letter of consolation arrived at the family home in Rosebery Road, Gaywood. It was from the surgeon who tried to save his life. He wrote:

> The Colonel came this morning to enquire after Captain Gamble. He told me that Captain Gamble had told him before he went in that he knew he would never come through. The Colonel said if he felt like that he had better not go. But Captain Gamble said: 'No: If the boys go I shall go too'. The Colonel spoke highly of Captain Gamble.

Mrs William Dean of Grove Hill, Middlesbrough, received the official news that her son, Second Lieutenant Thomas W. Dean, aged 28, had been killed in action. He was an old High School boy, had enlisted in the Royal Engineers and after serving in France for some months was offered and accepted a commission. He was a partner of the firm of Dean Brothers, builders, Middlesbrough. Mrs Dean's other two sons, Sergeant Turner Dean, Green Howards, and Second Lieutenant Harold Dean, Green Howards, were both on active service. Dean was a member of a well-known and a highly respected Wesleyan family. H.A.S. Prior, Lieutenant Colonel commanding 9/Yorkshire Regiment, writing to Mrs Dean, said:

> My Dear Mrs Dean – I am very grieved to be the bearer of bad tidings to you, but I fear there is no doubt that your son Second Lieutenant T.W. Dean must be accounted dead. My Information comes from Private Fagg [11817 Private Alfred E Fagg] of A Company of this Battalion, who tells me that he was with him when he died. He had been badly wounded both in the ankle and thigh with bullets and like the gallant fellow he was, was well in front of our front line at the time. Fagg says he was quite conscious before he died and asked that you should be told. I am making further inquiries as to his burial, and will let you know as soon as I hear further. The position was a very obscure and dangerous one, which accounts for the difficulty in obtaining information. I thought very highly of your boy, and he was in every sense of the word a gallant and fearless gentleman. We all mourn his loss and the loss of many of his brave comrades who fell with him on the morning of the 7th inst. With my very deepest and most heartfelt sympathy, believe me dear madam. Your Sincerely
>
> H.A.S Prior Lieut-Colonel
> Commanding, 9/Yorkshire Regiment.

Lieutenant Colonel Prior was never able to let Mrs Dean know where Thomas was buried for his remains were never found and today he is commemorated on the Ypres, Menin Gate Memorial to the Missing.

Second Lieutenant George C. Knowles was born in Wood Green, London, in 1897. He attended Brighton College and left in 1916 to join the army. He was commissioned into 3/Green Howards and was posted to the 9/Yorkshire Regiment in France. After his death his father passed copies of the letters he had received regarding George to Brighton College to enable them to include an obituary in the school magazine. One officer wrote:

> In difficult times in trenches and when at rest behind the lines, he was always doing something for the care of his platoon, and his boldness and absolute disregard of danger when in action was superb. You will be glad to know he died the most glorious death imaginable. He was bringing in one of his men from the open (the man had been badly wounded) when he was shot through the arm and fell. He got up again and tried to drag the man in, when he was shot through the shoulder. After a few

Second Lieutenant George Clarence Knowles, 9th Bn, died of wounds on 9 July 1917.

> minutes he once again tried to drag in the wounded man, when he received a bullet in the abdomen.

A senior officer, most likely Lieutenant Colonel Prior, wrote:

> Your son was one of the best and most gallant fellows it has ever been my privilege to meet; we all loved him and his loss will be keenly felt. He died, as he would have wished to die, from wounds received in the attempt to save the life of one of his men, an attempt in which he was successful.

George Kidson recalled the following about May and June 1917:

> Out of the trenches we were training for the Battle of Messines Ridge, 7 June 1917. The morning when the guns opened up we were blown up about a yard. Then we went forward. Our objective was a place called Battle Wood, we were held up by snipers, and our C.O. refused to go, that was a good job for us. We got relieved and we were in and out of the trenches until Passchendaele.

Private Edmund Staveley, from Hawes, died of wounds on 9 June 1917.

The dead of both battalions came from many different parts of the region. In Willington, County Durham, Mr and Mrs J. Little received the official notification that their son, Corporal Herbert Little MM, had been killed in action. He had enlisted a month after war had been declared and had been in France for twenty-two months in all. Before enlisting he had been a putter at Brancepeth Colliery. His parents received two further letters, the first from Captain W.F. Greenwood, writing from his hospital bed in London, where he was lying wounded, which said:

> It is with deepest sorrow that I have to write to you. You will have heard that your son Corporal H Little has been killed in action. Corporal Little's death was a blow to me as I had known him for a long time. As soon as I took over command of the Company, I made your son a non-commissioned officer in appreciation of his continuous good work and numerous qualifications and capabilities. Please accept this letter of deepest

sympathy on behalf of the NCOs and men of the Company. The Officers join me in the above message.

The second letter came from his Company Quartermaster, Sergeant William Jackson, who was also a miner. Although born in Castle Eden, he was employed at Wheatley Hill Colliery when he had enlisted on 1 September 1914. He wrote as follows:

> Sorry I am to write you in regard to your son 'Josh,' as he was known to the boys and myself. He fell in action on 7 June 1917. He did his duty, as he always did – with a good and a true heart. He died like a soldier. He was buried by his comrades, who put up a cross to their hero. Had he lived further honours awaited him.

A memorial service was held in the Presbyterian Church, Willington, on Sunday, 22 July 1917. Although his original grave was marked, it was lost in subsequent fighting and he is commemorated on the Menin Gate Memorial to the Missing in Ypres.

The casualties for both battalions were very different but had one thing in common: the vast number of those killed who were missing. The table below shows the place of burial or commemoration of those killed in action on 7–9 June 1917.

8/Yorkshire Regiment

Lijssenthoek Military Cemetery	Railway Dugouts Burial Ground (Transport Farm)	Ypres (Menin Gate) Memorial	Ypres Reservoir Cemetery
4	3	40	1

9/Yorkshire Regiment

Bedford House Cemetery	Hooge Crater Cemetery	Lijssenthoek Military Cemetery	Perth Cemetery (China Wall)	Woods Cemetery	Ypres (Menin Gate) Memorial
1	1	5	1	2	71

The large number of missing from 9/Yorkshire Regiment reveals the vicious nature of the fighting in Battle Wood. The burial in Bedford House Cemetery was carried out in February 1921, when the remains of Second Lieutenant Joseph A. Child, who was serving with 69 LTMB, were found. The remains buried in Perth Cemetery (China Wall) were those of 42007 Robinson Collin, whose body was exhumed in August 1919, and the grave in Hooge Crater

Cemetery is that of 43005 Private Hammil Howarth, formerly in the KOYLI, from Bottomboat near Wakefield. One of four bodies found at I.35.d.5.6., he was identified by his looking glass. One of the others had a 'York' shoulder title but nothing else to identify him. Lijssenthoek Cemetery, Woods Cemetery and Railway Dugouts were in use at the time of the battle, so have not been checked for reburials.

The one exhumation from 8/Yorkshire Regiment was 42554 Lance Corporal James Colton, whose body was found in May 1921. Identified by his identification disc, he was reburied in Ypres Reservoir (North) Cemetery.

The author's grandfather, Private Walter Sheen, never spoke much about the war but did relate that at Messines they had been issued Wrigley's chewing gum. This was to combat the dust of the explosions as they went over the top. He remembered this as it was the first time he had seen it; as a miner they were more used to chewing tobacco. In 2018, at a talk on the First World War in Coxhoe village hall, the author was talking to a relative of 17691 Private George Dring, who was killed with 9/Yorkshire Regiment. The story about the chewing gum was related and the lady said, 'You have just given me goose bumps.' 'Why?' 'Well we have all of George's personal effects and among them are some sticks of Wrigley's chewing gum and we could never figure out why it was there. Now we know!'

Indeed, the carriage of chewing gum to the men in the line by the Yukon pack men of 9/Yorkshire Regiment at Jackdaw Craters is mentioned in a later battalion operation order dated 17 September 1917.

The 9/Yorkshire Regiment were relieved in the front line on 9 June by 10/DWR. They moved into Brigade Reserve and two days later moved back to Vancouver Camp. On 13 June they went back even further to the Berthen area for divisional rest and reorganisation. Likewise, 8/Yorkshire Regiment moved by Lorries to Montreal Camp on the night of 12–13 June. At 4.30 p.m. a very tired but happy battalion marched to the Berthen area, where they arrived around 8.30 p.m. A and C Companies were accommodated in barns with the other two companies in tents. It was in glorious weather that the battalion spent the two next days cleaning up and refitting and replacing missing and damaged equipment.

Private George Dring from Ferryhill Station, died of wounds on 8 June 1917.

On 17 June there was a church parade and afterwards General Babington inspected the battalion. The general took the opportunity to thank the men for their fine and successful work on 7 June. Over the next day's specialist training started to replace those lost in the recent fighting; Lewis gunners, signallers and grenadiers all needed training. A new officer, Lieutenant Williams, East Lancashire Regiment, was attached to 8/Yorkshire Regiment on 19 June. The same day the divisional gas officer visited the battalion and inspected all gas helmets. Also that day in the afternoon, the 69 Infantry Brigade Horse show was held. The results were as follows:

In Class I, Pack Animals, 9/Yorkshire Regiment took first place.

In Class II, Lewis Gun Limber, 8/Yorkshire Regiment, took second place.

In Class III, neither battalion took anything.

In Class IV, Water Carts, 9/Yorkshire Regiment, were in first place, with 8/Yorkshire Regiment in second place.

In Class V, saw nothing for the Green Howards

In Class VI, Dismantling a S.A.A (small arms ammunition). limber, unhook and unharness the horses, 9/Yorkshire Regiment were once again in first place.

In Class VII, the challenge was driving a limber and pair through pegs, which saw 9/Yorkshire Regiment in joint second place with Brigade HQ.

In Class VIII, the officers' hurdle race was easily taken by Lieutenant Colonel Western, 8/Yorkshire Regiment, with Captain Atkinson of the same battalion in second place, while Lieutenant Middleton, 9/Yorkshire Regiment, was placed third.

In Class IX, which was added for fun, the mule race for NCOs and men was won by Driver Jennings, 9/Yorkshire Regiment.

On the whole a very good day for those of 9/Yorkshire Regiment that looked after the battalion horses and mules.

The 9/Yorkshire Regiment do not record anything until on 20 June, when they moved to Dickebusch and were employed on making roads. Here they were joined by B and C Companies, 8/Yorkshire Regiment.

On 23 June Second Lieutenants C.T. Hepworth, formerly a private in the 12th Lancers, and G.F. Pearce, previously a sergeant in the 9th Lancers, joined 8/Yorkshire Regiment, having been commissioned, and were posted to A and D Companies. The battalion less the companies working on the roads left the Berthen area at 4 p.m. on 28 June and marched via Godewaersvelde to Alberta

Camp, a mile south of Reninghelst, arriving there at 9 p.m. They were later joined by the other two companies. That night an advance party left for Hill 60 sector, during the night a lot of rain fell which did not improve the state of the trenches.

The next day eight new officers joined for duty on their first appointment, all second lieutenants, namely: Charles A. Bottomley, Edward Clegg, Richard. R. Crute, Leonard Dickens, William Lister, John H. McNicholas, James Morrison, Frank C. Vernon and James Mills. The last named was a former pony driver from Wheatley Hill and had been in France since July 1915 serving as a sergeant in 7/Yorkshire Regiment. Indeed, except for James Morrison, all the others had served in the ranks prior to being commissioned and brought much-needed experience to the battalion. For the battalion the day was spent in inspections and preparing to move back to the line. At 4.30 p.m. the battalion marched out of camp via Dickebusch to the trenches. At Dickebusch a halt was made for one hour in order to have tea, the relief being complete by 2.30 a.m. on 30 June. The battalion was shelled on the way up to the line and two men were wounded. All that day rain fell and at the trenches, which were slightly further on than those taken on 7 June, the front line was a series of posts. During the day a lot of rain fell, which made the trenches extremely wet. The 9/Yorkshire Regiment had also been on the move. They had been shelled out of their camp at Dickebusch and were in Brigade Reserve at the Triangular Spoil Bank.

However, one lucky man did not go into the line with 8/Yorkshire Regiment. No. 13093 Private Walter Sheen was given his first and only leave on 30 June, to have ten days at home in Durham. Bearing in mind that the family shared an alleyway with Mrs Inglis, he would have to speak to her about Harry's death. He dealt with the situation by giving her a Green Howards cap badge and telling her that was all that was picked up at the spot where Harry was hit. Of course, it was not the truth; Harry like everyone else would have been wearing a steel helmet. When the author met Harry Inglis' great nephew, before the author spoke, Ronnie Inglis said, 'Did you know your grandfather gave my Gran a Green Howards cap badge when he told her how Harry died.' So it was a true story!

Private Walter Sheen and Paddy Burke on leave, June 1917.

The other notable event on this leave was that he was reunited with Paddy Burke, who stood beside him on the platform at Durham Railway Station in September 1914. Posted to 10/Yorkshire Regiment, Paddy was at home recovering from being gassed in France while serving with his battalion.

No. 36415 Private Harry Severs was the servant to Major Charles Bolckow, serving in 9/Yorkshire Regiment. Wounded in the leg, he was evacuated to the same CCS as Major Bolckow, who had been evacuated sick. Concerned about a letter from home, he made this request:

> No 7 Canadian General Hospital
> Ward B.3
> Etaples
> 30 June 17
>
> Dear Sir
> Just a line to let you know how I am getting on. You will see I have got so far as the base. In the first instance I went to the C.C.S. where you and I were for those first days and then I came here the next day. I am going on very steady but I still have a lot of pain in my leg but I think it will be alright in time. I hope Sir your cold is better, no doubt it will start to hang on you while you are still under.
>
> The night I was at the C.C.S Fritz came over dropping bombs but luckily he did not damage me and having come to this beautiful ward here now I wonder Sir if you would be so kind as to see if there is any letters for me in the orderly room and have them forwarded to me if you are able. I am expecting one from home and I am rather anxious about it. If you would do that I should be very much obliged.
>
> I remain Yours Private H P Severs

By the time he received the letter Major Bolckow had been evacuated to No. 8 (Michelham) Home for Convalescent British Officers, APO S.8, France. This was based at Dieppe on the French coast. He wrote a letter (in a very poor hand) to Lieutenant Lionel Tinkler, who was formerly a sergeant in King Edward's Horse, and asked him to deal with Private Severs' request:

> 8/7/17
> My dear old Tinkler You must drop me a line + tell me how things are going – but I suppose I must forgive you as you won't have much time for writing in the unenvious position in which my cold blooded desertion has left you. Much to my surprise + quite undeservedly I have been awarded

by Medical Board 28 days at this really charming place & if I am not better under the time limit I should be as nothing horrid is done to me, and one lives like a Cock fighter. I heard from Hunnybun that you are due one. Whizzbangs and 4.5s are getting …….. galore. ………………… They shall have a company again. Major Goodison will be quite cheery again……… If old Madderson [Lieutenant H. Maddison] tell him my address, much appreciated seeing him. Re the enclosed letter from Pte Severs is forwarded to you. Will you ask our CQMS to see into it please. Also I want you to give him 5 F.F. for the mens teas at Mont des Cats. One other request, either Blake or Hunnybun paid for my six copies of equestrian photos which I have not squared up. Have you squared up my debt to the Company, if not let me know + I will send you back on ………… here. Re ………. Our copy of new trench orders I took down to CCS + and as far as the Ambulance train. I handed them to Christie to send them back by his servant to you. You should have it by now as Christie could not [the next six lines are scribbled and although some words can be made out they do not make sense.]

Yours Ever Charles Bolckow.[13]

Chapter 8

Menin Road Ridge, Polygon Wood, Passchendaele

The month of July stated quietly for 8/Yorkshire Regiment. The weather was fine and 10/DWR relieved the battalion who moved into Brigade Reserve at Larch Wood with A and B Companies in immovable support, C Company at Larch Wood and D Company at S.P.9. During daylight hours they rested but on the night of 2 July they provided large working parties. On the night of 3 July, after being relieved by a London battalion from 47th Division, the battalion marched to MicMac Camp, where they were under canvas. At 4 a.m. next morning a German aeroplane flew low over the camp and dropped two bombs. There were three casualties: 241534 Private John Husband, a resident of Church Street, Middlesbrough; and 23217 Private Edgar Winterflood, who hailed from Thornhill near Dewsbury. Both are commemorated on the Menin Gate Memorial to the Missing. The third man was wounded. 42576 Private Ernest Robertson from Newcastle, who had previously served in the Durham Light Infantry, was evacuated to No. 2 CCS at Bailleul, where he succumbed to his wounds and was buried there. The battalion left MicMac Camp at 11.30 a.m., marched to Ouderdom and entrained for Godewaersvelde. After leaving the train the marching continued to billets 2 miles north of Steenvoorde. Also moving on this route was 9/Yorkshire Regiment. Between 5 and 11 June units were refitting and training. Each battalion constructed an assault course as prescribed by 'Bullet and Bayonet Training'. All the battalions received drafts to replace the losses of June.

The training area was somewhat limited and 8/Yorkshire Regiment carried out their training by companies. All the old favourites took place in the morning: physical training, arms drill, bayonet fighting, musketry and the platoon in the attack, and of course the specialists did their own thing as always. Afternoons were given over to sport, football competitions etc. On 7 July General Babington visited the battalion and inspected a draft of 219 newly arrived other ranks. He also presented the ribbon of the Military Medal to twenty-five men for their gallantry at Messines. Of the 9/Yorkshire Regiment no information is included in their War Diary between 4 and 11 July 1917. On 10 July Babington returned to the 8/Yorkshire Regiment and presented the Ribbon of the Military Cross to Lieutenant J.P. Reed and Second Lieutenants J.P. Heron and A.T. Dudley. He also presented the ribbon of the DCM to 14770 Company Sergeant Major W. Mashender, 11577 Sergeant A. Knowles and 11751 Private A. Smith.

These inspections by General Officers were commented upon in the *Green Howards Gazette*:

> High up in the list of war's discomforts must be placed the G.O.C.s inspection. Periodically, the general officer commanding the division takes it into his head to liven up things, and, once having made up his mind, life becomes a misery for officer and man until he has been and gone.
>
> We have come out of the line, dirty and fed-up. The second day brigade sends the following message: 'The G.O.C. will inspect your battalion tomorrow 22 inst. At 11 a.m.; dress, full marching order. Company commanders will be mounted.' From such simple beginnings do troubles in the army arise.
>
> Breakfast is disposed of by 8 a.m., and the next few hours are marked by scenes of feverish activity. Company parade is at 9 a.m. The platoon commanders make a preliminary survey of their platoons and take this opportunity to tell them to answer to any name their officer gives them. (A platoon commander is supposed to know the name of all his men; but, of course occasionally doesn't.) O.C. Company then makes a detailed inspection of everybody. Glaring irregularities are painfully obvious, and the culprits put right. Pte 'Bill Jones' hasn't got an entrenching tool helve – one is salved from the quartermaster's stores. Two or three men need a haircut, the barber is only human, however, and he'd probably shaved over a hundred heads since the previous afternoon – too late to remedy this. Horror of horrors! – Pte 'Bloggins' hasn't shaved! There is time to remedy this, and he is forthwith packed off, to reappear in half an hour, respectable – to find himself booked for the next 'company orderly room.' Several 'hard cases' are not wearing the belt of the equipment on the hooks of their tunics! There is the inevitable man with the filthy equipment, and another with rusty ammunition.
>
> With sighs of resignation the company commander leads his men to the next stage of the ordeal, the Commanding Officer's inspection at 10 a.m. The latter realising just how good things can be made under existing conditions, examines each man fully, pointing out a few trifling matters to remedy. Stopping before a diminutive solder, who looks the picture of misery, 'Are you happy?' he enquires, and is powerless to check the resulting laugh. Such a little incident as this means a good deal, however, confidence and good humour are inspired, and this means smart drill.

Having seen all four companies, and brought them as near to perfection as possible, the C.O. awaits the G.O.C., and the battalion is paraded at 10.30 a.m. 'Dressing' is a long job, but is done at last, and we are left to 'stand easy.' which in full marching order is not so 'easy.'

Prompt at 11 a.m. the G.O.C. rides on to the scene supported by the Brigadier and the Brigade Major and four or five painfully smart staff officers. Much to the relief of the company commanders the G.O.C. dismounts and the rest of his staff do likewise. That dread of scattering one's own company is thus allayed. We have given him a general salute and – Allah be praised! – The man who dropped his rifle wasn't spotted. The fireworks now begin. The G.O.C. orders bayonets to be unfixed, saying with a wicked smile he would like to see a few rifles. No. 1 Platoon is the first to be inspected and with an occasional comment he passes on to No. 2, and then to No. 3. 'What's this man's name?' he asks pointing to 'Pte White.' 'Black, Sir,' is the prompt reply from the platoon commander and 'Pte White' gazes at his officer with respectful admiration. 'Let me see your rifle.' To a man in the rear rank. 'Humph! Quite good.' He passes on to No. 4 Platoon and pounces on a front rank man. 'Turn out your pack I would like to check your kit.' *The pack is emptied, and the wretched man hasn't got a spare pair of boot laces!* The platoon commander is severely censured, and with polite attention listens to a long list of his shortcomings, and as the G.O.C. and his following pass on to B Company catches a solemn wink from the Adjutant.

B Company has a similar experiences but the eagle eyed warrior spots a bayonet in its scabbard with the ring to the front! In No. 8 Platoon the general comes across an old friend. This is 'Pte Pepper', who fought with him in the Zulu war. They have a long chat, and highly pleased, the general passes on to C Company. Faults are hard to find, so he begins to criticise fingernails. The colonel is duly impressed with the necessity of seeing to this point. Otherwise C Company is good the G.O.C. is pleased to admit. D Company next. '*Do you use a tooth brush*? He enquires of a man in the front rank. 'Yes Sir.' '*How Often?*' 'Every time I clean my buttons sir.' The staff look pained but the old gentleman is tickled, and finishes off the battalion in quick style.

We have not done yet. He now mounts his charger, and delivers a short address, something after this fashion:

> '*I am very pleased to have had the opportunity of inspecting your battalion this morning.* B-r-r-r. *It is a very smart battalion – a very smart battalion indeed. I have inspected six battalions in my division this last week and*

this is the smartest I have seen. (Murmurs of astonishment.) *But I have not come to praise you* B-r-r-r. *In a few days our division will make a big attack and this battalion will have the honour of taking a leading part in the attack.* B-r-r-r. *I need not ask you to do your best – I know you will. Good bye, men and good luck!*

With a farewell salute the general rides away, closely followed by his glittering staff, and, tired and aching we march back to our billets and dismiss. We have been on parade, in full marching order from 9 a.m. until 1 p.m. – in short we have been inspected to death.[1]

The period of training over 69 Brigade moved to the Hubertushoek area on 12 July and commenced the relief of 68 Brigade in the Mount Sorrel, Hill 60 Sector. Leaving billets at 10 a.m., they followed the reverse route to Mimac Camp. C and D Companies did not stop, embarked on motor lorries and took over support positions from 12/DLI. At 7.45 p.m. on 12 July 8/Yorkshire Regiment moved forward and became the right front-line battalion. This relief was completed without casualties. However, the rain was falling hard and the trenches became impossible to move in. At dusk and dawn the enemy put down a heavy barrage including gas shells. On 14 July the Germans put a heavy barrage on the left company, which caused thirty casualties, five of whom were killed. Also Second Lieutenants Mills and Morrison were wounded. The weather improved but the Germans switched their fire to the right company headquarters and one man was killed. On the night of 16 July 11/West Yorks moved into the front line and 8/Yorkshire Regiment became the Brigade Support battalion. They were tasked with providing large working parties carrying food ammunition and trench stores to the line.

In the meantime, 9/Yorkshire Regiment had moved on 11 July to Hedge Street Tunnels, where they relieved 11/Northumberland Fusiliers. On 16 July 10/DWR replaced them and they moved back to support positions, A Company to Canada Trench, B Company to Rudkin House, C Company into Metropolitan Left, while HQ and D Company remained at Hedge Street Tunnels. After three days they went back into the line,

Corporal George Gregory Pearson, from Shildon. Killed in action 17 July 1917.

where on the night of 22–23 July German shelling caused the deaths of three men. On 23 July the whole of 69 Brigade commenced moving to the Berthen area. The weather was hot and on arrival the Brigade Commander inspected all the new drafts. On 25 July the weather turned very wet again, but despite this General Babington inspected every battalion in fighting order. At the time he inspected 8/Yorkshire Regiment he also presented the ribbon of the Military Cross to Second Lieutenant J.T. Lakin and that of the Military Medal to 14827 Private H. Guy, 18332 Private J. Wood, 18609 Private H. Dresser and 13388 Private S. Watson.

On 26 July orders were issued for a move to the II Army training area for musketry. As usual the battalion transport sections moved by road and those on foot moved via Fletre to Caestre and entrained for Saint-Omer, where they arrived at 6 p.m. A training programme was put into operation and a refresher class for sergeants was commenced under the RSM. Owing to heavy rain, the allotted ranges could not be used, so training was confined to billets. Over the first two weeks of August a lot of musketry and Lewis gun work was carried out. Each company had a day on the rifle range. On 7 August General Sir H.C.O. Plumer GCMG KCB ADC inspected the 69 Brigade on the training area, visiting each battalion in turn. On 9 August the whole brigade moved to the Éperlecques area, where the training continued. At this time 23rd Division was transferred from X Corps to XVIII Corps, which was commanded by General Sir Ivor Maxse. He wasted no time in visiting the division and addressed the combined officers of 68 and 69 Brigades on 11 August. A number of lectures

Large German Trench area.

and demonstrations were given by XVIII Corps school with a view to future operations. Each platoon gave a demonstration of the platoon in the attack at X Corps Grenade School at Inglinghem. This included Lewis guns, rifle grenadiers, heavy machine guns and Stokes mortars. During a short break in the training Brigadier Lambert presented the ribbon of the Military Medal to 12529 Private Joseph W. Cleminson. Although born in New Marske, in 1911 he was working as a coal putter in Birtley, County Durham. The second recipient was 41589 Private Samuel Hooker. Two new officers joined 8/Yorkshire Regiment at this time, Second Lieutenants P. Robinson and T.E. Hardcastle, along with two drafts of thirty-four and thirty-seven other ranks.

The final practice on 21 August was a full brigade attack with attention being paid to the independent attack by platoons against strong points.

In late July or early August 14806 Private John T. Collins wrote with news of his old platoon to Second Lieutenant Richard B. Wilson. In late August Private Collins had a reply from the officer:

9th Yorkshire Regt
Att 8th T.R. Batt.
Rugeley Camp
Staffs
26 Aug 1917

Dear Collins,
My many thanks indeed, for your letter. I was very sorry to hear how No. 10 has been cut up. Just my luck to be away when they went over. I knew they would do well. However I may be with you all again soon as I've just been passed G.D. I applied to be sent out here but the C.O. won't let me go. So I've written to Colonel Prior asking him to get me transferred. You might let me know if you hear anything at Batt' HQ.

As you see from my address I've left West Hartlepool. I am now close to home, I expect I shall pop over today. Sorry to hear about Mr Robson being wounded. Are you still round the same old spot? I expect its worse than ever. Still old Fritz is having a fairly hot time now.

What is the batt sniping like now, do they ever kill anyone? I hear nearly all our casualties were through sniping? Well Collins I'm sending a few cigarettes as I know you can always get rid of them. Hoping to see you all soon in the field & wishing you the best of luck.

Yours sincerely
R.B. Wilton[2]

On 23 August new orders were received transferring 23rd Division to II Corps the next day. This necessitated another move to the Wippenhoek area. The road parties set off on the afternoon of 23 August and the following day the rest of the brigade marched to Watten Station, where they entrained for Abeele. The trains were very late leaving and it was 5 a.m. on 25 August before the last units arrived. Both Yorkshire Regiment battalions were carried by motor lorries to the Dickebusch huts area. From there the companies were transported to the II Corps model of the front, where the next assault was planned. On 27 August reconnoitring parties went up the line to look at the positions to be taken over and to view the ground where the assault would take place. It was while he was doing this that the Commanding Officer of 8/Yorkshire Regiment Lieutenant, Colonel B.C.M. Western DSO, was severely wounded by a shell and Major Grellet had to assume command of the battalion. At 8.30 p.m. 8/Yorkshire Regiment vacated the camp at Dickebusch and took over the area near Château Segard. One company were in trenches and the others in bivouacs. The move took place in very heavy rain and bivouacs were erected with great difficulty. A Yukon pack detail was set up with fifty men under Second Lieutenant J.H. McNichol. They were accommodated in the school in Ypres and they were tasked with carrying SAA, flares, etc. to the forward dumps. The work of reconnoitring paying particular attention to the line Inverness Copse to Glencorse Wood continued but both battalions suffered casualties to carrying parties. The weather turned really wet again and this caused the cancellation of the planned operation.

This cancellation caused 69 Brigade to move back to the Lederzeele area; 9/Yorkshire Regiment moved on foot via Steenvoorde, while 8/Yorkshire Regiment, who also went via Steenvoorde, marched to Wulverdinghe. Almost two weeks was spent training, with special emphasis on taking strong points. Time was found for the usual sporting events on 6 September, when the officers played the sergeants of 8/Yorkshire Regiment at cricket, which the officers won by four runs. However, the sergeants took in the honours at football, beating the officers four goals to one. Range work was also carried out at this time, with the whole battalion firing, including the Lewis guns. On 10 September a move was made to the X Corps training area, where an area of ground had been marked out to resemble the area of the coming attack. On 12 September General Sir H. Plumer visited 69 Brigade and watched as the whole brigade practised an attack over the training area.

The preparations for the coming offensive had been going on for some time. On 20 August, 69 Brigade headquarters issued the following instruction:

Administration Order No. 1

1. The Brigade will be accommodated on X, Y and Z days as will be notified later.
2. Until further orders units will occupy the same transport limes as at present. Each unit will detail one mounted orderly to report to Brigade Transport Officer at Rear Brigade HQ by noon on Y day. The position will be notified later.
3. WATER

   Rear Supplies (Drinking).

Tank No. 60.	H.32.a.1.3.	5,000 gallons per day.
Tank No. 17.	H.26.a.4.7.	5,000 gallons per day.
Tank No. 13.	H.28.d.3.2.	15,000 gallons per day.
Tank No. 10.	H.23.a.6.7.	10,000 gallons per day.
Tank No. 9.	H.14.a.9.3.	10.000 gallons per day.

   Forward Supplies.

   Main supply is from 16,000 gallon tank at about I.22.b.8.2. Water requires boiling before drinking.

   Advanced points to take water filled petrol tins will be made in slits with splinter proof protection at about J.19.b.2.9., J.13.d.1.8 and in tunnels under the Menin Road. Tins will be dumped at each of those places.

   In addition a reserve of 100 tins will be kept at Brigade HQ (Dormy House) and 100 tins at Ritz Street Tunnels. Battalion and Company Commanders are responsible for the return of all tins when empty. Unless this is systematically done units will not be provided with water.
4. RATIONS.

   Each unit is in possession of a second day's ration (P.M. and biscuit). Instructions as to the consumption of this ration will be issued later.

   In addition there is a store of about 2,000 iron rations held in reserve in the Ritz Street Tunnels. These are held for use in an emergency and instructions for issue will only be given by Brigade HQ. Rations may be sent up to ration dump day. Each Transport Officer will reconnoitre all tracks and roads.
5. The system of supply of and establishment of dumps Small Arms Ammunition, Grenades etc. is set out in Appendix 'A'.
6. R.E. Arrangements.

   There is an advanced R.E. dump at Zillebeke (I.22.b.8.4.)

   Consolidation R.E. stores have also been dumped around the CULVERT and the MENIN Road.

Further small dumps will be formed approximately on line CLAPHAM – STIRLING CASTLE. Exact locations and contents of dumps will be notified later.

7. REINFORCEMENTS.
The arrangements regarding reinforcements have been notified in 23rd Division G.132/1/12 dated 25 August 1917, forwarded to units under this office B.W. 885/6 dated 27 August 1917.

8. MEDICAL ARRANGEMENTS.
Medical Arrangements are set out in 23rd Division are set out in 23rd Division Medical Arrangements No. 108 of 26 August 1917 forwarded to units.

9. Instructions regarding actual casualties are set out in 23rd Division Q.S 52 of 27 August 1917 – copy herewith.

Attention is directed to 'Estimated Casualties' para 111. Units will report estimated casualties to Advanced Brigade HQ by 4 p.m. daily or any additional estimated casualties contemplated by para (vii) by 5 a.m. daily.

Actual Casualties.
Particular attention is drawn to instructions contained in this office M/1855 dated 27 August 1917.

All actual casualties will be reported on proforma to Brigade Rear HQ via Brigade Advanced HQ the reports to reach Brigade Advanced HQ at 2 p.m. daily.

10. Attention is drawn to 23rd Division Q.S.52 of 27 August 1917, copies of which are issued to units herewith, which contain detailed information as to:-
(1) Provost Marshall Arrangements.
(2) Ordnance Stores.
(3) Veterinary Arrangements.
(4) Burial of Dead.
(5) Clearing the Battlefield.
(6) List of Cemeteries.
Detailed instructions will be issued later regarding (4) and (5).[3]

30 August 1917
Captain

Staff Captain
69th Inf Bde

The above arrangements seem to cover all areas of battalion and brigade administration. Of particular interest are the arrangements for supplying water to those in the front line. Also of interest are the medical arrangements, which are covered by separate documents. During the last tour of the trenches at the end of August, the division suffered eleven casualties with trench foot. All the men were interviewed and the ADMS Colonel R.J. Blackham reported:

In all cases the men were on outpost duty in shell holes and state that they spent the whole time (4 days) in water up to their knees.

They did not either change their socks or rub their feet. A second pair of socks was carried, but only one man effected a change.

Only one man states he had hot food during the period.

The state of the trenches owing to the rain approached winter conditions.

I would strongly recommend that when we next go into the line the Precautions against Trench Foot (copy attached) for ready reference, which were so successful last winter, be put in force.[4]

Colonel A.M.S
A.D.M.S. 23rd Division

Other medical arrangements included a complete list of Regimental Aid Posts, field bearer posts, divisional collecting posts, bearer relay posts, ambulance car loading points, ADS locations, lorry loading points, Main Dressing Station and Divisional Rest Station. X Corps also planned to run light railway services to evacuate casualties:

Service 1. An hourly service from Menin Road stopping if required at Woodcote house, Dunedin Street and delivering wounded at Remy Siding C.C.S.

Service 2. An hourly service, from Larch Wood to Remy stopping at Dunedin if required.

Service 3. An hourly service, from Chester Farm stopping near Spoil Bank to Kilmarnock Street.

Service 1 would consist of eight trucks and the other two of four trucks each. Each truck could carry twenty walking wounded or four stretcher cases. It speaks volumes for the confidence of the Army Medical Services that they could plan scheduled rail services to evacuate the wounded at this stage of the war.

On the training areas the battalions completed their training and started to move back towards Ypres. On 13 September 8/Yorkshire Regiment left Wulverdinghe and travelled the 20 miles to Steenvoorde on foot, where they arrived at 7 p.m. having only four stragglers. The 9/Yorkshire Regiment travelled the same route. Next day both battalions moved to camps in the Reninghelst area, 8/Yorkshire Regiment to Alberta Camp and 9/Yorkshire Regiment to MicMac Camp. Two days were spent here. On 16 September 8/Yorkshire Regiment moved to MicMac Camp. They paraded before dawn each day to practise forming up on a taped line in the dark. Some men got the chance to bathe before going up the line. Battle stores were issued and the Brigade Commander addressed the battalions about the forthcoming attack.

Before 69 Brigade moved forward a further brigade order was issued:

69 Infantry Brigade Order No. 140

1. The 23rd Division will take part in the operations of the SECOND and FIFTH Armies on a date to be known as 'Attack Day'. The task of the Division is to capture and hold the trench line running along the high ground from about J.21 central to J.15 central forming part of the Passchendaele Ridge. The task will be carried out in three successive phases known as the Red, Blue and Green Objectives.

   The 2nd Brigade of the First Australian Division will attack on the left of the 23rd Division and the 123 Brigade of the 41st Division will be on the right of the 23rd Division.
2. Dividing lines of Division and Brigades, objectives, strong points to be formed and the Headquarters of Units are shown in 69 Infantry Brigade Instructions No. 1 and the maps issued therewith. The positions of assembly of Units are shown in 69 Infantry Brigade Instructions No2 and addenda thereto.

   It is of great importance to secure observation of the Polderhoek Spur (J.16.c), the Reutelbeek Valley and if possible of the Scherriabeek Valley on the 69 Brigade Front.
3. The 68 Brigade will attack on the right of the 23rd Divisional Front and 69 Brigade on the left. 70 Brigade will be in Divisional Reserve.

   In consequence of the state of the ground opposite 68 Brigade front special instructions have been issued to enable part of 68 Brigade to advance through the Red and Blue areas allotted to 69 Brigade.

   The knoll 100 yards to the west of Herenthage Chateau and the ruins of the Chateau must be cleared by 11/West Yorks Regiment as quickly as possible to cover the left flank of 68 Brigade.

4. On 69 Brigade front the Red objective will be captured by 11/West Yorks Regiment, the Blue objective by 9/Yorkshire Regiment and the Green by 10/DWR and two companies of 8/Yorkshire Regiment. Headquarters and two companies of 8/Yorkshire Regiment will be in Brigade Reserve.
5. The advance of 11/West Yorkshire Regiment will commence at Zero plus three minutes, proceeded by a succession of creeping barrages nearly 1,000 yards in depth from Zero hour.

   84 18pdrs, 30 4.5 howitzers and 42 guns and howitzers of a heavier nature will support the attack on the divisional front.

   A pause of 45 minutes will be made on the Red objective. During this pause special arrangements will be made by O.C. 9/Yorkshire Regiment and O.C. 10/Northumberland Fusiliers to examine and prepare crossings over the Basseville Beek.

   At Zero plus 1 hour 28 Minutes 9/Yorkshire Regiment will pass through the Red Line to capture and consolidate the areas up to the Blue Line.

The instruction then goes on to cover the movement of battalions of 68 Brigade through 69 Brigade and the covering fire to be supplied by the machine gun companies and trench mortar batteries of 23rd Division:

11. Five Tanks will co-operate on the Brigade front, advancing from Clapham Junction at Zero. Two of these will move down the Menin Road to assist 68 Brigade on the Blue Line. Three will move on the north side of Inverness Copse to assist 69 Brigade.

Further instructions are then included regarding support by the Divisional RE and the Pioneer Battalion, 9/South Staffordshire Regiment.

Finally all troops were to be in their battle positions by Zero minus thirty minutes. Zero hour was to be notified at a later time.

On 16 September 8/Yorkshire Regiment moved to MicMac Camp. On the early afternoon of 19 September A and D Companies, 8/Yorkshire Regiment, left the camp for the line. At 7.30 p.m. the rest of the battalion followed. Shortly after they moved out it started to rain, which lasted until midnight. Having moved into position from where 69 Brigade were to attack Inverness Copse, 8/Yorkshire Regiment was committed piecemeal. A Company moved into a trench known as New Cut at Zero Hour plus fifteen minutes. That afternoon, at 2.30 p.m. the OC A Company was ordered to report to 10/DWR and was ordered by him to proceed to SP 'N' and support the right of the Green Line.

Two platoons dug in in front of SP 'N' and Second Lieutenant Sumerville, with two Lewis gun sections, was attached to A Company, 10/DWR. These dispositions remained unchanged until the company was relieved on the night of 21 September. C Company of 8/Yorkshire Regiment relieved the front-line company of 10/DWR referred to above. D Company was attached to 10/DWR for the attack on the final objective. They moved to Clapham Junction–Stirling Castle area on the night 19–20 September. The company lay out in the open behind the ridge until Zero on 20 September. Then they moved into Jasper Lane, where they remained until Zero plus three hours. They then advanced with the Australians on the left and the 10/DWR on the right. They took the final objective at about 11 a.m., where they dug in and consolidated the position. There was no attempt by the Germans to counter-attack.[5] However, that is contrary to the Official History, which states that the enemy counter-attacked up the Reutelbeek valley against the 1st Australian and 23rd Divisions. At 7.20 p.m. an intense barrage fell on the Germans, brought down by the firing of signal rockets, which burst into three colours: red, green and yellow.

The artillery answered the SOS in less than half a minute and for forty to sixty minutes the area in front of both divisions was combed and re-combed by fire.[6]

Later on the night of 23–24 September, D Company, 8/Yorkshire Regiment, was relieved by D Company of 9/Yorkshire Regiment.

At 11.30 a.m. C Company moved forward to the Blue Line to act as reserve to the Green Line. At 6.30 a.m. on 21 September they relieved B and C Companies of 10/DWR in the front line and were in turn relieved by the Sherwood Foresters at 9.30 pm, when they moved to Sanctuary Wood.

The night before the offensive, B Company rested in Wellington Crescent trench on Yeomanry Ridge, where they arrived at about 11 p.m. On the morning of 20 September they moved forward to the assembly positions in New Cut at Zero plus fifteen minutes, carrying with them the consolidation stores. On arrival additional stores were added to the already heavy loads. Then at Zero plus three hours B Company followed 10/DWR over the top, moving by platoons in artillery formation. They passed through the German counter-barrage laid down on Inverness Copse, although they did have some casualties. B Company reached its objective at four dugouts, near the Tower (S.P. 'I.'). These dugouts had been destroyed by the British barrage so the company dug in around them, forming a strong point. From there reconnoitring parties went forward to Northampton Farm and strong point 'C', to find out the situation and the position of the companies who had taken the Green Line. About an hour after they had arrived, the CO of 10/DWR ordered two platoons of B Company to reinforce the Green Line. No. 5 and 6 Platoons were ordered to move and on arrival they dug in. Nos 7 and 8 Platoons then formed Strong

Point 'N'. These two platoons also brought forward the stores brought up by the company. Consolidation carried on by those in the front line and by the morning of 21 September a continuous line had been dug. However, the Germans put a heavy barrage on the forward area and large numbers of enemy infantry were seen massing for a counter-attack. British Forward Observation Officers were alert and a barrage dispersed most of them. Lewis guns in the front line joining in also completed the dispersal. That evening B Company was relieved and moved back to Sanctuary Wood Craters. However, they had not finished and on 22 September they were employed as carrying parties, with those not carrying doing salvage work behind Clapham Junction–Stirling Castle.[7]

When all the companies had been relieved, 8/Yorkshire Regiment returned to Alberta Camp.

Meanwhile, what happened to 9/Yorkshire Regiment is well covered in the Commanding Officer's account of the action near Inverness Copse on 19–25 September 1917:

> The battalion left MicMac Camp at 1.10 p.m. on 18 September and proceeded to Railway Dugouts. Headquarters, A and B Companies remained here for the night of 18–19 September while C and D Companies, after being issued battle stores, proceeded at 5.30 p.m. to Sanctuary Wood where they dug themselves in. That night these two latter companies were shelled heavily with high explosives and gas and suffered twelve casualties. At 1 p.m. on 19 September HQ moved up to Clapham Junction under the Menin Road and A and B Companies moved up to the vicinity of Stirling Castle and Sanctuary Wood. At 9.30 p.m. the comp[anies] began to move into their assembly positions ready for the attack and they were all in position by 2.a.m. on 20 September. At Zero hour (5.30 a.m.) A and D Companies advanced towards Inverness Copse followed by B and C Companies. The morning was dark and there was a considerable mist. This combined with the dense clouds of smoke caused by the British Artillery barrage rendered the question of keeping direction extremely difficult.
>
> In spite of this and in spite of the fact that the ground over which they were advancing was pitted with shell holes and strewn with broken tree trunks and barbed wire, very little loss of direction occurred until the battalion had advanced about 150 to 200 yards into the Copse. Here according to arrangement a halt was called for about three quarters of an hour, troops taking advantage of shell holes and natural cover. Even in this early stage isolated instances of fighting occurred, individual Germans who had not been mopped up, bombing our men from the rear where the enemy also fired a Green S.O.S. Very Light.

During this phase troops were reorganised and the direction checked with the aid of compasses while the men were in the best of spirits, in spite of heavy artillery and machine gun fire, they were sat in shell holes, smoking German cigars, calmly waiting for the advance. Eventually at Zero Hour plus 1 Hour 2 Minutes the companies began to move forward and it was while advancing from this position to the Red Line that some of the heaviest fighting took occurred. Numerous small parties of Germans remained in the wood in dugouts and shell holes and many of these put up a strong resistance, attacking our men with bombs and causing many casualties by machine gun and rifle fire.

All these parties were however, successfully mopped up, at least 60 Germans being killed in the Copse. By this time however, the battalion had suffered considerable casualties both from Germans in the Wood, from machine gun fire from Strong Points beyond, and from hostile artillery barrage.

Before reaching the Red Line 8 out of 16 Company officers had already become casualties, including two Company Commanders. In spite of this, however, the men were formed up well under the barrage ready to go forward to the assault at Zero plus 1 Hour 28 minutes according to the programme.

As was previously anticipated, the main centres of German resistance were around the line of dugouts extending from the tower on the north, southwards to the small pond by the Menin Road. These dugouts had hardly suffered at all from our artillery barrage and around them the fighting varied considerably in intensity. Several hostile parties, as soon as they recognised that they were outflanked, abandoned their machine guns and weapons and came forward waving small pieces of white cloth which had obviously been prepared beforehand. Around several of the dugouts however, the fiercest hand to hand fighting occurred, the Germans holding out to the last and refusing to surrender. Our men here got well home with the bayonet and many Germans were killed both around the tower and in the actual passages of the dugouts themselves. In this part no fewer than ten machine guns were captured, some in concrete emplacements, others in open shell holes. Fifteen *Flammenwerfers*, five trench howitzers and four trench mortars were also taken in the vicinity.

While A and D Companies were thus engaged in mopping up these positions B and C Companies passed through them and advanced towards the Blue Line. Each of these companies had at this time only one officer left and one of these had been shot through the helmet and wounded in the hand. In spite of this, and notwithstanding the heavy losses they had

German infantry. The centre of resistance was a line of dugouts.

suffered earlier in the day both in N.C.O.s and men, so thoroughly did each man know his individual task which had been allotted to him, that formations and direction still continued to be well maintained and each section made independently for its own objective on the Blue Line, captured it, and commenced to consolidate it. At about 10.30 a.m. B Company of 8/Yorkshire Regiment under Captain Miller reported their arrival at the dugouts about 150 yards N.N.W. of the Tower as previously arranged. This company had brought up wire, stakes, tools and other material but had suffered severely en-route. Second Lieutenant John Lakin and fifteen other ranks from 8/Yorkshire Regiment were sent to Jackdaw Dump as Prisoner escorts; however, they acquired some mules and moved all the S.A.A. and bombs that had been left on the duckboards at the dump, closer to the front line.

Although this work of consolidation was much hampered by the fire of enemy machine guns and snipers, the ground was soft and all men worked intensively so that by the time the barrage moved forward to the Green Line every man had provided himself with good cover. While this consolidation was in progress an excellent target presented itself on our left front where a large number of the enemy were observed to be retiring over the ridge. Lewis gun and rifle fire was immediately brought to bear on these and it is thought that a number of casualties were inflicted on the enemy.

In the meanwhile Battalion HQ had moved up to an advanced position in the German Aid Post just south of the Menin Road at 9.15 a.m.

> Throughout the remainder of the day the positions occupied were improved and consolidated and stores brought up, so that when a heavy barrage was opened by the enemy during the afternoon and evening in conjunction with the counter-attacks of the Tower Hamlets Ridge very few casualties occurred.
>
> On the morning of the 21 September it was found advisable to thin out the posts in the vicinity of the Reutelbeek where the ground was very marshy, and to transfer these men to better positions on the right of the Blue Line. Our positions were shelled by the enemy throughout the day but with particular intensity during the afternoon and evening. On the afternoon of the 22 September as a result of heavy casualties in other battalions 9/Yorkshire Regiment was called upon to take over a portion of the Green Line. B and C Companies took over the positions previously occupied by A and D Companies. A Company took over the portion of the front line north of the Reutelbeek Road from the Australians, D Company took over the portion of the front line south of the Reutelbeek from 8/Yorkshire Regiment. Battalion headquarters moved to a dugout just south of the Tower. On the night of 24/25 September Battalion HQ and C Company were relieved by Battalion HQ and C Company, 2/5/ Worcestershire Regiment, D and B Companies were relieved by two companies of 4/King's Liverpool Regiment. The battalion on completion of the relief moved at 8.20 p.m. to Camp Area No. 1 near Dickebusch.[8]
>
> 25 September 1917
> R S Hart Lieutenant Colonel
> Commanding 9/Yorkshire Regiment

At the final position a light German *minenwerfer* was found with a good supply of ammunition. This was brought quickly into action by Second Lieutenant Bottomley, 9/Yorkshire Regiment, attached to 69 LTMB, and trained on a copse in which many parties of enemy were seen to be running as if massing there. The copse was kept under continued fire during the afternoon, over 200 shells being fired. The supply of shells to all teams was kept up entirely by small carrying parties that had been attached to 69 LTMB from infantry battalions some days previously. A load of four shells proved ideal, the men being able to move more quickly and make more journeys than when carrying six shells as on previous occasions. For men carrying parts of the gun, rifles again proved an encumbrance and there was a tendency to drop these on the chance of finding another at any time if necessary.[9]

Of the tanks detailed to assist in the reduction of strongholds, one failed to reach the objective but the others did all they could to assist the infantry. One received a direct hit on the Menin Road, the others helped to reduce one point of resistance but the main infantry advance was too quick for them and most of the work had already been finished. The ammunition they brought up was however, useful. Those men employed as Yukon pack-carrying parties, two NCOs and eighteen men from each battalion, earned special praise from the Brigade Commander, who wrote:

> The manner in which these men worked day and night for their comrades, trudging under heavy fire, regardless of casualties and cheerful to the last, is almost beyond description. If the value of the Yukon Pack requires further advertisement it can be sought in the record of what was done between the period 17–24 September. On the day of the attack I myself saw Yukon Pack men trudging stolidly and fearlessly right up to the front line over absolutely open ground to deliver water, s.a.a. and food to their comrades in need. This was not done by order as they were intended to go only as far as battalion headquarters,[10] but they went on their own initiative without an officer.

Eight officers were wounded: Major R.C. Grellet (Acting CO) and Lieutenant W.E. Bush (Adjutant), Second Lieutenants H.J. Smith, Thomas H.A. Bell, W.R. Parker John Heron, F.C. Vernon and William Cox.

The total battalion casualties for September are recorded in the Brigade War Diary as:

Killed		Wounded		Missing	
Off	O.R.	Off	O.R.	Off	O.R.
39	8	-	184	-	19

The CWGC records show that between 17 and 26 September 8/Yorkshire Regiment had forty fatalities. Of these, twenty-five men are commemorated on the Tyne Cot Memorial to the Missing. Five men who all died from wounds are buried in Lijssenthoek Military Cemetery. Two of these have known places of death: 16735 Private John McManus from Horden died at No. 10 CCS at Remy Sidings, while 42817 Private George Bedwell from Bury St Edmunds died at No. 2 Canadian CCS. Others that died from wounds were 33610 Private William Thomas Clare from Leighton Buzzard, formerly with the ASC. He died on 17 September and is buried at Voormezeele Enclosure No. 1 and No. 2. Another ex-ASC man was 33625 Private Harry Marshall from Newcastle upon Tyne, who is buried at Godewaersvelde. A Bradford lad, 202942 Private Joseph Hardy, who served in B Company, made it to a hospital to the west and is buried in Blargies Communal Cemetery Extension. Only one of the battalion died at a hospital on the coast, 13404 Private James Horton, who lived at South Bank, Middlesbrough. He is buried at St Sever Cemetery, Rouen. Seven men are battlefield exhumations. Three were found on 8 September 1919 in a small area at J.14.c.5.6., where the body of 241786 Private Isaac Rodgers from South Hetton was identified and although the others were identified as Yorkshire Regiment by their shoulder titles no other means of identification was found. The body of Sergeant George Fearnley from South Bank was discovered on 6 November 1919 at J.15.c.5.5., while 42646 Private John Hall from Shipley was also found the same day some 20 yards away at J.15.c.7.6. All five were taken to Hooge Crater Cemetery for reburial. The other two men appear to have died on the way back to the aid post as the location of the exhumations is very close to the Menin Road. No. 11916 Private Jerry Sheehan, whose home was in Grangetown, was found at J.14.c.6.3. and is now lying in Plot XLIII, Row F, Grave II of Tyne Cot Cemetery. The body of 14493 Private Joseph Eltringham, a coal miner from Ryhope, was not found until 31 May 1921 at J.13.d.9.9, which is just north of Clapham Junction, closer to Ypres than the others.

The War Diary of 9/Yorkshire Regiment gives a breakdown of the casualties from 16–30 September in a table format. See below. With that in mind, a check of the casualties revealed some interesting facts. Buried at Bedford House Enclosure No. 4 are the remains of 235239 Private Archibald H. Woath. Originally a Northumberland Fusilier, he died on 20 September 1917. His body was recovered at J.14.C.60.40. Second Lieutenant Lancelot Nicholson was an apprentice joiner in Seaham County Durham, in 1911 but by 1917 he was a lieutenant in 9/Yorkshire Regiment. He was killed in action on 20 September 1917. His body was recovered on 15 April 1919 at J.14.c.9.1 and reinterred at Hooge Crater Cemetery. Also there lie the remains of 28956 Private George Carter, whose body was found at J 14.c.2.2 on 11 April 1919. Two of the battalion were exhumed and reinterred at Tyne Cot Cemetery: 20679 Private Harold Cappleman from Scarborough was found at J.14.d.35.35 and 33651 Private H.J. Bamford was exhumed at J.14 d.35.3 and identified by his discs. The remaining exhumations were of 15355 Corporal George Thompson, a Scarborough resident, whose body was found at J13.c.11.61 on 6 June 1921 and identified by his chevrons and disc. The other man was 242713 Private Arthur Leslie Timms, who was born in Ellington, Yorkshire. His body was found at J.14.c.90.10 on 24 March 1921. Both were reburied in Ypres Reservoir Cemetery.

	Officers			Other Ranks		
	Killed	Wounded	Missing	Killed	Wnd	Missing
16/09/1917	-	-	-	-	1	-
18/09/1917	-	-	-	-	1	-
19/09/1917	-	-	-	-	10	-
20/09/1917	Lt N. Groom	Capt G.N. Hunnybun		19	139	27
	2/Lt H J. Bunker	Capt M.D.W. Maude				
	2/Lt L. Nicholson	Lt H. Dunclafe				
	2/Lt R.M. Matthews	2/Lt I.G. Evans				
		2/Lt R. Wood				
		2/Lt B Wahl				
21/09/1917	-	-	-	5	21	1
22/09/1917	-	-	-	2	18	-
23/09/1917	-	-	-	3	5	-
24/09/1917	-	-	-	3	3	-
	4	6	0	32	198	28

Of the 9/Yorkshire Regiment officers, Second Lieutenant Richard M. Matthew came from Walmer in Kent. He had five lines written about him in one local newspaper, which simply stated he had left an estate valued at £11,392 and had left £100 pounds to his old nurse.[11] However, in a second newspaper there is a long obituary:

> We much regret to record the death of Second Lieutenant Richard Malcolm Matthews of Yew Tree Cottage, Upper Walmer, fourth son of the late Mr John Matthews J.P. of The Old House, Walmer and a member of the firm of Messrs Thompson and Son Ltd. Lieutenant Matthews was killed in action in France on 20th inst, at the age of 38. He was educated at Charterhouse and after a year in Germany entered the business in 1905. In the early days of the war, he offered himself for service but being rejected on medical grounds he became a member of the Deal and Walmer V.T.V. on the formation of that body, taking a keen interest in the corps. He was

> subsequently passed for service and after a period of training was gazetted to the Yorkshire Regiment in July last, and within a month of joining his regiment he proceeded to France on active service. By a pathetic coincidence he was killed the day after the third anniversary of his brother Captain J.H. Matthews Northumberland Fusiliers and like him was within a few days of his birthday. From the time of his return to his native place Lieutenant Matthews was a member of the choir of St Mary's Parish Church, Walmer, and he took a keen interest in the promotion of cricket and other games for the choir boys and others in the village, taking an active part in the Walmer Cricket Club. For a short time he was secretary of the Walmer Musical Society, of which he was a member from the time of his return to Walmer. Mr Matthews was very highly regarded in the neighbourhood, and a wide circle of friends will deeply regret this further bereavement in a family which has taken an honoured part in local affairs for many years.[12]

Second Lieutenant Lancelot Nicholson was aged 24 when he died. On 4 September 1914 he had volunteered for the cavalry and joined a Hussar Regiment. He was then transferred to the 4th Royal Irish Dragoon Guards, however a shortage of infantry necessitated a transfer to the infantry and he was again transferred to the Dorsetshire Regiment. After completing training he landed in France on 29 July 1915. In 1917 he was sent home and received his commission on 29 May 1917. He had only been with the battalion nine weeks when he was killed in action.[13] Of Lieutenant Noel Groom and Second Lieutenant Harold Bunker nothing additional has come to light. A fifth officer was to die from the wounds he received on 20 September, Captain Michael D.W. Maude suffered a severe shrapnel wound in the thigh on 20 September 1917. He was safely evacuated via the Casualty Clearing system to a hospital on the French coast and from there to the Military Hospital at Dover. His obituary appears in the *Green Howards Gazette*:

Private Samuel Bailey, from Dawdon, was killed in action on 20 September 1917.

> Captain Maude who was born on Michaelmas Day 1899 was the son of Lieutenant Colonel W.W. Maude of The Fleets, Rylstone, near Skipton in Craven, He was educated at Sedbergh School and at Aspatria Agricultural College and was gazetted to a commission in the Special Reserve Battalion on 7 June 1913. Promoted

> Lieutenant 28 May 1914, he went to the front with the Seventh Division. Landing at Zeebrugge on 6 October 1914, he took part in the critical fighting near Ypres, until in November when he was invalided home seriously ill from ptomaine poisoning. He was promoted Captain on 1 February 1915. Re-joining the battalion at the Front, Captain Maude took part in much heavy fighting and was mentioned in Despatches after the Somme Operations. He had been recently attached to one of the service battalions with which he was serving when he was wounded. His loss to the Regiment is great. His remains were interred at Aldborough near Boroughbridge on 19 October with full Military Honours.[14]

His old school magazine, *The Sedberghian*, collated many tributes after his death, 'He was quite the best company commander I ever worked under.' 'The men of his company thought the world of him.' 'He had a very strong sense of duty.'[15]

On being relieved on the night of 24–25 September, 8/Yorkshire Regiment moved back to Alberta Camp. There they were inspected by General Babington, after which the rest of the day was spent cleaning up. With Major Grellet wounded, Major A.C. Barnes from 9/Yorkshire Regiment took over temporary command. Likewise, 9/Yorkshire Regiment moved out of the line and arrived at Wood Camp south of Westoutre on 25 September.

As General Plumer had foreseen, the Germans made desperate efforts to retake the lost ground and maintain their hold on the eastern edge of the Gheluvelt plateau. The 33rd Division, which had replaced the 23rd Division, in two days suffered almost 3,000 casualties. They had to be replaced and although 69 Brigade had only had two days rest they were ordered back to the line.

At 9 a.m. on 27 September 8/Yorkshire Regiment left Alberta Camp by bus and were carried to Café Belge, from where they marched to Scottish Wood. From there they moved to Sanctuary Wood on foot. The battalion moved in the dark into unknown positions but by careful study of maps and the help of the guides provided by the outgoing unit, all companies were in position by 11.30 p.m. A, B and D Companies manned the front line from about J.16.a.6.7. to J.15.d.5.5., with C Company in support in a trench in front of and south of Black Watch Corner. Next morning C Company was shelled heavily and suffered casualties. Enemy artillery fire fell in the vicinity of Black Watch Corner, south of Polygon Wood, and 8/Yorkshire Regiment lost about twenty-five men killed and fifteen wounded. The Germans mounted strong counter-attacks, which were seen forming up. These were driven off by rifle and machine gun fire.

Meanwhile, 9/Yorkshire Regiment had moved up to Stirling Castle where they remained, they did however supply a working party to assist the 33rd Divisional RE dig a new communication trench southern edge of Glencorse

Private Thomas Edward Ferguson won his Military Medal on 1 October 1917.

Wood. The night of 30 September was lit by a full moon and the battalion took over the front line from 8/Yorkshire Regiment. During their time in the front line they had captured thirty prisoners and four light machine guns. Having been relieved, the 8/Yorkshire Regiment moved back to the craters near Sanctuary Wood. Meanwhile, in the front line 9/Yorkshire Regiment plus an attached company of 10/DWR were in the following positions: A Company in support at Carlisle Farm, D Company I.15.d.50.45 to the Reutelbeek, B Company from the Reutelbeek to Jut Farm, D Company, 10/DWR, from Jut Farm to J.16.c.10.20. and C Company, 9/Yorkshire Regiment, on the left. At dawn on the morning of 1 October the forward positions of 69 Brigade from Polygon Wood to the Reutelbeek were shelled heavily by German guns of all calibres. The fire concentrated on the left of the Brigade front. C Company, 9/Yorkshire Regiment, as was stated previously, were holding this sector and suffered a number of casualties. Under the cover of the barrage they were attacked heavily. This point was where 23rd Division linked up with 15th (Scottish) Division and the Germans forced an entry, driving in the 69 Brigade posts occupied by C Company from Polygon Wood to Cameron Covert. On their right, D Company of 10/DWR stood firm and withstood all enemy attempts to penetrate their line. The Company Commander, Lieutenant Miles Bennison, along with Lieutenant Gibson of 69 LTMB, led a counter-attack and both were killed. The Germans came on again and the men of C Company were forced back some 150 yards. Seeing the Germans had gained a footing in a trench to his left, Second Lieutenant Herbert Lewis led a bombing party from his platoon and retook the trench, in so doing recovering his platoon's Lewis gun. Unfortunately this officer was shot dead by a German sniper shortly after the trench was retaken and a post established. This post was slightly in front of the line and it held out until every round of ammunition was fired and the last bomb had been thrown. As dusk fell it was withdrawn to the line held by D Company, 10/DWR, and all that were left of C Company, 9/Yorkshire Regiment. Throughout the day artillery fire was very heavy but no further infantry attacks took place. Relief arrived on 2 October in the shape of 1/East Surrey Regiment. The 9/Yorkshire Regiment moved back to Stirling Castle for the night and at 11 a.m. next day moved to Ridge Wood. They were then met by buses and transported to the Berthen area.

Second Lieutenant Richard B.W. Wilton was killed on 1 October 1917.

Over the next two day they were refitting but the good news was that the heavy casualties feared in C Company only amounted to one officer and ten men missing. It was now that the weather turned very wet and cold.

As well as the two officers already named, Second Lieutenants Hugh Graham from Scarborough and Richard Wilton, whose home was at Weeping Cross, Stafford, were killed, along with sixteen other ranks on 1 October and a further six the next day.

On 5 October, Mrs Lewis received the following letter from the battalion Adjutant, written on behalf of Lieutenant Colonel R.S. Hart:

> Dear Mrs Lewis,
> A few words to offer my deepest sympathy in the loss of your husband, who was killed near Polygon Wood on 1 October; gallantly holding a post that had been entrusted to him. On 20 September your husband did very good work in the attack on the enemy and took command of his company when all the other officers had become casualties and handled it with the greatest daring and skill. On 1 October the brunt of the German attack fell on your husband's company and he and all the other officers were killed gallantly holding on to the position that had been entrusted to them. It was their heroic conduct that prevented the enemy meeting with any success. Their names will be forever remembered in the Yorkshire Regiment.
> Lt Col R S Hart
> 9th Yorks[16]

Second Lieutenant H.O.R. Lewis, killed at Polygon Wood on 1 October 1917.

Captain Arthur Jardine also wrote to Mrs Lewis expressing the condolences of himself and the other officers:

> 8.XI.17
> Dear Mrs Lewis,
> Though a stranger I am taking the liberty of writing to you to sympathise with you in your recent loss. I knew your husband well. In the attack on the 20th of September he was the only

officer besides myself who survived to reach the Battalion's last objective. We were thrown together in the hour of doubt & danger and I found him ever cool under heavy fire & considering the welfare of his men before everything. I was a great admirer of your husband's qualities & I asked him to transfer to my Company a few days before he met his end. He refused to do so on the grounds that he had got used to 'C' Coy and didn't want to leave it. He died in circumstances of exceptional heroism. The enemy attacked three times & each time your husband's platoon drove them back with rifle and MG fire. Eventually the enemy got a footing on the left of your husband's platoon. Your husband immediately attempted to bomb the enemy out. He was throwing bombs when a sniper picked him off and he died a clean & painless death – he set an example of courage in the face of death & of determination to win which will not readily be forgotten by his company. Please convey to yours the sympathy of his brother officers in your great loss. Please do not trouble to acknowledge this.

Yours sincerely
A C Jardine
9th Yorkshire Regiment.[17]

Private George Esmond Hagie was born in Sunderland and had formerly served with the Durham L.I. He was killed on 2 October 1917.

Second Lieutenant Richard B. Wilton had before the war been employed alongside his father as a clerk to the Stafford Board of Guardians and the Rural District Council. At the age of 18, in November 1914 he had enlisted into the Argyll and Sutherland Highlanders and went to France the following April. He was gassed at Festubert in May and sent to England. When convalescent, he volunteered to go out again with a draft in October 1915 and was in the trenches when he received information that he had been granted a commission and was to go to England for instruction. He had a narrow escape leaving the trenches for the enemy had two machine guns trained on a weak part of the trench and fired several rounds as he went along. After completing his course, he went out in July 1916 and shared in the work on the Somme, taking part in the capture of Contalmaison and Le Sars. He moved to the scene of the present fighting in October the same year, and remained there until April last, during which time he acted as intelligence officer and was complimented by the CO on his good work. He was invalided home in April suffering from colitis. As soon as he was convalescent, he, with two other officers volunteered for the front and returned to France on 8 September. He was engaged in the big push on the 20th. In his last letter he said he was looking forward to the next advance. Almost his last words on leaving home were. 'I shall make good.' Lieutenant Wilton was educated at Stafford Grammar School.

The lieutenant colonel of the regiment wrote:

> A few words to offer my deepest sympathy at the loss of your son, who was killed in action south of Polygon Wood on 1 October 1917 gallantly defending a post of which he was in command. Your son's company was in a part of the line against which the Germans launched a desperate counter-attack, and it's thanks to their gallantry and devotion to duty that the enemy did not gain a footing. There were four officers in the company, all of whom died gallantly at their posts sooner than be driven back, and their names will be forever remembered by the Yorkshire Regiment.[18]

Second Lieutenant Hugh C. Graham was the younger son of Mr C.C. Graham, the Mayor of Scarborough. 'He was educated at Giggleswick School and later at Leeds University where he took his degree of BSc. He afterwards took up business in Hull and joined the army as a private on the outbreak of war. He took up a commission in the Yorkshire Regiment earlier this year.'[19]

With 8/Yorkshire Regiment Major Barnes relinquished command and Major M.R.C. Backhouse DSO, late Northumberland Hussars, assumed command. This battalion also moved to the Berthen area, where they too started cleaning up and refitting. A and D Companies went away to work on the light railway north of Ypres. The weather was interfering with training and parades. Over the next week a few small drafts arrived to replace the dead and wounded. On 9 October orders were received to standby for a move. At 3.05 p.m. on 10 October they moved to Ontario Camp at Reninghelst. In very wet and stormy weather a move was made to Hallebast Corner, where A and D Companies re-joined the battalion. Here they were able to bathe at Dickebusch and receive a clean change of clothing. Also that day, Second Lieutenant C.J. Roddam joined with another small draft of thirteen men.

On the night of 14–15 October the battalion took over the front line from 10/ Northumberland Fusiliers. Enemy aircraft were flying low over the front lines and strafing the soldiers in the trenches. There were very few British aeroplanes flying over that sector and along with this the German artillery was active all day. A patrol sent out by A Company to get in touch with the unit on the left was unsuccessful but another patrol sent to the right was able to establish contact with 10/Durham LI of 14th (Light) Division on the right. The next day there was very little shelling, but enemy aircraft were again flying low over the lines. On the night of 18–19 October 8/Yorkshire Regiment were relieved by 13/Durham LI. However, owing to enemy artillery making the relief difficult this was not completed until 7 a.m., when 8/Yorkshire Regiment proceeded to Railway Dugouts. The following night a battalion of the 21st Division relieved them and they moved back to MicMac Camp, then from there on 21 October by bus to the Boisdinghem area. Casualties during this tour were Lieutenant C.H. Sparshott, wounded but remained at duty, and Second Lieutenant T.E. Hardcastle, who was accidentally wounded. Furthermore, thirty-two men had been killed, forty-five wounded and one was missing.

In the meantime, 9/Yorkshire Regiment had been attached to 70 Brigade and on 11 October the CO and two Company Commanders (A and B) went up to reconnoitre the line. While they were doing this the battalion moved to Zillebeke Bund. They were not here long, for the very next day, in heavy rain, they relieved 8/York and Lancs in the front line. A and B companies were in the front line and C and D in support with battalion headquarters at the Butte. That night, the support companies were shelled heavily and again the following night with trenches blown in and several casualties including Captain A.C.H. Millar MC. It was not long, however, before 11/Sherwood Foresters arrived and the battalion moved back to support positions at Clapham Junction. Here they started the eternal round of cleaning up and refitting and by 19 October 9/Yorkshire Regiment had sent billeting parties to Boisdinghem. It rained heavily that morning but in the afternoon the GOC presented medal ribbons to those who had displayed gallantry in action. That night the battalion transport set off by road for Boisdinghem. On 20 October the battalion moved by train from Dickebusch to Boisdinghem, where they arrived at 9 p.m. In this location the battalion cleaned up and then training was carried out by companies. On 25 October General Babington returned and presented the ribbon of the Military Cross to two officers and two Distinguished Conduct Medals and seven Military Medals to other ranks of the battalion. On 26 October a route march was organised but had to be ended early owing to the very bad weather. New drafts arrived and were described as 'very poor', in the War Diary. At least on 31 October there was a fine day and the Commander in Chief of the BEF, Sir Douglas Haig KT GCB, inspected the 69 Infantry Brigade in drill order. After the inspection the brigade marched past in column of companies.

The award of the Military Cross to four officers, a Distinguished Conduct Medal to 15201 Corporal A. Danby, four bars to the Military Medal and twenty-three Military Medals was published in the War Diary of 8/Yorkshire Regiment. On 25 October the four officers and twenty-four of the other ranks were decorated by General Babington. The battalion organised an inter-company football competition in which C Company defeated B Company 8–0 and Headquarters defeated D Company 4–1. The whole battalion was able to bathe and every man received a fresh change of clothing. A service was held on 28 October in memory of the men who had been killed in action in the recent fighting and the War Diary lists 100 men by number, rank and name. Comparing this to the actual list of dead it appears that the War Diary lists those men known to be confirmed as dead. The names of those men missing are not included, presumably in the hope they may still be alive.

On 31 October the battalion was present with the rest of the brigade at the aforementioned parade for Sir Douglas Haig.

Over the period of the fighting at Menin Road and Polygon Wood the division had come in for several letters of congratulations. On 3 October General Babington wrote:

> SPECIAL ORDER
> The Divisional Commander most sincerely congratulates all ranks of the 69th and 70th Infantry Brigades on the highly satisfactory results of the last six days. Called upon to take over an important part of the battle front at short notice and with but little time to reorganise after the battle of 20 September and the events of subsequent days, these Brigades have firmly held the ground won against repeated and at times heavy attacks by the enemy, all of which were repulsed with great loss to him and comparatively small loss to themselves. This very marked success is due to the able dispositions made by the Brigade Commanders and subordinate commanders, to the gallantry of officers and men in their determination never to give ground, and to the confidence the men now have in their rifles and the use they made of them.
>
> It has been clearly demonstrated to the enemy that against good troops he stood no chance either in attack or defence.
>
> Divisional Headquarters
> 3 October 1917.[20]

On 7 October HQ Second Army sent information from captured German documents:

> The evidence gained from captured documents all tend to show that the enemy intended to launch a heavy attack on Second Army front on 3 October and that in order to gain a better footing a preliminary attack was made on 1 October.

> This was so heavily dealt with by 23rd Division that it so dislocated the further attack that General von Finckenstein, Commanding 4th Guard Division, who was in charge of operations, evidently decided to postpone his attack from 3 to 4 October.
>
> The result of this postponement is well known. The Army Commander wishes the 23rd Division to be informed of the far reaching results of their determined resistance and to congratulate and thank all ranks concerned on behalf of himself and Second Army.
>
> 7 October 1917[21]
> C.H. Harington
> M.G.G.S., Second Army.

Another letter of congratulations was received from HQ Second Army, via HQ X Corps on 12 October:

> The Army Commander has read the reports.
>
> The manner in which the line was held and the several counter-attacks repulsed reflects great credit on all the troops engaged.
>
> The Army Commander would like his appreciation of their action conveyed to all the units concerned.
>
> The Corps Commander will doubtless submit recommendations for immediate rewards for those officers and N.C.O.s and men who specially distinguished themselves.
>
> 12–10–17
> C.H. Harington
> M.G.G.S., Second Army

As October turned into November both battalions were well behind the line training. The 8/Yorkshire Regiment were using the rifle ranges, bayonet fighting was practised and rifle bombers were instructed in the use of the Mills No. 23 and Hales No. 24 Rifle Grenades. Another change of clothing was issued when the battalion bathed by companies at Acquin. The football competition continued, with A Company beating HQ 2–0. Second Lieutenant F.G. Parker arrived and was posted to B Company. On 4 November for those of the Roman Catholic faith a solemn requiem mass was held in memory of the officers and men of the division who had been killed during the war. Also that day a draft of sixty-one other ranks joined for duty. Next day there was a parade inspected by the Commanding Officer followed by a route march. On 7 October the battalion left Acquin and marched in fine weather to Longuenesse, where they arrived at noon. The 9/Yorkshire Regiment followed more or less the same training programme with range work and route marching, parades and inspections and presentation of medal ribbons to worthy recipients, until on 8 November when they too moved, marching to Saint-Martin-Au-Laërt that morning.

While 9/Yorkshire Regiment were moving, HQ C and D Companies of 8/Yorkshire Regiment and half of the battalion transport marched to Wizernes and entrained at 5p.m. The other two companies and the remainder of the transport arrived at the station at 12.15 a.m. and entrained at 2 a.m. Likewise, on 9 November, 9/Yorkshire Regiment made their way to Arques railway station, where the first half of the battalion entrained at 4.39 a.m. and the second half at 8.39 a.m. Why were they on the move? Where were they bound? Events far to the south on the Isonzo front in Italy required that France and Britain send reinforcements.

Chapter 9

The Italian Front, November 1917–July 1918

In northern Italy along the River Isonzo, the Italian and Austro-Hungarian Armies had been fighting since 1915. In August 1917, at the eleventh Battle of the Isonzo, the Italians had forced a withdrawal of the Austrians and the Austrian High command had decided to restore the situation by a counter-offensive against the Italian northern flank and to do so before winter set in. After various diplomatic moves, Germany agreed to make troops available to assist the Austrians and six divisions with various army troops attached formed the German Fourteenth Army, which under the command of General Otto von Bülow was ordered to the Italian Front. Plans were made and the Germans and Austro-Hungarian troops moved up to the front.

On 24 October 1917 in heavy rain and snow storms on the heights, in poor visibility the attack commenced and took the Italians by surprise. Using a combination of high-explosive gas and smoke the attacking force, using bombs and flamethrowers, broke through almost immediately and by the end of the first day had advanced almost 25km into the Italian lines. The Italian Army was forced to withdraw, having lost thousands of men killed and more taken prisoner. The scale of the defeat and the amount of casualties incurred forced the Italian Government to request help through the British and French Military Missions. The French agreed to send four divisions and so the British Government instructed Sir Douglas Haig to select a good man and later they instructed him to select two good divisions. His choice fell on Lieutenant General, The Earl of Cavan and the XIV Corps headquarters, along with the 23rd and 41st Divisions, as well as all the support troops, supply depots, Casualty Clearing Stations, hospitals, sanitary sections, field bakery, field butchery, pay units, veterinary hospital, mechanical workshops and a base post office unit needed to keep them in the field.

Rudolph Lambert, 10th Earl of Cavan, commanded XIV Corps on the Italian Front.

On 28 October warning orders were sent out and advance parties of corps and divisional staff consisting of eight officers and thirteen other ranks from XIV Corps headquarters and eight officers and fourteen other ranks from each division were ordered to reach Paris in time to catch the evening mail train for Italy. On 1 November units were warned that they would be moving by rail to an unknown destination shortly.

General Sir H. Plumer arrived in Italy in advance of his troops and issued an account of the position from his point of view:

> The Italian Army had just received a very severe blow, from which it was bound to require time to recover and reorganise … The Italian retreat had been arrested on the River Piave, but it was uncertain whether they could hold this line and in the first instance it was arranged that, in conjunction with the French, two of our divisions should move forward on arrival to the hills north and south of Vicenza, where a stand could certainly have been made. The forward march was well carried out. The marches were necessarily long as time was, or might have been, important … By the time we reached the above position the general situation had improved and it was suggested that we should take over the Montello sector with the French on our left, to which we agreed.[1]

The first troops of 23rd Division to leave on 8 November were 68 Brigade, who entrained some hours before 69 Brigade at the same stations.

The trains travelled through France via Paris, Lyons, Marseilles, Toulon and Cannes, stops were made for tea and food and for men to wash and shave. Along the Riviera the weather was beautiful and it brought new life into the men after the dreary bloody and muddy fields of Flanders. The time spent on the train allowed the men to clean up their uniforms to a better standard than they had for a long time.

Having crossed the border into Italy the trains moved via San Remo, Savena, Sampierdarena and Busalla. On 13 November the first train carrying 8/Yorkshire Regiment arrived at San Antonio at 9 a.m., where they detrained. They set off on foot via Mantova and Castellucchio to billets in Rivalta. The other half of the battalion detrained at Mantova at 2.30 p.m. and followed the others on the same route to the billets in Rivalta, where they arrived at 8 p.m. Following behind, 9/Yorkshire Regiment arrived at Mantova on 14 November. From there they moved on foot to Sarginesco, where they arrived at midnight. They were followed by the remainder of the battalion in the early morning of 15 November. The billets in Sarginesco were described by the diarist of 9/Yorkshire Regiment as 'very good'. After spending 16 November cleaning up, the next day they went on a route march, where on passing through villages they had a great reception. While they were route marching 8/Yorkshire Regiment was practising rapid deployment and attack formations. The officers also carried out a reconnaissance of the River Mincio from Rivalta to Bell'Acqua. They also found time to hold an all-denominations church parade, after which the GOC 69 Infantry Brigade awarded the bar of the Military Medal to Sergeant William McNally, a coal miner from Murton, County Durham. He also awarded the ribbon of the MM to Privates Plowman, 12785 Robson College, yet another coal miner from Murton, 28278 James Thackery and 19313 Lance Corporal Robert Jackson. Two other men mentioned as Military Medal winners that day were 11492 Sergeant Charles Broad and 11821 Lance Sergeant Benjamin Shires from West Hartlepool.

The march towards the front started on 20 November and 8/Yorkshire Regiment, with a strength of 33 officers and 775 men, joined the 69 Infantry Brigade from Rivalta to Gazzo, reaching their billets at 4 30 p.m. The 9/ Yorkshire Regiment moved at 7.40 a.m. arriving at Cade about 4 p.m. At 8.30 a.m. on 20 November their march continued; they travelled 16 miles and arrived at Sanquinetto around 4 p.m. For the next five days the marching continued. Each night they spent in a different village, until on 26 November 9/Yorkshire Regiment halted at S. Georgio-di-Brendi and started cleaning up. The battalion carried out training over the next two days. Each day the march continued, the villages passed through are mentioned and the distances travelled are recorded until on 28 November 9/Yorkshire Regiment moved off at 7 a.m. and formed the brigade advance guard to S. Florino:

The 8/Yorkshire Regiment were on a different rout and marched to Minerbe via Legnago. As the battalion moved through that last-named village, General Sir H. Plumer took the march past, with the battalion reaching billets at 2 p.m. More than thirty men, because of their physical condition, were marching behind the battalion under the command of Lieutenant Killacky. The battalion paraded under company arrangements and inspections of kit, rifles and gas helmets was carried out. On 28 November they left Bolzonella at 9.39 a.m. and moved top Valla via Castelfranco. Two men were carried by the Field Ambulance and five men marched in the rear owing to their physical condition. The march continued the next day but it was a short one, only 5 miles, arriving in billets at Edifizio at 1 p.m. Two letters were received as follows:

> The XIV Corps Commander, Lieutenant General the Earl of Cavan, having seen all arms of your Division at different points of its historical march congratulates you and all ranks on:- (i) The good march discipline maintained throughout. (ii) The smartness of the Transport. (iii) The fine

> spirit of the men in spite of their fatigue. F. Graythorne-Hardy Brig. Genl General Staff XIV Corps.

Added to this was a message from the GOC 23rd Division, General Babington:

> The G.O.C. feels proud to command a Division which has gained such praise and confidently relies on all ranks to maintain its reputation in any circumstances.

On the last day of the month the CO, Adjutant and Signals Officer visited the sector that the battalion was to take over. Since leaving France twenty-five men had been evacuated and seventy-three reinforcements had joined. The total strength of the battalion stood at thirty-five officers and 827 other ranks.

XIV Corps now took over the Montello Sector, where they faced initially the Austrian 13th Division and the German 12th Division. However, the German formation was replaced early in the month and the German 117th Division came into the line.[2] The 9/Yorkshire Regiment were in Brigade Reserve, having moved to Venegazzu. Here, they took over billets described as 'in very bad condition'. Therefore a great deal of time was spent cleaning up. Three companies of the battalion were moved into one very large billet. Training was carried out and work commenced on building a rifle range. The training taking place was adapted to the Italian front and foothill fighting attacking and defending, with the CO lecturing all officers, CSMs and sergeants, on 'Outposts'.

On 2 December 8/Yorkshire Regiment left Edifizio at 9.10 a.m. and marched towards Montebello. They halted for dinner at the southern foot of Montebello and for tea in sheltered ground near the summit. During the late afternoon they relieved the 135th Italian Infantry Regiment and by 6.15 p.m. A, C and D Companies manned the front line with B Company in support. Very few of the British officers and men spoke any Italian. Likewise, the Italian officers had almost no English. However, quite a number of the Italian other ranks had picked up English in America and they served as unofficial interpreters.[3] The following evening saw some light shelling, but a lot of work was required on the line, where sanitation, camouflage and dugout construction all required attention A patrol under Captain Miller of B Company tested the possibility of fording the River Piave on the extreme left of the battalion position. This was, however, found to be impossible. The following night Second Lieutenant Summerville led a patrol to a position opposite S. Margarite to test the possibility of fording the river. They found the third channel too deep and fast flowing to be forded. The work on sanitation, dugout construction and organisation of the defences continued over the next week. On 9 December the GOC 69

Brigade inspected the part of the brigade front held by 8/Yorkshire Regiment. The next day saw an escalation in the enemy artillery fire, which caused two casualties in A Company and two in D Company, all wounded. That night Second Lieutenant Summerville accompanied by 13874 Lance Corporal Henry Sewell from Boldon Colliery and 16396 Private George Prudhoe, a resident of Seaham, reconnoitred an island in the River Piave opposite A Company's position. As on the previous patrol, they were unable to cross to the far bank of the river owing to the depth and strength of the current. The battalion doctor, Lieutenant Noel Sherrard, RAMC, left the battalion on posting to 69 Field Ambulance and was replaced by Captain Picken. Then, on 15 December, Lord Cavan visited the front line.

The evening of 16 December saw 9/Yorkshire Regiment relieve 8/Yorkshire Regiment in the left sub-sector of the brigade front, and during the night there was a heavy fall of snow. One platoon of B Company, under Second Lieutenant Leonard Dickens, remained behind attached to 9/Yorkshire Regiment to work on tunnels and dugouts, most likely owing to the number of coal miners in the ranks. They continued the work started by 8/Yorkshire Regiment and like that battalion officer patrols also made a number of unsuccessful attempts to reach the other bank of the Piave. But by 23 December they did, however, manage to fix a wire between the British-held bank and the island. This allowed a boat to be used to cross to the island to look for enemy activity. Although one patrol spent more than three hours searching the island, no trace of the enemy could

Austrian gunners caused casualties to the men of the 8th Battalion.

be found. On Christmas day the weather was fine but dull and in the front line 9/Yorkshire Regiment made no mention of any work or of any special meal laid on for the men.

Out in support, 8/Yorkshire Regiment started a period of inspections of kit, boots and equipment. They also continued the work on the rifle ranges and that of a bullet and bayonet course. Specialist courses were started for signallers, stretcher-bearers and observers. Christmas Day was observed as far as possible as a holiday. In the morning there was a voluntary service at Battalion HQ followed by Holy Communion at 9.30 a.m. The GOC 23rd Division and the Brigade Commander both visited the battalion during the morning; however, there is again no mention of a special meal being laid on. On Boxing Day at 9.15 a.m., forty-five large enemy aircraft crossed the line flying from the north-east. When they reached the Montello they turned south. At noon a further fifteen machines crossed the lines and dropped bombs on Montebal,luna. These aircraft were engaged by anti-aircraft guns and it was reported that seven of them were brought down. Classes were commenced for battalion Lewis gunners and sergeants were given instruction in compass work.

That day behind the line at Venegazzu, Privates T. Stockton and H. Edwards were both tried by Field General Court Martial. In both cases the offence was ‘quitting or sleeping at their post’. Considering the gravity of this offence on active service, the punishment in both cases was twenty days’ Field Punishment No. 1.

They were not the only Courts Martial at this time: 17243 Corporal Joseph Manners from Murton and 19826 Sergeant George Orwin, who came from Byker, both of 9/Yorkshire Regiment, were found guilty of drunkenness and reduced to the ranks on 4 December 1917. The same sentence was handed down to 12970 Sergeant Donald Lynch a Washington man, on 5 December 1917. Earlier in the month Private W. Simpson of 9/Yorkshire Regiment was tried for desertion. In his case he was unlucky to be sentenced to death, however, his sentence was reduced to ten years’ penal servitude. Others were tried for a number of offences including striking a superior officer, desertion, disobedience and breaking out of barracks. All except one man were found guilty, the innocent man being 16186 Private Frederick Tindal, who lived at Horden Colliery. Charged with drunkenness, he was found not guilty.[4]

Furthermore, many men were lucky to avoid Court Martial, and only went in front of the Commanding Officer and were awarded Field Punishment No. 2. Among them was Private Walter Sheen, who had two lots of F.P. No. 2, ten and fourteen days. Then, in August, fourteen Days’ F.P. No. 1. The apparent ease with which it was possible to obtain *vino rosso* or *vino bianco* meant that drunkenness was a problem until after the end of the war and British troops left Italy.

In the front line the work on the trenches and dugouts continued and the GOC 70 Brigade and officers of the relieving units visited the line on reconnaissance of the positions. Meanwhile, out at 'rest' 8/Yorkshire Regiment sent 220 men under Lieutenant Roddam of C Company to replace the platoon employed as tunnellers working in the front line. Second Lieutenant C.A. Bottomley was struck off strength on posting to the 69/LTMB, and on 31 December Captain A.V. Richardson reported for duty along with a small draft of twenty-five other ranks. During the month one officer and eleven men had been evacuated and six officers and 132 men had joined. The strength of the battalion on 31 December 1917 stood at forty officers and 963 other ranks. At this time the Corps Commander sent a letter to all three divisions and to the infantry in particular:

1. The Corps commander is thoroughly aware of the amount and excellence of the work on defensive lines which has been carried out by all units in the Corps, and has no complaints to make on this head.
2. At the same time, everyone can learn, and he is of the opinion that the work done in the sector held by the 69th Infantry Brigade of the 23rd Division is in advance of anything that is being carried out at the moment, both as regards organisation of labour, and as regards the tactical dispositions.
3. He wishes all units of the Corps to study, and where possible to initiate, the system which is to be seen in this Brigade.

   He wishes therefore G.S.O.I and C.R.E. of Divisions and all Brigadiers to visit this sector at as early date as possible, and in any case before 3 January; the arrangements to be made direct with the G.O.C. 23rd Division.
4. There are many points of interest to be seen.
   Special attention is called to:-
   (a) The combined action of Machine and Lewis guns with Trench Mortars in Defence
   (b) The amount of tunnelling work which is carried out by men who are not trained tunnellers.

       Units have complained that they have no tunnellers available, but the G.O.C. 69th Infantry Brigade has proved that tunnellers can be produced from any unit.
   (c) The excellent interior economy and cleanliness. Every dugout has its rifle rack in which rifles are standing as clean as if in a barrack room.

5. If it were possible, and can be arranged with the G.O.C 23rd Division, the Corps Commander would like Battalion Commanders to visit these lines, in addition to the officers enumerated above.[5]

27/12/1917
F Gawthorne Hardy
B.G.G.S. XIV Corps.

This letter does the men of 69 Brigade great credit for their work improving the positions. However, Lord Cavan in his observations appears to have missed the fact that many of the brigade, both original members and reinforcements, came from mining districts and digging and shoring up tunnels would have been almost second nature to them. Likewise, 68 Brigade, with its Northumberland and Durham battalions, was equally well equipped for tunnelling operations. The 70 Brigade, on the other hand, may have had some miners, particularly in 8 and 9/Yorks and Lancs, but there was probably a good level of men from the woollen mills in the other battalions.

So 1917 turned into 1918 and at this time 9/Yorkshire Regiment had to send a number of men to the ADMS for medical inspection, who ordered that they be sent before a Corps Medical Board. These men were attached to the Divisional Supply Company for employment while they awaited the outcome of their medicals. On 4 January 9/Yorks and Lancs relieved 9/Yorkshire Regiment, who moved back to Montebelluna. Here the usual routine of cleaning up began and C Company provided a working party. That night enemy aircraft were overhead and bombs were dropped, one of which went through the roof of D Company billet. Fortunately there were no casualties. The training carried on as usual but divisional tactical schemes were also practised. On 7 and 8 January there was heavy falls of snow, but this was not allowed to stop the training and range work. On 18 January the battalion relieved 11/Northumberland Fusiliers in support at Serrggiotto.

The 8/Yorkshire Regiment had moved into the support area at C. Zantta Il Montello, where a platoon musketry competition was organised. This consisted of rapid and deliberate fire; Lewis gun and revolver completions were also organised. On 1 January Second Lieutenants Sydney Layfield and Kenneth Bruce joined for duty and were posted to A and B Companies respectively. On the third of the month they were relieved by 11/Sherwood Foresters and moved to Pederiva, where they became the Northern Battalion of the Reserve Brigade. The relief took place in fine but cold weather and was done very smoothly, with the battalion complete in their new billets by 9 p.m. The billets in the new location were not up to standard and time had to be spent cleaning them up as well as preparing equipment ready for parade. At 11.30 a.m. on 5 January the battalion paraded on the football field for inspection by the Commanding Officer. The rest of the day was spent cleaning the billets and some recreational training. The following officers arrived and were posted to companies as follows: Captain Frank Hiley, C Company; Second Lieutenant Frank S. Vernon, re-joined from being wounded, D Company; Second Lieutenant Douglas Fullerton, C Company; and Second Lieutenant F. Summerscale, C Company. The following day there was another parade, and this time the proclamation by King George V for a special prayer for victory was read. After that the GOC 69 Brigade presented the ribbon of the Military Medal to Sergeant Shires and Sergeant Broad at Biadene in the presence of their platoons. The next day saw A and B Companies using the brigade baths while D Company was on the ranges and C Company paraded under the Company Commander's arrangements. Also, the classes for specialists were organised. Lectures to officers were given by various senior officers from brigade and division. The battalion also set up an ironing room and a rest room for sick men and over the period every company had their blankets disinfected at the divisional baths. Company teams for a proposed divisional musketry meeting practised on the ranges.

A copy of a letter from the Rt Hon. A.J. Balfour OM MP was received at battalion HQ and recorded in the War Diary:

> Rome 8 Jan 1918.
> Sir:
> The following quite unsolicited testimonial as to the impression which British troops are making in Italy will undoubtedly be of interest. The President of the Council observed yesterday that they could not allow the opportunity to pass of expressing his unqualified admiration of the British Troops which had been sent to Italy. We had just come down from the front, and in saying what he felt he was echoing the opinion of General Diaz, and also the King of Italy. His Majesty said he could not find words to express adequately his appreciation of these troops. There has not been a single case of indiscipline or any subject of complaint. I have also seen a private letter from an Italian Officer unknown to me personally, to a friend of his, in which he writes:- '*I am at ____ at the district Headquarters where you may send me a few lines. I have almost all my time done service in the immediate neighbourhood of the British Troops. They are marvellous. I am not speaking of their discipline which is perfect, but of the singular delicacy of feeling which distinguished officers and soldiers. When they leave a billet which they have occupied, not a chair is out of its proper place. Their cleanliness is so great that you would not find a straw on the ground. So also with their camps, where hundreds of wagons and quadrupeds have*

stopped; They do not leave any trace of their passage. No one even takes a glass of water without asking leave.'

Such exemplary conduct cannot fail to have a most beneficial effect on relations and I feel most grateful to the Supreme Command in Italy for having inspired the forces sent to this country with such a high ideal of their obligations. I am sending a copy of this despatch to Sir Herbert Plumer. I have the honour to be, with the highest respect, Sir, Your most obedient servant,

The Rt. Hon. A.J. Balfour. O.M. M.P.[6]

General Armando Diaz, Commander in Chief in Italy.

On 18 January 8/Yorkshire Regiment relieved 13/Durham LI in the front line and became the left battalion of the left brigade in the line. C Company were on the right, D Company in the centre and B Company on the left, with A Company in support. Battalion HQ was located at Belvedere. The relief was done smoothly and without casualties, being completed by 9.30 p.m. There was very little artillery activity on both sides and every available man was at work on the defensive positions. Improvements were made to the support line, communication tranches and dugouts where needed. B Company sent out a patrol on the night of 19 January, however, there was nothing of interest to report. A large number of partly trained Lewis gunners and signallers were sent back to the transport lines for further training. On 21 January the enemy artillery started shelling the battalion front. A heavy shell landed in York Avenue and a number of lighter shells fell during the day. These caused the slight wounding of two soldiers but did not stop the work. Thirty-four men under Second Lieutenant Hart of A Company were sent to join the Divisional Pioneers, 9/South Staffordshire Regiment, to assist with dugout construction. The next night Second Lieutenant Frank Summerscales, of C Company, originally a private in the Leeds Pals, led a patrol and tried to cross the Piave. Although they crossed fifteen streams, the sixteenth was too fast, too deep and the current too strong. They were very quiet and did not see any enemy at all, although they could hear the sounds of them working. The next morning was misty and although the British heavy artillery bombarded the Austrian positions around Sernaglia between 11.30 a.m. and 11.42 a.m., the results could not be observed. However, no retaliation resulted, so the day passed off quite well. That night Second Lieutenant Kenneth Bruce, serving in B Company and from Sheffield, led another patrol to attempt a crossing of the Piave. This time they were successful. On reaching the enemy bank, as on the previous night, no enemy were seen but sounds of working troops was heard. The following night, having been successful once, Bruce, accompanied by Second Lieutenant Wilkinson of D Company, again crossed the Piave. However, they immediately encountered a strong enemy post, which opened heavy rifle fire. The British patrol returned fire and threw a number of bombs. They achieved a withdrawal without casualties. The night of 25 January was lit by bright moonlight and this ruled out any patrol activity. Then on the night of 26 January they were relieved by 9/Yorkshire Regiment.

We left the 9/Yorkshire Regiment relieving 11/Northumberland Fusiliers on 18 January and from then until 26 January their War Diary records almost the same as that of 8 Yorkshire Regiment. However, it does not include the fact that Second Lieutenant Claude H. Cooper died on 17 January. He was the son of John C. and Florence M. Cooper, and the husband of Mrs L. Cooper, of 43, Cranwich Road, Stamford Hill, London. He is buried at Plot I, Row C, Grave 6, at Giavera, British Cemetery. Furthermore, the *Green Howards Gazette* shows he was posted as 'missing believed drowned' and eventually his body was recovered for burial. It would seem he was lost on a patrol across the Piave but nothing is mentioned in the battalion War Diary. Work continued. The weather was lovely, then it snowed heavily, until on 26 January they took over the left sub-sector from 8/Yorkshire Regiment. Over the next week the battalion worked hard on the trenches, support line and communication trenches, putting in traverses and revetting where needed. On the night of 31 January, B Company sent out a fighting patrol. This was supposed to include eight Italians, however, they did not turn up in time and the patrol moved off without them.

Out at rest, 8/Yorkshire Regiment were busy, having spent the first day cleaning up and attending to the billets. The second day was spent bathing and special classes for specialists and junior NCOs under the RSM were started. Second Lieutenant E.E. Hirons reported for duty and was posted to A Company. Those selected for the battalion team in the divisional musketry meeting practised on the local ranges and those men free for employment were set to work hurdle making, cutting stakes and tunnelling. On 30 January Lieutenant W.J. Williams, 2nd East Lancashire Regiment attached, was struck off strength and evacuated to England sick. On the night of 31 January – 1 February enemy aircraft were very active and a large number of bombs were dropped. At the end of the month the battalion strength was forty-three officers and 940 other ranks.

During the month of February 9/Yorkshire Regiment was in and out of the line. On 3 February they were replaced by 8/Yorkshire Regiment, who in in turn were replaced by 9/Yorkshire Regiment on 11 February. They went into divisional rest at Riese on 18 February, where they trained in hill warfare until 23 February. The following day they started marching back towards the line. After two days marching they replaced 15/Hampshire Regiment in the St Urbana sub-sector. Here the Austrian Artillery were sending over chance shots and on 26 February four men were wounded and 40451 Private Wilfred Darnell from Grimsby was killed. He was a reinforcement from the 11th Reserve Cavalry Regiment and had previously been wounded twice at Ypres with the 13/Yorkshire Regiment.

Out at rest, 8/Yorkshire Regiment continued training and on 3 February divine services were held for the various denominations. There seems to be much more religious activity recorded in the War Diary since the transfer to the Italian Front. Having taken over from 9/Yorkshire Regiment on 3 February, each night they had a defensive patrol of one officer and six men out from one of the front companies, until on the night of 6 February a patrol of one officer and four men accompanied by two Italian privates tried to cross the Piave. They managed to cross three streams but the fourth was too deep and too fast. However, another Italian patrol was accompanied by two privates of 8/Yorkshire Regiment. This patrol set off from the same place and at the same time as the British patrol. On their return to the battalion position the two British soldiers reported that the Italian patrol had remained on the allied bank of the river. Over the next five days they manned the front line and every night patrols were out. Nothing of note was reported and no signs of the Austrian forces on the northern bank were seen. Good news was published in divisional routine orders announcing the awards of the Belgian Croix de Guerre to 17460 Sergeant George Blyth of Sunderland and 17142 Private Thomas Charlton.

The night of 11 February saw 9/Yorkshire Regiment arrive to take over the positions held by 8/Yorkshire Regiment, who in turn moved to the silk factory in Filanda Marcato. Two days later, on 13 February at about 9 a.m., Captain Frank Hiley, Commanding C Company, was inspecting the nose cap of an enemy shell, which had fallen and failed to explode, close to C Company billets. Evidence indicates that Captain Hiley dropped or threw away the nose cap. The cap was detonated and exploded with the result that the following casualties occurred: killed, Captain Hiley. Wounded, 14770 Company Sergeant Major William Mashender DCM MM (severely, right leg), 13899 Sergeant William Bottoms (severely, right shoulder), 15755 Sergeant John Wilson MM (right arm and leg), 42875 Private T. Owen (severely both feet). All four were evacuated and eventually discharged owing to their wounds. The warrant officer and two NCOs had been with the battalion since its formation in 1914. Private Tom Owen had been called up on 5 February 1916 and had only served with 8/Yorkshire Regiment. Captain Hiley's obituary was published in the *Green Howards Gazette* in March 1918:

> Captain Frank Hiley accidentally killed on 13 February was the youngest son of Councillor and Mrs T Hiley of the Greyhound Inn, Corn Market, Pontefract. Enlisting in the Grenadier Guards in the first month of the War he obtained a commission in one of our service battalions on 5 January 1915 and saw much active service in France. He was promoted Lieutenant 19 June 1916 and Captain 11 June 1917. When in action on the Somme he was completely buried by a shell explosion. Transferred recently to another theatre of war he met his death through the explosion of an enemy bomb which had been brought into the billet by another man. He was 23 years of age.

A strange accident occurred on 14 February when 47980 Private James Mason was walking towards a steam to collect water. From an east to south-easterly direction he was struck in the left leg just above the ankle by a revolver bullet fired by an unknown person. He was a farm worker from Sedbergh who had attested in 1916, but was not called up until 22 February 1917, when he reported for duty at Halifax. The wound necessitated his evacuation to England, but he was not declared fit again until later in the year and he joined the 9/Yorkshire Regiment in October 1918. With no rifle ranges in the vicinity of where he was wounded, the Court of inquiry could not identify anyone who could have fired the shot. This being so, Private Mason was found free of any blame.

Training and range work continued until 16 February. The 11/Queens (Queens Royal West Surrey Regt), 41st Division took over the support position, being complete by 7 p.m. The 8/Yorkshire Regiment started moving to Pederiva, where they arrived at 8.30 p.m. The next day's march via C Merlo, Busta, Caselle and Altivole took them to Brioni. A third morning March took the battalion to Loria via Riese. Arriving in billets by 1 p.m., the afternoon was devoted to hair cutting and cleaning up of billets. The morning of 19 February saw the issue of new clothing and essential equipment, followed in the afternoon by inspection of equipment and arms. It also saw the release of 23rd Division Routine Order No. 160, which read:

> The Divisional Commander has been desired by the Corps Commander to convey to all ranks of the Division, his sincere appreciation of the work they have done during the last two and a half months, both as regards

> organisation and the manner in which it has been carried out. The Corps Commander also considers the active spirit shewn by all Units in crossing the river is most praiseworthy. He wishes all ranks to be informed of his gratitude for their accomplishments. The Divisional Commander, in adding his congratulations, feels sure the Division will continue to merit the high opinion formed of them by the Corps Commander in any undertaking they may be called upon to carry out.

Over the next five days the training continued. Then on 23 February the CO, Assistant Adjutant and a representative of each company proceeded by motor lorry to Crepano to reconnoitre the newly constructed defensive line. The following day the battalion started marching back towards the line at 9.30 a.m., arriving in Brioni at 12.30 p.m. The 69 Brigade took over the front line from 122 Brigade, with 8/Yorkshire Regiment relieving 12/East Surrey Regiment as brigade support battalion at C Zannatta (Il Montello). In support the training continued as before.

Likewise, on 16 February 9/Yorkshire Regiment was relieved by 23/Middlesex Regiment and they too moved back to the divisional rest area at Reise. Although there is little detail in the battalion War Diary, they also carried out training and then moved back to the line, where on the night of 25–26 February they took over from 15/Hampshire Regt in the St Urbana sub-sector. On 26 February a chance shell wounded four men and killed 30347 Private Walter Daniels from Greenwich. The next day further enemy artillery caused the wounding of a further four men.

The situation in France was not good at this time. In the BEF divisional strengths were being reduced from twelve battalions to nine; furthermore, the establishment of the divisional pioneer battalion was being reduced from four companies to three. Lots of meetings were being held, in London at the War Cabinet and in France at Versailles, where the Executive War Board was in control of the General Reserve. The eventual outcome was that two British divisions and two French divisions would be brought back from Italy to France. There were some objections by the Italian Government and Haig was offered four Italian divisions but declined, stating he would prefer two British divisions. After some political and high-level arguments, on 1 March 41st Division and XI Corps HQ and Corps troops began to return to France.

Another loss to the British troops in Italy occurred on 10 March when General Plumer was recalled to the BEF and he took over Second Army again. However, he was ably replaced by Lord Cavan. It was not until 1 April that the British 5th Division began to return to France. Also moved back to France were three French divisions. Eventually the Italian II Corps, with the 3rd and 8th Italian Divisions under command, arrived in France between 18 and 27 April.

March started with 8/Yorkshire Regiment at C Zannatta (Il Montello). HQ, D and B Companies went to the brigade baths at Venegazzu and were issued with clean underclothing. The afternoon was taken up with range work, especially for the Lewis gun teams. Then in the evening the battalion took over the front line from 9/Yorkshire Regiment, reported complete by 9.30 p.m. and without casualties. In the line, B Company held the right sector, C Company was in the centre and A Company was positioned on the left, with D Company in support and Battalion HQ at Back House. The only action reported over the next few days was both British and Austrian artillery fire. However, compared to the barrages in France, only ten Austrian shells fell on 4 March and the same number fell around A Company HQ on 5 March. One man of 8/Yorkshire Regiment was wounded along with two men of Royal Engineers wounded and one Royal Engineer killed. On the night of 6–7 March 8/KOYLI of 70 Brigade took over the line and 8/Yorkshire Regiment moved into the Brigade Reserve area, in billets at Mercato Vecchio.

On 12 March 1918 XIV Corps headquarters issued a warning order that at the end of March the corps would take over a part of the front on the Asaigo Plateau from the Italian XXVI Corps. The sector would be divided up into two

9th Battalion officers in Italy, March 1918. (*Green Howards Museum*)

divisional sub-sectors: initially 23rd Division would take over the entire front, but after a few days the 7th Division would take over in the left sub-sector. Divisional staffs and commands of all divisions were directed to reconnoitre the new front, especially with a view to taking the offensive there, and to pay attention to training in mountain warfare.[7]

With these orders issued, both 8 and 9/Yorkshire Regiment started moving to the rear. Between 6 and 10 March 9/Yorkshire Regiment were in reserve billets in Montebelluna, where in pouring rain hill warfare was practised and some recreational training was undertaken. This was followed by daily moves, firstly to Treville, then St Pietro, arriving in Rampazzo on 13 March. Here battalion training started again. After eleven days in Rampazzo, during which the battalion transport won the silver medal during the brigade sports, The marching started again with a move to Noveledo. Then to Thiene, eventually reaching M. Cariola on 28 March, where they were accommodated in huts.

Using a different route, starting at 8.30 a.m. 8/Yorkshire Regiment marched from Mercato Vecchio to Castelfranco, where they arrived at 3.30 p.m. Only one man fell out. Next day they moved on to S. Pitero in Gu. This march was over 17 miles and although no one fell out they did not reach the new billets until 5 p.m. All battalions of the brigade were on the route this day and Lord Cavan drove past the column in his staff car. When he reached the head of

CO, 2IC and Adjutant, 9th Battalion in Italy, March 1918. (*Green Howards Museum*)

the column he stopped his car and congratulated the Brigade Commander on the turn out and march discipline of the brigade. Having had a long day on 12 March, the next day they only travelled 6 miles to Grantorte, where they were established in billets by 11 a.m. Here the battalion settled down to inspections and training. One aspect of the training was ceremonial drill and battalion drill under the Commanding Officer. Religious services were a feature of the stay here. On 17 March a joint Church of England service with 9/Yorkshire Regiment was held at Grantorto. The Roman Catholic service was at Grumolo Church and the nonconformists paraded for their service at Grantorto. There was also a paper chase for mounted officers, with the officers of 69 Brigade HQ, 11/West Yorks and 9/Yorkshire Regiment taking part. On 19 March the whole battalion attended the brigade sports day held in Gaianigo. On the subsequent day the battalion took part in a tactical scheme in which 11/West Yorks also participated. This took the form of a trench-to-trench attack, with A and C Companies attacking the first trench and then B and D Companies passing through to take the second objective. Part of the scheme involved a contact aeroplane flying over with the objective of establishing if contact could be made with the infantry by using small flags waved by them. This was similar to a scheme tried in Flanders; however, in Italy it proved a failure.

Over the next four days the usual parades, bathing, drill and sports all took place. Furthermore, on 23 March the Commanding Officer, Adjutant and Signals officer left by lorry to reconnoitre the area on the Asiago Plateau shortly to be taken over. While they were away church parades in the same locations were held. The Brigade Commander was present and immediately after the church parades the presentation of medal ribbons and sporting trophies won at the brigade sports took place. Afterwards another mounted paper chase was held. Moving off at 9.30 a.m. on 25 March, they moved on foot to Villaverla. They covered 17 miles and halted at 12.45 p.m. for dinner for one and a half hours, arriving in billets at 6.15 p.m. Despite the heat and bad roads not a single man of the battalion fell out. In this location time was spent cleaning up and there were kit inspections prior to taking over the line. The battalion transport was divided into A and B Echelons. A Echelon was to accompany the battalion into the mountains, while B would remain on the plains and they made their way to Fara under the command of Second Lieutenant E.E. Hirons.

To understand the position to be taken over, a brief description of the British sector is required. The Venetian Plain extends northwards to a line running east to west through Marostica, Breganze, Thiene and Schio. Just north of this line the ground rises up to 4,500ft. The Asiago Plateau is a natural basin in the Alps and is some 7 miles long from east to west and 3 miles from north to south. The central point of the plateau is the town of Asiago, which stands at

3,000ft above sea level. The plateau is bounded to the south by pine-covered mountains for about 4,000 yards to a point where the mountains slope steeply to the plain. To the north lies a higher and deeper range of mountains guarding the southern Trentino and merging gradually back into the high Alps. At the western edge the plateau narrows down to the gloomy ravine of Val d'Asse, where the opposing front trenches were close to one another on either side of an impassable gorge some 2,000ft deep. To the east the plateau again ends in the rugged heights on each side of the Brenta. The plateau itself consists of undulating, cultivated land freely sprinkled with villages and perfectly adaptable for ordinary military use. This was the only part of the whole Italian mountain front where the operations of ordinary attack were possible.[8]

Although these positions were in the mountains, water in the Asiago sector was scarce. There were some ponds fit for watering animals, but they dried up in summer; in that season the supply of water for the troops and animals was pumped by pipeline from the Astico river. Various reservoirs, tanks and standpipes were provided, catchment tanks were constructed by the RE and the supply of water was usually adequate; but owing to the danger of the pipeline being cut by shell fire, care was taken to husband water and it was rationed at a gallon a man per day for all purposes.[9]

The orders for the movement of the brigades of the division were issued on 22 March. Each brigade group was allotted 240 lorries, half British and half Italian, and were organised into sections of ten lorries each. Each vehicle carried fifteen men with their kit and the move began on 26 March. The 68 Brigade moved first and took over the left sub-sector from the 12th Italian Division. On 28 March 70 Brigade took over the right sub-sector from 11th Italian Division. The 69 Brigade, moving on 28 March, became Divisional Reserve in the Granezza area. That morning the battalion, less Transport embossed at 8.10 a.m. and were carried to the Granezza area. Unlike in France and Flanders, reliefs were taking place in daylight and on 29 March 8/Yorkshire Regiment relieved 2nd Battalion 27 Italian Regiment, at M Langebisa, which was completed smoothly without incident by 9 a.m. The new billets required a lot of cleaning and although signallers, observers and some NCOs attended classes, the majority of the battalion were cleaning up their company areas.

Likewise, 9/Yorkshire Regiment was conveyed by lorries to M Cariola, where they found billets in huts. They then moved to Magnaboschi on 29 March, where they relieved a battalion of the 12th Italian Division. The next day saw them move to support lines at Malga Fassa. April began with 9/Yorkshire Regiment manning the switch line running between Malga Fasa and Ville Del Barenthal. In rain and snow, on 2 April, A Company and a platoon of D Company took over part of the line held by 8/KOYLI. Then, on 11 April, 10/DWR arrived and took over the position held by 9/Yorkshire Regiment, who moved to the positions in the support line vacated by 10/DWR. During the time holding the forward positions three men were wounded. Nine days were spent in the support line before 7/R Warwickshire Regt relieved the battalion on 20 April. The 9/Yorkshire Regiment then moved to huts in Granezza en route for the training area, a march that took three days. The first day, marching in rain and snow took them to billets at Fara. The second day, the weather was fine and they bivouacked at Stecchin near Noveledo. However, it was not a night to be under canvas as the weather turned very wet. On day three, 23 April, the battalion marched to billets at Cornedo, where for the next week they underwent intensive training in all aspects of infantry work.

Meanwhile, on 1 April 8/Yorkshire Regiment officers and NCOs reconnoitred the approaches to the front and support lines. On 2 April a tunnelling platoon under Second Lieutenant Frederick G. Parker was formed for work on the support line at Kaberlaba. The officer was an original member of the First Hull Pals, who was resident in Hedon near Hull. After being wounded he had served with the 8/East Yorks and 3/Tyneside Scottish, Northumberland Fusiliers, prior to being commissioned. One day later, Lieutenant Harold Parker from Birmingham formed a platoon of one corporal and twenty-four men and was attached to 101 Field Company, Royal Engineers, for duty. These Yorkshireman worked on the mule track between Kaberlaba and Malgafassa under the supervision of the Royal Engineers. On 5 April Lieutenant Harold Parker was sent away to hospital and he was replaced by Lieutenant Frederick Waud, who had been commissioned from the Artists Rifles. The next four days continued in the same way until on the afternoon of 10 April, 8/Yorkshire Regiment relieved 11/West Yorks in the line in heavy snow and hailstorms. The handover was completed without incident by 5 p.m. In the line D Company was on the right, C Company on the left, B Company in Support and C Company in reserve. On the battalion's right was 3rd Battalion, 108 French Regiment, and to their left was 10/DWR.

Over the next few days the artillery was active but no casualties were recorded. On 12 April Captain F.C. Miller and Second Lieutenant L.C. Dickens led a patrol from B Company to the village of Ave, where they found a group of houses to be occupied by the enemy. A Company also had a patrol out under the command of Second Lieutenant S. Layfield. This patrol reconnoitred the approaches to the village of Sec. Here they came across an enemy working party just south of the village. The 13th saw an increase in enemy artillery activity, mainly on the back areas, but for those in the line it passed quietly enough. Captain F.C. Miller, this time accompanied by Second Lieutenant K.C. Bruce, on 14 April led another patrol back to the village Ave, where the houses occupied previously were found to be vacant. Likewise, A Company sent another patrol to the village of Sec. This patrol was commanded by Second Lieutenant Norman Miller, late trooper, Yorkshire Hussars. Here they came across two enemy working parties and quietly withdrew without attracting enemy attention. On the morning of 15 April, the reserve and support companies went to the divisional baths at Granezza, where having cleaned their bodies they were issued with clean clothing. That afternoon the two front line companies were relieved, with A moving into support and D Company into reserve. Throughout the day the Austrian gunners had kept up bursts of fire, particularly on the S Sisto road. On the subsequent night patrols from the front companies again went to Ave and Sec. Both villages appeared to be held strongly and the patrols withdrew during some artillery fire.

On the night of 17–18 April, under cover of artillery fire, Lieutenant Charles E. Sparshott led a patrol of one other officer and thirty other ranks from C Company. They endeavoured to enter the enemy trenches near Sec. However, the enemy wire was found to be too strong. Furthermore, their orders were that casualties were to be avoided. Given these facts, Lieutenant Sparshott had little option but to withdraw. Moreover, they had established that the Austrians considered the village to be tactically important. The next two days passed without incident and on the morning of 20 April 6/Warwickshire Regiment completed the relief of 8/Yorkshire Regiment by 11.30 a.m. In fine weather the latter battalion marched to the Granezza area. Overnight rain fell, then at 10.10 a.m. they descended the mountains in high winds, snow and hailstorms to Fara, where they arrived in billets at 4.30 a.m. Despite the conditions, not one man fell out of the column, which comprised twenty-three officers and 696 other ranks.

The marching continued to bivouacs south of Leva and on 23 April they continued on to billets in the villages of Grumo and Cereda. Lieutenant Colonel Backhouse left the battalion to attend an senior officers' course near Padova and Major A.V. Richardson assumed temporary command. The usual cleaning of equipment and billets was undertaken. This was followed by the issue of new underwear, and above all repairs to boots. On 26 April Second Lieutenant B. Ainsworth reported his arrival. At 10.30 a.m. on 28 April the Roman Catholics in the battalion paraded at Cereda Church for Holy Mass. At the same time the nonconformists paraded for their service at battalion headquarters. Those of the Church of England faith did not parade until 2.30 p.m. The remainder of the day was filled with billet and kit inspections. The day 29 April started with bad weather as the Commanding Officer, Intelligence Officer and three of the Company Commanders went off to reconnoitre the Velo Reserve line. On 30 April the battalion paraded in column of route at 9 a.m. and went for a route march via Castelgomberto. That afternoon Lieutenant Colonel Backhouse returned and took over command of the battalion. During April the strength of battalions on the Italian Front was reduced to thirty-four officers and 716 other ranks, which led to a number of men being sent to the reinforcement depot.

While all this was going on for 8/Yorkshire Regiment, between 1 and 18 May 9/Yorkshire Regiment remained in Cornedo training in mountain warfare. With the change of month came a change in the weather and throughout May it was very hot. On 18 May the battalion started back towards the Asiago Plateau. The first day took them to S Maria, then the following day's march took the battalion to Lugo Mare. In the early morning of 20 May, which was very hot, they reached Granezza where the battalion moved into hutments. It was not until 25 May that they took over the line from 11/Sherwood Foresters. They had only just been in the line four days when mountain fever broke out. Twenty men per day were falling to the illness, but fortunately the enemy were very quiet and no battle casualties were incurred.

On the training area 8/Yorkshire Regiment were busy carrying out tactical exercises. On one occasion B and D Companies, accompanied by pack transport, attacked a hill, during which special attention was paid to the use of covering fire by the Lewis gunners. The mules had carried fuel and cooking equipment and the men were fed in the field after the attack. Both the divisional and brigade commanders watched the attack, after which those that participated were marched to the brigade baths in Cornedo. Sergeants A.E. Piper and W. Wilson were posted to an officer cadet battalion for commissioning. The weather turned wet and owing to this the training was carried on under company arrangement in billets. On 7 May, the Company Sergeant Major of D Company, John H. Griffiths MM, and Sergeant F.M. Brough of B Company left for England for commissions. Over the next week the tactical exercises in conjunction with a section of D Company, 23rd Battalion Machine Gun Corps (23/MGC), and 69 LTMB continued. On 12 May the Brigade Hill Sports took place, with 8/Yorkshire Regiment winning the Yukon pack and pack mule competitions. This was followed, the next day, by a brigade tactical exercise. The plan was for the brigade to take the crest of M. Verdaldo and its western spur. The 9/Yorkshire Regiment took the knoll above Cornedo, while 10/DWR took the crest of Verlaldo. The 8/Yorkshire Regiment formed up behind 10/DWR, passed through them and attacked the western spur. On 14 May the battalion received the news that the Bandmaster, 3/8998 Sergeant Stephen Cannon, had died from an accident in hospital. A Wakefield man, he had originally joined 3/Yorkshire Regiment but on formation of the service battalions he was posted to 8/Yorkshire Regiment and crossed to France with it in August 1914. Sergeant

Canon had been Bandmaster since June 1915, when the brass band replaced the bugle band.[10]

Training continued until 17 May, when preparations to return to the line started. At 6.55 a.m. the following morning the battalion set off by march route from Grumo to Sarcedo, where they were in billets by 2 p.m. In spite of the heat and a long march the excellent march discipline of the battalion was maintained throughout. The next day's march took them to Lugo. Leaving at 8 a.m., they were reported all present by 10.30 a.m. An even shorter march was then undertaken when at 8 a.m. they left for the Mare area, arriving at 9 a.m. They 'rested' for three days at Mare, however, they were not idle as various training and hill fighting schemes were carried out. In the afternoon of 24 May, at 4 p.m. the battalion marched out of Mare and travelled on foot to the Granezza area, where they were in billets at 7 p.m.

News reached the battalion on 25 May that Brigadier General T.S. Lambert CMG GOC 69 Brigade had been appointed GOC 32nd Division. He arrived at 2.15 p.m. and inspected the battalion at Granezza. After the general salute he delivered an address and expressed his regret at leaving the brigade and his good wishes for the future. The battalion then gave three cheers for General Lambert. Immediately the parade was over 8/Yorkshire Regiment moved off and replaced 8/KOYLI as support battalion of the left brigade on M. Kaberlaba. In this new position the battalion was well spread out. Battalion HQ with C Company was on M Kaberlaba, D Company were positioned on M Torle, B Company were 500 yards west of Pria dell'Acqua, with A Company at Spiazze Croce.

On 26 May Brigadier General A.B. Beauman DSO took over command of 69 Infantry Brigade. The same day a Special Order of the Day was received from Brigadier General T.S. Lambert:

> In saying farewell to the Yorkshire Brigade with which he has had the honour to serve for more than two years, Brigadier T.S. Lambert desires to thanks all ranks for the manner in which they have supported him, for the great gallantry in action which they have always shewn, and for their behaviour at all times which have given the Brigade the reputation it holds. He knows that the reputation will never fail and that those who have served with him will always look back with pride to the days they have spent in the 69th Infantry Brigade, and share they have taken in its victories. He wishes all ranks the best of Good Luck. They know that his heart is always with them.

Over the next four days working parties were active on the tracks and the approaches to the front line. Enemy artillery was active but caused no casualties.

Despite the reduction of the battalion strength on the Italian Front on 31 May 1918 the strength of the 8/Yorkshire Regiment was forty-five officers and 840 other ranks.

The 9/Yorkshire Regiment were left holding the left sub-sector of the left front line, where on 2 June they were relieved by 10/DWR. They then moved to the advanced support positions, where they spent five days before being relieved by 11/Northumberland Fusiliers and they marched to huts and bivouacs in Cavalleto.

On 1 June 8/Yorkshire Regiment were in support at Kaberlaba providing working parties and preparing to take over the front line. This they did the following day, when they replaced 11/West Yorkshire Regiment as the right battalion of the left brigade. On 3 June they started work on three redoubts named Leeds, Sheffield and York. That night a patrol of thirty men under the command of Captain John Tilly MC reconnoitred the wire in the vicinity of Morar. The patrol encountered a large, superior enemy force, which was trying to outflank them. The patrol immediately opened fire and conducted an effective withdrawal, without incurring casualties. The night of 4 June found a patrol of D Company reconnoitring Morar. This time no enemy were encountered, but a number of white Very lights were sent up from the houses in the village.

The work on the redoubts was continued and although the British artillery was active, there was very little reply from the Austrian artillery. Then at 3 a.m. on 8 June D Company carried out a successful raid, the report of which, by 69 Brigade HQ, describes the operation:

> The raiding company was divided into three parties:- (a) Party under Captain J Tilly M.C. and Second Lieutenant Wilkinson consisting of two platoons. (b) Party under Second Lieutenant Lister, one platoon. (c) Party under Second Lieutenant Oldfield one platoon.
>
> By Zero ?(b) and (c) parties were assembled in their correct positions viz;- (b) at H.59.51 (c) at H.58.53. (a) party however, found a large enemy working party near their assembly point and being unwilling to disturb the enemy before Zero assembled on the south side of the Ghelpac. At Zero the Artillery successfully 'crashed' Morar and the raid commenced. The enemy were very alert – they were probably 'standing to' at the time – as practically as soon as our artillery opened, M.G. and rifle fire started from Morar and the enemy front line. T.M.s also attempted to put down a barrage round Morar from an un-located position.
>
> (a) Party appear to have become disconnected and somewhat lost direction as instead of attacking Morar from due east, the bulk of the party arrived at the S.E. corner of Morar. Here Captain Tilly was unfortunately

badly wounded. Second Lieutenant Wilkinson however, succeeded in getting through the wire with a small party and exterminated an enemy post of three men. (b) party made repeated and most gallant attempts to force an entrance from the south but the enemy put up a very strong resistance with bombs and machine gun fire, and the wire proved much stronger than expected. This party did most valuable work however, in keeping the garrison fully occupied thus giving (c) party a fine opportunity which they were not slow to take. (c) party which was handled with great dash and initiative by Second Lieutenant Oldfield forced a passage through the wire on the west of Morar. A sentry post was then met with, of whom one was killed and the other taken prisoner. The S.W. house was then rushed and ten more prisoners taken. As the time was now Zero plus 30 and the objectives of the raid were gained, Second Lieutenant Lister who was now the senior, thought it advisable to retire without making a further search of the houses. The retirement was successfully carried out in spite of a light barrage put down by the enemy Artillery.

I wish to place on record the deep regret felt by all ranks of this Brigade for the death of Captain J Tilly M.C. The success of the raid was largely due to his careful organisation and fighting spirit. This gallant officer met his end while going forward alone to reconnoitre a better line of approach to his objective when his party were held up by strong wire.[11]

Captain Tilly's obituary was printed on 17 June and stated:

The Official news has been received by Mr and Mrs Tilly of Seaton Carew that their youngest son Captain John Tilly M.C. Yorkshire Regiment was killed in action in Italy on the 8th inst. Captain Tilly was 31 years of age. He was educated at Ayesgarth School, Repton and Pembroke College, Cambridge, where he graduated B.A. in 1908. In 1911 he was admitted a solicitor of the Supreme Court and joined the staff of the firm of Turnbull and Tilly solicitors West Hartlepool. Immediately on the outbreak of war he applied and was recommended for a commission in the Yorkshire Regiment, but not hearing anything he enlisted as a private in the Public Schools Battalion on 5 September and in due course joined the battalion at Epsom for training, but within a week he obtained his commission in the Yorkshire

Captain John Tilly MC, killed 8 June 1918.

Regiment (Green Howards). In August 1915 he proceeded to the Western Front and since that date, except when home wounded, he has seen continuous active service. He was wounded in November 1915 and again (severely) in August 1916 in the Battle of the Somme. He was awarded the Military Cross for gallant conduct during the British offensive on 21 September 1917, and in the following November went with the first British Expeditionary to Italy.

Several points worth noting were listed at the end of the report:

(a) The enemy were very alert and considering the severity of the artillery fire shewed a good fighting spirit. Heavy though wild shooting was kept up by them for a considerable time after Zero.
(b) It is almost certain that heavy casualties were inflicted on the enemy by our artillery. Judging by the rifle fire and the number of very lights, their front line was very strongly held. AQs our artillery fire developed its full effect the rifle fire and very lights gradually died out.
(c) Red flares lit from our front line well to the flank of the raid proved a valuable guide for disconnected parties for the return journey.

Result of the Raid, Prisoners 11; Killed for certain 4
Our Casualties, Killed 1 Officer Slightly wounded 3 Other Ranks.
Signed A.B., Beauman Brigadier General

On 10 June 13/Durham LI relieved 8/Yorkshire Regiment, who marched back to Granezza and the march continued the following day to the Mare area in the foothills. Here they were visited by General Babington, who presented medal ribbons to those who took part in the raid. The Military Cross was awarded to Second Lieutenants H. Oldfield and W. Lister, the Distinguished Conduct Medal to 9475 Sergeant O. Bolland and 33399 Private E. Webb, Bar to the Military Medal to 18609 Lance Sergeant H. Dresser, and the Military Medal to 33580 Corporal J.F. Cox and 13659 Private H. Mackenzie. Lieutenant, Acting Captain F.G. Batty received the Military Cross in the King's Birthday Honours. On 12 June the award of the Distinguished Conduct Medal to 14006 CQMS J.P. Kelly and the Meritorious Service Medal to 14769 RQMS A.H. Bolton were announced. Both had been with the battalion since its formation.

On 14 June the battalion was placed under half an hour's notice to move back to the plateau.

The Austrians had been planning an offensive for some time and the attack opened at 3 a.m. on 15 June on the British positions on the Asiago. The

British had on the right 23rd Division, with 70 and 68 Brigades each with two battalions in the line one in support and one in reserve. On the left was the 48th (South Midland) Division. The 69 Brigade, as we have seen, was the Divisional Reserve in the foothills. The bombardment with gas, shrapnel and high explosive, even some armour-piercing shell, fell on the whole of the British front system, battery positions, divisional and brigade headquarters and other areas such as ammunition and stores dumps.[12]

In the attack on the 23rd Division front the enemy penetrated the line on the extreme right held by 11/Sherwood Foresters of 70 Brigade. Their right company lost all its officers and a number of men. The support company held a line of about 1,000 yards with four posts that the Austrians were unable to penetrate. The battalion Commanding Officer, Lieutenant Colonel C.E. Hudson, formed his battalion headquarters party and some Italian trench mortar gunners for a counter-attack. He then went forward and drove the enemy off the position they had taken. By abut by 2 p.m. the counter-attack had restored the position. In the sector held by 68 Brigade 13/Durham LI and 12/Durham LI held their line and even sent patrols forward to round up enemy wounded and those lying unwounded in no man's land. On the left, at the junction of 23rd and 48th Division where 11/Northumberland Fusiliers joined 1/4/Oxford & Bucks LI, the Austrians attacked powerfully and broke through. The 11/Northumberland Fusiliers formed a defensive flank along the Boscon Switch and sent patrols forward to keep the Austrians at a distance. This flank was reinforced by 10/Northumberland Fusiliers with two companies of 8/York and Lancs attached from 70 Brigade. Therefore, the left flank of 23rd Division remained secure.

With 69 Brigade in divisional support, 9/Yorkshire Regiment moved to temporary positions at Spiazzi Di Croce. They must have come under artillery fire. Three men were wounded and 13710 Corporal William Moss, a 25-year-old coalminer serving with C Company, from Houghton-le-Spring was killed. Two days later the battalion moved into the right sub-sector, where they relieved 8/York and Lancs. While they held this sector another four other ranks were wounded. Down on the plain, in Divisional Reserve, news of the attack reached 8/Yorkshire Regiment at 4 a.m. The battalion was ordered to move to Granezza immediately. By 7.20 a.m. the battalion had reached their destination, where orders were received to occupy a position known as the Marginal Line, immediately south of Granezza. These orders were carried out with the whole battalion in the line, from right to left D Company, C Company, B Company, HQ Company, A Company. Lewis gun and rifle posts were selected and a hot meal distributed to the men. Some information trickled back regarding the situation at the front. At 2 p.m. A and C Companies were ordered forward to reinforce 70 Brigade on the right. Then at 3.30 p.m. Battalion Headquarters with B and D Companies were ordered to report to 68 Brigade Headquarters on M Kaberlaba. They reached HQ 68 Brigade by 5.30 p.m. and here they were ordered to reinforce the left flank of the division at dusk. It took until 11 p.m. before they were in position in the second line on Kaberlaba, where they came under the orders of the Commanding Officer of 10/Northumberland Fusiliers. Major Boys was given command of the second line, and the garrison was comprised 8/Yorkshire Regiment less two companies and one company of 10/Northumberland Fusiliers. With the two companies attached to 70 Brigade, A Company was in support of 8/York and Lancs. C Company, on the other hand, reinforced the 9/York and Lancs, putting two platoons into the front line. They sent out patrols and one platoon brought in three machine guns and a number of prisoners. The 16 June was a quiet day, during which B Company were relieved by a company of 10/Northumberland Fusiliers. Lord Cavan sent the following message to all battalions of the corps. 'Owing to the staunchness of the 23rd Division, and determination of the 48th Division to lose no ground to the Austrians our positions have been maintained. My sincere thanks to all ranks. Cavan.' During the fighting five men were wounded and 47081 Private Frank Marshall, a 20-year-old reinforcement from Gainsborough, Lincolnshire, was killed. The fact that the enemy did not break into the 23rd Division positions was put down to the fact that the troops involved were Hungarian *Honved* troops of an inferior *Landwehr* class, that desisted, even panicked, after a few casualties.[13]

Having spent a week in support positions, 9/Yorkshire Regiment relieved 11/West Yorkshire Regiment and two platoons of 10/DWR in the right sub-sector of the right brigade front line, preparatory to a brigade attack on the Austrian positions between Ave and Sec. This attack was, however, cancelled. The last two days of June saw the Austrian artillery shelling the positions held by 9/Yorkshire Regiment, causing four slight casualties. The trench fever that had been causing a lot of casualties had by the end of the month died out. The usual patrols were busy and one from C Company captured an Austrian prisoner.

In Brigade Reserve 8/Yorkshire Regiment were providing working parties to wire the S. Sisto ridge, and they also reorganised and had kit inspections. On 22 June, Major J.C. Bull, 10/DWR, took over temporary command of the battalion. The wiring work continued until 26 June, when at 3 p.m. they started back towards the front line. The Battalion first line transport was moving with the column, and in charge of the second water cart was 17150 Private Michael Faragher, a 37-year-old coal miner from South Street in Durham. As his cart approached a traffic control point, the traffic sentry told Private Faragher to put his steel helmet on. The helmet was hanging on a hook on the side of the cart and, not wanting to slow the cart, he jumped up to retrieve his helmet. On landing he caught his heel on the wheel of the cart, which brought him to the ground. Lying there he was attended to by stretcher-bearers and evacuated to 69/Field Ambulance.

As in all cases of accidental injury, the RAMC unit had to forward a report to Brigade Headquarters, the last sentence of which could have been led to Private Faragher being charged stated, 'He did not ask the driver to stop the cart.'

However, Major Bull had obviously spoken to the transport officer, quartermaster and Private Faragher about the accident before forwarding the paperwork to Brigade Headquarters. He wrote:

> Herewith, A.F.B. 3428 in the case of No. 17150 Pte M Faragher.
>
> I should like to point out that in my opinion, the injury sustained was quite accidental. Private Faragher is an extremely good soldier. He came out with the Division in 1915 and has served continuously since then in charge of a water cart; under the circumstances I should be glad if his case could be dealt with as leniently as possible.
>
> J.C. Bull Major
> Commanding 8/Yorkshire Regt.

The statements and evidence were forwarded to the AA and QMG at HQ 23rd Division, who sent a brief one sentence reply that read, 'Please note that disciplinary action cannot be taken if in performance of military duty.'

When they arrived at the front, the battalion relieved 8/KOYLI in the left subsector of the Brigade front. B and C Companies were placed in the line, with A and D Companies in support. That night patrols were out covering the battalion front. The next day passed quietly but the hours of darkness were full of activity. An outpost was manned on Guardinalti Ridge and an offensive patrol reconnoitred Ave. On the night of 28 June B and C Companies turned the outpost on Guardinalti Ridge into two strong points, while A and D Companies provided covering patrols. On 29 June the Italians on the right attacked the Austrians, which brought down retaliatory artillery fire on to 8/Yorkshire Regiment, causing some casualties. No. 46862 Private Arnold Wood, who hailed from Kirkheaton near Huddersfield and had barely turned 18 when he was sent as a reinforcement to the battalion, died of his wounds at the Field Ambulance or CCS located at Granezza. Along with him, 14511 Private Thomas E. Cox, a butcher from Hendon in Sunderland, was killed in action.

At the end of the month the strength of 8/Yorkshire Regiment stood at forty-two officers and 802 other ranks. The casualties were one officer killed, two other ranks dead, eight wounded and thirty-six evacuated sick, with thirty-eight reinforcements being taken on strength.

Chapter 10

Italy to the Armistice, 4 November 1918

July 1918 started in the same way that June had ended in the front line. The 8/Yorkshire Regiment had an uneventful three days. The Austrians were very quiet and apart from sending out night patrols and working parties constructing strong points, nothing of interest was reported until on 4 July they were relieved by 13/Durham LI. Likewise, in the right sub-sector 9/Yorkshire Regiment were replaced by 11/Northumberland Fusiliers. Both Yorkshire battalions moved to the huts in Granezza. For the next six days both battalions carried out the usual training programmes. The 8/Yorkshire Regiment introduced a bayonet fighting and a physical training competition, each platoon submitting a team. Along with that the inevitable inter-platoon football competition was started. In the final of the physical training competition held on 8 July, D Company took the honours. But the bayonet fighting was won by B Company. The football competition was put on hold, for at 2 p.m. on 10 July the battalion started back towards the line, where they took over the left sub-sector of the left brigade front from 11 Sherwood Foresters. Here the battalion came under the orders of 70 Infantry Brigade, with A, B and D Companies in the line and

8th Battalion band in summer dress, Italy. Sergeant Poole is at the front, lying down. The Battalion Green Diamond Battle Patch can be seen on the left-hand side of the helmet. (*Green Howards Museum*)

Private John Roberts, from Oldham, had previously served with the DWR. He was posted missing on 20 July 1918.

C Company in support. The next day an Austrian shell fell in B Company's sector. It wounded one man and killed 235419 Private Herbert Haigh, who was born in Leeds but was living in Batley. He had served in France with 4/Northumberland Fusiliers prior to being transferred to the Yorkshire Regiment.

That day 9/Yorkshire Regiment travelled the same route up to the plateau and took over as the right support battalion in the left sub-sector from 8/KOYLI. By 12 June all battalions of the brigade had arrived and 69 Brigade Headquarters assumed command of the brigade sector. The weather was now so hot that khaki drill uniforms were issued to all ranks and service dress was returned to stores. With the issue of the tropical helmet the battalion battle patch normally worn in the centre of the back just below the collar was positioned on the left of the helmet stitched on to the pagari, with the cap badge mounted on the green diamond, that of 8/Yorkshire Regiment being horizontal and the diamond of 9/Yorkshire Regiment being vertical.

On the night of 19/20 July 9/Yorkshire Regiment carried out a raid. The following report appears in the battalion War Diary:

1. The night of the raid there was a very bright moon and in spite of this the raiding parties were formed up and ready by 11.50 p.m.
2. At midnight the barrage opened and at 12.04 a.m. the barrage lifted and the advance commenced.
3. The right party unfortunately became much disorganised during their advance up Notts Trench owing to shells bursting amongst them and also owing to rifle fire from a strong point in a loop holed ruined house. And for the most part lost direction. Eventually two officers, Captain W.F. Greenwood M.C. and Second Lieutenant Edwards-Crate, and two other ranks, Lance Corporal George Watts and Private Lowther, succeeded in making their way into the railway cutting. A party of the enemy had by now lined the southern rim of the cutting and were firing to their front. Captain W.F. Greenwood M.C. and his small party attacked them from the rear and inflicted heavy casualties on them with revolver and rifle. He also cleared out about 10 large shelters and dugouts, killing a considerable number of the occupants and driving

the rest out into the cutting where they surrendered. Unfortunately Lance Corporal Watts was shot dead at point blank range by one of the enemy and Captain Greenwood was left with only one man. This was quite inadequate for either completing the operation or extricating the large number of prisoners captured so Captain Greenwood was eventually obliged to retire with only 12 prisoners.

4. The left party encountered very strong opposition. In spite of heavy machine gun fire a party under Lieutenant W.A. Sharpe succeeded in entering the cutting and advanced 50 yards eastward where they were held up by and enemy bombing party and did not succeed in making further progress. Another party under Lieutenant E.G. Bingham M.C. failed to make progress towards Post Spur owing to heavy Machine Gun Fire and suffered considerable casualties. Lieutenant E.G. Bingham, himself being severely wounded. One prisoner was taken by this party.
5. Both parties retired about 12.30 a.m. under heavy machine gun fire.
6. The railway cutting is very thickly populated, the eastern end having a continuous line of bunked dugouts and shelters under the southern wall. Four mules were in the cutting at the time of the raid – three of these were killed during the fighting. Ration dumps were noticed and the ruined house is strongly held and loop holed.
7. Results of the Raid:-
   Prisoners captured. 13
   Enemy killed. Over 30
   Mules killed. 3
8. Casualties:-
   Officers wounded 1
   O.R.s
   Killed. 2
   Missing. 3
   Wounded. 14.

The results of the raid were probably not what the senior officers wanted. Indeed, for Captain Greenwood it must have been particularly galling. Having captured so many of the enemy only to leave them behind to fight again must have been very hard to take. The figures for the dead and missing in the report are one man short. The CWGC and SDGW record that 11607 Private John Duncan from Middlesbrough and 23792 Sergeant Albert Ratcliffe, a Knottingley man, were killed. However, there are four men recorded as missing on 20 July 1918: 47991 Private Arthur Hough, from Nottingham, 34491 Private Arthur Matthews, from Normanton, 266475 Private John Roberts, born in Oldham but living near Huddersfield, and of course, 23588 Lance Corporal George Watts, who came from Islington. The last named we know was killed inside the Austrian lines, so we must assume he was buried by the Austrians. He is, however, commemorated with the other three on the Giavera Memorial to the Missing, next to the village church south of the Montello ridge.

On 22 July battalions of 48 Division were arriving to relieve 69 Brigade. The 8/Worcestershire Regiment replaced 9/Yorkshire Regiment, while 6/Gloucestershire Regiment took over from 8/Yorkshire Regiment.

Owing to the heat during the day, the moves to the plains were largely done in the evening. Having been relieved, 8/Yorkshire Regiment moved to Granezza, where they arrived at 1 p.m. On 23 July they moved off at 4 p.m. and bivouacked at Fara about 7.30 a.m. On 24 July they left Fara at 8 p.m. and marched to Bergana Camp, being bedded down shortly after 10 p.m. The next day's trek started at 7 p.m. when they moved to billets at Brogliano, where at midnight they took over billets. It was with some pride that the officer recording the battalion's War Diary wrote, 'During these three days of marching not a man fell out.' The 9/Yorkshire Regiment followed the same route until on 28 July they moved to Cornedo, where they arrived at 2 a.m.

The next three days were spent there and the normal training started. During the month eighteen men had been wounded. The casualty list also included those killed and wounded during the trench raid.

On 26 July Major R.C. Grellet DSO re-joined 8/Yorkshire Regiment and took over command. Major J.C. Bull MC was appointed second in command, with Major E. Boys MC taking over command of A Company. The normal inspections of kit and billets took place but started at 6 a.m. and were finished by 10 a.m. Every type of drill, arms, gas, musketry and attack was undertaken and cumulated with the battalion firing Part I of the short musketry course, during which the shooting was recorded as fair. The end of July saw the strength of the battalion as forty-three officers and 786 other ranks.

For the first six days of August 8/Yorkshire Regiment carried out a lot of range work and tactical exercises. In the evenings they found time to have a battalion cricket team. On 3 August they played 9/Yorkshire Regiment and won by six runs. On 9 August the battalion team played 11/West Yorkshire Regiment and won by thirty-four runs. Other notable events during this period were as follows, On 3 August, for the first time since arriving abroad the battalion sergeants' mess held a regimental dinner at Brogliano. On 8 August the 69 Infantry Brigade musketry meeting was held on A Range. The 8/Yorkshire Regiment shot very well, as seen in the table below. Obviously the musketry practice had paid off and although they took no positions on events VI and IX, all the other positions showed how much the musketry of the British infantry had improved since 1916, when it was relying on the use of the grenade to take a position.

69 Infantry Brigade Musketry Competition Results
8/Yorkshire Regiment

Event	Battalion Position
I	2
II	1
III	1
IV	1
V	2
VI	Not entered
VII	2
VIII	1
IX	Not entered
X	2

Thus with ten events and placed in eight, 8/Yorkshire Regiment won the 69 Infantry Brigade Musketry Cup, given by Brigadier General A.B. Beauman DSO. Following this victory the battalion were straight away back on the range the following morning, while the afternoon saw all companies go to the baths and in the evening to the divisional horse show. The battalion cricket team was in fine form during this period of rest. On 11 August they defeated 11/Northumberland Fusiliers by 61 runs in the semi-final of the Divisional Cup and three days later they met the Divisional Headquarters team and a well-fought match ended in a draw. The cricket match over at 7.30p.m., they left Brogliano and marched to Beregana Camp, where they arrived at 2 p.m. They rested throughout the day and set off again at 7 p.m. for Camisino, arriving at 11 p.m. On both these marches only one man fell out. The third day was a rest day but at 6 a.m. on 17 August they were on their way once more. This was a very stiff climb, travelling by mule tracks back to the plateau. The weather was very hot and took a toll of the men, so much so that no fewer than eleven fell by the wayside. However, by 11 a.m. the battalion was in position on M. Serona. In the early hours of 18 August the battalion took over support positions from 20/Manchester Regiment. The next few days were very quiet until 22 August found them taking over the front line from 10/DWR. The British artillery made a deliberate destructive shoot on the Austrian line opposite the battalion and this caused a heavy retaliatory barrage. The War Diary for 26 August 1918 records: 'Today is the anniversary of the battalion embarking for France. At the present time there are 20 Officers and 167 Other Ranks who came overseas with the battalion in August 1915.'

The next morning 11/Northumberland Fusiliers relieved the 8/Yorkshire Regiment, who marched back to Serona Camp. Here they cleaned up and started practising the 'company in the attack'. They also had to find large working parties of twenty officers and 200 men for the Royal Engineers.

So August came to a close for 8/Yorkshire Regiment with a battalion strength of thirty-eight officers and 773 other ranks.

Meanwhile, 9/Yorkshire Regiment spent the first two weeks of August in Cornedo. However, what they actually did is unknown, for the War Diary simply states 'Training'. On 14 August at 7 p.m. the battalion left Cornedo for Beregana Camp. Travelling the same route as 8/Yorkshire Regiment but twenty-four hours behind, we therefore must assume the marching conditions were just as bad for 9/Yorkshire Regiment. When they reached the plateau, the battalion went straight into the line, where they replaced 2/Honourable Artillery Company. With one company manning the outpost line, over the next nine days the battalion had twelve men wounded. On 27 August 13/Durham LI relieved them and they moved to Brusabo Camp, where they were at the end of the month.

At the beginning of September orders were received from the War Office that the brigades on the Italian Front were to be reduced to three battalions. This had been carried out on the Western Front in February 1918 on the recommendation of the War Cabinet against the advice of the Army Council. Each of the divisions in Italy would lose three battalions; in the 23rd Division each brigade was to lose one battalion. Thus in 68 Brigade, 13/Durham LI were selected, in 69 Brigade the choice fell on 9 Yorkshire Regiment and finally in 70 Brigade 11/Sherwood Foresters were nominated.

On 3 September 9 Yorkshire Regiment became the Divisional Reserve and on 11 September they received orders to move into the front line. However, these were cancelled and the battalion moved to Centrale to await the orders to move to France. At 3.30 a.m. on 13 September B and C Companies entrained at Morano for France. They were followed at 7.30 a.m. by A and D Companies for a journey that would take three days. The reader will learn more of their activities in France in the next chapter.

Meanwhile, the 8/Yorkshire Regiment spent the first four days of September training and providing working parties. On the afternoon of 2 September the battalion held a boxing competition; this was described as a good meeting with plenty of entries, and this was followed in the evening by a very successful battalion concert in the Church Army tent. The following night at 7 p.m. the battalion moved to the line, where they relieved 8/KOYLI as the support battalion in the left sub-sector. From 3 September until 14 the enemy was very quiet. The only Austrian shelling took place on 6 September and the only casualties were two mules, one killed and one wounded. On the night of 15 September, at 8.30 p.m. 11/Northumberland Fusiliers took over and owing to the bright moonlight the relief was accomplished very quickly. By midnight 8/Yorkshire Regiment had arrived in camp at Carriola Point, having suffered no casualties during the tour. Over the next ten days the battalion carried out range work by companies, provided working parties and practised the company in the attack.

The weather held until 24 September, when it rained all day and the training was confined to lectures in billets. The following day at around noon the Italian 49th Regiment of the Parma Brigade arrived to take over Carriola Camp and 8/Yorkshire Regiment were moved by motor lorry to Beregana Camp, where they arrived at 5 p.m. The battalion marched out of the last-named camp at 7 p.m. the next evening and moved on foot to billets in Pagana near Vicenza, where they arrived at around 1.30 a.m. on 27 September. The battalion War Diary states, 'The Battalion marched extremely well – not a man fell out – Distance about 15 miles.' The last four days of September were spent cleaning up and training, Lieutenant Colonel M.R.C. Backhouse DSO re-joined from hospital and on 30 September inspected the battalion in 'Marching Order', the turnout being described as 'very good'. At the end of the month the strength of the battalion stood at thirty-six officers and 905 other ranks. They had received one officer and 140 other ranks as reinforcements and three officers and twenty-one men had either transferred or been evacuated sick.

At this time there were changes in the command structure on the Italian front and the British XIV Corps comprising the 7th and 23rd Divisions along with the Italian XI Corps made up of the 23rd Italian and 37th Italian Divisions formed the Tenth Army, which was commanded by Lord Cavan.[1]

The British divisions were moved by stages from the Asiago Plateau to the Piave Front, where the Italian Commander General Diaz was planning an offensive.

The 8/Yorkshire Regiment spent the first four days of October carrying out various forms of training. The box respirators of the battalion were refitted with updated eyepieces and tested. On 5 October a move was made to Montecchio Maggiore, followed by a move via Montebello to Ronca, where they received a very cordial welcome as the area had not been occupied by British troops before. That morning at 1 a.m., winter time came into force and the clocks were put back one hour. The weather turned wet and it rained heavily on 11 October, so all training was done in billets. The next day the battalion marched to Creazzo, where they arrived at 4 p.m. and were placed at one hour's notice to move. At

5.20 a.m. the next morning the battalion moved to Villaverla Station, where they entrained at 4 p.m. and left at 7 p.m. It had rained heavily during the march and although it cleared during the entrainment, the men were standing about in wet clothing most of the afternoon. Travelling through the night, they arrived at Mogliano at 08.30 a.m. The weather was wet but they did not leave until midday for Maerne, where they arrived at 3.30 p.m. Here they started the process of drying out clothing and equipment. However, four men reported sick with a feverish complaint similar to influenza and were despatched to hospital.

On 17 October a Special Order of the Day was issued on the occasion of Major General Babington relinquishing the Command of the 23rd Division to take up command of XIV Corps:

> It is with no ordinary feelings of regret that Major General Sir J.M. Babington K.C.M.G., C.B relinquishes Command of the 23rd Division, with whom he has served since it was embodied more than four years ago: no Commander has ever received more whole hearted support from all ranks than he has during that entire period. By their exemplary conduct in billets and most marked gallantry in the field, the Division has made a name for themselves of which they may well be proud; in more than three years of hard fighting they have never once failed to gain their objective in the attack or lost any ground in the defence. Major General Babington thanks all ranks from his heart for their devoted services and in bidding them farewell assures them that his pride in them is only equalled by his affection for them.

The influenza epidemic was starting to hit the army in Italy and on 18 October six more men of 8/Yorkshire Regiment were admitted to hospital. On 19 October Second Lieutenant F. Summerscale, Lieutenant A.T. Dudley and twenty-nine men were sent away, then each day twelve, and five men went to hospital. Soon the whole of XIV Corps was affected by the breakout. However, as soon as the men left billets and were bivouacking in the open air the breakout tended to disappear.[2]

Owing to the heavy rains, particularly in the mountains, the River Piave was swollen and the attack had to be delayed to let the fast-flowing current subside to enable the infantry to cross the river. By 23 October the preparations for the attack across the Piave were under way and the battalion sent forward reconnoitring parties and all battle stores were issued. At 5 p.m. on 24 October they moved forward to the front line, where it was intended to cross to the island of Lido, the jumping off point for the attack. The crossing was to be made by boat, but only A Company was able to cross owing to a shortage of these, and the remainder of the battalion had to return to billets. The next day further preparations were made by the battalion in billets, while A Company spent a very quiet day on the island. At 1 a.m. the remaining three companies marched from their billets to an embarkation point. The first stream was crossed by a footbridge and the second by boats ferried by Italians. However, as dawn was approaching D Company had once again to return to billets. On the island A, B, C Companies and Battalion HQ dug themselves in on the northern end of the island. They were in touch with 2/Royal Warwickshire Regiment of 7th Division on the right and although the Austrians shelled the island at dawn the battalion were well dug in and suffered no casualties. The Austrian defences consisted of two main lines of shallow trenches, as owing to the high water table the defenders could not dig very deeply. They did, however, have good wire defences and plenty of machine gun posts and trench mortar emplacements. The defenders were from the 17th, 38th and 132nd Regiments of the 7th (Hungarian) Division. This division along with 29th Austrian Division formed the Austrian XVI Corps. The Corps Commander, Field-Marshal Lieutenant Ritter von Berndt, stated that, 'The attack came as a complete surprise, it not being known that the British were in the line.'[3]

At 11.30 p.m. the preliminary barrage started, then at midnight D Company crossed and re-joined the battalion. Furthermore, the barrage brought retaliation on the north end of the island. By 3 a.m. the whole battalion was in its assembly positions and although there was some shelling there were few casualties.

Austrian soldiers in 1918. The defenders of the Piave.

At 5.20 a.m. the advance commenced, the crossing of the River Piave proved most difficult as the last stream to be crossed was quite deep and swift. Several men were drowned during this phase of the advance. The method adopted was for the men to link arms in chains. As dawn broke the artillery and machine gun fire became intense and along with the fact it was very cold and raining heavily it slowed the crossing. However, by 7 a.m., A and B Companies stormed and captured the Austrian line from Zandonadi to a point 400 yards westwards. The attack was pinned down and 13133 Private George Knaggs from Lazenby, under heavy machine gun fire, went back and found a Lewis gun and ammunition, which he brought up to the forward position. The gunner had difficulty in bringing the gun to bear on the Austrian position, so Knaggs stood up and put the barrel on his shoulder while the gunner brought fire down on the enemy. Attacking with B Company was 13093 Private Walter Sheen, but his section came across an Austrian pillbox and were held up. The usual tactic of the time was for the Lewis guns to keep the enemies' heads down while the riflemen made their way around the flank. Sheen made his way up to the right side of the position and eventually got his back against the wall of the pillbox. Taking a grenade from his pocket, he pulled the pin with his right hand and with his left hand pushed the grenade through the opening. As he did so, the gunner moved the barrel of his gun, and took the tops off Walter's little and ring fingers. The gunner was killed in the grenade blast but three men came out of the position and surrendered. B Company was held up in its advance by heavy machine gun fire from the vicinity of some buildings on the flank. Utterly regardless of personal safety, 13820 Sergeant William McNally, a coal miner from Murton Colliery, rushed the machine gun post single-handedly, killing the team and capturing the gun. Considerable opposition was met but was overcome, and by midday A and B Companies had reached their final objective the Tezze–Borgo Malanotte road, the former village being inclusive and the latter exclusive. Here they were in touch with the 7th Division. During the day 8/Yorkshire Regiment had taken 400 prisoners, six artillery pieces and thirty-six machine guns.

During the night C Company took over from B Company and D Company replaced A Company. At 12.30 p.m. the following day the advance resumed. Support fire was provided by the heavy artillery and apart from a few snipers, very little opposition was met with. By 3 p.m. the battalion had reached its objective and was consolidating its position. Then at 7 p.m. Second Lieutenant J. Summerville MC MM led a patrol of thirty men to seize a bridge over the river Monticano, about 5 miles north of the line the battalion was holding. The patrol reported all clear and A Company were sent forward. The town of Vazzola was searched and then A Company proceeded to the bridge, where they joined the patrol. Here they took nine prisoners and two field guns before they were joined by 1/South Staffordshire Regiment from 91 Brigade of 7th Division, who came up in support.

On 29 October at 8.30 a.m. the battalion continued the advance covered by a cyclist patrol from the 14/Cyclist Battalion. They reached Vazzola without opposition and found that the Corps Cavalry, the 1/1st Northamptonshire Yeomanry, were already in the town and had pushed patrols forward to the River Monticano. The 8/Yorkshire Regiment continued the advance up the Vazzola–Cesiol road and joined A Company at the bridge. It was then realised that they were at the wrong bridge, with the correct one about 800 yards further north of Vazzola. A patrol from the Northamptonshire Yeomanry then came in with the news that the north bank of the Monticano was held in great strength by the enemy. Immediately, B Company was sent forward and after some very stiff fighting was able to secure a foothold on the enemy-held bank. The Austrians, who had a large number of machine guns, opened fire on B Company's left flank. Sergeant William McNally immediately directed the fire of his platoon against the danger point, while he himself crept to the rear of the enemy position. Realising that a frontal assault would mean heavy losses, he rushed the position unaided, killing or putting to flight the garrison and capturing the machine gun.

D Company was sent to extend the line to the left. C Company was then ordered up in support, leaving A Company in reserve. It was now found that the 91st Brigade had been unable to come up on the right so two platoons of A Company had to be deployed as a flank guard. At this stage C Company had been absorbed into the line owing to the nature of the fighting. Most of the battalion were in the line. One platoon of B and two platoons of A Company were on the right, while three platoons of B Company and three platoons of D Company were with the whole of C Company in the centre. On the left one platoon of D Company was in touch with 11/West Yorkshire Regiment. Having crossed the bridge, the advance was able to continue for another 400 yards north of the bridge. D and C Companies deployed to the left and reached the village of C Campana, where they met with the platoon of D Company that had moved to the left and forded the river higher up. The 8/Yorkshire Regiment were under heavy fire from the right. Sergeant McNally's platoon were holding a newly captured ditch and were counter-attacked from both flanks. By his coolness and skill in controlling the fire of his party he frustrated the attack, inflicting heavy casualties on the enemy. Throughout the whole operation his innumerable acts of gallantry set a high example to his men and his leading was beyond all praise.

Although the left was secure, where they were in touch with 11/West Yorkshire Regiment, the right was unprotected owing to the fact that 7th Division had been unable to press their advance and the two remaining platoons of A Company under Captain J.T. Shaw were deployed to protect that flank and prolong B Company's line to the right. The battalion now came under a heavy artillery barrage fired by their own artillery, which forced them to withdraw for about 300 yards. At 2 p.m. an enemy counter-attack was launched. During this attack Second Lieutenant Summerville engaged an enemy machine gun and unfortunately lost his life. Around 3 p.m. 9/York and Lancs advanced in support of 8/Yorkshire Regiment and carried the final objective with D and C Companies of 8/Yorkshire Regiment advancing in close support. By this time 7th Division was in position on the right, although their final line was thrown back. As soon as the 9/York and Lancs advanced, A and B Companies of 8/Yorkshire Regiment moved forward to Cesiol to support 9/York and Lancs. Over the last three days of fighting the battalion had Second Lieutenant J.T. Summerville MC MM and seventeen other ranks killed and Captain C.H. Sparshott, Second Lieutenant H. Oldfield MC, Second Lieutenant J.H. Morrison, Second Lieutenant B. Ainsworth, Second Lieutenant L.C. Dickens, Second Lieutenant K.C. Bruce and ninety-seven other ranks wounded, with three other ranks missing.

On 30 October 23rd Division moved back to billets, where they became the corps reserve; the 7th Division and the Italians continuing the advance. During their advance the 23rd Division had taken 1,830 Austrian prisoners, which included thirty-one officers. They had also captured twenty-nine guns. The British XIV Corps was the only formation to achieve complete success on 27 October and on the following days had advanced 3,000 yards beyond the River Piave. Initially detailed as the flank guard of the Italian Eighth Army, XIV Corps had become the spearhead of the attack.[4]

Congratulatory messages were received on 31 October, the first from the Army Commander, the Earl of Cavan commanding Tenth Army:

> Once more I beg you to convey to all ranks my high appreciation and congratulations on the splendid advance today in spite of opposition, fatigue and difficulty of supply. It is a military feat of which they may well be proud.

The second message came from the Commander-in-Chief, General Armando Diaz, who wrote:

> I am well aware of the exhaustion of the two British Divisions and the cold nights and difficulties of sleep. I am sure that they will realise the necessity of completing the task that they began so heroically and I ask

> all ranks confidently to press forward. The XIV Corps must keep the lead after being easily first over the water.

The third letter of congratulations came from the Commander of XIV Corps, General Babington, who said:

> My very best thanks and congratulations to all ranks on the excellent work they have done and the great success they have obtained. I am more than proud to command such troops.

The final message came from Major General H.F. Thuiller, who had taken over command of 23rd Division on the promotion of General Babington. His message to 69 Brigade reads as follows:

> The Divisional Commander congratulates Brigadier General Beauman on the successful result of the operation and desires him to convey to all units engaged the Divisional Commanders cordial appreciation of the fine dash and spirit with which they overcame the difficult obstacles and opposition encountered.

As October ended the strength of 8/Yorkshire Regiment stood at twenty-eight officers and 710 other ranks. During the month the casualties had been seven officers and 117 men, while 111 other ranks had been evacuated sick and thirty-four reinforcements had joined the battalion.

On 1 November the battalion remained in billets at Bibano at three hours' notice to move and there was news of an armistice between the Allies and Turkey. At 10 a.m. on the next morning the battalion undertook a long and tiring March to Tamai, where they arrived at 5 p.m. Church parades were held on the morning of 3 November and at 2 p.m. they set off once more and marched to Palse. The whole of 69 Brigade was assembled here and addressed by the Brigade Commander, who thanked them for their fine work during the recent operations. On 4 November the official news was received that an armistice had been signed between the Allies and Austria-Hungary, which would take effect at 3 p.m. The most important message of congratulations to the Army Commander, Lord Cavan, was received from His Majesty the King, which read:

> With all my heart I congratulate you and the XIV Corps upon the splendid victory achieved fighting side by side with Italian troops of the Tenth Army resulting in the Armistice which takes effect from today. For your great services I thank you. George R.I.

With the war in Italy over, 8/Yorkshire Regiment moved over several days on foot and by train to the Vicenza area, where the news was received that an armistice with Germany had been agreed and that Kaiser Wilhelm II had abdicated. By 14 November the battalion was carrying out training with the idea of keeping the men fit. A number of sporting and fitness competitions were organised. A brigade inter-company football competition being one of the first. In the first round C Company beat D Company 3–2. Another competition held was in physical training and bayonet fighting, in which each platoon entered a team of twenty men. In the physical training A Company took first place, with B Company in second. In the bayonet fighting B Company were first, with C Company as runners-up. In the brigade inter-company football competition, A Company 8/Yorkshire Regiment lost 3–2 to A Company 11/West Yorkshire Regiment. A draft of 200 men, mainly young lads from training battalions in England, joined the battalion on 17 November. At the end of the month a long list of officers and other ranks who had been awarded gallantry medals was published in the battalion War Diary.

At the end of November 1918, the battalion had twenty-seven officers and 876 men on strength. One officer and 320 men had joined during the month and forty-six men had been evacuated.

The training continued, and on 1 December another 107 young lads arrived from England. On 5 December the whole brigade was assembled to witness

8th Battalion Warrant Officers and Sergeants, Arzignano, Italy, December 1918. (*Green Howards Museum*)

the presentation of medal ribbons earned during the Battle of the Piave. On 8 December the semi-final of the brigade inter-company football competition took place, with C Company 8/Yorkshire Regiment playing A Company of 11/West Yorkshire Regiment. In a keenly contested match, after extra time it was a goalless draw. The game was replayed the next day, once again after extra time the game was drawn, this time 1–1. The match was replayed two days later and won by the 11/West Yorkshire Regiment 3–2.

On 7 December the news was received that Sergeant William McNally had been awarded the Victoria Cross for his actions on the 27 October at the crossing of the Piave and for the actions on 29 October at Vazzola. During the rest of the month the training continued and sporting events were held. On 13 December the 23rd Divisional Concert Party gave a very successful performance for the battalion in the theatre at Arzignano. Various parades were held and there were a number of notifications of gallantry awards made to members of the battalion. On 23 December the first batch of twenty-eight miners left for England and demobilisation. These were all elderly men who had come out with the battalion in August 1915. On 31 December the strength of the battalion stood at twenty-eight officers and 980 other ranks. Eighty men had been struck off strength during the month and 184 reinforcements had joined.

The year 1919 started with nothing important to report, however sometime between 2 and 4 January a large draft of eighty-six coal miners left for England. Throughout the month the main themes of the War Diary were the lists of gallantry awards and the numbers of men leaving for demobilisation. Even the Commander of Tenth Army, the Earl of Cavan, was on his way home, and he sent this message to all ranks:

> Soldiers of the Italian Expeditionary Force
> Tomorrow I hand over the command to Lieutenant General Sir J. M. Babington after more than a year in Italy.
> I want to thank every officer, N.C.O. and man of you for your pride in your units which is the essence of discipline, and for all the unforgettable work that you have done in the mountains and on the plains.
> No Commander ever had his task made so easy for him, owing to the loyalty, steadfastness and enthusiasm of you all.
> I wish you all the happiest possible furlough on return to England – good football, good beer, good friends – and after a holiday a real good job.
> With all my heart I thank you, and I hope you will not forget the kindness and hospitality of our Italian friends.
> General Headquarters CAVAN General
> 17 January 1919 Commander in Chief, British Forces in Italy

On 22 January the Corps Commander inspected all ranks entitled to the 1914–15 Star. The 8/Yorkshire Regiment had nine officers and 104 other ranks on parade. Of course, a large number of the surviving original men, the coal miners, had already left for demobilisation. By the end of January the battalion strength had fallen to twelve officers and 412 other ranks.

February followed much the same pattern as the previous month, with training and education classes for those remaining in Italy. The Commanding Officer spoke to the battalion about the Army of Occupation and by 18 February two officers, Second Lieutenants E.E. Hirons and F.B. Harper, had volunteered along with 104 other ranks. They marched off in bad weather headed for Terrossa to be drafted to 8/York and Lancs in Fiume.

At the end of February the battalion had been reduced to eighteen officers and 210 other ranks. Seventeen man had re-enlisted for one year, nine for two years and three for three years. On 28 February the battalion was reduced to cadre, i.e. four officers and forty-six men. The remaining officers and men were to continue serving in the Army of Occupation.

On 4 April 1919 the Cadre of 8/Yorkshire Regiment arrived at Southampton and proceeded to Richmond, where the battalion was disbanded. At the end of March 1920 the battalion King's Colours, which were cased, of the 6th, 7th, 8th 10th, 12th, 13th and 16th (Service) Battalions and 1st Garrison Battalion of the Princess of Wales's Own Yorkshire Regiment, were taken to the parish church in Richmond. At the church the colours were uncased and placed in the chancel. The Reverend Canon Egerton-Leigh officiated and incorporated the consecration with the morning service. A short record of each battalion was read out and the priest gave an impressive address. The troops had marched down to the church under arms, which they piled in Frenchgate and after the service the men were formed up in open order in Frenchgate facing the entrance to the churchyard. The colour parties then marched on to parade, outwards turned and each colour party took up position on the opposite pavement facing the troops and opposite their eventual place in the line. Lieutenant Colonel Swan then ordered the Royal Salute, after which the colour parties marched to their place in the line and all marched back to barracks. The colours were carried by Captain Magee and Lieutenants Atkinson, Hawkins and Downes. The men, 80 per cent of whom were recruits with less than twelve weeks' training, were very steady on parade and handled their arms well.[5] So, came to an end the story of the 8th (Service) Battalion of Alexandra, Princess of Wales's Own Yorkshire Regiment (The Green Howards).

Chapter 11

9th Yorkshire Regiment Back in France

The two trains carrying 9/Yorkshire Regiment took three days to make the uneventful journey back to the battlefields of northern France. At 12.30 p.m. on 17 September 1918 the first train arrived at St Riquier, followed at 2 p.m. by the second train. The battalion detrained and marched to billets in Neuville and Oneux. Here, along with 11/Sherwood Foresters and 13/Durham LI, they became part of 74 Brigade of the newly reformed 25th Division. Between 18 and 26 September training was carried out and the battalion reorganised on the French establishment. It was soon time to return to the line and on 25 September the transport set off by road. The remainder of the battalion entrained at Saint-Riquier at noon on 27 September and travelled to Albert, where they arrived at 6 p.m. on 28 September. On detraining they marched to billets. The next move was to hutments and dugouts in Faviere Wood in the Maricourt area, where they remained until 2 October.

At about 1 p.m. on that day the battalion marched to the line south of Le Catelet. On the morning of 5 October at 6 a.m. the battalion commenced the attack on Beaurevoir. The enemy position at Beaurevoir was very strong: the village stood on a hill that gave complete command of the absolutely bare and exposed ground, while farm buildings and houses provided concealed firing positions for dozens of machine guns. The barrage was fired by six brigades of field artillery and the village itself was shelled until half an hour after the infantry had reached the railway, when the village was to be mopped up from north and south. The 9/Yorkshire Regiment was held up by machine gun fire. It was during this attack that 14509 Private James Sheen was wounded in the right foot. Initially he was evacuated to the Regimental Aid Post and from there to No. 20 Casualty Clearing Station. He then arrived at the No. 12 Stationary Hospital and on 9 October was embarked on HM Hospital Ship *Aberdonian*, from which, after landing he was sent to the 1st Southern General Hospital in Stourbridge.[1] Casualties among the battalion had been the highest since Passchendaele the previous November. No fewer than forty-seven men were killed or missing. Lieutenant George M. Wolstenhome MC and Second Lieutenant Percy Helms had both died. Percy Helms was aged 28 and the youngest son of the late John and Mrs E. Helms, of 27 Adnitt Road, Northampton. He was educated at the Town and County School, Northampton, and was on the Board of Agriculture for Scotland. He had enlisted in 1914 into the 9/Royal Scots (the Dandy Ninth) and crossed with them to France in February 1915.[2] Lieutenant George M. Wolstenhome MC was aged 21 when he was killed. He had enlisted in the Inns of Court OTC at the age of 18, had obtained a commission in the Yorkshire Regiment and went out to France in January 1917. The young officer was a great favourite and a very gallant soldier, and was awarded the Military Cross for 'bravery on the field'. Prior to enlisting he was engaged in business in his father's firm, Messrs Wolstenholme and Holland, one of the oldest cotton brokering firms in Liverpool. It was almost two years since his eldest brother, Captain R.F. Wolstenholme of the King's Liverpool Regiment, made the supreme sacrifice on 28 November 1916.[3]

Private James Sheen, from Durham, was wounded on 15 October 1918.

Beaurevoir was eventually taken by men of 75 Brigade.[4] After the village fell, 9/Yorkshire Regiment moved through the village and dug in in front of it. Here they remained for two days until a move was made back into support positions. They were only there one night and at 2.30 a.m. they moved forward through Beaurevoir again. The objective was reached and the battalion dug in on the railway line near Honnechy. While in this position cavalry passed through them and pushed forward against the enemy. There was no rest though and at 2 a.m. on 8 October the battalion moved off to attack the village of Saint-Benin. They reached a position west of the village and dug in. However, the attack was continued and by 3 p.m. the village was taken and 9/Yorkshire Regiment dug in just outside the village. The next day they were relieved by 2/Royal Munster Fusiliers and marched back to Honnechy. On 10 October a move was made to Premont.

In the early hours of 18 October a warning order was issued to all companies and the transport section of 9/Yorkshire Regiment:

1. The Battalion will be ready to move off at 10 minutes notice after 06.00 Hours tomorrow the 19th inst.

2. All blankets will be returned to the Q.M. Stores by 06.00, also officers kits and mess boxes.
3. On receipt of the word 'ADVANCE' Companies will fall in on the main road outside their billets.
   Pack animals loaded with Lewis Guns and ammunition in the rear of respective companies.
   Transport will parade in the rear of the battalion
   DRESS: Battle Order.
4. The Q.M. will make arrangements for the men to have breakfast at 05.30 hrs tomorrow, and for an issue of tea at 08.00 hrs should the Battalion not be required to move.
   18/10/18 C.L. Porter Lieut. A/Adjt
   9/Yorkshire Regiment.

At 6 a.m. on 19 October the battalion stood to and eventually at 1 p.m. marched off to Honnechy. Here they spent four days until at 3 a.m. on 23 October they moved off and dug in east of Le Cateau. The other brigades of 25th Division advanced in steady waves and reached the north edge of Bois l'Évêque, where 1/8/Worcestershire Regiment of 75 Brigade captured Tilleuis Farm and captured three mortars and a large party of Germans. In the meantime, 74 Brigade waited until the situation became clear. The advance continued and at 9 a.m. 9/Yorkshire Regiment dug in on the edge of Bois l'Évêque. The next objective was the German position known as Herman II, which was well covered with machine guns and lots of barbed wire.

Instructions for the next phase of the advance were issued on 29 October and stated:

1. The 25th Division will be prepared to carry out an operation on the morning of October 30 on receipt of orders today. The object of this operation is to secure ground in advance of the line now held to facilitate forthcoming operations.
2. The objective to be captured by the Division will be as follows;-
   Road between G.20.b.4.9 and G.21.a.7.9 – G.15.d.6.8. (on the light railway). – G.15.b.6.3. (where the railway crosses the Fontaine Au Bois – Landrecies Road) – G.15.b.8.7. – G.9.c.8.5. – G.9.c.1.9. to present line at G.8.b.5.3.
3. The attack will be carried out by 74 Infantry Brigade on the Right and 75 Infantry Brigade on the left. 7 Infantry Brigade will swing forward its right to link up with the left of 75 Infantry Brigade at G.9.c.1.9.

4. DIVIDING LINE BETWEEN BRIGADES
Landrescies – Fontaine au Bous running through G.15.b. – G.9.c. – G.8.d. inclusive to 75 Brigade.
5. DETAIL.
(a) The 9/Yorkshire regiment will be on the right.
(b) The 11/Sherwood Foresters will be on the left.
(c) The 13/Durham L.I. will be in support and at ZERO minus 2 hours will move to the vicinity of G.13.d. where they will dig in and be ready to support either 9/Yorks or 11/S.F.
6. ASSEMBLY POSITIONS. Battalions will assemble on line north and south grid line running through G.14. Central from G.20.b/0.6. – G.8.d.00.25. Tape will be laid out on this line under Brigade arrangements.
Battalions will see that they have gaps made in the hedges through which they will pass from Assembly Position to present Front Line. No posts will be east of the forming up tape at Zero minus 2 hours.
7. BARRAGE. The attack will be carried out under a creeping barrage. The barrage will come down at Zero on a line one hundred yards west of the north and south Grid Line between G.14 and G.15 and will remain for six minutes. A protective barrage will be put down beyond the final objective which will remain for thirty minutes after the time allowed for the capture of the final objective.
8. SYNCHRONISATION OF WATCHES. Brigade Signalling Officer will arrange to send two watches to battalions to have reached the last Battalion Headquarters by 5 a.m.
9. MACHINE GUNS. One section of 25th Machine Gun Corps is allotted to the Brigade. Two guns will take up a position at G.20.b.4.7. where they will remain. Remaining two guns cover the advance. When the Objective has been reached these two guns will take up a position about G.21.a.7.9.
10. ZERO HOUR. Zero Hour will be 8 a.m. October 30 1918.
11. Acknowledge.
Bagshaw
Captain. Brigade Major 74 Infantry Brigade

The 74 Brigade had been assembled along the eastern edge of the wood and at 4 a.m. the attack commenced. It was a bright moonlit night and as the troops emerged into the open, they came under heavy fire from the Germans in Herman II. The enemy fire was suppressed, the wire rushed and after some hand-to-hand fighting the position was taken.[5] Having reached and held their final objective, the battalion dug in and held their positions until relieved by 1/5/Gloucestershire Regiment on 31 October. The Battalion War Diary gives the following casualties for the whole of October:

	Officers	Other Ranks
Killed	6	63
Wounded	15	356
Missing		47

Of the officers killed, four have already been named, the other two were as follows: Major Gerald Norman Hunnybun, who had been with the battalion since joining as a second lieutenant in September 1914 and for some time was Adjutant. The local press in his home region carried these few lines. 'General sympathy is felt in the Thrapston district with Mr Gerald Hunnybun, the clerk of the Magistrates in the loss of his youngest son, Major Norman Hunybun.'[6] The other officer to die was Second Lieutenant Ronald Edwards-Crate from Doncaster, where he was employed by the Great Central Railway Company. Of the other ranks, all but two had joined the battalion as reinforcements at some stage. On 10 October 12125 Private Anthony Peacock of Middlesbrough was killed in action and then on 29 October 14208 Lance Corporal George Marsh of Burnhope Colliery fell too. Both had landed with the battalion on 25 August 1915.

Having been relieved by 1/5/Gloucestershire Regiment on 31 October, on the same day 9/Yorkshire Regiment moved to billets in Pommereuil, where they spent three days. At 8 a.m. on 4 November the battalion moved off from Pommereuil and took up positions outside of Malgani. It was a quiet morning and the positions were reached without being observed by the enemy. At 1 p.m. they set of from Malgani towards Landrecies, with 11/Sherwood Foresters leading as an advanced guard. No opposition was encountered and there was no shelling of any importance. The battalion crossed the canal north-east of Landrecies by means of a petrol tin floating bridge. Here they took up an outpost line and Battalion Headquarters occupied a farm that had been a German artillery headquarters. A battery of 4.2cm howitzers and one 8cm howitzer along with eight prisoners were captured. The next morning they moved off at 7 a.m. and the 11/Sherwood Foresters were once again the advanced guard. The 74 Brigade crossed the Petite Helpe River, which was some 20ft wide and largely unfordable, and here slight opposition was encountered. However, the Sherwood Foresters were able to push on. They reached Maroilles, entered the village and prevented the Germans blowing up a bridge. The 9/Yorkshire Regiment took up an outpost line astride the main Maroilles–Marbaix road.

On the morning of 6 November 9/Yorkshire Regiment became the brigade advanced guard. A Company under the command of Captain Wilfred L. Blow led the battalion and before they reached Marbaix they were held up by machine gun fire from both sides of the road. Number One Troop of B Squadron. the 12th Lancers. and two armoured cars assisted the advance and by 2 p.m. Marbaix had been occupied by A and C Companies. Throughout the village they had a running fight with the Germans but could not bring them into hand-to-hand fighting. Five prisoners and eight machine guns were taken. The Germans shelled Marbaix in the early evening, while 9/Yorkshire Regiment took up an outpost line outside the village. On the morning of 7 November 75 Brigade passed through the battalion and 9/Yorkshire Regiment moved back to billets in the village for the night. The next day took them to Bousies, where they started cleaning up and refitting. It was here that they learned the news that hostilities with Germany would cease at 11 a.m. on 11 November. On 13 November the battalion moved to billets in Le Cateau, where a draft of fifty other ranks joined the battalion. Salvage operations commenced on 22 November, two companies on salvage work and two training. A move to Saint-Vaast took place at the end of the month, when the War Diary records that casualties for the month had been:

	Officers	Other Ranks
Killed	0	3
Wounded	0	32
Missing	0	15

The War Diary for the whole of December simply records 'Saint Vaast – Salvage work'. The same is recorded for January until on 14 January one man is demobilised. Thereafter the daily numbers sent home for discharge are recorded until on 30 January Major General J.R.E. Charles CB DSO presented the King's Colour to the battalion. The colour was consecrated by the Reverend, Major Jenkin CF, was received by Lieutenant James S. Wood MC and the Battalion Guard was commanded by Lieutenant Colonel R.S. Hart DSO. The colour was then trooped through the ranks of the battalion. Throughout February the daily demobilisations are listed and then on 28 February the Diary simply ends with the note '70 other ranks for demobilisation'. No details of where surplus men were sent. Thus the story of the 9th (Service) Battalion of Alexandra, Princess of Wales's Own Yorkshire Regiment (The Green Howards) comes to an end.

Chapter 12

What Became of the Survivors?

The years after the war were not kind to the vast majority of the men. In the north-east and across the country mine owners wished to maintain their profits and the way they wanted to do this was a reduction in men's wages, coupled with longer working hours. This was rejected by the Miners Federation of Great Britain with the slogan, 'Not a penny off the pay, not a minute on the day'. The miners were supported by the Trade Union Congress. The Government set up a Royal Commission headed by Sir Herbert Samuel to look at the problems of the mining industry and consider its impact on other industries. The outcome was published on 10 March 1926 and recommended national agreements and sweeping reorganisation of the industry. Furthermore, it also recommended a reduction of miners' wages by 13.5 per cent. After publication of the report the mine owners declared that miners would be offered new terms of employment that included lengthening the working day and the reduction in wages. The final negotiations began on 1 May but ended without agreement. This led to the TUC declaring a General Strike 'in defence of miners' wages' and it began on 3 May at one minute to midnight. There was worry that the strike would bring in revolutionary elements, so the participation was limited to railway men, transport workers, printers, dockers, iron workers and steel workers as well as coal miners. The strike was called off on 12 May and although the miners held out for a few more months they were forced by their own economic means to return to work. For one ex-soldier this led to never working in the mines again. When Walter Sheen and other soldiers returned to the colliery in Durham, they were met by a manager who to say the least was obnoxious. As the men arrived for work he stood laughing at them and said, 'Look at the state of you, you couldn't wait to get away in 1914 and you didn't get a foreign holiday did you.' He then added, 'Serves you right, some of you were lucky to come back at all not like the silly b...... lying in France.' There was a loud murmuring and Walter stepped forward and knocked him down. He stayed down but said, 'You'll never work in the Durham coalfield again.' Walter moved to the Yorkshire coalfield for a time and by 1939 was laying runways at the De Havilland Factory in Hatfield, where two of his children Mary and Edward worked, manufacturing the Mosquito fighter-bomber.

The next thing to affect the survivors was the Depression of the 1930s and the hardest-hit areas were the heavy industrial and mining areas of the North of England, Scotland, Northern Ireland and Wales. Unemployment reached 70 per cent in some areas. Of course not long after this along came the Second World War.

To research all those that served with both of the battalions and survived would be a book in itself, but those men who were wounded at Contalmaison on 10 July 1916 and admitted to No. 34 CCS provides a good cross section of both battalions at that time.

Demographics of the Wounded Men

An analysis shows that within the group, the largest number were primarily recruited from the colliery villages of County Durham. This figure was followed by the thirty-two men from Middlesbrough. In civilian life, the latter group were largely from the foundries and iron and steel mills of the district along the south bank of the Tees from Middlesbrough to Redcar. Most of the recruits had responded to the owners and directors of those iron works, who had agreed that the family of each man who enlisted should receive half his wage every week so long as he was in the army.[1] Although the total number of other ranks traced to both battalions is 1,912, only 1,503 (78 per cent) have been traced to a town or village. A total of 244 have been traced to Middlesbrough, however, if the numbers for South Bank, North Ormesby, Eston, Grangetown Newport Redcar and Thornaby are included this figure goes up to 434 or 22.6 per cent of those traced.

Furthermore, to produce meaningful figures the soldier's place of residence has been taken as the reference point and not his place of birth. Thus a man born in Wales but living in Middlesbrough has been counted as a Middlesbrough man. What is more, the third largest group of wounded in those admitted to the 34 CCS were recruited from the villages around the ironstone mines situated on the North Yorkshire Moors not far south of Middlesbrough. There were two smaller groups: one comprised of miners from the Northumberland coalfield, with a similar group recruited in Sunderland. The latter group was made up of shipyard workers and coal miners, reflecting the two important industries of that town. In addition, there were smaller groups such as farm workers, sailors and dock workers. Only seven of the group were identified as skilled tradesmen. Most responded to Lord Kitchener's call for 100,000 men at the end of August and the beginning of September 1914. At the time of enlistment, 56 per cent of the selected men were under 24 years of age, with almost half of that figure being teenagers.

On 14 November 1914, Corporal Joseph Birtley stated on his enlistment forms (Army Form B. 2505) that he was 21 years and 9 months of age.[2] However, when Corporal Birtley was admitted to No. 34 CCS on 11 July 1916 he told the admissions clerk taking his details he was aged 20. However, a search of birth registrations found that his birth was registered in the March quarter of 1898. Joseph had added at least four years to his age at the time he enlisted. This in effect meant he was then aged 16. Therefore, along with Private William Strong mentioned in Chapter 6, and three 17-year-olds, they were not of recruiting age when they joined up.

Regarding older men, four men were in their forties when they enlisted. The oldest was Private John G. Durham, who may have taken four years off his age. To confirm this, searches of several classes of documents were made. The *Newcastle Journal* of Thursday, 24 August 1916 shows his home as West Cornforth, a mining village in County Durham. However, he had not registered as an absentee voter in 1918. Coupled with that fact there are several John Durhams living in the region it has proved extremely difficult to confirm the correct man. The most likely candidate, found on the 1911 Census, was born in 1866. This would have put him above the age for enlistment, which was 38 in 1914. The graph on page 48 illustrates that 57 per cent of the research group were under the age of 25. Many of the young recruits did not appreciate the dangers of enlistment and this is reflected in the statement by Private Michael Manley, 'We thought it would be a good holiday and a chance to see different countries.'[3]

Soldiers with Previous Military Service

A search of soldiers' documents (WO363) and pension documents (WO364), traced documents for fifty-two of the 126 being researched. Of these, seven of the fifty-two had previous service. It is significant that three were NCOs as these men brought some level of experience to the volunteers. Corporal John Ryder was a serving regular soldier when war broke out. At the time of the 1911 Census, he was a bandsman based at Strensall Barracks in York. However, he did not embark for France until 1916, when he joined the 8th Battalion Yorkshire Regiment and was posted to C Company. On recovering from his wounds, he was transferred to the 2/6th South Staffordshire Regiment and was killed in action on 27 March 1917.[4] Sergeant Charles Ogden had twelve years' experience in the Regular Army. Ogden served with the band of the 1st and 2nd Battalions, Yorkshire Regiment. As a boy he enlisted in 1899, transferring to the reserve in 1911.[5] He re-joined to the Regimental Depot in early August 1914 and was in France with the 2nd Battalion by November 1914. Furthermore, Private Samuel

Stephenson, who came from Newcastle, had served for twelve years with the 2nd Battalion of the Northumberland Fusiliers.[6] Private Walter Williams originally enlisted into the 4th Militia Battalion of the Yorkshire Regiment in 1906.[7] On 23 March 1915 he joined the 2nd Battalion in France. He was reported wounded in *The Times* Daily Casualty list of 27 July 1915. Once fit he returned to France and was posted to the 8th Battalion. Unfortunately, the wound to his left knee at Contalmaison on 10 July 1916 ended his military career and he was discharged on 3 July 1917.[8] Three of the men had previous service in the Territorial Force, all coal miners. Two from the Rainton area of County Durham had served in the 2nd Durham Royal Garrison Artillery, Territorial Force (RGA), and one from Bedlington had served in the Northumberland RGA.

Arrival in France

The perception of New Army divisions on the Somme is that they were entirely made up of 'Kitchener Volunteers'. Not all of those of the study group wounded on 10 July 1916 were original enlistments to the two battalions of the Yorkshire Regiment that landed in France on 25–26 August 1915. Some had served in France from early in the war, others had been wounded at Gallipoli and some had been wounded at Loos. When fit these wounded soldiers had returned to the front and were posted to the battalions in 69 Brigade. Also among those studied are 1916 enlistments under Lord Derby's recruiting scheme.

Absence and Desertion

Following their combat experience at Contalmaison, within the group studied there were issues with absenteeism and desertion. Three soldiers, Privates John W. McKenzie, Matthew Manning and William Savage, all deserted at different stages. Furthermore, Privates Samuel Stephenson, Anthony Hunter and Luke Carroll were all posted AWOL but apprehended before they were classed as having deserted.

Private John W. McKenzie became a habitual absentee and deserter. Having been discharged from hospital after treatment to the gunshot wound (GSW) to his left arm, McKenzie was absent without leave (AWOL) between 17 and 22 September and again between 4 October and 9 November. Again, on 11 December, he was declared a deserter until apprehended by the Military Police on 9 February 1917. His charge sheet read, 'When under orders for active service deserting His Majesty's Service'. He was sentenced to 112 days' detention but the sentence was remitted so he could join the 13th Battalion, Yorkshire Regiment in France. Wounded a second time, Private McKenzie was admitted to the 2nd Southern General Hospital, Birmingham, on 8 June 1917. He was again absent from 6 to 18 August 1917. He re-joined the 3rd (Reserve) Battalion Yorkshire Regiment at West Hartlepool on 28 November and the absenteeism started again. He was AWOL from 30 March 1918 until 4 April 1918 and 21 May until 16 August. Detained by the Military Police at West Hartlepool Railway Station on 16 August, McKenzie was tried by District Courts Martial on 23 August 1918. Unfortunately, this sentence has not survived in his documents.[9]

Private Anthony Hunter went AWOL on 9 December 1916, only to be apprehended on 14 January 1917. He broke out of the guardroom and escaped on 27 January 1917 but was again caught and then tried by District Courts Martial. He was sentenced to twelve months' detention, however, the sentence was remitted and on 1 March 1917 he was returned to France. Despite the absence, he ended the war with the rank of sergeant. Perhaps the fact that these absentees and deserters had been wounded on the Somme justifies their reluctance to return to France.

Commissioned from the Ranks

Two of the selected group became commissioned as second lieutenants. Private Robert Coulson Robinson was commissioned into the Durham Light Infantry (DLI) on 31 October 1917. When he registered as an absentee voter in 1918 he was serving at South Shields with the 3rd (Reserve) Battalion, DLI. Sergeant Joseph William White MM received a commission into the Manchester Regiment on 29 May 1918 and served with its 52nd Battalion. It is remarkable that both men were at the time of the 1911 Census aged 17 and were 'putters' (hand filling coal tubs underground) in their local collieries. At the end of the war, Robinson returned to coal mining and was still employed as such in 1939.

It proved more difficult to trace Lieutenant White. Several avenues of research were followed, such as early death and emigration records. Consideration was also given to the fact he may have joined the Auxiliary Division of the Royal Irish Constabulary, the infamous 'Black and Tans'. However, in a search of those records, there was no trace of a J.W. White, late Manchester Regiment, serving with them. Subsequent research showed that in 1917 he had been awarded the Military Medal and by 1939 he was employed as a colliery blacksmith in a small village near Bishop Auckland in County Durham.

Furthermore, another three of the group were awarded the Military Medal. However, it is evident that being commissioned or being awarded a gallantry medal had not given the men any great advantage for life post-war.

What Became of the 126 Soldiers?

Whatever the treatment the men received at No. 34 CCS, all of them survived their wounds of 10 July 1916. Some were transferred to munitions work and those transferred to other regiments. The largest group of twenty-five men were discharged either sick or wounded before the end of the war. Three men, who were physically unfit for further service, were transferred to Class P Reserve. Twenty-one men of the group, those still serving in the Yorkshire Regiment at the end of the war, were transferred to Class Z Reserve. The graph also shows that sixteen of them returned to the front and were killed in action or died of wounds before the end of the war. This was followed by twelve men transferred to the Labour Corps. However, these men were transferred as individuals, not as part of a draft. The soldiers transferred to the Royal Irish Regiment (RIR), ten of those researched, were transferred as part of a larger draft. All their new numbers in the RIR are very close together. Research into the medal rolls of the RIR showed that over 100 men of the Yorkshire Regiment in France were transferred to the RIR in Salonika. One soldier of the study group, Private Thomas Hunwick, probably through sickness became detached from the draft to the RIR. It is unlikely he went to Salonika as an individual reinforcement. He eventually joined the 6th Battalion of the Connaught Rangers, where he was renumbered 6293. He was killed in action with his new unit on 21 June 1917.[10] Thomas is buried in the British Military Cemetery at Struma in Salonika.[11] Nine individuals were transferred to other regiments, so are shown collectively as one group.

Post-War Employment

The next avenue of research was to examine what the survivors did for a living after the war. To achieve meaningful figures on this group the 1939 Register of England and Wales was consulted. By the time the 1939 Register was completed thirty-eight of the men had been killed or died. It proved to be a challenge to identify accurately twenty of the remaining men who were still alive. However, sixty-eight were traced and identified in the 1939 Register. The majority of those traced were employed in coal mining, general labouring, iron and steelworks and iron ore mining, thus following their trade prior to enlistment in 1914.

A free passage scheme to the Dominion of the ex-serviceman's choice was set up in 1920 and they had to fulfil certain criteria to be eligible. In 1919 the Government estimated some 405,000 men would emigrate, however, by March 1923 only 86,027 had taken advantage of the scheme. Three men of the group studied are known to have emigrated, but they did not do so until after the

Government scheme had closed. One of them, William Hunter, a coal miner from Murton Colliery, went on to serve in the Australian Army in the Second World War.[12] With the number of men untraced, another point to consider is that others may have also emigrated.

One man, Private John Batty, a steel mill labourer, identifies himself in 1939 as an invalid unable to work. Despite extensive searches, however, no personal nor pension records appear to have survived and no evidence has been traced of any incapacity, neither was he awarded a 'Silver War Badge' for being discharged sick or wounded. Private Sandy McKenzie described himself as an 'incapacitated war pensioner'. In his case, he was awarded a Silver War Badge, having been discharged sick on 31 January 1919 and in 1922 he spent some time in hospital owing to neurasthenia.

Post-War Deaths

One, Private Albert Barclay from Leeds, was transferred to the 2/8th Battalion, Royal Scots on 30 December 1916. He was home on leave from Dublin when he was admitted to East Leeds Hospital on 4 July 1917. Diagnosed with pulmonary tuberculosis, he was discharged on 5 April 1918. He received a War Pension of 27 shillings and sixpence a week, died in May 1920 and is buried in Leeds Cemetery.[13]

Although not part of the study group, Quartermaster Sergeant J. Wadsworth died on 6 August 1925.

Between 1930 and 1970 sixty-five men died. The numbers were fairly equal in each decade, until with the passage of time, they became smaller as those surviving reduced. Possibly the last to die was Sergeant Anthony Hunter, whose death was recorded in the December quarter of 1988 at the age of 93. However, this may not be accurate as there are twenty deaths that could not be confirmed owing to common first and surnames. The second graph illustrates the age of the men when they died post-war. Many had been wounded more than once. It was expected that most would have died soon after the war ended. However, the research shows that the majority lived until old age. Whether they died of war-related injuries is unknown as it would be economically prohibitive to purchase the death certificate for each man.

This has been an attempt to examine the health and social outcomes of 126 soldiers wounded during the attack on Contalmaison on 10 July 1916, and to understand the post-war lives of those who survived. The soldiers under study came from pre-war regulars, regular reservists, special reservists, pre-war Territorials, Kitchener Volunteers and those who enlisted under Lord Derby's recruiting scheme. Among those researched are at least five young boys – two 16-year-olds and three aged 17 – who were under recruiting age when they enlisted and there was also one soldier who was over the age of enlistment, none of whom should have been in the army. There are four gallantry award winners. However, there are a number of absentees and deserters. Furthermore, others were commissioned from the ranks to command men in the field. Yet, the majority of those in the study were average soldiers ready to do what was required of them. Some, having recovered from their wounds, returned to the front, only to be killed in action or die of wounds later in the war. In other cases, they were wounded a second or even a third time. Most of the soldiers were 'Kitchener Volunteers', and are considered to have patriotically answered Kitchener's call for volunteers. The truth may well be many had enlisted to escape the conditions of employment in the steelworks and the iron mines of Teesside and the coal fields of Northumberland and Durham. Others would have been encouraged to enlist by offers of half their wage paid to families as long as they were in the army. The research evidence shows that lightly wounded men were often very quickly returned to service at the front and some were killed in action. However, the longevity of most of the group was a surprising factor, with 40 per cent living beyond retirement age. Thirty-two per cent died before retirement age. Deaths for 15 per cent could not be traced and only 13 per cent were war deaths.

As was stated earlier, a total of 1,912 other ranks were traced as having enlisted into or embarked with both battalions in August 1915, with 926 found in the 8th Battalion and 964 in the 9th Battalion. A further twenty-two men were traced as landing on 25 August 1915, but their records do not indicate their original battalion. Most of these transferred to the Royal Flying Corps. Of the original total, 515 men were killed, died of wounds or sickness before the war ended; that is 26.9 per cent. Five hundred and forty-seven men were discharged or transferred to various reserve categories or 28.6 per cent. Those transferred to Class Z Reserve made up the largest group: 732 of the original men who embarked remained to be classed as fit enough to be called up if needed, that is 38.2 per cent. The remainder are made up of various small categories. Thus, thirty men who had deserted were still missing and fifteen were still serving at the time the medal rolls were compiled in 1920. Thirty-one had been commissioned from the ranks. Research carried out in the Ministry of Pension ledgers revealed that a number of men died from their wounds and disabilities during the 1920s. Some men applied for pensions and had their claims rejected, but the record cards give no indication as to why this was.

For some there may have been the opportunity to meet with old comrades through either the Regimental Old Comrades Association or a battalion OCA. However, research in the Regimental Museum reveals one photograph of a meeting of the 8th Battalion old comrades. This took place in May 1958. Searches of the local press between 1920 and 1939 record many meetings, particularly of the Territorial OCA, but like all old soldiers the 8th and 9th Battalions simply faded away.

Old Comrades Association, 8th Battalion, 1958.

Gallantry Awards to Officers, NCOs and Men of the 8th and 9th (Service) Battalions of Alexandra, Princess of Wales's Own Yorkshire Regiment, The Green Howards

Victoria Cross

Temporary Second Lieutenant Donald Simpson Bell, 9th Battalion, Horseshoe Trench, 5 July 1916

For most Conspicuous bravery. During an attack a very heavy enfilade fire was opened on the attacking company by a hostile machine gun. Second Lieutenant Bell immediately, and on his own initiative, crept up a communication trench, and then followed by a Corporal Colwill and Private Batey rushed across the open under very heavy fire and attacked the machine gun, shooting the firer with his revolver and destroying the gun and personnel with bombs.

This very brave act saved many lives and ensured the success of the attack. Five days later this gallant officer lost his life performing a similar act of bravery.

Lieutenant Donald Simpson-Bell VC, 9th Battalion.

12067 Private William Short, 8th Battalion, Munster Alley, 6 August 1916

For most Conspicuous bravery. He was foremost in the attack, bombing the enemy with great gallantry when he was severely wounded in the foot. He was urged to go back, but refused and continued to throw

Private William Short VC, died 7 August 1916.

bombs. Later his leg was shattered by a shell and he was unable to stand, so he lay in the trench adjusting detonators and straightening the pins of bombs for his comrades.

He died before he could be carried out of the trench. For the last eleven months he had always volunteered for dangerous enterprises and has always set a magnificent example of bravery and devotion to duty.

13820 Sergeant William McNally MM and Bar, 8th Battalion, River Piave and Vazzola, 27–29 October 1918

For most conspicuous bravery and skilful leading during the operations on 27 October 1918 across the Piave, when his company was most seriously hindered in its advance by heavy machine-gun fire from the vicinity of some buildings on a flank. Utterly regardless of personal safety, he rushed the machine-gun post single handed, killing the team and capturing the gun. Later, at Vazzola on 29 October 1918, when his company, having crossed the Monticano River, came under heavy rifle fire and machine gun fire. Sergeant McNally immediately directed the fire of his platoon against the danger point while he himself crept to the rear of the enemy's position. Realising a frontal attack would mean heavy losses, he unaided, rushed the position, killing or putting to flight the garrison and capturing the machine-gun. On the same day, when holding a newly captured ditch, he was strongly counter-attacked from both flanks. By his coolness and skill in controlling the fire of his party, he frustrated the attack, inflicting heavy casualties on the enemy. Throughout the whole operations his innumerable acts of gallantry set a high example to his men and his leading was beyond all praise.

Sergeant Billy McNally VC MM & Bar. (*Murton History Society*)

CBE Military Division

Major and Brevet Lieutenant Colonel Temp Brigadier General H.G. Holmes, *London Gazette* (LG), 3 June 1919

Distinguished Service Order

Lieutenant Colonel Miles Roland Charles Backhouse DSO, Northumberland Hussars, Commanding 8th Battalion, Yorkshire Regiment

Bar to the Distinguished Service Order

Major Anthony Barnes, 9th Battalion, LG, 14 November 1916
For conspicuous gallantry in action, when in command of two companies he held his own with great determination for thirty-six hours and later recaptured a lost position.

Bar to the Distinguished Service Order, LG, 3 June 1918
Birthday Honours. No citation available.

Captain William F. Greenwood, 9th Battalion, LG, 2 December 1918 (Italy)
For conspicuous gallantry and devotion to duty when in charge of a raiding party. The main body losing direction, he penetrated the enemy's position with two men. He cleared out a number of dug-outs and shelters, killing all who resisted, and eventually returned with twelve prisoners. By his personal initiative and daring he prevented the raid being a failure and achieved a partial success.

Major Reginald Charles Grellet, 9th Battalion, LG, 18 March 1918
He led his battalion through heavy shell fire and assisted both in the capture and defence of the furthest objective. By his determination and by his energy, coolness and judgement, he raised the highest enthusiasm among his men. As a result of his organisation, the Battalion within a short period took over and maintained with the highest spirit, a new portion of the line under most difficult conditions.

Major (acting Lieutenant Colonel) Reginald Seton Hart, Notts & Derby Regiment, Commanding 9th Battalion, Yorkshire Regiment, LG, 18 March 1918
When in command of the Battalion, by his personal intervention at critical moments, by his energy and courage and by the excellent arrangements and determination, the hostile defence was broken and the position captured and maintained against counter-attacks. Owing to his fine skill and organising powers, his battalion was, after a short period, ready to take over a portion of the line well beyond the original objective.

Bar to the Distinguished Service Order, LG, 8 March 1919
For conspicuous gallantry during the attack on Beaurevoir on 5 October 1918, the advance on Honnechy 9 October and the capture of St Benin on 10 October. Throughout the whole operations from 5 to 11 October 1918, he led his battalion with great skill and judgement. On more than one occasion when his battalion was held up by strong enemy resistance, he personally led his men in the attack, and the success of the operations was largely due to his leadership.

Lieutenant (Acting Captain) Bertram Lamb Pearson MC, 8th Battalion, LG, 25 August 1917

For conspicuous gallantry and devotion to duty in leading his Company to their objective with great skill over difficult ground. He personally killed four of the enemy with his revolver and after being wounded for the second time, he lay in a shell hole giving all the necessary orders until he fainted from loss of blood. He set a fine example of pluck and skilful leadership.

Captain Joseph T. Shaw, 8th Battalion, LG, 2 April 1919 (Italy)

No citation available.

Major (Temp Lieutenant Colonel) Philip Edmund Vaughan, Worcestershire Regiment, Commanding 8th Battalion, LG, 22 September 1916

For conspicuous gallantry in action. After a long advance under very heavy fire, his Battalion was held up by wire, but with another Officer he forced his way through, got his men into a village, consolidated and held his position there and captured over 150 prisoners and ten machine guns.

Captain (temp Major) Bertram Charles Maximilian Western, East Lancashire Regiment attached 8th Battalion, LG, 22 September 1916

For conspicuous gallantry in action. After a long advance over the open under heavy machine gun fire, he assisted his CO to force a way through wire. They led the men on to their position there capturing over 150 prisoners and ten machine guns.

Military Cross

Captain E.E. Appleyard, General List, Late 9th Battalion, LG

No citation available.

Second Lieutenant William Harold Armitage, 9th Battalion, LG

For conspicuous gallantry. He led out a wire cutting party before an attack on the enemy trenches, and although hampered by the enemy's searchlights and 'Very' lights, successfully cut the wire. Two nights previously he had helped a wounded man back from the wire.

Lieutenant F.G. Batty 8th Battalion, LG, 3 June 1918

Birthday Honours. No citation available.

Captain Wilfred Lawrence Blow, 9th Battalion, LG, 8 March 1919
At Belle view Farm on 5 October 1918, he led his company with great skill and gallantry, capturing the farm and taking 30 prisoners. On 9 October at St Benin, he made a most daring and valuable reconnaissance of the line, getting across and only returning when held up by an enemy post.

Captain Charles Henry Blyth Botting, 9th Battalion
For conspicuous gallantry in action. He led his men with great courage and initiative to their objective. Later he led a daring bombing attack, killing 60 of the enemy and capturing 120 prisoners.

Captain Evelyn Boys, 8th Battalion, LG, 19 November 1917
In an attack he captured, consolidated and held some strong points with his company and when his Commanding Officer and Adjutant were wounded he took over command of his Battalion. He showed great courage and ability.

Captain John S.A. Bunting, Special Reserve attached 8th Battalion (after leaving the 8th Battalion)
For conspicuous gallantry and devotion to duty. When in command of a Company, he resisted for twenty-four hours repeated attacks of the enemy, inflicting great losses on them. In the rear guard action on subsequent days he rallied his men with skill and courage until finally wounded.

Lieutenant (Temp Captain) W.E. Bush, 8th Battalion, LG, 1 January 1918
New Year's Honours award. No citation available.

Bar to the Military Cross, LG, 2 April 1919
No citation available.

Lieutenant Peter Miles Courage, 9th Battalion, LG, 25 November 1916
For conspicuous gallantry in Action. Accompanied by one man he rushed six of the enemy and took them prisoners. He has on many previous occasions done very fine work.

Bar to the Military Cross, LG, 20 December 1916
For conspicuous gallantry in Action. He led a clearing party with great courage and skill, single handed, capturing 12 prisoners in a cellar. He has on many previous occasions done very fine work.

Second Lieutenant Ian R. Edwards-Crate, 9th Battalion, LG, 2 December 1918
For conspicuous gallantry and resource during a raid. His party having become scattered by artillery fire at the commencement, he eventually found himself in the enemy's front line, where he killed a number of the enemy singlehanded. Prior to the raid, he had done excellent patrolling up to the enemy's defences and brought back information of great value to his Commanding Officer in forming plans for the raid. He did splendidly.

Second Lieutenant Walter Rayes Gamble, 9th Battalion, LG
For conspicuous gallantry in Action. He led the assault with the greatest dash and courage after his senior officer had been wounded.

Second Lieutenant Thomas Richard Gibson, 8th Battalion, LG, 25 November 1917
For conspicuous gallantry and devotion to duty. During heavy shelling and repeated counter-attacks, he behaved with utmost gallantry reorganising his men and leading them to counter-attack. Though wounded he again collected men for a fresh attack which he gallantly led until disabled by a second wound.

Captain William Foster Greenwood, 9th Battalion, LG, 1 January 1918
New Year's Honours. No citation available.

Second Lieutenant Lawrence Hart 8th Battalion, LG, 3 June 1919
Birthday Honours. No citation available.

Second Lieutenant Charles Thomas Hepworth, 8th Battalion, LG, 12 November 1917
He showed great courage in patrol work after the occupation of the objective. Later, with a working party he dug a long communication trench under continuous shell fire and, by his foresight and leadership, got his party back without casualties.

Second Lieutenant Harold Spurgeon Hobby, Special Reserve attached 9th Battalion, LG
For conspicuous gallantry and devotion to duty in taking charge of his company and completely reorganising it after the Commander had become a casualty. Although twice wounded, he refused to leave the line and remained until the Battalion was retired, displaying great ability and cheerfulness in spite of his wounds and setting a splendid example to his men.

Captain Gerald Norman Hunnybun, 9th Battalion, LG, 1 Jan 1918
New Year's Honours. No citation available.

Lieutenant Arthur Clament Jardine, 9th Battalion, LG
He took over command and handled his company with great ability, when his Company Commander was wounded, and reached the objective under heavy shell fire and made a strong point. He greatly inspired his men by his cheerfulness in the face of great difficulties.

Second Lieutenant Charles William Jones, Special Reserve attached 8th Battalion, LG
For conspicuous gallantry and devotion to duty. He went out in broad daylight and carried out a lengthy reconnaissance, furnishing a valuable report. He has on many previous occasions done fine work.

Second Lieutenant John Thomas Lakin, 8th Battalion, LG, 25 August 1917
For conspicuous gallantry and devotion to duty in commanding his Company, when all the Officers had become casualties. He showed great ability and initiative in organising his men and consolidating the captured position; and the following day, when his trenches were almost obliterated by hostile shell-fire, he exposed himself recklessly, encouraging his men by his disregard of danger.

Lieutenant (Temp Captain) Eric Noel Lampart, Special Reserve attached 8th Battalion, LG
Birthday Honours. No citation available.

Second Lieutenant Herbert Owen Rowland Lewis, 9th Battalion, LG
He led his company with great courage and success when the other officers became casualties; he repaired a strong point. He proved himself to be a very gallant leader throughout the operations.

Second Lieutenant George Muschamp Lister, 8th Battalion, LG, 26 September 1916
For conspicuous gallantry during operations. He led a party of volunteers into the enemy's position, bombed his way along the trench and captured an important point. He inflicted considerable losses on the enemy and took some prisoners before he was wounded.

Captain Frederick Currer Miller, 8th Battalion, LG, 19 November 1917
He led his company with conspicuous skill and courage and set his men a splendid example. He rendered valuable service to the Battalion when his commanding Officer and Adjutant were wounded.

Bar to the Military Cross, LG
Second Lieutenant Norman M. Miller, 8th Battalion, LG

Second Lieutenant H. Oldfield, 8th Battalion, LG, 13 September 1918
For conspicuous gallantry and devotion to duty in command of one platoon of a raiding party composed of his own and two other parties. When the other two parties were checked, this officer led his party with great skill and initiative and managed to enter his objective from the rear. This completely changed the situation and directly resulted in the capture of eleven prisoners who were taken by this officer personally. Throughout the operation he showed marked gallantry and powers of leadership.

Lieutenant Bertram Lamb Pearson, 8th Battalion, LG
For conspicuous gallantry in action. He reorganised and consolidated the position under very heavy fire, greatly assisting in repulsing three enemy counter-attacks. He set a splendid example to his men.

Lieutenant John Philip Reed, 8th Battalion, LG, 25 August 1917
For conspicuous gallantry and devotion to duty. He led his company in the attack with exceptional skill and courage, consolidating under heavy machine-gun fire and maintaining cheerfulness under trying circumstances, which fully inspired the morale of his men.

Captain Arthur Valentine Richardson, 8th Battalion, LG, 1 January 1917
New Years Honours. No citation available.

Bar to the Military Cross, LG, 25 May 1917
For conspicuous gallantry and devotion to duty. He rushed the enemy's position with great dash and succeeded in capturing sixty prisoners. Later, with a few men he cut off 100 of the enemy who surrendered.

Second Lieutenant Arthur Beverley Hepworth Roberts, 9th Battalion, LG
For conspicuous gallantry. He was one of a party which successfully raided the enemy trenches, and showed great coolness and judgement in directing his men. Two nights previously he had done good work reconnoitring the enemy's position. He also helped two wounded officers to get back to our lines.

14958 Company Sergeant Major Archibald Robson, 8th Battalion, LG, 26 September 1916
For conspicuous gallantry and good work during operations. He organised a continuous supply of bombs, sandbags etc. for the captured position. He was for five hours under heavy shell-fire and at times exposed to rifle and machine gun fire. Later he did other fine work.

Second Lieutenant Maurice Geoffrey Robson, 9th Battalion, LG, 18 July 1917
For conspicuous gallantry and devotion in command of a raid on enemy trenches. His party being held up by hostile wire, he proceeded with one man only and under heavy fire, along the enemy trench. His personal courage and coolness in patrol work has always been of great encouragement to his men.

Bar to the Military Cross, LG, 25 August 1917
For conspicuous gallantry and devotion to duty in advancing again and again under deadly machine-gun fire and rifle fire in order to ascertain the position of our line. He also went forward under similar heavy fire and brought in a wounded man at whom hostile snipers were firing. Whilst doing so he was twice wounded.

Second Lieutenant Joseph Summerville, 8th Battalion, LG
Bar to the Military Cross, LG, 18 January 1918, Citation, LG, 23 April 1918
For conspicuous gallantry and devotion to duty in making two separate reconnaissances in daylight of enemy strong points, 700 yards in front of our wire. On each occasion he brought back valuable information.

Second Lieutenant George William Sutcliffe, 9th Battalion, LG, October 1919
At Beaurevoir on 5 October 1918 when his Company Commander was killed, he assumed command and handled his Company with the greatest skill and gallantry, consolidating his line under very heavy machine-gun fire.

Second Lieutenant Leonard Johnson Taylor, 9th Battalion, LG, Oct 1919
At Beaurevoir on 5 October 1918 when his Company Commander was killed and he received orders to with draw from an untenable position, he displayed marked skill and gallantry, consolidating his line under very heavy machine gun fire. During the period 5–10 October during which time the Battalion was constantly in action, his conduct was of a very high order.

Captain John Tilly, 8th Battalion, LG, 19 November 1917
When in command of his Company, he held the line under very heavy fire. He showed great coolness and resource during enemy counter-attacks.

Captain George Kenneth Thompson, 9th Battalion, LG, 14 November 1917
For conspicuous gallantry and ability. Although hampered by searchlights and 'Very' lights, he led, with great dash and determination, a successful attack on the enemy trenches.

Bar to the Military Cross, LG, 16 September 1918
For conspicuous gallantry and devotion to duty. This Officer displayed splendid initiative and skill as Intelligence Officer throughout the fighting until wounded. He worked his scouts with ability and by personal reconnaissances obtained important information. On one occasion after he had under heavy fire taken important information to Brigade Headquarters, he found and rallied seventy men and took up a position on the high ground protecting a threatened flank which enabled the line to hold on till the evening.

Captain Arthur Ravesley Thomson, 8th Battalion, LG
For conspicuous gallantry in action. He rallied his men, led a bombing attack and showed great coolness and skill in holding his particular part of the defences against all opposition.

Second Lieutenant Clement Watson, 8th Battalion, LG
For conspicuous gallantry during operations. After being shelled heavily all night he repulsed an attack on a sap-head. When attacked again two hours later, he waited till the enemy were within thirty yards and then destroyed a party of fifty of them. Later he did other fine work and set a splendid example of courage and determination throughout.

Second Lieutenant J.W. Wilkinson, 8th Battalion, LG
No citation available.

Second Lieutenant George Mellor Wolstenholme, 9th Battalion, LG, 19 November 1917
He was in charge of a party carrying material to the front line and, in spite of heavy hostile fire, by his personal example and energy, he succeeded in delivering all the material.

Distinguished Conduct Medal

17805 Private Jonathan A. Aspinall, 8th Battalion, LG, 22 September 1916, Sunderland

For conspicuous gallantry during an advance. Although twice wounded he continued to push on until wounded a third time. He exhibited the greatest bravery and devotion and set a fine example to all with him.

16784 Private Joseph Batey, 9th Battalion, LG, 22 September 1916, Spennymoor

For conspicuous gallantry and devotion. An Officer observing that an enemy machine gun was holding up a company during an attack, Private Batey crept out with the officer and another man, under heavy fire and over open ground and put the gun and team out of action, thus saving the situation.

14979 Private Walter Beardmore, 8th later 13th Battalion, LG, 3 September 1918, Leamside

For conspicuous gallantry and devotion to duty. This man with another was a stretcher-bearer. These two continually crossed an open gap of about 50 yards, swept by fire, attending to wounded and carrying them away. On another occasion they volunteered to fetch water from a water point exposed to fire, and although a water can was shot out of their hands while filling it, they managed to bring back three cans full to their company, who were urgently in need of it.

13704 Company Sergeant Major George Bird, 9th Battalion, LG, 6 February 1918, Brandon Colliery

For conspicuous gallantry and devotion to duty. He maintained communication between the battery and an observation post throughout the operations. The line was continuously cut, but he repeatedly went out and repaired it, often under a heavy barrage. It was entirely owing to his courage and resource that valuable information was sent back at a critical period.

3/9475 Sergeant Orlando Bolland, 8th Battalion, LG, 30 October 1918, Northallerton

For conspicuous gallantry and devotion to duty during a raid. He rendered his platoon commander great assistance in reorganising the right party, which had become scattered by heavy rifle and machine-gun fire. He then went on with his platoon commander and attacked and killed an enemy post of three men. He then joined the centre party, who were meeting with heavy resistance, and rendered great help. Throughout the raid he showed great courage and ability.

14496 Private Edward E. Brick, 9th Battalion, LG, 15 March 1916, Battersea
For conspicuous gallantry. Corporal Hodgson and Private Brick were with a party which most successfully raided the enemy's trenches, although hampered by searchlights and 'Very' lights. About twenty of the enemy were killed.

13778 Private Charles Chapman, 8th Battalion, attached 176th Tunnelling Coy, RE, LG, 27 July 1916, South Bank
For conspicuous gallantry. When the enemy exploded a mine which buried an officer and some men, he at once ran up without arms or equipment, regardless of heavy fire and bombing and succeeded in rescuing three men. He only ceased his gallant work when ordered back.

13873 Private Robert W. Codling, 8th Battalion, LG, 22 January 1916, Tyne Dock
For conspicuous gallantry near Rue Du Bois 21 December 1915, when, under heavy fire and in the face of rifle grenades he returned to a wounded comrade and brought him in. Later in the day he joined a patrol and searched under heavy fire for his platoon officer, who had failed to return.

13055 Company Sergeant Major William Coleman MM, 9th Battalion, LG, 2 December 1919, Eston
At Honnechy crossing on 9 October 1918, he displayed great gallantry and courage in attacking the position under heavy machine-gun fire. It was largely due to his behaviour that his company reached their objective successfully. Subsequently, at St Benin on 10 October, he led his men with great dash through a heavy barrage of shell fire, and showed great ability in assisting to consolidate the position after it was captured.

15958 Lance Corporal Harrison Colwill, 9th Battalion, LG, 22 September 1916, Hetton-le-Hole
For conspicuous gallantry and devotion. An Officer observing that an enemy machine gun was holding up a company during an attack, Lance Corporal Colwill crept out with the officer and another man, under heavy fire and over open ground and put the gun and team out of action, thus saving the situation.

13364 Sergeant Ernest Crowther, 9th Battalion, LG, 15 March 1916, Bradford
For conspicuous gallantry when he was one of a party which though hampered by the enemy's searchlights and 'Very' lights, successfully cut the enemy wire previous to a raid on his trenches. He also joined in the raid with great dash.

15201 Corporal Alfred Danby, 8th Battalion, LG, 6 February 1918, Acomb
For conspicuous gallantry and devotion to duty when in charge of the battalion signallers and runners. He carried an important message to all the companies of his battalion immediately before the attack under heavy shell fire, and afterwards kept the lines repaired under continuous fire. He set a splendid example of indifference to danger.

12381 Company Sergeant Major George E. Dent, 8th Battalion, LG, 3 September 1919, Sheffield
During the period 26 February to 14 September 1918 he has performed his duties with a zeal which cannot be too highly praised. On 15 June 1918 and on several separate occasions during raids when the company has been in the line he has, at great personal risk, visited the company posts, etc., during severe enemy retaliatory bombardments. He is most efficient when out of the line, and under fire inspires confidence by his exceptional coolness.

13272 Private John Dixon, 9th Battalion, LG, 15 March 1916, Middlesbrough
For conspicuous gallantry when he was one of a party which though hampered by the enemy's searchlights and 'Very' lights, successfully cut the enemy wire previous to a raid on his trenches. He also joined in the raid with great dash.

14927 Sergeant Arthur Dockray, 9th Battalion, LG, 11 December 1916, Leeds
For conspicuous gallantry in action. With three men he rushed and enemy machine-gun, thereby ensuring the success of the Infantry attack.

3/9005 Sergeant William Gardner, 8th Battalion, LG, 21 October 1918, Middlesbrough
For conspicuous gallantry and devotion to duty, and good work both in and out of the line, for the past three years. He invariably displayed the greatest coolness and courage, and his devotion to duty has been at all times most marked.

11984 Private Arthur Gething, 9th Battalion, LG, 15 March 1916, Middlesbrough
For conspicuous gallantry when he was one of a party which though hampered by the enemy's searchlights and 'Very' lights, successfully cut the enemy wire previous to a raid on his trenches. He also joined in the raid with great dash.

3/8899 Company Sergeant Major John Goodison, 9th Battalion, LG, 1 January 1919, Middlesbrough
During the period 26 February to 14 September 1918, he has always displayed conspicuous gallantry in action and has rendered excellent service by his

example of leadership. He has rendered invaluable service to the battalion by his personal example.

Bar to the Distinguished Conduct Medal, LG, 26 February 1920
At Beaurevoir on 5 October 1918 he showed conspicuous gallantry in leading his men under very heavy machine-gun fire. After his company officers had been killed he assumed command of his company and led them to the objective with great dash. Throughout the operations he set a fine example of cheerful courage.

17889 Corporal William Hodgson, 9th Battalion, LG, 15 March 1916, Wheatley Hill
For conspicuous gallantry. Corporal Hodgson and Private Brick were with a party which most successfully raided the enemy's trenches, although the advance was hampered by searchlights and 'Very' lights. About twenty of the enemy were killed.

11525 Company Sergeant Major Edward L. Homer MM, LG, 25 February 1920, Middlesbrough
During the period 26–29 October 1918 in the Piave Battle, he showed great skill and conspicuous gallantry in carrying out his duties. When all Officers of his company except his Company Commander had become casualties, he took over the duties of second in command. On one occasion he personally led an attack on a strongly fortified post and succeeded in killing or capturing the garrison.

17447 Private Lewis Horton, 9th Battalion at LTMB, LG, 3 September 1918m Radford
For conspicuous gallantry and devotion to duty while in charge of a Stokes mortar in a forward position at the outbreak of an enemy attack. He continued firing his gun at the advancing enemy until they were at very close quarters, and bayoneted two of them who reached his emplacement. Also, he later went back under heavy fire, to the trench and carried back his officer who had been wounded.

243279 Private Stephen C. Husband, originally 11988 9th Battalion, DCM with 5th Battalion, LG, 3 September 1918, Marton
For conspicuous gallantry and devotion to duty. During a heavy engagement he made three journeys for ammunition, although warned that the journey was too hazardous to attempted until dusk. It was due to his courageous conduct that his company was enabled to retain superiority of fire, giving the men confidence and assisting materially in the conduct of the defence.

27486 Private Charles Jefferson, 8th Battalion, LG, 11 March 1920, Bradford
During the period 15 September to 4 November 1918, he has shown great gallantry and devotion to duty. He was especially noticeable during the operations on the Piave. He has never spared himself since joining the battalion in July 1916, and did especially good work in the Ypres salient.

14006 Sergeant, A/CQMS James P. Kelly, 8th Battalion, LG, 21 October 1918, Washington Station
For conspicuous gallantry and devotion to duty, and exceptionally good service for over three years in the field. He always displayed the greatest courage and resource, and set a splendid example to all of devotion to duty.

11546 Private Charles W. Kett, 9th Battalion, LG, 15 March 1916
For conspicuous gallantry when he was one of a party which though hampered by the enemy's searchlights and 'Very' lights, successfully cut the enemy wire previous to a raid on his trenches. He also joined in the raid with great dash.

13133 Private George Knaggs, 8th Battalion, LG, 25 February 1920, Lazenby
In the Piave battle 27–29 October 1918, he showed most conspicuous gallantry throughout the advance. When his company was held up he went back under heavy machine-gun fire and brought up a Lewis gun. Finding difficulty in bringing fire to bear on the enemy he stood and held the gun on his shoulder while it was fired. Later he was wounded but carried on and continued to do most valuable and gallant work.

11577 Sergeant Albert Knowles, 8th Battalion, LG, 25 August 1917
For conspicuous gallantry and devotion to duty. Although wounded in the foot, he remained at duty for sixty hours without rest or sleep, maintaining communication between Brigade and Battalion Headquarters. He has on numerous occasions displayed the utmost fearlessness and devotion to his work, passing frequently through intense barrages to establish communications. Much of the success of his battalion has been due to his splendid initiative under very difficult circumstances.

203156 Private William H. Lowther, 9th Battalion, LG, 15 November 1918, South Bank
For conspicuous gallantry and devotion to duty during a raid. With an officer and party of three he penetrated the enemy's main position. He attacked a large party of the enemy and killed a number of them both with rifle fire and bayonet. He then assisted his officer to clear up two large enemy dug-outs, killing all who

resisted, and afterwards helped him bring back twelve prisoners. Throughout this operation this young Private showed a magnificent fighting spirit and the utmost contempt of danger.

14770 Company Sergeant Major William A. Masheder, LG, 25 August 1917, Pallion, Sunderland
For conspicuous gallantry and devotion to duty. He continually crossed a railway cutting under an intense barrage to carry messages and orders to two detached platoons. He constantly attended wounded under the heaviest fire, and, in short, wherever the bombardment was heaviest or the line being pressed, there was this warrant officer to be found cheering and encouraging the men by his splendid personal example.

12001 Company Sergeant Major William R. Parker, 8th Battalion, LG, 22 September 1916, Hornsea
For conspicuous gallantry and resource in leading his men during an attack after his company officer had been killed and two other officers wounded.

14091 Corporal James Riddle, 9th Battalion, LG, 6 February 1918, South Shields
For conspicuous gallantry and devotion to duty. He showed great initiative in collecting his men under hostile fire and attacking and capturing a strong point, which was held by a large number of the enemy. Throughout twelve days of fighting his courage and determination were a splendid example to his platoon.

14958 Regimental Sergeant Major Archibald Robson MC, 8th Battalion, LG, 3 September 1919, Seaton
During the period 26 February to 14 September 1918, he has shown an unrelaxing keenness in the execution of his duty. Both in the lines and out his personal example has imbued all the NCOs and men with a great regard for spirit-de-corps, courage and devotion to duty. Since joining this battalion in August 1914 he has never missed one day's duty and has held the following appointments: CSM until August 1916, RSM since August 1916 to present date.

11751 Private Arthur Smith, 8th Battalion, LG, 25 August 1917, Newbottle
For conspicuous gallantry and devotion to duty. After taking a leading part in the advance, he assumed command when the final objective was reached, all officers and nearly all NCOs being casualties, reorganised the men, and made all necessary dispositions. Although wounded, he twice carried messages to the forward command post under heavy shell fire, and finally helped a wounded officer to the dressing station before going to the casualty clearing station

on account of his own wounds. He displayed magnificent courage and very great initiative.

16071 Sergeant Marshall Smith MM & Bar, 9th Battalion, LG, 10 January 1920, Snaith, Yorkshire
On 24 October 1918, at Malgani, he behaved with conspicuous gallantry when leading his platoon to attack an enemy strong point. It was chiefly due to his fine example under heavy fire that the enemy were driven out of a strongly prepared position which was holding up the advance.

13277 Corporal Ernest Tewson, 9th Battalion, LG, 4 March 1918, Eston
For conspicuous gallantry and devotion to duty. When the enemy gained a temporary footing on his flank and were threatening his rear, he gallantly held on to his post after his platoon commander had been killed, and only withdrew when the situation was secure and all his ammunition and bombs had been expended. His gallant conduct saved the whole line being turned.

14233 James Thirtle, 8th Battalion, LG, 26 September 1916, West Herrington
For conspicuous gallantry during operations. He was one of a party of volunteers who carried out a bombing attack. He threw bombs with great accuracy, and, when wounded in the leg and hand stuck to his post and threw bombs, though repeatedly urged to go to the dressing station.

33399 Private Ernest H. Webb, 8th Battalion (Formerly Suffolk Regiment), LG, 30 October 1918, Leyton, Essex
For conspicuous gallantry and devotion to duty in a raid. For two nights previously he reconnoitred the ground, often fired at by the enemy and within bombing distance of them, his reports were of the greatest value to the raiding party. In the raid itself he acted as guide for the left party and took a prominent part in the capture of the eleven prisoners. He did splendid service.

Military Medals Awarded to the 8th Battalion of the Yorkshire Regiment

33310	Pte	Ager Reginald A.	LG 17 Dec 1917
12361	Sgt	Appleton John Parker	LG 17 Dec 1917
13108	Pte	Armstrong Edward	LG 16 Aug 1917
12620	Pte	Battle Harry	LG 14 Sep 1916
11569	Pte	Binns David	LG 9 Dec 1916
23366	Pte	Boycott Leonard	LG 9 Dec 1916
12898	Cpl	Boyle Edward	LG 16 Aug 1917

Private Robson MM, kneeling centre. Killed on 9 October 1918. (*Murton History Society*)

Private William Suggitt MM, from Murton. Killed 8 October 1916.

13548	Pte	Breheny James	LG 25 Jan 1918
11492	Sgt	Broad Charles	
12652	Cpl	Burdon Surtees	LG 19 Dec 1917
12838	Cpl	Carroll Thomas	LG 16 Aug 1917
12363	Sgt	Cautley Laurence	LG 9 Dec 1916
12199	L/Cpl	Chamberlain Richard	LG 21 Sep 1916
13489	Cpl	Clarke George	LG 16 Aug 1917
12785	Pte	College Robson	LG 25 Jan 1918
27279	Pte	Currey Ernest L.	LG 17 Dec 1917
16101	Pte	Dobson Heath	LG 17 Dec 1917
241402	Pte	Douglas John R.	LG 29 Mar 1919
241623	Pte	Dowey John M.	LG 17 Dec 1917
16299	Pte	Dowie Robert	LG 17 Dec 1917
42637	Pte	Downie John C.	LG 17 Dec 1917
18609	L/Sgt	Dresser Harold	LG 16 Aug 1917
	Bar		LG 18 Oct 1918
30474	Pte	Drury John W.	LG 17 Dec 1917
21146	Pte	Dryden Edward	LG 29 Mar 1919
11069	Pte	Dryden John	LG 10 Sep 1918

11959	L/Cpl	Duffy John A.	LG 16 Aug 1917
3/8875	Pte	Duffy Thomas	LG 11 Nov 1916
12815	CSM	Farrelly George	LG 29 Mar 1919
25951	Sgt	Gamble John W.	LG 25 Jan 1918
15744	Pte	Gill Albert	LG 56 Jan 1917
9216	A/CSM	Gower E.	LG 30 May 1919
235509	Sgt	Gregory Harry F.	LG 29 Mar 1919
14244	Pte	Hanlon John	LG 16 Aug 1917
17804	Pte	Hendry William	LG 17 Dec 1917
10872	L/Cpl	Hill John	LG 14 Dec 1917
13333	Cpl	Hill Joseph	LG 23 Aug 1916
41589	Pte	Hooker Samuel	LG 17 Sep 1917
11525	CSM	Homer Edward L.	LG 9 Dec 1916
42563	L/Cpl	Humphrey William H.	LG 29 Mar 1919
19313	Cpl	Jackson Robert	LG 16 Aug 1917
17800	Pte	Kennedy John	LG 9 Dec 1916
12047	Sgt	Lane George R.	LG 14 Sep 1916
	Bar		LG 28 Sep 1917
26401	Pte	Lee Herbert	LG 29 Mar 1919
14089	Cpl	McCallum Simon	LG 21 Nov 1919
18630	Pte	McLean Frank W.	LG 9 Dec 1917
	Bar		LG 17 Dec 1917
13820	Sgt	McNally William	LG 23 Aug 1916
	Bar		LG 23 Feb 1918
42876	Pte	Middleton Hilton	LG 17 Dec 1917
14759	Sgt	Miller Zachariah	LG 3 Jun 1919
14068	Pte	Mitchell Jack	LG 29 Mar 1919
12757	L/Cpl	Morgan William A.	LG 1 Sep 1916
13986	Pte	Orton Joseph	LG 17 Dec 1917
14611	Sgt	Parkin John M.	LG 14 Sep 1916
26256	L/Cpl	Peacock James S.	LG 29 Mar 1919
26136	Pte	Pickard Frederick	LG 9 Dec 1916
22959	Pte	Plowman Henry	LG 30 January 1918
8462	Pte	Poulter Charles	LG 29 Mar 1919
41590	L/Cpl	Ranger Norman F.L.	LG 29 Mar 1919
34169	Pte	Robinson Thomas	LG 29 Mar 1919
24383	Pte	Storr Percy W.	LG 17 Dec 1917
11811	Pte	Saul Charles D.	LG 16 Aug 1917
265802	Pte	Saverton Joseph	LG 29 Mar 1919
13874	Pte	Sewell Henry	LG 1 May 1917

10757	L/Cpl	Sharp John R.	LG 8 Dec 1916
11821	Sgt	Shires Benjiman	LG 4 Feb 1918
240862	Cpl	Smithson Charles	LG 29 Mar 1919
12662	Pte	Suggitt William	LG 21 Sep 1916
27415	Pte	Sutcliffe Walter	LG 29 Mar 1919
28278	Pte	Thackery James	-----
17572	Cpl	Thompson Thomas	LG 29 Mar 1919
11551	Cpl	Turner James A.	LG 14 Dec 1917
13388	Pte	Watson Stephen G.	LG 16 Aug 1917
12110	Cpl	Williams Thomas	LG 14 Aug 1917
25846	Pte	Williamson R.	LG 29 Mar 1919
14602	Pte	Wilkinson John T.	LG 15 Aug 1916
18332	Cpl	Wood John W.	LG 16 Aug 1917
	Bar		LG 29 Mar 1919
16739	Cpl	Young Thomas	LG 17 Dec 1917

Military Medals Awarded to the 9th Battalion of the Yorkshire Regiment

34370	Pte	Adams Walter J.	LG 22 Jul 1919
36010	L/Cpl	Allison J.S.	LG 24 Jan 1919
266575	Pte	Barrow Edgar R.	LG 24 Jan 1919
34242	Pte	Bassett James S.	LG 24 Jan 1919
15769	Cpl	Bower Alexander	LG 16 Aug 1917
35894	Pte	Brown Thomas	LG 22 Jul 1919
202995	Pte	Buck George	LG 24 Jan 1919
3/8036	Pte	Cannings George F.	LG 24 Jan 1919
	Bar		LG 22 Jul 1919
235473	Sgt	Caygill Richard	LG 22 Jul 1919
33058	L/Cpl	Clark David B.	LG 17 Oct 1919
35898	Pte	Clennell Hugh	LG 19 Aug 1919
12555	Pte	Coleby William S.	LG 17 Dec 1917
13055	CSM	Coleman William	LG 18 Jul 1917
25949	Sgt	Collins Cecil	LG 22 Jul 1919
15908	Pte	Collinson Frederick G.	LG 23 Aug 1916
19788	Sgt	Collinson Joseph H.	LG 17 Dec 1917
	Bar		LG 17 Dec 1917
	Second Bar		LG 17 June 1919
23257	Cpl	Connell Harry	LG 19 Jun 1919
38192	L/Cpl	Copely George F.	LG 22 Jul 1919
10610	L/Cpl	Craddock Thomas	LG 19 Dec 1916

28275	Sgt	Dawson Bertie	LG 19 Jun 1919
3/9065	Sgt	Dolan James	LG 12 Sep 1916
12918	Pte	Doughty Alfred	LG 17 Dec 1917
17691	Pte	Dring George	LG 23 Aug 1916
17883	Pte	Dyson Albert E.	LG 22 Jul 1919
17794	Pte	Ferguson Thomas E.	LG 17 Dec 1917
20291	Pte	Flint James W.	LG 16 Aug 1917
38954	Pte	Geggie Robert	LG 22 Jul 1919
15234	Pte	Gillespie Hector	LG 17 Dec 1917
29727	Pte	Gilmore George H.	LG 22 Jul 1919
53584	Pte	Guest Clarence	LG 22 Jul 1919
38490	L/Cpl	Harland William	LG 17 Dec 1917
15465	Pte	Harling Bertram	LG 14 Aug 1917
15321	Pte	Heptinstall Henry	LG 17 Dec 1917
28122	Sgt	Hewgill George	LG 22 Jul 1919
15987	Pte	Hitchen Alfred	LG 23 Aug 1916
42049	Pte	Hobson Ernest	-----
16491	Pte	Hodgson Lionel	LG 25 Jan 1918
3/8686	Cpl	Hoffman Frederick W.	LG 9 Dec 1916
17447	Pte	Horton Lewis, DCM	LG 24 Jan 1919
18233	Pte	Hughes George	LG 17 Dec 1917
28109	L/Cpl	Huller John W.	LG 22 Jul 1919
13992	Pte	Ingleby John H.	LG 25 Jan 1918
38026	Pte	Kidson George W.	LG 19 Jun 1919
13722	Pte	Kirkup Joseph	LG 23 Aug 1916
38476	L/Cpl	Leete Fred	LG 17 Oct 1919
14205	Pte	Little Herbert	LG 12 Sep 1916
17892	Sgt	Lyall John W.	LG 8 Dec 1916
	Bar	CSM	LG 30 May 1919
24372	Pte	Mantle Richard	LG 16 Aug 1917
28175	Pte	Martin Mark	LG 16 Aug 1917
17252	L/Cpl	Maughan John	LG 16 Aug 1917
28228	Pte	McBean John R.	LG 17 Dec 1917
14689	Cpl	Meredith George	LG 9 Dec 1916
14552	Sgt	Messenger Albert	LG 16 Aug 1917
27090	L/Cpl	Mounsey Clifford	LG 16 Aug 1917
33108	Cpl	Nunn Edward	LG 17 Dec 1917
	Bar		LG 17 Dec 1917
3/8839	Sgt	Oglesby Richard	LG 8 Dec 1916
34493	Cpl	Oliver Thomas	LG 19 Jun 1919

3/8430	L/Sgt	Quinn Edward	LG 17 Dec 1917
24931	Pte	Robinson John T.	LG 17 Dec 1917
34278	Pte	Saint George J.	LG 22 Jul 1919
42460	Pte	Sanders Elias	LG 18 July 1917
17901	Sgt	Shields John J.	LG 14 Sep 1916
13274	A/Sgt	Shields Richard T.	LG 19 Jun 1919
14996	L/Sgt	Simpson W.	LG 14 Dec 1917
39279	Pte	Sissons James R.	LG 14 Dec 1917
16071	Sgt	Smith Marshall	LG 16 Aug 1917
	Bar		LG 24 Jan 1919
34394	CQMS	Smith Herbert	LG 16 Dec 1919
15620	Sgt	Stainton John W.	LG 19 Aug 1919
14321	L/Cpl	Stead Frank	LG 22 Jul 1919
38500	Pte	Steel Harold V.	LG 17 Dec 1917
34514	L/Cpl	Stendall John T.	LG 22 Jul 1919
15985	L/Sgt	Stephenson Reginald H.	LG 22 Jul 1919
28187	Pte	Sutcliffe Albert	LG 21 Aug 1917
34518	L/Cpl	Sutton Thomas	LG 17 June 1919
10526	Cpl	Sweetman Thomas	LG 17 Dec 1917
3/8858	CSM	Tait William T.	LG 19 Aug 1919
14445	Pte	Thompson Joseph	LG 12 Dec 1917
12511	Pte	Thompson Ernest	LG 1 Sep 1916
14153	Pte	Turnbull William	LG 16 Aug 1917
	Bar		LG 17 Dec 1917
12595	Cpl	Walker Frederick W.	LG 16 Aug 1917
15267	Sgt	Wilkinson George H.	LG 14 Sep 1916
8470	Sgt	Wilkinson William	LG 22 Jul 1919
11808	Sgt	Williams Albert	LG 18 Oct 1917

Nominal Roll of Officers Known to Have Served with the 8th (Service) Battalion, Alexandra's Princess of Wales's Own, Yorkshire Regiment, The Green Howards

Rank	Name	Initials / First	Commissioned	Remarks	Home
Second Lieutenant Lieutenant	Addinsell	Thomas A.A.	23-Nov-14	F&F 11 Nov 15	Harrow on the Hill
Second Lieutenant	Ainsworth	B.			
Second Lieutenant, Major	Anne	Cawthorne E.I.C.	17-Sep-14	Trf before embarkation Royal Flying Corps. Died 15 Apr 1917, Mikra Memorial Greece	Malton
Second Lieutenant, Lieutenant	Armstrong	J.L.	01-Jan-16	Joined for duty 4 May 17. Wnd 7 Jun 17	
Second Lieutenant, Lieutenant	Ayton	Herbert	20-Sep-16	Formerly 4048 Honourable Artillery Coy F&F 27 Oct 15 Wnd 10 Oct 16	
Captain	Atkinson	Reginald G.H.	15-Mar-15	NWFrontier 2 Dec 14 1/ Yorkshire Regt, O.C. C Company until att 69 Bde H.Q. 8 Jan 18	Green Howards Depot
Major, Lieutenant Colonel	Backhouse	Miles R.C.	03-Oct-14	F&F 5 Oct 1914, Assumed command 1 Oct 17	Norwich
Second Lieutenant	Bailey	H.R.B.	26-Jan-16	Bayonetted by sentry 1 Sept 16. 1917 att 2/5 RW Kent Regt	
Captain	Barmby	A.J.	20-Feb-17	F&F 1 Jul 15, with 7th Lt MiD 4 Jan 17 Army List Nov 18 shows with 8th, MIC shows 2nd 6 Mar 19	Covent Garden Hotel Strand WC 2
Second Lieutenant, Lieutenant	Barrowcliff	Frank	07-Jul-16	F&F 25 Aug 16, Wnd 1 Jan 17. From Artists Rifles PoW 12 Aug 18	

Rank	Name	Initials / First	Commissioned	Remarks	Home
Lieutenant, Captain	Batty	F.G.	06-Nov-15	F&F 2 Oct 15 MiD 11 Dec 17. MC	Birkenhead
Lieutenant, Captain	Bawtree	David E.	27-Mar-15	F&F 4 Oct 15 Relquished Commission 3 Feb 16	Colchester
Second Lieutenant	Bell	Thomas H.A.	20-May-16	F&F 5 Oct 1914, 9468 Cpl 2nd Yorks, St. Sever Cemetery, Rouen DoW 17 Oct 17	Norwood, born Newcastle
Lieutenant	Bennison	Miles	30-Jan-16	KiA 1 Oct 17 Tyne Cot	Middlesbrough
Lieutenant, Captain RE	Besley	E.M.	03-Feb-15	MiD LG 11 Dec 17, Trf Royal Engineers 5 Fld Coy, POW 30 Mar 1918	
Second Lieutenant	Binns	Raymond L.	22-Apr-15	3rd Bn att KiA 10 Jul 16 Becourt Mil Cem	Worcester
Second Lieutenant, Lieutenant	Blunden	William S.	03-Mar-15	F&F 30 Sep 15, Joined 9 Oct 15 trf 11th R Warwickshire Regt	Brighton.
Second Lieutenant, Lieutenant	Bottomley	Charles A.	25-Apr-17	Egypt 6 Dec 15 Formerly Cpl 16/786 1st Bradford Pals, Joined for Duty 29 June 17. Att 69/LTMB	Bradford
Captain, Major	Boys	Evelyn	07-Feb-18	War Diary 16 June 1918. MiD MC	Warford, Kent
Second Lieutenant, Captain	Bright	Harold N.	20-Feb-15	F&F 4 Oct 15	Green Howards Depot
Second Lieutenant	Bruce	Kenneth C.	29-Aug-17	Joined for Duty 23 Oct 17, rejoined 1 Jan 18	Sheffield

Rank	Name	Initials / First	Commissioned	Remarks	Home
Second Lieutenant	Buckle	William	07-Jul-16	DoW 07 Jun 17 Lissjenthjoek Mil Cem	Middlesbrough
Second Lieutenant	Bunting	John S.A.	25-Sep-15	MC to 2nd Battalion	Hampstead
Second Lieutenant	Bush	Hamilton B.	06-May-15	F&F 19 Oct 15, Wnd 21 Sep 16 MC	Highgate, London
Second Lieutenant	Bush	W.E.	26-Jan-16	MC & Bar	
Second Lieutenant	Carr	William G.	20-May-15	F&F 24 Jan 15 Pte 1099 5/ London Regt, F&F 12 Oct 15	Bradford
Second Lieutenant	Clegg	Edward	25-Apr-17	F&F 1 May 16 formerly 104359 Pte R Engineers Joined for Duty 29 June 17. SOS to R Engineers 18 Oct 17	Bradford
Lieutenant	Cole	Ernest	05-Jan-16	DoW 8 Aug 16	Bristol
Lieutenant, Captain	Comber	Norman M.	03-Feb-15	SWB	Leeds University
Lieutenant	Cox	William D.	08-Jul-17	MiD LG 11 Dec 17	Middlesbrough
Lieutenant, Captain and Adjutant, Major	Cranko	Albert C.W.	17-Sep-14	F&F 26 Aug 15, West Indies Regt att	Buckfastleigh
Second Lieutenant	Crichton	Charles J.W.	11-Jan-15	F&F Aug 15 Major 55 TDS RAF	Leamington Spa
Second Lieutenant	Cruit	Kenneth	05-Nov-15	F&F 25 July 16 Trf King's African Rifles,	Liverpool

Rank	Name	Initials / First	Commissioned	Remarks	Home
Second Lieutenant	Crute	Richard R.	26-Apr-17	Formerly 39617 Durham L.I. Joined for Duty 29 June 17	Sunderland
Second Lieutenant	Darling	Alan H.	23-Apr-15	From Northbld Fusiliers, KiA 10 July 16 Buried Becourt Military Cemetery	South Shields
Lieutenant & QM, Captain QM	Delaney	Michael	25-Aug-15	F&F 26 Aug 15. Att HQ 16th Group RAF Captain. Died 29 Mar 1919 Buried Sheffield St Michaell's RC Cem	Middlesbrough
Second Lieutenant	Delius	John Daniel	12-Sep-14	Trf before embarkation 4th Queen's Own Hussars Captain	Harrogate
Second Lieutenant	Dickens	Leonard C.	26-Apr-17	Joined for Duty 29 June 17. Formerly 1341 Cpl 10 London Regt	Wilesden
Second Lieutenant, Captain	Dodgson	Francis	18-Oct-14	F&F 26 Aug 15, C Company, KiA 10 Jul 16	Bovingdon, Herts
Second Lieutenant	Dudley	Arnold T.	29-Jun-16	From Artists Rifles, Wnd 9 Jun 17 MC Wnd 23 Jun 18	York
Lieutenant	Elliston	George S.		F&F 28 Feb 17, R.A.M.C att joined for duty 19 Apr 1918. MC	London W.C. 1
Second Lieutenant, Major	Emerson	Henry O.	24-Nov-14	F&F 26 Aug 15, Trf Machine Gun Corps Major	Thornaby on Tees
Second Lieutenant	Evers	R.		In Regt History not in April 1915 Army List	

Rank	Name	Initials / First	Commissioned	Remarks	Home
Second Lieutenant	Fenton	William V.	08-Feb-15	DoW 16 Sep 15	Heston, Middlesex
Second Lieutenant	Fullerton	Douglas	29-Aug-17	F&F 11 Oct 17, Joined for duty 15 October 17	Gateshead
Second Lieutenant	Gibson	Thomas R.	20-Sep-16	MC	West Hartlepool
Second Lieutenant, Lieutenant	Goldsbrough	Robert W.	30-Nov-14	Captain 38th Bn MGC	Normanton
Second Lieutenant	Graham	Hugh C.		KiA 1 Oct 17 Tyne Cot	Scarborough
Second Lieutenant Lt Colonel	Grellet	Reginald C.	02-Dec-14	F&F 26 Aug 15, DSO, MiD L.G. 4 Jan 17-11 Dec 17.	West Hartlepool
Second Lieutenant	Gregory	James L.		Killed in Ypres 13 May 1917 att 101 Fld Coy RE.	Bradford
Second Lieutenant	Hardcastle	Thomas E.	27-Jun-17	F&F 18 Apr 15 2147 Cpl 5/Yorks, Comm 3/Yorks Wounded accidentally.	Malton
Second Lieutenant	Harper	Frank B.	21-Apr-15	F&F 20 Aug 14, TS/2059 ASC, 1900 L/Cpl 2nd King Edwards Horse, To Army of Occupation 18 Feb 1919.	Lincoln
Lieutenant	Harper	Harry C.	05-Jul-15	F&F 26 Aug 15	
Second Lieutenant	Hart	Lawrence	29-Aug-17	Formerly 4338 & 201485 Seasforth Highlanders, F&F March 16, Joined for Duty 23 Oct 17 MC	Shipley, Yorks
Second Lieutenant, Captain	Helmer	Roy H.	18-Dec-14	MC Trf General List, MiD L.G. 29 May 17, Royal Engineers att Army Signals	Louth, Lincolnshire

Rank	Name	Initials / First	Commissioned	Remarks	Home
Second Lieutenant	Hepworth	Charles T.	19-Jun-17	M.C. F&F 15 Aug 1914, L/ Cpl 3791 12 Lancers. joined for Duty 23 Jun 17.	Norwich
Second Lieutenant, Lieutenant	Heron	John P.	23-Nov-15	M.C. F&F 17 Apr 15, Pte 2099 4/Green Howards, 11th 8th Bns, Patrol 22 Sep 16	Middlesbrough
Second Lieutenant, Captain	Hiley	Frank	05-Jan-15	Formerly Grenadier Guards F&F 4 Oct 15, KiA 3 Feb 18.	Pontefract
Second Lieutenant	Hirons	E.E.	25-Sep-17	Egypt 12 Jul 15 Formerly 40514 Sergeant R Engineers, joined for duty 28 Jan 1918. posted to A Coy. To Army of Occupation 18 Feb 1919	Wellesbourne, Warwick
Second Lieutenant, Lieutenant	Hume Wright	Maurice G.	04-Nov-14	Enl Hampshire Carabineers Aug 1914, F&F 26 Aug 15, KiA 10 Jul 16	Ash Vale, Surrey
Second Lieutenant	Jackson	Albert P.	20-Sep-16	F&F 26 Aug 15 C/Sgt 12433 Wnd 10 Oct 16, Captain Labour Corps	Barry Port, S Wales
Second Lieutenant	James	Arthur	24-Jul-15	To 7th Bn, Died 5 Jan 1917, Guards Cem LesBoeufs	NoK Res Paris
Second Lieutenant, Captain	Jennings	Percy	14-Jan-15	F&F 12 Mar 16, Yorks Regt att RE, South Staffs Regt, R Corps of Sgnals	Harrogate
Second Lieutenant	Jennings	Sidney	14-Jan-15	F&F 26 Aug 15, Lieutenant R.A.F.	Harrogate

Rank	Name	Initials / First	Commissioned	Remarks	Home
Second Lieutenant, Lieutenant	Jennings	Thomas N.	14-Jan-15	F&F 4 Oct 15, Posted to 2nd Bn, Trf East Yorks Regt & R.F.C. R.A.F.	Harrogate
Lieutenant	Jessop	Bernard	03-Feb-15	F&F 26 Aug 15 Trf R Engineers Major	Ilkeston, Derbyshire.
Second Lieutenant, Captain	Jones	Charles W.	12-Oct-15	MC, 3rd Bn att	Bristol
Second Lieutenant, Lieutenant	Killacky	Patrick J.	14-Apr-15	Wnd 21 Sept 16, rejoined 8 May 17	Dublin
Second Lieutenant	Kennington	Alfred E.	29-Aug-17	King's R Rifle Corps, Comm Yorks Regt	Pickering
Second Lieutenant	Lakin	John T.	01-Mar-17	MC Formerly 43794 L/Cpl R Engineers	Banbury
Lieutenant, Captain	Lambert	Eric N.	08-Mar-16	3rd Bn att. MiD L.G. 4 Jan 17, KiA 7 Jun 17	Hove
Second Lieutenant	Larner	Donald St H.	05-May-15	3rd Bn att, SWB. Joined 7 Oct 15	Brixton
Second Lieutenant	Layfield	Sydney		F&F 15 Apr 15, Formerly 2184 Pte 4/Yorkshire Regt. joined for duty 1 Jan 18 posted to A Coy. E131	
Second Lieutenant	Lewis	Herbert O.	24-Apr-17	F&F 14 Jul 16 Formerly 448 5 London Regt. MC	Finchley
Second Lieutenant, Captain	Lister	George M.	22-Jan-15	F&F 26 Aug 15 MC, r4ejoined from Wnds 2 February 17	Sunderland
Second Lieutenant	Lister	William	26-Apr-17	M.C. Joined for Duty 29 June 17	B Scarborough Res Harrogate

Rank	Name	Initials / First	Commissioned	Remarks	Home
Captain	MacDonald	P.B.	05-Dec-14	Relinquished Commission owing to ill health 16 Apr 1915	
Second Lieutenant	Maclean	D. Pyman	22-Nov-16	F&F 5 Jan 17, SWB LG 29 Mar 19	Sleights, N Yorks
Second Lieutenant	McCulloch	Alfred G.		Joined for duty 4 May 17. Later att 8/West Yorkshire Regt	
Second Lieutenant	McNicholas	John H.	25-Apr-17	Joined for Duty 29 June 17. Formerly 26200 Cpl 2nd & 8th Green Howards	Grangetown
Second Lieutenant, Captain	Miller	Frederick C.	08-Feb-15	Led Trench Raid 20 February 17, Trf R Army Medical Corps, Lieutenant Colonel. MC	
Second Lieutenant	Miller	Norman M.	28-Aug-17	F&F 15 Apr 15 Formerly 2121 Tpr Yorkshire Hussars, Joined for duty 17 Oct 17 MC	Middlesbrough
Lieutenant	Millhouse	George	15-May-17		Acton W.3
Second Lieutenant	Mills	James	25-Apr-17	F&F 13 Jul 15 Formerly 14730 Sgt 7/Yorkshire Regt, Joined for Duty 29 June 17. Wnd July 17	Wheatley Hill Co Durham
Captain, Major.	Mintoft	T.C.	28-Dec-14	1st Bn in India 1914, Took command 15 February 17, CO on leave.	York

Rank	Name	Initials / First	Commissioned	Remarks	Home
Second Lieutenant	Mitchell	Wilfred H.	22-Nov-16	F&F 5 Jan 17, To 1st Yorks Afghistan 1919	Linthorpe, Middlesbrough
Major	Monk	John M.	15-May-16	From 1/Worcestershire Regt, F&F 5 Nov 1914, MiD LG 1 Jan 16, MC, att Staff, 197 Bde, Died 24 Oct 1920. Buried Khartoum War Cemetery	Goudhurst, Kent.
Second Lieutenant	Morrison	James H.	26-Apr-17	Joined for Duty 29 June 17	Gateshead
Second Lieutenant	Morton	J.H.	13-May-15		
2nd Lt, Lt, Captain	Nichols	S.K.	01-Feb-15	MC, MiD L.G. 4 Jan 17, 6 Jan 1919 Staff	
Second Lieutenant	Nicholson	C.	27-Sep-15		
Second Lieutenant	Oldfield	H.	29-Aug-17	Joined for Duty 23 Oct 17. MC	
Second Lieutenant Captain	Oakley	Harry L.	20-May-15	MBE, F&F 18 Oct 15 Joined 7 Oct 15. Rejoined from Wnds 2 Feb 17. rejoined 15 Oct 17	York
Second Lieutenant	Oakley	Reginald C.	26-Aug-15	F&F 12 Jul 16, KiA 25 Aug 16	York
Major	Paget	J.B.	23-Sep-14	F&F 26 Aug 15 Railway Transport Officer	Army & Navy Club SW1
Second Lieutenant	Parker	Frederick G.	29-Aug-17	Sgt 10/1367 10/East Yorks & 38693 Northumberland Fus	Hedon Nr Hull

Rank	Name	Initials / First	Commissioned	Remarks	Home
Lieutenant	Parker	Harold	08-Jun-17	F&F July 16, MiD 11 Dec 17 att 101 Fd Coy RE 3 Apr 18 with 1 Cpl +24 Men MiD 11 Dec 17	Birmingham
Second Lieutenant Captain	Parker	William R.	17-Dec-16	F&F 26 Aug 15, Formerly 12001 CSM 8/Yorkshire Reg, DCM Wnd 20 Sep 17	Hornsea
Second Lieutenant	Pearce	George F.	22-Jun-17	F&F 15 Jun 15, Formerley Sgt 4672 9th Lancers, Joined for Duty 23 Jun 17	London
Second Lieutenant	Pearce	H.B.	22-Dec-14		
Captain	Pearson	Bertram L.	19-Nov-16	DSO MC MiD 11 Dec 17	
Second Lieutenant	Pebody	Edward A.	29-Aug-17	Balkans 10 Aug 15 formerly 3198 Pte Bedfordshire Regt, joined for duty 10 Jan 18	Olney, Bucks
Second Lieutenant	Pellow	Edward C.	26-Apr-17	Egypt 30 Aug 15, Cpl 2756 2/London Regt, To York and Lancaster	Par, Cornwall.
Second Lieutenant	Peters	A.J.			
Captain	Picken	Samuel E.	09-Oct-15	R.A.M.C. att joined for duty 14 Dec 17 MC MiD 29 May 17 Posted to 70 Fld Amb 19 Apr 17	Belfast
Second Lieutenant, Lieutenant	Pickering	E.C.	18-Dec-14	F&F July 15 Trf General List	Mansfield
Second Lieutenant, Captain	Player	Eric N.	04-Nov-14	F&F 26 Aug 15, KiA 6 Jun 16	Abberley, Worcester
Captain	Reed	John P.	15-May-17	MC	

Rank	Name	Initials / First	Commissioned	Remarks	Home
Captain, Major	Richardson	Arthur V.	23-Dec-14	F&F 26 Aug 15, MC Trf Royal Munster Fusiliers Major	Wimbourne, Dorset
Lieutenant and Quartermaster	Ridsdale	C.	22-Sep-14	Trf R Defence Corps & Royal Air Force.	Selby
Captain	Riky	J.	24-Sep-14	B Company	
Second Lieutenant	Robinson	P.	09-Jan-15		
Captain	Robinson	Swinburne	18-Oct-14	D Company, To Labour Corps	Haswell, Co Durham
Second Lieutenant	Roddam	Cyril J.	08-Nov-15	F&F 13 Jul 16 Joined for duty 14 Oct 17	Darlington
Lieutenant, Captain	Ross	Alic Wm	08-Jul-17	F&F 25 July 16, Patrol 22 Sep 16, Wnd 10 Oct 16 Rejoined 8 May 17	Sutton Surrey
Second Lieutenant	Rowley	Newton	18-Dec-14	Formerly Private 9484 5th London Regt, KiA 10 Jul 16, Becourt Cem	New Barnet
Second Lieutenant, Captain	Shaw	Joseph T.	17-Jul-16	Joined for duty 4 May 17. DSO	Shipley
Lieutenant,	Sherrard	Noel S.	31-Oct-16	R.A.M.C. att posted to 69 Fld Amb 14 Dec 17	Beccles
Lieutenant, Captain	Simpson	Clifford S.	24-Nov-14	Adjutant 16. KiA 10 Jul 16, Becourt Mil Cem	Liverpool
Second Lieutenant	Smith	H.J.	09-Apr-17	Wnd 20 Sep 17	
Lieutenant, Captain	Sparshott	Charles H.	15-Jul-15	F&F 22 Mar 17, Wounded at Duty 21 Oct 17	

Rank	Name	Initials / First	Commissioned	Remarks	Home
Lieutenant Colonel	Spottiswoode	Charles J.	01-Oct-14	Bt Colonel, First Commanding Officer, resigned owing to ill health.	
Lieutenant Colonel	Stephen	A.J.	12-Oct-14	MiD L.G. 15 Jun 16	
Lieutenant	Storey	Nevill E.O.	14-Oct-15	Formerly Pte 24648 13th Bn Canadian Infantry. 15th Bn att 8th wnd 10 Oct 16	Faynes Co Limerick
Second Lieutenant	Summerscale	Frank	29-Aug-17	F&F 22 Dec 1915 Joined for Duty 23 Oct 17. Formerly 15/860 Private West Yorkshire Regiment	Leeds
Second Lieutenant	Summerville	Joseph	26-Apr-17	F&F 9 Oct 15, Formerly 22504 CSM Durham LI Inverness Copse 17 KiA 29 Oct 1918. MC & Bar	Annfield Plain
Second Lieutenant	Swain	Thomas	24-Sep-15	F&F 16 Jun 16, Died of Wounds 25 July 16 Buried Northallerton	Northallerton
Second Lieutenant	Swain	William	16-Dec-15	F&F 25 Jul 16, 14th Bn att 8th KiA 22 Sep 16	Northallerton
Lieutenant, Captain	Thomson	Arthur R.	16-Apr-15	F&F 26 Aug 15, MC Trf RAF	Wimbledon
Second Lieutenant, Captain	Tilly	John	22-Sep-16	F&F 26 Aug 1815MC KiA 8 Jun 18	Seaton Carew
Major, Lieutenant Colonel	Vaughan	Philip E.	18-Jun-16	Worcester Regt att, F&F Sept 14, MiD LG 4 Jan 17, DSO	London N.W.1.

Rank	Name	Initials / First	Commissioned	Remarks	Home
Second Lieutenant	Vernon	Frank S.	26-Apr-17	Formerly 2478 & 200501 4 KOYLI F&F 13 Apr 15, Joined for Duty 29 June 17, Wnd 20 Sep 17	Wakefield
Second Lieutenant	Wahl	Blauckenberg	01-Mar-17	F & F 27 July 17, To East Yorkshire Regt	Kenhardt Cape Province
Lieutenant	Walker	Leonard	01-Jul-17	F&F 16 Jun 16, Formerly 3244 Pte OTC	Woking
Captain	Walter	Weever K.	03-Dec-15	3rd Bn att 2nd & 8th Bns, F&F 4 Jan 15	Cape Province SA
Second Lieutenant	Watson	Clement V.	07-May-15	F&F 20 Oct 15 Joined 7 Oct 15	
Second Lieutenant, Lieutenant	Waud	Frederick C.	12-Jan-16	From Artists Rifles, Capt Comdg Prisoner of War Coy 1/11/1918	Caton Hall, Lancaster
Captain	Webb	Thomas L.	14-Nov-14	A Company	Richmond, N Yorks
Major, Lieutenant Colonel	Western	Bertram C.M.	22-Aug-16	DSO, 2nd East Lancashire Regt att. F&F 6 Nov 14.	Elgin, Cape Province, S Africa
Second Lieutenant	Wellesly	Eric G.	01-Feb-15	KiA 21 Dec 15	Honiton, Devon
Second Lieutenant	Wheeler	George H.	01-Mar-17	Joined for duty 29 May 17	Stoke Newington
Second Lieutenant	Whitehead	G.M.C.	16-Sep-14	Relinquished Commission 25 Aug 1915	
Second Lieutenant	Whitehead	M.J.	25-Jan-17		
Lieutenant	Whiting	H.J.	01-Jul-17		
Lieutenant	Widdowson	S.W.	01-Jul-17		

Rank	Name	Initials / First	Commissioned	Remarks	Home
Second Lieutenant	Wilkinson	J.W.		D Company Patrols Piave 24 Jan 18 MC	
Lieutenant	Williams	W.J.		2nd East Lancashire Regt att, Joined for duty 17 June 17 to B Coy. To UK Sick 30 Jan 1918	Kennsington
Second Lieutenant	Withington	Arthur G.	23-Nov-16	Formerly 4790 4/Yorkshire Regt F&F 20 Jan 17Wnd 14 Apr 17	Redcar
Second Lieutenant	Wilson	R.F.	07-Jul-16	Wnd 10 Oct 16	

Nominal Roll of Officers Known to Have Served with the 9th (Service) Battalion, Alexandra's Princess of Wales's Own, Yorkshire Regiment, The Green Howards

Rank	Name	Initials / First	Commissioned	Remarks	Home
Second Lieutenant, A/Capt	Almgill	David B.	06-Jan-16	Wnd 7 June 1917	Easingwold
Second Lieutenant	Appleyard	Edward E.	22-Feb-15	MC	Harrogate
Second Lieutenant, Lieutenant	Armitage	William H.		MC KiA 22 May 1916, Tranchee de Mecknes Cemetery, Aix-Noulette	Sheffield
Second Lieutenant, Captain	Atkey	Freeman A.H.	29-Jan-15	KiA 05 Jul 1916, Becourt Mil Cem	Woodford
Lieutenant, Captain, Lt Colonel	Barnes	Anthony C.	15-Dec-14	DSO	Caterham, Surrey
Second Lieutenant, Lieutenant	Barraclough	Clive	19-Sep-14	Served with D Coy MiD 15 June 1916	Leeds
Second Lieutenant	Barraclough	John C.	29-Jan-16	France 14 Feb 1916 RFC & RAF	Lowestoft
Second Lieutenant, Captain	Bass	Harold J.	12-Dec-14	F&F 6 Oct 1915 MC MiD LG 15 June 1916, KiA 24 Apr 1918 Att W Yorks Regt	
Second Lieutenant	Bedford	Albert E.	26-Apr-17		Rotherham
Captain, Major	Becket	Victor L.S.	22-Oct-14	KiA 14 Jul 1916, Heilly Station Cemetery, Mericourt-l'Abbe	Fly, Cambridgeshire
Second Lieutenant	Bell	Donald S.	10-Jun-15	Victoria Cross 5 Jul 1916, KiA 10 Jul 1916	Harrogate
Captain	Benke	L.L.	02-Dec-15	3rd Bn F & F 6 Nov 14 to 9th Bn att E Lancashire Regt	Northwood, Middlesex
Lieutenant	Bennison	Miles	30-Jan-16	KiA 1 Oct 1917, Tyne Cot Memorial	Middlesbrough
Second Lieutenant	Bethell	Richard C.		DoW 22 May 1916, Fosse No. 10 Communal Cemetery Extension, Sains-en-Gohelle	
Lieutenant, Captain	Bingham	Edmund G	29-Jan-16	F&F 15 Jun 1916, Wnd 10 July 1916. MC	Sheffield

Rank	Name	Initials / First	Commissioned	Remarks	Home
Second Lieutenant	Blore	Samuel	05-Jan-17	Wnd 7 June 1917	
Captain	Blow	Wilfred L.	22-Dec-15	2365 Colour Sergeant 4/Yorkshire Regt	Richmond, Yorks
Major	Bolckow	Charles F.H.	20-Apr-16	F&F 30 Apr 17	Nunthorpe
Captain	Botting	Charles H.B.	30-Apr-16	F&F 25 Jul 16, MC	Stamford Hill N.16
Captain	Bowmaker	H.			
Second Lieutenant	Boyce	G.	08-Nov-15		
Second Lieutenant	Brass	Percival	30-Jan-16	14565 Sgt DLI F&F 11 Sep 1915 Comm Yorks to RFC	Goole
Second Lieutenant, Lieutenant	Brown	William	26-Apr-17	From Artist Rifles	
Second Lieutenant	Bullmer	Samuel	27-Sep-15	F&F 18 Mar 1916 Trf Royal Engineers	Res Ypres 1925
Second Lieutenant	Bunker	Harold J.	28-Apr-17	KiA 28 Sep 1917, Tyne Cot Memorial	Forest Hill, London
Lieutenant	Caffin	Ernest G.	23-Dec-07	F&F 26 Aug 1915, Lt Col Northbld Fus MiD L.G. 15 Jun 1916	Northallerton
Second Lieutenant	Carr			Royal Free Hospital, Gray's Inn Road, March 1916	Bradford
Second Lieutenant	Catton	W.J.	26-Apr-17	Tpr South African Bde 6577 Lt Yorks R Wnd July 1917	Heytherville S. Africa
Second Lieutenant, Lieutenant	Christie	Ralph L.	13-Jun-17	F&F 17 Jan 1917, Wnd July 1917	Durie, Fife
Second Lieutenant	Christmas	H.R.		Wnd 10 Oct 16	
Major	Chambers	J.W.	11-Dec-16		
Second Lieutenant	Child	Joseph A.	24-Dec-16	11269 C/Sgt F&F 13 Jul 1915, KiA 7 Jun 1917 att 69 LTMB	Cleckheaton

Rank	Name	Initials / First	Commissioned	Remarks	Home
Second Lieutenant, Lieutenant	Collier	Edwin	19-Sep-14	Captain att King's African Rifles	
Second Lieutenant	Cooper	Claude H.		GS/723 Sgt 9 R Fusiliers Drowned 17 Jan 1918	Stamford Hill N.16
Second Lieutenant	Corfeld	G.F.C.	10-Dec-14		
Second Lieutenant, Lieutenant	Courage	Peter M.	19-Sep-14	F&F 1/9/1915 MC	Tidworth 4th D.G.
Second Lieutenant, Lieutenant	Crawford	Gerald B.	20-Nov-17	Italy Dec 1917, Att West African Frontier Force	Leeds
Captain	Crawley-Boevey	Leslie	22-Oct-14	Egypt 2 Mar 16, Captain Liverpool Regt Trf Yorks Regt	Depot Richmond
Second Lieutenant	Daniels	Alfred	20-Nov-15	F&F Jul 16, 3031 Cpl 4th Res Bn Trf RFC & RAF Wnd 10 Oct 16	Leigh on Sea
Second Lieutenant	Dean	Thomas W.		DoWnds 7 June 1917	Middlesbrough
Second Lieutenant	Dixon	Harry	15-Aug-16	F&F 12 Oct 16 KiA 6 Oct 18	Middlesbrough
Lieutenant	Dudley	A.T.	26-Mar-18	MC	
Lieutenant	Duncalfe	H.	14-Dec-15		Nottingham
Second Lieutenant	Eaton	Robert T.	25-Jan-17	F&F 16 Mar 17 Wnd 7 June 1917. Trf MGC	Glasgow
Second Lieutenant	Ecob	William A.	24-Nov-14	F&F 25 Aug 15, Trf RAF	Radcliffe on Trent
Second Lieutenant	Edwards-Crate	Ian R.	28-Aug-17	17984 L/Sgt KOYLI M.C. DoW 11 Oct 1918	Bossingham Kent
Second Lieutenant	Ellis	W.T.	22-Jun-17		
Second Lieutenant	Evans	I.G.	26-Apr-17		
Second Lieutenant, Lieutenant	Finn	Wilfred	01-Oct-15	F&F 2 Jul 16, Edinburgh University OTC	Bridlington

Rank	Name	Initials / First	Commissioned	Remarks	Home
Second Lieutenant	Francis	D.J.			
Second Lieutenant, Captain	Gamble	Walter R.	06-Feb-16	F&F 17 Aug 1914 Pte 3119 16 Royal Irish Lancers M.C. MiD June 1916, Wnd 7 June 1916	King's Lynn
Second Lieutenant, Lieutenant	Gibson	John	13-Nov-14	KiA 5 July Thiepval Memorial	Hull
Second Lieutenant	Graham	H.C.	30-May-17		
Second Lieutenant, Captain	Greenwood	William F.	22-Sep-14	F&F 26 Aug 15, Trench Raid 22 Apr & 21 May 1917 MiD 11 Dec 17. DSO MC	Hebden Bridge
Second Lieutenant	Grimsley	William H.	12-Jan-16	From Artist Rifles KiA 6 Oct 18	Bicester
Second Lieutenant, Lieutenant	Groom	Noel	06-Jul-16	F&F 17 Nov 1915 Formerly PS/427 Sgt Middlesex Regt Killed in Action 20 Sep 1917	
Second Lieutenant	Gutteridge	J.F.	26-Apr-17		
	Halliwell	Wilfred .N.		DoW 21 Sep 1916	
Second Lieutenant	Hart	Edgar O.	07-Oct-15	Enl 4th (West Riding Howitzer Bde in Sep 1914, F&F 22 Apr 16, KiA 10 Jul 16	Richmond Yorkshire
Lieutenant Colonel	Hart	Reginald S.	16-Aug-17	Gallipoli 8 Jun 15, Capt att 9 Yorks, MiD 2 Dec 17, DSO	1st Sherwood Foresters Blackdown 1921
Second Lieutenant	Helms	Percy		F&F 24 Feb 1915 L/Cpl 9 Royal Scots, DoWs 5 Oct 1918	Northampton
Lieutenant	Hermiston	Frank	15-Dec-14	F&F 28 Aug 15, KiA 5 Jul 16	Crouch End
Second Lieutenant	Hobby	Harold S.		MC, F&F 6 May 16, Wnd 7 June 1917	Macclesfield

Rank	Name	Initials / First	Commissioned	Remarks	Home
Major, Lieutenant Colonel	Holmes	H.G.	18-Oct-14	F&F 14 Aug 1915. Brigadier Comdg No 2 Section Tyne Garrison	Nenagh, Co Tipperary
Second Lieutenant, Lieutenant	Horner	K.W.R.	11-Jul-17	Wnd Oct 16	
Second Lieutenant, Captain and Adjutant	Hunnybunn	Gerald N.	19-Sep-14	KiA as Major 23 Oct 1918	Godmanchester
Second Lieutenant	Jacobs	A.R.	25-Aug-15	Att R Lancaster Regiment 1917	Wimbledon
Second Lieutenant	James	Sidney G.	30-May-17	Formerly 2261 & 470383 Sgt 12/ London Regt F&F 24 Dec 14	Antwerp, Belgium
Second Lieutenant	Jardine	Arthur C.	23-Feb-15	MC	Richmond, Surrey
Second Lieutenant	Johnson	A.B.	21-Sep-16	Employed Ministry of Munitions Dec 18	
Second Lieutenant	Keall	H.W.	26-Apr-17		
Second Lieutenant	Kemp	R.C.	07-Dec-14		
Second Lieutenant	Knight	R.J.	29-Aug-17		
Lieutenant, Captain	Knott	William R.	29-Sep-15	MC	Lewisham
Second Lieutenant	Knowles	George C.	16-Aug-16	Wnd 7 June 1917, DoW 10 Jun 1917, Lijssenthoek Mil Cem	Palmers Green London
Second Lieutenant	Lampshire	L.F.	12-Dec-15	F&F 9 May 15 3321 Pte 28 London Regt (Artists Rifles)	Wallington, Surrey
Second Lieutenant	Laycock	J.	11-Dec-14		
Second Lieutenant	Lee	L.G.	29-Nov-14		
Second Lieutenant	Lewis	Herbert O.R.	26-Apr-17	From 448 Pte 5/London Regt, MC, Tyne Cot Memorial 1 Oct 1917	Finchley
Second Lieutenant	Lister	William	26-Apr-17	F&F June 1917,	Harrogate
Second Lieutenant	Maddison	Herbert	23-Apr-16	F&F 13 Jul 1915 12845 Sgt 7th Bn, MiD 11 Dec 17	Middlesbrough

Rank	Name	Initials / First	Commissioned	Remarks	Home
Second Lieutenant	Matthews	Richard M.	05-Apr-17	Formerly 8901- 762906 Artists Rifles killed in action 20 Sep 1917	Walmer, Kent
Captain	Maude	Michael D.W.	01-Feb-15	3rd Bn att F&F 6 Oct 14, Wnd 20 Sep 1917 Died 14 Oct 1917	Boroughbridge
Second Lieutenant, Captain Major	McCall	Maurice G.T.	18-Dec-14	F&F 25 Aug 15	London E.C.3
Second Lieutenant	McKinnell	S.R.	29-Aug-17		
Second Lieutenant, Lt, Captain	Middleton	Hugh	26-Feb-15	F&F 25 Aug 15 MiD 22 May 17	Worthing
Second Lieutenant	Miles	Gordon		KiA 7 Oct 16	Weymouth
Second Lieutenant, Captain	Miller	A.C.H.	04-Aug-15	MiD 4 Jan 17	
Second Lieutenant	Nicholson	Lancelot	29-May-17	Enl 4 Sep 14 Hussars trf to R Irish D Gds to 13591 Cpl Dorsetshire Regt Ent F&F 29 July 1915, Killed in Action 20 Sep 1917	Seaham Harbour
Second Lieutenant	Neill	C.V.	01-Mar-17		Southport
Second Lieutenant, Captain	Parry	A.C.L.	22-Oct-14	MiD 28 Nov 17	
Captain	Pettle	Richard G.	15-Dec-14	To General List for employment as Brigade M.G. Officer	
Second Lieutenant	Pomfrey	James A.	28-Aug-17	Egypt 23 Dec 1915, Sgt 11/937 11 East Yorks	Hull
Major, Lt Colonel	Prior	Harold A.S.	22-Oct-14	F&F 24 Aug 16, MiD June 1916 From 8th Battalion	Hyde Park
Second Lieutenant	Randall	Herbert E.	08-Nov-15	F&F 21 Jul 15 S2965 Sgt Rifle Bde, 11th Yorkshire Regt to RAF	Hooley, Surrey
Second Lieutenant	Ransome	H.N.	28-Aug-17	F&F 7 Sep 1915, 113241 Cpl R Engineers, MiD	Felixstowe

Rank	Name	Initials / First	Commissioned	Remarks	Home
Second Lieutenant	Read	Charles	25-Jan-17	10994 Private 5th Royal Fusiliers, F&F 16 Mar 17, Wnd 7 June 1917. KiA 5 Oct 18	Leeds
Second Lieutenant	Regge	Robert G.B.	28-Dec-14	Relinquished commission owing to ill health 29 Aug 1915	
Second Lieutenant, Captain	Roberts	Arthur B.H.	22-Sep-14	F&F 25 Aug 1915 MC	Wakefield
Second Lieutenant	Robinson	A.F.	08-May-15	Employed Conv Hosp 1916	
Second Lieutenant, Lieutenant	Robinson	C.H.	12-Jun-16		
Second Lieutenant	Robson	Maurice G.	05-Aug-16	F&F 18 Apr 15 1793 Pte 4/ Yorks Led Raids on 22 Apr & 21 May 1917. Wnd 7 June 1917 MC To RAF	Hebden Bridge
Major	Ross	C.E.	30-Sep-14	Late Indian Army Relinquished owing to ill health 23 Mar 1915	
Second Lieutenant	Salmon	Harold J.	26-Apr-17	F&F 26 Aug 15 Formerly 14518 Sgt 9th Bn, Acc Wnd July 1917 MM Trf RAF	
Second Lieutenant	Scott	H.G.		Wnd 13 Feb 1917	
Second Lieutenant	Selch	Frederick W.	29-Aug-17	63989 Sgt R.G.A. 9th Bn att 7/East Yorkshire Regt	West Hartlepool
Second Lieutenant	Sharpe	W.A.	29-Aug-17		
Second Lieutenant	Sutliffe	George W.	26-Apr-17	Formerly 13660 10/Essex Regt F&F 25 Jul 15	London E 5
Second Lieutenant	Thompson	Gerald	15-Dec-14	F&F 18 Apr 1915, MC & Bar	Beverley
Second Lieutenant	Thornton	Harry E.	28-Dec-16	From 1774 Sgt 24 Coy MGC MC, to 2/96 Infantry Indian Army as Capt	Darlington

Rank	Name	Initials / First	Commissioned	Remarks	Home
Second Lieutenant Captain	Tinkler	Lionel M.	23-Feb-17	F&F 1 Jun 15 Formerly 405 Sgt King Edwards Horse MC OBE in South Russia	Liverpool
Second Lieutenant, Captain	Tolson	Robert H.	15-Dec-14	Wnd Dec 1915, June 1917	Leeds
Second Lieutenant, Lieutenant	Tomlinson	George E.	05-Aug-16	Formerly PS/3304 R Fusilier, F&F 14 Nov 15, att 51st Leicestershire Regt	Castle Bromwich
Second Lieutenant	Tomlinson	S.	30-May-17		
Second Lieutenant	Venables	Charles E.	15-Jan-16	F&F 13 Jan 15 32887 Private RAMC. Comm 14/Yorkshire Regimment, DoW 12 Oct 16 Buried Dernancourt Com Cem	Middlesbrough
Colonel, late Indian Army	Vincent	H.C.F.		First Commanding Officer until 14 October 1914	
Lieutenant and quartermaster, Captain and quartermaster	Wall	Robert E.	22-Sep-14	F&F 21 Aug 15, MiD 22 May 17	Southampton
Second Lieutenant, Lieutenant	Wahl	Blaukenburg	01-Mar-17	F&F 27 Jul 17, To East Yorkshire Regt	Cape Province
Second Lieutenant	Ward	R.	25-Jan-17		
Second Lieutenant	Wareham	E.H.			
Second Lieutenant, Lieutenant	Waugh	John W.	29-Aug-17	F&F 18 OCT 17	Newcastle
Second Lieutenant	Weeks	J.R.	29-May-15		
Second Lieutenant	Whittaker	William A.	30-May-17	725 Private Welsh Fld Amb att Cheshire Regt, F&F 14 Feb 15	Newport, Mon.
Lieutenant	Whittingham	W.	18-Dec-14		
Second Lieutenant	Wilkinson	Bernard J.	20-Nov-14	F&F 6 May 16	

Rank	Name	Initials / First	Commissioned	Remarks	Home
Captain	Wilkinson	William T.	15-Dec-14	Enl Public Schools Bn Aug 1914, KiA 5 July 1916, Becourt Mi Cem	Vancouver Island
Second Lieutenant	Wilton	Richard B.	16-Nov-15	F&F 1 May 15 formerly 2551 Argyll & Sutherland Highlanders KiA 1 Oct 17 Tyne Cot	Stafford
Second Lieutenant, Lieutenant	Wolstenholme	George M.	20-Nov-16	F&F 18 Jan 1917 MC MiD, KiA 5 Oct 1918	Birkenhead
Lieutenant	Wood	James S.	26-Apr-17	F&F 21 Jun 17 att 9/ Northumberland Fus. As 2nd Lt. Received Bn Colour 31 Jan 1919	Huddersfield
Second Lieutenant	Wood	R.	27-Jun-17		
Second Lieutenant	Wood	Thomas T.	23-Jan-16	F&F 28/9/15 14271 Cpl Shropshire LI DoW 14 July 1916	Bebington, Cheshire.
Lieutenant	Wright	Herman M.	11-Sep-14	From 6431 L/Cpl Inns of Court OTC, to 2nd Yorks Regt KiA 2 Apr 17, Buried Henin Com Cem Ext.E52	Reading
Captain	Wright	T.	06-Jul-16		
Second Lieutenant	Wyld	Cyril G.	05-Mar-16	F&F 14 Jul 15, 14990 Corporal Notts & Derby Regt Kia 5 Jul 16	Skegness, Lincolnshire.

Nominal Roll of Other Ranks that Served with 8th (Service) Battalion, Alexandra's Princess of Wales's Own Yorkshire Regiment, The Green Howards, and Landed in France with the Battalion on 25 or 26 August 1915 or Died or Left the Battalion Prior to Embarkation

Number	Rank	Name	First Name	Home Town	Bns served with	Reported Wounded	Discharged	MR Comment
12716	Pte	Ablett	Frank	Middlesbrough	8th, 4/Tank Corps 75719 Sgt			
11798	Pte	Adams	John E.	Middlesbrough	8th, Labour Corps 31848	MDG 9/08/1916	22/03/1919	Class Z Reserve
	Pte	Akers	Raymond		8th, 6th, 2nd		19/09/1919	Class Z Reserve
13181	Pte	Alder	Samuel	Middlesbrough	8th		11/07/1916	Dead
11940	Pte	Alderson	John E.		8th	Dis Sick Died 01/06/1916	08/05/1916	Discharged
19377	Pte	Allday	Robert	Eston	8th	DL 4/09/1916	18/04/1917	Discharged
19339	Pte	Allen	Francis		8th, 2nd, 6th, 6th		24/09/1919	Class Z Reserve
14381	Pte	Almond	William		8th, 8th		13/03/1919	Class Z Reserve
16705	Pte	Anderson	George	Ferryhill	8th, East Yorkshire Regt 30018	DL 18/10/1917		Class Z Reserve
17128	Pte	Anderson	John W.	Hetton le Hole	8th, Labour Corps 604662	DL 28/08/1917	08/02/1919	Class Z Reserve
14015	Pte	Angus	John	Southwick	8th	DL 04/02/1916	02/04/1917	Dead
14043	Pte	Angus	Norman	Fencehouses	8th, 11th, 8th	Docs, DL 17/11/1915. DL 09/08/1916	31/03/1919	Class W Reserve
11545	Pte	Appleton	John E.	Middlesbrough	8th		11/07/1916	Dead
12361	Sgt	Appleton	John P.	Skirhaugh	8th, L/Cpl 22/09/1914, Sgt 14/10/1914, 8th. FGCM Drunk 06/08/1918	MM 17/12/1917	12/03/1919	Class Z Reserve
11921	Pte	Archbold	John B.	Middlesbrough	8th, Depot 16/04/1916 3rd 28/08/1916, 8th 06/10/1916	Shrapnel Wnd R Arm at Duty 20/05/1917	27/03/1919	Class Z Reserve
16730	Sgt	Archer	Walter E.	Kimblesworth	8th, Sgt 6/8/1917 10th, 2nd.02/02/1918 Sgt POW 08/05/1918	GSW Arm 22/07/1917	02/04/1919	Class Z Reserve

Number	Rank	Name	First Name	Home Town	Bns served with	Reported Wounded	Discharged	MR Comment
13108	Pte	Armstrong	Edward	Middlesbrough	8th,MM 16/08/1917 8th. FGCM Italy 22/05/1918 84 Days F.P. No 1.		23/04/1919	Class Z Reserve
11408	Pte	Armstrong	George	Sunderland	8th Originally 6th to 8th 9/1914	Not Overseas	28/10/1914	Discharged
14454	Pte	Armstrong	Harry		8th, Labour Corps 223034		23/02/1919	Class Z Reserve
13996	Pte	Ash	James	Washington	8th	DL 19/08/1916	10/07/1916	Dead
12254	Pte	Ashfield	John C.	Middlesbrough	8th		24/09/1915	Dead
12208	Sgt	Ashton	Alfred	Middlesbrough	8th, 8th	MDG 22/08/1916, DL 19/08/1916, DL 23/10/1917	18/03/1919	Class Z Reserve
4	Pte	Aspinall	Jonathan A.	Sunderland	8th		10/07/1916	Dead
19399	Pte	Atkinson	Thomas		8th, 8th Renumbered 67062		14/03/1919	Class Z Reserve
13196	Pte	Bage	J. W.		8th	reported wnd twice in GHG but no other trace		
13783	Pte	Bail	Alfred J.	South Bank	8th, Depot, 3rd, 10th Trg Res, 6th, 13th , Depot, 3rd, 6th, 301, 387 Home Service Lab Coy, 17/08/1918 Labour Corps 562329	Bayonet Wnd Chest 10/07/1916, Wnd 23/11/1917. DL 27/12/1917	26/04/1919	Class Z Reserve
12064	Pte	Bailes	John H.	South Bank	8th	MDG 22/08/1916, DL 19/08/1916	11/07/1916	Dead
14281	Pte	Bailey	James		8th, 8th	DL 02/02/1916	Still Serving Mar 1920	Still Serving Mar 1920
14561	Pte	Baker	Henry	Sunderland	8th, 8th		02/03/1919	Class Z Reserve

Number	Rank	Name	First Name	Home Town	Bns served with	Reported Wounded	Discharged	MR Comment
11841	Pte	Barclay	Albert		8th, Royal Scots 326251	DL 26/08/1916	05/04/1918	Discharged
12698	Pte	Barker	Isaac A	Eston	8th, 7th. Class W Reserve 25/03/1917 Iron Mines.	GSW R Shoulder 10/07/1916, DL 19/08/1916	01/02/1919	Discharged
14140	Cpl	Barker	William	Easington Colliery	8th	DL 13/04/1916	31/03/1916	Dead
3/7425	Sgt	Barrs	Alfred	Sheffield	3rd, 2nd, Depot, 8th, Chinese Labour Corps 425418	Wnd l Hand Mar 15, GSW R Leg Dec 15. Originally Entered France 14/11/1914 Posted to & Embarked with 8th Bn 26/08/1915	18/03/1919	Class Z Reserve
7506	Pte	Bates	Harry		8th, 11th, 6th, 4th renumbered 202930		29/01/1919	Discharged
12620	Cpl	Battle	Harry	Middlesbrough	8th	Newcastle Journal 18/08/1916 DL 18/08/1916	30/08/1917	Discharged
13314	Cpl	Batty	George W.	Halifax	8th, 2nd, 5th	DL 16/08/1916	24/07/1918	Dead
13782	Pte	Batty	John		8th	DL 19/08/1916	31/01/1919	Discharged
13818	Pte	Baxter	Matthew	New Herrington	8th	Sunderland Echo 16/08/1916	10/07/1916	Dead
14979	Pte	Beardmore	Walter	Leamside	8th, 13th to 5th Duke of Wellingtons Regt		12/02/1919	Class Z Reserve
11846	Cpl	Beaumont	Lloyd	Huddersfield	8th		10/01/1917	Dead

Number	Rank	Name	First Name	Home Town	Bns served with	Reported Wounded	Discharged	MR Comment
11953	L/Cpl	Bedford	Thomas A.	Leeds	8th, 4th 29/Durham LI 101684	GSW Thigh & Testicle 10/07/16	22/02/1919	Class Z Reserve
11906	Pte	Bell	Alan	Guisborough	8th, Depot 15/02/1917, 3rd, Class W Res Munitions Iron Mines	GSW R Arm 09/02/1917	03/01/1919	Discharged
12101	Pte	Bell	Alfred	Middlesbrough	8th, 8th		23/02/1919	Class Z Reserve
13737	Pte	Bell	Charles	Grangetown	8th. Widow claims a pension			Discharged
3/9176	RSM	Bell	Fred	Sheffield.	8th. A/C/Sgt 08/10/1914, CSM 15/10/1914, RSM 25/08/1915, Reduced to CSM 24/08/1916Depot 05/09/1916, 3rd. A/RSM 20/12/1918, To Army of the Rhine 01/02/1919	Formerly 4888 1st Yorkshire Regt Enl 02/05/1895. Discharged as C/Sgt 16/06/1913	06/06/1919	Class Z Reserve
13406	Pte	Bell	John T.	North Ormesby	8th. L/Cpl 01/08/1915, 11th, 3rd, Class P Res 10/01/1917 Munitions	Bomb Wnd L Groin & Abdomen 26/05/1916	10/01/1917	Discharged
13736	Pte	Bell	Lancelot	North Ormesby	8th		03/10/1916	Dead
14569	Pte	Bell	Robert		8th, Labour Corps 446687		10/03/1919	Discharged
12530	Pte	Bell	Thomas		8th, 8th, 8th		21/02/1919	Class Z Reserve
16679	Pte	Bell	William	Sunderland	8th		10/07/1916	Dead
13387	Pte	Bellamy	William	Ormesby	8th, Machine Gun Corps 124205, Royal Engineers WR 204780	DL 19/07/1916 MDG 19/06/1916		
16819	Pte	Bennett	James	Grangetown	8th. Enl Connaught Rangers Trf 8th Yorks 10/03/1915, Unfit 09/12/1915	GSW Head 02/11/1915	14/03/1919	Class Z Reserve

Number	Rank	Name	First Name	Home Town	Bns served with	Reported Wounded	Discharged	MR Comment
15720	Pte	Bennett	Michael	Grangetown	8th, 10, 5th		14/07/1918	Dead
12037	Pte	Bennett	Stephen	Grangetown	8th		14/04/1916	Dead
16673	Pte	Beresford	Thomas	Henbode Shropshire	8th, East Yorkshire Regt 30634		25/04/1918	Dead
14579	Pte	Berry	John	Byker	8th		24/09/1915	Dead
14292	Pte	Berry	William J.	South Shields	8th, 8th, 10th	GSW Ankle, GSW Head & Shouilder	14/10/1918	Discharged
14341	Pte	Bewick	Thomas W.	New Herrington	8th		14/07/1916	Dead
11569	Pte	Binns	David	Grangetown	8th, Depot 14/10/1916, 8th. 11/06/1917, 9th 03/07/1917 Depot 04/08/1917, Class W Res Munitions 22/08/1917		31/01/1919	Discharged
11849	Cpl	Birkby	Michael E.	Bradford	8th		10/07/1916	Dead
16830	Pte	Bivens	Thomas	Spennymoor	8th, 2nd		18/10/1916	Dead
13233	Pte	Black	William	Middlesbrough	8th, Labour Corps 420907		13/07/1918	Discharged
12622	Pte	Blackburn	William	North Ormesby	8th Cpl 17/12/1914 Reverted 29/05/1915, 8th		12/02/1919	Class Z Reserve
13132	Pte	Blades	Walter	Middlesbrough	8th, L/Cpl 30/10/1917, 8th		16/04/1919	Class Z Reserve
13615	Pte	Blakelock	Joseph	Murton	8th		05/08/1916	Dead
13956	Pte	Blakey	William		8th		19/05/1916	Discharged
19405	Pte	Bland	Ernest		8th		31/01/1919	Discharged
13386	Pte	Blenkey	Christopher	Middlesbrough	8th, Depot 03/01/1916, 11th 12/03/1916	GSW Hand & Knee 31/12/1915	02/05/1916	Discharged
13185	Cpl	Blenkinsop	George W.	Middlesbrough	8thCpl 27/08/1916. 10th Trg Res Bn	MDG 09/08/1916	01/03/1919	Class Z Reserve

Number	Rank	Name	First Name	Home Town	Bns served with	Reported Wounded	Discharged	MR Comment
13343	Pte	Blewitt	Ernest	Hetton le Hole	8th, Depot 24/09/1916 2nd	GSW Wnd Mild 24/09/1916 GSW Severe 31/07/1917, DL 10/09/1917	01/04/1918	Discharged
19334	Pte	Blunt	Thomas	New Lambton	8th		16/09/1916	Dead
17760	Sgt	Blyth	George M.	Deptford	8th, 8th.		29/10/1918	Dead
11507	Pte	Boddy	Timothy	Middlesbrough	8th, Depot 14/07/1916, Discharged to Munitions 16/12/1916	GSW L Arm Shrapnel Elbow & Face 08/01/1916 DL 27/01/1916, GSW L Ankle DL & MDG 09/08/1916	20/08/1917	Discharged
14769	L/Sgt	Bolton	Albert H.		8th, Reenlisted RASC 30/04/1919 A/450466 WO II		24/09/1919	Discharged
16742	Pte	Booth	Lawrence	Lingdale	8th	GSW Rt shoulder with fracture	21/04/1917	Discharged
19374	Pte	Boothby	Jesse		8th, 6th, 13th		11/01/1919	Discharged
12123	Pte	Bostock	George W.		8th to 23rd Divisional Cyclist Coy, Trf ACC 3490		10/03/1919	Class Z Reserve.
13899	Sgt	Bottoms	Wilfred	Usworth	8th, 11th, 2nd, 8th, 8th		19/06/1918	Disc harged
12153	Pte	Bowman	Ernest	North Ormesby	8th		10/07/1916	Dead
3/8766	Sgt	Bowman	William		8th, 8th		Still Serving Mar 1920	Still Serving Mar 1920
15603	Pte	Boyes	Frank	Scarborough	8th 21/11/1914, 9th 26/08/1915, To Hosp Sick 21/04/1916, 2nd 10/07/1916, [illegible]	Tuberculosis 26/12/1916	12/03/1917	Discharged

Number	Rank	Name	First Name	Home Town	Bns served with	Reported Wounded	Discharged	MR Comment
11936	Pte	Boyle	Owen	South Bank	8th, Depot 15/07/1916, Class W Res Munitions 19/02/1917	GSW R Thigh 10/07/1916	13/01/1919	Discharged
12898	Cpl	Boyle	Edward	Hetton Colliery	8th, Cpl 07/05/1917, Depot 14/06/1917, 3rd A/Sgt 01/04/1918	GSW L Hand 07/06/1917	11/01/1919	Class Z Reserve
13122	Pte	Bradbury	Charles	Middlesbrough	8th, Depot 16/07/1916, 81st Trg Res Bn 20/12/1916	GSW L Thigh10/07/1916, MDG 11/08/1916	04/05/1917	Discharged
14706	Pte	Bradford	James		8th, 8th		28/01/1919	Class Z Reserve
13318	Pte	Bradford	John	Ryhope	8th	GSW L Shoulder	27/01/1919	Discharged
15727	Pte	Bradley	Thomas	Trimdon Colliery.	8th, Depot 13/07/1916, Reenlisted 5th Durham LI 08/07/1928 4446982.	GSW R Foot 10/11/07/1916	25/12/1917	Discharged
13408	Pte	Braithwaite	Richard	Middlesbrough	8th, Labour Corps 219532	DL 11/08/1916, Traumatic Neurasthenia	28/12/1917	Discharged
17113	Pte	Bramwell	Thomas W.	Howden le Wear	8th, 8th.		28/01/1919	Class Z Reserve
17726	Pte	Breeze	Michael	Yarmouth	8th.		08/08/1916	Dead
13548	Pte	Breheny	James	South Shields	8th, West Yorkshire Regt 63132	DL 19/02/1917		Class Z Reserve
12005	Pte	Bricklebank	Charles Wm.	Hull	8th, Depot 12/02/1916.	Evac Rheumatism	23/07/1916	Discharged
13240	Pte	Brighton	Alfred	Lazenby	8th, Labour Corps L/Cpl 32177		25/03/1919	Discharged
15077	Clr Sgt	Bristoll	Harry J.		8th		26/09/1917	Discharged to Commission Lancashire Fusiliers

Number	Rank	Name	First Name	Home Town	Bns served with	Reported Wounded	Discharged	MR Comment
16672	Pte	Britton	Albert H.	Sacriston	8th, Depot 13/07/1916	GSW R Arm	28/05/1917	Discharged
11492	Sgt	Broad	Charles		8th, 10th, 8th, 8th		02/03/1919	Class Z Reserve
13766	Pte	Brockson	John W.	Eston	8th	MDG 18/08/1916	10/07/1916	Dead
15719	Sgt	Brooks	Ernest	Grangetown	8th Sgt 04/10/1915, Depot 15/07/1916, 51st Liecester Regt TR/6/30062, Att Nigerian Regt	GSW L Thigh 10/07/1916	03/07/1919	Class Z Reserve
3/9175	Pte	Brown	Albert		8th		05/03/1919	Class Z Reserve
19394	Pte	Brown	Ernest	Darlington	8th		28/09/1917	Dead
13379	Pte	Brown	Frank H.	North Ormesby	8th, 8th		28/03/1919	Class Z Reserve
13811	Pte	Brown	George H.	Grangetown	8th, 13th, 8th, 9th		17/07/1918	Discharged
9024	CQMS	Brown	Henry		8th, Lincolnshire Regt 23831		04/02/1919	Class Z Reserve
16724	Pte	Brown	James A.	East Rainton.	8th, Depot 11/06/1917	GSW L Hand Amputation of thumb, Index and Middle Fingers	22/08/1917	Discharged
13880	Pte	Brown	James A.D.	Southwick	8th		10/07/1916	Dead
13405	Sgt	Brown	John W.		8th		09/03/1919	Class Z Reserve
14836	Pte	Brown	Matthew	Trimdon Colliery	8th		27/01/1919	Discharged
11497	Pte	Brown	Thomas W.		8th, 8th		06/03/1919	Class Z Reserve
14309	Pte	Brown	William	Jarrow	8th, 6th		14/08/1917	Dead
11897	Pte	Brown	Morris W.		8th		27/01/1919	Discharged
16369	Pte	Brownless	George	Castletown	8th	GSW L Arm	24/08/1917	Discharged

Number	Rank	Name	First Name	Home Town	Bns served with	Reported Wounded	Discharged	MR Comment
12412	Pte	Brunskill	John T.	Middlesbrough	8th, 5th, renumbered 243312 15/01/1917, To UK Iron miner 22/05/1917	GSW R Knee, MDG 11/08/1916	30/01/1919	Discharged
3/9142	Pte	Bryan	Harry	Leeds	8th, Depot 17/02/1916	Discharged owing to Double Hernia.	20/07/1916	Discharged
13425	Cpl	Buckley	Wiliam	South Hetton	8th, 8th		04/02/1919	Class Z Reserve
14876	Pte	Buckton	Stephen		8th, 6th, 8th		17/01/1919	Discharged
13784	Pte	Bullock	Albert	Grangetown	8th	GSW L Forearm 4/10/1916	04/04/1917	Discharged
13265	Pte	Bulmer	Sydney	Great Ayton	8th, Labour Corps 638764		12/03/1919	Class Z Reserve
12652	Pte	Burdon	Surtees		8th, Machine Gun Corps 161304		15/01/1919	Class Z Reserve
15735	Pte	Burgham	Arthur	Boldon Colliery	8th, 912 AE Coy Labour Corps 417770, 43rd Royal Fusiliers GS/101020	Bronchitis	08/02/1919	Discharged
11345	Sgt	Burlison	Edgar	Bradford	8th		06/08/1916	Dead
17745	Pte	Burn	Bertram	Easington Colliery	8th		04/10/1916	Dead
13334	L/Cpl	Burn	Robert T.		8th, Northumberland Fus TR/5/127146		11/02/1919	Discharged
14239	Pte	Burns	David	Hendon	8th, 8th	ICT R Thigh 13/10/1918	07/03/1919	Class Z Reserve
11923	Pte	Burns	William E.		8th, East Yorkshire Regt 30019			Class Z Reserve
15732	Pte	Bush	Andrew S.	New Washington	8th, 25th DLI 48996, R Engineers WR273268	GSW Left Hand	13/04/1919	Discharged

Number	Rank	Name	First Name	Home Town	Bns served with	Reported Wounded	Discharged	MR Comment
8532	Sgt	Butler	Joseph	Middlesbrough	8th		28/05/1916	Dead
11848	Pte	Butson	Charles E.	Bradford	8th		20/09/1917	Dead
14917	A/ CSM	Butterley	Thomas	South Shields	8th, 2nd, 8th		08/03/1919	Class Z Reserve
13136	Pte	Butterwick	John G.	Middlesbrough	8th, 21st Northld Fus 55334, 1st NF, 19th NF, 1st NF	MDG 09/08/1916 para 392 xvia	26/04/1919	Discharged
14379	Pte	Bycroft	William	Middlesbrough	8th		17/11/1915	Dead
13496	Pte	Cable	William T.	Bedlington Station	8th	Injury to big toe	17/01/1919	Discharged
13378	Pte	Cahill	Thomas	Middlesbrough	8th		20/05/1916	Dead
14382	Pte	Caily	Frederick		8th, Royal Irish Regt 5081		22/04/1919	Class Z Reserve
12107	Cpl	Callaby	George W.	North Ormesby	8th		30/01/1919	Discharged
17383	Pte	Campbell	John	Newcastle	8th	Sickness 392 xvi	30/01/1919	Discharged
13799	Pte	Campion	Pearson	Whitby	8th, 8th	GSW L Foot 08/01/1916. GSW L Thigh 06/08/1916, DL 02/02/1916	18/03/1919	Class Z Reserve
13235	Pte	Cannell	James E.	Grangetown	8th		22/01/1916	Dead
3/8998	Sgt	Cannon	Stephen	Wakefield	8th, 8th	Died from an accident	11/05/1918	Dead
11828	Pte	Carey	Roy	Guisborough	8th, 11th, 6th, 4th Renumbered 7513		25/10/1916	Dead
12261	Pte	Carney	John	Newtown Monmouth	8th, 8th		27/10/1918	Dead

Number	Rank	Name	First Name	Home Town	Bns served with	Reported Wounded	Discharged	MR Comment
14070	Pte	Carr	Cleasby	Seaham	8th Depot 20/01/1916 , 11th, 6th 09/09/1916, 4th 19/09/1916, 8th 15/10/1916, 4th 09/11/1917. 3rd 4/10/1918	Bomb Wnd R Thigh 13/01/1916, GSW Abdomen 13/04/1918. DL 02/02/1916	03/03/1919	Class Z Reserve
12578	Pte	Carr	George	Spennymoor	8th, Machine Gun Corps 23124	KR 392 xvia Wounds	14/12/1918	Discharged
13814	Pte	Carroll	Philip	Monkwearmouth.	8th, Depot 25/10/1917, 3rd 08/01/1917	Rep Missing 06/08/1916 Not missing 13/08. GSW Back 21/10/1917	24/03/1919	Class Z Reserve
12270	Pte	Carroll	Luke		8th, Labour Corps 619681		20/03/1919	Class Z Reserve
12838	Cpl	Carroll	Thomas		8th	AO 11 10/08/1917 2, b, 1	04/01/1918	Discharged
14090	Pte	Carter	William	Easington Colliery	8th	MDG 18/08/1916	10/07/1916	Dead
12020	Pte	Cartman	Charles E.		8th, 8th		21/02/1919	Class Z Reserve
12096	Pte	Cartman	William	Manchester	8th	GSW Chest 11/06/1916, GSW L Arm 07/08/1916	21/02/1919	Class Z Reserve
19402	Pte	Carver	Fred	Boosbeck,	8th		10/07/1916	Dead
11553	A/Cpl	Cassidy	Matthew	Middlesbrough	8th, 9th. Army Pay Corps 21393	Sickness 392 xvi	11/08/1917	Discharged
13779	Pte	Caulfield	David		8th, Machine Gun Corps		02/03/1919	Class Z Reserve
12363	A/ CSM	Cautley	Laurence	Hedon Yorks	8th, 8th		28/10/1918	Dead

Number	Rank	Name	First Name	Home Town	Bns served with	Reported Wounded	Discharged	MR Comment
14409	Pte	Cecil	Tom	Redcar	8th Depot 05/03/1916, 11th, 3rd, 5th Renumbered 243313 POW 25/03/1918	GSW Both Legs	31/05/1919	Class Z Reserve
3/8962	Pte	Chadwick	John		8th		03/02/1919	Discharged
13315	Sgt	Chadwick	Walter	Leeds	8th		10/07/1916	Dead
12199	Sgt	Chamberlain	Richard	Todmorden	8th	GSW R Foot 21/09/1917	02/04/1919	Class Z Reserve
13778	Pte	Chapman	Charles A.	South Bank	8th att 176 Tunn Coy R.E. to Depot6, 11th Bn, Trf 176 Tunn Coy R Engineers 156434, 01/07/1916	Tried by DCM sentenced to 112 Days detention 3/2/1915.	15/03/1919	Class Z Reserve
13661	Pte	Champley	James		8th, 8th		12/02/1919	Class Z Reserve
13329	Pte	Chapman	James	Sunderland	8th		13/10/1916	Dead
17142	Pte	Charlton	Thomas	Shotton Colliery	8th, 8th		31/12/1918	Class Z Reserve
13200	Pte	Chelton	Edward	Barrow in Furness	8th		25/09/1915	Dead
13947	Pte	Chilvers	George	Washington Station	8th, 8th		17/03/1919	Class Z Reserve
15717	Pte	Christie	Joseph	Middlesbrough	8th		07/06/1917	Dead
13013	Sgt	Clarey	John	Sunderland	8th, 8th, Depot 18/10/1918.		21/02/1919	Class Z Reserve
17176	Pte	Clark	John	Southwick	8th, Depot 21/11/1916, 13th, 6th	GSW L Forearm & R Thigh 14/11/1916	11/02/1919	Class Z Reserve
14863	Pte	Clark	John R.	South Shields	8th		08/10/1916	Dead
14063	Pte	Clark	John W.	Trimdon Colliery	8th	GSW 02/10/1917	04/05/1918	Discharged

Number	Rank	Name	First Name	Home Town	Bns served with	Reported Wounded	Discharged	MR Comment
11909	Pte	Clarke	Ernest	Hull	8th, Reenlisted Labour Corps 30/05/1919		23/03/1919	Class Z Reserve
13489	Pte	Clarke	George	South Shields	8th, 8th Sgt FGCM 23/05/1918 Drunk. Reduced to Pte. Depot 29/04/1919.	GSW R Ankle DoW Plymouth	18/07/1919	Discharged
17182	Sgt	Clarkson	Thomas	Sherburn Colliery	8th, Depot 17/03/1917 8th, 11/06/1917, 8th	ICT Finger 17/03/1917	09/02/1919	Class Z Reserve
14821	Pte	Claydon	Charles R.	North Ormesby	8th		18/05/1916	Dead
12529	Pte	Cleminson	Joseph W.	New Marske	8th, 8th		28/01/1919	Class Z Reserve
13882	Pte	Clennell	Foster	Dawdon	8th, 7th		13/05/1917	Dead
11952	Pte	Close	Thomas W.	Middlesbrough	8th	MDG 18/08/1916	10/07/1916	Dead
17148	Pte	Clough	George	Durham City.	8th, Depot 02/12/1915, 11th 15/04/1916, 8th 28/08/1916, Class W Reserve 02/12/1916	ICT R Knee 20/11/1915	18/09/1917	Discharged
19348	Pte	Cockerill	William J.	Pickering	8th	GSW Face 24/03/1916, GSW L Thigh 10/07/1916	09/01/1918	Discharged
13873	Pte	Codling	Robert W.	Tyne Dock	8th		13/10/1916	Dead
12785	Pte	College	Robson	Murton	8th, 8th		29/10/1918	Dead
13146	Pte	Collins	Thomas	Lackenby	8th. Munitions Ironstone miner 06/10/1916		17/01/1919	Discharged
13144	Pte	Conroy	Joseph	Middlesbrough	8th, Labour Corps 184865	MDG 09/08/1916	13/03/1919	Class Z Reserve
13967	Pte	Conway	George	Washington	8th, Depot 15/07/1916	Wnd 10/07/1916	23/10/1917	Disc harged
13978	Sgt	Conway	James		8th, 51st Grad Bn Leicester Regt, Att King's African Rif		03/07/1919	Class Z Reserve

Number	Rank	Name	First Name	Home Town	Bns served with	Reported Wounded	Discharged	MR Comment
13162	Pte	Cook	James		8th, Royal Irish Regt 5135		15/02/1919	Class Z Reserve
18966	Pte	Cook	Sydney	Peckham S.E.	8th, Depot 14/07/1916 10 Trg Res Bn, 3rd, 7th, 6th	ICT R Leg 27/05/1916, GSW 10/07/1916 GSW Abdomen Wall 25/10/1917	23/01/1918	Discharged
3/9163	Pte	Cooling	William	Kennington	8th		10/07/1916	Dead
11943	Cpl	Cooper	Alfred	Middlesbrough	8th, Depot 31/05/1916	GSW L Arm WL 19/06/1916	26/06/1918	Discharged
14614	Pte	Cooper	Francis S.		8th, Labour Corps Sgt 658665		21/03/1919	Class Z Reserve
13412	Pte	Cooper	Frederick H.	Durham City	8th, 8th		08/10/1918	Dead
16399	Pte	Cooper	George	Durham City	8th, 8th		04/02/1919	Class Z Reserve
13823	Pte	Cooper	John J.	Southwick	8th, 6th, 4/Royal Fusiliers 100064	NJ 11/08/1916		
13785	Pte	Cooper	William J.	South Bank	8th	Wnd Chest & Foot, MDG 09/08/1916	27/08/1917	Discharged
16728	Pte	Coote	John W.	Willington Durham	8th	GSW L Foot	26/10/1916	Discharged
11572	Pte	Cope	Albert	North Ormesby	8th	MDG 18/08/1916	10/07/1916	Dead
14012	Pte	Corbrick	George W.		8th, 8th		04/02/1919	Class Z Reserve
14870	A/Sgt	Corkhill	William G.G.		8th, 12th, 8th		18/03/1919	Class Z Reserve
13743	Pte	Coser	Ernest	Whitby	8th	MDG 22/08/1916	10/07/1916	Dead

Number	Rank	Name	First Name	Home Town	Bns served with	Reported Wounded	Discharged	MR Comment
15093	Sgt	Cottam	George	Plymouth	8th		10/07/1916	Dead
12028	Cpl	Cowell	Ernest	Grangetown	8th	DL 16/02/1916	07/06/1917	Dead
14462	Pte	Cowling	William	Boldon Colliery	8th, Machine Gun Corps 23127		27/09/1917	Dead
14511	Pte	Cox	Thomas	Hendon	8th, 8th		29/06/1918	Dead
13345	Pte	Coyles	John W.	Murton	8th, 6th, 5th Renumbered 243410		19/04/1919	Class Z Reserve
13649	Pte	Cragg	George H.	West Hartlepool	8th, Labour Corps 413302	Myalgia	04/03/1919	Class Z Reserve
12246	Pte	Cragie	Charles	Middlesbrough	8th		21/07/1916	Dead
44	Pte	Craig	John	Usworth Colliery	8th, Depot 24/06/1917	GSW Forearm Severe.	11/12/1917	Discharged
13883	Cpl	Crake	William	Ryhope	8th, 6th, 4th, 8th, 8th	DL 04/02/1916	04/02/1919	Class Z Reserve
19400	Pte	Crawley	William D.		8th		13/01/1919	Discharged
12111	Pte	Cregan	Joseph	Middlesbrough	8th	MDG 18/08/1916	10/07/1916	Dead
13112	Pte	Critchley	Thomas	Middlesbrough	8th	GSW L Thigh serious 06/10/1915	09/06/1916	Discharged
17189	Pte	Croft	James		8th, 1st GB North Staffs 43235, 94 Coy & 954 Coy Labour Corps 519983, 43/ Royal Fusiliers			
17762	Pte	Cuings	Stephen	Easington Colliery	8th, 6th, 1/East Yorkshire Regt 30771	WL 27/10/1917	27/04/1918	Dead
16708	Pte	Cunnah	Joseph	West Cornforth	8th		05/10/1916	Dead
16798	Pte	Cunningham	Frederick G.		8th, 2nd, 6th, 7th.		11/03/1919	Class Z Reserve

Number	Rank	Name	First Name	Home Town	Bns served with	Reported Wounded	Discharged	MR Comment
17241	Pte	Curry	Edward	Horden	8th, Depot 23/10/1915, 7th 07/04/1916, Depot 17/05/1917	GSW R Thigh Accidental 05/1917	09/09/1919	Discharged
15004	Pte	Daglish	Joseph	Murton	8th, 7th, 9th, 9th, 9th		28/01/1919	Discharged
13734	Pte	Dalby	Edward	Normanby	8th. Munitions Cleveland Iron Works 13/03/1917		03/01/1919	Discharged
13059	Pte	Dale	John R.	Normanby	8th, 11th, 10th		03/07/1916	Dead
15208	Pte	Dale	William	York	8th		16/04/1916	Dead
15723	Pte	Daley	Owen	Grangetown	8th, 5th Labour Battalion, Labour Corps 153727		17/01/1919	Discharged
15201	Pte	Danby	Alfred	Acomb	8th, 8th		21/02/1919	Class Z Reserve
13307	Pte	Davies	Arthur		8th, 12th, 868 Coy Labour Corps 406018, 43/Royal Fusiliers GS/104902			
13599	Pte	Davies	John W.	Haswell Plough	8th		13/10/1915	Dead
13368	Pte	Davies	Morgan	Middlesbrough	8th	DL 16/02/1916	25/04/1918	Discharged
13891	Pte	Davis	John		8th		26/12/1916	Discharged
13924	Pte	Davis	William	North Ormesby	8th		11/07/1916	Dead
14265	Pte	Davy	William	South Shields	8th		05/08/1916	Dead
16720	Pte	Dawson	Edward	Houghton le Spring	8th, Depot 02/12/1916, 3rd 26/04/1917, 9th 17/05/1917, 8th 15/08/1917	Bullet Wnd Scalp 20/09/1915	09/02/1919	Class Z Reserve
13163	Pte	Dawson	George	Cargo Fleet	8th, 8th		18/03/1919	Class Z Reserve
7516	Pte	Dawson	Percy H.	Middlesbrough	8th, 11th, 6th, 4th renumbered 202937		25/04/1917	Dead
12539	Pte	Daynes	Charles		8th, 8th		23/04/1919	Class Z Reserve

Number	Rank	Name	First Name	Home Town	Bns served with	Reported Wounded	Discharged	MR Comment
3/8654	Pte	Daynes	James	Guisborough	8th		18/10/1917	Dead
16810	Pte	Dent	John T.	Northallerton	8th, Labour Corps 679803		22/02/1919	Class Z Reserve
13131	Pte	Dent	Thomas		8th, Machine Gun Corps 11919		24/06/1919	Class Z Reserve
12381	CSM	Dent	George E.	Sheffield	8th, 8th	GSW L Arm	14/03/1919	Class Z Reserve
13301	Pte	Dermody	Daniel	Washington Station	8th		10/10/1917	Discharged
16740	Pte	Devlin	John	Sunderland	8th		10/07/1916	Dead
12281	Pte	Dickinson	Wilfred	Armley, Leeds	8th, Labour Corps 341269		05/07/1919	Class Z Reserve
14828	Pte	Dinning	George	Seaham Harbour	8th, 2/West Yorkshire Regt 63577	DL 23/10/1917	17/01/1919	Class Z Reserve
15716	Pte	Dinning	Walter	Seaham	8th, 8th	GSW L Thigh 26/05/1916, GSW Side	04/02/1919	Class Z Reserve
13157	Pte	Dinsdale	John R.	Hawes	8th, 8th, 3rd Res, 5th		27/05/1918	Dead
11512	Pte	Ditchburn	Isaac R.	Boosbeck,	8th. Depot 16/03/1917 Class W Res Iron stone Miner 25/03/1917		17/01/1919	Discharged
13300	Pte	Dixon	Andrew	Washington Station	8th	Died 16/06/1922	12/03/1917	Discharged
15013	Pte	Dixon	George	South Shields	8th, 10th	GSW Right Arm	17/03/1919	Deserted 19/09/1917
14772	Pte	Dixon	James	Monkwearmouth	8th		11/07/1916	Dead
12159	Pte	Dixon	John	South Bank	8th, 8th		03/03/1919	Class Z Reserve
19506	Pte	Dixon	Joseph	New Penshaw	8th, Labour Corps 118906		06/03/1919	Class Z Reserve

Number	Rank	Name	First Name	Home Town	Bns served with	Reported Wounded	Discharged	MR Comment
15033	Pte	Dixon	Joseph B.		8th, 8th		21/02/1919	Class Z Reserve
16818	Pte	Dixon	Thomas	Fencehouses	8th		06.07.1916	Dead
12266	Pte	Dixon	John	Washington Station	8th, Labour Corps, 412543		31/12/1917	7/03/1919
13938	Pte	Dobson	Alexander	Barmston	8th, 3rd Res, 5th		17/07/1917	Dead
17106	Pte	Dobson	Henry	Southwick	8th, 8th		21/02/1919	Class Z Reserve
11515	Pte	Dobson	William		8th	DL 16/08/1916	20/01/1917	Discharged
15736	Pte	Dodds	Thomas	North Ormesby	8th, Depot 18/10/1916	GSW R Ankle 4/10/1916 Lower leg Amputated	09/05/1917	Discharged
13022	Pte	Dodds	William	Easington Lane	8th	MDG 18/08/1916	11/07/1916	Dead
14382	Pte	Dolan	Arthur		8th, 6th, 2nd		Still Serving Mar 1920	Still Serving Mar 1920
13768	Pte	Dooley	Peter	Grangetown	8th		28/02/1919	Class Z Reserve
13139	Pte	Dowd	Patrick A.	Middlesbrough	8th, Depot 14/07/1916, Deserted 09/09/1918, 7th 05/03/1917, 5th 26/03/1917, Deserted 22/6/1918	GSW L Forearm 10/07/1916, GSW L Leg 23/04/1917	Still AWOL 1919	Deserted 22/6/1918
13513	Pte	Dowell	Jacob	Fencehouses	8th, 8th		04/10/1916	Dead
15045	Pte	Drury	Edward		8th, 8th		23/02/1919	Class Z Reserve
11861	Pte	Dryden	George		8th, 8th		21/02/1919	Class Z Reserve
13455	Pte	Duffy	James		8th, 8th		04/02/1919	Class Z Reserve
16729	Pte	Dunn	Edward	Ushaw Moor	8th		10/07/1916	Dead
11487	Pte	Dunn	Harold P.	Guisborough	8th	DL 19/08/1916	10/07/1916	Dead

Number	Rank	Name	First Name	Home Town	Bns served with	Reported Wounded	Discharged	MR Comment
15746	Pte	Durkin	Frank	Bradford	8th		11/07/1916	Dead
14825	Sgt	Dwyer	James E.	Durham City	8th		14/05/1917	Dead
14423	Pte	Earl	John E.	Leeds	8th, 6th, 5th renumbered 5689 then 243023	DL 23/10/1917	14/12/1919	Discharged
11898	Pte	Easby	Richard		8th, 5/Royal Irish Regiment 5072	GSW IV 10/07/1916 3 CCS 12/07/1916	02/03/1919	Class Z Reserve
11873	Cpl	Edwards	Harry	Boosbeck	8th, Depot 17/03/1917 , Class W Reserve Ironminer 25/03/1917	GSW Head 29/08/1916	17/01/1919	Discharged
14384	Pte	Ellis	James	Grangetown	8th.		09/12/1915	Dead
11521	Pte	Elvidge	Fred	Guisborough	8th, Depot 25/06/1917 Class W Reserve Ironstone miner 02/07/1917	GSW Knee 11/07/1916, DL 19/08/1916	15/01/1919	Discharged
14495	Pte	Ely	Alfred	Redcar	8th, Depot 15/07/1916 8th Class W Reserve 14/12/1916	GSW Both legs 10/07/1916	01/02/1919	Discharged
13728	Pte	English	Peter	Blaydon	8th	GSW Shoulder & R Knee Edinburgh War Hosp	07/04/1916	Discharged
12056	Pte	Evans	George	Grangetown	8th, 6th, 13th	MDG 09/08/1916	10/01/1919	Discharged
17772	Pte	Evans	Henry V.	Scampton Yorks	8th		10/07/1916	Dead
11946	Pte	Evans	Robert	Middlesbrough	8th, 6th, 7th		14/09/1917	Discharged
17807	Pte	Evans	Samuel B.		8th, 7th, 12th Bns, to 12th K O Yorkshire LI 62826		15/01/1919	Class Z Reserve
13401	Pte	Evetts	Walter H.	South Bank	8th		24/03/1916	Dead

Number	Rank	Name	First Name	Home Town	Bns served with	Reported Wounded	Discharged	MR Comment
12897	Pte	Falconer	Daniel	Sunderland	8th	GSW Lower extremities	28/01/1917	Discharged
17150	Pte	Faragher	Michael	Durham City.	8th, 8th		28/01/1919	Class Z Reserve
12259	Pte	Farquharson	Alexander	Middlesbrough	8th		11/07/1916	Dead
11904	Pte	Fawns	Albert	Guisborough	8th, Class W Reserve Munitions Iron miner 06/10/1916		16/01/1919	Discharged
13787	Pte	Fearnley	Fred	South Bank	8th, Class W Reserve Munitions Iron miner 05/08/1917	ICT Heel 01/04/1916	7/03/1919	Discharged
13786	Sgt	Fearnley	George	South Bank	8th	DL 16/02/1916	20/09/1917	Dead
11606	Pte	Felgate	Arthur	Middlesbrough	8th, 8th		18/03/1919	Class Z Reserve
13212	Pte	Fellows	Samuel C.	Middlesbrough	8th		08/06/1917	Dead
19352	Pte	Fenton	Francis		8th, 8th	GSW L Axiller	06/03/1919	Class Z Reserve
12550	Pte	Fincham	George	Guisborough	8th, 8th		08/02/1918	Discharged
13327	Pte	Fitzjohn	George E.	Middlesbrough	8th, Depot 15/07/19166th, 2nd		21/03/1919	Class Z Reserve
16737	Pte	Flanagan	Wiliam	Horden	8th, West Yorkshire Regt 63237			Class Z Reserve
13434	CSM	Fleming	James A.		8th. To R Engineers 333644		16/06/1917	Discharged
13609	Pte	Fleming	Thomas		8th, 4th, 1/King's Liverpool Regt 105688		16/12/1918	Deserted 16/02/1918
14310	Pte	Fletcher	Henry	Fatfield	8th		01/07/1916	Dead
13130	Pte	Fletcher	Thomas	Middlesbrough	8th, Depot 16/05/1917 8th, 8th 16/08/1917		23/02/1919	Class Z Reserve

Number	Rank	Name	First Name	Home Town	Bns served with	Reported Wounded	Discharged	MR Comment
12482	Pte	Foggin	William		8th, 6th Bn, 5th renumbered 5690 renumbered 241267 to 9th.		14/03/1919	Class Z Reserve
12452	Cpl	Forkin	John		8th, 2nd, 8th.		27/05/1919	Class Z Reserve
14003	Pte	Forster	William	Barmston	8th.		14/08/1916	Dead
12369	Pte	Fortune	Thomas		8th, 8th.		06/03/1919	Class Z Reserve
17147	Pte	Francis	Joshua	Fencehouses	8th, Depot 17/07/1916, Deserted 20/02/1917 10th.	GSW L Hand 10/07/1916	27/01/1919	Discharged
11585	Pte	Fraser	William	Middlesbrough	8th, Depot 13/10/1915 11th 02/01/1916, Class W Reserve Munitions Steel Works 02/03/1916.	Evac Sick Sec Exzma	06/02/1919	Discharged
11601	Pte	Freeman	Ernest		8th, 8th.		31/01/1919	Class Z Reserve
12338	Pte	French	Charles A.	Leeds	8th.		30/10/1917	Discharged
13111	Sgt	French	George W.	Middlesbrough	8th.		11/07/1916	Dead
14987	Sgt	Frobisher	Herbert	Castleford	8th, 6th.		20/02/1919	Class Z Reserve
3/8887	Sgt	Frost	Charles W.		8th.		28/01/1919	Class Z Reserve
3/8904	Pte	Fuller	George W.		8th, 8th.		21/02/1919	Class Z Reserve
11490	Pte	Gadsby	Matthew	Skinningrove	8th, Depot Class W Reserve Iron stone miner 23/05/1916		31/01/1919	Discharged
12480	Pte	Gaffney	George	South Bank	8th, 4th.	MDG 09/08/1916		Discharged
15193	Pte	Gall	P.		8th, R Welsh Fus 9/07/17, Labour Corps 28/06/1918, Army Service Corps M/414891		10/06/1919	Class Z Reserve

Number	Rank	Name	First Name	Home Town	Bns served with	Reported Wounded	Discharged	MR Comment
12034	Pte	Gallacher	Thomas H.	Middlesbrough	8th, 8th, FGCM Drunk 25/06/1918	DL 23/10/1917	27/03/1919	Class Z Reserve
14021	Pte	Gallagher	James	Houghton le Spring	8th		17/01/1919	Discharged
12446	Pte	Gallagher	Michael	Darlington	8th		10/07/1916	Dead
13780	Pte	Gallagher	Thomas		8th		06/02/1919	Discharged
25951	Pte	Gamble	John W	Guisborough	8th, 8th		14/02/1919	Class Z Reserve
13287	Pte	Gardner	Thomas G.	Middlesbrough	8th, Depot 28/06/1916, 11th 15/08/1916, Class W Res Munitions, Iron works 20/10/1916	Synovitis R Knee	06/02/1919	Discharged
13775	Pte	Garland	Thomas	South Bank	8th, 8th		11/03/1919	Class Z Reserve
14612	Sgt	Gee	Arthur F.	Brotton	8th, 8th		01/03/1919	Class Z Reserve
17175	Pte	George	Charles A.	Monkwearmouth	8th		27/09/1915	Dead
13867	Pte	Gibbons	Michael	Newbottle	8th		20/03/1919	Deserted 09/03/1917
15352	Sgt	Gibson	William H.		8th, Labour Corps 632993		03/07/1919	Class Z Reserve
13994	Sgt	Gibson	Robert		8th, 8th		04/02/1919	Class Z Reserve
11858	Pte	Gilbraith	Robert W.	Stockton	8th, Depot 11/08/1916 7th 06/03/1917, 5th 26/03/1917	GSW Back, Arm & Buttock, GSW Severe 23/04/1917	02/02/1919	Class Z Reserve
13120	Pte	Gill	Trevor		8th 6th, 5th Renumbered 243409		31/03/1919	Class Z Reserve
15744	Pte	Gill	Albert	Yarm	8th, 8th		09/03/1919	Class Z Reserve

Number	Rank	Name	First Name	Home Town	Bns served with	Reported Wounded	Discharged	MR Comment
15234	Pte	Gillespie	Hector	Thornaby	8th, 8th, 9th 03/07/1917, 9th, 9th	GSW R Chest 10/07/1916, GSW Hip 5/10/1918. DL 22/11/1917	02/02/1919	Class Z Reserve
11589	Pte	Gillings	John	Middlesbrough	8th		10/07/1916	Dead
11564	Cpl	Gillings	Thomas	Middlesbrough	8th, Depot 15/07/1916, 3rd 28/08/1916, 8th 06/10/1916, Reenlisted 6th West Yorks 26/03/1925 - 31/03/1937, 4350906	GSW L Side 10/07/1916	22/02/1919	Class Z Reserve
19811	Pte	Gillis	James L.	Edinburgh	8th, Depot , 7th 17/02/1917	GSW Thigh 27/01/1916, GSW R Knee 14/11/1917	28/01/1919	Discharged
13237	Pte	Glasper	George A.	Middlesbrough	8th, 8th. Reenlisted R Corps of Signals 23/01/1922	Shell Shock 07/08/1916	11/05/1919	Class Z Reserve
13227	Cpl	Goddard	George	Middlesbrough	8th		05/10/1916	Dead
11944	Pte	Goodchild	William		8th		12/03/1919	Class Z Reserve
14380	Pte	Goodman	Hugh	Middlesbrough	8th		13/07/1919	Discharged
16714	Pte	Gorman	Hugh	Middlesbrough	8th	MDG 18/08/1916	10/07/1916	Dead
17095	Pte	Gowland	Matthew		8th, Royal Scots 202190	DL 04/02/1916	03/10/1918	Discharged
13399	Cpl	Graham	Albert E.	North Ormesby	8th		27/10/1916	Dead
14662	Pte	Graham	George		8th		Still Serving Mar 1920	Still Serving Mar 1920
15374	Pte	Graham	Richard B.	Middlesbrough	8th, 8th		06/05/1919	Class Z Reserve
14834	Pte	Grainger	Thomas E.	Station Town Durham	8th, 8th	GSW Right Foot	26/03/1919	Discharged

Number	Rank	Name	First Name	Home Town	Bns served with	Reported Wounded	Discharged	MR Comment
14467	Pte	Green	Charles W.S.	Monkwearmouth	8th, Labour Corps Sgt 615690	GSW Calf	17/02/1919	Discharged
13679	Pte	Greener	John J.		8th, 8th		01/02/1919	Class Z Reserve
14401	Pte	Gregson	James	Redcar	8th, 11th, 9th	MDG 11/08/1916	05/02/1919	Discharged
12068	Pte	Grieves	Thomas W.	Middlesbrough	8th		01/02/1919	Discharged
14652	Pte	Groombridge	William	Boldon Colliery	8th		22/07/1916	Dead
19398	Pte	Gunn	Norman	Middlesbrough	8th, Nottinhamshire & Derbyshire Regt TR/6/9035		14/12/1918	Discharged
13886	Pte	Guy	Arthur	Seaham Harbour	8th, 8th		04/02/1919	Class Z Reserve
14827	Pte	Guy	Henry	Seaham	8th		17/01/1919	Discharged
12205	Cpl	Haddock	Samuel	Hunslet	8th, DLI 54471			Discharged
15156	Pte	Haell	John G.	Keighley	8th		10/07/1916	Dead
13354	Pte	Hagan	Thomas		8th, 8th		11/02/1919	Class Z Reserve
14595	Sgt	Haggerston	William	South Shields	8th, 8th		28/02/1919	Class Z Reserve
19456	Pte	Hall	Charles	Old Hunwick Durham	8th, 7th, 13th		10/01/1916	Class Z Reserve
13068	Pte	Hall	Charles N.	Eston	8th	MDG 18/08/1916	11/07/1916	Dead
14443	Pte	Hall	George	Whitby	8th	Not Overseas	10/10/1914	
3/9380	Cpl	Hall	Henry S.	Grangetown	8th		16/02/1919	Class Z Reserve
12969	Sgt	Hamill	John	Middlesbrough	8th		01/05/1919	Class Z Reserve
15750	Pte	Hamilton	Arthur	Gateshead	8th, Depot 01/11/1916, DCM Desertion 01/06/1917, 9th, 13th, 4th	GSW Chest 01/10/1917	17/03/1919	Deserted 18/06/1917
14610	Sgt	Hampshire	Harold	Liversedge	8th, 7th, 8th		18/10/1917	Dead

Number	Rank	Name	First Name	Home Town	Bns served with	Reported Wounded	Discharged	MR Comment
13389	Pte	Hannar	Charles		8th, Labour Corps 636715		19/03/1919	Class Z Reserve
12946	Pte	Hanratty	Peter J.		8th, 1/5/ Manchester Regt 201848			Discharged
12996	Pte	Haond	John G.	Sunderland	8th		11/07/1916	Dead
12231	Pte	Harbord	Ernest		8th, Machine Gun Corps 148269		18/03/1919	Class Z Reserve
13069	Pte	Harburn	Joseph T.		8th		05/07/1916	Discharged
15158	Pte	Hardcastle	George E.	Dewsbury	8th	GSW R Shoulder	05/02/1918	Discharged
13214	Pte	Harker	Francis		8th, 6th		02/03/1919	Class Z Reserve
17112	Cpl	Harker	Joseph	Nettlesworth	8th		07/06/1917	Dead
11797	Pte	Harkin	Charles H.	Middlesbrough	8th, Depot 06/02/1917,	GSW R Foot 20/01/1917	10/05/1918	Discharged
11922	Pte	Harman	John T.	Middlesbrough	8th, Depot 13/07/1916, 11th, 3rd, 10th, 5th Missing 28/03/1918 POW	GSW L Arm MDG 11/08/1916	14/03/1919	Class Z Reserve
11863	Pte	Harris	Henry	Middlesbrough	8th	MDG 18/08/1916	10/07/1916	Dead
3/8929	Sgt	Harrison	John	Thornaby	8th		07/06/1917	Dead
14414	Sgt	Harvey	Alec or Alexander		8th		19/02/1919	Class Z Reserve
15724	Cpl	Harvey	Robert W.	South Bank	8th, Depot 17/07/1916, 2nd 03/03/1917, 7th 20/03/1917	Shrapnel Wnd R Arm 10/07/1916	18/02/1919	Class Z Reserve
13756	Pte	Hastings	David	South Bank	8th, 8th	WL 27/08/1917	16/02/1919	Class Z Reserve
13393	Pte	Hastings	Robert	Spring, Richmond Yorks	8th, Labour Corps L/Cpl 544479		19/02/1919	Class Z Reserve

Number	Rank	Name	First Name	Home Town	Bns served with	Reported Wounded	Discharged	MR Comment
12097	Pte	Haughey	Edward	North Ormesby	8th, 8th, 6th, 8th		21/02/1919	Class Z Reserve
13477	Cpl	Havelock	George	Ryhope	8th.		06/10/1916	Dead
12842	Pte	Hawes	Robert	Fulwell	8th, Depot 31/05/1916, 11th, 3rd, 6th, 13th	Evac Enteric 31/05/1916	31/01/1919	Discharged
9028	Sgt	Hawkins	Stephen	North Kensington	8th, Labour Corps Sgt 564792		05/05/1919	Class Z Reserve
12704	L/Cpl	Hawkswell	Arthur	Whitby	8th		26/03/1916	Dead
20675	Pte	Hayes	Charles		8th, 13/R Inniskilling Fusiliers 47496			
14471	Pte	Healer	John T	Murton Colliery	8th, Depot 10/10/1916, 9th 11/06/1917, 8th 15/08/1917, 8th	GSW Leg & Abdomen, 10/1916, GSW R Chest R Foot, R Forearm 03/1917	31/01/1919	Class Z Reserve
14282	Pte	Hellam	Norman S	Tyne Dock	8th, Labour Corps 124228	GSW Rt Thigh	22/05/1919	Class Z Reserve
14577	Pte	Henderson	Watson	New Herrington	8th, Depot 19/07/1916, 10thj Trg Res Bn 17/10/1916	GSW L Cheek	31/12/1917	31/12/1917
11830	Pte	Henderson	Charles	Middlesbrough	8th. Did not Serve Overseas.		27/10/1914	Discharged
17804	Pte	Hendry	William	Grangetown	8th, 8th. Military Medal 17/12/1917	GSW Scalp 28/05/1917, ICT R Thigh 14/10/1918	11/03/1919	Class Z Reserve
17162	Pte	Hetherington	George	Wingate	8th		08/10/1916	Dead
17092	Pte	Hetherington	Herbert	Spennymoor	8th		06/07/1916	Dead
14961	Pte	Hewison	Matthew	Penshaw	8th		22/09/1915	Dead
14312	Pte	Hewison	Thomas W	Shiney Row	8th. Depot 31/07/1916	GSW R Thigh	10/01/1919	Class Z Reserve

Number	Rank	Name	First Name	Home Town	Bns served with	Reported Wounded	Discharged	MR Comment
8956	Pte	Hewitson	Francis		8th, Labour Corps 701949		04/02/1919	Discharged
13680	Pte	Hewitt	Robert		8th, 8th		21/02/1919	Class Z Reserve
13374	Pte	Hick	John E	Whitby	8th, Depot 02/06/1916	Evac VDH 26/05/1916	13/10/1916	Discharged
19356	Pte	Hicks	George		8th, Labour Corps 284756			
13774	Pte	Higgins	Michael	Eston	8th		04/10/1916	Dead
12275	Pte	Higgins	Peter	Middlesbrough	8th, Labour Corps 418428	Neurasthenia Defective Vision	06/06/1920	Discharged
13949	Pte	Hill	James	Washington	8th 3rd 10/04/1916, Depot 23/07/1916	Wounds & Sickness 392 xvi	03/01/1917	Discharged
13332	Sgt	Hill	Joseph	Murton	8th, 8th		28/01/1919	Class Z Reserve
13877	Pte	Hind	Robert	Shotton Colliery	8th, Labour Corps 27/12/1917 479272	GSW L Hand 11/04/1917 GSW L Forearm 31/07/1917, DL 10/09/1917	03/03/1919	Discharged
12219	Pte	Hodson	Thomas	Leeds	8th, Depot 31/03/1917, 3rd, 12th, 5th,Durham LI 29th, 20th 101750	GSW L Foot 04/11/1917	20/03/1919	Class Z Reserve
19454	Pte	Hogg	Arthur E	West Auckland	8th		15/08/1919	Discharged
14613	Pte	Hoggarth	Arthur		8th, 8th		06/03/1919	Class Z Reserve
13243	Pte	Hoggett	Henry	Eston	8th		18/09/1915	Dead
13984	Pte	Holden	Andrew	Barmston	8th, Royal Irish Regt 5119		26/03/1919	Class Z Reserve
13066	Pte	Holdsworth	John Wm	Normanby	8th		23/01/1916	Dead
11934	Pte	Hollywood	Michael	Middlesbrough	8th, 8th	DL 23/10/1917	23/04/1919	Class Z Reserve

Number	Rank	Name	First Name	Home Town	Bns served with	Reported Wounded	Discharged	MR Comment
17738	Pte	Holman	Henry	Seaham Harbour	8th, 8th		01/02/1919	Class Z Reserve
14306	Cpl	Holt	George	Jarrow	8th		10/07/1916	Dead
14197	Pte	Holt	Josiah	Burnley	8th		Still AWOL 1919	Deserted 27/12/1916.
13297	Pte	Holt	Stephen	Newbottle	8th, Depot 15/07/1916, 3rd 04/11/1916, 7th, 6th, 2nd	GSW L Thigh 10/07/1916	31/01/1919	Class Z Reserve
11525	CSM	Homer	Edward L.	Middlesbrough	8th , 8th, 8th.		09/03/1919	Class Z Reserve
13795	Pte	Hood	John W.		8th, 8th		03/02/1919	Class Z Reserve
14531	Pte	Hope	John E.	Sunderland	8th, 18th Gloucestershire Regiment 53469	GSW Left Hand	16/01/1919	Class Z Reserve
17131	Pte	Horn	Stanley		8th, Royal Irish Regt 5118			Class Z Reserve
12542	Pte	Hornby	Robert	Eston	8th		24/01/1916	Dead
12540	Pte	Hornby	Thomas	Eston	8th	DL 16/02/1916	24/01/1916	Dead
13809	Pte	Horton	Charles	Sunderland	8th, Depot 14/07/1916, Class W Reserve 22/01/1917 Munitions	GSW VIII Upper Extremities	03/01/1919	Discharged
13404	Pte	Horton	James W.	South Bank	8th		26/09/1917	Dead
11948	Cpl	Hotchkiss	Albert E.	Middlesbrough	8th		21/03/1918	Dead
13148	Cpl	Huby	Charles F.	Middlesbrough	8th, Depot 17/10/1916	GSW R Knee	06/03/1919	Class Z Reserve
15031	Pte	Hughes	John	Ryhope	8th	9/11/1916 Leeds Mercury		Discharged
13377	Pte	Hughes	Joseph		8th, 8th		28/03/1919	Class Z Reserve

Number	Rank	Name	First Name	Home Town	Bns served with	Reported Wounded	Discharged	MR Comment
12063	Pte	Hugill	Edward	Haverton Hill, Res South Bank	8th, Depot 19/07/1916, Trg Res 13 29/11/1916, 8th 30/07/1917, Oxford & Buckinghamshire LI 2nd Gar Bn 35648	GSW Back	01/04/1919	Class Z Reserve
13676	Pte	Hull	George	Wheatley Hill	8th		06/07/1916	Dead
13804	Pte	Hull	John	Hendon	8th, Depot 26/10/1917, 13th. AWOL 30/03/1918 - 18/07/1918 DCM Desertion 6 Mnths Detention, remitted	GSW L Arm 25/03/1916, GSW Both Legs 12/10/1917	02/08/1919	Deserted 18/07/1918,
13942	Pte	Humble	Joseph	Fatfield	8th		10/07/1916	Dead
16741	Pte	Humphrey	James	Hendon	8th, 8th		14/03/1919	Class Z Reserve
13051	Pte	Hunt	Richard J.	Normanby	8th	MDG 18/08/1916	10/07/1916	Dead
16709	Pte	Hunter	James C.	West Cornforth	8th		09/07/1916	Dead
14299	Pte	Hunter	John		8th, 8th		01/03/1919	Class Z Reserve
16669	Pte	Hunter	Percy	Esh Winning	8th, 7th, 8th, 8th	Shrapnel Wnd R Eye 27/07/1916	08/03/1919	Class Z Reserve
16680	Pte	Hunter	Samuel W.	Sunderland	8th, East Yorkshire Regt 51130	GSW L Arm		Discharged
12269	Pte	Hunter	Thomas		8th, Royal Irish Regt 5071		06/04/1919	Class Z Reserve
14064	Pte	Hush	Thomas	Felling	8th		15/07/1916	Dead
13101	Pte	Inglis	Henry	Durham City	8th		10/07/1916	Dead
14219	Pte	Ironside	Frank	Monkwearmouth	8th, 8th		17/03/1919	Class Z Reserve
14377	Pte	Jackson	Ernest		8th, 8th		14/03/1919	Class Z Reserve
13800	Pte	Jackson	George E.	Wakefield	8th, 8th		03/02/1919	Class Z Reserve

Number	Rank	Name	First Name	Home Town	Bns served with	Reported Wounded	Discharged	MR Comment
11949	Pte	Jackson	Herbert	Redcar	8th, 8th		22/02/1919	Class Z Reserve
14773	Pte	James	William		8th		17/01/1919	Discharged
14492	Pte	Jefferson	George	Richmond	8th, 13th 6th		26/09/1917	Dead
10573	Cpl	Jefferson	John		8th		Still Serving Mar 1920	Still Serving Mar 1920.
13416	Pte	Jerverlund	Frank	Middlesbrough	8th		01/07/1916	Dead
13463	Pte	Jobling	James A.	Whitburn	8th, 8th		04/02/1919	Class Z Reserve
15376	Pte	Jobling	Robert H.	Yarm	8th, 8th		12/03/1919	Class Z Reserve
15032	Pte	Jobling	Thomas	Monkwearmouth	8th	Rheumatism	06/04/1918	Discharged
19347	Pte	Johnson	Albert E.		8th, 2nd, 5th		04/03/1919	Class Z Reserve
13110	Pte	Johnson	John		8th, Labour Corps 702546		21/04/1917	Discharged
14720	Pte	Johnson	Jonathon	Ryhope	8th	GSW Right Foot	20/08/1917	Discharged
12690	Pte	Johnston	William	Fencehouses	8th.Depot 17/07/1916, Reenlisted R Field Artillery 13/10/1930	GSW L Wrist 10/07/1916	22/05/1917	Dicharged
12088	Sgt	Jones	James	Middlesbrough	8th, Depot 13/07/1916, 9th, 8th	GSW L Buttock 10/07/1916	20/02/1919	Class Z Reserve
14682	Pte	Jones	James R.	Rotherhithe,	8th, Depot 09/11/1916, 8th		14/02/1919	Class Z Reserve
25966	Pte	Jones	John	Middlesbrough	8th	GSW Chest 01/10/1917	06/03/1919	Class Z Reserve
13760	Pte	Jones	Thomas H.		8th, K O Yorkshire LI 62922		14/03/1919	Class Z Reserve
13232	Cpl	Jones	William	Middlesbrough	8th	GSW Shldr & L Arm 09/06/1917	02/03/1919	Class Z Reserve
16799	Pte	Jordan	William C.		8th, 8th		19/03/1919	Class Z Reserve

Number	Rank	Name	First Name	Home Town	Bns served with	Reported Wounded	Discharged	MR Comment
14303	Cpl	Judson	William	Seaham	8th	GSW R Hip & Leg, GSW Face serious Acc at Bomb school 13/11/1915	24/03/1920	Class Z Reserve
13990	Pte	Kane	John	Jarrow	8th, Labour Corps 397456, King's Royal Rifle Corps 58409		03/06/1919	Class Z Reserve
13825	Pte	Kavanagh	William	Hetton le Hole	8th, 2/Royal irish Regt 5080	GSW R Thigh 10/07/1916, Daily List: 11th August 1916, M/Bro Dly Gaz Fri 11/8/1916 P 6 Col 3, Also Newcastle Journal 11/8/1916 page 6 Col 5 Durham Chronicle 18/8/1916 Page 3 Col 5	03/03/1919	Class Z Reserve
13755	Pte	Kearns	Daniel		8th		17/01/1919	Discharged
14342	Pte	Kears	John E	Wallsend	8th		10/07/1916	Dead
19340	Pte	Keating	James	Fencehouses	8th		22/09/1916	Discharged
13070	A/Sgt	Keegan	James	Middlesbrough	8th, Depot 18/05/1916, 6th 21/09/1916, 2nd	Shell Wnd Arm 13/05/1916, GSW L Thigh 09/10/1917	08/03/1919	Class Z Reserve
13320	Pte	Keenan	Fred	Sunderland	8th. Depot 13/02/1917 Class W Reserve Munitions	Docs in Bradford Docs	06/01/1918	Discharged

Number	Rank	Name	First Name	Home Town	Bns served with	Reported Wounded	Discharged	MR Comment
19337	Pte	Kelbett	Ernest	Fencehouses	8th		17/01/1919	Discharged
14006	Sgt	Kelly	James P.	Washington Station	8th, 8th		26/03/1919	Class Z Reserve
17173	Pte	Kemp	William	Carlin How	8th, 7th		26/04/1917	Dead
17800	Pte	Kennedy	John	Grangetown	8th, Depot 11/10/1916 Military Medal 09/12/1916	GSW R Arm	16/10/1917	Discharged
13407	Pte	Kennington	Arthur	Manchester	8th, Depot 23/11/1914, 8th 04/02/1916, Depot 07/08/1916, 2nd 07/04/1917, 2nd	ICT Both Legs 21/11/1915 GSW 07/08/1916 Wnd Burried Shell 31/07/1917, Gassed 20/05/1918	21/02/1919	Class Z Reserve
14146	Pte	Keogh	Cornelius	Ludworth	8th		04/02/1919	Class Z Reserve
13983	Pte	Keoghan	Patrick A.	Great Usworth	8th, 8th, 8th	Died 23 Jan 1922	29/01/1919	Discharged
12234	Pte	Kilburn	Thomas	Leeds	8th		10/07/1916	Dead
13936	Pte	King	Joseph		8th, 8th		04/02/1919	Class Z Reserve
3/8896	Pte	King	Peter	Haverton Hill	8th		12/07/1916	Dead
16813	Pte	King	Robert	Washington Station	8th, Enlisted Border Regt trf 8th Yorks Regt 31/01/1915, Depot 14/07/1916, 6th 18/11/1916	GSW L Arm & Back 10/07/1916, GSW Buttock, L Thigh L Shldr 27/09/1917	20/03/1918	Discharged
13982	Pte	King	Bernard	Washington Station	8th, Depot 02/08/1916, 6th 17/02/1917, 2nd Bn 16/05/1918	Wnd Slight 10/07/1916 DL 04/09/1916	02/02/1919	Class Z Reserve

Number	Rank	Name	First Name	Home Town	Bns served with	Reported Wounded	Discharged	MR Comment
12090	Pte	Kirton	George		8th, Machine Gun Corps 23123		19/03/1919	Class Z Reserve
13133	Pte	Knaggs	George	Lazenby	8th, 8th		10/02/1919	Class Z Reserve
11552	Clr Sgt	Knight	James H.		8th, 8th		18/03/1919	Class Z Reserve
15737	Pte	Knowles	William	North Shields	8th, Labour Corps 284881		17/01/1919	Discharged
11577	Clr Sgt	Knowles	Albert		8th, 8th		20/03/1919	Class Z Reserve
15722	Pte	Lagan	Joseph	Grangetown	8th To Loyal North Lancashire Regiment 43009		26/03/1919	Class Z Reserve
13870	Pte	Lamb	James R.	Jarrow	8th, Labour Corps 207871	Died 05/11/1920 Wife's Pension refused married after discharge	17/02/1919	Discharged
15945	Pte	Lanaghan	James	Jarrow	8th, Depot 17/07/1916	GSW L Foot 10/07/1916	07/02/1917	Discharged
13113	Pte	Lancaster	William	Middlesbrough	8th, Labour Corps 25976	Amputation of Right Index Finger	16/03/1919	Class Z Reserve
12047	Pte	Lane	George R.		8th, 8th , 10th Commission 4/02/1919	MiD June 1916	02/02/1919	Discharged to Commission
17806	Pte	Langan	Richard	Horden	8th	Evac Septic Leg 01/04/1916	05/02/1918	Discharged
14276	Pte	Laws	Wilfred	Shiney Row	8th, 8th, 10th, 2nd	GSW Chest	10/04/1919	Class Z Reserve
14717	Pte	Lawson	Benjamin	Monkwearmouth	8th	Died 10/10/1924	09/01/1919	Discharged
16690	Pte	Lawson	David S	Hebburn Colliery	8th		10/07/1916	Dead

Number	Rank	Name	First Name	Home Town	Bns served with	Reported Wounded	Discharged	MR Comment
11956	Cpl	Lawson	George	Flamborough	8th	Ploegsteert Memorial	25/09/1917	Discharged to Commission 10/ Yorks Regt
12715	Pte	Lazenby	Robert T.	South Bank	8th	DoW 38th CCS	11/07/1916	Dead
12714	Pte	Leach	Alfred	North Ormesby	8th		17/07/1917	Dead
13745	Pte	Lee	Alick	Halifax	8th, Depot 07/04/1916, 6th, 4th, 8th, 8th.	GSW R Knee Bomb explosion 13/11/1915, GSW Shrap Wnd Legs 27/12/1915, GSW L Wrist 27/03/1916	23/02/1919	Class Z Reserve
15199	Pte	Lee	Thomas B.A.		8th, 1st			Class Z Reserve
17123	Pte	Lee	Andrew	Haswell	8th, 6th		27/08/1917	Dead
13771	Pte.	Lenaghan	Michael	South Bank	8th	Evac Chronic Bronchitis exposure	27/08/1917	Discharged
12630	Pte	Lenton	Henry J.	Middlesbrough	8th, Depot 11/06/1917, 7th 08/09/1917, 4th 10/02/1918, 9th 26/10/1918, Depot 11/11/1918	ICT L Foot 18/04/1916, GSW Severe Abdomen 11/06/1917, GSW R Eyebrow	26/02/1919	Class Z Reserve
13166	Pte	Lester	Henry E.	Middlesbrough	8th		05/10/1916	Dead
13369	Sgt	Lewis	Arthur R.	Stockton	8th	DoW 1/2nd South Midland Fld Amb RAMC	29/07/1916	Dead

Number	Rank	Name	First Name	Home Town	Bns served with	Reported Wounded	Discharged	MR Comment
12030	Pte	Lewis	John	Grangetown	8th, Depot 15/07/1916, Class W Reserve 12/03/1917 Munitions	GSW Thigh 10/07/1916, MDG 11/08/1916	13/01/1919	Discharged
11474	Pte	Lickess	William H.	Stockton	8th	No 2 Gen Hosp Le Havre	19/07/1916	Dead
11491	Cpl	Lier	John T.	Guisborough	8th		10/07/1916	Dead
16401	Pte	Lindoe	Henry	Coxhoe	8th		21/01/1919	Discharged
15269	Pte	Linley	Frank		8th, Labour Corps 570624		28/03/1919	Class Z Reserve
8939	Pte	Livingstone	David	Middlesbrough	8th, 7th, 2nd, 2nd 266th POW Coy Labour Corps 619955, Northmbld Fus 98007	DL 24/08/1916	18/03/1919	Discharged
13697	Pte	Lobbin	William J.	Hendon Sunderland	8th, Wiltshire Regiment, Bedfordshire Regt 59824	GSW Both Thighs	05/04/1919	Class Z Reserve
14392	Pte	Long	Dennis		8th, 8th		28/01/1919	Class Z Reserve
13218	Pte	Looney	John	Pendleton, Manchester	8th, 8th		02/10/1919	Class Z Reserve
11358	Pte	Lowe	George		8th, Royal Engineers 82671			Class Z Reserve
13757	Pte	Lowery	Joseph	South Bank	8th		12/07/1916	Dead
16670	Pte	Lumley	Thomas W.	Waterhouses	8th, Depot 19/07/1916, Labour Corps 23/06/1917 284655	Shell Shock 10/07/1916	20/01/1919	Class Z Reserve
13868	Pte	Luther	Walter		8th, 2/ West Yorkshire Regt 63328		11/01/1919	Class Z Reserve
12472	Pte	Lyle	David	Stockton	8th	Died at Home	06/07/1918	Dead
12970	Pte	Lynch	Donald	Washington	8th, Sgt 28/11/1914 03/12/17, 8th	Shell Shock 31/07/1916	06/03/1919	Class Z Reserve

Number	Rank	Name	First Name	Home Town	Bns served with	Reported Wounded	Discharged	MR Comment
11715	Pte	Lynch	Thomas	Middlesbrough	8th, Labour Corps 485147	Shell Shock MDG 18/08/1916	20/06/1919	Class Z Reserve
13135	Pte	Lyon	Charles	Eston	8th		12/07/1916	Dead
15048	Cpl	MacKay	Malcolm J.	Sunderland	8th, East Yorkshire Regt 27707 L/Sgt Educated Bede College Durham	GSW Left Arm	06/04/1919	Class Z Reserve
8984	Pte	MacKenzie	Arthur	Catterick	8th, Royal Sussex Regt G/22555		20/03/1918	Dead
13763	Pte	Mackin	Owen	Middlesbrough	8th	R Forearm amputated 10/07/1916	29/11/1916	Discharged
11823	Pte	Mackin	Thomas	South Bank	8th		10/05/1917	Dead
14865	Pte	Macknay	John	Seaham Harbour	8th, 8th	Bronchitis	04/02/1919	Class Z Reserve
12999	Pte	Manders	Benjamin	Middlesbrough	8th, Depot 10/05/1916, Class W Reserve Munitions	Evac Debility	18/08/1917	Discharged
11556	Pte	Manders	Patrick	Middlesbrough	8th, 11th, 9/South Staffordshire Regt 43366	DL 01/09/1917		
17759	Cpl	Mann	John W.	Southwick	8th, Depot 18/03/1917, Class W Reserve Munitions	Trench Foot 01/03/1917	16/01/1919	Discharged
11529	Pte	Manning	Dennis	Middlesbrough	8th		22/03/1916	Dead
16738	Pte	March	William	Witton Park	8th, Depot 31/05/1916, 7th, 16/12/1916, 8th, 30/07/1917, 8th	Evac sick 13/05/1916	27/01/1919	Discharged
13176	Pte	Marney	Patrick	Middlesbrough	8th, Royal Army Medical Corps 137737 18/2/18	6/9/15 R Hand, 5/7/16 R Thigh, 16/11/1917 Wnd S		Reenlisted Northhbld Fus 23/02/1920

Number	Rank	Name	First Name	Home Town	Bns served with	Reported Wounded	Discharged	MR Comment
17240	Pte	Marr	Henry	Sunderland	8th, Depot 25/03/1916, 11th 22/04/1916	Evac Infl Middle Ear	05/07/1916	Discharged
17096	Pte	Marriott	Ernest	Northampton	8th, Labour Corps 223074	Bronchitis	04/03/1919	Class Z Reserve
12264	Pte	Marron	James	Middlesbrough	8th, 6th	MDG 11/08/1916	27/08/1917	Dead
13179	Pte	Martin	James W.	Middlesbrough	8th, Northld Fus	DL 02/02/1916		Class Z Reserve
19338	Pte	Martin	Robert	Fencehouses	8th, Depot 06/02/1916, Highland LI 33082 5/11/16, Labour Corps 382139 23/1/1917	Wnd Severe 02/1916	13/03/1919	Discharged
14732	Sgt	Martindale	Arthur C.		8th		26/06/1917	Discharged to Commission Northblnd Fus
11982	A/Sgt	Martindale	George H.	Hull	8th, Depot 21/08/1916, 261st Inf Bn 16/07/1917, 51st Leicester regt 01/12/1917	Paralysis R Arm 17/08/1916	01/03/1919	Class Z Reserve
14770	CSM	Mashender	William	Sunderland	8th, 8th	Multiple shell wounds.	29/01/1919	Discharged
14007	Pte	Mason	Hedley	Washington	8th, Depot 15/07/1916, 3rd 01/12/1916	Wnd Contusiuons Back 10/07/1916	08/01/1919	Class Z Reserve
15740	Pte	Mason	James W.	Eston	8th, Depot 05/10/1916 Class W Reserve Ironstone miner 06/10/1916		07/01/1919	Discharged
15715	Clr Sgt	Mason	Richard		8th		20/09/1916	Discharged to Commission 13/ Yorkshire Regt
15036	Pte	Mather	John	Glasgow	8th		18/10/1917	Dead

Number	Rank	Name	First Name	Home Town	Bns served with	Reported Wounded	Discharged	MR Comment
7667	Pte	Matthews	Charles	Hull, Res Custom House, London	8th, 2nd, 4th, renumbered 203077		23/04/1917	Dead
13316	Pte	Matthews	James	Sunderland	8th, Labour Corps 614266	Bronchitis	15/02/1919	Class Z Reserve
3/8367	Pte	Matthews	John	South Bank	8th		15/06/1916	Dead
13394	Pte	Maude	John	Grangetown	8th, West Yorkshire Reg 72498		30/09/1919	Class Z Reserve
16814	Pte	Maughan	Anthony	Hetton le Hole	8th, Attested for 7th Border Regt Trf 8th Yorks Regt 05/02/1915, Depot 13/07/1916, 2nd, 7th	GSW Scrotum 10/07/1916 MDG 09/08/1916, Fractured Ankle 12/1917, MDG 09/08/1916, DL 28/08/1917	10/01/1919	Class Z Reserve
14484	Pte	McAdams	Francis S.	Washington Station	8th Ex 1st Border Regt Time expired	Trench Mortar Wnd Back & R Arm 14/01/1916	26/07/1916	Discharged
12880	Pte	McCabe	Charles	Sunderland	8th, Depot 30/03/1916, 7th, 16/12/1916, 9th 18/06/1917	Evac Sick 03/1916, Shell Wnd L Leg 21/09/1917	17/04/1918	Discharged
14089	Cpl	McCallum	Simon		8th, 8th			Class Z Reserve
14884	Pte	McCartney	Bernard		8th, 7th, 12th, 5th Duke of Wellington's Regt 34486		09/02/1919	Class Z Reserve
12268	Pte	McCluskey	James		8th, 8th		25/02/1919	Class Z Reserve
13207	Pte	McCracken	John J.	Middlesbrough	8th		31/01/1916	Dead
3/8836	Pte	McCulloch	John	Clydebank Glasgow	8th	Bronchitis	08/03/1919	Class Z Reserve
13954	Cpl	McDermott	Thomas		8th, 8th, 8th		03/02/1919	Class Z Reserve

Number	Rank	Name	First Name	Home Town	Bns served with	Reported Wounded	Discharged	MR Comment
12487	Pte	McDonald	Thomas		8th		14/01/1919	Discharged
12106	Pte	McGill	John	Middlesbrough	8th, Labour Corps 514550, Border Regt 31074	Neurasthenia	09/12/1919	Discharged
12156	Pte	McGuiness	Patrick		8th, 8th, 8th.. AWOL 27/08/1918 - 05/09/1918		23/02/1919	Class Z Reserve
14835	Pte	McKenna	William	Kelloe, Durham	8th	Bronchitis	02/05/1916	Discharged
13808	Pte	McKenzie	John W.	Sunderland	8th, Depot 14/07/1916 Deserter 11/12/1916, 8th, 13th	GSW L Arm 10/07/1916	26/02/1919	Deserted 06/03/1917
15034	Pte	McKenzie	Michael	Easington Colliery	8th, Labour Corps 263587	Neurasthenia, Died 07/11/1925	10/03/1919	Class Z Reserve
19416	Pte	McKenzie	Sandie	Boosbeck	8th	GSW L Shldr, Neurasthenia.	31/01/1919	Discharged
16735	Cpl	McManus	John	Horden	8th		22/09/1917	Dead
12948	Pte	Meaburn	James W.	Eston	8th, 8th	GSW L Knee	23/03/1919	Class Z Reserve
18978	Pte	Mead	Henry H.	Whitby	8th, Depot 21/05/1917	GSW Back Frac Vertibrea Spine 05/1917	10/12/1917	Discharged
12435	Sgt	Mellor	Joshua		8th	Did not serve overseas	20/07/1915	Discharged
14391	Pte	Middleton	John E.	Grangetown	8th, 6th, 4th, 8th		17/01/2019	Discharged
14567	Pte	Milburn	John		8th		17/01/1919	Discharged
11869	Pte	Miller	Frederick	Hull	8th	Sickness 392 xvi, V.D.H.	09/09/1916	Discharged

Number	Rank	Name	First Name	Home Town	Bns served with	Reported Wounded	Discharged	MR Comment
14487	Pte	Miller	John	Washington	8th, Depot 14/06/1917 5th Missing 27/05/1918 POW	GSW L Hand 07/06/1917	31/03/1919	Class Z Reserve
13892	Pte	Miller	Robert		8th, 8th		28/01/1919	Class Z Reserve
14759	Sgt	Miller	Zachariah	Ryhope Colliery	8th, 8th, FGCM 12/04/1918 AWOL 22/03 - 28/03/1918	Acc Wnd Hand 25/09/1915, ICT Face 17/05/1917	04/02/1919	Class Z Reserve
13738	Pte	Mills	William	Wansford, Cheshire,	8th, Depot 12/12/1915, 2nd 07/04/1917, 8th 14/09/1917, 8th	ICT R Thigh 19/11/1915	18/03/1919	Class Z Reserve
13863	Pte	Minto	Matthew S.	Hebburn	8th, Somerset LI 52502, Lab Corps, R Irish R, Rifle Bde		22/03/1919	Class Z Reserve
14010	Pte	Mitchell	Gordon	Seaham Harbour	8th, 8th		28/01/1919	Class Z Reserve
14068	Pte	Mitchell	Jack		8th, 8th		28/01/1919	Class Z Reserve
13330	Pte	Moir	Arthur W.	Sunderland	8th, Royal Engineers, 29th Durham LI 101780		11/01/1919	Class Z Reserve
13072	Pte	Molyneux	John	Leamside	8th, Depot 26/05/1916, Renumbered 243398		05/02/1918	Discharged
19823	Pte	Monaghan	Thomas	Bedlington	8th, To Depot 29/06/1917	Shell Wnd Chest 15/10/1916' GSW Leg & Back L Thigh Amputated 07/06/1917	30/12/1917	Discharged
11851	Pte	Money	Herbert	Leeds	8th, 8th, 10th		11/04/1917	Dead
14494	Sgt	Moody	Alfred	South Bank	8th, 8th		06/05/1919	Class Z Reserve
13549	Cpl	Moody	John T.	Hartlepool	8th.Class P Reserve 26/04/1918 Shipbuilding	GSW L Shldr & Arm 09/1917	27/01/1919	Discharged

Number	Rank	Name	First Name	Home Town	Bns served with	Reported Wounded	Discharged	MR Comment
11517	Pte	Moore	Thomas J.	Eston	8th.	DL & MDG 09/08/1916	26/05/1917	Discharged
15152	Pte	Moore	Walter	Darlington	8th.		07/07/1916	Dead
12544	Pte	Moore	William		8th		13/01/1919	Discharged
16717	Pte	Morgan	John	Fencehouses	8th, 8th, 10th, 4th.		23/03/1918	Dead
12445	Pte	Morgan	Osborne	Grangetown	8th.	MDG 09/08/1916	17/01/1919	Discharged
12757	Pte	Morgan	William A.	Battersea	8th.		10/07/1916	Dead
12911	Sgt	Morris	James V.		8th		11/05/1919	Class Z Reserve
13742	Pte	Morris	John T.		8th, 1st.			Class Z Reserve
12240	Pte	Morris	Robert H.	Scarborough	8th		10/07/1916	Dead
13209	Pte	Morrison	Thomas	Middlesbrough	8th.		10/04/1916	Dead
11286	Pte	Mortimer	Clifford	Leeds	8th, 6th.	DL 09/08/1916	07/12/1916	Dead
12184	Pte	Mortimer	Edward	Beeston	8th, 2nd.		31/07/1917	Dead
12541	Pte	Mortimer	Frank		8th, Royal Irish Regt 5070			
14645	Pte	Morton	John	Shadforth Durham	8th.	GSW Lsft Forearm	26/11/1918	Discharged
17115	Cpl	Moses	Jacob	Howden le Wear	8th, 2nd, 12th, 5th.		27/05/1918	Dead
12943	Pte	Moy	John	Grangetown	8th, Depot 15/07/1916, 2nd 16/03/1917, 13th 21/11/1918.	Shrapnel Wnd R Leg 07/1916	29/03/1919	Class Z Reserve
15009	Pte	Mulligan	Andrew	Ryhope	8th, 7th.		08/02/1917	Dead
14348	Pte	Muncaster	Robert W.	Lanchester	8th, 2nd.		06/11/1918	Dead
15751	Pte	Munro	Joseph J.	Leeds	8th, 8th.	ICT Hand 26/09/1915	27/03/1919	Class Z Reserve

Number	Rank	Name	First Name	Home Town	Bns served with	Reported Wounded	Discharged	MR Comment
14534	Pte	Murdy	Thomas	Monkwearmouth	8th, Depot 28/11/1916, 7th 25/11/1917, 8th 30/04/1918		02/02/1919	Class Z Reserve
12724	Pte	Murphy	Timothy	Middlesbrough	8th, 5th Renumbered 243264	MDG 09/08/1916		Deserted 17/08/1917
12076	Pte	Murray	James		8th		06/02/1919	Discharged
11590	Pte	Musgrove	Robert		8th		06/01/1919	Discharged
14227	Sgt	Mussett	Alfred	Monkseaton	8th	Neurasthenia	31/03/1917	Discharged to Commission 3/ Northld Fusiliers
17232	Cpl	Mustard	Christopher	Sunderland	8th, 8th		04/02/1919	Class Z Reserve
9056	CSM	Myers	Edward W.	Latchingdon Essex	8th, Labour Corps CQMS 317978	Died 16/10/1919, Nephritis.	03/06/1919	Class Z Reserve
17091	Pte	Myers	Joseph	Spennymoor	8th, Depot 14/07/1916, 2nd 03/03/1917, 7th 20/03/1917 Depot 29/03/1918	GSW L THIGH 10/07/1916, GSW L Leg severe	21/09/1918	Discharged
14709	Cpl	Naylor	James	Sunderland	8th	DL 04/02/1916	30/08/1917	Discharged
11902	Pte	Naylor	Joseph E.	Guisborough	8th		17/01/1919	Discharged
12325	Pte	Nelson	Albert	Middlesbrough	8th, R Irish Regt 11806	MDG 09/08/1916	14/09/1918	Discharged
12242	Sgt	Nelson	Walter	Burton Salmon Yorks	8th, 8th, Depot 07/06/1918 To OCB	Scalp Wnd & Shock 05/10/1916	06/02/1919	Class Z Reserve
3/9003	Sgt	Nelson	Fred		8th, 8th		21/02/1919	Class Z Reserve
13187	Pte	Newby	Charles	Middlesbrough	8th		11/07/1916	Dead
19335	Pte	Newman	Robert	Fencehouses	8th, Labour Corps 118619	Neurasthenia	25/11/1918	Discharged
14017	Pte	Newstead	Alexander	Hetton le Hole	8th, Labour Corps 387983	GSW Right Upper Arm	22/04/1918	Discharged

Number	Rank	Name	First Name	Home Town	Bns served with	Reported Wounded	Discharged	MR Comment
11925	Pte	Nichols	Charles	Middlesbrough	8th, 8th		16/03/1919	Class Z Reserve
15203	Pte	Nicholson	Charles	York	8th		10/07/1916	Dead
13323	Pte	Nicholson	John B.	Murton Colliery	8th, South Staffordshire Regt 43361			Class Z Reserve
14444	Pte	Noble	Frank	Hunslet	8th, 8th, 10th		25/09/1917	Discharged
13246	Pte	Noble	Richard	Middlesbrough	8th	Bomb Wounds Bothn eyes	02/12/1916	Discharged
13816	A/Cpl	Nolan	Michael	Monkwearmouth	8th		07/06/1917	Dead
3/9127	Sgt	Normandale	George	Scarborough	8th, 24/10/1914 9th Sgt 01/11/1914, Depot 16/07/1916 81st Trg Res Bn 14/09/1916	GSW L Foot 10/07/1916	22/05/1919	Class Z Reserve
13748	Pte	O'Brien	Mark	Grangetown	8th		24/03/1916	Dead
14189	Pte	O'Connell	John W.	Middlesbrough	8th. CSM 10/10/1914 Reverts to Sgt 04/01/1915, Depot 15/05/1916, 51st Liecestershire Regt 01/12/1917 CSM 11/12/1917	Evac Nephritis 05/1916	07/02/1919	Class Z Reserve
16800	Pte	O'Donnell	John	Hull	8th, Depot 15/07/1916, 8th 01/02/1917, Depot 01/03/1917 att 53rd YS Durham LI	Laceration R Leg 10/07/1916	06/03/1919	Class Z Reserve
11508	Pte	Olford	Arthur W.	Eston	8th	DoW No 2 Stationary Hosp	08/07/1916	Dead
16821	Pte	Oliffe	Percy	Upton Park, London	8th		10/07/1916	Dead
14573	Pte	Oliver	John	North Ormesby	8th, Labour Corps Cpl 376068	MDG 09/08/1916	21/02/1919	Class Z Reserve

Number	Rank	Name	First Name	Home Town	Bns served with	Reported Wounded	Discharged	MR Comment
9376	Pte	Oliver	Tom	Scarborough	8th, Depot 03/10/1917 Labour Corps 407 Ag Lab Coy 26/12/1917 503675	Injury to shldr Dug-out collapsed 08/1915	21/03/1919	Class Z Reserve
13753	Pte	O'Marra	Thomas	Grangetown	8th	MDG 11/08/1916	25/04/1917	Discharged
17808	Pte	O'Neill	Thomas	Middlesbrough	8th	DoW 70 Fld Amb RAMC	31/12/1915	Dead
13636	Sgt	Ord	Robert H.	Haswell	8th		28/02/1919	Class Z Reserve
14066	Pte	Owens	Robert	Trimdon Colliery	8th, Labour Corps 285 Area Employment Coy 370004	V D H	26/03/1918	Discharged
12861	Pte	Oxley	Hercules	South Bank	8th, 6th, 6th, 2nd	MDG 09/08/1916+H610	18/03/1919	Class Z Reserve
15027	Pte	Oxley	Robert A.	Monkwearmouth	8th, 8th		10/07/1916	Dead
13939	A/Sgt	Palmer	Harold S.G.	West Pelton	8th		07/10/1916	Dead
15729	Pte	Park	Ralph	Houghton le Spring	8th, Depot 15/06/1917	GSW R Thigh & 4th Finger R hand 06/07/1917	27/01/1919	Discharged
14830	Pte	Parker	James	Cold Hesledon	8th, 8th		04/02/1919	Class Z Reserve
15757	Pte	Parker	John	South Shields	8th, Depot 19/07/1916, Class P Reserve 31/05/1917	GSW Back 10/07/1916	31/05/1917	31/05/1917
12001	Clr Sgt	Parker	William R.	Hornsea	8th. DCM LG 22/09/1916 ended war as a Captain Yorks Regt		17/12/1916	Discharged to Commission 8/ Yorks Regt
12462	Pte	Parkin	Edward T.		8th, 8th		28/03/1919	Class Z Reserve
17121	Pte	Parkin	Thomas	Horden	8th, 2nd, 9th, 9th, 9th		05/10/1918	Dead
14611	Sgt	Parkin	John M.	Horden	8th, 9th, 9th, 8th, 8th, 10th,	DL 23/10/1917	01/04/1919	Class Z Reserve

Number	Rank	Name	First Name	Home Town	Bns served with	Reported Wounded	Discharged	MR Comment
13109	Pte	Parry	Christopher	Middlesbrough	8th, 6th	MDG 11/08/1916	17/01/1919	Discharged
13195	Pte	Pattison	Albert		8th, 8th		12/03/1919	Class Z Reserve
14710	Pte	Pattison	Cuthbert	Sunderland	8th, 8th		18/03/1919	Class Z Reserve
14574	Pte	Pattison	George		8th, 8th		18/04/1919	Class Z Reserve
12081	Pte	Pattison	John		8th, South Staffordshire Regt 36259		28/04/1919	Class Z Reserve
14763	Pte	Pattison	John J.	Easington Colliery	8th		14/02/1917	Dead
11905	Pte	Pattison	Wilfred	Middlesbrough	8th, 6th, 5th Renumbered 243916		21/02/1919	Class Z Reserve
11825	Cpl	Paylor	Arthur	Guisborough	8th		10/07/1916	Dead
13950	Pte	Perkins	John T.	Washington Station	8th		13/07/1918	Disc harged
16690	Pte	Pescod	James		8th 7th, 4th, 43 Garr Bn Royal Fusiliers 83820			
13625	Pte	Philips	Thomas W.		8th	DL 02/02/1916	20/02/1919	Discharged
12783	Pte	Pickering	John G.	Eston	8t		16/07/1916	Dead
11605	Pte	Pigg	Ernest J.	Thornaby	8th		28/09/1915	Dead
14793	Cpl	Piper	Cuthbert W.	Stockton	8th MM		31/07/1917	Discharged to Commission Northblnd Fus
11918	Cpl	Pitchers	Frederick		8th, 8th, 8th		01/02/1919	Class Z Reserve
12210	Pte	Pitchers	James H.		8th, 8th		16/02/1919	Class Z Reserve
16452	Pte	Plant	John W.	Brandon Colliery	8th Labour Corps 411228		07/03/1917	Discharged

Number	Rank	Name	First Name	Home Town	Bns served with	Reported Wounded	Discharged	MR Comment
14570	Pte	Plumpton	George	Monkwearmouth	8th, 7th		26/04/1918	Deserted 13/02/1917
11604	Pte	Pollard	William		8th, 8th		21/02/1919	Class Z Reserve
11998	Pte	Poole	Charles	Eston	8th, Depot 25/03/1916, 6th 09/09/1916, 8th 11/07/1917		19/03/1919	Class Z Reserve
14667	Sgt	Poole	George	Pickering	8th, 8th		14/02/1919	Class Z Reserve
13116	Pte	Porthouse	George	Middlesbrough	8th, 8th, 2nd		06/05/1918	Dead
11907	Pte	Postgate	Ernest	Guisborough	8th, Depot 17/03/1917 Class W Reserve Ironestone miner 25/03/1917		17/01/1919	Discharged
14018	Pte	Potts	John	Bishop Auckland	8th, Depot 13/07/1916, 8th, 8th	ICT L Thumb	09/02/1919	Class Z Reserve
12495	Pte	Potts	John L	North Shields	8th		21/09/1917	Dead
12038	Pte	Pounder	Harry		8th		13/01/1919	Discharged
19350	Pte	Price	George E	Middlesbrough	8th, Labour Corps 570437		10/04/1919	Class Z Reserve
13258	Pte	Price	John	Middlesbrough	8th	7/12/1915, 21 July 1916 Wnd	22/03/1918	Dead
13826	Pte	Price	John	Hetton le Hole	8th		10/07/1916	Dead
12017	Pte	Price	Thomas H	Warrenby	8th, 8th		21/02/1919	Class Z Reserve
16671	Pte	Proud	A		8th, RAF		30/11/1918	Discharged
12725	Cpl	Proud	James		8th 1/5/Manchester Regt 201881	GSW Right Buttock		Class Z Reserve
16396	Pte	Prudhoe	George A	Seaham Harbour	8th, Depot 04/12/1916 12th, 8th, 8th		27/02/1919	Class Z Reserve

Number	Rank	Name	First Name	Home Town	Bns served with	Reported Wounded	Discharged	MR Comment
14238	Pte	Pullan	Robert L.		8th, 23 Div Sig Coy Royal Engineers 312600 21/09/1917		18/03/1919	Class Z Reserve
15059	Pte	Pullman	Christopher	South Bank	8th	GSW Chest & Left Ankle	07/12/1917	Discharged
11519	Pte	Purdy	William	Guisborough	8th, 8th Depot 18/02/1918 FGCM AWOL 02/07/1918, 8th. Reenlisted 4th 08/08/1921		23/02/1919	Class Z Reserve
19455	Pte	Pybus	Henry O.	West Auckland	8th, 8th		14/03/1919	Class Z Reserve
16809	Pte	Quinn	Patrick	Sunderland	8th, 8th.	GSW Scalp 03/10/1918	27/02/1919	Class Z Reserve
3/8938	Sgt	Rabey	Frank	Upton Park, London	8th		05/10/1916	Dead
13299	Pte	Rae	Alexander D.		8th, 8th		07/03/1919	Class Z Reserve
19383	Pte	Reay	Harold		8th	DL 22/02/1916	28/03/1919	Class Z Reserve
14372	Pte	Redman	David		8th, Royal Irish Regt 5063		28/03/1919	Class Z Reserve
14776	Pte	Reed	Edward	Ryhope	8th, Labour Corps 239059		30/01/1919	Discharged
15741	Pte	Reed	John W.	Shiney Row	8th	GSW Right Eye, Widow claims pension 1935	09/12/1916	Discharged
13125	Pte	Reevell	Thomas W.K.	North Ormesby	8th, Machine Gun Corps 148271		19/03/1919	Class Z Reserve
14014	Pte	Reid	Charles	Hetton Downs	8th, Labour Corps L/Cpl 19540	GSW L Ankle	04/06/1919	Discharged
11917	Sgt	Renals	Ernest	Middlesbrough	8th, Depot 14/07/1916, 9th 09/02/1917 , 9th, 9th	GSW R Thigh, 10/07/1916, MDG 09/08/1916	14/03/1919	Class Z Reserve

Number	Rank	Name	First Name	Home Town	Bns served with	Reported Wounded	Discharged	MR Comment
15061	Pte	Renney	Thomas H.	Monkwearmouth	8th		10/07/1916	Dead
14873	Pte	Richardson	John	Boldon Colliery	8th		09/08/1917	Discharged
14955	Pte	Richardson	John J.	Boldon Colliery	8th, 8th, 5th	Died whilst a POW	10/10/1918	Dead
14133	Cpl	Richardson	William		8th		27/12/1916	Discharged
19406	Pte	Richardson	William	Newcastle	8th		23/04/1916	Dead
12247	Pte	Ripley	William	Middlesbrough	8th		10/07/1916	Dead
13750	Pte	Risborough	James	Eston	8th		09/01/1919	Discharged
13303	Pte	Ritchie	Ernest	Sunderland	8th	DoW No 13 Gen Hosp Boulogne	16/07/1916	Dead
7651	Pte	Roberts	Frederick J.	Bingley	8th, 4th, renumbered 203061		11/12/1918	Discharged
11541	Cpl	Robertson	John H.	Birmingham	8th, Trf Army Cyclist Corps 14/02/15 back to 8th		19/03/1919	Class Z Reserve
12367	Pte	Robertson	William L.		8th, 8th		22/05/1919	Class Z Reserve
13129	Pte	Robinson	Albert	Middlesbrough	8th, Depot 05/07/1916, Class W Reserve 19/12/1916		04/01/1919	Discharged
11498	Pte	Robinson	George		8th Renumbered 66461		07/02/1918	Discharged
19376	Pte	Robinson	George W.		8th, 7th		28/01/1919	Discharged
13866	Pte	Robinson	John		8th, Labour Corps 502668		12/03/1919	Discharged
14715	Pte	Robinson	John G	Ryhope	8th, Labour Corps 219429	9/11/1916 Leeds Mercury	13/12/1917	Discharged
17105	Pte	Robinson	Joseph	Monkwearmouth	8th, Depot 17/07/1916 2nd 07/04/1917	GSW R Leg	01/05/1919	Discharged
12059	Pte	Robinson	Samuel	Eston	8th. Depot 08/07/1916		04/04/1919	Discharged
19460	Cpl	Robson	Alexander B.	Crook	8th, 8th		24/04/1919	Class Z Reserve

Number	Rank	Name	First Name	Home Town	Bns served with	Reported Wounded	Discharged	MR Comment
14537	Pte	Robson	Lawson	South Shields	8th		17/03/1919	Class Z Reserve
11939	Pte	Robson	Stanley	Thornaby	8th, 8th		26/02/1919	Class Z Reserve
12206	Pte	Robson	Thomas	Brandon Colliery	8th		16/01/1918	Discharged
14022	Pte	Robson	William	Fencehouses	8th, 6th, 9th, 8th, 6th, 2nd		09/04/1919	Class Z Reserve
14958	CSM	Robson	Archibald	Seaton	8th, 8th		05/05/1919	Class Z Reserve
13821	Pte	Rochester	George	Seaham Harbour	8th, Duke of Wellington's Regt 30321, Labour Corps 238294		05/03/1919	Discharged
12074	Pte	Rodway	William	Rodingham Lincs	8th		10/07/1916	Dead
11994	Pte	Rogers	Alfred		8th, Royal Irish Regt 5046		30/04/1919	Class Z Reserve
12621	Sgt	Rooke	Joseph	Middlesbrough	8th. Depot 19/07/1916	GSW L Knee 10/07/1916 Amputated	21/11/1917	Discharged
13180	Pte	Rooney	John T.	Middlesbrough	8th	GSW Left Elbow	17/04/1918	Discharged
15734	Pte	Rose	Clement	Monkwearmouth	8th		13/10/1915	Dead
12681	Pte	Rose	John G.	Monkwearmouth	8th, 2nd	Fraudulently enlisted in RFA as 238951 Geo Ross DCM Connaught district in Ireland 17/09/1917	23/04/1919	Fraudulent Enlistment
13846	Pte	Ross	James S.	Haswell	8th		27/01/1919	Discharged
11979	Pte	Routh	Harry M.	Drypool Hull	8th, Depot 15/07/1916, 6th 13/10/1916, 2nd 16/05/1918	Bullet Wnd R Arm 10/07/1916, GSW R Leg	31/03/1919	Class Z Reserve
17152	Pte	Rowan	John	Fencehouses	8th, 2nd		18/10/1916	Dead

Number	Rank	Name	First Name	Home Town	Bns served with	Reported Wounded	Discharged	MR Comment
13607	Pte	Rudd	John		8th, 8th		28/01/1919	Class Z Reserve
13830	Pte	Rumney	Frederick W.	West Rainton	8th, 8th		07/03/1919	Class Z Reserve
12062	Pte	Rushton	George		8th, Tank Corps 75963		25/01/1917	Discharged
11932	Pte	Russell	Thomas	Middlesbrough	8th, Depot 18/05/1916, Reenlisted 4th 11/04/1921	Evac sick 05/1916	22/09/1916	Discharged
13172	Pte	Rutley	William	Middlesbrough	8th		16/12/1915	Dead
11592	Pte	Ryan	James	Middlesbrough	8th	GSW Scalp 19/10/1917	26/03/1919	Class Z Reserve
12165	Pte	Ryan	Michael		8th, 6th, 2nd		11/03/1919	Class Z Reserve
11976	Pte	Ryder	Harry	Drypool Hull	8th		12/12/1915	Dead
12116	Pte	Rymer	James	North Ormesby	8th	MDG 18/08/1916	10/07/1916	Dead
12241	Pte	Salt	Philip	Birmingham	8th		10/07/1916	Dead
11811	Pte	Saul	Charles D.	Middlesbrough	8th		27/03/1919	Class Z Reserve
13339	Pte	Savage	William	Murton Colliery	8th, 8th	MDG 11/08/1916	19/02/1919	Deserted 22/11/1916
14397	Pte	Sayers	Robert	Hebburn Colliery	8th , Labour Corps Cpl 654602		19/02/1919	Class Z Reserve
13945	Pte	Scott	John	Washington	8th, East Yorkshire Regt 51140			Discharged
17556	Pte	Scott	John	Coopers Quay Blyth	8th		18/07/1916	Dead
12157	Pte	Scott	John E.	Middlesbrough	8th, 8th		09/03/1919	Class Z Reserve
13096	Pte	Scott	John T.	Witton Gilbert	8th, RFC 30/08/1917, RAF 133055		18/02/1919	Deserted 30/12/1914
15005	Pte	Scottow	Henry		8th, 7th, Deserted Renumbered 66460		Still Serving Mar 1920	Deserted 27/02/1917

Number	Rank	Name	First Name	Home Town	Bns served with	Reported Wounded	Discharged	MR Comment
19346	Pte	Sedman	Tom	Scarborough	8th	DL 19/08/1916	24/10/1917	Discharged
13874	Pte	Sewell	Henry	Boldon Colliery	8th, 8th. Mil Medal & Medal Militaire de Guerre	GSW L Leg 07/03/1918		Class Z Reserve
14686	Pte	Shakeshaft	George	South Bank	8th		21/03/1916	Dead
14215	Pte	Sharp	Alfred	Murton Colliery	8th		07/10/1916	Dead
12204	Pte	Sharples	Albert	Middlesbrough	8th, 8th. Reenlisted 4th Bn 02/07/1921	ICT Face 06/07/1916	25/02/1919	Class Z Reserve
11916	Pte	Sheehan	Jerry	Grangetown	8th	DL 22/10/1917	20/09/1917	Dead
13093	Pte	Sheen	Walter	Durham City.	8th, 8th	Shell Shock 06/08/1916, GSW L Forearm 05/11/1916, GSW L Hand 27/10/1918	02/02/1919	Class Z Reserve
13216	Pte	Sheffield	Arthur H.	Wolverhampton	8th 7 days FP 05/06/1915, 11th 04/09/1915 9th, Labour Corps 474772		14/03/1919	Class Z Reserve
13789	Pte	Sherwood	Henry		8th		13/01/1919	Discharged
11821	Sgt	Shires	Benjamin	West Hartlepool	8th, FGCM 14/01/1917 21 Days FP No 1, Reenlisted 4th Bn 09/01/1925 - 09/01/1939		31/03/1919	Class Z Reserve
13749	Pte	Shore	Albert	Thornaby	8th, Depot 15/07/1916, 6th 13/11/1916 , 9th 16/05/1917, 2nd 03/06/1917 Class W Reserve 13/07/1917 Steel worker	GSW Face 24/03/1916, GSW L Thigh 10/07/1916	01/01/1919	Discharged

Number	Rank	Name	First Name	Home Town	Bns served with	Reported Wounded	Discharged	MR Comment
16674	Pte	Short	George T.	Willington	8th, Depot 13/07/1916, 9th 22/10/1916, Depot 12/12/1916	GSW R Arm	12/04/1918	Discharged
17219	Pte	Short	William	Hetton Le Hole	8th		1507/1916	Dead
12067	Pte	Short VC	William	Grangetown	8th		07/08/1916	Dead
13298	Pte	Shotton	John C.	Shiney Row	8th, 8th		03/02/1919	Class Z Reserve
12079	Pte	Shutt	William		8th, 8th		02/03/1919	Class Z Reserve
15753	Pte	Simpson	James	North Ormesby	8th		10/02/1919	Deserted 18/5/1916
16677	Pte	Simpson	John	Sunderland	8th, 8th		04/02/1919	Class Z Reserve
15743	Pte	Sis	Robert	South Bank	8th, 10th Lincs Lab Coy 46520, 49th Lab Coy Labour Corps 29184	GSW L Forefinger & Buried 10/07/1916	14/05/1919	Class Z Reserve
11892	Pte	Skeet	George	West Hartlepool	8th, Depot 12/03/1917 Class W Reserve Ironstone miner 25/03/1917		22/01/1919	Discharged
14102	Cpl	Slassor	Charles A.	Newbottle	8th, Depot 14/07/1916		19/02/1919	Discharged
12415	Pte	Smallwood	Thomas	Marske	8th	2nd Western Gen Hosp Manchester	21/08/1916	Dead
13348	Pte	Smith	Albert	Hetton le Hole	8th, Depot 26/01/1916, Class W Reserve 18/08/1916	Shrapnel Wnd L Eye, Jaw & Face 14/01/1916 DL 04/02/1916	02/08/1917	Discharged
13396	Pte	Smith	Charles B.		8th, 8th		14/03/1919	Class Z Reserve
13331	Pte	Smith	George W.	Pallion	8th, 6th, 2/West Yorkshire Regt 63114	DL 09/08/1916, GSW Left Leg & Back	14/04/1919	Class Z Reserve

Number	Rank	Name	First Name	Home Town	Bns served with	Reported Wounded	Discharged	MR Comment
15742	Cpl	Smith	John	Washington Station	8th, 8th		31/10/1918	Dead
12061	Pte	Smith	John G.	Grangetown	8th, Depot 07/1916	MDG 11/08/1916	10/02/1919	Discharged
15947	Pte	Smith	Joseph	Jarrow	8th		18/05/1916	Dead
16802	Pte	Smith	Joseph H.	Middlesbrough	8th, 6th, 2nd	MDG 22/08/1916	22/03/1918	Dead
13769	Pte	Smith	Matthew	South Bank	8th		24/09/1917	Dead
11941	Pte	Smith	Nathaniel	South Bank	8th, Labour Corps 124224		03/04/1919	Class Z Reserve
17154	Pte	Smith	Ruben	Skinningrove	8th, Depot 15/07/1916	Shrapnel Wnd R hand Severe 10/07/1916, MDG 11/08/1916 Thumb amputated	24/10/1916	Discharged
13219	Pte	Smith	Samuel		8th, Labour Corps 416325		20/01/1917	Discharged
17145	Pte	Smith	William	Bishop Auckland	8th, Labour Corps 599594	MDG 09/08/1916	03/03/1919	Discharged
11499	Pte	Smith	George W.	Guisborough	8th		20/09/1917	Dead
13177	Cpl	Smitheringale	Harry	Middlesbrough	8th, 8th	GSW Back & Shldr 07/06/1917	21/02/1919	Class Z Reserve
13337	Pte	Smithson	George	Hetton le Hole	8th, Depot 21/07/1916 Class P reserve 31/05/1917	GSW Bomb Acc 13/11/1915, GSW R Leg & Face serious 10/07/1916	31/05/1917	31/05/1917
13398	Sgt	Smithson	Marmaduke	Middlesbrough	8th Bn To Northumberland Fusiliers A/CSM 94078		Still Serving Mar 1920	Srtill Serving 1920
12312	Pte	Softley	James		8th		06/02/1919	Discharged
13476	Pte	Somerville	Samuel	Bishopwearmouth	8th, 8th		11/07/1916	Dead

Number	Rank	Name	First Name	Home Town	Bns served with	Reported Wounded	Discharged	MR Comment
13336	Pte	Soppitt	John S.	Hetton le Hole	8th, Depot 11/08/1916, Class P Reserve 31/05/1917	GSW L Forearm fracture	31/05/1917	31/05/1917
13328	Pte	Southern	James	Deptford, Sunderland	8th, Labour Corps 476729		10/02/1919	Class Z Reserve
15147	Pte	Southwell	J.A.		8th, Army Service Corps M/353667 11/12/1917		13/05/1919	Class Z Reserve
11947	Cpl	Sparks	John	Middlesbrough	8th, Depot 14/10/1916, 2nd 20/01/1917 Depot 14/06/1917	MDG 09/08/1916	03/03/1919	Class Z Reserve
13067	Pte	Spencer	Charles H.	Normanby	8t	MDG 18/08/1916	10/07/1916	Dead
12050	Pte	Spencer	George	Grangetown	8th		10/07/1916	Dead
12702	Cpl	Spencer	George	Grangetown	8th		29/08/1916	Dead
13268	Pte	Spencer	John	Normanby	8th		27/07/1917	Discharged
15758	Pte	Spencer	William		8th, King's Own Scottish Borderers 46916, Labour Corps 476579		27/02/1919	Demobilised
13063	Pte	Spencer	Edwin I.		8th, Labour Corps 387984		13/02/1919	Discharged
14308	Cpl	Spoors	William	Jarrow	8th		10/07/1916	Dead
13705	Cpl	Steele	James C.	Fencehouses	8th	GSW Left Thigh	10/01/1919	Class Z Reserve
17235	Pte	Stephenson	Frederick	Scarborough	8th, Depot 08/04/1916 8th, 8th	GSW 01/11/1915 Evac Flu 28/03/1916	23/03/1919	Class Z Reserve
17900	Pte	Stewart	John W.	North Shields	8th, Labour Corps L/Cpl 599522	Missing Newcastle Journal 08/08/1916		Class Z Reserve
13647	Clr Sgt	Stillwell	Herbert S		8th		06/06/1919	Class Z Reserve

Number	Rank	Name	First Name	Home Town	Bns served with	Reported Wounded	Discharged	MR Comment
13012	Pte	Stockdale	John	Seaham Harbour	8th, Depot 16/07/1917	GSW R Leg WL 07/08/1917	02/11/1918	Discharged
11999	Cpl	Stockton	Frank	North Ormesby	8th, 8th		13/03/1919	Class Z Reserve
3/8857	Pte	Stockton	John	West Hartlepool	8th, 2nd		03/08/1917	Dead
13284	Sgt	Storey	George R.	Middlesbrough	8th, Depot 26/09/1917	Shell Shock 08/07/1916, Shell Wnd L Shldr 09/1917	19/06/1919	Class Z Reserve
8798	Pte	Storr	Arthur H.	Eston	8th, Royal Irish Rifles 40696	GSW Left Forearm, Died 11/03/1925	29/03/1919	Class Z Reserve
13474	Pte	Stothard	Charles H.	Fulwell	8th	DL 04/02/1916, 10/6/1916 Shields Gaz	10/07/1916	Dead
17233	Pte	Stoves	William	Horden Colliery	8th, Depot 31/05/1917 8th 08/09/1917, 5th 19/09/1917 Depot 11/11/1917	GSW R Elbow severe, GSW R Leg & L Thigh 31/10/1917	27/01/1919	Discharged
17217	Pte	Straughan	Henderson	Easington Lane	8th, Labour Corps 234844	GSW Abdomen.	06/03/1918	Discharged
17188	Pte	Strickland	Henry	West Hartlepool	8th, Royal Defence Corps 65187	Neurasthenia	01/06/1918	Discharged
17231	Pte	Strong	William	New Seaham	8th	Shell Shock MDG 28/08/1916	27/01/1919	Discharged
12947	Pte	Stubbings	James	North Ormesby	8th, 8th	Shell Shock 10/07/1916, GSW R Arm 06/08/1916	11/05/1919	Class Z Reserve
12546	Pte	Sturdy	John	Guisborough	8th	V.D.H.	27/09/1916	Discharged

Number	Rank	Name	First Name	Home Town	Bns served with	Reported Wounded	Discharged	MR Comment
12662	Pte	Suggitt	William	Murton Colliery	8th		08/10/1916	Dead
15745	Pte	Surtees	Albert	Benwell, Newcastle	8th	Dementia	14/05/1918	Discharged
13490	Pte	Suthern	John		8th, 8th		04/02/1919	Class Z Reserve
14466	Pte	Sweeney	John	Durham City.	8th		07/06/1917	Dead
14023	Sgt	Tankard	John	Hetton Le Hole	8th	MDG 22/08/1916	11/07/1916	Dead
14082	Pte	Tate	William	Easington	8th, Depot 06/04/1916, 6th 13/10/1916, 6th Depot , 2nd 16/05/1918	GSW R Arm 29/03/1916 WL 21/04/1916, GSW Shell Cont Back 27/09/1917 WL 27/10/1917	26/02/1919	Class Z Reserve
12265	Cpl	Taylor	Banjamin T.		8th, Labour Corps 631971		20/03/1919	Class Z Reserve
13248	Pte	Taylor	James	Middlesbrough	8th, 8th		03/03/1919	Class Z Reserve
14108	Pte	Taylor	William	Shiney Row	8th, 8th.		18/05/1918	Dead
13134	CSM	Taylor	William H.	Darlington	8th. Military Medal 09/12/1916		14/03/1919	Class Z Reserve
11833	Pte	Temple	James	Guisborough	8th, Depot 11/08/1916 Class W Reserve Ironstone miner 20/02/1917	GSW Head	05/02/1919	Discharged
12326	Pte	Tester	Amos H.	Middlesbrough	8th	Sickness 392 xvi, Nephritis	17/06/1916	Discharged
12951	Pte	Tewson	Thomas E.	Eston	8th		23/10/1915	Dead
14355	Pte	Thexton	John	Belmont	8th, Depot 26/07/1916, 2nd, 03/01/1917, Depot 21/06/1917 Class W Coal miner	GSW L Arm & Buttock	05/12/1918	Discharged

Number	Rank	Name	First Name	Home Town	Bns served with	Reported Wounded	Discharged	MR Comment
14233	Pte	Thirtle	James	West Herrington	8th, Depot 11/08/1916 4th 09/11/1917 Missing 27/05/1918 POW, DCM 26/09/1916	GSW Self Inflicted Hand 03/1916, GSW Hand & Leg, 10/07/1916, Wnd Chest 23/03/1918, Gassed	31/03/1919	Class Z Reserve
16801	Pte	Thomas	David W.	Grangetown	8th, 10th Trg Res 05/10/1916, 5th renumbered 5714 Class W Reserve Steel Works 17/01/1917	GSW 10/07/1916 MDG 09/08/1916	15/02/1919	Discharged
11983	Pte	Thomas	George H.	Eston	8th, Depot 11/07/1916 9th 09/02/1917 Depot 22/09/1917	GSW R Shoulder 10/07/1916 GSW L Shoulder 20/09/1917	13/01/1919	Discharged
13767	Clr Sgt	Thomas	Joseph	Grangetown	8th, 8th		25/02/1919	Class Z Reserve
16380	Pte	Thomas	W.		8th, Army Service Corps S4/232742 15/09/1916		03/07/1919	Class Z Reserve
17781	Pte	Thomas	Walter	Horden Colliery	8th, Depot 09/04/1916, Class W Reserve Coal miner	Evac DAH & Rheumatism 04/1916	10/12/1917	Discharged
17097	Pte	Thompson	Benjamin	Tow Law	8th. Depot 13/07/1916, Class P Reserve 05/02/1917	Bullet Wnd R Foot 10/07/1916	05/02/1917	Discharged
14403	Pte	Thompson	John W.		8th		01/02/1919	Discharged
12244	Pte	Thompson	Ralph	West Hartlepool	8th		29/09/1916	Dead
11822	Pte	Thompson	William H.	Middlesbrough	8th		07/08/1916	Dead
12894	Pte	Thorne	Laurence	Hebburn	8th		10/07/1916	Dead

Number	Rank	Name	First Name	Home Town	Bns served with	Reported Wounded	Discharged	MR Comment
15189	Pte	Thorpe	Ned	Hunslet	8th, Depot 07/04/1916, 11th AWOL 27 July 1916, 6th, 4th, 19/09/1916 renumbered 7552 then 202966	Evac Boils 04/1916, Wnd 23/04/1917	09/02/1919	Class Z Reserve
16806	Pte	Thurgood	John	London	8th, 8th		29/03/1919	Class Z Reserve
16394	Pte	Thurlbeck	William R.	Seaham Harbour	8th, 8th		26/01/1919	Class Z Reserve
12031	Pte	Tierney	James		8th, Labour Corps 387984		03/03/1919	Class Z Reserve
11603	Pte	Todd	Frederick	Stockton	8th	not overseas	17/10/1914	Discharged
14367	Pte	Todd	Frederick	Hendon	8th		12/07/1916	Dead
11860	Pte	Tones	George H.	Guisborough	8th, 7th		28/12/1916	Dead
11862	Pte	Tones	Thomas E.	Guisborough	8th, Depot Class W Reserve Iron stone miner 07/06/1917		20/01/1919	Discharged
12987	Pte	Topham	Thomas	Haswell Plough	8th, West Yorkshire Regt 63527	DL 22/02/1916,GSW Head, Died 10/07/1924	10/01/1919	Discharged
13184	Pte	Topliss	Samuel	Middlesbrough	8th, Labour Corps L/Cpl 387984	GSW Right Hand, Left Foot & Head	30/03/1919	Class Z Reserve
11503	Pte	Towle	Alfred	Guisborough	8th, Depot 02/05/1916, 1st Garr Bn South Staffordshire Regt 34729	]	26/11/1919	Class Z Reserve
11238	Pte	Townend	Charles	Grimsby	8th	DoW 70 Fld Amb RAMC	14/11/1915	Dead

Number	Rank	Name	First Name	Home Town	Bns served with	Reported Wounded	Discharged	MR Comment
17227	Pte	Townsend	William T.	North Ormesby	8th, Depot 16/07/1916, 7th 29/11/1916, Depot 19/02/1917, Lab Corps 31/07/1917, Royal Army Medical Corps 25/08/1917 132406	GSW Shldr 10/07/1916 GSW R Hand, R Thigh & Left Leg 08/02/1917	19/03/1919	Class Z Reserve
12155	Pte	Trilk	Albert	Middlesbrough	8th, 8th		28/01/1919	Class Z Reserve
13269	Pte	Trinder	William H.		8th		21/01/1919	Discharged
13762	Cpl	Turnbull	Harry J.	Newcastle	8th, 8th		02/03/1919	Class Z Reserve
13940	Cpl	Turnbull	Robert	Barmston	8th. 8th	Died 24/06/1921	26-Feb-19	Class Z Reserve
13752	Pte	Turner	Charles H.		8th		02/01/1919	Discharged
12040	Cpl	Turner	James	Redcar	8th, Depot 10/05/1916	Evac Arttyhritis & Myalgia 09/05/1916	09/04/1918	Discharged
11551	A/Sgt	Turner	James A.	Middlesbrough	8th, 8th		02/03/1919	Class Z Reserve
14564	Pte	Tweddell	Wilfred	Sunderland	8th. Depot 22/06/1917	GSW Head 10/07/1916, GSW L Knee 7/6/1917 to England HS Grantully Castle.20/6/1917	26/06/1918	Discharged
13210	Pte	Tweddle	Stephen	Middlesbrough	8th, 11th, 6th, 4th renumbered 7551		12/11/1916	Dead
15731	Pte	Urwin	Robert	Barmston	8th, 8th		20/12/1918	Dead
11874	Pte	Vallely	John	Middlesbrough	8th, Labour Corps 407290	GSW L Hand	05/03/1919	Class Z Reserve
14691	Sgt	Vincent	Matthew M.	West Hartlepool	8th,		23/11/1918	Discharged

Number	Rank	Name	First Name	Home Town	Bns served with	Reported Wounded	Discharged	MR Comment
3/8835	Pte	Wainwright	John	Sheffield	8th West Yorkshire Regt 63305	Alias Joh Flowers, GSW Left Ankle, Died 23/07/1929	06/12/1918	Discharged
12126	Cpl	Waland	Charles		8th, 8th		Still Serving Mar 1920	Still Serving Mar 1920
13317	Pte	Walker	George	Hetton Le Hole	8th		10/07/1916	Dead
13203	Pte	Walker	John	Middlesbrough	8th, 8th		06/05/1919	Class Z Reserve
14833	Pte	Walker	John G.	Trimdon Colliery	8th, Labour Corps 636658		23/01/1919	Class Z Reserve
13764	Pte	Walker	John W.	South Bank	8th, Depot 8th 29/08/1916 Class W Reserve Iron works 24/10/1916		06/02/1919	Discharged
12402	Pte	Walker	Frederick	Bradford	8th		31/08/1917	Discharged
12003	Clr Sgt	Walker	Harry	Hornsea	8th		30/10/1917	Discharged to Commission
7554	Pte	Wallace	John G.	Spennymoor	8th, 11th, 6th, 4th renumbered 202968		23/04/1917	Dead
17715	Pte	Waller	Ernest	Redcar	8th, Depot 26/06/1916 Class W Reserve Steel Works 27/06/1916		06/02/1919	Discharged
11986	Pte	Walsh	James	Middlesbrough	8th, 7th, 6th	No 3 CCS 10 Jan 16 GSW Buttocks	17/03/1918	Dead
13171	Pte	Walsh	William	Dublin	8th, 8th		19/02/1917	Dead
15748	Cpl	Walton	Charles V.	Redcar	8th		10/07/1916	Dead
13302	Pte	Ward	Arthur	Old Penshaw	8th		11/07/1916	Dead

Number	Rank	Name	First Name	Home Town	Bns served with	Reported Wounded	Discharged	MR Comment
12215	Pte	Ward	James	Hunslet	8th, Depot 06/06/1917 Army Service Corps 1/12/1917 M/353266	Trench Fever	24/01/1919	Class Z Reserve
19397	Pte	Waters	Jonathan R.	Darlington	8th	Shell Shock MDG 28/08/1916	10/06/1918	Discharged
11995	Pte	Waters	William	Middlesbrough	8th, Depot 21/11/1915	GSW R Thigh paralysis of the leg 01/11/1915	27/05/1916	Discharged
17803	Pte	Watson	Ernest	Tyne Dock	8th, 8th		16/02/1919	Class Z Reserve
13283	Pte	Watson	Francis	Eston	8th, North Staffordshire Regt 44741	Mystagmus	08/11/1918	Discharged
14504	Pte	Watson	George	Belmont	8th, Labour Corps 449808	DL 03/05/1917	06/03/1918	Discharged
15197	Pte	Watson	James		8th, 8th		01/02/1919	Class Z Reserve
3/9379	Pte	Watson	James	Armley	8th		15/03/1919	Class Z Reserve
14129	Pte	Watson	Richardson	Seaham Harbour	8th		10/07/1916	Dead
16743	Pte	Watson	Thomas	Ryhope	8th, 6th, 2nd			Dead
12972	Pte	Watson	William		8th, 8th		15/02/1919	Class Z Reserve
13388	Pte	Watson	Stephen G.	Winlaton	8th	ICT L Hand 31/03/1916	02/03/1919	Class Z Reserve
12945	Pte	Weatherill	Charles W.	Thornaby	8th, 8th		12/03/1919	Class Z Reserve
14566	Pte	Webster	James	Sunderland	8th, 4th		27/05/1918	Dead
12066	Cpl	Webster	William L.	South Bank	8th, 7th 12/08/1917	GSW L Hand 06/07/1916, MDG 09/08/1916, Shell Wnd L Hand 21/09/1917	01/02/1919	Class Z Reserve

Number	Rank	Name	First Name	Home Town	Bns served with	Reported Wounded	Discharged	MR Comment
15047	Sgt	Webster	William		8th,		21/02/1919	Class Z Reserve
14829	Pte	Weddell	Philip		8th, 8th	DL 04/02/1916	21/02/1919	Class Z Reserve
14530	Pte	Welburn	William		8th, 8th.		28/01/1919	Class Z Reserve
15754	Pte	Welch	William	Penshaw	8th, Labour Corps 284688	GSW Left Knee	12/04/1919	Class Z Reserve
13385	Pte	Wells	Charles R.	Middlesbrough	8th	DoW Ontario Mil Hosp Orpington	03/08/1916	Dead
13735	Pte	Wells	William	Middlesbrough	8th. Depot 13/07/1916, Class W Reserve Steel works 25/01/1917	GSW Legs & R Hand Middle Finger amputated 10/07/1916 MDG 11/08/1916	01/01/1919	Discharged
15150	Pte	Westerman	Arthur	Tingley	8th		09/11/1915	Dead
13186	Pte	Westwood	James W.	Middlesbrough	8th, 8th	Died shortly after discharge	23/04/1919	Class Z Reserve
17130	Pte	Wetherell	Joseph	East Rainton	8th, 8th	GSW R Shldr 10/07/1916	11/01/1919	Class Z Reserve
13153	Cpl	Wheatley	Edward	Middlesbrough	8th, 8th		09/05/1919	Discharged
14179	Pte	Wheatman	Nicholas	Ryhope	8th		10/07/1916	Dead
19378	Pte	Wheetman	Benjamin	West Hartlepool	8th	Committed suicide at Folkestone.	14/04/1915	Committed Suicide
14831	Pte	White	Albert E.	East Boldon	8th, 7th		13/05/1917	Dead
13178	Cpl	Whittle	Francis	Middlesbrough	8th, Depot 15/11/1915 Class P Reserve 18/12/1916	GSW L Hand 09/11/1915	18/12/1916	Discharged
3/9092	Pte	Whyley	Frederick		8th, 8th		18/02/1919	Class Z Reserve
13228	Pte	Wiles	Frederick	Middlesbrough	8th, 8th		12/03/1919	Class Z Reserve

Number	Rank	Name	First Name	Home Town	Bns served with	Reported Wounded	Discharged	MR Comment
12041	Pte	Wilkinson	John H.		8th		03/01/1919	Discharged
13765	CSM	Wilkinson	Robert		8th		30/04/1918	Discharged to Commission 3/ Yorkshire Regt
14062	Pte	Wilkinson	John T.	Trimdon Grange	8th, 10th	WL 06/08/1917	29/01/1919	Discharged
11808	A/Sgt	Williams	Albert		8th, 6th, 8th		06/05/1919	Class Z Reserve
12110	Sgt	Williams	Thomas	Middlesbrough	8th		29/09/1917	Dead
19351	Pte	Willie	Robert		8th, 2nd, 5th, Renumbered 243324		04/03/1919	Class Z Reserve
11927	Pte	Wilson	Ira Israel	Spennymoor	8th		07/06/1917	Dead
3/9006	Pte	Wilson	James R.		8th		06/02/1919	Discharged
15755	Sgt	Wilson	John	Washington	8th, 8th, 8th		17/01/1919	Discharged
12121	Pte	Winch	Alfred	Middlesbrough	8th. Depot 11/02/1916	Bomb Wnd Knee & Eye severe 13/11/1915 Dangouresly ill	07/04/1917	Discharged
12574	Pte	Winterton	Charles	Saltburn	8th, 8th		27/03/1919	Class Z Reserve
14918	Pte	Wolfe	Robert	Hebburn Colliery	8th, 7th, 13th		26/03/1919	Dead
12093	Pte	Wood	Ernest	North Ormesby	8th, Cpl 19/08/1916, 8th, FGCM Drunk Italy 07/04/1918 Red to Pte		12/03/1919	Class Z Reserve
3/8196	CQMS	Wood	Fred	Leeds	8th, Ex 2nd Bn Reenlisted 3rd Bn WO II Comm 4th RWF Lt & QM		18/04/1916	Discharged to Commission.
16395	Pte	Woodhall	Ernest	Fatfield	8th		31/03/1919	Class Z Reserve

Number	Rank	Name	First Name	Home Town	Bns served with	Reported Wounded	Discharged	MR Comment
11972	Pte	Woodhall	Joseph	Middlesbrough	8th, 8th		12/03/1919	Class Z Reserve
11942	Pte	Woods	James A.	Middlesbrough	8th	GSW R Thigh, R Leg, R Arm 10/07/1916.	24/11/1916	Discharged
11513	Pte	Wright	Ernest	Guisborough	8th, Class W Reserve 19/03/1917 Steelworks	GSW R Thigh two heavily discharging wnds 10/07/1916, DL 16/08/1916	27/02/1919	Discharged
12232	Cpl	Wright	John	Marske	8th		10/06/1917	Dead
14240	Cpl	Wright	Richard	Seaham Harbour	8th, Depot 16/04/1916 6th 09/03/1917 , 2nd 16/05/1918	GSW R Thigh R Hand & GSW L Thigh 29/03/1916, GSW R Arm 07/11/1918	27/02/1919	Class Z Reserve
3/8730	Pte	Wyles	Harry G.		8th, 8th			Special Reserve 12/03/1919
15148	Pte	Yates	Joseph T.		8th, 8th		09/02/1919	Class Z Reserve
11527	Pte	Youles	William D.	South Bank	8th, 2nd, 9th 26/02/1917, 1st East Yorkshire Regt 31/03/1918 29993 POW 23/04/1918		02/10/1918	Dead
13828	Pte	Young	David P.		8th, 8th		29/01/1919	Class Z Reserve
16739	Cpl	Young	Thomas	Horden Colliery	8th, 8th		28/01/1919	Class Z Reserve
13380	Cpl	Youngs	Richard B.	North Ormesby	8th	GSW R Shldr & Arm 07/06/1917	10/01/1918	Discharged

Nominal Roll of Other Ranks that Served with the 9th (Service) Battalion, Alexandra's Princess of Wales's Own Yorkshire Regiment, The Green Howards, and Landed in France with the Battalion on 25 or 26 August 1915 or Died or Left the Battalion Prior to Embarkation

Number	Rank	Name	First Name	Home Town	Bns served with	Reported Wounded	Discharged	MR Comment
13282	Pte	Abell	Maurice	Eston	9th		07/06/1917	Dead
15470	Cpl	Adams	Alfred	Scarborough	9th.9th.9th, Depot, 3rd 19/11/1918	GSW Hand, 10/11/1916	06/03/1919	Class Z Reserve
16819	Pte	Adams	William		9th, South Lancashire Regt 63049 Lab Corps 878458		16/01/1919	Class Z Reserve
12635	Pte	Addinall	Richard M.	York	9th, Depot 10/06/1917 Royal Defence Corps 15/09/1917 65241. Ex Regular served in India & South Africa Enl 1894 Dis 1910	GSW Scalp 1916, GSW L Hand Severe. DL 18/01/1916	30/11/1917	Discharged
17271	Pte	Addison	Thomas		9th, Machine Gun Corps 152645	DL 16/02/1916	16/07/1919	Class Z Reserve
15906	Cpl	Agar	Cyril E.	Scarborough	9th. C/Sgt 19 Officer Cadet Bn, Commission 3/West Riding Regt.		31/07/1917	Discharged to Commission.
3/9114	Pte	Agar	John W.	Boosbeck	9th		30/08/1915	Dead
15924	Pte	Agar	Thomas	Boosbeck	9th		06/10/1916	Dead
17875	Pte	Alison	William	Middlesbrough	9th, Alleged Self Inflicted Wnd 3/11/1916, 9th, Cpl 3/12/1917 9th, Reduced to Pte 27/04/1918	GSW Little finger. DL 16/11/1916	09/03/1919	Class Z Reserve
13017	Pte	Allan	Charles	Linton, Lincs	9th	Not Overseas	06/10/1914	
15097	Pte	Allan	Fred		9th		09/03/1919	Class Z Reserve
12434	Pte	Allatt	Percy A.		9th	DL 16/02/1916	10/03/1917	Discharged

Number	Rank	Name	First Name	Home Town	Bns served with	Reported Wounded	Discharged	MR Comment
17945	Pte	Allcock	Charles	Low Walker	9th	DL 18/10/1917	06/03/1918	Discharged
13280	Pte	Allday	Francis	Eston	9th, 36th Northumberland Fus 54136	Shell Shock 19/05/1916, Blown up by German mine at Souchez	26/02/1919	Discharged
3/8693	Pte	Allen	Charles		9th		21/04/1917	Discharged
15457	Pte	Allgood	Charles F.	Cambridge	9th. Depot, 11th, 10th, 3rd,		31/01/1919	Trf Army Res Munitions 01/01/1917
3/9079	Pte	Amer	William		9th, 9th, 9th		29/03/1919	Class Z Reserve
17946	Pte	Amos	Walter E.	Alfreton	9th		10/07/1916	Dead
14056	Pte	Anderson	Joseph	Seaham Harbour	9th, Labour Corps 364120	DL 16/08/1916	28/01/1919	Class Z Reserve
16092	Pte	Anderson	Nicholas	Hetton Le Hole	9th, Depot 03/03/1916.	Sickness 392 xvi	20/06/1916	Discharged
15766	Sgt	Ankers	Benjamin	Byker	9th	Reduced to the Ranks, Misconduct 04/06/1916	10/07/1916	Dead
18664	Pte	Applegarth	George		9th	DL 16/08/1916	30/10/1917	Discharged to Commission Northblnd Fus
13255	Pte	Archer	Alfred	Grangetown	9th, To Munitions Clarence Iron Works 02/04/1916.		17/05/1919	Discharged
13421	Pte	Archer	Thomas N.	Middlesbrough	9th	DL 24/08/1916, DL 03/04/1917	17/06/1918	Dead

Number	Rank	Name	First Name	Home Town	Bns served with	Reported Wounded	Discharged	MR Comment
15937	Pte	Archer	Walter	Durham City.	9th, 6th, 5th Renumbered 243250	DL 02/08/1916	31/03/1919	Class Z Reserve
15989	Cpl	Arkley	Robert	Silksworth	9th. Cpl 08/06/1916. Alder Hey Hosp 16/04/1917	GSW R Forearm 10/07/1916	07/05/1917	Discharged
17947	Pte	Armstrong	George E.		9th	Posted Missing GHG Jul 16, Shell Shock DL 16/11/1916	27/01/1919	Class Z Reserve
12058	Pte	Armstrong	Harry	Hetton Le Hole	9th	Contusions Back (Shell) 24/02/1916, Shell Shock 10/03/1916, DL 22/02/1916	10/06/1916	Discharged
15362	Pte	Armstrong	John		9th, att 19 Ordnance Depot, 879 Lab Coy, Labour Corps 408456, 43rd Royal Fusiliers GS/103354			
17927	Sgt	Armstrong	John H.	Seaham Harbour	9th, Previous service 1st Northblnd Fus. Sgt 26/10/1914, Reenlisted labour Corps 709964 11/06/1919. Reenlists RHA & RFA Territorial Force 29/09/1921 742973	Shell Shock & Gassed	20/01/1919	Class Z Reserve
17948	Pte	Armstrong	John T.	Hebburn	9th	DoW No 45 CCS	08/10/1916	Dead

Number	Rank	Name	First Name	Home Town	Bns served with	Reported Wounded	Discharged	MR Comment
19845	Pte	Armstrong	William		9th, 9th, 9th		24/02/1919	Class Z Reserve
13960	Clr Sgt	Ashford	Thomas	Thornley	9th, 9th, 9th		11/05/1919	Class Z Reserve
13064	Pte	Atkinson	John H.	Middlesbrough	9th	DL 24/08/1916	10/07/1916	Dead
15991	Pte	Atkinson	Joseph	Middlesbrough	9th, Depot 14/07/1916	Bullet Wnd R Heel, DL 16/08/1916	06/12/1917	Discharged
15767	Pte	Aylieff	Edgar W.	Clapham Common	9th	DL 22/08/1916	20/01/1917	Discharged
12258	Pte	Bacon	Ernest	Middlesbrough	9th, 9th	DL 22/10/1917, DL 21/11/1917	03/02/1919	Class Z Reserve
14777	Pte	Bainbridge	George	New Silksworth	9th, Depot 15/09/1916 10th Training Res Bn 21/10/1916, Class W Reserve 30/11/1916 Coal Miner	Shrapnel Wnd Back 05/07/1916, DL 02/08/1916	21/12/1916	Discharged
15913	Pte	Baldam	Ernest		9th, 9th, 9th.		16/03/1919	Class Z Reserve
23052	Pte	Baldwin	Tom	Leeds	9th, 7th, Labour Corps 193 Lab Coy 17/09/1917 421312	DL 30/10/1916	17/01/1919	Discharged
17949	Pte	Bamford	John	Newsham	9th, Enlisted Northbld Fus Trf Yorks Regt 10/09/1914, 9th, Depot, 37th IBD, 6th, Depot, 3rd. 2nd	GSW Left Arm 10/07/1916 GSW R Hand & Leg 30/08/1918. DL 24/08/1916	10/01/1916	Class Z Reserve
13409	Pte	Banes	George H.		9th, Machine gun Corps 23739, Royal Engineers WR/266685			

Number	Rank	Name	First Name	Home Town	Bns served with	Reported Wounded	Discharged	MR Comment
3/8937	RSM	Bannard	Francis P.	Bexley Heath	9th		16/02/1919	Class Z Reserve
14624	L/Cpl	Barker	Wilfred G.	Thirsk	9th, Labour Corps 395218		02/04/1919	Class Z Reserve
12696	Pte	Barkess	Ralph	Houghton le Spring	9th	DoW No 2 Canadian Stat Hosp	07/07/1916	Dead
13714	Pte	Barkess	Thomas	Houghton le Spring	9th		05/07/1916	Dead
14840	Pte	Barnes	George R.		9th, 6th 2/West Yorkshire Regt 63122	DL 16/11/1916	28/02/1919	Class Z Reserve
14440	Pte	Barron	John R.	Durham City.	9th	DL 06/11/1916	13/10/1916	Dead
13592	Pte	Barron	Joseph W.	Durham City.	9th		05/07/1916	Dead
15954	Pte	Barron	Thomas W.	Eston	9th, 7th, 6th, 2nd	DL 16/08/1916, DoW Warrington War Hosp	27/09/1918	Dead
15469	Pte	Barstow	John	Scarborough	9th, 9th. 3rd		12/03/1919	Class Z Reserve
16022	Pte	Barton	Alfred	Station Town	9th, att 176 Tunn Coy RE 06/09/1917, 7th, 12th, 6th (Russian Exp Force)	Between 09-11/04/1918	24/09/1919	Class Z Reserve
3/8951	Pte	Bates	Frank		9th	DL 02/08/1916	29/03/1919	Discharged
17931	Pte	Bates	Joseph	Kimberworth, Rotherham	9th, Depot 02/04/1916 Munitions. Originally 10918 number duplicated.		06/02/1919	Discharged
10863	Pte	Bates	George W.		9th		07/03/1919	Class B Reserve
16748	Pte	Batey	Joseph	Spennymoor	9th	DL 22/11/1917	26/01/1919	Deserted 26/07/1918
14794	Pte	Batty	George E.		9th, 10th, 4th, 6th		26/07/1919	Class Z Reserve

Number	Rank	Name	First Name	Home Town	Bns served with	Reported Wounded	Discharged	MR Comment
15360	Pte	Bayliss	William	Stockton	9th		17/10/1915	Dead
12513	Sgt	Bee	Ralph	Brandon Colliery	9th, 9th, 9th	DL 24/08/1916	14/01/1919	Class Z Reserve
7509	Pte	Beeforth	Fred	Guisborough	9th, Depot, 11th, 6th, 4th 19/09/1916 renumbered 202933	To England Sick 04/05/1916	29/01/1919	Discharged
15270	Sgt	Bell	Albert	York	9th, 12th, 9th.8th 05/10/1918	To England Sick 02/06/1917	05/05/1919	Class Z Reserve
14058	Pte	Bell	Fred	Langley Park	9th		06/10/1916	Dead
15993	Pte	Bell	George	North Ormesby	9th, 8th 05/10/1918	Wounded Contusions 07/06/1917, DL 22/10/1917	28/03/1919	Class Z Reserve
14502	Pte	Bell	John		9th, Labour Corps 629238	DL 02/08/1916	27/02/1919	Class Z Reserve
13062	Pte	Bell	Joseph	Eston	9th. Munitions 07/10/1916	DL 17/06/1916	03/01/1919	Discharged
14163	Pte	Bell	Martin	Langley Moor	9th, 9th. Depot 15/10/1918		27/02/1919	Class Z Reserve
19173	Pte	Bell	Thomas	Stockton	9th		04/10/1917	Dead
3/9064	Pte	Bell	William		9th		11/02/1919	Discharged
14065	Pte	Bennett	John		9th, 10th, 5/Royal Irish Regt 5054		02/02/1919	Class Z Reserve
13041	Pte	Bennett	Richard	Willington	9th		08/10/1916	Dead

Number	Rank	Name	First Name	Home Town	Bns served with	Reported Wounded	Discharged	MR Comment
14027	Sgt	Bennett	Tom	Witton Gilbert	9th, 9th Sgt 01/01/1917, 9th. FGCM Drunk 26/06/1918	GSW R Leg 09/11/1918	28/01/1919	Discharged
15304	Pte	Bennington	George	Thornaby	9th. FGCM 19/07/1916 Self Inflicted Wnd, FGCM 28/05/1917 Desertion Not Guilty, Guilty of AWOL	GSW Left Hand 09/07/1916, Wnd 28/09/1917	03/12/1918	Discharged
9106	Sgt	Bennison	William		9th, Labour Corps 608159		20/02/1919	Class Z Reserve
3/8725	Pte	Bentley	Arthur	Eston	9th, 7th		05/11/1916	Dead
11930	A/Cpl	Benton	Frederick	South Bank	9th, Depot 29/09/1917	GSW L Forearm 20/09/1917 Ypres	07/02/1918	Discharged
12915	Sgt	Benton	Thomas	South Bank	9th	Sharnel Wnd R Ankle 22/03/1917	14/11/1917	Discharged
15994	Cpl	Best	Alfred	Sunderland	9th, Depot 11/11/1915, 7th 07/04/1916, Depot 29/11/1916	Sickness owing to cold & exposure	29/06/1917	Discharged
13704	Sgt	Bird	George	Brandon Colliery	9th, 9th, 9th		14/01/1919	Class Z Reserve
15955	Sgt	Birtley	Joseph	Hetton le Hole	9th, 22/11/1914 Lance Corporal 1/6/1915, Corporal 6/4/1916. Depot 15/7/1915 To Trg Res Bn 26/9/1916 to 6th Bn 25/11/1916 cancelled to 9th Bn 9/12/1916. 9/3/1918 Being in posession of a forged pass at King's X Railway Station RTO Discharged 27 Dec	GSW Arm R 10/07/1916	24/01/1919	Class Z Reserve

Number	Rank	Name	First Name	Home Town	Bns served with	Reported Wounded	Discharged	MR Comment
14425	Pte	Blagdon	Joseph	Durham City	9th		04/06/1917	Dead
15582	Pte	Blenkinsop	John C.		9th, Labour Corps Sgt 611005		21/03/1919	Class Z Reserve
13400	Pte	Bollen	John	West Hartlepool	9th		10/07/1916	Dead
14819	Pte	Bounes	Charles E.	Carlin How	9th		07/06/1917	Dead
17795	Pte	Bourne	Samuel J.E.	Darlington	9th, Depot 31/12/1915, 8th, 8th		30/03/1919	Class Z Reserve
14035	Pte	Bousfield	Thomas	Willington	9th		05/07/1916	Dead
15769	Sgt	Bower	Alexander	Cowpen Village	9th L/Cpl 6/11/1915, Cpl 05/04/1917 Sgt 07/06/1917, 9th		20/01/1919	Class Z Reserve
11516	Pte	Bowes	John W.	Boosbeck	9th, Depot 11/08/1916 Munitions Iron Stone Mines 04/05/1917	GSW Heel	03/01/1919	Discharged
15907	Pte	Bowker	Frank	Middlesbrough	9th, Depot 06/01/1916 Munitions		05/02/1919	Discharged
13222	Pte	Boyd	Anthony		9th, 7th. Re-enlisted 429891		Still Serving Mar 1920	Deserted 10/8/1917
11520	Pte	Boyes	William	Guisborough	9th	DL 16/08/1916, DL 10/09/1917	23/04/1918	Discharged
3/8805	Pte	Boyle	John	Middlesbrough	9th		03/02/1916	Dead
15623	Pte	Brack	Francis W.	Skinningrove	9th, 7th, 9th		20/09/1916	Dead
12524	Pte	Bradley	James	Durham City	9th	DL 18/10/1917	05/03/1919	Class Z Reserve
13238	Pte	Bradley	John	Middlesbrough	9th, East Yorkshire Regt 51144			Class Z Reserve

Number	Rank	Name	First Name	Home Town	Bns served with	Reported Wounded	Discharged	MR Comment
9039	Pte	Bradley	Frederick		9th, Labour Corps 418973		22/03/1919	Class Z Reserve
15604	Pte	Brandling	Thomas S.	Wheatley Hill	9th	MDG 25/08/1916 KR 392 xvi wounds	11/04/1917	Discharged
15458	Pte	Brandling	William		9th		31/05/1917	Discharged
13213	Pte	Brannigan	Bartley	Middlesbrough	9th, 8th, 4th	Moved to Glasgow 1922, GSW Rt Shoulder, DAH	14/03/1919	Class Z Reserve
14280	Pte	Breen	Tom	Halifax	9th, 9th		07/09/1917	Discharged
14496	Pte	Brick	Edward E.	Battersea	9th, 2nd, 9th		07/06/1917	Dead
14455	Pte	Briggs	George C.	Wheatley Hill	9th, Royal Engineers 147745	Gas Poisoning 392 xvia	30/12/1918	Discharged
14816	Cpl	Brighton	Charles		9th, 9th, 9th		28/01/1919	Class Z Reserve
3/8910	Pte	Brine	Fred		9th, 6th, 7th		03/02/1919	Discharged
11526	Pte	Brodie	Dixon		9th, 9th, 9th		01/03/1919	Class Z Reserve
11819	Pte	Broomfield	Samuel	Middlesbrough	9th, Depot 04/01/1916	Wounds 392 xvi	22/09/1916	Discharged
17951	Pte	Brotherston	Christopher	Lesbury, Alnwick	9th, Depot 25/10/1915	GSW L Leg 10/07/1916	10/07/1916	Discharged
17876	Pte	Brown	Charles		9th, Training Res 4386, Royal Engineers WR 203974			Class Z Reserve
12523	Pte	Brown	Edward	Darlington	9th		06/06/1917	Discharged
3/8748	Pte	Brown	James	Boosbeck	9th		10/07/1916	Dead
17686	Pte	Brown	James T.	Middridge, Co Durham	9th, 9th, att 1786 Tunn Coy RE 06/09/1917		20/01/1919	Class Z Reserve

Number	Rank	Name	First Name	Home Town	Bns served with	Reported Wounded	Discharged	MR Comment
12577	Pte	Brown	John	Durham City.	9th, 6th		13/02/1917	Dead
19315	Pte	Brown	Joseph	West Rainton	9th, 10th, 4th, 9th		05/11/1918	Dead
11632	Pte	Brown	Robert	Newcastle	9th		10/07/1916	Dead
19842	Pte	Brown	William		9th 10th, 5th		12/02/1919	Class Z Reserve
15314	Pte	Brown	George A.		9th, 9th, 9th		23/02/1919	Class Z Reserve
15770	Pte	Brown	William	Bedlington	9th, 7th		18/01/1918	Deserted 11/08/1917, Dead
15956	Pte	Brown	Thomas		9th, 12th then 11th Bns West Yorkshire Regiment 43646		28/01/1919	Class Z Reserve
19284	Pte	Bruce	Alfred A.	West Hartlepool	9th, Depot 06/10/1916, 3rd 14/2/1917, Class A Res	GSW L Hand Amputation of Thumb.	22/05/1917	Discharged
14676	Pte	Bruce	Henry	Leamside	9th, Depot 26/12/1915, FGCM SIW Not Guilty	GSW Foot Severe 24/10/1915	12/05/1916	Discharged
13270	Pte	Brundall	Robert W.	Eston	9th		05/07/1916	Dead
15305	Pte	Buckle	George	Scarborough	9th, 9th, 9th	GSW Thigh 27/01/1916	09/03/1919	Class Z Reserve
13730	Pte	Buckley	Hugh	Middlesbrough	9th, Depot 05/01/1916, 11th June 8th 30/06/1916, 8th FGCM Drunk 24/08/1916	GSW Arm & Leg 01/01/1916, AWOL 11th 20/05/1916	14/09/1916	Discharged
14969	Sgt	Bullock	Donald K.	Newbottle	9th, 9th, 9th	GSW Neck 05/07/1916	20/01/1919	Class Z Reserve
15613	Pte	Bullock	William	South Shields	9th, 8th, 10th		01/01/1917	Dead

Number	Rank	Name	First Name	Home Town	Bns served with	Reported Wounded	Discharged	MR Comment
17692	Cpl	Bulman	Ronald	Bishop Middleham	9th	Shell Shock 05/07/1916	12/04/1917	Discharged
17777	Pte	Bunting	John	Sunderland	9th		07/08/1916	Dead
12857	Pte	Burke	John	Middlesbrough	9th	To 70 FA then 3CCS 19/10/15	20/10/1915	Dead
19303	Pte	Burkin	Albert E.		9th		05/02/1919	Discharged
15333	Pte	Burnett	George	Leeds	9th, 2nd		22/03/1918	Dead
15996	Pte	Burnett	Richard	Sunderland	9th	Dow 3rd Northern Gen Hosp Sheffield	06/10/1916	Dead
17930	Pte	Burney	William	Newcastle	9th		05/07/1916	Dead
13230	Pte	Burnside	William	Middlesbrough	9th	DL 18/10/1917	02/04/1919	Class Z Reserve
15768	Pte	Burrell	John		9th, 7th, 2/West Yorkshire Regt 63067		06/03/1919	Class Z Reserve
15899	Pte	Burton	Alfred		9th, Labour Corps 374215		15/03/1919	Class Z Reserve
12585	Pte	Butler	Edward	Durham City.	9th, 9th	GSW Chin 05/07/1916, GSW L Hand 31/07/1916, GSW L Knee 10/10/1918	27/01/1919	Class Z Reserve
14936	Sgt	Butler	George		9th, 9th, 9th		16/03/1919	Class Z Reserve
3/8866	CSM	Buxton	John		9th, 9th, 9th		07/03/1919	Class Z Reserve
11495	Pte	Byers	John W.	Guisborough	9th. Munitions 11/02/1917, Class W Reserve 25/03/1917		17/01/1919	Discharged

Number	Rank	Name	First Name	Home Town	Bns served with	Reported Wounded	Discharged	MR Comment
15621	Pte	Cain	Joseph	Jarrow	9th, 9th, 2nd	DL 10/09/1917	24/01/1919	Discharged
11058	Pte	Caisley	Joseph		9th, 21st Northld Fus 39053, 14th NF		02/03/1919	Class Z Reserve
16026	Pte	Cann	Arthur J.	Normanby	9th		20/09/1917	Dead
17953	Pte	Carden	Anthony		9th, 9th, 9th		04/03/1919	Class Z Reserve
15114	Pte	Carnell	John		9th, 6th, 9th, 8th, 8th		18/03/1919	Class Z Reserve
15109	L/Cpl	Carney	Thomas		9th, 7th, 12th, 17th Worcestershire Regt 64894 Sgt		12/02/1919	Class Z Reserve
13138	Pte	Carr	John	Port Clarence	9th		10/07/1916	Dead
14673	Pte	Carr	John	Brandon Colliery	9th, 9th, 9th, 8th	GSW L Arm 14/07/1916	12/01/1919	Class Z Reserve
14556	Pte	Carr	Percy	Sheffield	9th		15/10/1917	Dead
15118	CSM	Carter	Arthur C.		9th, 13th, 7th, 13th, 13th.		02/08/1919	Class Z Reserve
11223	A/Sgt	Carter	William	South Bank	9th, 11th, 10th, 23rd Northld Fus, 40756		24/01/1919	Discharged
17943	Sgt	Cartwright	Ronald	Nottingham	9th		09/01/1916	Dead
19627	Pte	Casey	Matthew	Dublin	9th		29/12/1915	Dead
13716	Pte	Cassidy	James		9th, Labour Corps 633310	DL 16/02/1916		Class Z Reserve
11509	Pte	Catterick	Thomas H.	Middlesbrough	9th. Labour Corps HS Lab Coy 30/06/1917, Yorks Regt Depot 25/12/1917		20/02/1919	Class Z Reserve
17878	Pte	Cawkwell	Arthur	Bedale	9th, 7th		30/09/1918	Dead

Number	Rank	Name	First Name	Home Town	Bns served with	Reported Wounded	Discharged	MR Comment
15349	Pte	Chadwick	Leonard	Leeds	9th, Depot 17/07/1916, 6th 27/09/1916, 5th Renumbered 241265 08/12/1916 Missing 27/05/1918	GSW Back 10/07/1916, GSW Face 26/06/1917	28/02/1919	Class Z Reserve
14160	Pte	Chambers	John R.	Willington	9th, Depot 17/06/1917	GSW Both Legs, Rt Leg Amputated below the knee	14/11/1917	Discharged
8073	Pte	Chandler	Simon		9th, Labour Corps 462872		17/08/1918	Discharged
13118	Pte	Chaney	Samuel	Middlesbrough	9th, Labour Corps 167125 L/Cpl, DLI 110357 1/9th. 2/7th Bns	Contusions R Side		Class Z Reserve
3/9099	Pte	Chapman	Albert	Old Malton	9th		25/09/1916	Dead
15288	Pte	Chapman	James	North Shields	9th, 2/West Yorkshire Regt 63071		02/03/1919	Class Z Reserve
17954	Pte	Chapman	John		9th, 21st Northld Fus 39054, 14th NF		04/03/1919	Class Z Reserve
15123	Pte	Charnock	Ernest	Scarborough	9th, Depot 08/07/1916, 2nd 20/01/1917 - 18/04/1917, Labour Corps 16/10/1917 395195	GSW Fingers L Hand, GSW L Forearm	06/02/1918	Discharged
14510	Pte	Chicken	Joseph	Durham City.	9th, West Yorkshire Regt 63322			Class Z Reserve
15914	Pte	Chilvers	George W.		9th, 9th, 9th		21/02/1919	Class Z Reserve

Number	Rank	Name	First Name	Home Town	Bns served with	Reported Wounded	Discharged	MR Comment
14005	Pte	Chilvers	Thomas J.	Washington Station	9th, - 15/1015, 10th 01/06/1916 - 06/07/1916 , Labour Corps 284727 Royal Defence Corps 76886	GSW Hand	27/03/1919	Discharged
15350	Pte	Christian	Albert V.	Leeds	9th, Depot 13/04/1916 11th, 37th IBD, 6th 09/09/1916, 4th 19/09/1916, Royal Engineers 364487	Bomb Wnd R Hand 23/10/1916, GSW R Shoulder & L Leg 01/08/1917	28/03/1919	Class Z Reserve
11755	Pte	Clarke	George T.	Jarrow	9th Bn		23/07/1916	Dead
15605	Pte	Clemens	Walter		9th, 7th, 6th			Class Z Reserve
15998	Pte	Clifford	Arthur H.	Houghton Le Spring	9th. FGCM Drunk 09/11/1915, Munitions Houghton Colliery 18/04/1917	ICT Ankle 06/10/1915	21/05/1917	Discharged
17765	Pte	Clish	William	Wheatley Hill	9th, Labour Corps 31895	GSW Left Hand 09/07/1916, Wnd 28/09/1917	04/03/1919	Discharged
14201	Sgt	Close	William	Lanchester	9th, Depot, 10/10/1917	ICT L Knee 10/03/1916, GSW R Leg 05/07/1916, Shell Wnd Arm Amputated 20/09/1917	08/05/1918	Discharged
7659	Pte	Cockburn	John	Fencehouses	9th renumbered 15957, 2nd, 4th renumbered 203069		23/04/1917	Dead

Number	Rank	Name	First Name	Home Town	Bns served with	Reported Wounded	Discharged	MR Comment
3/8964	Sgt	Cockcroft	Sam		9th, 9th		20/03/1919	Class Z Reserve
13175	Cpl	Cockerill	Arthur	Middlesbrough	9th, 9th	GSW L Elbow 10/07/1916, DL 22/11/1917	15/08/1919	Discharged
17279	Pte	Codling	George T.	Loftus	9th, Depot 20/07/1916, Trg Res Bn 26/09/1916, 6th, 5th, 7th, POW 23/04/1917. Renumbered 241266		28/03/1919	Renumbered 241266
15772	Pte	Cole	William G.G.	Ashington	9th, Labour Corps 584259	DAH	18/02/1919	Class Z Reserve
12555	Pte	Coleby	William S.		9th, 9th		08/03/1919	Class Z Reserve
13055	Pte	Coleman	William	Eston	9th, 9th		12/04/1919	Class Z Reserve
15261	Pte	Colledge	Herbert	Leeds	9th, Depot 12/03/1917, 8th 06/10/1916, Depot 20/11/1916	GSW Face & Eyes 14/11/1916	23/04/1917	Discharged
12516	Sgt	Collings	Jonathan	Tudhoe Village	9th, 10th, 5th		21/08/1918	Discharged
14806	Pte	Collins	John T.		9th, 9th, 9th		Still Serving Mar 1920	Still Serving
12558	Pte	Collins	William		9th, 9th		25/01/1919	Class Z Reserve
17955	L/Cpl	Collinson	Wiliam	Middlesbrough	9th		16/10/1915	Dead
15908	A/Cpl	Collinson	Frederick G.	Middlesbrough	9th		07/06/1917	Dead
15958	Pte	Colwill	Harrison	Hetton le Hole	9th, Depot 15/07/1916	GSW L Leg 10/07/1916	07/01/1919	Class Z Reserve
11933	Pte	Conway	James	Middlesbrough	9th, Depot 08/07/1916, 3rd 09/09/1916, Trg Res		09/08/1917	Discharged

Number	Rank	Name	First Name	Home Town	Bns served with	Reported Wounded	Discharged	MR Comment
3/8915	Pte	Cook	Edward		9th, 9th, 9th		25/03/1919	Class Z Reserve
13413	Pte	Cook	Frederick	Middlesbrough	9th, Depot 21/07/1916	GSW L Arm 10/07/1916	17/01/1919	Discharged
14037	Pte	Cook	John G.	Willington	9th, 9th, 9th		01/02/1919	Class Z Reserve
15583	Pte	Cook	William		9th, 1st Royal Irish Regt 5125, Royal Engineers WR/286003			
12517	Pte	Cooney	John		9th, 9th, 9th		01/02/1919	Class Z Reserve
15132	Pte	Cooper	Arthur		9th		Still Serving Mar 1920	Still Serving Mar 1920.
13085	Pte	Cooper	John	Upper Norwood	9th		10/07/1916	Dead
15940	Pte	Coote	Elijah	Willington	9th, Depot 1916, 2nd 17/03/1917, 5th 28/03/1917 POW	GSW Foot 10/07/1916	24/03/1919	Class Z Reserve
14805	Pte	Cordery	Charles	Grangetown	9th, 7th	GSW Left Foot	17/04/1918	Discharged
14841	Pte	Cornforth	James	Carlin How	9th	Fractured Pelvis, VDH, Bronchitis.	10/04/1917	Discharged
15606	Pte	Costello	George R.	Scarborough	9th		10/07/1916	Dead
15760	Pte	Costigan	William	Sunderland	9th, 21st Northld Fus, 25th Northld Fus 39052		23/03/1918	Dead
14053	Pte	Coulson	Thomas		9th		17/01/1919	Discharged
12891	Pte	Coultas	Arnold	Scalby	9th		05/07/1916	Dead
3/8643	Pte	Coultate	George	Northampton	9th		22/05/1916	Dead
3/8758	Pte	Coultate	Lawrence	Leeds	9th		26/02/1919	Class Z Reserve

Number	Rank	Name	First Name	Home Town	Bns served with	Reported Wounded	Discharged	MR Comment
14571	Pte	Cowan	Thomas	Sherburn	9th		05/07/1916	Dead
15763	Pte	Cowen	William		9th, 9th, 9th		10/02/1919	Class Z Reserve
15908	Pte	Cowling	William	Stockton	9th, 1st Garr Bn West Yorkshire Regt, 1/8th West Yorks 27409		13/07/1918	Discharged
15959	Pte	Cowlishaw	John E.	Fencehouses	9th		10/11/1915	Dead
13671	Cpl	Crabtree	George B.		9th, 10th, 9th, 2nd, 9th			Class Z Reserve
15462	Pte	Craven	Joseph		9th, Labour Corps 375453		26/03/1919	Class Z Reserve
24403	Pte	Craven	Thomas	Scarborough	9th, 6th, 8th, 9th, 9th, 9th	DL 24/08/1916	05/10/1918	Dead
13620	Pte	Cross	James		9th, 7th, 8th, 8th		02/02/1919	Class Z Reserve
13364	Sgt	Crowther	Ernest	Bradford	9th	DCM, MC with W Yorks	08/08/1916	Discharged to Commission West Yorks
15960	Pte	Crozier	George	Houghton le Spring	9th, West Yorkshire Regt 63351			Class Z Reserve
15024	Sgt	Crute	Stanley	Sunderland	9th		05/07/1916	Dead
14797	Pte	Cryer	Richard	Carlin How	9th		31/01/1917	Dead
14463	Pte	Cuin	Mark	Murton	9th		05/07/1916	Dead
13551	Pte	Cuings	Edward	Brandon Colliery	9th		31/01/1917	Dead
15584	Pte	Cunningham	Harry		9th, 9th, 9th		14/03/1919	Class Z Reserve
15608	Pte	Curran	Philip P.	Leeds	9th, Depot 09/07/1916, 3rd 26/10/1916		20/08/1917	Discharged

Number	Rank	Name	First Name	Home Town	Bns served with	Reported Wounded	Discharged	MR Comment
17956	Pte	Curry	William	North Sunderland	9th, 10th		04/10/1917	Dead
19850	Pte	Cusick	George	Gateshead	9th		13/01/1919	Discharged
17957	Pte	Cuskin	Patrick	Shotton Colliery	9th	Mordus Cordus (Heart Disease), Died 18/11/1931	10/04/1917	Discharged
3/8885	Pte	Cusworth	John	Rotherham	9th		10/07/1916	Dead
13420	Pte	Cusworth	William	Rotherham	9th		11/09/1917	Discharged
15607	Pte	Cutcliffe	Frederick S.		9th, Labour Corps 258159		10/04/1919	Class Z Reserve
15624	Pte	Cuthbert	George		9th, 7th, 13th	Wnd Head & Foot	06/03/1919	Class Z Reserve
11903	Pte	Dale	Frank	Guisborough	9th, Depot 17/07/1916. 3rd 13/01/1917 Munitions Iron Mines 03/03/1917, Reenlisted 4th 04/12/1925	GSW L Shoulder	07/01/1919	Discharged
15307	Pte	Dale	John E.	Sunnington, Yorks	9th, Labour Corps 502158		03/04/1919	Class Z Reserve
15901	Cpl	Daniel	Olous E.	Haverton Hill	9th	DL 16/02/1916	16/10/1917	Dead
3/8747	Pte	Darby	Alfred	Sedgeley Staffs	9th		09/01/1916	Dead
14558	Pte	Davey	Sidney	Pitsmoor	9th, 2nd, 6th		10/10/1917	Dead
16217	Pte	Davies	John T	Spennymoor	9th		07/06/1917	Dead
13208	Pte	Davies	Joseph	Guisborough	9th		23/12/1915	Dead
14738	Pte	Davies	Joseph	West Hartlepool	9th		02/02/1916	Dead

Number	Rank	Name	First Name	Home Town	Bns served with	Reported Wounded	Discharged	MR Comment
3/9002	Pte	Davies	Richard L.		9th, 9th, 9th		04/05/1919	Class Z Reserve
15776	Sgt	Davison	George C.	Felling	9th, Depot 07/10/1917, 3rd 15/03/1918. 2nd, Att MGC	GSW Neck, GSW Buttock, GSW Arm	01/03/1919	Class Z Reserve
16218	Cpl	Davison	John W.	Station Town	9th. Class W Reserve Munitions miner 05/06/1917		17/01/1919	Discharged
13857	Pte	Dee	James E.		9th, 9th			Class Z Reserve
12832	Pte	Degnan	Charles	Darlington	9th, 9th, 9th		04/03/1919	Class Z Reserve
11576	Pte	Dent	Henry	Cargo Fleet	9th, 9th, 9th	GSW Face	05/02/1919	Discharged
11575	Pte	Dent	John	Middlesbrough	9th		12/12/1915	Dead
3/8916	Sgt	Dent	James	Leicester	9th, 9th, 9th, 9th		06/10/1918	Dead
11236	Pte	Devine	Daniel	South Bank	9th, Depot 08/07/1916 7th 11/06/1917 Class W Res Munitions Steel Works 22/08/1917. Previously served 3rd DLI 1909	Bullet Wnd L Arm & L Hand DL 02/08/1916	01/02/1919	Discharged
15777	Pte	Devlin	Joseph		9th, 7th		08/01/1919	Class Z Reserve
14560	Pte	Dick	Aaron	Ryhope	9th		05/03/1919	Discharged
17958	Pte	Dick	Cuthbert F.	North Shields	9th, Labour Corps 583400	DAH, Died 06/05/1924	17/03/1919	Class Z Reserve
12706	Pte	Dilworth	Thomas	Middlesbrough	9th, Depot 20/06/1916 3rd 23/03/1917	GSW R Thigh in two places with compound fracture	22/05/1917	Discharged

Number	Rank	Name	First Name	Home Town	Bns served with	Reported Wounded	Discharged	MR Comment
12603	Pte	Dinsley	Edward	New Coundon	9th, 20/10/1916 Class P Reserve	Compound Frac Skull loss of R Eye. 07/09/1916	27/12/2016	Discharged
17865	Pte	Dixon	David	Bishop Auckland	9th, 6th		28/03/1919	Class Z Reserve
13272	Pte	Dixon	John	Middlesbrough	9th, 11th AWOL 20/07/1916 Labour Corps 351668		07/03/1919	Class Z Reserve
3/9247	Pte	Dixon	John		9th, 9th		04/03/1919	Class Z Reserve
15902	Pte	Dixon	Joseph	South Bank	9th, Depot 03/05/1916, Class W Reserve		03/01/1919	Discharged
15341	Pte	Dixon	Robert W.	Wheatley Hill	9th		10/07/1916	Dead
12092	Pte	Dixon	Thomas A.	Middlesbrough	9th, 6th, 2nd, 13th	DL 22/02/1916, Tuberculosis	31/05/1917	31/12/1917
13251	Pte	Dixon	Alfred O.	Grangetown	9th	Died 07/07/1924	06/03/1919	Class Z Reserve
15910	L/Cpl	Dobson	Edmund		9th, West Yorkshire Regt 43645 Sgt 12th Bn		26/06/1917	Discharged to Commission 3/West Yorks
15299	Pte	Dobson	Joseph	Stockton	9th		09/11/1915	Dead
17959	Pte	Dobson	Nicholson		9th, 9th, 8th		09/02/1919	Class Z Reserve
14927	Sgt	Dockray	Arthur	Leeds	9th		25/04/1917	Discharged to Commission Yorkshire Regt
14623	Pte	Dodsworth	John		9th		04/03/1919	Class Z Reserve
14934	Pte	Doherty	John	Middlesbrough	9th		05/07/1916	Dead

Number	Rank	Name	First Name	Home Town	Bns served with	Reported Wounded	Discharged	MR Comment
3/9065	Sgt	Dolan	James	Middlesbrough	9th		11/12/1916	Discharged
12586	Pte	Donaldson	Harry		9th, 9th, 9th, 9th	wounded	12/03/1919	Deserted 16/6/1917
17728	Pte	Donaldson	Henry	South Shields	9th		05/07/1916	Dead
10523	Pte	Donoughe	John	Huddersfield	9th, 7th	Pension Records show second number as 2822.	17/01/1919	Discharged
17882	Pte	Dooley	John	Fishergate, York	9th	Died 1931	23/04/1918	Discharged
12918	Pte	Doughty	Alfred	Thornaby.	9th, 9th, 8th		18/03/1919	Class Z Reserve
17766	Pte	Dove	Albert W.	Wheatley Hill	9th		06/10/1916	Dead
19305	Pte	Dowey	Thomas A.	Grosmont	9th, 2nd		31/07/1917	Dead
12806	Pte	Downs	Albert E.		9th, 9th, 9th		18/03/1919	Class Z Reserve
12733	A/Sgt	Drew	Alfred	Cork	9th, 9th, Depot 03/09/1918	Bullet Wnd R Shoulder 20/07/1918	26/02/1919	Class Z Reserve
13065	Pte	Drew	Thomas	Eston	9th		05/07/1916	Dead
17691	Cpl	Dring	George	East Howle	9th		08/06/1917	Dead
11959	Sgt	Duffy	John A.	Middlesbrough	9th, 2nd, 8th, 8th		29/10/1918	Dead
11151	Pte	Dunn	Charles T.	Middlesbrough	9th. Depot 15/07/1916	GSW L Leg amputated DL 24/08/1916	11/07/1917	Discharged

Number	Rank	Name	First Name	Home Town	Bns served with	Reported Wounded	Discharged	MR Comment
19316	Pte	Dunning	Henry	West Rainton	9th, Duke of Wellington's Regt	Daily List: 18th August 1916, Newcastle Journal Fri 18/8/1916 P 6 col 5, Weekly Casualty list 30/10/1917 p 11. Weekly Casualty list 11 June 1918 page 38. Durham Chronicle 25/8/1916 Page 8 Col 4	29/11/1918	Discharged
14799	Pte	Dunning	William F.		9th, 9th, 9th		16/03/1919	Class Z Reserve
8955	Pte	Durham	John G.		9th, 21st Northld Fus 39055, 14th NF	DL 24/08/1916		Class Z Reserve
15262	Pte	Durkin	Michael	Bradford	9th, 6th, to 3 East Yorks 27687, 1st 6th E Yorks to Duke of Cornwall's LI 056		21/03/1919	Class Z Reserve
17883	Pte	Dyson	Albert E.		9th		21/02/1919	Class Z Reserve
15941	Pte	Dyson	George W.	Esh Winning	9th	Mitral Disease Not Overseas	19/06/1915	Discharged
12099	Sgt	Earl	John T.	North Ormesby	9th, Depot 30/09/1916, 13th 01/11/1917, 9th	GSW R Arm & Back 19/09/1916 , Shell Shock	18/02/1919	Class Z Reserve
3/9049	Sgt	Eaves	Albert W.	North Ormesby	9th		10/07/1916	Dead

Number	Rank	Name	First Name	Home Town	Bns served with	Reported Wounded	Discharged	MR Comment
7519	Pte	Eden	Alfred	Seaham	9th, Renumbered 13128, Depot 31/3/16, 11th, 9/7/16, 6th, 4th 9/9/16 renumbered 202939	PoW 29/05/1918	08/05/1919	Class Z Reserve
17960	Pte	Edes	Samuel	Cold Hesleden	9th		02/02/1919	Class Z Reserve
3/8975	Pte	Edwards	James W.	Glamorgan	9th		24/05/1916	Dead
15764	Pte	Elderwick	Frederick	Hetton le Hole	9th Depot 20/05/1916, 10th Trg Res Bn, 6th, 2nd		20/03/1919	Class Z Reserve
14724	Pte	Elgie	Percy	Bedale	9th, 1/5/ Manchester Regt 201869		28/01/1919	Class Z Reserve
17747	Pte	Ellemor	William	Silksworth	9th		14/05/1916	Dead
16003	Cpl	Ellershaw	Sidney	Scarborough	9th		05/07/1916	Dead
15276	Sgt	Elliott	Wilfred	Sheffield	9th, Durham Light Inf Trg Reserve, Northbld Fus Trg Reserve TR/5/530		18/04/1918	Discharged
19320	Pte	Ellis	Hugh	Haswell	9th		10/07/1916	Dead
14820	Pte	Elwick	Thomas	Scarborough	9th, 6th, 13th.		03/06/1918	Discharged
13271	Pte	English	John E.	Eston	9th, 23 Div Cyclist Coy 9th, 9th	GSW R Hip 10/07/1916	14/12/1919	Class Z Reserve
11859	Pte	Evans	Richard G.	Middlesbrough	9th		10/07/1916	Dead
11817	Pte	Fagg	Alfred E		9th, 8th, 9th renumbered 66450		13/01/1919	Discharged
12443	Pte	Fairbank	Walter	Hedon Yorks	9th, 9th, 9th		05/10/1918	Dead

Number	Rank	Name	First Name	Home Town	Bns served with	Reported Wounded	Discharged	MR Comment
13158	Pte	Fairbridge	William	Middlesbrough	9th		16/10/1917	Dead
14253	Pte	Falkous	Thomas	Mason Hall Nthbld	9th		17/01/1919	Discharged
15271	Cpl	Farndale	William		9th, 9th		24/04/1919	Class Z Reserve
17885	Pte	Farr	Arthur	Leeds	9th, Depot 22/07/1916, 2nd, 4th 06/05/1917, 13th	GSW Shoulder R Leg 10/07/1916, GSW 06/12/1917	22/08/1919	Deserted 22/07/1918,
12057	Pte	Farrell	William	Thornaby	9th	MDG 29/08/1916	08/06/1917	Dead
12815	CSM	Farrelly	George	Murton	9th, 8th 24/11/1917	Dangerousley ill Para typhoid 1/04/1916	09/02/1919	Class Z Reserve
15903	Pte	Fearon	John	Middlesbrough	9th	L Leg & Face, Wounds 392 xvi	05/07/1916	Discharged
15427	Pte	Fenn	Alfred		9th, 7th		20/08/1917	Discharged
12978	Pte	Fenn	William	Sunderland	9th			Class Z Reserve
3/8945	Pte	Fenwick	William	Middlesbrough	9th, 2nd, 7th	MDG 25/08/1916	04/03/1919	Discharged
7652	Pte	Ferguson	James	Tantobie	9th, 2nd, 4th renumbered 203062		19/11/1918	Dead
14505	Pte	Ferry	George	Durham City.	9th, 15th South Lancashire Regt 64007	Died 09/11/1920	04/04/1919	Class Z Reserve
12836	Pte	Finlay	Robert	Middlesbrough	9th, 8th		20/09/1917	Dead
13042	Pte	Firth	Laurence	Crook	9th		10/07/1916	Dead
18433	Pte	Flack	Robert W.	Woodford Bridge Essex	9th, Labour Corps 649384		16/03/1919	Class Z Reserve

Number	Rank	Name	First Name	Home Town	Bns served with	Reported Wounded	Discharged	MR Comment
15325	Pte	Flanagan	James	Middlesbrough	9th, 11th AWOL 15/07/1916, Durham LI 54497			Discharged
11992	Pte	Flanagan	Thomas	Middlesbrough	9th, 9th.		03/04/1919	Class Z Reserve
13003	Cpl	Fleming	Lewis R.	Middlesbrough	9th, Depot 30/03/1916 Munitions Steel works		06/02/1919	Discharged
19366	Pte	Fletcher	John J.	Spennymoor	9th		07/06/1917	Dead
11801	Pte	Flynn	James	Middlesbrough	9th		30/01/1917	Discharged
8663	Pte	Foley	William		9th, Labour Corps 370271		21/02/1919	Class Z Reserve
17961	Pte	Ford	Alma	North Shields	9th		02/02/1919	Class Z Reserve
13390	Pte	Ford	Michael		9th, 9th, 9th		03/03/1919	Class Z Reserve
15778	Pte	Forster	Joseph	Barmston	9th		14/08/1916	Dead
13518	Pte	Foster	Aaron H.	Sedgefield	9th. Depot 09/05/1916	GSW L Shoulder seriously ill 18/04/1916	24/10/1916	Discharged
13540	Pte	Foster	William		9th, 10th, 5th		06/04/1919	Class Z Reserve
11341	Pte	Foulis	Albert	Leeds	9th	DL 02/08/1916, DoW No 36 CCS	09/07/1916	Dead
15323	Pte	Fox	Sidney E.	West Hartlepool	9th, 6th, 2nd		27/01/1919	Discharged
17962	Pte	Fox	Thomas		9th		16/03/1919	Discharged
16750	Pte	Francis	Michael	Bishop Auckland	9th. Military Medal 24/08/1916	Died 14/12/1925, Neurasthenia	25/08/1916	Discharged
15190	Pte	Frearson	William		9th, 9th, 9th		19/02/1919	Class Z Reserve

Number	Rank	Name	First Name	Home Town	Bns served with	Reported Wounded	Discharged	MR Comment
13249	Pte	Fretter	John L.	Middlesbrough	9th, 7th		04/07/1917	Discharged
3/8935	Pte	Fry	Charles		9th, 9th, 8th		20/02/1919	Class Z Reserve
15311	Pte	Fryer	George	Leeds	9th		04/04/1917	Discharged
3/9025	Pte	Gaffighan	Henry	North Ormesby	9th, 9th, 9th, 8th		01/02/1919	Class Z Reserve
14045	Pte	Gaines	George	Coundon	9th, Labour Corps L/Cpl 619662		06/03/1918	Discharged
15779	Sgt	Gair	William	Bedlington	9th, Depot 15/07/1916, Class W Reserve 27/01/1917 Miner	GSW L Hand 10/07/1916	30/07/1917	Discharged
17963	Pte	Gall	James C.	Longhaugh	9th, Labour Corps 527570		21/03/1919	Class Z Reserve
3/8979	Pte	Gallagher	James		9th		11/02/1919	Discharged
15361	Pte	Gardner	Thomas	Stockton	9th		05/07/1916	Dead
3/9005	Pte	Gardner	William	Middlesbrough	9th, 9th, 8th		20/02/1919	Class Z Reserve
5693	Pte	Garry	John T.	Trimdon Grange	9th, 6th renumbered 243258		26/06/1917	Dead
17964	Pte	Gascoyne	James	Alfreton	9th	DoW King George Hosp London	18/06/1917	Dead
17887	Sgt	Gatehouse	Walter		9th, Labour Corps 258164		25/02/1919	Class Z Reserve
7522	Pte	Gaunt	Arthur		9th, 11th, 6th, 4th, 8th, renumbered 202941		21/02/1919	Class Z Reserve
11984	Pte	Gething	Albert	Middlesbrough	9th, Depot 14/06/1917 3rd 31/12/1917	ICT Feet 5/10/1916	09/11/1919	Class Z Reserve

Number	Rank	Name	First Name	Home Town	Bns served with	Reported Wounded	Discharged	MR Comment
3/8638	Pte	Gettings	Edward	Middlesbrough	9th, 9th	GSW Shoulder & Thigh	30/08/1918	Discharged
14161	Pte	Gibson	Joseph	Bishop Auckland	9th	WL 19/06/1916 GSW R Leg Died 07/11/1939	25/05/1917	Discharged
19317	Pte	Gibson	Robert		9th, Northumberland Fus 87642			Class Z Reserve
15574	Pte	Gibson	Sidney		9th, Royal Irish Regt 5109		25/03/1919	Class Z Reserve
14563	Cpl	Giles	Ernest	Easington Colliery	9th, 9th	GSW Back, Died 29/01/1925	22/11/1918	Discharged
16006	A/Clr Sgt	Glaister	John		9th		11/12/1917	Discharged to Commisiion KOYLI
17886	Pte	Goodall	Francis W.	Plumstead	9th, 7th		26/12/1916	Dead
3/8899	Sgt	Goodison	John	Middlesbrough	9th, 9th		09/02/1919	Class Z Reserve
15322	Pte	Goodwill	Richard	Boosbeck	9th, Labour Corps 382873		05/02/1919	Class Z Reserve
14223	Sgt	Gornall	Norman	Hemlington Row	9th Depot 01/10/1915, 11th 31/10/1915, 7th 23/12/1917	ICT Slight Wnd 23/09/1915, GSW Arm 01/07/1916	11/07/1917	Discharged
17740	Pte	Gould	Frederick	Fencehouses	9th, 9th		15/10/1917	Dead
14055	Sgt	Goulder	Albert		9th, Leicestershire Regt 64311		15/10/1919	Class Z Reserve
13050	Pte	Graham	John F	Eston	9th		17/10/1915	Dead
13155	Pte	Graham	Robert	Stockton	9th		10/07/1916	Dead

Number	Rank	Name	First Name	Home Town	Bns served with	Reported Wounded	Discharged	MR Comment
13415	Sgt	Grainger	Francis	Middlesbrough	9th, FGCM Stricking a superior 28/10/1917	GSW Hand 11/10/1918	26/04/1915	Class Z Reserve
13142	Pte	Grayson	Charles	Great Ayton	9th		09/11/1915	Dead
14041	Pte	Grayson	Joseph W.		9th, Labour Corps Cpl 444330		03/03/1919	Discharged
15401	Pte	Green	Robert		9th, 1/R Scots Fusiliers 203092, Yorkshire Regt 66721	London Gen Hosp Aug 1916	Still Serving Jul 1920	Still Serving Jul 1920
19812	Pte	Green	Frank	Saxondale, Notts	9th	DoW Whalley Mil Hosp	27/04/1916	Dead
14632	Pte	Green	George	Skinningrove	9th	Died No 5 Gen Hosp Amiens	21/07/1916	Dead
14030	Pte	Grenwell	Mosley	Willington	9th, Connaught Rangers 6292		25/01/1919	Class Z Reserve
11550	Pte	Grimes	Bernard	Middlesbrough	9th, Depot 23/09/1915	Sickness 392 xvi	13/06/1916	Discharged
11588	Pte	Grinnell	Frederick	Guisborough	9th, 7th		01/07/1916	Dead
15120	Pte	Gunn	William		9th, 9th, 9th		14/03/1919	Class Z Reserve
15477	Pte	Gurden	Walter	York	9th		10/07/1916	Dead
15962	Pte	Guy	James	Houghton le Spring	9th, Labour Corps 384303		18/03/1919	Class Z Reserve
15587	Pte	Haddaway	James	Middlesbrough	9th		27/01/1916	Dead
46593 (14443)	Pte	Hall	George	Guisborough	9th. Class W Reserve Munitions Ironstone miner 24/07/1917	Bomb Wnd R Thigh20/05/1917	15/01/1919	Discharged

Number	Rank	Name	First Name	Home Town	Bns served with	Reported Wounded	Discharged	MR Comment
13353	Pte	Hall	Matthew	Haverton Hill	9th, Depot 02/04/1916 Munitions		06/02/1919	Discharged
15588	Sgt	Hall	Randall V.	Stainton in Cleveland	9th		25/03/1918	Discharged
13143	Pte	Hall	Robert	Middlesbrough	9th	DL 16/02/1916	05/07/1916	Dead
11885	Pte	Hall	Thomas	Jersey C.I.	9th		05/07/1916	Dead
15942	Pte	Hall	Thomas	West Hartlepool	9th		10/07/1916	Dead
13777	Pte	Hamer	Thomas	Manchester	9th, FGCM SIW 1-01/01/1916, Depot 13/07/1916, Durham LI 05/05/1917 Labour Corps 574 Agric Coy 238110	GSW R Foot Toe Amputated 01/01/1916, GSW Arm & Forearm	27/03/1919	Class Z Reserve
17721	Pte	Hanson	Alfred	Skelton	9th, Labour Corps 368838	Died 12/02/1926	12/10/1919	Class Z Reserve
12594	Pte	Hanson	Stephen	Bearpark Colliery	9th, Royal Irish Regt 5110	Died 1921	08/02/1919	Class Z Reserve
15099	Pte	Hammond	Thomas		9th, 8th, 9th, 9th 9th		02/03/1919	Class Z Reserve
17702	Pte	Harding	Robert	Sunderland	9th, Army Service Corps T/386904	Wnd Head	23/02/1919	Class Z Reserve
14787	Sgt	Hardisty	James	York	9th, 13th,	GSW L Leg 10/07/1916	29/04/1918	Dead
12188	Pte	Hardy	Herbert	Leeds	9th		16/10/1917	Dead
14050	Pte	Hardy	William	Langley Moor	9th		10/07/1916	Dead

Number	Rank	Name	First Name	Home Town	Bns served with	Reported Wounded	Discharged	MR Comment
13281	Pte	Harker	James	Shotton Colliery	9th		18/09/1916	Dead
13275	Cpl	Harland	Tom	Guisborough	9th, 6th	GSW Wrist 05/07/1916	15/01/1919	Discharged
15465	Pte	Harling	Bertram	West Hartlepool	9th, Labour Corps527 HS Emp Coy 659466 MM LG 16/08/1917, Black Watch 31417	Evac PUO 28/09/1917	03/04/1919	Reenlisted Black Watch
14702	Pte	Harn	Michael	Hartlepool	9th, Labour Corps 407406		17/02/1919	Discharged
12253	Pte	Harrington	Frank	Middlesbrough	9th	GSW R Foot	01/06/1917	Discharged
19813	Pte	Harris	Percy		9th, 9th		12/03/1919	Class Z Reserve
15589	Cpl	Harrison	George G.	Grangetown	9th, Depot 13/04/1916, 13th	GSW Thigh & Leg 23/02/1918	29/11/1918	Discharged
15409	Pte	Harriman	Arthur	Thornley	9th, 1/5/Manchester Regt 201874			Class Z Reserve
13049	Pte	Harvey	John		9th		17/01/1919	Discharged
12509	Pte	Harvey	Marshall A.	Sacriston	9th, East Kent Regt 7th Bn 13/08/1918 G/14611	GSW Finger 18/09/1918	31/01/1919	Class Z Reserve
15783	Pte	Harwood	Frederick W.	North Shields	9th	GSW L Hand Amp of Middle Finger	08/06/1917	Discharged
15018	Cpl	Hastings	George	Murton	9th		18/02/1919	Class Z Reserve
13145	Pte	Haw	James W.	Middlesbrough	9th, Depot 10/10/1916, Lincolnshire Regt, Labour Coy 06/02/1917, 32204	GSW L Forearm 02/10/1916	27/03/1919	Class Z Reserve

Number	Rank	Name	First Name	Home Town	Bns served with	Reported Wounded	Discharged	MR Comment
15347	Pte	Hawkins	John F.	Leeds	9th, Depot 10/07/1916, 6th	ICT L Leg 09/03/1916	12/05/1917	Discharged
15915	Pte	Hawksby	James T.	Middlesbrough	9th, 7th 17/07/1916, Reenlisted Labour Corps 29/05/1919 699919 18th Labour Coy 19/06/1919 Dis 26/04/1920	Evac Septisimia 01/01/1917	03/08/1917	Discharged
3/9022	Cpl	Hawkswell	Thomas	Scarborough	9th. Sgt 21/07/1916	GSW L Arm & Chest	11/04/1917	Discharged
11582	Pte	Haworth	Nathaniel	Lanchester	9th Cpl 09/02/1915, 6th 29/08/1915	Wounds 392 xvi	28/04/1916	Discharged
13381	Pte	Hawthorne	John V.R.		9th, Royal Irish Rifles 40681			Class Z Reserve
19814	Pte	Hayes	Joseph	Bedlington	9th, Depot 23/09/1917	GSW Severe L Hand	13/12/1917	Discharged
3/9007	Pte	Hazel	Joseph	East Hartlepool	9th		10/07/1916	Dead
19852	Pte	Heaney	William	Walker	9th, 7th, 5th		23/04/1017	Dead
14722	Pte	Hebdon	Albert	Thirsk	9th, Depot 12/01/1916	Evac Bronchitis 04/01/1916	09/06/1916	Discharged
19342	Pte	Helm	Ernest	Northallerton	9th, 11th, 24th MG Coy 14/7/16, 57th MG Coy 9/8/17	R Hand, R Foot, GSW Thigh Springburn Woodside Hosp Glasgow 2/12/6	25/09/1917	Dead
15612	Pte	Henderson	Horace H.	Middlesbrough	9th, Durham LI 66290	GSW Left Shoulder	02/04/1919	Class Z Reserve

Number	Rank	Name	First Name	Home Town	Bns served with	Reported Wounded	Discharged	MR Comment
12027	Pte	Henderson	Charles		9th, 26/8/15 - 17/6/17, 29/DLI 3/7/18 - 19/8/18, 43/R Fusiliers 23/8/18 - 19/11/1918			
9110	Cpl	Henderson	Edward	Ferryhill	9th		14/10/1914	Dead
15339	Pte	Henning	Herbert J.		9th, 6th, 9th, 9th, 8th		14/03/1919	Class Z Reserve
15321	Pte	Heptonstall	Henry	Pontefract	9th, 9th. Military Medal 17/12/1917	GSW R Arm 10/10/1918	30/01/1919	Class Z Reserve
11887	Pte	Herbert	John E.	St lements, Jersey C.I.	9th		05/07/1916	Dead
3/9001	Pte	Hewett	William		9th	Died 22/09/1924	25/02/1919	Class Z Reserve
15296	Pte	Hick	John		9th, Labour Corps 444715		25/03/1919	Class Z Reserve
12711	Pte	Hill	John G.	Middlesbrough	9th, 9th FGCM 05/11/1917 Desertion 3 Yrs Penal Servitude suspended 9th	GSW L Fingers 07/06/1916 Evac Wounded 25/10/1918	01/10/1919	Deserted 05/11/1917
15781	Pte	Hill	Robert	Bedlington	9th, Depot 15/07/1916, 3rd Res, 4th 21/05/1917	GSW L Calf 10/07/1916	15/05/1919	Class Z Reserve
12695	Pte	Hill	Walter H.		9th, East Yorkshire Regt 30769 Cpl		24/01/1919	Class Z Reserve
14026	Pte	Hill	James W.	Durham City.	9th, Labour Corps 401744 245 Div Emp Coy		04/03/1919	Discharged
15590	Pte	Hinchey	Joseph	Scarborough	9th. 11th Off Cadet Bn 08/04/1917	Wnd 20/09/1916	01/08/1917	Discharged to Commission West Riding Regt

Number	Rank	Name	First Name	Home Town	Bns served with	Reported Wounded	Discharged	MR Comment
13107	Pte	Hind	John H.	Middlesbrough	9th, Depot 16/01/1916 11th, 8th 30/06/1916, 10th 07/09/1916, Labour Corps 15/01/1918 479401	WGSW Hand Severe 01/1916,	01/02/1919	Discharged
13086	Pte	Hinds	John G.	West Hartlepool	9th att 69 Coy MGC	Abrasions R Leg 05/07/1916	11/12/1916	Deserted 11/12/1916.
15987	Cpl	Hitchin	Alfred	Haverton Hill	9th Military Medal 10/07/1916	GSW L Leg 28/09/1917	20/04/1919	Class Z Reserve
15626	Pte	Hodge	Thomas	Skinningrove	9th, Durham LI 54510	Rheumatic Fever	09/01/1918	Discharged
17779	Pte	Hodgson	George W.		9th, 6th West Yorkshire Regt 63135		17/01/1919	Class Z Reserve
17758	Pte	Hodgson	John N.	Gateshead?	9th, Royal Irish Regt 5108		17/02/1919	Class Z Reserve
15100	Pte	Hodgson	William	Leeds	9th, Labour Corps 271897		25/04/1919	Discharged
16491	Pte	Hodgson	Lionel	Carlin How	9th		01/10/1917	Dead
17889	Cpl	Hodgson	William	Wheatley Hill	9th, 11th Class W Reserve 11/08/1916	Evac Nephritis	24/10/1917	Discharged
3/8686	Cpl	Hoffman	Frederick W.	Sheffield	9th		13/03/1918	Discharged
13373	L/Cpl	Hoggard	Harry		9th, Machine Gun Corps 23133		07/03/1919	Class Z Reserve
17274	Cpl	Holligan	Alfred	Stockton	9th, Depot 11/07/1916, 10th, 9th		26/02/1919	Class Z Reserve
18501	Pte	Hollingsworth	William V.	Scarborough	9th, 9th		09/03/1919	Class Z Reserve

Number	Rank	Name	First Name	Home Town	Bns served with	Reported Wounded	Discharged	MR Comment
13278	Pte	Hollinshead	Sion G.	Eston	9th		05/07/1916	Dead
13229	Pte	Holmes	Alexander	Port Clarence	9th, Depot 11/11/1915 11th, Munitions 19/06/1916	Shell Wnd L leg severe 07/11/1915	06/02/1919	Discharged
14175	Pte	Holmes	Hugh	Leiterim Ireland, Res Wakefield (Time Exp Regular.	9th, Depot 11/08/1916, 3rd, 18th 03/05/1917		17/07/1917	Discharged
12120	Pte	Holmes	Robert	Gateshead	9th		07/06/1917	Dead
13205	Cpl	Holsey	Herbert G.	Normanby	9th		07/06/1917	Dead
3/9118	Pte	Hopton	Joseph E.	Middlesbrough	9th		10/07/1916	Dead
13362	Pte	Horner	William	Thirsk	9th		20/10/1917	Discharged to Commission 3/West Yorks & RAF
15591	Pte	Horseman	Charles H.	Middlesbrough	9th		07/06/1917	Dead
14791	Sgt	Hudon	George		9th, 9th, 9th		15/02/1919	Class Z Reserve
15471	Pte	Hudson	Harry	Scarborough	9th.9th.9th	GSW R Leg Severe	24/02/1919	Class Z Reserve
12109	Pte	Hudson	Robert F.	Middlesbrough	9th		10/07/1916	Dead
12252	Pte	Hudson	Thomas E.		9th.2nd	Adm 4th Stat Hosp, Scabies 28/07/1916 to Duty 14/08/1916	06/03/1919	Class Z Reserve
15297	Pte	Hughes	Michael		9th, 9th, 9th		16/03/1919	Class Z Reserve
15096	Pte	Humble	Robert	Walbottle	9th, 9th	Wnd July 16	04/03/1919	Class Z Reserve

Number	Rank	Name	First Name	Home Town	Bns served with	Reported Wounded	Discharged	MR Comment
7672	Pte	Humphrey	Sidney	Hull	9th, 2nd, 4th renumbered 203082		23/04/1917	Dead
12225	Pte	Hunt	Albert	Leeds	9th		08/07/1919	Class Z Reserve
13043	Pte	Hunter	Anthony	Willington	9th, Depot 15/07/1916, 7th, 13th, 4th	GSW R Arm 10/07/1916	11/03/1919	Class Z Reserve
3/9076	Pte	Hunter	John J	Leeds	9th, 5th		27/05/1918	Dead
17888	Pte	Hunter	John W.	Lanchester	9th, 2nd, 6th	ICT Leg 14/05/1916	10/01/1919	Discharged
14428	Cpl	Hunter	Thomas		9th.Renumbered 65904		06/03/1919	Class Z Reserve
19385	Pte	Hunter	William A.	Murton Colliery	9th, 7th	GSW L Side 10/07/1916	05/10/1917	Discharged
11991	Pte	Hunwick	Thomas	Marton, Cleveland	9th, Connaught Rangers 6293	GSW L Shldr 10/07/1916	21/06/1917	Dead
15925	Pte	Husband	Joseph G.	Lingdale	9th		01/01/1916	Dead
11988	Pte	Husband	Stephen C.	Eston	9th, Depot 08/07/1916, 81st Trg Res Bn, to 2nd, 5th Bns Renumbered 243299	GSW L Elbow 10/07/1916	02/04/1919	Class Z Reserve
11568	Pte	I'Anson	George H.		9th, 6th, 5th 7529, 5th Durham LI 245108, POW Lab Coy 604996, Yorkshire Regt 66715		Still Serving Jul 1920	Still Serving Jul 1920.
14549	Sgt	Ibberson	Nelson	Sheffield	9th, Depot 08/07/1916, 13th 13/10/1916	GSW Head Penetrating, Back, Shldr#, Arm Severe. DL 01/09/1917	18/10/1917	Discharged

Number	Rank	Name	First Name	Home Town	Bns served with	Reported Wounded	Discharged	MR Comment
13992	Pte	Ingleby	John H.	Low Pittington	9th, 9th, 9th		05/10/1918	Dead
14328	Pte	Jack	Robert A.	Stockton	9th, 23rd Div Cyclist Coy 3501		07/10/1916	Dead
12433	C/Sgt	Jackson	Albert P.	Barry Port, S Wales	9th Second Lt 8th Bn, Capt Labour Corps		10/09/1916	Discharged to Commission
14620	Pte	Jackson	Frederick		9th		11/04/1917	Discharged
13918	Pte	Jackson	John T.	Blackhall	9th, Depot 20/06/1916, D Court Martial 19/10/1917 Desertion 7th		20/02/1919	Deserted 09/08/1918
19313	Pte	Jackson	Robert	Murton Colliery	9th, 8th		22/09/1917	Dead
13547	Cpl	Jackson	William J.	Wheatley Hill	9th. To UK for Commission 22/01/1917 Deserted FGCM 31/12/1917 Reduced to Pte	Shellshock 07/10/1916, GSW Shldr 26/10/1918	25/03/1919	Class Z Reserve
19359	Pte	Jeffrey	George		9th, Labour Corps 436302		05/02/1919	Class Z Reserve
15943	Pte	Jennings	Alfred	Harrogate	9th, Depot 11/07/1916, 6th 30/10/1916. 2nd 16/05/1918	GSW L Shldr 05/07/1916 Appendicitis 24/11/1917	20/02/1919	Class Z Reserve
17278	Pte	Jennison	George W.	Whitby	9th, 9th, 9th		09/03/1919	Class Z Reserve
15944	Pte	Jepson	Ernest	Pontefract	9th, 2nd, 8th, 9th, 9th, 9th		21/01/1919	Class Z Reserve

Number	Rank	Name	First Name	Home Town	Bns served with	Reported Wounded	Discharged	MR Comment
17773	Cpl	Johnson	Alfred	Stokesley	9th, 9th, 9th. Reenlisted 5th 05/07/1921		14/03/1919	Class Z Reserve
15459	Pte	Johnson	Henry	Wheatley Hill	9th.9th.9th		05/10/1918	Dead
17934	Pte	Johnson	John		9th, 6th		02/03/1919	Discharged
14254	Pte	Johnson	William H.	Seaham Colliery	9th, Labour Corps 603724		04/03/1919	Discharged
15786	Pte	Jolly	Charles J.		9th, Army Service Corps 14/12/1917 T/384531		11/05/1919	Class Z Reserve
14942	Pte	Jones	Alfred E.	Middleton Yorks	9th		15/05/1916	Dead
8950	Pte	Jones	George		9th, Labour Corps 646346		23/02/1919	Class Z Reserve
12104	Pte	Jones	Joseph	Middlesbrough	9th, 9th		11/03/1919	Class Z Reserve
3/8940	Pte	Jones	Joseph		9th, 9th		15/04/1919	Class Z Reserve
13173	Pte	Jones	Walter	Middlesbrough	9th, Depot 04/12/1916, 7th 06/03/1917, Labour Corps 477250	MDG 30/08/1916 Not Missing Wnded, ICT Buttocks 09/05/1916, ICT Foot Right 05/07/1916	20/03/1919	Class Z Reserve
13220	Pte	Jordan	John H.		9th Labour Corps 475499		04/04/1919	Class Z Reserve
12075	Pte	Jowers	Robert	Middlesbrough	9th, 9th, 9th		14/02/1919	Class Z Reserve
12375	Pte	Judson	Robert P.	Boosbeck	9th		31/01/1919	Discharged

Number	Rank	Name	First Name	Home Town	Bns served with	Reported Wounded	Discharged	MR Comment
19172	Pte	Kane	Thomas	Middlesbrough	9th, 9th.		01/02/1919	Class Z Reserve
15313	Clr Sgt	Kaye	Frank H.	Lenthwaite	9th, 9th. 13 Officer Cadet Bn, Returned to Unit 02/12/1918		16/05/1919	Class Z Reserve
12078	Pte	Keany	James	Middlesbrough	9th		19/10/1915	Dead
15615	Pte	Keegan	Philip	Middlesbrough	9th, Royal Engineers WR/277390			
14631	Pte	Kennedy	Robert		9th, Royal Irish Regt 5122	GSW L Arm 10/07/16 MDG 25/08/1916, WL 23/04/1918	06/05/1919	Class Z Reserve
15137	Cpl	Kennedy	Thomas	Dawdon	9th		11/12/1915	Dead
13964	Pte	Kent	George	Trimdon	9th		05/07/1916	Dead
19590	Pte	Kerss	Peter	Seaton Delaval	9th, Royal Irish Regt 5062, Labour Corps 388423	Malaria	06/06/1919	Class Z Reserve
14439	Pte	Kerwin	Andrew	Durham City.	9th		10/07/1916	Dead
12712	Pte	Kerwyn	Thomas W.	Witton Park	9th		10/07/1916	Dead
11546	Pte	Kett	Charles W.	Middlesbrough	9th, 6th, East Yorkshire Regt 44806			Class Z Reserve
14735	Pte	Kirby	William	Thornley	9th, 9th, 9th		24/01/1919	Class Z Reserve
13722	Pte	Kirkup	Joseph	Croxdale	9th att 69th TMB, Depot 01/02/1917, 6th, 2nd	Wnd in Face accident with Trench Mortar 27/01/1917, GSW L Arm 21/03/1918	28/01/1919	Class Z Reserve

Number	Rank	Name	First Name	Home Town	Bns served with	Reported Wounded	Discharged	MR Comment
3/9061	Pte	Kisby	Thomas	Monkwearmouth	9th	Died in Frensham Mil Hosp	15/06/1915	Dead
11893	Pte	Knaggs	George	Guisborough	9th, Class W Reserve Munitions Ironstone Miner 03/10/1916		16/01/1919	Discharged
13052	Pte	Knaggs	Thomas		9th, Royal Irish Regt 5121		06/05/1919	Class Z Reserve
13372	Pte	Knight	Richard	Middlesbrough	9th, Labour Corps 450776		14/04/1919	Class Z Reserve
19820	Pte	Knowles	William	North Shields	9th	GSW Face & Jaw, Died by June 1922	12/05/1917	Discharged
15965	Pte	Laidler	George W.	East Rainton	9th		10/07/1916	Dead
12103	Pte	Laing	Wallace		9th, 7th		19/03/1919	Class Z Reserve
15787	Pte	Lally	John	Jarrow	9th, Depot 11/07/1916	GSW L Arm Fractured 05/07/1916	20/08/1917	Discharged
17314	Pte	Lambert	George	Swalwell	9th		10/07/1916	Dead
3/9295	Sgt	Lanagan	Joseph Henry	Tynemouth	9th	Shorncliffe Mil Hosp	14/04/1915	Dead
9295	Sgt	Lanaghan	Joseph	Tynesmouth	9th	Died in Shorncliffe Mil Hosp Bronchitis, Heart Failure	11/05/1915	Dead
14790	Cpl	Lane	Albert E.		9th, 9th, 9th.		18/02/1919	Class Z Reserve
7534	Pte	Laverick	Thomas	Middlesbrough	9th, Depot 24/04/1916, 11th, 6th, 4th renumbered	Evac Synovitis R Knee	29/01/1919	Discharged

Number	Rank	Name	First Name	Home Town	Bns served with	Reported Wounded	Discharged	MR Comment
15354	Cpl	Laws	Philip J.	King's Lynn	9th.	DoW Lahore Brit Gen Hosp Calais	15/01/1916	Dead
14115	Pte	Lawther	John		9th, 9th, 9th		29/08/1919	Class Z Reserve
13167	Pte	Layburn	Fred	Middlesbrough	9th, 6th, 5th Bns renumbered 5540		11/01/1917	Dead
15988	Pte	Lazenby	Robert	South Bank	9th, East Yorkshire Regt 30619			Discharged
12257	A/Cpl	Lazenby	William	North Ormesby	9th		10/07/1916	Dead
13622	Pte	Le Count	Lionel	Durham City.	9th, 9th, 9th		05/10/1918	Dead
13491	Pte	Leigh	James	St Helens	9th, Depot 03/04/1916, Labour Corps 19/11/1918 584729	Evac Scabies 03/04/1916	17/01/1919	Class Z Reserve
15592	Pte	Leonard	Charles		9th, Royal Engineers WR/267459			
3/8952	Pte	Leonard	Michael	Middlesbrough	9th	MDG 09/08/1916	15/03/1919	Discharged
16038	Pte	Leonard	Nelson	Wingate	9th	Rheumatic Fever	20/07/1917	Discharged
14615	Sgt	Lightfoot	George A.	Kilkenny Barracks	9th,Depot 05/02/1916, Leicestershire Regt Trg Res 5/31284	Functional Paralysis, Shell Shock & Bruises 19/12/1915	14/12/1918	Discharged
15897	Pte	Lightfoot	Major	Skinningrove	9th 9th, 9th		14/03/1919	Class Z Reserve
17891	Pte	Linehan	William	South Bank	9th. Depot 15/07/1916	GSW L Arm 10/07/1916	04/05/1917	Discharged
14203	Pte	Lintern	Archibald	Willington	9th, Depot 28/04/1916	Evac PUO 17/04/1916	30/01/1919	Class Z Reserve
14205	A/Cpl	Little	Herbert	Willington	9th		07/06/1917	Dead

Number	Rank	Name	First Name	Home Town	Bns served with	Reported Wounded	Discharged	MR Comment
11510	Pte	Loftus	Albert	Scarborough	9th, 1st Royal Irish Regt 5069		10/03/1918	Dead
14590	CSM	London	George T.		9th		08/05/1919	Class Z Reserve
13431	Sgt	London	James N.	Whitburn	9th, Depot 14/07/1916		14/01/1919	Class Z Reserve
15121	Pte	Longman	John W.		9th, 9th, 9th		24/07/1919	Class Z Reserve
17771	Pte	Loughren	Charles	Wheatley Hill	9th, 25th Durham LI 11/04/1917 20256, Labour Corps 19/08/1917, 169587	GSW Loss of L Eye (enemy action)	02/04/1918	Discharged
19318	Pte	Lovenson	James		9th , Lab Corps 371599 291 Lab Coy Yorks Regt 66607		Still Serving Mar 1920	Reenlisted as 66607 Deserted 30/04/1919
13972	Pte	Lowe	James	South Shields	9th		05/07/1916	Dead
13972	Pte	Lowery	James	Middlebrough	9th		05/07/1916	Dead 05/07/1916
12794	Pte	Lowery	Robert E.		9th, 8th, K O Yorkshire LI 80188. GSM Iraq 1/ KOYLI 4682197		14/12/1918	Discharged
7666	Pte	Luccock	William	South Hetton	9th, Depot 19/08/1916, 4th, 15/01/1917 renumbered 203076		22/01/1919	Class Z Reserve
17892	CSM	Lyall	John W.	Thornaby	9th, Depot 03/10/1917, 9th 07/04/1918, 9th	GSW R Foot 20/09/1917	15/02/1919	Class Z Reserve
15762	Pte	Lynch	James		9th, 10th, 2nd	Wnd L Leg	24/01/1919	Discharged
13140	Pte	Lynch	John		9th, 2/East Yorkshire Regt 27673. Royal Fusiliers GS/140325			Class Z Reserve

Number	Rank	Name	First Name	Home Town	Bns served with	Reported Wounded	Discharged	MR Comment
12520	Pte	Madden	Andrew		9th, 7th, 6th		16/02/1919	Class Z Reserve
14507	Pte	Maddison	John G.		9th, 2nd, 6th, 2nd		14/07/1919	Class Z Reserve
11973	Pte	Magee	Patrick		9th, Northumberland Fus 79612			Deserted 27/10/1917
7539	Pte	Malcolm	Thomas W.	Fencehouses	9th, 6th, 4th, renumbered 202956	Gassed	28/06/1918	Discharged
19591	Pte	Malton	Arthur	Seaton Delaval	9th		29/03/1916	Dead
15294	Pte	Malton	Fred	Scarborough	9th, 6th 18/01/1917, 4th Bn 19/09/1917, Labour Corps 10/05/1918 650340	Gassed July 1918	11/04/1919	Class Z Reserve
14814	Pte	Manix	John	Grangetown	9th, Northumberland Fus 40772	Died 24/01/1924	20/09/1918	Discharged
11951	Pte	Mann	Joseph	Middlesbrough	9th	DoW Alex Pk Hosp Stockport	24/07/1916	Dead
15312	Pte	Mannall	Gordon W.	York	9th, 6th, 7th.		09/05/1917	Dead
17243	Pte	Manners	joseph	Murton Colliery	9th, FGCM Drunk 03/12/1917 9th, 9th		10/01/1919	Class Z Reserve
3/8931	Pte	Manning	John	Middlesbrough	9th	DL 22/11/1917	03/02/1919	Discharged
11089	Pte	Manning	Matthew	Bishopwearmouth	9th, Depot 15/07/1916, DCM Deserter 18mnths remitted 22/01/1917, 9th 09/02/1917	GSW R Hand 10/07/1916, DL 24/08/1916	04/03/1919	Class Z Reserve
13252	Pte	Mannion	John R.		9th, 9th, 9th		14/03/1919	Class Z Reserve
16262	Pte	Markham	Henry	Darlington	9th		18/10/1917	Dead

Number	Rank	Name	First Name	Home Town	Bns served with	Reported Wounded	Discharged	MR Comment
17746	A/Sgt	Marlee	Jonas J.	Sunderland	9th		31/07/1917	Discharged to Commission Northblnd Fus
3/9071	Pte	Marsden	William	Scarborough	9th, Ex 1st Bn Time expired. Depot 16/07/1916	Right Leg Amputated 10/07/1916	30/06/1917	Discharged
14208	Pte	Marsh	George	Burnhope Colliery	9th, 9th, 9th		29/10/1918	Dead
3/8365	Sgt	Marsh	John J C.	North Ormesby	9th	Died 14/01/1922	10/04/1918	Discharged
14554	Pte	Martin	Hugh C.	Sheffield	9th, Depot 18/03/1917	Evac Tuberculosis	19/11/1917	Discharged
14166	Pte	Martin	James	Willington.	9th, Depot 11/06/1917	Shell Wnd Back 07/06/1917, WL 06/08/1917	12/12/1918	Discharged
17928	Pte	Martin	James	Blyth	9th		10/07/1916	Dead
19846	Pte	Mason	Alfred	Kilsby Leics	9th		25/01/1916	Dead
13629	Sgt	Mason	John H.		9th, 9th, 9th		19/02/1919	Class Z Reserve
14622	Pte	Mason	John W.	Thirsk	9th	GSW Slight 19/11/1915, GSW 05/07/1916 GSW 20/10/1917	23/04/1918	
24357	Pte	Mason	John W.	West Hartlepool	9th, 7th, 7th, 8th, 9th	GSW L Arm 01/07/1916	23/04/1918	Discharged
3/8999	CSM	Mason	Michael H.	Whitechapel	9th		20/02/1919	Class Z Reserve
13657	Pte	Mason	Henry	Howden le Wear	9th, 11th		01/10/1919	Deserted 07/05/1916
13397	Pte	Matsell	Robert E.	Middlesbrough	9th, West Yorkshire Regt 63479			Class Z Reserve

Number	Rank	Name	First Name	Home Town	Bns served with	Reported Wounded	Discharged	MR Comment
11900	Pte	Matthewman	John	Eston	9th, Depot 14/07/1916, 6th 17/11/1916, 2/West Yorkshire Regt 63093	GSW L Arm 10/07/1916, Shrapnel Wnd L Knee 10/1917, GSW R Shlder 13/10/1918	19/03/1919	Class Z Reserve
15983	Pte	Maude	John H.	Whitby	9th, Depot 02/10/1916	GSW Arm 02/10/1916	05/03/1919	Discharged
17252	Pte	Maughan	John	Hetton le Hole	9th. Military Medal 17/10/1918	Wnd Shell 03/11/1915, GSW£ L Arm 09/10/1918	30/01/1919	Class Z Reserve
15113	Pte	Maw	Harold		9th, 9th, 9th.		24/07/1919	Class Z Reserve
15133	Pte	Maw	John N.	Cloughton Yorks	9th, 9th, 9th.	Died Sep 1988	14/03/1919	Class Z Reserve
15934	A/Sgt	Maxwell	William	Stockton	9th	Evac Nephritis 07/04/1916	14/03/1919	Discharged
15792	Pte	McAll	John J C.	Tynesmouth	9th	DL 04/02/1916	07/06/1917	Dead
11865	Pte	McArdle	Denis	Gateshead	9th.		20/09/1916	Dead
15917	Pte	McCann	John	Middlesbrough	9th, 9th, 9th Depot 17/10/1918.	GSW R Eye sever 09/10/1918	15/03/1919	Discharged
12444	Pte	McCarthy	Eugene		9th, Labour Corps 658985		12/03/1919	Class Z Reserve
15791	Pte	McCluskey	John	Alston	9th, Depot 21/10/1916, Class W Reserve Munitions 21/01/1917	Shrapnel Wnd R Shldr 05/07/1916	14/12/1917	Discharged
17893	Pte	McClusky	Anthony	North Ormesby	9th. Depot 13/07/1916		09/01/1918	Discharged

Number	Rank	Name	First Name	Home Town	Bns served with	Reported Wounded	Discharged	MR Comment
14296	Pte	McCormack	Joseph	Jarrow	9th, Machine Gun Corps 23132	Phithiasis	17/06/1918	Discharged
12596	Pte	McDermott	Thomas	Bearpark	9th		24/05/1916	Dead
15364	Pte	McGee	James		9th, Labour Corps 377999		16/03/1919	Class Z Reserve
3/8816	Pte	McGin	John E.	Newport, Middlebrough	9th, 2nd	GSW Arm with Fracture	02/09/1918	Discharged
15472	Pte	McGrath	Lawrence	Leeds	9th, Labour Corps 206472		11/12/1919	Discharged
13204	Pte	McGrother	John	Middlesbrough	9th		10/07/1916	Dead
15789	Pte	McGuire	James		9th, East Yorkshire Regt 27669		26/04/1919	Class Z Reserve
13631	Pte	McKean	James	Hull	9th	GSW R Arm amputated	30/05/1917	Discharged
17693	Pte	McKee	Edward	Jarrow	9th		10/07/1916	Dead
12117	Pte	McKegney	Arthur	Middlesbrough	9th, 2nd, 8th. Renumbered 66456		29/03/1919	Class Z Reserve
13137	Pte	McKenna	John	Middlesbrough	9th, Depot 08/07/1916, 7th 01/03/1917, Depot 27/09/1917 DCM AWOL 17 - 20/12/1917 avoiding embarkation, 9th	GSW L Wrist 05/07/1916, Contusions Back 1918	14/01/1919	Deserted 31/12/1917
15793	Pte	McKenzie	John D.	Dundee	9th		10/07/1916	Dead
15794	Pte	McLellan	Thomas	Jarrow	9th	DL 16/02/1916	05/07/1916	Dead
15619	Pte	McLynn	John		9th		05/02/1919	Discharged

Number	Rank	Name	First Name	Home Town	Bns served with	Reported Wounded	Discharged	MR Comment
12045	Pte	McManus	John		9th, Labour Corps 264038		28/04/1919	Class Z Reserve
11235	Pte	McMillan	Hugh	South Bank	9th, Labour Corps 264111	Debility, Died 26/04/1926	24/12/1917	Discharged
13047	Sgt	McNamara	Andrew	Durham City.	9th, 8th 3rd Res, att Nigeria Regt		09/01/1919	Dead
12726	Pte	McPartland	Peter	Middlesbrough	9th, Depot 02/03/1916, 11th, 8th 30/06/1916 , 7th 20/07/1916	Evac Flu 01/03/1916 GSW Scalp	08/05/1919	Class Z Reserve
15476	Pte	McPartland	Peter		9th, Labour Corps 368713		25/02/1919	Discharged
14024	Pte	McPherson	Allan	Bearpark	9th, 3rd Res	Shrapnel Wnd R Lung, & R Leg 04/07/1916	21/08/1918	Discharged
15363	Pte	McPhie	William	Hutton Rudby	9th		26/01/1916	Dead
13060	Pte	Meaburn	John G.		9th, East Yorkshire Regt 30025			Class Z Reserve
16085	Pte	Meadows	George	Station Town	9th, 13th, 12th, Class P Reserve 07/12/1918		29/01/1919	Discharged
14689	Sgt	Meredith	George	West Hartlepool.	9th, 13th	DL 23/10/1917, DL 22/11/1917	05/07/1919	Class Z Reserve
14552	Sgt	Messenger	Albert	Sheffield	9th		23/09/1917	Dead
15359	Pte	Middleton	Jonathon	Stockton	9th, Depot 12/02/1917	Evac Infl Glands in Neck	19/12/1917	Discharged
11523	Pte	Milburn	Ernest	Guisborough	9th, Depot 28/07/1916, 9th 09/02/1917, Class W Munitions 23/05/1917	GSW Chest severe, Foot & Hand DL 02/08/1916	31/01/1919	Discharged

Number	Rank	Name	First Name	Home Town	Bns served with	Reported Wounded	Discharged	MR Comment
15478	Pte	Mildenhall	John W.	York	9th, Labour Corps 442325	Bronchitis Died 1953	25/02/1919	Class Z Reserve
15788	Pte	Miller	Michael R.	Bedlington	9th, 7th, 12th 5th, 2/4th Duke of Wellington's Regt 34591	Gastritis	15/03/1919	Class Z Reserve
3/9011	Sgt	Mitchell	Thomas	Brompton	9th		02/05/1917	Dead
15618	Cpl	Mole	George A.	Wheatley Hill	9th, 9th, 9th	GSW Legs 20/09/1916, GSW Legs 07/06/1917	05/02/1919	Class Z Reserve
3/9012	Cpl	Molloy	George E.		9th, Northumberland Fus 79544			Self Inflicted Wnd 8/11/1917
15795	Pte	Monaghan	Thomas P.	Hebburn	9th FGCM 22/01/1916 Disobedience, FGCM 16/01/1917 Drunk		13/03/1919	Class Z Reserve
19824	Pte	Moon	Arthur	Canterbury	9th		19/09/1916	Dead
15386	Pte	Moon	Claude L.	Banques Guernsey	9th, 14th K O Yorkshire LI 41699, Labour C 706475		09/01/1918	Discharged
14298	Pte	Moore	Matthew	Jarrow	9th. Depot 10/12/1914 Shipbuilding 11/01/1916	ICT R Arm 21/11/1915	05/02/1919	Discharged
17776	Pte	Moran	John	Ludworth	9th		28/01/1917	Dead
16013	Sgte	Mordey	Christopher	Hendon	9th, 9th, 9th		20/02/1919	Class Z Reserve
15966	Pte	Morley	William G.	West Rainton	9th	GSW in action severe 10/1916	25/01/1917	Discharged
15287	Pte	Morring	Frank		9th, 9th		09/03/1919	Class Z Reserve

Number	Rank	Name	First Name	Home Town	Bns served with	Reported Wounded	Discharged	MR Comment
15301	Pte	Morrison	James	Middlesbrough	9th, 9th		15/10/1918	Deserted 25/10/1917, Dead
13711	Pte	Moss	Albert	Fencehouses	9th	DoW Hosp Aberdeen	24/07/1916	Dead
15119	Cpl	Moss	Arthur	Nottingham	9th		21/09/1917	Dead
13710	Cpl	Moss	William	Houghton Le Spring	9th, 8th, 9th, 9th		15/06/1918	Dead
12160	Pte	Moulds	Thomas		9th		05/02/1919	Discharged
13038	Pte	Mount	James	Norfolk	9th, 6th 27/11/1916, 5th 03/12/1916	Sprained Ankle 03.07/1916	16/04/1918	Discharged
19319	Pte	Moyle	George W.	Houghton Le Spring	9th		13/04/1918	Dead
15796	Pte	Mullholland	John	Byker	9th, Army Reserve Class W 11/06/1917 Shipbuilding		03/01/1919	Discharged
14032	Sgt	Muncaster	Daniel	Leeholme	9th, 9th, 9th		05/02/1919	Class Z Reserve
15265	Pte	Mundy	Charles		9th, 4th		06/03/1919	Class Z Reserve
3/8720	Pte	Murphy	Arthur		9th		09/03/1919	Class Z Reserve
19593	Pte	Murphy	Hugh	Spennymoor	9th		05/07/1916	Dead
13341	Sgt	Murphy	James	South Bank	9th, Depot 19/12/1916, Class W Reserve Munitions 09/1916	Shell Shock MDG 29/08/1916	21/01/1919	Discharged
3/9010	Pte	Murphy	John	Middlesbrough	9th		10/07/1916	Dead
11331	Clr Sgt	Murray	Arthur	Leeds	9th, Att The Guards Off Cadet Bn 09/03/1917		26/06/1917	Discharged to Commission Royal Lancster Regt

Number	Rank	Name	First Name	Home Town	Bns served with	Reported Wounded	Discharged	MR Comment
15124	Pte	Murray	Arthur	Scarborough	9th, depot 21/07/1916, Labour Corps 20/06/1917 297 Coy, South Staffordshire Regt 01/12/1918 60142	GSW Thigh 05/07/1916	27/04/1919	Class Z Reserve
14031	Sgt	Musgrave	Matthew H.	Coundon	9th, Leicestershire Regt Trg Res5/36034	Chronic Sinoitis Died 08/12/1964	14/12/1918	Discharged
15414	Pte	Musther	Harold	Stranton	9th		10/07/1916	Dead
10867	Pte	Naven	Richard		9th		18/02/1919	Class Z Reserve
17706	Pte	Neal	William		9th, 9th		20/01/1919	Class Z Reserve
11829	Pte	Nelson	John H.	Middlesbrough	9th, Labour Corps 573340	GSW Knee	27/03/1919	Class Z Reserve
19358	Pte	Nelson	John T.		9th		28/01/1918	Discharged
17280	Pte	Nendick	John W.	Middlesbrough	9th, 2nd		07/11/1918	Dead
15122	Cpl	Nettleton	John C.		9th		30/10/1917	Discharged to Commission West Yorks Regt
3/8829	Pte	Newby	David		9th		03/02/1919	Discharged
14044	Pte	Newby	John	Sherburn Durham	9th, 9th, 9th		03/02/1919	Class Z Reserve
14804	Pte	Newell	Herbert	Redcar	9th	GSW R Arm Frac Humerous	23/06/1918	Discharged
12251	Pte	Newland	Alfred		9th		28/04/1916	Discharged
12525	Pte	Nice	Walter	Langley Park	9th		19/07/1918	Dead

Number	Rank	Name	First Name	Home Town	Bns served with	Reported Wounded	Discharged	MR Comment
19825	Pte	Nicholson	Norman	Bedlington	9th, Depot 13/07/1916, 8th 17/12/1916, Depot 11/06/1917, Deserter 10/12/1917 DCM 08/02/1918, 13th 02/04/1918	Shell Wnd L Thigh	24/09/1919	Class Z Reserve
15594	Pte	Nicklin	Elijah		9th, 7th, 8th, 8th	DL 16/02/1916	24/03/1919	Class Z Reserve
3/8897	Pte	Nickling	Daniel	Middlesbrough	9th, Labour Corps 124011	DL 30/11/1915, DL 01/03/1916, GSW Back	16/02/1919	Class Z Reserve
15926	Pte	Noble	Thomas	Boosbeck	9th, Depot 12/03/1917 Class W Reserve 25/03/1917 Ironstone miner	Wnd 05/07/1916	17/01/1919	Discharged
12072	Pte	Nuttall	Bernard	E Kinton Derbyshire,	9th		07/06/1918	Discharged
14933	Pte	O'Brien	Edmund	Middlesbrough	9th, 8th		18/10/1917	Dead
15918	Pte	O'Connor	Thomas	Middlesbrough	9th, Labour Corps, 614688	GSW Neck	24/05/1919	Class Z Reserve
14327	Sgt	Oddy	John	Staincliffe, Res Cleckheaton	9th, 9th, 9th		07/02/1919	Class Z Reserve
3/8839	Cpl	Oglesby	Richard	Loftus	9th		24/09/1917	Dead
13266	Pte	O'Leary	Cornelius	Middlesbrough	9th, Labour Corps 238526	VDH, GSW R Buttock	20/09/1919	Discharged
13707	Pte	Oliver	David H.	Sunderland	9th, Depot 19/06/1916, Class W Reserve 23/12/1916 Eppleton Colliery 06/01/1917	Shell Wnd Back 24/05/1916	17/01/1919	Discharged

Number	Rank	Name	First Name	Home Town	Bns served with	Reported Wounded	Discharged	MR Comment
19826	Pte	Orwin	George N.	Byker	9th Sgt 01/12/1916, Depot 14/07/1916	GSW R Thigh 10/07/1916, GSW Leg & Arm 09/10/1918	06/03/1919	Class Z Reserve
14550	Cpl	Outram	George H.	Burngrave	9th		05/07/1916	Dead
12890	Cpl	Overin	Willie	Leeds	9th. Depot 15/0-7/1916 10 Trg Res 21/10/1916	GSW L Forearm & L Thigh 10/07/1916	09/02/1919	Class Z Reserve
15595	Pte	Page	James	Rotherham	9th	GSW R Arm Moved to Canada	26/02/1918	Discharged
12598	Cpl	Palmer	Hugh	Bishop Auckland	9th		18/09/1916	Dead
14943	Cpl	Palmer	Sidney		9th	Wounds 392 xvi	15/12/1916	Discharged
17894	Pte	Panks	Arthur W.	Darton Yorks	9th, 2nd, 9th, 2nd	GSW R Hip Died 09/01/1924	08/02/1919	Class Z Reserve
14054	Pte	Parker	Bertram		9th, West Yorkshire Regt 63170			Class Z Reserve
13034	Pte	Parker	Tom		9th, 6th, 5th Renumbered 243267		13/04/1919	Class Z Reserve
12091	Pte	Parkes	John T.	Worcester	9th, Depot 01/08/1916		30/08/1916	Discharged
3/8971	Clr Sgt	Parkin	Harold	Sheffield	9th	GSW Thigh	10/04/1917	Discharged
15968	Pte	Parkin	William E.	Houghton le Spring	9th, 6th		27/01/1919	Discharged
19360	Pte	Parkinson	George A.	Howden le Wear	9th, 9th, 29/Durham LI 101802	DL 23/10/1917		Class Z Reserve
12882	Pte	Parkinson	William	York	9th, Class W Reserve Munitions Ironstone		16/01/1919	Discharged

Number	Rank	Name	First Name	Home Town	Bns served with	Reported Wounded	Discharged	MR Comment
3/8832	Sgt	Parsons	Thomas	Middlesbrough	9th.		31/03/1917	Discharged
14206	Pte	Pattinson	Luke	Willington	9th, Depot 11/04/1916, 2nd 14/01/1917, 4th 14/01/1917	GSW Back	23/08/1919	
13151	Pte	Pattison	George E.	Middlesbrough	9th, 7th		19/04/1917	Dead
13391	Pte	Pattison	James	Middlesbrough	9th, 2nd	GSW Back	31/03/1919	Class Z Reserve
17895	Pte	Paver	John W.	York	9th, Depot 27/09/1917	GSW Back Severe 09/1917	02/03/1919	Class Z Reserve
15332	Pte	Payne	George	Cassington	9th	DL 28/08/1917	30/10/1917	Discharged
15302	Pte	Payne	James S	Leeds	9th	L Arm Amputated	05/09/1918	Discharged
12125	Pte	Peacock	Anthony	Middlesbrough	9th, 9th, 9th		10/10/1918	Dead
14802	Pte	Peacock	Thomas	Saltburn	9th, 9th, 8th	Neurasthenia, moved to Glasgow	29/03/1919	Class Z Reserve
12582	Pte	Peacock	William		9th, Machine Gun Corps 23135		07/03/1917	Discharged
15610	Pte	Pearson	Hugh	Jarrow	9th. 11th 17/08/1916, 4th 01/09/1916, 7th 20/03/1917	GSW Chest Severe	02/01/1919	Discharged
13037	Pte	Pearson	Thomas	Bearpark	9th		14/10/1914	Discharged
17922	Pte	Pearson	Thomas	Willington	9th	Original number crossed out ~~13037~~	14/10/1914	Discharged
15799	Pte	Peart	Albert	North Shields	9th		27/04/1918	Discharged
14935	Pte	Pease	Edward		9th, 9th, 9th		14/03/1919	Class Z Reserve

Number	Rank	Name	First Name	Home Town	Bns served with	Reported Wounded	Discharged	MR Comment
14453	Cpl	Peddle	Albert E.	Sheffield	9th, Depot 14/07/1916 25th Durham LI 17/04/1917, Labour Corps 170038	GSW Abdomen & R Hand 10/07/1916	06/12/1917	Discharged
12406	Pte	Pennock	Harold T.	Saltburn	9th	DL24/08/1916	10/07/1916	Dead
15428	Pte	Pentith	Harry H.	Hull	9th	DoW 38th CCS	02/07/1916	Dead
13018	Sgt	Petch	Joseph	Sutton in Ashdale Notts	9th	DoW 26th Field Amb RAMC	20/01/1916	Dead
22858	L/Cpl	Pickard	John F.	Pickering	9th Labour Corps 458594		21/03/1919	Class Z Reserve
15969	Pte	Pickering	George	Houghton le Spring	9th, East Yorkshire Regt 51139			Discharged
11919	Cpl	Pinchbeck	John R.	South Bank	9th, FGCM Drunk 27/04/1918 Reduced Pte 9th	GSW Back Severe 24/10/1918	20/02/1919	Class Z Reserve
15320	Pte	Platt	Norman	Leeds	9th		07/06/1917	Dead
7542	Pte	Plews	George	Langley Park	9th,renumbered 12515 11th, 6th, 4th renumbered 202958		23/04/1917	Dead
15798	Pte	Plummer	Alfred	Newcastle	9th, 11th West Yorkshire Regt 82351	GSW R Arm		Class Z Reserve
12114	Pte	Pollock	Alexander	Middlesbrough	9th, Depot 22/09/1916 Class W Reserve Marine Fitter 25/09/1916		06/02/1919	Discharged
3/9044	Pte	Poskett	John G.	Middlesbrough	9th, 7th		22/12/1917	Dead
15104	Pte	Postlethwaite	Morris		9th, 9th		14/03/1919	Class Z Reserve

Number	Rank	Name	First Name	Home Town	Bns served with	Reported Wounded	Discharged	MR Comment
15111	Pte	Potter	Alfred C.	Middlesbrough	9th, East Yorkshire Regt 27679	Malaria.	13/02/1919	Class Z Reserve
14929	CSM	Potter	George	Leeds	9th		07/11/1915	Dead
17774	Pte	Pratt	Norman	Horden	9th, Depot 02/08/1916	Wnd in action 05/07/1916	27/01/1919	Discharged
17277	Pte	Preston	Walter	York	9th, 9th		16/01/1920	Discharged
19828	Pte	Pringle	Thomas	Newcastle	9th	GSW Ankle, Calf & L Buttock	01/10/1917	Discharged
14222	Cpl	Pyle	Thomas	Wheatley Hill	9th, 6th, 7th	MDG 25/08/1916, DL 24/08/1916	08/02/1917	Dead
3/9031	Pte	Raby	John	Norwich	9th, att 53 HG Rly Op Coy as Batman 23/09/1917		12/03/1919	Class Z Reserve
15289	Pte	Raby	Robert	Carlton in Cleveland	9th, 9th, 9th		25/02/1919	Class Z Reserve
12205	Pte	Radigan	Thomas	Middlesbrough	9th	DoW 2nd Western Gen Hosp Manchester	07/06/1916	Dead
13781	Pte	Rafferty	Michael		9th, Labour Corps 632510		31/03/1919	Class Z Reserve
17762	Cpl	Raffle	William	Wheatley Hill	9th, Depot 14/06/1917	GSW L Leg 07/06/1917	10/01/1919	Class Z Reserve
19624	Pte	Raine	Sidney	Suffield Nr Scarborough	9th	Shell Shock GSW L Arm 09/10/1918	05/04/1919	Class Z Reserve
12625	Pte	Raison	Frank	North Ormesby	9th		02/10/1917	Dead

Number	Rank	Name	First Name	Home Town	Bns served with	Reported Wounded	Discharged	MR Comment
17896	Pte	Ramsay	George		9th, 21st Northld Fus, 25th Northld Fus, 3rd Northld Fus 39056		29/03/1919	Class Z Reserve
15597	Pte	Ramshaw	John	South Bank	9th, Labour Corps 480433	GSW Chest	11/03/1919	Discharged
15952	Pte	Rawden	Alfred	Scarborough	9th, Labour Corps Sgt 124223	GSW R Shoulder	09/04/1919	Class Z Reserve
3/8974	Pte	Raywood	Charles	South Bank	9th, 3rd		08/07/1918	Dead
15801	Pte	Reay	Alfred S.	Tynemouth	9th, Depot 14/07/1916 2nd, 2nd, 6th, 6th, 2nd	GSW L Thigh, 10/07/1916, GSW R Thumb 11/08/1918, DL 03/05/1917	16/02/1919	Class Z Reserve
12602	Pte	Reay	Joseph	Easington Lane	9th		08/06/1917	Dead
17897	Pte	Reddington	Thomas		9th, Labour Corps 609319		12/04/1919	Class Z Reserve
3/8884	Cpl	Reilly	James	Sheffield	9th		05/07/1916	Dead
15932	Pte	Reilly	John	Richmond	9th, Labour Corps 227899		24/03/1919	Class Z Reserve
12408	Clr Sgt	Rennison	Charles E.		9th		15/03/1919	Class Z Reserve
15919	Pte	Rich	John H.	Middlesbrough	9th, Depot 07/08/1917 Class W Munitions		01/02/1919	Discharged
3/8973	Pte	Richards	John C.		9th, 9th, 9th		24/02/1919	Class Z Reserve
12323	Cpl	Richardson	Joseph H.		9th, 9th, 9th		04/02/1919	Class Z Reserve
15802	Pte	Richardson	Matthew	West Stanley	9th, 2nd		31/07/1917	Dead

Number	Rank	Name	First Name	Home Town	Bns served with	Reported Wounded	Discharged	MR Comment
19829	Pte	Richardson	Stephen	Spennymoor	9th, Depot 09/02/1918 Ex 1st Buffs 1892 - 1904		11/03/1918	Discharged
14040	Pte	Richardson	Thomas	Brandon Colliery	9th, 7th, 5th		23/04/1917	Dead
11561	Pte	Riley	John	West Hartlepool	9th, Att 23rd Div HQ, 9th Att XIV Corps HQ		27/05/1919	Class Z Reserve
13340	Pte	Riley	Peter	Oldham	9th	DL 24/08/1916	10/07/1916	Dead
13231	Pte	Ritting	William	South Shields	9th, 9th, 9th		24/02/1919	Class Z Reserve
6792	Pte	Roach	Isaac	Bradford	9th		Still Serving Mar 1920	Still Serving Mar 1920.
16050	Pte	Roberts	Christopher	Sunderland	9th	GSW Neck 05/07/1916	04/03/1919	Class Z Reserve
15800	Pte	Robertson	Thomas A.	Bedlington	9th Depot 04/10/1915, 8th 12/12/1915 FGCM 17/02/1918 SIW	GSW Scalp 02/10/1915, Self Inflicted Wnd negligence 17/02/1918	04/02/1919	Class Z Reserve
15330	Pte	Robinson	Arthur		9th		20/01/1917	Discharged
19855	Pte	Robinson	Frederick	Whickham	9th, Ex 2nd Bn 12 Yrs Svc time expired		20/01/1919	Class Z Reserve
15346	Pte	Robinson	George	Kirkleatham	9th		10/07/1916	Dead
15804	Pte	Robinson	George	Bedlington	9th, att 69 MG Coy, Depot 20/10/1917 Deserter 23/03/1918 rejoined 10/05/1918, Escaped still AWOL 07/02/1920		22/05/1920	

Number	Rank	Name	First Name	Home Town	Bns served with	Reported Wounded	Discharged	MR Comment
12151	Pte	Robinson	George W.	Middlesbrough	9th		14/11/1916	Dead
15338	Pte	Robinson	Joseph	North Ormesby	9th	Wnd 01/01/1916, GSW Rt Knee, Both Arms Rt Shldr, R Eye	02/10/1916	Discharged
14437	Pte	Robinson	Robert C.		9th, 6th	DL 24/08/1916	30/10/1917	Discharged to Commision Durham LI
15927	Cpl	Robinson	William	Lingdale	9th, Class W Reserve Ironstone miner 17/10/1917	DL 24/08/1916	01/01/1919	Discharged
15291	Pte	Robinson	Samuel	Scarborough	9th, 2nd		02/04/1917	Dead
13965	Pte	Robson	Nicholas	Ludworth	9th, 6th, 9th, 6th		09/05/1918	Dead
17933	Pte	Robson	Thomas W.	Brandon Colliery	9th, 2nd 30/07/1916 Depot 29/05/1917	GSW L Shldr 05/07/1916 , GSW L Leg 09/04/1917	24/11/1917	Discharged
12383	Cpl	Rodgers	Charles		9th, 2nd		01/02/1919	Class Z Reserve
14875	Sgt	Rooney	Andrew T.		9th		26/06/1917	Discharged to Commission 3/ Yorkshire Regt
14568	Cpl	Rooney	Edward	Horden Colliery	9th, Labour Corps 443621	Myalgia, Died 1930	24/01/1919	Class Z Reserve
13382	Pte	Rooney	Edwin	Middlesbrough	9th	Missing Newcastle Journal 08/08/1916	31/10/1917	Dead
19830	Pte	Routledge	Thomas	Bedlington	9th		22/04/1916	Dead

Number	Rank	Name	First Name	Home Town	Bns served with	Reported Wounded	Discharged	MR Comment
18969	Pte	Rowland	Thomas	Horden Colliery	9th, Labour Corps 370331 946 Area Emp Coy	Deafness	11/03/1919	Discharged
13363	Pte	Rowley	James	Jarrow	9th, 9th, 9th	Trench Feet 11/1915	15/03/1919	Class Z Reserve
14792	Pte	Rowse	John	Millom Cumb	9th		05/07/1917	Dead
12856	Pte	Ruddick	Edward	Sunderland	9th	Shrapnel Wnds L Leg & R Knee, Died 21/01/1926	09/10/1916	Discharged
19851	Pte	Rutter	James W.	Winlaton	9th, Depot 24/10/1917	Wnd 10/1917	14/06/1918	Discharged
11866	Pte	Rye	James A.	Guisborough	9th, Depot 17/07/1916 Class W Reserve Ironstone miner	GSW Face & Scalp 08/05/1916 at Duty, GSW L Arm 10/07/1916	02/04/1918	Discharged
14224	Pte	Sach	Leonard	Burnhope	9th	GSW Fracture	17/05/1917	Discharged
20641	Pte	Sadler	Robert W.	Richmond	9th, Joined 11th 04/08/1915, Labour Corps 643114		20/02/1919	Class Z Reserve
16015	Pte	Salkeld	Joseph	Jarrow	9th, 9th att Senior Officers School Aldershot 09/04/1917		01/02/1919	Class Z Reserve
14518	Sgt	Salmon	Harold S.G.		9th. To RAF		25/04/1917	Dis to Commision Yorkshire Regt
15598	Pte	Saunders	Reuben		9th		21/01/1919	Discharged
14060	Pte	Sayers	Ernest	Gilling West	9th		22/09/1916	Dead
13673	Pte	Sayers	Robert	Wheatley Hill	9th, 9th, 9th	Stomach Disorder	01/02/1919	Class Z Reserve
3/9373	Sgt	Scott	Adam		9th		04/02/1919	Class Z Reserve

Number	Rank	Name	First Name	Home Town	Bns served with	Reported Wounded	Discharged	MR Comment
17898	Pte	Scott	Albert G.	Wideopen, Nthbld	9th, Durham LI 194735, Labour Corps 194735	GSW & Fracture of Leg, Died 08/01/1924	12/07/1918	Discharged
15970	Pte	Scott	George A.	Fatfield	9th, Depot 20/07/1916, 2nd. Declared a Deserter 08/1918	Wnd 10/07/1916, GSW 03/1918	18/08/1918	Deserted 18/08/1918
13448	Pte	Scott	John T.	Ryhope	9th	Pension for Wife and 4 Childresn	08/06/1917	Dead
14812	Pte	Semper	John	Redcar	9th, 9th, 8th		15/02/1919	Class Z Reserve
13428	L/Cpl	Shaw	John	Murton Colliery	9th, Labour Corps Sgt 515968	GSW R Shoulder, Bronchitis	21/01/1919	Discharged
14509	Pte	Sheen	James	Durham City.	9th, 9th, 9th	ICT Feet 05/10/1916, Shrapnel Wnd R Foot, 05/10/1918	10/02/1919	Class Z Reserve
17901	Cpl	Shields	John J.	Jarrow	9th		10/07/1916	Dead
11565	Pte	Shields	Thomas W.	Middlesbrough	9th	DL 24/08/1916, GSW L Knee, Died 19/10/1925	04/02/1919	Discharged
13274	A/Sgt	Shields	Richard	Middlesbrough	9th, 2nd, 12th, 6th, 9th, 12th	WL 27/08/1917	07/11/1918	Dead
19831	Pte	Short	William D.		9th, 7th, 12th to 12th K O Yorkshire LI 62881		11/03/1919	Class Z Reserve
15920	Pte	Sidwell	John	Liverpool	9th	DoW No 2 Stationary Hosp Rouen	19/04/1916	Dead

Number	Rank	Name	First Name	Home Town	Bns served with	Reported Wounded	Discharged	MR Comment
17687	Sgt	Simpson	Fred		9th, 9th, 8th		04/02/1919	Class Z Reserve
19384	Pte	Simpson	George E.	Seaham Colliery	9th, 6th	Shrapnel Wnd L Thigh	02/05/1918	Discharged
13953	Pte	Simpson	James	Middlesbrough	9th		08/02/1915	Discharged Misconduct
13634	A/Cpl	Simpson	Arthur		9th		20/01/1917	Discharged
14996	Sgt	Simpson	William	Wheatley Hill	9th, 9th, 9th	Debility	24/01/1919	Class Z Reserve
13311	Cpl	Sinclair	Herbert	Spennymoor	9th, Depot 09/06/1916 , Class W Reserve 05/12/1916 Miner at Trimdon Grange Colliery	Evac Sick Rheumatism 06/1916	12/10/1917	Discharged
10602	Sgt	Skipper	John W.	King's Lynn	9th	DoW No 45 CCS	09/10/1916	Dead
12357	Pte	Sloan	Henry T.		9th, 9th, 9th		Still Serving Mar 1920	Still Serving Mar 1920
19832	Pte	Smart	Andrew	Wooler	9th	DL 16/02/1916, Fomerly 12028 Northbld Fus	05/07/1916	Dead
14118	Pte	Smith	Alexander	Middlesbrough	9th		17/11/1915	Dead
11566	Pte	Smith	Arthur	Middlesbrough	9th, Depot 05/10/1916	Acc Inj L Hand fingers amputated	14/05/1917	Discharged
12250	Sgt	Smith	Edward		9th, 9th		21/03/1919	Class Z Reserve
15468	Pte	Smith	Harold	Scarborough	9th,Depot 14/07/1916, 2nd 20/01/1917, 7th 17/02/1917, Depot 17/05/1917	GSW Legs & Abdomen	20/09/1918	Discharged

Number	Rank	Name	First Name	Home Town	Bns served with	Reported Wounded	Discharged	MR Comment
15971	Pte	Smith	job J.	Middle Rainton	9th, Depot 09/07/1916, 6th 07/08/1917, FGCM 2 Yrs Hard Labour 26/04/1918, 8th Bn 18/09/1918	GSW Head 11/1915, GSW Leg 05/07/1916, GSW R Thigh 19/10/1917	08/05/1919	Class Z Reserve
19849	Pte	Smith	John		9th, Labour Corps 233070		23/03/1919	Class Z Reserve
15972	Pte	Smith	John R.	Houghton le Spring	9th	DoW No 36 CCS	11/07/1916	Dead
17899	Pte	Smith	Richard	Darlington	9th, Depot 09/06/1917	Wnd Severe 06/1917	16/04/1918	Discharged
12557	Pte	Smith	Stephen		9th, 7th, 10th, 8th	DL24/08/1916	09/02/1919	Deserted 19/9/1917
15973	Pte	Smith	Thomas R.	Houghton le Spring	9th, Labour Corps 642624		10/03/1919	Discharged
15328	Pte	Smith	Thompson		9th, 9th, 9th		17/04/1919	Class Z Reserve
7543	Pte	Smith	William F.		9th, 11th, 6th, 4th, 2nd renumbered 202959		16/03/1919	Class Z Reserve
	Pte	Smith		Leeds	9th, Discharged unlikely to become efficient			Discharged
17767	Pte	Smith	Joseph W.	Cassop Colliery, Durham	9th	GSW Shoulder & Buttock	01/04/1918	Discharged
14096	Sgt	Snaith	James	Wheatley Hill	9th,Depot 05/16 11th 04/07/1916 9th 28/08/1916, 9th		11/02/1919	Class Z Reserve
15319	Pte	Southern	Charles W.J.	Eversham Gloucestershire	9th,Depot 14/07/1916, Durham LI 101824			Class Z Reserve

Number	Rank	Name	First Name	Home Town	Bns served with	Reported Wounded	Discharged	MR Comment
15351	Pte	Spence	Harry	Leeds	9th, 2nd 01/01/1917, 2nd 31/08/1917, 2nd 28/11/1918	Wnd Arm & Wrist 09/04/1917, Wnd 09/10/1917	20/03/1919	Class Z Reserve
14798	A/Cpl	Spence	Joseph	Grangetowm	9th		17/07/1916	Dead
17867	Pte	Spoors	Thomas	Tow law	9th, Depot 30/07/1916, 10th Trg Res Bn 05/10/1916 , 2nd 15/04/1917, Missing 22/03/1918, POW	Evac Impetigo 29/07/1916	21/03/1919	Class Z Reserve
15948	Pte	Spurr	Harry	Pontefract	9th, Depot 14/07/1916, 6th 17/11/1916, 7th, 2nd 16/05/1918	GSW R Ankle 10/07/1916, GSW L Leg 9/11/1918	12/03/1919	Class Z Reserve
14811	Pte	Stainton	Ernest	Middlesbrough	9th		05/07/1916	Dead
15620	Pte	Stainton	John W.		9th, Labour Corps Sgt 710737		29/02/1920	Discharged
14033	Pte	Staley	William	Coundon	9th		18/09/1916	Dead
15463	Pte	Stapylton	George D.	Sowerby	9th, Depot 23/10/1916, 2nd 07/04/1917, 6th 14/07/1918	Evac Myalgia 10/1916, GSW R Hand Severe 02/08/1917, GSW Back 30/03/1918, DL 10/09/1917	23/08/1919	Class Z Reserve
14321	Pte	Stead	Frank	Heckmondwyke	9th		13/02/1919	Class Z Reserve
3/8944	Pte	Steadman	Lawrence		9th		03/02/1919	Discharged
12122	Cpl	Stephenson	Frank	Cargo Fleet	9th, 13th 9th		08/06/1917	Dead
15984	Cpl	Stephenson	Henry C.	Scarborough	9th		20/09/1916	Dead

Number	Rank	Name	First Name	Home Town	Bns served with	Reported Wounded	Discharged	MR Comment
17269	Pte	Stephenson	James	Kimblesworth	9th		07/06/1917	Dead
15986	Pte	Stephenson	Richard	Heysham Lancs	9th		20/09/1916	Dead
17902	Pte	Stephenson	Samuel	Byker	9th, Ex 2nd Bn Northbld Fus 12 Yrs Svc time expired, Depot 17/01/1916, Class W Reserve Newcastle Tramways 16/03/1917, Reenlisted labour Corps 710282 10/06/1919	Evac Bronchitis 01/1916	10/08/1917	Discharged
13206	Pte	Stephenson	Thomas R.	South Bank	9th, Depot 25/09/1915, 2nd 16/12/1915, Class W Steel works 21/12/1916		11/01/1919	Discharged
15326	Pte	Stephenson	William	Scarborough	9th, 9th, 9th		14/02/1919	Class Z Reserve
15985	Cpl	Stephenson	Reginald H.	Scarborough	9th, 9th, 9th		08/03/1919	Class Z Reserve
15074	Pte	Stone	John T.	Langley Park	9th	GSW Throat	05/02/1919	Discharged
15929	Pte	Stonehouse	Albert E.	Lingdale	9th, Depot 19/05/1917 Class W Reserve Ironstone miner		20/01/1919	Discharged
15930	Pte	Stonehouse	Richard	Lingdale	9th, Class W Reserve Ironstone miner 01/06/1917		24/01/1919	Discharged
14810	Sgt	Stonehouse	William	South Bank	9th		07/10/1916	Dead
15103	Pte	Stott	Mark	Leeds	9th, Royal Defence Corps 73160, Reenlisted RASC 1/12/1919 EMT/46729	KR para 392 XVI Sick, VDH	14/11/1918	Discharged

Number	Rank	Name	First Name	Home Town	Bns served with	Reported Wounded	Discharged	MR Comment
12580	A/Cpl	Strong	George	Durham City.	9th		05/07/1916	Dead
15622	Pte	Stubbs	Fred		9th, 6th To East Yorkshire Regiment 59276		Still Serving Jun 1920	Class Z Reserve
15949	Sgt	Sullivan	Arthur	Scarborough	9th		07/06/1917	Dead
15599	Pte	Sullivan	Timothy	Grangetown	9th		21/12/1915	Dead
15308	Pte	Swales	Zachariah	Guisborough	9th. Depot 12/03/1917, Class W Reserve Ironestone miner		21/01/1919	Discharged
13410	Pte	Tait	Albert M.	Billingham	9th, 69th MG Coy MGC 72682, Military Foot Police P/13814,	Trench Fever	31/05/1919	Class Z Reserve
12850	Sgt	Tait	Charles E.	Durham City.	9th		06/05/1919	Class Z Reserve
3/8858	Sgt	Tait	William T.	Monkseaton Nthbld	9th, 9th, 9th		20/03/1919	Class Z Reserve
3/9130	Pte	Talbot	George	London	9th, Ex 3rd Bn Time Expired, Depot 15/07/1916	GSW L Chest 10/07/1916, DL 24/08/1916	07/04/1917	Discharged
12384	Pte	Tankard	Frank	Sheffield	9th, 6th, 5th Bns renumbered 243416	GSW L Foot DL 02/08/1916	15/02/1919	Discharged
11959	Pte	Taylor	Albert	Loftus	9th, 6th, 1/4th, 5th Duke of Wellington's Regt 34909	MDG 25/08/1916	13/09/1918	Dead
14506	Pte	Taylor	Ernest W.	Brancepeth	9th		18/02/1919	Class Z Reserve
14255	Pte	Taylor	George		9th, Labour Corps 211181		23/12/1918	Discharged

Number	Rank	Name	First Name	Home Town	Bns served with	Reported Wounded	Discharged	MR Comment
8645	Sgt	Taylor	Gilbert		9th, Labour Corps 564544	DL 18/08/1916	14/04/1919	Class Z Reserve
14625	Pte	Taylor	Henry	Lowestoft	9th		01/08/1916	Dead
15974	Pte	Taylor	Luke	Hetton Le Hole	9th, 6th, 4th 27/09/1916, renumbered 7547 then 202963	Evac Myalia 06/05/1916, ICT Hand 17/11/1916, GSW L Foot 28/03/1918	28/01/1919	Class Z Reserve
15975	Pte	Taylor	Thomas	Hetton Le Hole	9th, Labour Corps 227698	MDG 09/08/1916	17/01/1919	Discharged
15976	Pte	Tempest	Robert	Hetton Le Hole	9th. 7th 18/09/1917, 13th 12/02/1918		13/03/1919	Class Z Reserve
13277	Sgt	Tewson	Ernest	Eston	9th, 9th, 9th		04/02/1919	Class Z Reserve
14630	C pl	Theaker	Luke	Brotton	9th, Depot 04/06/1917 Class W Reserve Ironstone miner 12/06/1917		20/11/1919	Discharged
15921	Pte	Thirkell	George W.	Middlesbrough	9th		09/10/1917	Dead
19596	Pte	Thompson	Charles E.	North Ormesby	9th, Depot 24/10/1918	GSW Head & L Thigh 24/10/1918	01/02/1919	Class Z Reserve
12511	Pte	Thompson	Ernest		9th, Labour Corps 430284		27/02/1919	Discharged
15273	Pte	Thompson	George		9th, York & Lancaster Regt 59705		03/04/1919	Discharged
19595	Pte	Thompson	George F.	North Ormesby	9th, Depot 06/03/1917 Class W Reserve Steel Works	Transferred to UK on Compassionate Grnds	11/01/1919	Discharged

Number	Rank	Name	First Name	Home Town	Bns served with	Reported Wounded	Discharged	MR Comment
14807	Pte	Thompson	James C.		9th, 9th		17/03/1919	Class Z Reserve
15140	Sgt	Thompson	John T.	Rillington Yorks	9th, 9th, 10th, 9th, 9th, 9th	GSW unspecified	17/04/1918	Discharged
14029	Pte	Thompson	Nichol P.	Langley Moor	9th, Depot 13/07/1916, Class P Reserve 02/06/1917	GSW L Foot 10/07/1916	02/06/1917	Discharged
14025	Pte	Thompson	Robert H.	Bearpark	9th, 9th		02/02/1919	Class Z Reserve
17932	Pte	Thompson	Thomas		9th, East Yorkshire Regt 4336155		Still Serving Mar 1920	Still Serving Mar 1920.
15355	Cpl	Thompson	George	Scarborough	9th, 9th		20/09/1917	Dead
14445	Pte	Thompson	Joseph	Brandon Colliery	9th		12/10/1917	Dead
14796	Pte	Thurlwell	Harold		9th, 1st Garrison Bn West Yorkshire Regt, 1/7th Bn, 46101			Class Z Reserve
16186	Pte	Tindle	Frederick	Horden Colliery	9th, 9th, 9th Depot 15/10/1918	GSW R Arm, GSW L Forearm	22/01/1919	Class Z Reserve
14198	Pte	Tis	James	Willington	9th, 9th, 9th		27/01/1919	Class Z Reserve
11901	Pte	Towle	Percy	Guisborough	9th, Depot 24/07/1917 29/Durham LI 20/06/1918 101835	Wnd R Arm at Duty 10/07/1916, GSW R Hand 20/11/1916, Cont L Thigh 13/07/1917, Bullet Wnd L Arm 01/10/1918	10/03/1919	Class Z Reserve
16265	Pte	Tremble	Cornelius	Middlesbrough	9th. Depot Class P Reserve 31/03/1917	GSW L Thigh	31/03/1917	Discharged

Number	Rank	Name	First Name	Home Town	Bns served with	Reported Wounded	Discharged	MR Comment
12779	Pte	Trevane	Frederick	St Helens	9th, S Staffs 37539, Trg Res, TR5/4391, Labour Corps 211181, K Liverpool 102822	GSW Hand, Injury to Spine, Died 04/07/1924	19/02/1919	Class Z Reserve
3/8942	Pte	Trimble	James		9th, 9th		06/03/1919	Class Z Reserve
13502	Pte	Trotter	Robert T.	Ryhope	9th		03/02/1916	Dead
15475	A/Sgt	Tudor	Charles	Middlesbrough	9th, 10th, 9th	DL 22/02/1916	07/06/1917	Dead
12977	Pte	Tunstall	George R.	Middle Rainton	9th	not overseas	22/12/1914	Discharged
15317	Pte	Tunstall	Joseph	Leeds	9th		10/07/1916	Dead
15318	Pte	Tunstall	Samuel	Leeds	9th	DL 24/08/1916	10/07/1916	Dead
3/8934	Sgt	Turnbull	Pearson		9th, 8th, 9th		27/02/1919	Class Z Reserve
14153	Pte	Turnbull	William	Willington	9th, 9th	VDH	26/01/1919	Class Z Reserve
15095	Pte	Turner	Marshall	Kirbymoorside	9th, 9th, 9th		04/10/1918	Dead
13201	Pte	Turner	William	Middlesbrough	9th	Missing Newcastle Journal 08/08/1916	05/07/1916	Dead
15110	Pte	Tyson	Christopher	North Ormesby	9th	GSW L Forearm	03/05/1919	Discharged
15978	Pte	Unsworth	Ralph	Houghton le Spring	9th, Labour Corps 569656		28/03/1919	Discharged
15403	Pte	Uren	Edmond J.	Loftus	9th		01/02/1919	Discharged
13538	Pte	Urwin	Frederick	Jarrow	9th, 9th, 9th		17/03/1919	Class Z Reserve
17741	Pte	Vardy	William	New Herrington	9th, 2nd West Yorkshire Regt 63559	Wnd 1917	14/01/1919	Class Z Reserve
19594	Pte	Varty	Ernest	Byers Green	9th, Depot 08/07/1916, 7th 16/12/1916. 9th 30/10/1917	GSW 02/01/1916, GSW Arm 05/07/1916, GSW	06/02/1919	Class Z Reserve

Number	Rank	Name	First Name	Home Town	Bns served with	Reported Wounded	Discharged	MR Comment
7553	Pte	Venables	Alfred W.	Wheatley Hill	9th, 11th, 6th, 4th renumbered 202967		29/06/1917	Dead
14726	Pte	Vickers	William	Langley Park	9th	Shrapnel Wnd L forearm & Shoulder 10/07/1916	20/02/1918	Discharged
19363	Pte	Vickerstaff	Robert	Spennymoor	9th, 2nd, 9th		07/06/1917	Dead
11888	Pte	Vitel	Peter M.	St Hellier CI	9th		22/03/1918	Dead
3/9548	Clr Sgt	Wadsworth	James		9th	Died 06/08/1925	15/02/1919	Class Z Reserve
19833	Pte	Wainwright	John	Belton Station	9th		27/01/1919	Discharged
14727	Pte	Waites	John		9th, 2nd, 8th, 9th		26/09/1917	Discharged
14105	Pte	Wake	William		9th	Died 07/03/1925		Discharged
13048	A/Sgt	Waldon	Alfred	Eston	9th, 6th, 9th	Bullet Wnd Back Knee 21/05/1917	21/02/1919	Class Z Reserve
17903	Pte	Walker	Joseph	North Shields	9th Renumbered 243241 released Class W Reserve Ship building 18/05/1918	GSW R Hand 01/02/1916, DL 22/02/1916	17/02/1919	Discharged
19361	Pte	Walker	William	West Cornforth	9th, 6th, 2nd	DL 24/08/1916 GSW L Elbow	09/03/1919	Class Z Reserve
12595	Sgt	Walker	Frederick W.	Grange Villa	9th, Depot 07/10/1916 2nd 30/01/1917 9th 26/02/1917, 9th		24/01/1919	Class Z Reserve
3/9119	Pte	Walker	George W.	Thornaby	9th, 10th, 2nd		08/05/1918	Dead
11931	Pte	Walsh	John	Middlesbrough	9th, 9th, 9th		06/03/1919	Class Z Reserve
15344	Pte	Walters	Albert V.	Scarborough	9th		16/10/1915	Dead

Number	Rank	Name	First Name	Home Town	Bns served with	Reported Wounded	Discharged	MR Comment
13279	Pte	Wanless	William	Eston	9th.		05/10/1916	Dead
15293	Pte	Ward	Bert	Robin Hood's Bay	9th, Depot 09/07/1916, East Yorkshire Regt 30773 03/04/1918 Missing 23/04/1918	Shell Wnd R Thigh 05/07/1916	25/04/1918	Dead
15898	Pte	Ward	James	North Ormesby	9th, Royal Engineers 255 Tunn Coy197784	Wnd Foot & Chest	31/07/1917	Dead
8902	Cpl	Ward	Michael		9th, 5/Durham LI 21444, 15/K O Yorkshire LI 64398		15/02/1919	Class Z Reserve
15404	Pte	Wardell	Sidney M.		9th	Injuries 392 xvi	05/09/1916	Discharged
18317	Pte	Waring	John	Sunderland	9th	DoW Hosp Woolwich	07/09/1916	Dead
14028	Pte	Warrant	John		9th, West Yorkshire Regt 63196			Class Z Reserve
3/9035	Pte	Waters	Leonard R.	Thornaby	9th	Alias William Jefferson	03/10/1916	Accidently Killed
14801	Sgt	Watson	George F.	Grangetown	9th		05/07/1916	Dead
15309	Cpl	Watson	James	Armley	9th		10/07/1916	Dead
15979	Pte	Watson	John		9th, 9th		14/12/1919	Class Z Reserve
17684	Pte	Watson	Ralph	Greatham	9th	DL 24/08/1916	10/07/1916	Dead
13662	Pte	Waugh	Christopher	Wheatley Hill	9th, Labour Corps 370051		11/03/1919	Class Z Reserve
17906	Sgt	Waugh	Septimus	Carlisle	9th		07/06/1917	Dead

Number	Rank	Name	First Name	Home Town	Bns served with	Reported Wounded	Discharged	MR Comment
19837	Cpl	Weatherburn	James	Cowpen Blyth	9th, Depot 03/12/1915 Class W Reserve Coal miner 02/12/1916	Synovitis R Knee 02/12/1915	22/01/1919	Discharged
15922	Pte	Weatherill	Henry P.		9th, 9th, 9th		09/03/1919	Class Z Reserve
14817	Pte	Webster	Ernest	Attleborough	9th		27/01/1916	Dead
8882	Pte	Welling	John W.		9th, Labour Corps 579911		05/03/1919	Class Z Reserve
10572	Pte	Wells	George H.		9th	DL24/08/1916	07/03/1917	Discharged
14501	Pte	Welsh	Fred	Durham City.	9th		13/07/1919	Discharged
3/9050	CSM	Westgarth	William W.	Eston	9th	DAH	13/02/1919	Discharged
3/9020	Pte	Wheatley	George H.	Childs Hill N.W.2	9th	Died 21/10/1932	20/06/1918	Discharged
12601	Pte	Wheatley	Robert	Coundon	9th, East Yorkshire Regt 27678		08/03/1919	Class Z Reserve
12600	Pte	Wheatley	Thomas	Coundon	9th		13/07/1916	Dead
19622	Pte	Whelan	James	North Ormesby	9th		12/07/1916	Dead
19628	Pte	White	John D.	Fencehouses	9th		10/07/1916	Dead
8536	Pte	White	John W.	Thornaby	9th, Labour Corps 31664	Varicous Veins	19/02/1919	Class Z Reserve
14750	L/Cpl	White	Joseph W.	Brandon Colliery	9th, 2nd. Manchester Regiment 52nd Bn		28/05/1918	Discharged to Commission Manchester Regt 28/05/1918
15337	Pte	White	Richard	Middlesbrough	9th, 9th, 7th, 6th, 7th	DL24/08/1916, GSW L Thigh, Died 25/06/1924	23/05/1918	Discharged

Number	Rank	Name	First Name	Home Town	Bns served with	Reported Wounded	Discharged	MR Comment
19629	Pte	White	Thomas D.	Ryhope	9th	DL 16/02/1916	15/01/1919	Discharged
15283	Sgt	White	William	Ryhope	9th		20/09/1916	Dead
15310	Pte	Whitehead	Archibald	Scarborough	9th, 2nd 19/01/1917	Shrapnel Wnd L Toes 05/07/1916, Gassed & Trench Fever	06/03/1919	Class Z Reserve
3/8809	Pte	Whitehead	John T.	Middlesbrough	9th		16/10/1915	Dead
19838	Pte	Whitening	James	Bedlington	9th	DL 24/08/1916	17/01/1919	Discharged
11896	Pte	Whitfield	Charles	Guisborough	9th		11/01/1916	Dead
12512	Cpl	Whitfield	Watson E.	Sacriston	9th		10/10/1916	Dead
15460	Pte	Whittaker	George	Gateshead	9th.9th.9th		19/04/1919	Class Z Reserve
19839	Pte	Widdrington	Ralph	Walker	9th		20/02/1917	Dead
15600	Pte	Wigglesworth	Joseph	Leeds	9th, East Yorkshire Regt 29967		27/02/1919	Class Z Reserve
14325	Pte	Wilkinson	Stanley		9th, 8th, 9th, 9th, 9th		20/02/1919	Class Z Reserve
17748	Cpl	Wilkinson	Thomas	Silksworth	9th, 9th, 9th, 9th	ICT L Leg 13/10/1917	20/01/1919	Class Z Reserve
17904	Pte	Wilkinson	William J.	Middlesbrough	9th, Deserter 08/10/1916, DCM 20/03/1917, 2nd 07/04/1917 FGCM 27/05/1917	GSW L Shldr, GSW R Buttock	31/12/1917	Discharged
15267	Sgt	Wilkinson	George	Boston	9th		20/09/1916	Dead
15272	Pte	Willerton	Samuel	Scarborough	9th, 7th, 9th		13/03/1918	Discharged
16018	Pte	Williams	Ernest	Sunderland	9th, 7th	DL 24/08/1916,	03/04/1918	Discharged

Number	Rank	Name	First Name	Home Town	Bns served with	Reported Wounded	Discharged	MR Comment
17742	Pte	Williams	Randolph	East Herrington	9th. Depot 11/08/1916	Ruptered Cartlidge R Knee, Fel from Transport horse 02/03/1916	06/01/1917	Discharged
17698	Pte	Williams	Robert	Roker	9th, Depot 14/06/1917 3rd Res 14/09/1917	Bullet Wnd R Hand 07/06/1917 GSW L Arm 22/04/1918	14/01/1919	Deserted 22/01/1918,
11806	A/Cpl	Williams	William H.	Newport, Monmouth.	9th, 2nd	GSW L Arm	08/01/1918	Discharged
17273	Cpl	Williamson	Leonard	Stockton	9th, 9th, 9th		08/02/1919	Class Z Reserve
13688	Pte	Willis	Alexander	Hartlepool	9th, 9th		08/02/1917	Dead
11926	Pte	Wilson	Gabriel	Middlesbrough	9th, Depot 20/07/1916, 2nd 30/01/1917, 9th 26/02/1917 Depot 04/08/1917, Class W Reserve Steelworks 22/08/1917. Reenlisted Labour Corps 31/05/1919 to BEF 20/06/1919 18th Lab Coy Dis 28/04/1920 699916	GSW Heel slighht 01/01/1916, GSW Scrotum 10/07/1916, DL 24/08/1916	11/05/1918	Discharged
15980	Pte	Wilson	John	High Moorsley	9th, 10th		02/04/1917	Dead
15981	Pte	Wilson	Robert	Houghton le Spring	9th, 6th, 9th, 2nd		01/02/1919	Class Z Reserve
17905	Pte	Wilson	John	Byker	9th, Labour Corps 32265	Left Wrist & Chronic Bronchitis	15/02/1919	Discharged

Number	Rank	Name	First Name	Home Town	Bns served with	Reported Wounded	Discharged	MR Comment
19341	Pte	Wilson	John E.		9th, Labour Corps 514236	Wnd Left Foot	13/04/1919	Class Z Reserve
13654	Pte	Wilson	Thomas	West Hartlepool	9th		10/12/1915	Dead
17272	Sgt	Wood	Roger		9th	DL 22/02/1916	26/06/1917	Discharged to Commission Yorkshire Regt
17778	Pte	Wood	Frederick	Seaham Colliery	9th		10/07/1916	Dead
3/9070	Pte	Woodrow	George E.	North Ormesby	9th, 9th	GSW L Thigh 10/10/1916	26/02/1919	Class Z Reserve
8821	L/Cpl	Woods	Dennis	Tottenham	9th, 1/5/Manchester Regt 201878		20/10/1918	Dead
15951	Pte	Woolams	Robert	Middlesbrough	9th, Depot 15/09/1916, 7th 01/03/1917, Depot 17/05/1917 8th 26/09/1917, 8th	Shell Shock MDG 29/08/1916 Evac Haemoroids 03/1917, DL 24/08/1916	22/02/1919	Class Z Reserve
14436	Pte	Worthy	William	Durham City.	9th, 2nd, 5th, 8th, 8th	DL 16/02/1916, GSW R Shoulder Spinal Caries	12/02/1919	Class Z Reserve
15466	Pte	Worton	John		9th, 9th		18/02/1919	Class Z Reserve
13073	Pte	Wray	Arthur	Hovingham	9th		07/10/1916	Dead
13754	Pte	Wright	Cecil E.	Workington	9th, Class P Reserve 31/03/1917	Trench feet 24/04/1916	31/03/1917	Discharged
15912	Pte	Wright	Ernest N.	Stockton	9th, RFC 02/01/1916, RAF 01/04/1918 19895		15/02/1919	
14619	Pte	Wright	John O.	Thirsk	9th	DoW No 22 CCS	13/05/1916	Dead

Number	Rank	Name	First Name	Home Town	Bns served with	Reported Wounded	Discharged	MR Comment
19841	Pte	Wright	William E.	Ashington	9th, 6th, 2/4th Duke of Wellington's Regt 34917		13/09/1918	Dead
13347	Pte	Wynn	Robert	Sunderland	9th, DCM 10/07/1915 AWOL 56 Days Detention Remitted to embark, Depot 09/02/1916 11th Deserted	Contusions R Arm 01/02/1916	14/09/1916	Deserted 14/06/1916
13029	Pte	Yard	Sidney	Burnopfield	9th, 9th, 9th, 8th 05/10/1918		30/01/1919	Class Z Reserve
13030	Pte	Yard	Walter		9th, Machine Gun Corps 148267		20/04/1919	Class Z Reserve
13124	Pte	York	Henry W.	Middlesbrough	9th, Depot 07/06/1916	GSW Both Legs & Back 07/04/1916 GSW Forearm 07/06/1916	02/01/1917	Discharged
13040	Pte	Young	William	Willington	9th	DL 24/08/1916	10/07/1916	Dead

Notes

Chapter 1

1. *Middlesbrough Daily Gazette*, Monday, 27 July 1914, p.3 col. 3.
2. *Middlesbrough Daily Gazette*, Tuesday, 4 August 1914, p.2 col. 5.
3. Colonel H.C. Wylly CB, *The Green Howards in the Great War* (Richmond, 1926), p.147.
4. *Middlesbrough Daily Gazette*, 5 August 1914, p.4 col. 3.
5. *Middlesbrough Daily Gazette*, 10 August 1914.
6. *Middlesbrough Daily Gazette*, Monday, 24 August 1914.
7. *Sunderland Echo*, Thursday, 27 August 1914, p.2 col. 3.
8. *Middlesbrough Daily Gazette*, Tuesday, 8 September 1914.
9. *Surrey Advertiser*, Thursday, 19 September 1914, p.7.
10. *Sunderland Echo*, Wednesday, 26 September 1914, p.4.

Chapter 2

1. The *Green Howards Gazette*, October 1924, p.118.
2. Green Howards Museum, unpublished manuscript 2019.24.
3. *Surrey Advertiser*, 14 October 1914.
4. *Chester-le-Street Chronicle*, Friday, 2 October 1914, p.2 col. 4.
5. *Green Howards Gazette*, October 1914, p.131.
6. *Surrey Advertiser*, 14 November 1914.
7. Charles Fair, *Marjorie's War* (Brighton, Menin House Publishers, 2012), p.23.
8. *The Sportsman*, 4 January 1915.
9. Unpublished part of a letter dated 12 January 1915. Courtesy Charles Fair.
10. Lt Col H.R. Sandilands CMG DSO, *The 23rd Division 1914–1919* (London, William Blackwood and Sons, 1925), p.12.
11. *Marjorie's War*, p.26.
12. *Green Howards Gazette*, May 1915, p.33.
13. *Marjorie's War*, p.27.
14. *Green Howards Gazette*, April 1915, p.14.
15. *Folkestone Express*, 6 March 1915, p.10 col. 3.
16. *Folkestone Advertiser*, Saturday, 13 March 1915, p.2 col. 4.
17. *Folkestone Herald*, Saturday, 20 March 1915, p.6 col. 2.
18. *Folkestone Advertiser*, Saturday, 27 March 1915, p.9 col. 3.
19. *Folkestone Herald*, Saturday, 20 March 1915.
20. Green Howards Museum, unpublished manuscript 2019.24.
21. *Folkestone Herald*, Saturday, 3 April 1915.
22. *Folkestone Herald* 17 April 1915.
23. *Folkestone Herald*, Saturday, 17 April 1915.
24. *Folkestone Herald*, Tuesday, 20 April 1915.
25. *Folkestone Advertiser*, Saturday, 24 April 1915, p.9 col. 3.
26. *Green Howards Gazette*, May 1915, p.33.

27. Lt Col H.R. Sandilands CMG DSO, *The 23rd Division 1914–1919* (London, William Blackwood and Sons, 1925), p.16.
28. *Marjorie's War*, p.34.
29. *Green Howards Gazette*, June 1915, p.53.
30. TNA, WO/339 Personal Documents of 13347 Private Robert Wynn 9/Yorkshire Regiment.
31. *Marjorie's War*, pp.36–37.
32. The *Green Howards Gazette*, August 1915, p.93.
33. *Marjorie's War*, p.40.

Chapter 3

1. TNA, WO/95/2183, War Diary 69 Brigade HQ, 25 August 1915.
2. TNA, WO/95/2184 War Diary 8/Yorkshire Regiment Yorkshire Regiment, 26 August 1915.
3. TNA, WO/95/2184 War Diary 9/Yorkshire Regiment Yorkshire Regiment, 26 August 1915.
4. *Marjorie's War*, p.84.
5. *Green Howards Gazette*, October 1924, p.119.
6. Green Howards Museum, unpublished manuscript 2019.24.
7. *Marjorie's War*, p.85.
8. War Diary, 5 September 1915.
9. *Marjorie's War*, p.87.
10. TNA, War Diary 2nd Cameron Highlanders, 11 September 1915, WO 95/2264.
11. War Diary 8th Yorks, 19 September 1915.
12. Green Howards Museum, unpublished manuscript 2019.24.
13. Unpublished letter, Lieutenant Francis Dodgson to his mother, Courtesy Charles Fair.
14. Ibid.
15. Ibid.
16. *Middlesbrough Daily Gazette*, 15 October 1915, p.5.
17. *Marjorie's War*, p.94.
18. *Marjorie's War*, p.94.
19. *Marjorie's War*, p.96.
20. *Marjorie's War*, pp.98–100.
21. *Marjorie's War*, p.101.
22. *Marjorie's War*, p.102.
23. TNA, MH106/308 Admission and Discharge Register Number 3 CCS, 19 October 1915.
24. *Middlesbrough Daily Gazette*, 31 Oct 1915.
25. Ibid.
26. *The 23rd Division 1914–1919*, p.34.
27. TNA, MH106/308.
28. TNA, WO/339 Soldiers Burnt Documents 12121 Private Alfred Winch.
29. *Aberdeen Express*, Thursday, 18 November 1915, p.4 col. 4.
30. TNA, War Diary 69 Infantry Brigade Headquarters WO95/2183.

Chapter 4

1. TNA, War Diary 9/Yorkshire Regiment The Yorkshire Regiment WO95/2184, Report on Trench Raid, 1 January 1916.
2. TNA, War Diary HQ 23rd Division WO 95/2167 Report on Trench Raid, 1 January 1916.
3. Ibid.
4. TNA, MH106/309 Admission & Discharge Register, No. 3 CCS.
5. *Marjorie's War*, p.130.
6. TNA, WO95/2183, War Diary 69 Infantry Brigade.
7. *Marjorie's War*, p.131.

8. *Marjorie's War*, pp.131–132.
9. Captain Francis Dodgson, unpublished letter dated 19 March 1916.
10. TNA, War Diary 69 Infantry Brigade WO/95/2183, 31 March 1916.
11. TNA. WO95/2183 War Diary, HQ 69 Infantry Brigade.
12. TNA. WO95/2184 War Diary, 8/Yorkshire Regiment Yorkshire Regiment.
13. TNA. WO95/2184 War Diary, 10th Duke of Wellington's Regiment.
14. Unpublished manuscript, Green Howards Museum.
15. *Marjorie's War*, p.169.
16. *Unpublished manuscript* Green Howards Museum.
17. 13942 Private Joseph Humble from Fatfield, County Durham, killed in Action, 10 July 1916.
18. Only one man of this name served in the regiment and his medal roll shows only service with the 12th Battalion.
19. *Marjorie's War*, pp.176–177.

Chapter 5

1. TNA, WO95/2183 Operation Order No. 63 dated 5 July 1916.
2. *Leeds Mercury*, 24 August 1916, p.5 col. 4.
3. TNA, WO95/2167, Intelligence summary 23rd Division 4–5 July 1916.
4. Green Howards Museum RICGH.2013.148. Letter to 14806 Pte J.T. Collins from J. Sydney Wilkinson.
5. *Green Howards Gazette*, Vol. XXIV July 1916, p.44.
6. Unpublished letter courtesy of the Green Howards Museum.
7. Brigadier General Sir James E. Edmonds, *Military Operations France and Belgium 1916 Vol. I* (London: Macmillan and Co., 1932), p.373.
8. John Sheen, *Tyneside Irish* (Barnsley: Pen & Sword, 2010 [1997]), p.101.
9. Brigadier General Sir James E. Edmonds, *Military Operations France and Belgium 1916 Vol. II* (London: Macmillan and Co., 1938), p.34.
10. TNA, WO95/2167, War Diary, Headquarters General Staff 23rd Division. 8 July 1916.
11. Colonel H.C. Wylly CB, *The Green Howards in the Great War 1914–1919 (*London: Butler & Thomas Ltd, 1926), p.255.
12. TNA, WO95/2170, War Diary, Commander Royal Artillery HQ 23rd Division, Appendix XXI Artillery Programme 10 July 1916.
13. TNA, WO95/2183 Appendix VI(b) 10/July 1916.
14. TNA. WO95/2167.
15. Edmonds, *Military Operations France and Belgium 1916 Vol. II,* p.55.

16 TNA, WO95/2179, War Diary of 69 Field Ambulance, RAMC, 7–10 July 1916.

17. TNA, WO95/2167, War Diary Headquarters 23rd Division, 10 July 1916.
18. TNA, MH106/690 Admission & Discharge Register No. 34 CCS, 10 July 1916.
19. TNA, WO95/2167.
20. *Leeds Mercury*, 24 August 1916, p.5 col. 4.
21. TNA, WO364, Soldiers Pension Documents, 13783 Private Albert Bail Yorkshire Regiment.
22. *The Surrey Advertiser*, Monday, 31 July 1916, p.2 col. 2.
23. TNA, WO95/2167.
24. Brigadier Sir James E. Edmonds, *Military Operations France and Belgium, 1916, Vol. II* (London MacMillan & Co., 1938), pp.54–55.
25. *Military Operations 1916, Vol. II*, p.60.
26. Major T.J. Mitchell, *History of the Great War, Medical Services, Casualties and Statistics* (Uckfield: Naval & Military Press reprint, 2010), p.147.
27. Andrew Davidson, *Fred's War, A Doctor in the Trenches* (London: Short Books, 2013), p.116.
28. Blackwood, 'Treatment of wounds from Fire', p.230.

29. Blackwood, 'Treatment of wounds from Fire', p.230.
30. Davidson, *Fred's War,* p.116.
31. Army Medical Service Expeditionary Force, *Field Service Manual 1913*, reprinted 1914, p.80.
32. Blackwood, 'Treatment of wounds', p.236.
33. Blackwood, 'Treatment of wounds from Fire Trench to Field Ambulance', p.232.
34. TNA, WO95/2179, War Diary of 69 Field Ambulance, RAMC, 7–10 July 1916.
35. TNA, WO95/2172, War Diary Assistant Director of Medical Services 23rd Division, 6 July 1916.
36. Niall Cherry, 'The RAMC on the Somme, 1916', Stand To! *The Journal of the Western Front Association,* April 2002, No. 64, p.38.
37. Mark Harrison, *The Medical War* (Oxford: Oxford University Press, 2010), p.22.
38. Mark Harrison, *The Medical War*, p. 8
39. W.G. Macpherson, *History of the Great War Medical Services General History Vol. II* (London: HMSO, 1923), p.42.
40. TNA, WO95/2172, War Diary ADMS 23rd Division, Operation Order Number 4, 4 July 1916.
41. TNA, WO95/695, War Diary DDMS III Corps, 11 July 1916.
42. TNA, WO95/695, War Diary DDMS III Corps, Operation Order No. 2 17 June 1916.
43. TNA, WO95/411, War Diary No. 21 Motor Ambulance Convoy, 639 Company Army Service Corps, 10–11 July 1916.
44. Mark Harrison, *The Medical War*, p.22.
45. Edith Appleton, *A Nurse at the Front*, *The First World War Diaries of Sister Edith Appleton*, ed. Ruth Cowen (London: Simon & Schuster, 2013 [2012]), p.166.
46. WO95/2182 Report on Operations 69 Brigade, 10–11 July 1916.
47. *Newcastle Journal*, 18 July 1916, p.6 col. 2.
48. *Middlesbrough Daily Gazette*, Wednesday, 26 July 1916, p.4 col. 1.
49. H.M.W. Gray, *The Early Treatment of War Wounds* (London: Henry Frowde, 1919), pp.56–64.
50. TNA, MH106/690, Admission and Discharge Register 34th Casualty Clearing Station, 11 July 1916.
51. *Soldiers Died in the Great War, Part 24. Alexandra, Princess of Wales's Own* (Yorkshire Regiment) (London: His Majesty's Stationery Office, 1921).
52. TNA, MH106/691, Admission and Discharge Register 34th Casualty Clearing Station, 11 July 1916.
53. WO/363 Service Records 1914–1920, 19353 Private Robert Brown Young.
54. Lieutenant Colonel C. Gordon Watson, G.M.G., F.R.C.S. RAMC, 'Gas Gangrene in Gunshot Wounds', *British Journal of Nursing*, No. 1462, Vol. LVI, 8 April 1916, p.310.
55. TNA, WO364, Soldiers Pension Documents, 11942 Private James A Woods, Yorkshire Regiment.
56. H.M.W. Gray, 'General Treatment of infected Gunshot Wounds', *British Medical Journal.* 1 January 1916, p.2870.
57. Ian R. Whitehead, *Doctors in the Great War* (Barnsley: Pen & Sword 2013 [1999]), p.168.
58. Ibid.
59. TNA, WO363, British Army First World War Service Records 1914–1920, 16670 Private T.W. Lumley, Yorkshire Regiment.
60. TNA, WO364, Soldiers Pension Documents, 17231 Private William Strong, Yorkshire Regiment.
61. The National Archives, 1939 Register of England, Seaham Urban District.
62. England & Wales, Civil Registration Death Index 1976.
63. Captain J.E.H. Roberts, the 'Treatment of Gunshot Wounds of the Head', *British Medical Journal*, 2 October 1915, p.498.
64. Gary Sheffield, *War on the Western Front: In the Trenches of World War* (Oxford: Osprey Publishing, 2007), p.227.

65. TNA, WO363, British Army First World War Service Records 1914–1920, 14423 Private John Ernest Earl.
66. TNA, WO363, British Army First World War Service Records 1914–1920, 14564 Private Wilfred Tweddle.
67. *Soldiers Died in the Great War, Part 24. Alexandra, Princess of Wales's Own* (Yorkshire Regiment) (London: His Majesty's Stationery Office, 1921).
68. *Soldiers Died in the Great War, Part 24. Alexandra, Princess of Wales's Own* (Yorkshire Regiment) (London: His Majesty's Stationery Office, 1921).
69. The Green Howards Museum, Richmond, Yorkshire, Recruiting Register 1915.
70. The National Archives, 1939 Register of England, Durham Rural District.
71. England & Wales, Civil Registration Death Index 1969.
72. TNA, WO364, Soldiers Pension Documents, 13783 Private Albert Bail Yorkshire Regiment.
73. Lieutenant H.H. Sampson, Address to III Corps Medical Society, *JRAMC*, Vol. XXVI, p.93.
74. TNA, WO364, Soldiers Pension Documents, 13783 Private Alfred James Bail, Yorkshire Regiment.
75. *Sheffield Daily Telegraph*, Thursday, 20 July 1916, p.3 col.2
76. *Stockton and Thornaby Herald*, 29 July 1916, p.5 col. 4.
77. *Stockton and Thornaby Herald*, 5 August 1916, p.1 col. 8.
78. Ernst Mugge, *Das Wurttembergerische Reserve Infantry Regiment Nr 122 im Weltkreig 1914–1918* (Stuttgart, Ehe Belsersche Buchhandlung, 1922), p.16.
79. Mugge, p.24.
80. Ibid., p.25.
81. Holger Ritter, *Historien om Schleswig-Holsteinischen Infanterie-Regiment Nr. 163* (Hamburg, Leuchtfeuer Verlag, 1926), p.75.

Chapter 6

1. TNA, WO95/2183.
2. TNA, WO329, Burnt documents 13093 Private Walter Sheen.
3. TNA, WO95/2172, War Diary ADMS 23rd Division, July 1916.
4. TNA, WO95/2183.
5. *The London Gazette*, 9 September 1916.
6. *The Middlesbrough Daily Gazette*, Saturday, 9 September 1916, p.4 col. 4.
7. *Official History Somme Vol. II*, p.188.
8. TNA, WO95/2183.
9. *Yorkshire Post*, Friday, 1 September 1916, p.4. col. 6.
10. TNA, WO95/2183.
11. TNA, WO95/2183.
12. TNA, WO95/2183.
13. *Middlesbrough Daily Gazette*, Monday, 30 October 1916, p.3 col. 7.
14. *Middlesbrough Daily Gazette*, Wednesday, 1 November 1916, p.3 col. 7.
15. TNA, WO95/2172 *War Diary ADMS 23rd Division*, 4 November 1916.
16. *Middlesbrough Daily Gazette*, 21 November 1916, p.3 col. 7.
17. TNA, WO95/2184 8th Battalion War Diary.

Chapter 7

1. Unpublished manuscript Private George Kidson, Courtesy of Green Howards Museum.
2. Ibid.
3. *Hartlepool Northern Daily Mail*, 13 February 1917, p.3 col. 4.
4. TNA, WO95/2184.
5. TNA, WO95/2168 23rd Division Intelligence Report No. 7, 15 April 1917.

6. TNA, WO95/2168 23rd Division Intelligence Report No. 14, 22 April 1917.
7. TNA, WO95/2184 9 Yorkshire Regiment Operation Orders for Raid, 21/22 April 1917.
8 TNA WO95/2173 War Diary ADMS 23rd Division Defence Scheme, 25 April 1917.
9. TNA, WO95/2168 HQ 23rd Division Instructions for the Battle of Messines, May 1917.
10. TNA, WO95/2184, 8/Yorkshire Regiment Report on Operations 6–12 June 1917.
11. TNA, WO95/2184, 9/Yorkshire Regiment Report on the attack, 7 June 1917.
12. TNA, WO339 Personal documents Captain E.N. Lambert, 8th Yorkshire Regiment.
13. Both letters and a single envelope in the author's collection.

Chapter 8

1. *Green Howards Gazette.*
2. Green Howards Museum RICGH:2013.148 Letter to 14806 Pte J.T. Collins from Second Lieutenant R.B. Wilton.
3. TNA. WO95/2183.
4. TNA. WO95/2173 War Diary HQ ADMS, 23rd Division. 2 September 1917.
5. TNA, WO952184.
6. Brigadier Sir James E. Edmonds, *Military Operations France & Belgium 1917 Vol. II*, p.274.
7. TNA. WO95/2184 War Diary, 8 Battalion, Yorkshire Regt.
8. TNA. WO95/2184.
9. TNA, WO95/2183.
10. Ibid.
11. *Kent Messenger & Gravesend Telegraph*, 8 December 1917, p.4 col. 7.
12. *Deal, Walmer and Sandwich Mercury*, 29 Sep 1917, p.3 col. 3.
13. *Sunderland Echo*, 29 Sep 1917, p.6 col. 4.
14. *Green Howards Gazette*, Oct–Nov 1917 issue, p.77.
15. Sedbergh School Roll of Honour.
16. Green Howards Museum RICGH:1972.5.2 Letter to Mrs Lewis from Lt Col R.S. Hart.
17. Green Howards Museum RICGH:1972.5.3 Letter to Mrs Lewis from Captain A.C. Jardine.
18. *Staffordshire Advertiser*, Saturday, 13 October 1917, p.4 col. 3.
19. *Yorkshire Post*, 9 October 1917, p.4 col. 3.
20. TNA. WO95/2183.
21. Ibid.

Chapter 9

1. Wylly, p.268.
2. Brigadier Sir James Edmonds CB CMG, *Military Operations Italy 1915–1919* (HMSO London, 1949), p.105.
3. Ibid., p.106.
4. TNA, WO213/19 Judge Advocate Generals Office, Courts Martial Registers, pp.76, 111, 161, 335.
5. TNA. WO95/4238 War Diary 9/Yorkshire Regiment, Italy, 31 December 1917.
6. TNA. WO95/4238.
7. Edmonds, *Military Operations Italy*, p.162.
8. Wylly, Chap XIII, p.273.
9. Edmonds, *Military Operations Italy*, p.173.
10. TNA, WO95/4238.
11 TNA. WO95/4328.
12. Edmonds, *Military Operations Italy*, p.199.
13. Edmonds, *Military Operations Italy*, p.217.

Chapter 10

1. Edmonds, *Military Operations Italy 1915–1919*, HMSO London, 1949.
2. Ibid., p.268.
3. Ibid., p.274.
4. Edmonds, *Military Operations Italy*, p.294.
5. *Green Howards Gazette*, Vol. XXVIII April 1920, p.8.

Chapter 11

1. TNA, WO363 Personal Records 14509 Pte James Sheen, 9/Yorkshire Regiment.
2. *Northampton Mercury Friday*, 11 October 1918, p.11 col. 1.
3. *Birkenhead News*, Wednesday, 16 October 1918, p.3 col. 5.
4. Brigadier Sir J.E. Edmonds, *Military Operations France and Belgium* 1918 *Vol. V* (HMSO London, 1947), p.177.
5. Edmonds, *1918 Vol. V*, p.373.
6. *Northampton Mercury*, Friday, 8 November 1918, p.6 col. 2.

Chapter 12

1. Peter Simkins, *Kitchener's Army, The Raising of the New Armies 1914–1916* (Barnsley: Pen & Sword Military 2007), p.65.
2. WO/363 British Army First World War Service Records 1914–1920, 15955 Sergeant Joseph Birtley, Yorkshire Regiment.
3. John Sheen, *Tyneside Irish*, p.6.
4. *Soldiers Died in the Great War Part 42, The South Staffordshire Regiment* (London: His Majesty's Stationery Office, 1921).
5. TNA, WO363, British Army First World War Service Records 1914–1920, 6037 Sergeant Charles Ogden, Yorkshire Regiment.
6. TNA, WO364 Pension Documents, 17902 Private Samuel Stephenson.
7. Yorkshire Regiment Militia Recruiting Book 1906, Green Howards Museum, Richmond, Yorkshire.
8. TNA, WO329 Silver War Badge List, Roll B, Sheet No. Y/252, 8489 Private Walter Williams.
9. TNA, WO329, Personal Documents, 13808 Private John W. McKenzie, Yorkshire Regiment.
10. *Soldiers Died in the Great War Part 69, The Connaught Rangers* (London: His Majesty's Stationery Office, 1921).
11. Commonwealth War Graves Commission, Cemetery Register, Struma Military Cemetery, Plot VI, Row H, Grave 15.
12. Murton Local History Group.
13. Leeds Cemetery Register, Entry 68204, 8 May 1920.

Bibliography

Newspapers

Aberdeen Express
Chester le Street Chronicle
Birkenhead News
Deal, Walmer and Sandwich Mercury
The Durham Chronicle
Folkestone Advertiser
Folkestone Express
Folkestone Herald
Hartlepool Northern Daily Mail
Kent Messenger & Gravesend Telegraph
Leeds Mercury
The London Gazette
Middlesbrough Daily Gazette
Newcastle Journal
Northampton Mercury
The Sportsman
Sheffield Daily Telegraph
Staffordshire Advertiser
Stockton and Thornaby Herald
Sunderland Echo
Surrey Advertiser
Yorkshire Post

Medical Histories

'The RAMC on the Somme, 1916', Stand To! *The Journal of the Western Front Association*, April 2002, Number 64, Niall Cherry
The Early Treatment of War Wounds, M.W. Gray (London: Henry Frowde, 1919)
History of the Great War, Medical Services, Casualties and Statistics, Major T.J. Mitchell (Uckfield: Naval & Military Press reprint, 2010)
Fred's War, A Doctor in the Trenches, Andrew Davidson (London: Short Books, 2013)
Army Medical Service Expeditionary Force, *Field Service Manual 1913*, reprinted 1914
'Treatment of wounds from Fire Trench to Field Ambulance', Blackwood
The Early Treatment of War Wounds (London: H.M.W. Gray, Henry Frowde, 1919)
The Medical War (Mark Harrison Oxford: Oxford University Press, 2010)
History of the Great War Medical Services General History Vol. II, W.G. Macpherson (London: HMSO, 1923)
Doctors in the Great War, Ian R. Whitehead (Barnsley: Pen & Sword, 2013 [1999])
'Gas Gangrene in Gunshot Wounds', Lieutenant Colonel C. Gordon Watson, GMG, FRCS RAMC, *British Journal of Nursing*, No. 1462, Vol. LVI

Military Histories

The *Green Howards Gazette 1914–1920*

The 23rd Division 1914–1919, Lt Col H.R. Sandilands CMG DSO (London: William Blackwood and sons, 1925)

The Green Howards in the Great War, Colonel H.C. Wylly CB (Richmond: 1926.)

Marjorie's War, Charles Fair (Brighton: Menin House Publishers, 2012)

War on the Western Front: In the Trenches of World War One, Gary Sheffield (Oxford: Osprey Publishing, 2007)

Tyneside Irish, John Sheen (Barnsley: Pen & Sword 2010 [1997])

Military Operations France and Belgium 1916 Vol. II, Brigadier Sir J.E. Edmonds, *Military Operations* (London: MacMillan & Co., 1938)

Military Operations France & Belgium 1917 Vol. II, Brigadier Sir J.E. Edmonds (London: HMSO, 1948)

Military Operations France and Belgium 1918 Vol. V, Brigadier Sir J.E. Edmonds (London: HMSO, 1947)

Military Operations Italy 1915–1919, Brigadier Sir J.E. Edmonds (London: HMSO, 1949).

National Archives, War Diaries and Related Documents

TNA WO95/695, War Diary DDMS III Corps

Edith Appleton, *A Nurse at the Front, The First World War Diaries of Sister Edith Appleton*, ed. Ruth Cowen (London: Simon & Schuster, 2013 [2012])

TNA MH106/308 Admission and Discharge Register No. 3 CCS

TNA MH106/690 Admission & Discharge Register No. 34 CCS

TNA WO/339 WW1 Soldiers Personal Documents

TNA WO339 Officers Personal documents

TNA WO/339 Soldiers Burnt Documents

TNA,WO364, Soldiers Pension Documents

TNA WO 95/2167 War Diary HQ 23rd Division

TNA WO95/2168 23rd Division Intelligence Report

WO95/2170, War Diary, Commander Royal Artillery HQ 23rd Division

TNA, WO95/2172, War Diary Assistant Director of Medical Services 23rd Division

TNA WO95/2173 War Diary ADMS 23rd Division

TNA WO/95/2184 War Diary 8/Yorkshire Regiment

TNA WO/95/2184 War Diary 9/Yorkshire Regiment

TNA WO95/4238 War Diary 9/Yorkshire Regiment Italy

TNA. WO95/2184 War Diary 10th Duke of Wellington's Regiment

TNA WO 95/2264 War Diary 2nd Cameron Highlanders

WO95/2179, War Diary of 69 Field Ambulance, RAMC

TNA, WO95/411, War Diary No. 21 Motor Ambulance Convoy, 639 Company Army Service Corps

TNA, WO213/19 Judge Advocate Generals Office, Courts Martial Registers

1939 Register of England, Durham Rural District

Murton Local History Group

Sedbergh School Roll of Honour

German Sources

Das Wurttembergerische Reserve Infantry Regiment Nr 122 im Weltkreig 1914–1918. Ernst Mugg (Stuttgart Ehe Belsersche Buchhandlung. 1922)

Historien om Schleswig-Holsteinischen Infanterie-Regiment Nr. 163 Holger Ritter. (Hamburg, Leuchtfeuer Verlag, 1926)